THE POLISH CRISIS AND RELATIONS WITH EASTERN EUROPE, 1979–1982

Documents on British Policy Overseas
Series III, Volume X

Edited by Isabelle Tombs and Richard Smith

Routledge
Taylor & Francis Group
LONDON AND NEW YORK

WHITEHALL HISTORIES: FOREIGN AND COMMONWEALTH OFFICE PUBLICATIONS

Series Editors: Patrick Salmon and Richard Smith

ISSN: 1471-2083

FCO historians are responsible for editing *Documents on British Policy Overseas (DBPO)* and for overseeing the publication of FCO Internal Histories.

DBPO comprises three series of diplomatic documents, focusing on major themes in foreign policy since 1945, and drawn principally from the records of the Foreign and Commonwealth Office. The latest volumes, published in Series III, are composed almost wholly of documents from within the thirty-year 'closed period', which would otherwise be unavailable to the public.

Since the early 1960s, several Internal Histories have been prepared by former or serving officers, the majority of which concentrated upon international developments and negotiations in which the UK has been directly involved. These were initially intended for use within the FCO, but some of the more substantial among them, studies that offer fresh insights into British diplomacy, are now being declassified for publication.

Published DBPO volumes:

SERIES I: 1945-1950

Volume I: The Conference at Postdam, July-August 1945
0 11 591682 2
Volume II: Conferences and Conversations, 1945: London, Washington and Moscow
0 11 591683 0
Volume III: Britain and America: Negotiation of the US Loan, 3 August-7 December 1945
0 11 591684 9
Volume IV: Britain and America: Atomic Energy, Bases and Food, 12 December 1945-31 July 1946
0 11 591685 7
Volume V: Germany and Western Europe, 11 August-31 December 1945
0 11 591686 5
Volume VI: Eastern Europe, August 1945-April 1946
0 11 591687 3
Volume VII: The UN, Iran and the Cold War, 1946-1947
0 11 591689 X

Volume VIII: Britain and China, 1945-1950
Volume IX: The Nordic Countries in the Early Cold War, 1944-51
978-0-415-59476-9
Volume X: The Brussels and North Atlantic Treaties, 1947-1949
978-0-415-85822-9
Volume XI: European Recovery and the Search for Western Security, 1946-1948
978-1-138-18369-8

SERIES II: 1950-1960

Volume I: The Schuman Plan, the Council of Europe and Western European Integration, May 1950-December 1952
0 11 591692 X
Volume II: The London Conference: Anglo-American Relations and Cold War Strategy, January-June 1950
0 11 591693 8
Volume III: German Rearmament, September-December 1950
0 11 591694 6
Volume IV: Korea, June 1950-April 1951
0 11 591695 4

SERIES III: 1960-

Volume I: Britain and the Soviet Union, 1968-1972
0 11 591696 2
Volume II: The Conference on Security and Co-operation in Europe, 1972-1975
0 11 591697 0
Volume III: Détente in Europe, 1972-1976
0 7146 5116 8
Volume IV: The Year of Europe: America, Europe and the Energy Crisis, 1972-1974
0 415 39150 4
Volume V: The Southern Flank in Crisis, 1973-76
0 7146 5114 1
Volume VI: Berlin in the Cold War, 1948-1990
978-0-415-45532-9
Volume VII: Britain and German Unification 1989-1990
978-0-415-55002-4
Volume VIII: The Invasion of Afghanistan and UK-Soviet Relations, 1979-1982
978-0-415-67853-7
Volume IX: The Challenge of Apartheid: UK–South African Relations, 1985-1986
978-1-138-92482-6
Volume X: The Polish Crisis and Relations with Eastern Europe, 1979-1982
978-1-138-68878-0

DOCUMENTS ON BRITISH POLICY OVERSEAS

Series III, Volume X

The Polish Crisis and Relations with Eastern Europe, 1979–1982

First published 2017
by Routledge
2 Park Square, Milton Park, Abingdon, Oxon OX14 4RN

and by Routledge
711 Third Avenue, New York, NY 10017

Routledge is an imprint of the Taylor & Francis Group, an informa business

British Library Cataloguing-in-Publication Data
A catalogue record for this book is available from the British Library

Library of Congress Cataloging-in-Publication Data
A catalog record for this book has been requested

ISBN: 978-1-138-68878-0 (hbk)
ISBN: 978-1-315-19714-2 (ebk)

Typeset in Times New Roman
by Wearset Ltd, Boldon, Tyne and Wear

CONTENTS

PREFACE

This volume charts the formulation of British policy towards the countries of Eastern Europe[1] during the eventful years 1979-82. It acts as a companion to *Documents on British Policy Overseas, Series III, Volume VIII: The Invasion of Afghanistan and UK-Soviet Relations, 1979-82*. After coming to power in 1979, the Conservative Government of Margaret Thatcher reaffirmed a policy of 'differentiation' between the Soviet Union and the rest of Eastern Europe, and between individual countries; concurrently it encouraged states to exercise a limited amount of independence. This policy was soon put to the test when in 1980 *Solidarność*, the Solidarity trade union led by Lech Wałęsa, challenged the power of the Party state in Poland. Political demands, social unrest and economic crisis culminated in the imposition of martial law in December 1981, finally suspended in December 1982 when this volume ends. The volume maps the UK response, in consultation with Western partners, to the unfolding crisis in Poland, the threat of Soviet intervention and the impact on other Communist states in Europe. The volume also provides a flavour of bilateral UK relations with Albania, Bulgaria, Czechoslovakia, the German Democratic Republic (GDR), Hungary, Romania and Yugoslavia;[2] highlighting themes such as human rights and trade. The documents show policy-makers grappling with a number of dilemmas: how to support opposition to Communism without dangerously destabilising the whole region; how to promote human rights without provoking a repressive crackdown; how to promote British trade without strengthening Communist regimes; how to encourage national independence within the Communist bloc without provoking Russian intervention; how to maintain links with opponents to a regime without alienating the government; how to promote reform without seeming to interfere excessively; and finally how to maintain unity among Western Allies who held a range of views, in particular the US following the election of Ronald Reagan in 1981.

Policy of differentiation

In the immediate aftermath of the Second World War it became obvious to British policy-makers that the Soviet Union was attempting to draw the countries of Eastern Europe politically and economically into their 'sphere of influence'. The background to these events is covered in *Documents on British Policy Overseas, Series I, Volume VI: Eastern Europe August 1945-April 1946* and *Series I, Volume XI: Economic Recovery and the Search for Western Security 1946-48*. The British Government knew it had few levers to check this drift given the Soviet Union's geopolitical and military preponderance in the region. A Foreign Office memorandum of March 1946 observed: 'The best we can do is to hold the door open—or to hold enough doors open—for the East Europeans to catch frequent glimpses of a more attractive and prosperous world in the West and be encouraged, when the occasion offers, to pass through'.[3] The establishment of the Cominform

[1] We use the term current at the time, which also covered countries in Central and South Eastern Europe.

[2] All these countries were covered by the FCO's Eastern European and Soviet Department, except the GDR which was covered by the Western European Department.

[3] *DBPO: Eastern Europe*. Appendix I. Foreign Office Memorandum of 12 March 1946 on Soviet Economic Policy: Central and South Eastern Europe.

in 1947 and the Warsaw Pact in 1955 brought Eastern Europe further under the control of Moscow, although Tito's Yugoslavia and Enver Hoxha's Albania managed to retain independence of action. Soviet dominance was challenged at various intervals—most notably in Hungary in October 1956 and Czechoslovakia in Spring 1968—but ultimately suppressed by military intervention. The Soviets justified the invasion of Czechoslovakia by claiming 'socialist' countries had the right to intervene in other 'socialist' countries, by force if necessary, in order to maintain or restore 'socialism'. The 'Brezhnev doctrine', as this justification was termed, affirmed that the Soviet Union would not allow an Eastern European country to revert to a non-socialist form of government.[4] Since East European governments were unrepresentative and imposed by force on a largely unwilling population, the British Government were determined to do nothing that would encourage or strengthen these regimes, or anything that could be interpreted as approval of them. Official contacts were kept to the bare minimum. But a distinction was drawn between governments and peoples, with expressions of friendship and goodwill extended to the latter. There was no hindrance to non-governmental contacts, although nothing was done to encourage or finance them.[5]

During the 1960s the Foreign & Commonwealth Office (FCO) began to look for a less passive role towards the region. An appraisal of policy in 1968 recognised the increasing diversity amongst the countries of Eastern Europe and the fact that potential for early change was much greater than in the Soviet Union. It was decided to extend existing political bilateral contacts, but also to look in other fields—trade, technology, science and culture—for more tangible results. Increases in the number of visits would not be restricted to ministers but include parliamentarians, intellectuals, administrators, cultural leaders, business men and the youth. It concluded: 'The growth of links with Western countries could make an important contribution not only to the evolution of the eastern European countries but, in the longer run, may well influence the policies of the Soviet Union itself both in Europe and in the rest of the world.'[6] This policy of pursuing better relations and closer contacts continued into the 1970s.[7] However, the economic and political troubles resulting from the energy crisis of 1973-5 threatened to check economic growth in Western Europe. The FCO thought that a consequence might be a diminution of Western influence in the Soviet satellites. The 'magnetic attraction' which Western Europe had exercised upon the countries of the East would no longer be reinforced by a rise in material prosperity as rapid as that of the previous decades; and it was possible that 'economic depression and its social repercussions might dim the lustre of Western Europe while increasing the economic dependence of Eastern Europe on the Soviet Union'.[8]

The Helsinki Final Act of 1975, the culmination of the Conference on Security and Co-operation in Europe (CSCE), effectively acknowledged the *status quo* in Europe by guaranteeing the inviolability of frontiers and non-interference in the internal affairs of states. But at the same time the West obtained commitments

[4] See *DBPO: Soviet Union, 1968-1972*, No. 62.

[5] Foreign Office memorandum: 'Special Conditions applying to contacts with the Satellites', 10 October 1956; FO 371/122073/N1026/7.

[6] *DBPO: Soviet Union, 1968-1972*, No. 11: 'Memorandum by the Secretary of State for Foreign Affairs on Relations with the Soviet Union and Eastern Europe', 17 June 1968.

[7] See *DBPO: Soviet Union, 1968-1972*, No. 89: 'Memorandum by Sir A. Douglas-Home on policy towards the Soviet Union and Eastern Europe', 29 February 1972.

[8] *DBPO: Détente*, No. 54: 'Planning Paper on Future Policy towards Eastern Europe by the Foreign and Commonwealth Office', 12 February 1974.

from the Soviet Union relating to respect for human rights, expansion of contacts between Eastern and Western Europe, freedom of travel, cultural exchanges and freedom of the press. The hope was to widen the channels through which Western ideas and objective information could reach the citizens of the Soviet Union and Eastern Europe.[9] A reduction in jamming of Western broadcasts, for instance, gave greater scope for BBC operations directed towards Eastern Europe. Whilst accepting that change might take a generation to occur, the Government was keen to use the CSCE Final Act to induce it. Foreign Secretary James Callaghan reasoned that the more links of all kinds—economic, cultural and human—that could be developed between Eastern and Western Europe, the more difficult it would become for the Soviet Union abruptly to sever them should they move away from détente. In addition, using the individual, national aspirations of the East European countries gradually to enlarge the area within which they could assert separate identities would make it harder for the Soviet Union 'to treat the countries of Eastern Europe as a drill squad'.[10]

Successive US administrations also followed a policy of differentiation between Eastern European countries. US President Jimmy Carter reaffirmed this policy in a Presidential Directive in September 1977 which stated that the United States would 'demonstrably show its preference for Eastern European countries that were either relatively liberal internally or relatively independent internationally'. Poland and Romania were to continue to receive preferential treatment, and relations with Hungary were to be improved. Meanwhile relations between the United States and Bulgaria, Czechoslovakia and the GDR were to remain limited.[11]

In 1979 the new Conservative Government was keen to reassess existing UK policy towards the Soviet bloc. Domestic political difficulties during the premiership of James Callaghan (1976-79) meant that Ministers had been unable to travel as extensively as they might have wished, particularly in Eastern Europe, whilst the Conservatives in opposition had often accused the Labour government of taking a too benign view of the Soviet Union. The present volume opens with an assessment of the concept of 'differentiation' between countries by Richard Parsons, Ambassador in Budapest, in advance of the October 1979 Heads of Mission Conference on the Soviet Union and Eastern Europe. He noted that governments of the Warsaw Pact were 'totalitarian and dominated by Marxists collaborating with the Soviet Union and essentially opposed to Western aims'. Yet he argued that 'each country has its own history and national aspirations' and that 'our aim should be to weaken the Soviet grip on Eastern Europe by encouraging existing centrifugal movement' without destabilising the region (No. 1). The October Heads of Mission Conference outlined the major themes of UK policy towards Eastern Europe (No. 2). Peter Blaker, Minister of State for Foreign and Commonwealth Affairs, declared that 'our major political goal in Eastern Europe was to encourage the states of the area to exercise the limited amount of independence they could achieve' as well as seizing trade opportunities. All ambassadors wanted closer UK relations with their respective countries to be encouraged. However, they differed on the potential impact of religious and human

[9] For the negotiation of the Act see *DBPO: CSCE*.

[10] *DBPO: Détente*: No. 87, Mr. Callaghan to Sir H. Smith (Moscow) 'The Conference of HM Ambassadors in the Soviet Union and Eastern Europe, 17-19 November 1975', 11 March 1976.

[11] *Foreign Relations of the United States*, 1977–1980, Volume XX, Eastern Europe, 1977–1980, eds. Carl Ashley and Mircea A. Munteanu (Washington: Government Printing Office, 2015), Document 16: PD/NSC–21 'Policy Towards Eastern Europe', 13 September 1977.

rights groups, as some thought it might push the Soviet Union to tighten its grip. Peter Male, Ambassador in Prague, was in favour of denouncing repression privately at the highest level. Peter Foster, Ambassador in East Berlin, doubted that this would be effective, and favoured publicising through the media repressive measures of Eastern European governments, as they were conscious of their image abroad. Kenneth Pridham, Ambassador in Warsaw, commented that in Poland it was the Roman Catholic Church—more than dissidents—who exercised influence.

On 7 December 1979, differentiation was restated by the Foreign Secretary, Lord Carrington, as official UK policy in a despatch on 'British Policy in East-West Relations' which noted: 'A major purpose is to do what we can to undermine Soviet power by encouraging the existing tendencies towards diversity within the Warsaw Pact, tendencies exemplified by Romania's foreign policy, Hungary's new economic mechanism and Poland's particular brand of pluralism'. Contacts and trade were to be two principal levers in achieving this aim. Contacts would enable the UK to learn more about those countries, to explain its own policies to the East, to broker trade deals and explore shared interests. It went on, 'We have no interest in provoking a crisis in the area, which would again be ended by invasion if the Russians thought it necessary. But the East European countries are generally the best judges of what contacts with the West are safe for them to take'.[12] The policy withstood an early test—the Soviet invasion of Afghanistan in December 1979.[13] Lord Carrington affirmed that a distinction between the USSR and Eastern Europe should be made, so as to avoid associating the latter with this Soviet act of aggression. Normal contacts and exchanges were to be maintained as a means of encouraging independence and diversity. Ambassadors in Budapest, Warsaw, Sofia and especially Bucharest were instructed to indicate 'that we recognise that the countries concerned have not toed the Soviet line' and to try to foster their concerns about the implications, 'in the hope of encouraging them to use helpfully any influence they may have in Moscow' (No. 4).

Poland

The country the British Government was most keen to discriminate in favour of was Poland. Not only had it periodically displayed its discontent with one-Party Communism but there were strong links between both countries. There was a large Polish community in the UK and memories of fighting together during the Second World War. There were also good trade links, worth nearly £300 million a year, with a balance in the UK's favour. By the end of 1979 the country was showing signs of discontent. A difficult economic situation and food shortages brought widespread unrest. Mr Pridham believed that 'sparks' were possible but less so a conflagration or a change of leadership (No. 3). From the beginning of July 1980, a crisis developed in two phases: the first centred on economic demands by strikers across the country and the second centred on political strikes in the Lenin Shipyard in Gdańsk. On 14 August, it climaxed with 16,000 workers stopping work at the shipyard and presenting economic and political demands. On 31 August the Government and the strikers at Gdańsk and Szczecin signed epoch-making agreements, which the Warsaw embassy interpreted as huge concessions made in writing and publicly: in effect they recognised the right to strike and to establish free trade unions. The agreements also covered relaxation of censorship, release of

[12] See *DBPO: Afghanistan*: No. 1.
[13] See *DBPO: Afghanistan*.

political detainees, and better access to the media for the Church. Mr Pridham commented that the new trade unions 'can hardly fail to become a force in the country parallel to the Party/Government and the Church'. He suggested that the regime's best hope was to learn to accept the situation and offer some genuine power-sharing (No. 19). In a despatch to Lord Carrington, he summed up: 'Poland will never be the same again . . . boundaries which Gierek said were uncrossable have been crossed' (No. 21, note 2).

President Carter considered that the best outcome would be accommodation between the authorities and the Polish people leading to a more liberal and democratic system. He thought that the West was right to express sympathy for Polish efforts to reform and urge restraint, and also to stress that the matter was for the Poles to decide without foreign interference (No. 23, note 2). Similarly, on 3 September, Lord Carrington instructed posts 'to regard events in Poland as a strictly internal Polish matter to be settled by the Polish authorities and people themselves' (No. 21). This remained the Government's line throughout. Mrs Thatcher wrote to President Carter that 'the concessions . . . are of enormous potential consequence, not only for Poland itself but for Eastern Europe as a whole' and reaffirmed the UK's policy of a 'careful and restrained attitude in public' (No. 23).

The summer of unrest was followed by further demands, as predicted in the FCO, in particular for the registration of Solidarity, which was agreed by the Supreme Court on 10 November. The British Embassy reported that Solidarity enjoyed widespread support. David Joy, Counsellor, commented: 'the average man (or woman) in the *Gdańsk* omnibus certainly sees Solidarity as a panacea for accumulated woes and frustrations. It seems at least doubtful whether even Russian tanks could reverse this' (No. 36, note 8). In December Mrs Thatcher spoke to the Polish Deputy Prime Minister, on a visit to London, of 'a change of a kind that had not occurred in a socialist state in the last 60 years'. She said that the socialist system had succeeded in suppressing the human spirit for a surprisingly long time but that she had always been confident that eventually there would be a break through (No. 41).

January 1981 saw further tensions, with Solidarity threatening widespread strikes to ensure the Gdańsk agreements were implemented. In February, the Polish Prime Minister, Józef Pińkowski, resigned after five months and was replaced by the Defence Minister, General Wojciech Jaruzelski. Mr Pridham recommended to the Foreign Secretary that Britain should encourage moderation, including on the part of Solidarity. He advised that the West—especially the incoming President Reagan who had praised Solidarity—should make clear that 'while we have the greatest sympathy with the aspirations of the Polish people, if Poland is to be saved they must have regard to political reality and not seek to do everything at once' (No. 47). The Cabinet discussed the situation several times in January and February and adopted a cautious stance. The Prime Minister congratulated General Jaruzelski on his appointment (No. 49). In July 1981 the new Ambassador, Kenneth James, commented on the success and popularity of Jaruzelski, 'a stiff, buttoned-up but respected figure, who is becoming the guardian of Poland's national spirit' (No. 71).

Nevertheless, the 'sparks' predicted by Mr Pridham in October 1979 regularly threatened to set fire to the political landscape. A turning point was the Bydgoszcz episode in March 1981, where farmers demanded the legalisation of rural Solidarity. The protest was violently repressed, which led to the threat of a general strike (No. 53). The summer and autumn of 1981 saw further unrest and strikes, and Mr James reported to Lord Carrington that talks between the Government and an intransigent Solidarity had broken down: the 'Government had its back to the wall' (No. 73). Mr James hoped that the forces of moderation, especially the Church, would encourage dialogue. In September 1981 the Solidarity Congress in Gdańsk demanded the implementation of the August 1980 agreements. They looked forward to the elimination of poverty, exploitation, fear and lies; better food supplies; genuine workers self-management; free elections to the Sejm and people's councils; equality before the law; and the release of political prisoners (No. 77 & 79). The Congress adopted an uncompromising programme—Solidarity becoming a '*de facto* opposition' (No. 87, note 5)—and elected Mr Wałęsa as leader—a 'living legend' as Mr James put it (No. 91). Mr James's analysis was that 'Solidarity is not a trade union. It is a political and social force on a national scale'. On 15 September, Lord Carrington told the Cabinet that Solidarity appeared to have gone 'considerably further than previously' (No. 79, note 5). General Jaruzelski replaced Stanisław Kania as First Secretary of the Central Committee of the Polish United Workers' Party on 18 October 1981. Mr James dispelled as misleading 'the idea that he is a soldier's soldier'. He considered him as a party man, but argued that 'no-one seems to doubt that he is essentially a moderate man who wishes to avoid the use of force' (No. 93). Yet the fear of a state of emergency was never far from Mr James's mind, and at the end of October he posed the question directly to Józef Czyrek, the Polish Foreign Minister, who replied that it would depend on 'the sense of realism of Solidarity' (No. 94). Following a strong reaction by the authorities to end a Fire School strike in Radom, Solidarity issued a statement on 3 December, which for the first time demanded democratic elections to People's Councils at all levels and therefore a change of the system (No. 111). Indeed Mr Czyrek retrospectively told Mr James that Martial Law should not have come as a complete surprise as it was clear after the demands made by Solidarity at Radom and Gdańsk that, in his view, 'Solidarity was leading Poland to anarchy, economic breakdown and destabilisation' (No. 149).

Aid for Poland

At the start of the 1980s economies in Eastern Europe were faltering with slow growth, a decline in living standards and an increase in foreign indebtedness. Many were dependent on continued access to Western capital (No. 67) and there was no longer any confidence that the Soviet Union would act a lender of last resort (No. 55). Julian Bullard, Deputy Under-Secretary for Europe at the FCO, drew up a list of five, now defunct, 'illusions' that had been held in the 1970s about the development of East-West trade: (i) the belief that economic growth in Western and Eastern Europe would always continue; (ii) that Western banks would always be willing to lend money to finance East-West trade; (iii) that Western governments/tax payers would always be willing to subsidise credit for East-West trade; (iv) that governments in Eastern Europe could be trusted to judge what was a safe level of borrowing; (v) that if ever they miscalculated, the Soviet Union would put up an umbrella to minimise the consequences (No. 101).

Poland was one of the most heavily exposed countries. With a hard currency debt of $22 billion in 1980 and rising, Poland needed to reschedule its debt and access external credits to stay afloat until the economy recovered. However the chances of recovery were hampered by industrial unrest. The UK Treasury wished to limit the further expansion of officially guaranteed credits and wanted any requests for refinancing to be handled multilaterally. There was also a desire not to see UK economic assistance going towards shoring up an unreformed system. Against this the FCO set the political arguments in favour of maintaining at least a certain level of credits for Poland: good bilateral relations; the value of Poland as an export market in the longer term; Western interest in Poland's stability and the maintenance of a degree of independence from the USSR (Nos. 15, 31, 46). In April 1981 the Government did agree to a package of economic aid, including debt relief and new credits (No. 57) but this was soon followed by a request from the Polish Government for a further loan of $500m from the West. As the Polish economy worsened and the Government struggled to contain the socio-economic forces unleashed by Solidarity it became harder for the FCO to argue for further support. The Bank of England did not believe that additional Western assistance could bring the Polish economy round within a reasonable time and argued that it would only create dangerous precedents for dealing with other bankrupt countries (No. 65). Lord Carrington pushed his international partners for a political and economic assessment, covering both what the West might be able to do to put the Polish economy back on the right track and the consequences of doing or not doing so, but the results failed to move the argument on (Nos. 72, 75). In September 1981 he discussed the situation with Mr Czyrek in New York, and told him frankly that the indications of economic help required by Poland in the longer term were more and more alarming: 'If things went on in that way the West might not have the capacity to help' (No. 83).

Lord Carrington continued to argue in the Oversea and Defence Committee that *Odnowa*—the Polish Renewal inaugurated by the strikes of August 1980—represented the most serious challenge the Soviets had faced in their East European empire: 'By helping Poland at this juncture we shall be doing what lies in our power to secure a political shift in Europe of lasting benefit to ourselves and to the West' (No. 99). Support came from other quarters. The TUC's General Secretary wrote to Mrs Thatcher in November 1981 arguing that it would be in the UK's and EC's interests to provide food aid—to be distributed by Solidarity—to avoid massive unrest, and invited the Prime Minister to give the lead at the forthcoming European Council (Nos. 105, 108). However the imposition of martial law in December 1981 changed the situation and whilst arguments were made for humanitarian assistance, further credits were withheld (No. 146).

Contagion

Events in Poland prompted much analysis regarding potential 'contagion' to the rest of Eastern Europe. There were some differences of opinion in the FCO. In December 1980 Gloria Franklin, from the Planning Staff, foresaw the 'infection' spreading quickly, especially if Poland succeeded in its peaceful evolution. She concluded that the UK should continue to encourage the East Europeans to 'move slowly and quietly, and preferably in harness with one another. The quickest way out for them is for the Russians to be beleaguered on so many fronts that they simply give up and go home. That I believe will happen soon, but they will go with a whimper rather than a bang' (No. 43). But the prevailing feeling was that the contagion was unlikely to spread quickly or simultaneously. Historical references to previous crises in Eastern Europe were often made. In April 1981 Mr Foster observed that 'the build-up of tensions in different countries has never synchronised: 1953 East Berlin, 1956 Hungary, 1968 Czechoslovakia, 1980/81 Poland and so on' (No. 58).

In September 1981 the Solidarity Congress in Gdańsk sent a defiant message to East European workers—effectively inviting them to support the first post-war independent trade union movement. Ramsay Melhuish, Counsellor in Warsaw, asked rhetorically: 'if Solidarity can get away with it in Poland, why should there not be free trade unions elsewhere?' (No. 80, editorial note). By October 1981 the FCO's overall assessment was that the immediate risk of contagion seemed small. But with time and a little economic success, 'the Polish heresy might exert a powerful attraction for its neighbours' (No. 89). A Planning Staff paper of November 1981, examining the crisis in Eastern Europe, thought few regimes in the region could afford to be entirely confident about the future. The most vulnerable country was thought to be Romania, where Polish events coincided with an indigenous economic crisis and where the repressive regime had engendered increasing resentment. In Hungary, there was some possibility that liberalising trends could lead to increased popular demand for change. And although the GDR was comparatively well managed, it was very difficult for the regime to appeal to nationalism, and the attractions of West German life made the authorities anxious. In Czechoslovakia, with its strong syndicalist tradition and widespread corruption, a responsive chord could be struck by Solidarity's success in defending the interests of the workers and removing corrupt officials. Bulgaria seemed relatively quiescent (No. 102). In early December 1981, just before martial law was declared, the Joint Intelligence Committee (JIC) reported that in spite of the dissimilarities between Poland and their own countries, East European leaders reacted with varying degrees of alarm to events there. In the short term, the impact of Polish developments had been relatively slight and had even antagonized public opinion in parts of Eastern Europe, aggravating historic antipathies. The JIC gauged that Polish developments did not appear to have stimulated dissident activities in Eastern Europe or affected the handling by regimes of the dissident problem (No. 107).

Possible Soviet intervention

With memories of the invasion of Afghanistan still fresh, the attitude of the Soviet Union was uppermost in many minds. Sir Curtis Keeble, Ambassador in Moscow, thought that Poland, however intractable, was an essential element in Soviet defence policy and vital for dominance of Eastern Europe as a whole. It thus followed that the Soviet leadership would want to see the rot stopped and he predicted 'rough politics between Moscow and Warsaw in which Soviet threats, intrigue and persuasion will be directed to limiting the damage' (No. 22). The big question was whether the Soviet Union would invade Poland to defend the *status quo* and what could the West do to prevent this. President Carter was clear that Soviet military intervention would be a development of the utmost gravity, striking at the root of détente and creating an entirely new situation in East-West and international relations (No. 30). The view of the British Government was that the Poles should be left to sort out their own problems without any external interference. But although both public and private warnings against intervention were made to Moscow, there was a sense in the FCO that Western policy consisted of not much more than waiting upon events and hoping for the best. The FCO explored a short-lived suggestion that 'back-channels' to Moscow be opened to minimise the international consequences (No. 38). Some discussion took place within the FCO as to whether the UK had a common interest in ensuring stability in Eastern Europe and whether a Soviet invasion was preferable to Polish volatility threatening the security of Europe (No. 37). Mr Pridham worried about the section of Polish opinion that wanted a World War III to rescue Poland (No. 47).

The Western Alliance began to work out a catalogue of measures to be taken in the event of an outright Soviet invasion of Poland (No. 42). The possibility of an embargo on exports to the Soviet Union brought the FCO into conflict with the Treasury and the Department of Trade (Nos. 51, 60). The FCO were wary of the more hard-line economic sanctions proposed by the US and the consequences it might have on Alliance relations (No. 68). Concern remained throughout 1982 as the Polish Government failed to deal decisively with Solidarity. The FCO continued to consider potential constraints the West could use to deter the Soviets: from renewed dialogue with the Americans, to a visit by Mrs Thatcher to Poland (No. 63). But Sir Curtis Keeble believed that the Soviet authorities were profoundly reluctant to intervene: 'I think that they may well be looking to a time when growing economic misery and despair may make a 'strong' solution more possible' (No. 89).

The imposition of martial law

Fears of a State crackdown against Solidarity grew at the beginning of December 1981. Mr James noted an escalation in General Jaruzelski's description of the situation from 'worsening' to 'critical' on 9-10 December (No. 111). In the early hours of Sunday 13 December martial law was declared, troops were deployed in the streets of Warsaw and other major towns, and Solidarity leaders were arrested. The new Military Council of National Salvation suspended many civil liberties, banned trade unions and dissolved the Sejm. The Embassy provided lively reporting of events but found it difficult to obtain information from the provinces as telephone and telex facilities had been cut. Inopportunely, Mr James was hospitalised during this period following a heart attack, but Mr Melhuish rose to the occasion providing vivid reports (No. 112). He recommended a change of policy from that of non-interference to 'vigorous denunciation' of the 'deliberate and callous suppression' (No. 119, note 2). The Embassy predicted that the state of emergency would go on for weeks, unless the situation worsened even further and the Soviet Union intervened. For some time the whereabouts of Mr Wałęsa were uncertain. Mr James reported that access to him had been difficult, including for his wife and his priest (No. 160). At least 5,000 people had been interned but it soon became clear that Solidarity had survived underground and the Embassy was therefore sceptical that there had been a return to work in mines, shipyards and factories as the Polish authorities had declared. In mid-January 1982, Lord Carrington formulated a damning indictment: 'Thirty six years of communist government have led to martial law, internment camps, special courts, food shortages, economic bankruptcy, and a political dead end. The socialist system has been shown to be a political and economic failure' (No. 133).

The response of the West

Martial law sparked an intense debate amongst members of the Western Alliance over how best to respond. The UK's immediate reaction was to express concern at the suspension of civil liberties and the imprisonment of trade unionists, but to avoid acting in a way which might inflame the situation further. It was hoped that the crisis would be kept under control, that Poland would solve its own problems without outside interference, and that the democratic gains of the last 17 months would not be permanently lost even if they were temporarily halted or reversed (No. 119). The initial response from the European Community was perceived by some as weak and a strong speech by Lord Carrington to the European Parliament in Strasbourg helped secure a tougher condemnation on 17 December (No. 117). The UK was also called to play a key role as president of the European Council and subsequently made a démarche to Warsaw on behalf of the Ten.

The administration of US President Ronald Reagan, armed with intelligence which they said proved that martial law had been caused by Soviet pressure, advocated a hard line that included sanctions against both Poland and the Soviet Union (Nos. 116, 124, 125). But the UK read the situation differently. Mrs Thatcher and Lord Carrington thought the US had overreacted and was 'playing the sanctions card' too soon (Nos. 118, 125). In a letter to President Reagan, sent on 22 December, the Prime Minister merely noted the difficult situation and the need for a clear and united response from the West. At the UN, Sir Anthony Parsons, UK Permanent Representative, advised the US delegation against taking the issue to the Security Council and believed that the Americans were in danger of making a mess of the question 'out of their desire to demonstrate instant activity' (No. 120). Lord Carrington thought that the Americans were focused more on East-West relations than on Poland, which had become a pawn in the wider US-Soviet relationship (Nos. 121, 125). Whilst the US pressed for immediate action others, such as the French, dragged their feet. Their loud criticism of Moscow was not followed by action and they made difficulties over Lord Carrington's attempts to arrange a meeting of EC Foreign Ministers, much to his and Mrs Thatcher's annoyance (No. 123). The FRG were also reluctant to react too strongly (No. 134). However an EC meeting on 4 January and a meeting of NATO Foreign Ministers on 11 January 1982 did much to bring US and European reactions into line. There was general agreement on three objectives—the ending of martial law, the release of detainees, and the renewal of dialogue between the State, Church and Solidarity—and on the Soviet Union's complicity (Nos. 127, 133). The Soviet Ambassador was subsequently summoned to the FCO to explain why they were jamming the BBC's Polish broadcasts (No. 129).

The British Government's strategy within NATO was to concentrate on the real crisis in Poland rather than letting itself be diverted by differences among partners (No. 130). They were willing to impose measures on Poland and the Soviet Union, to satisfy the US, which signalled displeasure without necessarily doing great harm to British interests (Nos. 131, 137, 142). Economic sanctions were considered by David Manning of the Eastern European and Soviet Department (EESD) as 'the one really effective weapon in the Western armoury' and the best way of forcing Jaruzelski to accept a measure of reform in Poland and forcing the Soviet system to bear the whole economic burden of the crisis. But in Warsaw Mr Melhuish warned that they would cause hardship to the Polish people, and that the authorities would attempt to blame Western governments. He also argued that it would increase Poland's economic and political dependence on the USSR (No. 132, note 3). In reality the measures the UK introduced (Lord Carrington preferred to use the term 'measures' as 'sanctions' was too loaded) were as much about maintaining Alliance cohesion as they were about trying to influence Poland or the USSR (No. 133). Transatlantic discord threatened to return in October 1981 when the Polish Government introduced new trade union legislation banning Solidarity. The FCO anticipated the 'risk of emotion taking over in the American camp' and the UK

Permanent Representative to NATO was instructed to maintain Alliance solidarity and ensure that any national or joint action by NATO governments in response to events was taken 'on a rational basis and related to considered objectives' (No. 182).

Taking stock

A month after martial law, the time had come to take stock. Between January and March 1982 Mr Melhuish provided a retrospective assessment in four dramatically titled despatches: 'The Gathering Storm'; 'Rise and Fall of Solidarity'; 'Darkness and Silence'; and 'After the War' (Nos. 138, 140, 144 and 147). In 'Darkness and Silence' (16 February), he gave a lively account of the first fortnight of martial law with its 'clinically efficient imposition' which stunned the population for a day or two and was followed by a uncoordinated wave of sit-in strikes which were crushed ruthlessly. By the time he wrote the despatch, he detected 'a false calm' hiding underlying tensions. Workers, even if not officially on strike, did minimum work resulting in a 30-40% drop in productivity. Localised sit-in strikes continued—including in the Lenin shipyard in Gdańsk. Rumours of deaths circulated, which the authorities did not admit. Mr Melhuish reported that Solidarity had gone underground. He concluded that 'in the absence of a constructive solution to the crucial problem of what political structure comes next in Poland, I believe that martial law is likely to remain in force here for a long time' (No. 144). He thought that Solidarity shared some responsibility for martial law: the trade union had won so many concessions that some elements indulged in 'over-confidence' and Mr Wałęsa had lost control over extremists. The foundation of KOR (the Committee for the Defence of the Workers) in 1976 had changed the character of the unrest centred in Gdańsk. For the first time in the history of the Polish protest movement, 'the brawn of industrial muscle was allied to the guile of experienced anti-government dissenters'. In addition, Mr Wałęsa displayed an unaffected piety which epitomised the union's close association with the Polish Church.

In what Mr Melhuish described as a second phase, from the events at Bydgoszcz in April 1981 to the end of the first Solidarity Congress in September, Solidarity had become more politicised and clashed with the Government over the control of the economy. The grass roots had increasingly supported radicals, who dominated the Congress. Yet although Mr Wałęsa had been weakened, there was no real challenger for the presidency. Solidarity had transformed itself from 'an amorphous, sprawling, ill-organised and often bickering movement' into an organised political movement. In this second despatch, Mr Melhuish asserted that ultimately the aims of Solidarity were irreconcilable with the political requirements of the Polish Government and the ideological concepts of the Communist Party. It demanded a pluralist democratic framework with secret voting and an unlimited list of candidates to replace the existing totalitarian system. This had taken Poland further away from the path of orthodox Communism than any other Eastern European country, as Solidarity made clear in a confident slogan: 'the winter may be theirs; the summer will be ours' (No. 140). The Communist Party—divided and disoriented—found itself paralysed, unable to adopt a position in favour of or against *Odnowa*. Solidarity had managed to infiltrate the Party locally, making it 'not so much the natural opposition to Solidarity as a vehicle for it' (No. 138).

In the fourth and concluding despatch, which looked at the likely strategy of the Polish leadership, Mr Melhuish assumed that General Jaruzelski would retain supreme power at least until the end of 1982. He commented that 'whether from Western or Polish (or indeed Soviet) points of view, little comfort could be derived if Jaruzelski fell from power'. He portrayed Jaruzelski as a general at heart who intended to permit no active opposition and was likely to keep Poland quiet with 'his road blocks, his curfew and his military courts' He concluded: 'The Polish crisis may yet surprise us all by how long it is going to last' (No. 147).

As for the Church, the UK had always recognised its importance as 'the undying symbol of Poland, past and future. The churches are full. Any visitor to Poland notices this immediately he goes for a walk on a Sunday morning' (No. 95). During the difficult months over the summer of 1981, after Cardinal Wyszyński's death on 28 May and his replacement by Archbishop Glemp in July, an assessment was carried out both by EESD and by the Embassy. Alan Montgomery of the EESD commented in August that although Archbishop Glemp might not equal Cardinal Wyszyński's stature, if he proved more flexible it might not necessarily be a bad thing (No. 76). After the election of Mr Wałęsa as president of Solidarity, Mr James commented: 'The Church see Wałęsa's victory as immensely important. They believe it is a guarantee that Solidarity will stay on a moderate course and not be over-political' (No. 91). On 27 February 1982, the Church took a bold step in publicising a hard-hitting document, 'Social Agreement', which contained a formidable list of criticisms of the Government and martial law. It called for dialogue between the authorities and the Church, the reactivation of Solidarity on an apolitical basis, the release of internees, an amnesty for those convicted for non-criminal acts, permission for the Catholic press to resume its activities and separate elections for local councils. The document warned of 'the great and deepening chasm between society and the authorities'. In a guidance telegram in April 1982, the FCO acknowledged that 'The Church in recent weeks has taken an increasingly militant stand in condemning martial law and the infringement of human rights. It continues however to urge its followers against violence and confrontation and the authorities no doubt assess that the Church will remain a moderating force whose support may be enlisted' (No. 153). And the Pope remained one of the key figures on the Polish scene, especially as he was due to visit in the summer of 1982—a visit eventually postponed.

The reappraisal of policy towards Poland and the end of martial law

At the end of January 1982, once the immediate crisis had passed, the FCO Planning Staff concluded that a return to *Odnowa* was highly unlikely. The West's objectives were now varied and included the continuation of reform 'which will carry with it the hope of gradual reform in other Eastern European countries', the continued cohesion of the Western Alliance, and taking sufficiently strong action towards Poland and the Soviet Union to deter Soviet expansionism (No. 139). By May 1982 none of the three Western conditions laid down for the restoration of normal relations with Poland had been met and Mr James wondered whether the policy needed revising in the face of reality (No. 157). Nevertheless, in July 1982 Sir Anthony Acland, Permanent Under-Secretary at the FCO, reiterated to the Polish Ambassador the British hope for a lifting of martial law, and told him that: 'Poland was the keystone to East-West relations. Events there had thrown a shadow over the totality of our relationships' (No.167). However, on 31 August there was a new wave of unrest. The Embassy reported rioting in Warsaw, which the authorities were ready to repress with tear gas and water cannons. Next to the Embassy, where Solidarity had its headquarters, there were 'internal security troops with fixed bayonets (fixed on the spot under our noses) . . . [and] several armoured personnel carriers just around the corner' (No. 172).

The new Foreign Secretary Francis Pym, who succeeded Lord Carrington after the latter's resignation in April 1982 over the Falklands War (No. 152), met officials in September to discuss policy in Poland. They decided that they should think in terms of a graduated response to any improvement that might occur in Poland rather than no change until all three conditions were fulfilled (No. 174). The outlawing of Solidarity in October and the resulting strikes violently repressed in Gdańsk further added to the impression that the three criteria were redundant. Nigel Broomfield, Head of EESD, argued to the Political Director at the FCO that Western pressure would never succeed in turning a one-party state into a pluralist democracy and argued for the adoption of a long-term policy aimed at evolutionary, not revolutionary, change. But he also recognised that to drop any mention of Solidarity would be seen as an act of political betrayal (No. 184). In October 1982 the UK Permanent Representative to NATO was instructed to explore the possibility of the Alliance taking a fresh look at policy towards Poland. But many in NATO showed caution about changing Allied policies or public positions (Nos. 182, 184, note 4). In discussions at the Quai d'Orsay the French scoffed at the prospect of the West attempting to lift sanctions without losing face a year after imposing them 'in righteous indignation' (No. 188). A further opportunity for change came with the decision to release Mr Wałęsa in November 1982 and to suspend martial law from 31 December 1982. But in the end, after what had been a bruising year for Alliance relations over the fate of European involvement in the Siberian gas pipeline project,[14] Mr Pym decided the overriding aim must be to maintain Alliance unity. The actions of the Polish authorities were to be judged by their practical effects and until these assessments were complete there could be no question of lifting measures which would only send the wrong sort of signal to both the Soviets and the Poles (No. 194).

Other countries

A common theme in reporting by British diplomats was how the peoples of Eastern Europe were attracted by the bright lights of the West, in contrast to the drab monotony of their own countries. Chronic shortages of food and other material goods were apparent, vividly illustrated by several documents. One, entitled 'Ceaușescu goes to market', recounts a visit by the Romanian leader to food markets in Bucharest, 'to show official receptivity, concern for living standards and for the wishes and convenience of the people in the wake of Poland'. In a country where the standard of living was one of the lowest in Eastern Europe, the Romanian Communist Party's newspaper reported 'without apparent conscious humour' according to the Embassy: 'this morning, Obor market received large quantities of meat, meat products, milk, cheeses, fruit and vegetables' (No. 25). Bryan Cartledge, Ambassador in Budapest, on a visit to Prague contrasted Czechoslovakia's relative success in exporting while shops were painfully empty. 'The pyramids of tinned fish in many shop windows, through the chinks of which one could discern empty shelves behind, were reminiscent of Moscow' (No. 173). Mr James described a typical day for a Polish woman, who spent an average of

[14] For the pipeline problem see *DBPO: Afghanistan*: Nos. 124, 126, 127, 129, 165.

four to five hours shopping, and concluded that there existed 'a cultural brain drain born of the frustrations of life here' (No. 95).

Diplomats also reported how the people of Eastern Europe craved Western books, magazines and films. They observed the creation of a generation gap, with potential implications for Communist parties who failed to sell Communism to their increasingly alienated youth. In July 1982, the Embassy in Sofia highlighted a series of press articles attacking discotheques as 'meeting places for feckless lay-abouts' who were 'unable or unwilling to do a decent day's work, who were happier to spend their afternoons drinking and gossiping, with Bony M blaring in the background' rather than building 'real socialism in Bulgaria' (No. 163). Within this prevailing drabness, Eastern European countries had some significant differences which affected the attitudes of British policy-makers towards them. The main issue regarding Yugoslavia was its diplomatic independence; for Hungary, its economy; for Romania, its foreign policy; for Czechoslovakia, its dissidents. The more orthodox regimes of the GDR, Bulgaria and Albania constituted a pretty impenetrable area and so bilateral relations were low key or non-existent.

Yugoslavia

Yugoslavia had benefited from special treatment on the part of the UK on account of its break from the Soviet Union after the Second World War. But Marshal Tito's fading health meant uncertain times for Yugoslavia and many feared the break-up of the country, opening the way for Soviet intervention. On the eve of Tito's death, in April 1980, the outgoing Ambassador, Robert Farquharson, reflected that bilateral relations were good—based on relations with the Partisans during the war: 'With Tito, this will pass into legend, and remain valuable.' But the UK had to find a continuing steady way to express its interest and influence: 'It is expected and will be valued' (No. 7). A month later the new Ambassador, Sir Edwin Bolland, attended Tito's funeral. He thought that beneath the unity of national mourning the country faced serious economic problems, latent national differences and the challenge of maintaining an independent foreign policy: 'A friendly, helpful, but not interfering West could help them in this daunting task' (No. 10). Mrs Thatcher gave new impetus to relations by making the first ever visit by a British Prime Minister to Yugoslavia in September 1980 (No. 28). Demonstrations and disorder in Kosovo in April 1981 highlighted an intractable problem in Yugoslavia's multi-national society. Bolland reported that it was the classic situation of the irresistible force of nationalism meeting the immovable object of official policy and wrote that: 'Something, somewhere has to give: Yugoslavia's problem is to decide what'. The underlying problem of Albanian nationalism in Kosovo was one to which there was no easy solution (No. 59).

The other challenge to Yugoslavia's stability was its difficult economic situation. Poor financial judgement and mistakes in the 1970s had left the country with too great a reliance on foreign credits. Now creditors had to be paid at a time when high interest rates and a world recession made it more difficult for Yugoslavia to meet its obligations (No. 64). As in Poland economic reform needed time and support from the West: the acceptance of more Yugoslav exports and the provision of credits to help meet the heavy repayments and to pay for essential imports. But as Mr Broomfield noted: 'The Yugoslavs have chosen a bad time to go broke.' There were 'severe constraints' upon what the UK could do materially to help as the problems in Poland and Romania and the Hungarian liquidity crisis had 'soured Western attitudes and created a much chillier climate than the Yugoslavs either expected or deserved to meet with in the West' (No. 179, note 5). In his valedictory despatch of October 1982 Sir Edwin Bolland posed the question whether it was still in Britain's interest to continue to support Yugoslavia as it advanced along 'Tito's path'. He reflected that Yugoslavia certainly remained Communist and, even in its modified form, stopped well short of Western systems. But by refusing to accept Moscow's diktat, Yugoslavia had made, and continued to make an important contribution to weakening the Soviet Union as a world force. He believed it was still in the UK's interest to strengthen links and help it remain stable, united and independent, even under a Communist government: 'In the East-West confrontation, which remains the most serious threat to world peace and freedom, Yugoslavia is essentially on our side' (No. 179).

Hungary

Hungary was one of the countries with which the UK was most eager to engage. This was on account of Hungarian economic reforms of the late 1960s—the New Economic Mechanism—which had proved successful in decentralising economic decision-making and freeing prices from central control. Whilst the Hungarian authorities could still take a tough line against dissidents (No. 193) and adopted a Soviet world view (No. 32, note 3) their economic experiments verged on the free market economy. It was a style of freedom Malcolm Rifkind, Parliamentary Under-Secretary of State for Foreign and Commonwealth Affairs, thought the UK should seek discreetly to sustain as it was more likely to prove infectious than the radicalism of Poland. It provided a valuable model of the market-orientated approach to economic management to which other East European countries might turn as a way of solving their own economic problems (No. 164). By 1982 Hungary was suffering from the domino effect of the Polish debt crisis and a rapid withdrawal of funds had led to a major liquidity problem. Hungarian leaders worried that Western governments and banks might deem them a bad financial risk, in the same category as Poland, Romania and Yugoslavia. Mr Broomfield thought that Hungary would find it more difficult to get credit in future (No. 145). Hungary was in the process of joining the World Bank, having just joined the International Monetary Fund, and had the prospect of substantial support in the future but needed help in the short-term. Mr Rifkind argued for assisting as 'economic reform and increasing economic freedom are the most likely route by which lasting political change will occur in Eastern Europe, even if there may be a time lag of some years'. The Hungarian economic initiatives were showing the Soviet Union and other Communist states that rigid, centralist socialist policies would 'provide bread queues and political discontent but a decentralised, profit-orientated market system in agriculture and industry actually produces the goods. We should do what little we can to help this process' (No. 164). Mr Pym took up the cause with the Treasury arguing, as with Poland, that the long-term political gains outweighed the short-term economic costs. If reform failed, he warned, 'Soviet-style orthodoxy can be the only winner, with all that this means in political as well as economic terms for Eastern Europe as a whole' (No. 176).

Romania

'Romania is an unpleasant dictatorship' was Mr Rifkind's verdict following a visit in 1982. But he also thought that its independent foreign policy was an 'embarrassment' to the Soviet Union and 'a reproof to the more docile Communist regimes such as the GDR and Czechoslovakia'. Therefore it continued to be 'of some limited use to us to encourage this grey sheep in the Soviet flock' without identifying too closely with the current regime (No. 180). It was generally thought worthwhile devoting some time and energy to satisfying the Romanian need for visible links with important Western countries, and Lord Carrington visited in 1980. But a constantly improving relationship was not thought possible or desirable, especially if it required a State visit (No. 9). Nicolae Ceauşescu's attempt to establish himself (and Romania) as an indispensable factor for peace and stability in the world, was considered a diversionary tactic to stave off trouble at home. Serious distortions in the Romanian economy were becoming evident, stemming from over-investment in certain sectors and the relative neglect of agriculture. 'If I were Ceauşescu,' wrote Colin Munro from the Embassy in Bucharest, 'what would worry me most would be the fact that no country which counts for something in the world feels strongly enough to be genuinely interested positively or negatively in Romanian foreign policy initiatives: we are all much too busy monitoring Romania's faltering economic performance and wondering if, when, and how Romania will repay its mounting debts' (No. 151). There was also debate over whether Romania was the country most likely to go the way of Poland. But it was concluded that, while there was frustration and discontent, Romanian workers did not seem to consider the wider political implications of Polish events as relevant to their situation and many of the crucial conditions which sustained the Polish 'renewal' did not exist in Romania. With largely cosmetic measures Mr Ceauşescu would probably succeed in heading off any potential pressure for reform in Romania (No. 69).

Czechoslovakia

Following a visit to Prague in June 1982, Alan Goodison, Assistant Under-Secretary at the FCO, reflected that although the regime was too unsavoury for the Government to contemplate an official visit, 'we should, as far as we can, nurture the good instincts of the Czechoslovaks so that they can flower in their own good time'. However, he did not feel that 'we have the powers to induce the kind of change the Czechoslovaks produced themselves in 1968 or that it would be wise to do so if we could. I am afraid of proposals to unravel Eastern Europe now' (No. 162). Some improvement in relations was nevertheless envisaged, especially after the resolution in early 1982 of a longstanding issue involving the return of gold to Czechoslovakia looted by Nazi Germany (and held by the Bank of England) in return for the settlement of various outstanding UK claims (No. 148). In July 1982, Mr Montgomery noted that if a way could be found to improve relations, it might be possible to make more effective interventions on behalf of the victims of human rights abuses and perhaps keep alive the concept that Czechoslovakia belonged as much to the traditions of the West as to the East (No. 166). For the time being, though, hopes were muted.

The major bilateral issue was the Czech government's poor record on human rights and persecution of organisations like Charter 77 and VONS, the Committee for the Defence of the Unjustly Prosecuted. Whenever they met, UK ministers and officials reminded their Czech counterparts of international agreements such as the UN Charter, Human Rights covenants and the Helsinki Final Act. At the Heads of Mission conference in October 1979, Mr Blaker had encouraged embassies to step up their contacts with dissidents. But this policy was not without its difficulties. Caroline Elmes, First Secretary in Prague, reported that the efforts which the

Embassy made to cultivate dissidents received a mixed response as they drew unfavourable attention from the authorities (No. 14). The Embassy also monitored trials, on which very little official information was disclosed, such as those of religious dissidents held in the autumn of 1981. It advised against attempting to influence trials through bilateral action or public statements and instead favoured a confidential démarche to the Czech authorities through the UK's Presidency of the EC. However, officials in London wanted to be consistent with the strong position the UK had taken over dissidents in the CSCE meeting at Madrid in November 1980. They judged that not protesting would send the wrong signal to the Czechoslovak authorities. Eventually démarches were made in London and Prague which the Czechs predictably dismissed as interference in their internal affairs (No. 88). The country's human rights record remained poor. The FCO's assessment in 1982 was that there were no signs of a likely improvement in the near future. But they advised against major public attack on the Czech authorities, as they continued to believe that more could be achieved by taking up human rights issues confidentially (No. 141).

German Democratic Republic

The United Kingdom's relations with East Germany were poor, due largely to the contested status of Berlin and the GDR's rigid orthodoxy. In June 1980 Mr Foster wrote: 'the system is, by democratic standards, nasty, fundamentally hostile to Western interests and externally the more dangerous in not needing to rely on naked terror' (No. 24, note 1). Polish strikes did not prove contagious because, as the Ambassador noted, a 'distasteful but fundamentally stable balance between oppression and discontent' had been established. He argued that East Germans knew perfectly well that the *Stasi*, underpinned by the massive Soviet military presence, was strong enough to frustrate any organised resistance or isolated outbreaks of dissatisfaction. Besides, the country did not encounter the same economic problems as Poland. Yet East Germans saw the FRG as a model, which deeply corroded the solidity of the regime's ideology (No. 24). In April 1981 Foster judged that 'by and large there was and is no chance . . . of rapid and dramatic change' in the GDR (No. 58).

In the autumn of 1981 Peter Maxey, the new Ambassador, redefined British priorities. He advised that the UK should keep up pressure on the GDR to be more forthcoming over trade in exchange for some development of political relations. He also suggested that a visit by the Secretary of State the following year might benefit British commercial interests, even if the state of the British economy made winning large contracts unlikely. He advised reconsidering the issue at the end of the year, when the prospect of trade improvement could be assessed (No. 84). Officials in London agreed that it was difficult to impose more stringent conditions for commercial contracts upon the GDR than for example upon Czechoslovakia, which had no better a record on human rights. It was also believed that by then the GDR shared the general desire to maintain the current calm in Berlin. A ministerial visit could be turned to advantage if tensions continued over Poland, by providing an opportunity for the UK to remind the GDR of the need for strict non-interference in Poland's affairs. The FCO concluded that the GDR was the most significant country for the Foreign Secretary to visit in 1982, as he had visited Poland, Romania and Hungary in 1980. If an invasion of Poland were to take place with the GDR's active support, cancellation of the visit would be one more way of indicating HMG's disapproval.

Lord Carrington agreed that the option of a visit should be kept open, even if HMG should continue to stall for the time being and hint strongly at the need for substantial improvement in commercial relations to balance improvements on the political side (No. 90). In March 1982 he agreed to visit the GDR in November. However following his resignation in April, his successor, Mr Pym, decided not to visit in 1982. It was decided that out of courtesy such a visit should become a priority the following year, especially as the GDR, if offended, could exercise considerable influence within the Eastern bloc to make life difficult for the UK (No. 170).

Bulgaria

Some countries were seen has having few positive elements worth encouraging. Bulgaria was in this category due to her 'self-appointed role as Moscow's most obedient and willing acolyte' (No. 150, note 12). In fact, more than one Ambassador wondered openly if it was worth bothering with Bulgaria at all. John Cloake admitted there was not much substance to relations, which just simmered away quietly (No. 13), whilst Giles Bullard said: 'It is permissible to ask what the British taxpayer gets in return for the £600,000 a year it costs to run this Embassy' (No. 150). But there was general agreement that a presence was useful to attempt to exert Western pressure on the Soviet Union through Sofia, or to be 'on the spot' in order to steer any changes in Bulgaria in a favourable direction. As in other Communist countries a gap was discerned between those who had fought Fascism, those who built Socialism and the next generation who saw 'the startling gap between the pretence of Communist hyperbole and the reality of the mess around them', as the failings of the State became increasingly apparent through foreign trade, wider cultural contacts and the influx of Western tourists (No. 163).

Yet Bulgaria was still capable of causing diplomatic headaches. Lyudmilla Zhivkova, the President's daughter and minister for culture, was invited to visit the UK in 1981 in conjunction with Bulgaria's 1300th Anniversary celebrations. But there had been great reluctance as memories of the murder of the dissident Georgi Markov in London in 1978 were still fresh. Instructions from Ministers were to keep the visit low-key and linked specifically to culture. However, it became clear that the Bulgarians were thinking that Mme Zhivkova should meet Mrs Thatcher for a discussion on political and economic questions, and also pay a courtesy call on The Queen. Brian Fall, Head of EESD, noted that it would be 'a very brave man who sought to persuade the Prime Minister that she should receive Mme Zhivkova' (No. 48). The urge for recognition, through high-level exchanges, was considered one of the principal motivations of Bulgarian foreign policy and their professed desire for friendship was thought to be sincere. The Bulgarian deputy Prime Minister complained to Lord Carrington that no British secretary of state had ever visited Bulgaria in 100 years of bilateral relations (No. 35). But it was thought a long and hard process to get them to appreciate 'that their practices were often not calculated to achieve their proclaimed goals'.

Albania

Although the UK recognised Albania it did not have diplomatic relations with the country. Relations were complicated by longstanding disputes. The Albanians wanted delivery 'with interest' of gold allocated to them in partial compensation for the much larger sum looted by the Germans during the Second World War and held in the Bank of England on behalf of the Tripartite Commission for the

Restitution of Monetary Gold. The British wanted Albania to pay the damages awarded to the UK by the International Court of Justice following the Corfu Channel incident in 1946, when two Royal Navy ships were mined with loss of life.[15] In 1980 Britain dropped the settlement of damages as a pre-condition for the resumption of relations but the Albanians continued to demand that the gold question be settled first. And there the matter rested: each country believing the ball was in the other's court (Nos. 97 & 135).

Conclusion

In September 1982 a review of policy towards Eastern Europe concluded that it should continue to be based on the principles of positive discrimination and the encouragement of evolution of more open societies (No. 174). However, in a paper discussed at the review there was an acknowledgement that the Polish crisis had chilled the atmosphere in which differentiation was practised and reduced any room for manoeuvre East European Governments might have had, whilst the problem of indebtedness had curtailed commercial relations. Nevertheless, the paper argued that building and developing contacts at all levels should continue. Although such exchanges were frequently sterile, they exposed Eastern decision-makers to Western thinking, and East European regimes prized visits as a mark of recognition. As such, visits by the Secretary of State could be used more sparingly, as a mark of favour to the specially deserving. And although economic problems meant that trade was no longer likely to be the mainspring of relations, the cultural field offered excellent opportunities. Young people watched events in the West with particular attention and identified far more closely with the European tradition than with the Soviet Union (No. 170).

Yugoslavia remained top of the UK's list by virtue of its independent stance. Hungary also deserved special consideration for its continuing economic experiments. Ceauşescu's personality cult and repressive regime meant that Romania no longer deserved the degree of special treatment accorded to her in the past. But the contacts that existed were to be maintained to encourage the preservation of a degree of independence in foreign policy. Czechoslovakia, the GDR and Bulgaria still provided few grounds for discriminating in their favour. However, the resolution of the gold question with the Czechs created a positive climate for the development of cultural and trade links. And as for Poland, once the situation settled, what predominated was the wish to restore and strengthen its political and cultural links with the West in order to consolidate 'the uniquely antipathetic character of the Polish State within the Soviet Empire' (No. 170).

[15] See *DBPO: Western Security*: Chapter 5.

Acknowledgements

In accordance with the Parliamentary announcement cited in the Introduction to this Series, the editors have had the customary freedom in the selection and arrangement of documents, including full access to all classes of documentation. There has been no instance in this volume when it has been necessary for security reasons to excise any passages from selected documents.

Documents quoted or cited in footnotes have only been accorded a file reference where it differs from that of the printed document to which they refer. Telegrams have been given the date on which they were sent. Omitted from the headings and formulations at the end of documents are some classifications regarding administration and circulation but the main security classifications are included. The spelling and punctuation of names in the documents remain as in the original. Some minor typing errors have been corrected.

We should like to thank Sir Simon McDonald, Permanent Under-Secretary of State and Head of the Diplomatic Service, Colin Martin-Reynolds, Chief Information Officer, and Robert Deane, head of the Knowledge Management Department, for their support. For assistance in providing documents we are grateful to colleagues in the Archives Management Team at Hanslope Park, headed by Martin Tucker, and staff at The National Archives. We are grateful to those members of FCO Historians who have helped with the volume, in particular Patrick Salmon, Chief Historian. Additional assistance has also been provided by Jim Daly, Tara Finn, Ann Herd, Martin Jewitt and Giles Rose. We are grateful, above all, to Gill Bennett, former Chief Historian of the FCO, for her valuable advice.

ISABELLE TOMBS　　　　　RICHARD SMITH

September 2016

ABBREVIATIONS FOR PRINTED SOURCES

Cmnd.	Command Paper (London)
DBPO: Afghanistan	*Documents on British Policy Overseas: Series III, Volume VIII: The Invasion of Afghanistan and UK-Soviet Relations, 1979-1982* (London: Routledge, 2012)
DBPO: CSCE	*Documents on British Policy Overseas: Series III, Volume II: The Conference on Security and Co-operation in Europe, 1972-1975* (London: HMSO, 1997)
DBPO: Détente	*Documents on British Policy Overseas: Series III, Volume III: Détente in Europe, 1972-1976* (London: Frank Cass, 2001)
DBPO: Eastern Europe	*Documents on British Policy Overseas, Series I, Volume VI: Eastern Europe, August 1945-April 1946* (London: HMSO, 1991)
DBPO: Soviet Union, 1968-1972	*Documents on British Policy Overseas: Series III, Volume I: Britain and the Soviet Union, 1968-1972* (London: HMSO, 1997)
DBPO: Western Security	*Documents on British Policy Overseas: Series I, Volume XI: European Recovery and the Search for Western Security, 1946-48* (London: Routledge, 2016)
Parl. Debs., 5th ser., H. of C.	*Parliamentary Debates (Hansard), Fifth Series, House of Commons, Official Report* (London, 1909f.)
Parl. Debs., 5th ser., H. of L.	*Parliamentary Debates (Hansard), Fifth Series, House of Lords, Official Report* (London, 1909f.)
Public Papers: Reagan (1981, 1982)	*Public Papers of the Presidents of the United States: Ronald Reagan* (Washington, 1982-83)

ABBREVIATED DESIGNATIONS

ACDA	Arms Control and Disarmament Agency
AFP	*Agence France-Presse* (French Press Agency)
APS	Assistant Private Secretary
AUS	Assistant Under-Secretary of State
BAOR	British Army of the Rhine
BCP	Bulgarian Communist Party
BIS	Bank for International Settlements
BOTB	British Overseas Trade Board
BTU	British thermal unit
CBI	Confederation of British Industries
CBM	Confidence building measures
CC	Cabinet Conclusions
CC	Central Committee
CDE	Conference on Disarmament in Europe
CGT	*Confédération Générale du Travail* (French Trade Union Confederation)
CIA	Central Intelligence Agency
CMEA	Council for Mutual Economic Assistance
COCOM	Coordinating Committee for Multilateral Export Controls
COI	Central Office of Information
COMECON	Council for Mutual Economic Assistance
COREU	EU Telegram
CPSU	Communist Party of the Soviet Union
CRD	Cultural Relations Department, FCO
CSCE	Conference on Security and Cooperation in Europe
CTB	Comprehensive Test Ban
DDR	*Deutsche Demokratische Republik* (see also GDR)
DEI	Department of Economic Intelligence, MOD
DOD	US Department of Defense
DOP	Cabinet's Oversea and Defence Committee
DOT	Department of Trade
DUS	Deputy Under-Secretary of State
EC	European Community
ECD(E)	European Community Department (External), FCO
ECGD	Export Credit Guarantee Department
EEC	European Economic Community
EESD	Eastern European and Soviet Department, FCO
EETC	East European Trade Council
ERD	Economic Relations Department, FCO
ESID	Economic Service (International Division)
ESSD	Energy Science and Space Department, FCO
FCO	Foreign and Commonwealth Office
FDP	*Die Freie Demokratische Partei* (Free Democratic Party, FRG)
FRD	Financial Relations Department
FRG	Federal Republic of Germany
FRUS	Foreign Relations of the United States
GATT	General Agreement on Tariffs and Trade
GDR	German Democratic Republic (see also DDR)
GSP	Generalised Scheme of Preferences
HE	His Excellency
HMA	Her Majesty's Ambassador
HMRR	Her Majesty's Representative
HMT	Her Majesty's Treasury
HSWP	Hungarian Socialist Workers' Party
IAEA	International Atomic Energy Agency
ICBM	Intercontinental ballistic missile
IFT	Immediate Following Telegram
ILO	International Labour Organization

IMF	International Monetary Fund
INF	Intermediate range nuclear forces
IRD	Information Research Department, FCO
JIC	Joint Intelligence Committee
KIK	*Inteligencji Katolickiej Warszawa* (Catholic Intellectual Clubs)
KOR	*Komitet Obrony Robotników* (Workers' Defence Committee)
KPN	*Konfederacja Polski Niepodległej* (Confederation of Independent Poles)
LCC	League of Communists of Croatia
LCY	League of Communists of Yugoslavia
LDC	Less developed countries
LPS	Lord Privy Seal
MED	Middle East Department, FCO
MEP	Member of European Parliament
MBFR	Mutual and Balanced Force Reductions
MFA	Ministry of Foreign Affairs
MIFT	My Immediately Following Telegram
MIPT	My Immediately Preceding Telegram
MOD	Ministry of Defence
MPLA	*Movimento Popular de Libertação de Angola* (Popular Movement for the Liberation of Angola)
MVD	Migration and Visa Department
NAC	North Atlantic Council (NATO)
NAM	Non-Aligned Movement
NATO	North Atlantic Treaty Organisation
NEM	New Economic Mechanism
NENAD	Near East and North Africa Department, FCO
NNA	Neutral and Non-Aligned
NOFUN	No First Use of Nuclear Weapons
NSC	US National Security Council
OD	Cabinet's Oversea and Defence Committee
ODA	Overseas Development Administration
OECD	Organisation for Economic Cooperation and Development
OID	Overseas Information Department, FCO
OPEC	Organisation of Petroleum Exporting Countries
PAP	*Polska Agencja Prasowa* (Polish News Agency)
PDRY	People's Democratic Republic of Yemen
PESC	Public Expenditure Survey Committee
PLO	Palestine Liberation Organization
POCO	Political Cooperation (EU)
PPS	Principal Private Secretary
PQ	Parliamentary Question
PRON	*Patriotyczny Ruch Odrodzenia Narodowego* (Patriotic Movement for National Rebirth)
PS	Private Secretary
PSBR	Public sector borrowing requirement
PUS	Permanent Under-Secretary of State
PUWP	Polish United Workers' Party
PZPR	*Polska Zjednoczona Partia Robotnicza* (Polish United Workers' Party)
RCP	Romanian Communist Party
RDF	Rapid Defence Force
ROPCO	*Ruch Obrony Praw Czlowieka i Obywatela* (Movement for the Defence of Civil and Human Rights)
RSFSR	Russian Socialist Federative Soviet Republic
SACEUR	Supreme Allied Commander Europe
SALT	Strategic Arms Limitation Treaty
SCG	Special Consultative Group (NATO)
SCR	Security Council Resolution (UN)
SED	*Sozialistische Einheitspartei Deutschlands* (Socialist Unity Party of Germany, GDR)
SLBM	Submarine-launched ballistic missile

SPC	Senior Political Committee (NATO)
START	Strategic Arms Reduction Talks
Stasi	*Ministerium für Staatssicherheit* (Ministry for State Security, GDR)
TASS	*Informatsionnoye agentstvo Rossii* (Russian News Agency)
TCC	Solidarity Temporary Coordinating Committee
Telno	Telegram number
TNF	Theatre Nuclear Forces
TRED	Trade Relations and Export Department, FCO
TUC	Trade Union Congress
TUR	Telegram under reference
UIP	United International Press
UKDEL	United Kingdom Delegation
UKMIS	United Kingdom Mission
UKREP	United Kingdom Permanent Representative
UND	United Nations Department, FCO
UNDP	United Nations Development Programme
UNHCR	United Nations High Commission for Refugees
UNSSOD	United Nations Special Session on Disarmament
USA	United States of America
USSR	Union of Soviet Socialist Republics
VONS	*Výbor na obranu nespravedlivě stíhaných* (Committee for the Defence of the Unjustly Persecuted)
VS	Verbatim Series, COI
WRON	*Wojskowa Rada Ocalenia Narodowego* (Military Council of National Salvation)
ZASP	*Związek Artystów Scen Polskich* (Polish Stage Actors' Union)
ZNAK	Association of lay Catholics in Poland
ZOMO	*Zmotoryzowane Odwody Milicji Obywatelskiej* (Polish para-military police)
ZZAP	*Związek Artystów Scen Polskich* (Polish Association of Stage Actors)

LIST OF PERSONS

Abrassimov, Petr, Soviet Ambassador, Berlin, 1962-71, 1975-83
Acland, Sir Antony, Permanent Under-Secretary, FCO, 1982-86
Adamek, Józef, Czech printer, Charter 77 signatory, detained, 1979, sentenced to 20 months' imprisonment, 1981
Alexander, Michael, Prime Minister's Private Secretary for Overseas Affairs, 1979-81
Allan, James, Head of Overseas Information Department, 1978-80
Amin, Hafizullah, Prime Minister and President of Afghanistan, Sept-Dec 1979
Andréani, Gilles, Director of the Policy Planning Staff, French MFA
Andrei, Stefan, Romanian Minister of Foreign Affairs, 1978-85
Arafat, Yasser, Chairman of the Palestine Liberation Organisation, 1969-2004
Aristov, Boris, Soviet Ambassador, Warsaw, 1978-83
Armstrong, Robert, Secretary of the Cabinet, 1979-87
Arthur, Michael (later Sir), Private Secretary to Lord Privy Seal, 1981-82 and to Minister of State, FCO, 1982-84
Al-Assad, Hafez, President of Syria
Atkins, Sir Humphrey, Lord Privy Seal, 1981-82
Axen, Hermann, GDR member of Central Committee of the SED and Chairman of its Foreign Affairs Committee, 1971-90
Babiuch, Edward, Deputy Chairman of the Polish Council of State, 1976-80; Prime Minister of Poland, 18 Feb-24 Aug 1980
Bafia, Jerzy, Polish Minister of Justice, 1976-81
Baibakov, Nicolai, Chairman of the Soviet State Planning Committee, 1965-85
Bakarić, Vladimir, Croatian communist and Yugoslav politician
Baldridge, Malcolm, United States Secretary of Commerce, 1981-87
Balmer, Michael, Commercial Secretary, Warsaw, 1981-84
Banks, Joseph, Principal Research Officer, FCO, 1972-91
Barcikowski, Kazimierz, member of Polish State Council, 1980-85; Government chief negotiator with striking workers in Szczecin, 1980
Barnett, Robin, Third Secretary, British Embassy, Warsaw, 1982-85
Barrass, Gordon, Planning Staff, FCO, 1979-82
Bartoszewski, Władysław, Polish historian, activist and journalist, lecturer at Flying University, member of Solidarity, 1980-81; detained Dec 1981-April 1982
Battěk, Rudolf, Czech sociologist, co-founder of VONS and spokesman for Charter 77 from 1980, sentenced to five and a half years' imprisonment for subversion, 1980
Battiscombe, Christopher, Assistant Head, Eastern European and Soviet Department, FCO, 1978-80
Bednářová, Otta, Czech journalist, arrested and tried 1979
Beel, Graham, Research Department, Soviet Section, FCO, 1972-94
Begin, Menachem, Prime Minister of Israel, 1977-83
Bence, György, Hungarian university professor, philosopher and human rights activist
Benda, Václav, Czech mathematician, philosopher and Charter 77 spokesman, 1979; arrested May 1979, sentenced Oct 1979 to four years' imprisonment
Biffen, John, Secretary of State for Trade, Jan 1981-Jan 82
Birch, John, Counsellor and Head of Chancery, Budapest, 1980-83
Bisztyga, Jan, Polish Ambassador, London, 1978-83
Blackwill, Robert, Deputy Assistant Secretary for European Affairs, 1982-83

Blaker, Peter, Minister of State for Foreign and Commonwealth Affairs, 1979-81
Bolland, Sir Edwin, HM Ambassador, Belgrade, 1980-82
Bölling, Klaus, FRG Permanent Representative in the GDR, 1981-82
Bone, Roger, APS to the Secretary of State for Foreign and Commonwealth Affairs, 1982-84
Braine, Sir Bernard, Conservative MP for Essex, 1950-92; President of the UK Committee for the Defence of the Unjustly Prosecuted (VONS), 1980-88
Braithwaite, Rodric, Head, Planning Staff, FCO, 1979-80; AUS, FCO, 1980-82
Brandt, Willy, Leader of the SDP, 1964-87; Chancellor, FRG, 1969-74
Brezhnev, Leonid, General-Secretary of the CPSU, 1964-82
Bridges, Thomas Edward, 2nd Baron Bridges, DUS, FCO, 1979-83
Brittan, Leon, Minister of State for the Home Office, 4 May 1979-5 Jan 1981; Chief Secretary to the Treasury, 5 Jan 1981-11 June 1983
Bromke, Adam, Polish-born political scientist, editor of Free Europe newsletters, emigrated to Canada, 1950
Broomfield, Nigel, Head, Eastern European and Soviet Department, FCO, May 1981-85
Brown, Judith (Macgregor from 1982), First Secretary, British Embassy, Belgrade, 1978-81; Eastern European and Soviet Department, FCO, 1981-86
Browning, Rex, Under-Secretary, Commercial Relations and Exports Division, Department of Trade, 1979-80
Bujak, Zbigniew, electrician and trade unionist at the Ursus tractor factory; Solidarity chairman, 1980; leader of Solidarity underground for Warsaw region, 1981
Bull, Peter, economist at the Bank of England, 1964-84
Bullard, Giles, HM Ambassador, Sofia, 1980-83
Bullard, Julian (later Sir), DUS Europe, FCO, 1979-82; Political Director and Deputy to the Permanent Under-Secretary, FCO, 1982-84
Burns, **(Robert) Andrew**, Private Secretary to the Permanent Under-Secretary, 1979-82
Burtica, Cornel, Romanian Minister of Foreign Trade, 1969-82
Butler, Sir Michael, UK Permanent Representative to the EC, Brussels, 1979-85
Callaghan, James, Prime Minister, 1976-79
Camdessus, Michel Jean, Deputy Director of the Treasury, France, 1974-82
Cameron, Fraser, First Secretary, British Embassy, Bonn, 1980-84
Campbell, Richard, Eastern European and Soviet Department, FCO, 1978-82
Carington, Peter, 6th Baron Carrington, Secretary of State for Foreign and Commonwealth Affairs, 1979-April 1982
Carstens, Karl, President of the FRG, 1979-84
Carter, James Earl 'Jimmy', President of the United States, 1977-81
Cartledge, Bryan, HM Ambassador, Budapest, 1980-83
Casey, William, US Director of Central Intelligence, 1981-87
Ceaușescu, Nicolae, General Secretary of the Romanian Communist Party, 1965-89; President of Romania, 1967-89
Cheysson, Claude, French Foreign Minister, 1981-84
Chojecki, Mirosław, publisher, co-founder of KOR, Solidarity member
Clark, Sir Terence (Joseph), Counsellor, British Embassy, Belgrade, 1979-82
Cloake, John, HM Ambassador, Sofia, 1976-80
Coles, (Arthur) John, Prime Minister's Private Secretary for Overseas Affairs, Dec 1981-84
Collett, Joanna, Information Officer, British Embassy, Warsaw, 1981-84
Cotterill, Kenneth, Deputy Head, Export Credit Guarantee Department, 1976-81
Couzens, Sir Kenneth, joint Second Permanent Secretary (Overseas Finance), HMT, 1977-83
Cox, Norman, HM Ambassador, Mexico City, 1977-81

Cresson, Edith, French Minister of Agriculture, 1981-83
Cummins, Rodney, Eastern European and Soviet Department, FCO, 1980-82
Czyrek, Józef, Polish Foreign Minister, 1980-82
Dąbrowski, Jerzy, Auxiliary Bishop of Gniezno, Poland, 1982-91
Dejmek, Kazimierz, actor, manager of Teatr Nowy in Łódź, 1974-81, and of Teatr Polski in Warsaw from 1981
Dienstbier, Jiří, Charter 77 Spokesman, 1979; arrested, May 1979; sentenced to three years' imprisonment, Oct 1979
Djilas, Milovan, Yugoslav author and human rights activist
Djuranović, Veselin, Yugoslav Prime Minister, 1977-82
Dobrosielski, Marian, Polish Deputy Foreign Minister, 1978-82
Dolgov, Vyacheslav, Minister-Counsellor, Soviet Embassy, London, 1982-84
Doronjski, Stevan, President of the Central Committee of the LCY, 1979-80
Dubček, Alexander, General-Secretary of the Czechoslovak Communist Party, 1968-69
Dufourcq, Bertrand, Director of the Europe Department, French MFA, 1979-84
Duka, Dominik, designer at Škoda and underground theology teacher; jailed, 1981-82
Dupont, Jacques, Political Deputy-Director, French MFA, 1979-82
Eagleburger, Lawrence, US Assistant-Secretary of State for European Affairs, 1981; Under-Secretary of State for Political Affairs, 1982-84
Elmes, Caroline, First Secretary, British Embassy, Prague, 1978-81
Erhard, Ludwig, Minister for Economics, 1949-63; Chancellor of the FRG, 1963-66
Evans, Sir Richard, AUS, 1979-82; DUS, FCO, 1982-83
Facey, Robert, Eastern European and Soviet Department, FCO, 1979-83
Fall, Brian, Head, Eastern European and Soviet Department, FCO, 1980-81; PPS to the Secretary of State for Foreign and Commonwealth Affairs, May 1981-84
Fallaci, Oriana, Italian journalist
Farquharson, Robert, HM Ambassador, Belgrade, 1977-80
Fell, William, First Secretary, British Embassy, Warsaw, 1979-82
Fergusson, Ewen, AUS (Europe), FCO, 1978-82
Fischer, Oskar, Minister of Foreign Affairs, GDR, 1975-90
Flesher, Timothy, Private Secretary to the Prime Minister, 1982-86
Foot, Michael, Leader of the Opposition, 1980-83
Foster, Peter, HM Ambassador, East Berlin, 1979-81
Franklin, Gloria, Planning Staff, FCO, 1979-81
François-Poncet, Jean, French Minister of Foreign Affairs, 1978-81
Fretwell, Sir John, HM Ambassador, Paris, 1982-87
Fuller, S. W. J., Privy Council's Office
Furness, Alan, Counsellor and Head of Chancery, British Embassy, Warsaw, 1982-1985
Gandhi, Indira, Prime Minister of India, 1980-84
Garton Ash, Timothy, British historian and journalist; author of *The Polish Revolution: Solidarity* (1983)
Gaus, Günter, FRG Permanent Representative in the GDR, 1973-81
Genscher, Hans-Dietrich, Foreign Minister and Vice-Chancellor, FRG, 1974-92
Geremek, Bronisław, historian, trade union activist and adviser to Solidarity; interned, Dec 1981-Dec 1982
Gierek, Edward, First Secretary of the PUWP, 1970-80
Gilmour, Sir Ian, Lord Privy Seal, 1979-81
Giosan, Nicolae, President of the National Assembly of Romania, 1974-89
Giscard d'Estaing, Valéry, President of the French Republic, 1974-81
Gladstone, David, Head, Western European Department, FCO, 1979-82

Glemp, Józef, Archbishop of Warsaw, 1981-2006
Gomersall, Stephen, Private Secretary to the Lord Privy Seal, 1979-82
Gomułka, Władysław, General Secretary of the PUWP, 1956-70
Goodall, Arthur, Minister, British Embassy, Bonn, 1979-82
Goodison, Alan, AUS, FCO, 1981-83
Grabski, Tadeusz, Polish Deputy Prime Minister, Aug-Oct 1980
Graham, Sir John, DUS, FCO, 1980-82; UK Permanent Representative to NATO, 1982-86
Gray, Charles, Third Secretary, British Embassy, Warsaw, 1976-79
Green, Andrew, Economic Relations Department, FCO, 1979-82
Gromyko, Andrei, Soviet Foreign Minister, 1957-85
Grudzień, Zdzislaw, member of the Politburo of the PUWP until Sept 1980
Grzyb, Zofia, Solidarity member of the Politburo of the PUWP, 1981-86
Guofeng, Hua, Chairman of the Communist Party of China, 1976-81
Gutmann, Francis, Secretary-General, French MFA, 1981-85
Gwiazda, Andrzej, Polish co-founder of the Baltic Free Trade Unions, April 1976
Haberer, Jean-Yves, Director of the Treasury, France, 1978-82
Haig, Alexander, US Secretary of State, 1981-July 1982
Hájek, Jiří, Czech co-founder and leading spokesmen of Charter 77; arrested and charged, May 1981
Halliday, John, PPS to the Home Secretary, 1980-83
Hardie, Alexander, First Secretary, British Embassy, Bucharest, 1979-81
Harrison, Alistair, Third and then Second Secretary, British Embassy, Warsaw, 1979-82
Havel, Václav, Czech playwright, co-founder of Charter 77; co-founder of VONS, 1979; interned, 1979-83
Havers, Sir Michael, Attorney-General, 1979-87
Heath, Sir Mark, Minister, 1980-82 and then HM Ambassador, Holy See, 1982-85
Henderson, Sir Nicholas, HM Ambassador, Washington, 1979-82
Hibbert, Sir Reginald, HM Ambassador, Paris, 1979-82
Himsworth, Katherine, Second and then First Secretary, East Berlin, 1977-79; First Secretary, FCO, 1981-84
Holmer, Paul, HM Ambassador, Bucharest, 1979-83
Holmes, John, APS to the Secretary of State for Foreign and Commonwealth Affairs, 1982-84
Honecker, Erich, General Secretary of the Socialist Unity Party, GDR, 1971-89
Hormats, Robert, US Assistant Secretary of State for Economic and Business Affairs, 1981-82
Howe, Sir Geoffrey, Chancellor of the Exchequer, 1979-83
Hoxha, Enver, First Secretary of the Party of Labour of Albania, 1944-85
Hulse, Christopher, Defence Department, FCO, 1981-83
Hume, Cardinal Basil, Archbishop of Westminster, 1976-99
Hurd, Douglas, Minister of State, FCO, 1979-83
Husák, Gustáv, First Secretary of the Communist Party of Czechoslovakia, 1969-87 and President of the Czechoslovak Republic, 1975-89
Hutton, Alasdair, MEP (Conservative), South Scotland, 1979-89
Jabłonski, Henryk, Chairman of the Council of State of the People's Republic of Poland, 1972-85
Jagielski, Mieczysław, Polish Deputy Prime Minister, 1970-July 1981; member of the Politburo of the PUWP, 1971-81 and of its Central Committee, 1959-July 1981
James, (Cynlais) Kenneth, HM Ambassador, Warsaw, 1981-83

Jankowski, Henryk, Polish Roman Catholic Priest, Provost of St Bridget's Church in Gdańsk, Lech Wałęsa's priest, member of Solidarity
Jaroszewicz, Piotr, Prime Minister of Poland, 1970-80
Jaruzelski, General Wojciech, Prime Minister of Poland, 1981-85 and First Secretary of the PUWP, 1981-89
Jay, Michael, Planning Staff, 1981-82, Private Secretary to the Permanent Under-Secretary of State, 1982-85
Jenkins, Richard, Research Department, Eastern European section, FCO, 1979-83
Johnson, David, Assistant Head (Soviet Union), Eastern European and Soviet Department, FCO, 1978-82
Joseph, Sir Keith, Secretary of State for Industry, 1979-81
Joy, David, Counsellor and Head of Chancery, British Embassy, Warsaw, 1978-82
Kádár, János, General Secretary of the Hungarian Communist Party, 1956-88
Kania, Stanisław, First Secretary of the PUWP, 1980-81
Karkoszka, Alojzy, Deputy Premier of Poland, 1975-76
Karmal, Babrak, Prime Minister, 1979-81 and President of Afghanistan, 1979-86
Keeble, Sir Curtis, HM Ambassador, Moscow, 1978-Sept 1982
Khrushchev, Nikita, First Secretary of the CPSU, 1953-64
Kirkpatrick, Jeane, US Ambassador to the UN, 1981-85
Kisiel, Henryk, Deputy Prime Minister of Poland and Chief of the Planning Commission, Aug 1980-June 1981
Kiszczak, General Czesław, Polish Minister of Interior, 1981-90
Knighton, William, Deputy Secretary, US Department of Trade, 1978-83
Kociołek, Stanisław, Polish Ambassador, Moscow, 1981-85
Kohl, Helmut, Chancellor of the FRG, 1982-98
Komorek, Wladyslaw, mechanical engineer and Solidarity member; interned, Dec 1981-Feb 1982
Kordík, Josef, Czech Catholic priest and Charter 77 signatory; sentenced to one year's imprisonment (suspended for two years), Sept 1981
Kosygin, Alekei, Premier of the USSR, 1964-80
Kostic, Peter, Yugoslav Minister of Finance, 1978-82
Kowalczyk, Edward, Vice-Premier of Poland, 1981-1985
Kreisky, Bruno, Chancellor of Austria, 1970-83
Krolikowski, Werner, Deputy Chairman of the National Council of Ministers, GDR, 1976-88
Krumpholc, Jan, Czech dissident sentenced to three years' imprisonment for producing and distributing unofficial religious literature, Sept 1981
Kubiak, Hieronim, Polish sociologist; Secretary of the Central Committee of the PUWP, responsible for higher education and culture, and member of the Politburo, 1981-86
Kulikov, Marshal Viktor, Soviet Commander-in-Chief of the Warsaw Pact, 1977-89
Kuroń, Jacek, Polish co-founder of KOR, main adviser to Solidarity and Lech Wałęsa
Kyncl, Ivan, Czech photographer, dissident and son of Karel Kyncl; emigrated to London, 1980
Kyncl, Karel, Czech journalist and signatory of Charter 77; imprisoned, May 1981-March 1982; emigrated to London, 1983
Lahnstein, Manfred, Head of Chancellery, 1980-82; Minister of Finance, FRG, April-Oct 1982
Lautenschlager, Hans Werner, State Secretary, MFA, FRG, 1979-84
Leprette, Jacques, French Permanent Representative to the UN and President of the Security Council, 1976-81

Lever, Paul, APS to the Secretary of State for Foreign and Commonwealth Affairs, 1978-81
Lipiński, Edward, Polish economist, co-founder of KOR and adviser to Solidarity
Lipski, Jan Józef, Polish historian, KOR activist and member of Solidarity; arrested, 4 Dec 1981 and charged with organising a protest
Lis, Bogdan, Polish co-founder of the Inter-Enterprise Strike Committee, 1980; vice-chair of Solidarity Founding Committee; a leader of underground Solidarity
Lizna, Frantisek, Czech Jesuit priest and Charter 77 signatory; sentenced to 20 months' imprisonment, Sept 1981; tried and sentenced to an additional seven months, Jan 1982
Loehnis, Anthony David, Associate Director (Overseas), Bank of England, 1980-81
Longworth, Peter, Head of Chancery and HM Consul, Sofia, 1981-84
Lowson, Robert, PPS to the Minister of Agriculture, 1982-83
Luce, Richard, Parliamentary Under-Secretary of State, FCO, 1979-81; Minister of State, FCO, 1981-82
Lukanov, Andrej, Bulgarian Deputy Prime Minister, 1976-86
Macgregor, John, Private Secretary to Lord Trefgarne and Malcolm Rifkind, 1981-83
Macharski, Franciszek, Archbishop of Kraków, 1979-2005
McIntyre, Colin, Reuters' chief correspondent for Austria and East Europe
McMahon, Christopher, Deputy Governor, Bank of England, 1980-86
Makepeace, Richard, Press Secretary, British Embassy, Prague, 1981-85
Male, Peter, HM Ambassador, Prague, 1977-80
Mallaby, Christopher, Head of the Eastern European and Soviet Department, FCO, 1979-80; Head of Planning Staff, FCO, Sept 1980-82
Manning, David, Eastern European and Soviet Department, FCO, 1980-83
Marden, Nicholas, First Secretary, Warsaw, Sept 1982-85
Marsden, William, Counsellor, UKREP Brussels (European Parliament), 1981-85
Marshall, Peter, UK Permanent Representative to the UN, Geneva, 1979-83
Mauroy, Pierre, French Prime Minister, 1981-84
Maxey, Peter, HM Ambassador, East Berlin, 1981-84
Maxwell, Robert, publishing and media mogul
Mayhew, Michael, Second Secretary, British Embassy, Prague, 1978-81
Meehan, Frank, US Ambassador, Warsaw, 1980-83
Melhuish, Ramsay, Counsellor (Commercial), British Embassy, Warsaw, 1979-82
Michnik, Adam, Polish co-founder of Flying University, 1979; adviser to Solidarity
Milewski, General Miroslaw, Minister of the Interior, Oct 1980-July 1981, Secretary of the Central Committee of the PUWP, 1981-85
Mitterrand, François, President of the French Republic, 1981-85
Mladenov, Petar, Bulgarian Foreign Minister, 1971-89
Moczar, Mieczysław, member of the Central Committee of the PUWP, 1965-81, and of its Politburo, 1980-81
Montgomery, Alan, Eastern European and Soviet Department, FCO, 1981-82
Mountfield, Peter, HM Treasury, 1980-91
Mroczyk, Piotr, founder, 1980, and chairman of Solidarity for Polish Radio and Television; interned, 1981-82
Munro, Colin, Private Secretary to Peter Blaker, FCO, 1979-Jan 1981; Head of Chancery, British Embassy, Bucharest, Jan 1981-82
Murray, Lionel (Len), General Secretary of the TUC, 1973-84
Murrell, Geoffrey, Research Department, Soviet Section, FCO, 1978-83
Muskie, Edmund, US Secretary of State, 1980-81
Nagy, Imre, Chairman of the Council of Ministers, Hungary, July 1953-April 1955 and Oct 1956-Nov 1956; executed for treason, 1958

Němcová, Dana, Czech psychologist, signatory of Charter 77, co-founder of VONS; interned for six months, 1979; sentenced to two years' imprisonment, Oct 1979
Nichols, John, Second, later First Secretary, British Embassy, Budapest, 1979-July 1982
Nier, Kurt, Deputy Foreign Minister, GDR, 1973-89
Nott, John, Secretary of State for Trade, 1979-81; Secretary of State for Defence, 1981-83
Odstrcil, Jan, Czech dissident; sentenced to 10 months' imprisonment, Sept 1981
O'Flaherty, Stephen, First Secretary and HM Consul, Prague, 1981-84
Olechowski, Tadeusz, Polish Deputy Foreign Minister, 1980-83
Olszowski, Stefan, member of the Politburo of the PUWP, 1970-85; Central Committee Secretary for ideology and media, Aug 1980-July 1982; Foreign Minister, 1982-85
Onyszkiewicz, Janusz, press spokesman of the First National Congress of Solidarity, 1980-81; interned 1981-82; arrested, April 1983; released under amnesty, July 1983
Ozdowski, Jerzy, Polish Deputy Prime Minister, 1981-82
Palliser, Sir Michael, Permanent Under-Secretary, FCO, 1975-82
Palka Grzegorz, member of Solidarity Regional Executive Committee, Łódź, and of the Presidium of its National Committee
Papandreou, Andreas, Prime Minister of Greece, 1981-89
Parkinson, Cecil, Minister for Trade, 1979-81; Paymaster General, 1981-83; Chancellor, Duchy of Lancaster, 1982-83
Parsons, Sir Anthony, UK Permanent Representative to the UN, 1979-82
Parsons, Richard (later Sir), HM Ambassador, Budapest, 1976-79
Patočka, Jan, Czech philosopher and co-founder of Charter 77; died after an eleven-hour interrogation, 1977
Pattison, Michael, Private Secretary to the Prime Minister, 1979-82
Paye, Jean-Claude, Director of Economic and Financial Affairs, French MFA, 1979-84
Pestell, Catherine, Cabinet Office, 1978-80
Pfeffer, Franz, Political Director, MFA, FRG, 1981-85
Pińkowski, Józef, Polish Prime Minister, 1980-81
Plaschke, Herbert, Head, Western European Department, MFA, GDR, 1975-84
Popov, Viktor, Soviet Ambassador, London, 1980-86
Pridham, Kenneth, HM Ambassador, Warsaw, 1978-81
Puja, Frigyes, Hungarian Foreign Minister, 1973-83
Pym, Francis, Secretary of State for Defence, 1979-81; Secretary of State for Foreign and Commonwealth Affairs, April 1982-83
Raison, Sir Timothy, Minister of State, Home Office, 1979-83
Rakowski, Mieczyslaw, Polish Deputy Prime Minister, 1981-88
Rejchrt, Miloš, Czech Protestant Church Minister; Charter 77 spokesman, 1980
Reagan, Ronald, President of the United States, 1981-89
Regan, Donald, US Secretary of the Treasury, 1981-85
Rennie, Peter, Research Department, Eastern Europe Section, FCO, 1977-84
Rich, John, HM Ambassador, Prague, 1980-85
Richards, Francis, APS to the Secretary of State for Foreign and Commonwealth Affairs, 1981-2
Rifkind, Malcolm, Parliamentary Under-Secretary of State, FCO, 1982-83; Minister of State, FCO, 1983-86
Rulewski, Jan, Solidarity leader for Bydgoszcz region, 1980-81; interned during martial law
Šabata, Jaroslav, Czech psychologist and political scientist; spokesman for Charter 77, 1978-81
Šabatová, Anna, daughter of Jaroslav Šabata, wife of Petr Uhl and co-founder of VONS
Sakharov, Andrei, Soviet nuclear physicist and human rights activist

Schmidt, Helmut, Chancellor of the FRG, 1974-82
Scott, Kenneth, HM Ambassador, Belgrade, 1982-85
Sebastian, Tim, BBC Eastern Europe correspondent, 1979-82
Sharansky, Anatoly, Soviet-Israeli human rights activist
Shultz, George, US Secretary of State, July 1982-89
Sikorski, General Władysław, Polish Prime Minister, 1939-43
Siwak, Albin, Member of the Politburo of the PUWP, 1981-86
Sliwinski, Krzystof, leader of the international section of Solidarity in Warsaw, 1980-82; interned, 1981-82
Słowik, Andrzej, Solidarity activist in Łódż and member of Solidarity Presidium, 1981; sentenced to four years' imprisonment, 1981
Smahel, Rudolf, Czech Jesuit priest; sentenced to two years' imprisonment for producing and distributing unofficial religious literature, 1981
Sokołowski, Antoni, Polish co-founder of the Baltic Free Trade Unions, April 1976
Solesby, Tessa, Counsellor, British Embassy, East Berlin, 1978-82
Spasowski, Romuald, Polish Ambassador, Washington, 1978-81; defected, Dec 1981
Stagg, Richard, Third Secretary, British Embassy, Sofia, 1979-82
Staniszewski, Stefan, Polish Ambassador, London, 1981-86
Stoessel, Walter, US Ambassador, Bonn, 1976-81; Under-Secretary of State for Political Affairs, 1981-82; Deputy Secretary of State, 1982; Secretary of State ad interim, 1982
Stoph, Willi, Prime Minister of the GDR, 1976-89
Štrougal, Lubomír, Czech Prime Minister, 1970-88
Stubbs, Claire, Western European Department, FCO, 1979-83
Summerscale, Peter, Head, CSCE Unit, FCO, 1976-77; Deputy Leader, UK Delegation, CSCE Belgrade Review Meeting, 1977-78; Visiting FCO Research Fellow, RIIA, Chatham House, 1979-81
Tait, Michael, Deputy Head, UK Delegation, CSCE Madrid Review Meeting, 1980-82
Taylor, Sir John, HM Ambassador, Bonn, 1981-84
Tebbit, Kevin, Eastern European and Soviet Department, FCO, 1982-84
Thatcher, Margaret, Prime Minister, 1979-90
Thom, Ian, Commercial Secretary, British Embassy, Warsaw, 1980-83
Thomas, Richard, Counsellor and Head of Chancery, British Embassy, Prague, 1979-82
Thompson, E.P., British historian and supporter of the Campaign for Nuclear Disarmament
Tigrid, Pavel, Czech author; exiled in Paris, 1960-89
Tímár, Mátyás, Governor of the Hungarian National Bank, 1975-88
Tindemans, Leo, Belgian Minister for Foreign Affairs, 1981-89
Tito, Josip Broz, President of Yugoslavia, 1953-80
Tomášek, František, Cardinal Archbishop of Prague, 1977-91
Tomin, Julius, Czech philosopher and Charter 77 signatory; emigrated to Britain, 1980; deprived of Czech citizenship
Toms, Edward, Overseas Labour Attaché, FCO, 1981-83
Trefgarne, Lord, Parliamentary Under-Secretary of State, FCO, 1981-82
Uhl, Petr, Czech activist and co-founder of VONS; husband of Anna Šabatová
Ulbricht, Walter, General Secretary of the Central Committee of the SED, 1950-71
Urban, Jerzy, Polish Government spokesman and Press Secretary to General Jaruzelski, 1981-89
Verdet, Ilie, Romanian Prime Minister, 1979-82
Vereker, Peter, Assistant Head, Western European Department, FCO, 1978-1982
Veselý, Antonin, Vicar-General of the Archdiocese of Olomouc, Czechoslovakia

Vlček, Jozef, Czech dissident; sentenced to 20 months' imprisonment for producing and distributing unofficial religious literature, Sep 1981
Vrhovec, Josip, Yugoslav Minister for Foreign Affairs, 1978-82
Wade-Gery, Sir Robert, Deputy Secretary of the Cabinet, 1979-82
Walden, George, PPS to the Secretary of State for Foreign and Commonwealth Affairs, 1978-82; Head of Planning Staff, FCO, July 1982-83
Walentynowicz, Anna, crane operator, member of the Free Trade Unions of the Coast and of Solidarity; editor of *Robotnik Wybrzeża* (The Coastal Worker); interned for nineteen months for organising strikes in Gdańsk, Dec 1981
Wałęsa, Lech, electrician; co-founder of Solidarity and Chairman of its National Coordinating Committee
Waliszewski, Leszek, Chairman of Solidarity for the *Silesia-Dąbrowski* region, 1980-83
Walker, Peter, Minister for Agriculture, Fisheries and Food, 1979-83
Watson, Richard, Burges, Head, Trade Relations and Export Department, FCO, 1978-81
Watt, David, journalist, *The Times*
Weinberger, Caspar, US Defense Secretary, 1981-87
Whitelaw, William, Home Secretary, 1979-83
Whitmore, Clive, PPS to the Prime Minister, 1979-82
Wiatr, Jerzy, Director, Marxist-Leninist Institute of the PUWP, 1981-1984
Wilberforce, William, Head, UK Delegation, CSCE Madrid Review Meeting, 1980-1982
Wilkes, Kathy, Lecturer in philosophy, Oxford, 1973-2003; co-founder of the Jan Hus Foundation
Williams, Anthony, Head, UK Delegation, CSCE Madrid Review Meeting, 1982-83
Williamson, Martin, Economic Adviser, ESID, FCO, 1981-84
Wilson, Fraser, Eastern European and Soviet Department, FCO, 1980-83
Wilson, Sir Harold, Prime Minister, 1964-70 and 1974-76
Wilson, William, Labour MP for Coventry South, 1964-83
Wojciechowski, Adam, Polish lawyer and human rights activist; member of Amnesty International and of KOR
Wojna, Ryszard, Member of the Central Committee of the PUWP
Wood, Andrew, Counsellor and Head of Chancery, British Embassy, Moscow, 1979-82
Wright, David, Private Secretary to the Secretary of the Cabinet, 1980-82
Wright, Sir Oliver, HM Ambassador, Bonn, 1975-81; and Washington, 1982-86
Wyszkowski, Krzysztof, Polish co-founder of the Baltic Free Trade Unions, April 1976
Wyszyński, Stefan, Primate of Poland, 1948-81; Cardinal Archbishop of Gniezno and Warsaw, 1953-81
Wyzner, Eugeniusz, Polish Ambassador to the UN, 1981-82
Zabłocki, Janusz, journalist, lawyer and Catholic activist; member of the Sejm, 1965-85 and Znak, 1977-81; Chairman of the Polish Catholic Social Union, 1981-84
Zawadski, Sylwester, Polish Minister of Justice, June 1981-Nov 1983
Zhivkov, Todor, First Secretary of the BCP, 1954-89
Zhivkova, Lyudmilla, President of the Bulgarian Committee for Art and Culture, 1975-81; daughter of the Bulgarian President

DOCUMENT SUMMARIES

	NAME	DATE	MAIN SUBJECT	PAGE
15	MR MALLABY EESD FCO	9 July	Submission to Mr Fergusson on Poland's economic problems.	49
16	MR PRIDHAM Warsaw Tel. No. 236	15 Aug	Reports labour unrest in Poland.	51
17	TO MR LEVER Helsinki Tel. No. 158	21 Aug	Reports the unfolding situation in Poland.	52
18	MR PRIDHAM Warsaw Tel. No. 277	3 Sept	Reports the agreements reached on 31 August between the Polish Government and striking workers.	54
19	MR PRIDHAM Warsaw Tel. No. 278	3 Sept	Comments on the events reported in No. 18.	56
20	MR PRIDHAM Warsaw Tel. No. 279	3 Sept	Additional comments following No. 19.	57
21	TO HM REPRESENTATIVES OVERSEAS Guidance Tel. No. 92	3 Sept	Conveys lines to take on events in Poland.	58
22	SIR C. KEEBLE Moscow	3 Sept	Despatch entitled: 'The Soviet Union, Poland and Eastern Europe'.	60
23	MRS THATCHER Prime Minister	3 Sept	Letter to President Carter on the situation in Poland.	65
24	MR FOSTER East Berlin	4 Sept	Letter to Mr Goodall (Bonn) commenting on Mr Foster's despatch entitled: 'How Orwellian is the GDR?'	66
25	MR HARDIE Bucharest	8 Sept	Letter to Mr Cummins on President Ceauşescu's visits to food markets in Bucharest.	68
26	MR MALLABY EESD FCO	23 Sept	Submission to Mr Fergusson commenting on No. 22.	69
27	Sir A. Parsons UKMIS New York Tel. No. 1357	25 Sept	Reports a meeting between Lord Carrington and the Polish Foreign Minister, in New York.	70
28	MR BOLLAND Belgrade Tel. No. 274	25 Sept	Reports a visit by Mrs Thatcher to Belgrade.	72
29	MR PRIDHAM Warsaw	16 Oct	Despatch entitled: 'The Polish Crisis: Should We Help?'	74

	NAME	DATE	MAIN SUBJECT	PAGE
		1981		
45	MR FALL EESD FCO	7 Jan	Minute to Mr Mallaby outlining various scenarios around potential Soviet intervention or a continuation of the present situation.	113
46	TO MR FALL EESD FCO	15 Jan	Letter from Mr Loehnis (Bank of England) setting out arguments against providing economic assistance to Poland.	116
47	MR PRIDHAM Warsaw Tel. No. 92	6 Feb	Warns that Solidarity also has a role to play in helping to prevent a Soviet invasion of Poland.	118
48	TO MR G. BULLARD Sofia	6 Feb	Letter from Mr Fall on a proposed visit by Madame Zhivkov to the UK.	119
49	TO MR PRIDHAM Warsaw Tel. No. 83	18 Feb	Provides guidance for Mr Pridham's forthcoming meeting with the Polish Prime Minister.	121
50	MR GLADSTONE WED FCO	19 Feb	Minute to Mr Fergusson following remarks made by Herr Honecker on German reunification.	123
51	LORD CARRINGTON Secretary of State	10 Mar	Minute to the Prime Minister on contingency planning in Poland and British trade.	124
52	MR BIRCH Budapest	12 Mar	Letter to Mr Facey on Hungarian aid to Poland.	126
53	MR PRIDHAM Warsaw Tel. No. 204	23 Mar	Reports a flare-up between local authorities and Solidarity in Bydgoszcz.	127
54	MR PRIDHAM Warsaw	23 Mar	Letter to Mr J. Bullard on policy towards Poland.	129
55	EESD FCO	26 Mar	Paper entitled: 'The Umbrella Theory: Soviet reaction to the possibility of a Polish default'.	130
56	SIR C. KEEBLE Moscow Tel. No. 182	1 Apr	Reports on Soviet policy towards Poland and the question of intervention.	134
57	CABINET DEFENCE & OVERSEA POLICY COMMITTEE OD(81)8th meeting	15 Apr	Discussion on the subject of Polish debt.	136
58	MR FOSTER East Berlin	15 Apr	Letter to Mr Mallaby offering his thoughts on change in Eastern Europe.	138
59	MR BOLLAND Belgrade	24 Apr	Despatch assessing recent trouble in Kosovo.	142

	NAME	DATE	MAIN SUBJECT	PAGE
119	TO SIR N. HENDERSON Washington Tel. No. 1974	21 Dec	Conveys lines to take when discussing the Polish situation.	285
120	SIR A. PARSONS UKMIS New York Tel. No. 1614	23 Dec	Reports on conversations with the US Mission over tactics to adopt in the UN over Poland.	288
121	TO SIR N. HENDERSON Washington Tel. No. 1990	24 Dec	Reports a conversation with Mr Eagleburger on the situation in Poland.	290
122	TO MR WHITMORE 10 Downing Street	24 Dec	Letter from Mr Fall giving an update on the situation in Poland and the reaction of Western allies.	291
123	NOTE OF CONVERSATION	27 Dec	Transcript of a telephone conversation between Lord Carrington and Mrs Thatcher on events in Poland.	293
124	SIR N. HENDERSON Washington Tel. No. 3941	28 Dec	Reports a conversation with Mr Haig on the attitude of the US administration towards Poland.	296
125	NOTE OF CONVERSATION	29 Dec	Note of a telephone conversation between Lord Carrington and Mrs Thatcher on the Western response to Poland.	299
126	TO MR WHITMORE 10 Downing Street	31 Dec	Letter from Mr Fall providing an update on the Western response to events in Poland.	300
		1982		
127	TO SIR N. HENDERSON Washington Tel. No. 5	5 Jan	Reports an informal meeting of EC Foreign Ministers in Brussels on Poland.	302
128	SIR A. PARSONS UKMIS New York Tel. No. 16	6 Jan	Advises on tactics to use over Poland in the UN.	304
129	RECORD OF MEETING	6 Jan	Record of a meeting between Lord Trefgarne and Mr Popov to discuss Soviet jamming of the BBC in Poland.	306
130	TO MR COLES 10 Downing Street	6 Jan	Letter from Mr Fall providing an update on the Western response to events in Poland and proposals for possible sanctions against the Soviet Union.	307
131	MR COLES 10 Downing Street	8 Jan	Letter to Mr Fall reporting a meeting with Mrs Thatcher to discuss proposals in No. 130.	311
132	MR BROOMFIELD EESD FCO	14 Jan	Submission to Mr J. Bullard on economic sanctions against Poland and the Soviet Union.	313

	NAME	DATE	MAIN SUBJECT	PAGE
164	MR RIFKIND Minister of State	22 June	Minute to Mr Pym reporting a visit to Hungary.	400
165	MR FELL Warsaw	2 July	Letter to Mrs Macgregor on the re-establishment of the Polish Stage Actors Union.	401
166	MR MONTGOMERY EESD FCO	7 July	Minute to Sir J. Bullard on UK-Czechoslovak relations.	402
167	SIR A. ACLAND AND MR STANISZEWSKI	14 July	Record of a meeting with the Polish Ambassador on the situation in Poland.	403
168	MR PYM Secretary of State	27 July	Minute to Mr Brittan (HM Treasury) on Polish refugees.	404
169	TO MR JAMES Warsaw	29 July	Letter from Mr Montgomery on the political and economic situation in Poland.	406
170	EASTERN EUROPEAN & SOVIET DEPARTMENT FCO	6 Aug	Paper on policy towards Eastern Europe.	408
171	MR FURNESS Warsaw	20 Aug	Letter to Mr Broomfield reporting the latest situation in Poland.	412
172	MR FURNESS Warsaw	3 Sept	Letter to Mr Broomfield reporting mass demonstrations on 31 August.	414
173	MR CARTLEDGE Budapest	6 Sept	Letter to Mr Montgomery giving his impressions of Czechoslovakia following a familiarisation visit.	416
174	EASTERN EUROPEAN & SOVIET DEPARTMENT FCO	15 Sept	Summary of points agreed at a meeting with Mr Pym on relations with the Soviet Union and Eastern Europe.	419
175	FOREIGN & COMMONWEALTH OFFICE	20 Sept	Briefing on Poland for a European Political Cooperation meeting of Foreign Ministers.	421
176	MR PYM Secretary of State	22 Sept	Minute to Sir G. Howe (Chancellor of the Exchequer) on the possibility of a loan to Hungary.	423
177	MR FURNESS Warsaw	22 Sept	Letter to Mrs Macgregor noting a conversation with Bishop Dąbrowski.	424
178	MR STAGG Sofia	23 Sept	Letter to Mr Wilson on preparations for a forthcoming Warsaw Pact exercise: Shield '82.	427
179	MR BOLLAND Belgrade	4 Oct	Valedictory despatch: 'Britain's stake in Yugoslavia'.	428

CHAPTER I

'Differentiation' and the emergence of Solidarity 18 September 1979 — 10 December 1981

No. 1

Note by Mr Parsons[1] (Budapest) for Mr Mallaby,[2] 18 September 1979
Confidential (FCO 28/3702, EN 400/2)

The East European Dimension[3]

1. Generalisations about Eastern Europe are dangerous since each country has its own history and national aspirations. Nevertheless a certain common pattern can be detected in the attitude of the Governments of the Warsaw Pact countries other than the Soviet Union, though Romania may sometimes be the odd man out.

2. The regimes in all these countries are dominated by Marxists who are prepared to collaborate with the Soviet Union. They would not be in power if they did not hold this view. It is probably fallacious to distinguish between 'good' Communist Governments (Poland, Hungary) and 'bad' ones (Czechoslovakia, East Germany, Bulgaria). Some of these Governments present a more smiling face owing to the accidents of history and geography and the inter-play of individual personalities. Some Governments are clearly more successful than others in controlling their populations without using too many measures of repression. But the leaders generally must be regarded as essentially opposed to Western aims in the political and military sphere. At heart all the regimes are totalitarian and there is no blinking the fact.

3. Nevertheless these Governments are essentially nationalistic, however slavishly some of them may appear outwardly to echo Soviet foreign policy. Without wishing to rock the Kremlin boat, they all strive for a greater measure of flexibility and national autonomy.

4. It is greatly in the interest of the West to encourage this tendency. Indeed highly placed East European nationalists can be a greater worry to the Kremlin than individual dissidents. These regimes are not monolithic and our aim should be to weaken the Soviet grip on Eastern Europe by encouraging existing centrifugal movement.

[1] HMA, Budapest.

[2] Christopher Mallaby, Head of the Eastern European and Soviet Department (EESD).

[3] This document was circulated in advance of the Heads of Mission Conference on the Soviet Union and Eastern Europe on 18 October (No. 2). In a covering letter Mr Parsons noted that the East European dimension was only one aspect of East-West relations, ultimately likely to depend on the Super Powers' relationship. In a reply dated 4 October Mr Mallaby agreed that the interest of the West was to encourage 'individualistic and nationalist' tendencies of the Warsaw Pact countries but at the same time not to provoke an uncontrollable outburst, which would be crushed by the Soviet Union (FCO 28/3679, EN 021/2).

5. It follows that attention paid by us to these Governments at senior Ministerial level would be well worth while. In several Eastern European countries we are now lagging noticeably behind the Germans, French, Italians and Americans (and even the Benelux and Scandinavian countries) in the display of high-level political interest.

6. Another area worth developing further is the encouragement of people who do not necessarily occupy governmental positions but exert influence in fields such as business, scholarship and the arts. Some of these are not members of the Communist Party and, without being overt dissidents, can be assumed to be working for a greater degree of national independence. In Middle Europe even poets and musicians have their political significance.

7. These aspects should be taken account of in our relationship with the Soviet Union, where different considerations often apply. For example, laying strong emphasis on the principles of human rights (as distinct from negotiation over individual cases) can have the counter-productive effect of making it easier for the Soviet Union to close the ranks and so strengthen her grip on her European allies. The same consideration could apply to Common Market trading policy with Eastern Europe unless handled with adequate regard for national sensitivities. It is sad to hear 'Europe' being described in Britain as synonymous with the EEC. What about the lands of Tolstoy, Chopin and Kodaly, not to mention those of Mozart and Sibelius?

8. Our policy in this area will inevitably be limited by the influence of the backward-looking British public opinion which perhaps takes undue account of past history and is suspicious of overt displays of friendship with alien regimes. For example, London is now perhaps the only major capital where a visit by János Kádár[4] of Hungary would be regarded as a political liability. But Ministers can give a lead by showing the practical advantages of contacts with Eastern Europe, e.g. in the field of trade. At the same time we can hardly argue publicly that our cultivation of Eastern Europe is designed primarily to break up the Communist monolith. This is tricky to manage as a declared aim. Ideological competition is part of the rules of the game, but not de-stabilization with its attendant risks.

9. The United States cannot always be relied upon to exert wise leadership in this area. Washington is handicapped on occasion by strong ethnic and émigré influences (e.g. Polish, Jewish) both within and outside the Administration.

10. Our European allies also have their own fish to fry (German *Ostpolitik*; the French Atlantic-to-Urals concept; Italian sensitivity to their own Communist Party). But in general there are good opportunities for concerting policy in this field with our EEC partners, provided that the vital importance of American defence backing is of course not forgotten (NATO consultations could be more effective than they are).[5] Britain will speak with a stronger voice in this respect when our senior Ministers have been able to exchange visits with countries of Eastern Europe.

[4] General Secretary of the Hungarian Communist Party.

[5] On 25 September Mr Parsons in a postscript to Mr Mallaby suggested going beyond bilateral relations by ensuring reciprocal information between missions and multilateral bodies in order to contribute to the UK's multilateral diplomacy (FCO 28/3772, ENH 026/2). On 2 October Mr Burns, of the PUS's office, minuted that it would be too time-consuming for missions to keep up-to-date with all global international gatherings, but that it would be useful for posts to understand their countries' attitudes towards issues discussed multilaterally, which would motivate the leaderships of the two countries concerned (FCO 28/3679, EN 021/2).

11. The CSCE[6] process is valued in East Europe where it provides a respectable umbrella for bilateral contacts with the West. We need to keep it going and avoid Russian attempts to sabotage it through diversionary tactics. Before the Madrid meeting it will be essential to try to reach a better understanding between the West Europeans and the Americans than was attained before Belgrade. But the uncertainties of American politics make this difficult at the moment. It is no coincidence that the greatest enthusiasm comes from countries like Yugoslavia, Finland, Austria, Romania and even Hungary, which have most to gain from an intensification of contacts between East and West. Their objection to Super-Power diplomacy is understandable and needs to be treated sympathetically by the Americans and their allies.

RICHARD PARSONS

[6] The Conference on Security and Cooperation in Europe began in 1972 and culminated in the Helsinki Final Act in 1975, signed by 35 States, and followed by major review meetings in Belgrade (October 1977 - March 1978), Madrid (November 1980 - September 1983) and Vienna (November 1986 - January 1989). The agenda was divided into three 'baskets': security in Europe, co-operation in the fields of economics, science and technology and the environment; and humanitarian issues (see *DBPO*: *CSCE*).

No. 2

Draft record of the Heads of Mission Conference on the Soviet Union and Eastern Europe, 18 October 1979[1]

Confidential (FCO 28/3701, EN 400/2)

Morning session: Political relations

1. *Mr Blaker*[2] opened the discussion by commenting on the Planning Staff's informal paper 'Managing Russia'.[3] He was surprised by the suggestion that Soviet motivations were largely defensive, formed by Russia's inferiority complex and fear of invasion. Though he recognised that these influences played their part, he saw Soviet motivations as largely expansionist. Russia had been expanding for centuries, and there was no evidence to suggest its expansionism had ceased. It remained the Soviet ambition to spread its power by any means short of major war. This view was the only explanation for the growth in the Soviet fleet; the military build-up in Europe could be explained as defensive but the expansion of the fleet could not. Events in Angola had shown that the Russians were prepared to exploit

[1] Those present included Mr Blaker, Mr Bullard, Sir C. Keeble, Mr Cloake, Mr Farquharson, Mr Foster, Mr Holmer, Mr Male, Mr Parsons, Mr Pridham, Mr Fergusson, Mr Mallaby, Mr Braithwaite, Mr Tait, Mr Vereker, Mr Murrell, Mr Beel, Mr Rennie, Mr Watson, Mr Allan, Mr Knighton, Mr Browning, Mr Cotterill, Miss Pestell, Mr Bull, Mr Morrison. This draft record was sent by Mr Mallaby to the Heads of Mission who attended for comment by 16 November. As the final record has not been found, amendments sent to Mr Mallaby have been included in footnotes.

[2] Peter Blaker, Minister of State, FCO.

[3] Not printed. This paper, circulated in July 1979, concluded that the Soviet threat needed to be kept in proportion and was perfectly manageable by a healthy united West. It noted that 'more constructively, it still makes sense to pursue the overall aim which lay behind the more sober definitions of détente in the early 1970s: the creation of a network of practical East-West relationships, in which the Soviet Union has a material stake, and which multiplies the links between the two sides, reinforcing the trend when the overall relationship is improving, and cushioning the shock when it deteriorates, as it is bound to from time to time' (FCO 28/3702, EN 400/2).

every opportunity. There was a major difference between pre-revolutionary Russian expansionism and the Soviet brand: the latter was ideologically based, and allowed the Russians to exercise a strong influence at a distance, for example in Cuba and areas of the Third World.

2. Mr Blaker found it difficult to accept the argument in paragraph 22 of the paper that the current nuclear debate in NATO had come about less because of the Soviet arms build-up than because the Alliance had 'set itself a manhood test'. However, he agreed that the West needed to demonstrate the political will which had been lacking in recent years in its relations with the East. The success we had in managing our own problems—economic problems, growth, the future of the EEC, for example—were naturally relevant. But Western political will itself was an important factor, particularly in the influence it could have in the Third World in buttressing resistance to communist expansion.

3. There were some major requirements in our relations with the USSR and Eastern Europe. The first priority was, of course, to maintain our defences, which the Government believed had been run down over recent years. We should look with scepticism on President Brezhnev's initiatives and attempt to ensure that Theatre Nuclear Force modernisation was not handled in the same way as the neutron bomb issue.[4] We should meet the challenge of the ideological struggle and recognise the influence that could be exerted through contacts of all kinds. On specific visits, Mr Blaker mentioned that Mr Gromyko had indicated in his talk with the Secretary of State in New York on 26 September[5] that he might wish soon to visit Britain. Visits by Brezhnev or Kosygin were unlikely, and the Prime Minister had not yet decided her own programme of foreign visits.

4. Our major political goal in Eastern Europe was to encourage the states of the area to exercise the limited amount of independence they could achieve. Visits were important means to this end; the Government recognised that our record on visits had been poor in recent years. This was largely because of the Parliamentary balance under the previous administration, which had limited visiting world-wide, not only in Eastern Europe. Mr Blaker reported that he would be visiting Poland and Yugoslavia in November and hoped to make further visits next year.[6] There were continuing trade opportunities in Eastern Europe, especially in the export of heavy machinery. These opportunities were, however, related to the debate over credit terms, and our desire to avoid competition with our Allies in the provision of credit facilities.

[4] Following protests against deploying warheads in Europe, in 1978 President Carter postponed the development of the neutron bomb, which had been tested in the 1960s. President Reagan restarted production in 1981. On 6 October 1979 Mr Brezhnev offered to negotiate limits on Soviet medium-range missiles (the SS-20s) if NATO halted its plans. On 12 December 1979 NATO Foreign and Defence Ministers took the 'twin-track' decision to modernise its Theatre Nuclear Forces by deploying Pershing II rockets and Cruise missiles in Western Europe, to start in 1983, as an appropriate response to the Warsaw Pact military build-up. To counteract the Russians seizing the moral high ground of the disarmament debate, 1,000 US nuclear warheads were to be withdrawn from Europe. NATO also offered immediate talks with Moscow on limiting TNF on the condition that it would be at par and adequately verifiable.

[5] They met at the United Nations General Assembly. Lord Carrington reported: 'This was only my second meeting with Gromyko and it left me in no hurry for the third', noting that in his speech to the General Assembly, Gromyko had been 'pooh-poohing talks of a Soviet-Cuban threat, accusing others of meddling in Afghanistan . . . With me he was by turns jocose, hectoring and disagreeable' (UKMIS New York tel. No. 1127 of 26 September; FCO 28/3691, EN 026/3).

[6] Mr Blaker visited Poland and Yugoslavia from 18 to 21 November 1979.

5. *Sir Curtis Keeble*[7] suggested that the 'expansionist' and 'defensive' theses about Soviet motives were not mutually exclusive. The USSR was a major imperial power, which at present found itself rather over-extended, but would take every opportunity to expand further if this could be done with security. The Russians did nonetheless have many current worries—about China and its invasion of Vietnam, about events on their Southern flank, especially in Afghanistan and Iran, about their loss of influence in the Middle East, and the continuing need to control the countries of Eastern Europe, at a time when the West appeared to be recovering a little of its assertiveness.

6. In managing Russia he agreed that there was a need for robustness so that the Russians did not think they were expanding into a vacuum. There was also a need for consistency in our policies; Soviet leaders had a remarkably limited view of world issues and a rather vague impression of others' policies, which made consistency important.

7. Soviet policy in regard to Eastern Europe was clear; they were totally determined to maintain military control, and had demonstrated this by military action on three occasions since the War. They also wished to achieve the maximum political and economic integration of Eastern Europe within the Warsaw Pact system. The energy problems of Eastern Europe brought the disadvantage that the Soviet Union was having to shoulder the burden of supply, but also the advantage of providing further leverage on Eastern Europe. A new leadership in Moscow would be more likely to tighten than loosen Soviet control of Eastern Europe. British policy should be to encourage assertions of independence of East European states, but only up to a certain limit, given that the Soviet Union would intervene militarily to prevent any true destabilisation of the area.

8. *Mr Pridham*[8] pointed out that Mr Blaker's remarks on the expansionism of the Soviet Union did not apply to Eastern European states or to Poland in particular. *Mr Male*[9] commented that the USSR took many more initiatives than the West in international affairs which were, at least superficially, attractive to Third World audiences. Western nations—with the exception of France—tended to react rather than act on the East/West scene.

9. *Mr Parsons* said that Eastern Europe, being the primary foreign policy concern of the USSR, was potentially useful as an area of leverage for the West. The military grip of the Soviet Union was here for the foreseeable future but our policy should be to encourage the centrifugal tendencies which existed in other fields. The meeting should discuss the potential for this of Ministerial visits, the CSCE, human rights issues, and economic policy. He was convinced that there was further scope for long-term evolution in Eastern Europe, not brought about by outright dissidents so much as by reformist elements in the establishments and governments themselves. All governments were coalitions, especially those in one-party states, and even if they contained no 'doves' there were 'hawks' and 'super hawks' and the less hard line could be cultivated. There were also important members of the establishment—for example in Hungary the Cardinal of the Roman Catholic Church or the President of the Academy of Sciences—who were potential 'dissidents' or free-thinkers outside the orthodox party line. The dangers of exploiting these opportunities were clear. We should not appear to be attempting to destabilise Eastern Europe. On the other hand, we should not be seduced by

[7] HMA, Moscow.
[8] HMA, Warsaw.
[9] HMA, Prague.

Eastern European representations suggesting that a softer line towards the Soviet Union would assist them in securing a degree of independence. Our defence policy should, of course, be based solely on our view of our national interest.

10. *Mr Blaker* asked whether we were achieving any progress in encouraging independent action by Eastern European states and which of those states were the more independent. *Mr Pridham* pointed out the importance of nationalism on the Polish scene; even leading communists saw themselves very much as Polish patriots. Poland was very important to Britain in trade terms and over £300 million worth of trade annually[10] and a sizeable balance in our favour. The Poles were heavily in debt but were unlikely to default. An essential element in Polish politics was the 'German factor'. The Poles were terrified of German re-unification, not least because the creation of a unified and demilitarised Germany might mean the transfer of Soviet forces to Poland. The Poles were forced into a close relationship with the USSR by their nervousness about Germany. There was no possibility therefore of the Poles adopting a Romanian-type independent foreign policy.

11. *Mr Foster*[11] agreed that we should not overdo our attempt to encourage independent attitudes on the part of East European governments. However, we were certainly not over-doing this at present. The CSCE was a prime example. We had accepted the prospect which the CSCE appeared to offer of a battle of ideas,[12] which we saw as inevitably in our favour; but so far the advantage seemed to lie more with Eastern Europe. This was partly because our effort was largely uncoordinated, both within our own national system, and between the Western allies. This lack of coordination was reflected in the trade field where one Western partner was played off against another, while in general propaganda the West was doing rather badly, for example in the neutron bomb debate and among the non-aligned. The East were employing the old technique of big lies repeatedly asserted, which the West had largely abandoned as unseemly. The East had forced a number of compromises and the adoption of terms which were in themselves victories for communist aims.

12. *Mr Cloake*[13] said that Bulgaria had the closest ties of any of the East European states with the Soviet Union, and indeed a strong friendship with the Russians. The USSR had no forces in Bulgaria; they did not need them. However, there had been in the last few years a notable growth of Bulgarian nationalism. This was not directly anti-Soviet, but it did operate against giving automatic priority to the Soviet alliance. A recent example was the decision to celebrate the 1300th anniversary of the Bulgarian state in 1981. The USSR was reported to be irritated by this decision, which flaunted the longer pedigree of Bulgaria. There was absolutely no chance[14] of confrontation between the Bulgarians and the Russians but where possible the Bulgarians wished to demonstrate their autonomy, and there were opportunities for us to encourage these centrifugal tendencies.

13. *Mr Male* said that Czechoslovakia was unique in its long-standing industrial development. Czechoslovaks now resented being overtaken by other members of

[10] Mr Pridham suggested the following amendment: '. . . nearly £300 million worth of exports last year'.

[11] HMA, East Berlin.

[12] Mr Foster suggested the following amendment: 'line 6 *et seq*: "battle of ideas, because we were confident that our ideas were better than theirs: but the unequal way in which the competition was proceeding threatened nevertheless to give the advantage to the Communist countries."'

[13] HMA, Sofia.

[14] Mr Cloake suggested: 'In paragraph 12 insert "for compelling economic reasons" before "There was absolutely no chance"'.

the Warsaw Pact, but Czechoslovakia was in an economic straitjacket because of its limited energy resources. It had low-grade coal and no gas, and was therefore heavily dependent on the USSR. Czechoslovakia had no iron ore but produced 15 million tons of steel each year, importing all its ore from the USSR. Similarly with textiles, Czechoslovakia's cotton, which previously came from Egypt, was now imported from the USSR. The Czechoslovaks recognised their need for imports from the West to help modernise their industry and the consequent need to export to Western countries. But they would be increasingly tied to the USSR, especially because they were now primarily responsible for the manufacture of equipment for 23 nuclear power plants for the CMEA.[15]

14. *Mr Holmer*[16] said Romania was in many ways a special case, above all in foreign policy. Romania's foreign policy was not simply a gimmick by Ceaușescu, but a product of long-term developments in Romania, for example the struggle between the Moscow-trained and the indigenous Communist leaders. There was no real prospect of a major diversion from this policy. Increasing economic dependence on the USSR might slow its development, but would not reverse it. Romania was in any case less economically dependent on the USSR than most East European countries; in the past the Romanians had imported no oil from the Soviet Union, but indications were that they would take 300,000 tons this year and 1 million next. The other side of the coin of Romania's independent foreign policy was, of course, its peculiarly strict internal regime. The USSR's tolerance of Romanian idiosyncrasy in foreign policy might be lessened if this internal policy were relaxed. Britain could attempt to exercise some influence on Romanian internal affairs, primarily in personal cases in which there was a strong British connection. On more general internal issues, there was a need for caution.

15. *Mr Pridham* gave four reasons for encouraging contacts with Eastern Europe:

(i) to increase trade;

(ii) the East European leaders had some influence in Moscow and probably were a factor for moderation;

(iii) to encourage the 'demonolithisation' of the Soviet bloc;

(iv) to encourage human rights and the more general improvement in the quality of life.

16. *Mr Blaker* asked whether too much Western pressure on Eastern European countries on human rights and religion would have the effect of forcing them back into the grip of the Soviet Union. *Mr Male* said that as far as Czechoslovakia was concerned, the Charter 77[17] movement probably had sympathy but not much support. The Czechoslovak authorities had reacted first harshly and then more leniently. But they were now bringing six dissidents to trial. There seemed to have

[15] Founded in 1949 in Moscow, the Council for Mutual Economic Assistance, or Comecon was an economic organisation led by the Soviet Union and including mostly countries from the Eastern Bloc, which aimed at strengthening their economic relationship by coordinating their activities. A response of the Soviet Union to the Marshall Plan, it wanted to limit imports from the West and avoid 'capitalist control'.

[16] HMA, Bucharest.

[17] Charter 77 was a combination of a statement and a petition denouncing violations of human rights by the Czechoslovak Government. Signed by more than 200 people, it referred to the covenant of the UN and the Helsinki Accord on human rights, considered as the framework of civilized life in the twentieth century. The signatories, of different faiths, opinions and convictions, considered their role as a civic duty, not as an opposition against the regime. The three major spokesmen were Messrs Jan Patočka, Václav Havel and Jiří Hájek.

been disagreement among the leaders; the present moment was a particularly delicate one at which to be conducting the trial. Perhaps the Czechoslovak authorities did not care about this, since they had also staged a major trial in the midst of the Belgrade Conference. But they might have wanted to have the trial earlier but had been restrained by the Soviet Union. The Charter 77 movement was divided between those who thought that support from the West gave them protection and those who thought it was no help. Mr Male thought it probably did help those who were prominent but not those who were less well known. He thought it was right that something should be said when people acting within the law were subject to repression. In general this should be done fairly privately and at the highest possible level. Public statements were of little value. The effect was enhanced if we could act in common with our partners in the Nine.[18] The best grounds for complaint were not the severity of the sentences, but the fact that people were being put on trial at all. *Mr Foster* said that no Government in Eastern Europe could take risks with its internal security. Naturally they took action against dissidents, but there were constraints. They now took a more flexible view than under Stalin and some grumbling was tolerated provided it was not organised. Moreover, the regimes were conscious of potential damage to their images abroad. But they were unlikely to take account of governmental representations unless they could use them as a bargaining counter. By and large they were not motivated to be more liberal by high-level interventions. But the impact of their image was significant and we should therefore make sure that their actions were widely known through the media.

17. *Mr Parsons* said that there were naïve people in the West who believed that the Russians were democrats who had gone astray. The Hungarian authorities did not have to take action against dissidents because there were no public dissident activities. The Hungarians said in private that they were opposed to the Czechoslovak trials and argued that the West should not take action, e.g. in multilateral fora, which would put Hungary in the position of having to support the Czechoslovaks. The question of how representations about dissidents should be made was essentially technical. Multilateral approaches obliged the members of the Warsaw Pact to stand up and be counted; this argued against a blanket approach at Madrid. *Mr Blaker* said HMG faced the difficulty that MPs and public opinion expected the Final Act to mean something and thought we should call on other countries to honour it. It might not be possible to avoid saying something in Parliament.

18. *Mr Pridham* said that dissident movements in Poland did not have significant influence. But the Roman Catholic Church did. If a community of interest between the dissidents, the Church and the workers arose on a specific issue, the Government would have to give way. The Pope's visit to Poland had given the Church new confidence.[19] It did not feel the need to hurry or to press matters. It was not sympathetic to the dissidents, many of whom were Marxists. It would try to work slowly for more concessions from the Government.

19. *Sir Curtis Keeble* thought that in the end the Soviet regime would crumble as a result of internal dissent, but the dissidents who would win in the long run were not the dissidents of today. The latter did not have significant influence on policy, though their activities and their contact with the Western press would have

[18] The nine EC Member States.

[19] John Paul II (born Karol Józef Wojtyła) visited Poland from 2 to 10 June 1979.

been unthinkable under Stalin. The need to avoid trouble during the Olympic Games[20] could cause a swing back to repression. As for our own policies, the main areas of our activity should be culture and information, including the BBC and imported books and newspapers. Visits could also open up Soviet society gradually. This was more important than support for individuals, which enabled the Russians to brand them as traitors. Official representations about individual cases, to have any chance of effect, should be undertaken in private at a high level.

20. *Mr Blaker* said that dissidents had told him they hoped the West would keep up the pressure. They thought it helped. Why was this? *Sir Curtis Keeble* thought public pressure protected well-known dissidents like Sharansky, but it was hard to see its effects further down the line. *Mr Male* commented that sentences were now much less than in the late 40s and early 50s. *Mr Cloake* said that there was no evidence of organised dissent in Bulgaria. There was the safety valve of grumbling, and anyway people were now better off. There were no Western press correspondents in Bulgaria with whom dissidents could make contact.

Mr Parsons commented that there were dissidents at the other end of the spectrum who thought that the East European Governments were not sufficiently pro-Moscow.

Mr Fergusson[21] said that there were different levels of dissent. The impact of Western criticism however focussed only on a small band of intellectuals. In the Soviet Union dissent was regarded as anti-Russian, so Western intervention was unlikely to evoke any effective response. *Mr Male* said that the Czechs would not regard dissenters as anti-patriotic since the whole tradition of the Czech lands favoured quiet dissent.

Information

21. *Mr Blaker* referred to Mr Foster's earlier remarks about the inadequacy of our information effort, especially in the Third World. He asked for practical examples of Soviet successes. *Mr Foster* said that the West was not doing very well in the ideological struggle. There was a lack of organisation in making our influence felt in the developing countries. The Western position had slipped over the years and there was an impression that we had contracted out, leaving the field to the Russians by default. There had been a steady drift over the years in the meaning of 'non-alignment'.[22] Marxist terminology was now second nature to many Third World leaders. The primitive Soviet sales technique had had a cumulative effect.[23] We also failed even to brief people visiting Communist countries adequately. The Communists used professionals where we used amateurs. A double standard was practiced against us on the question of

[20] The Moscow Summer Olympics took place from 19 July to 3 August 1980. They were boycotted by 65 countries led by America in protest against the 1979 Soviet invasion of Afghanistan. See *DBPO*: *Afghanistan*.

[21] Ewen Fergusson, Assistant Under-Secretary of State (Europe).

[22] Mr Foster suggested the following amendment: 'Expand sixth sentence: "in the meaning of non-alignment": "in the wake of the Havana Conference the non-aligned were even talking of the need for a compromise between the extremes of Tito and Castro."'

[23] Mr Foster suggested inserting here: 'But of more direct concern to East European posts was the lack of effective co-ordination within and between Western countries in exploiting opportunities in the context of the final act to exert influence in Communist countries, while the latter took full advantage of our open societies. We could not expect to achieve complete symmetry. But we could do more with our existing resources to reduce the present asymmetry. We failed even to brief'.

development aid.[24] *Sir Curtis Keeble* thought that this was a shade too pessimistic. The Russians no longer escaped altogether on the question of development aid. But he did not dissent from the philosophy behind Mr Foster's remarks. *Mr Blaker* asked whether we were now less good at propaganda than when IRD[25] existed. *Mr Pridham* said that there were now no letters to *The Times* inspired by IRD. Many people on the left praised Marxism while dismissing the Soviet Union. They cherished the thought that there could be another kind of Marxism. *Mr Parsons* agreed that the West must not play football with only one goal. We must recognise that there was an ideological struggle and expose the other side of our way of life. The other side was much better than we at spreading the idea of comradeship. It has used this to capture the thinking of the local establishments, to generate affection for 'struggling peoples' and to make propaganda about people being mistreated in far-away places. The old Commonwealth idea had had a certain value but some Third World countries were themselves now dictatorships. The West had to think of better ways of selling its product and should not cut out ways of disseminating information. Mr Blaker agreed that democracy was not always attractive to autocratic Third World rulers.

22. *Mr Foster* agreed that the Russians were very successful in adopting popular causes abroad and posing as the champions of liberation movements. *Mr Cloake* mentioned the area of apparent disarmament initiatives where the Russians so often had successfully put us on the defensive. *Mr Blaker* said that Southern Africa was a very relevant factor which needed to be borne in mind. Our relations with Southern Africa were likely to be a source of propaganda for the other side for some time to come. Meanwhile, we needed to expose the nature of the Soviet system more effectively.

23. When the discussion turned to the CSCE *Mr Parsons* said that there was a myth about the Belgrade Meeting that if President Carter had made less fuss about human rights, an agreement might have been reached allowing the Helsinki watchers to operate in the Soviet Union and Eastern Europe. The West had done the right thing for the wrong reasons. It had been wrong to think that major new measures could be achieved at Belgrade, but right to call attention to areas of the Final Act which had not been implemented. CSCE was important to the small countries of Eastern Europe and to the Neutrals and Non-Aligned. It was a gospel on which to base bilateral contacts. Madrid should keep the process going as background for our other activities, but we should not aim too high. There should be a frank and sensible review of implementation. The need was to get implementation of the existing provisions rather than more provisions. *Sir Curtis Keeble* said that the Russians would hope by advancing ideas on the military side,

[24] Mr Foster suggested moving this sentence to the end of paragraph 21. In a letter to Mr Bullard on 23 October, he suggested a more interventionist UK policy, but Mr Johnson argued that while the 'struggle of ideas' was bound to work to the West's disadvantage, it was unacceptable to imitate the GDR's methods, as the West's strength rested on the freedom of citizens. He added that in any case, freedoms of thought, expression and movement were exercising a positive impact on the Soviet bloc.

[25] The Information Research Department of the Foreign Office was set up in 1948 to counter Soviet propaganda, disseminating information globally through writers, politicians and trade unionists, and supporting anti-Communist publications. See FCO History Note 9, *Origins and Establishment of the Foreign Office Information Research Department, 1946-48* (FCO, 1995) available at www.issuu.com/fcohistorians. The department was closed down in 1977 by the Foreign Secretary, David Owen.

to slide out of the review process, but this would not, in his view, make them *demandeurs* at Madrid.

24. Sir Curtis Keeble referred to the influence of books on Soviet Society. Some modest success had been achieved and this could continue if there were further expenditure. Influence could be exercised through the BBC and, to some extent, through publications. We should encourage scientific, cultural and educational exchanges. Greater access to books and newspapers was a worthwhile objective in the CSCE context. Mr Pridham said that many Poles listened to the BBC. The authorities' excuse for their failure to import Western books was financial. The Germans and French did quite a lot with publications but Britain did not. *Mr Cloake* said that the best ways of exercising influence were the BBC and tourism. In Bulgaria there was the same financial problem as in Poland. Was there some way in which we could help Eastern European countries to meet the currency problem? *Mr Parsons* said that the Embassy in Budapest had tried to make its Library more accessible but financial cuts would mean that it would be open for four hours per week.[26] He recalled that parts of Eastern Europe could receive Western TV and radio programmes. *Mr Foster* said that West German Television covered 70% of the GDR but the GDR authorities were very strict about Western published material and Embassy reading rooms. It was against the law for a GDR citizen to visit a Western Embassy without permission. This made the importance of the BBC all the greater. It also heightened the need for unofficial visitors to the GDR to be intelligently briefed.

Conclusions

25. *Mr Bullard*[27] said that he sensed a high degree of concurrence with the papers which had been circulated in advance, including Mr Blaker's minute of 9 August.[28] East/West contacts should be encouraged to the limit of the constraints such as limits on Ministers' time. He would not dissent from the 4 reasons which Mr Pridham had put forward for encouraging contacts, but thought that 'demonolithisation' was more feasible in Eastern Europe than in the Soviet Union. Additional reasons were the need to learn more about the European communist countries and the need to develop our Embassies' contact with people who took decisions, e.g. in the trade field. He was struck by the recurrence of debate about the need to strike a balance between the two extreme views of Eastern Europe: that the countries were 100% satellites or that they were striving for independence. We were perhaps in danger of erring in the latter sense. The phenomena which pointed in this direction were of a fairly superficial nature. The East European Governments almost certainly had not been consulted about Brezhnev's speech in East Berlin[29] (with the possible exception of the GDR) and the Poles had not yet been consulted by the Russians about Madrid. The East Europeans had been disappointingly like the Russians at Belgrade. This helped one to see the prospects for East European independence in the proper perspective. Moreover, the East

[26] Mr Parsons asked for this to be amended to 'fewer hours per week'.

[27] Julian Bullard, Deputy Under-Secretary of State (Europe).

[28] Not printed. His minute, sent to the Foreign Secretary, defined the approach he thought the UK should adopt towards the Soviet Union and its allies. In the face of Soviet ambition in Eastern Europe, Blaker advised increasing Western defences, encouraging Eastern European States to exercise a limited amount of independence, and differentiating 'between the Soviet Union and Eastern Europe, and between one East European and another'. He suggested an active programme of visits and exchanges and a continuation of the CSCE process (FCO 28/3679, EN 021/2).

[29] On 6 October 1979 President Brezhnev on a visit to East Berlin had given a 35-minute address to the East German Parliament.

European need for Soviet energy, and indeed the Western recession, might well increase the division of Europe.

26. Mr Bullard agreed that coordination was weak in the West. Neither NATO nor the Nine were very good at it. This was not for want of trying. The Nine had to proceed by consensus, which was difficult to achieve, even on a subject as obvious as credit. The East-West struggle had been compared to a very bad game of tennis in which the only points were double faults. The neutron bomb episode was not a triumph for Soviet propaganda but a failure of US decision making. Fortunately this failure appeared to have been taken into account in planning US decisions on TNF modernisation.

27. It was a serious weakness that the non-aligned movement was not really non-aligned. There had been a failure of US policy in this area. But some of the contributions to the debate had been reminiscent of those who in 1939 had thought that the war would be won by propaganda. The best course for the West was to manage its own affairs better. The National Income of the GDR might be higher than that of the UK but there was no sign of people wanting to cross the wire in the reverse direction. The West should beware of becoming more like the GDR.

28. On human rights, it would be important to maintain consistency between policy towards the East and towards other countries. The right note could only be decided in the FCO with proper reference to public opinion. Anything done by the Nine would inevitably be the highest common factor on which agreement could be reached. Human rights were only one element in East-West relations.

Afternoon session: economic affairs

29. *Mr Parsons* summing up this morning's discussion said that there were two views about relations with Eastern Europe. No-one knew which would turn out to be right, but there were advantages in looking at things optimistically since pessimism led to inactivity.[30] Mr Parsons then turned to Hungary's dependence on imported energy. Hungary had gone in for high technology, capital intensive industries (e.g. pharmaceutical, petro-chemicals). These required large energy inputs, but the Hungarians had no energy resources of their own. Hungary's oil was all imported, above all from the Soviet Union. Mr Parsons suggested that in Eastern Europe except Romania the Soviet Union was unlikely to need to use troops to maintain a hold; the economic lever was sufficient. Some 50% of the Hungarian economy was represented by foreign trade; of that 50% was with non-Communist countries; and of that 50% was with the EEC. Trade with non-Communist countries had been deliberately increased. However the Hungarians were now having to expand trade with the Soviet Union again, to offset oil purchases. The New Economic Mechanism[31] was now 10 years old and had proved very effective. The Hungarians had a high standard of living, though not up to Western standards. The Russians had not objected to a system based on the profit motive; there was no reason why they should. The question was whether the West should make it easier or more difficult for the Soviet Union to provide oil to Hungary and other Eastern European states. Was it in our interests to starve the

[30] Mr Parsons suggested: 'change end to read "since pessimism led to failure to exploit opportunities"'.

[31] In 1968 Mr Kádár introduced a comprehensive plan of economic reforms, called the New Economic Mechanism. It partially decentralised economic decision-making and freed some prices from central control.

Soviet Union of oil thus putting pressure on supplies to Eastern Europe? Or was a fat Communist better than a thin one?

30. *Mr Cloake* said that 80% of Bulgaria's foreign trade was with the CMEA, including 50% with the Soviet Union. 80% of Bulgaria's fuel and 90% of her oil were imported from the Soviet Union. This year the Bulgarians had borrowed Hungary's economic mechanism in an attempt to improve efficiency. Industry in future would have to be profitable. The standard of living in Bulgaria had improved due to rapid industrialisation. But the cost and availability of oil supplies would make it difficult to maintain progress. It appeared that the Soviet Union had pressed Bulgaria to place more emphasis on the one resource it possessed—good land. This would suggest a stand-still or even reversal in the standard of living. Until now the Bulgarians had been insulated from consumer price rises, but these were on the way. Mr Cloake thought they would create no internal problems.

31. *Mr Pridham* said that Poland had no oil but did have 200 million tons of coal. 80% of Poland's oil came from the Soviet Union. The Polish authorities had three ideas for alleviating the energy problem; these were conservation, alternative sources and technological processes (e.g. coal liquification). Mr Pridham said that Polish imports of technology would probably slump, due as much to lack of foreign currency as to energy difficulties. He thought that in the final analysis the Soviet Union would bail Poland out but would extract a price for doing so. He felt that Poland would have some difficulty in paying its hard currency debts.

32. *Mr Holmer* said that Romania's extraction of oil had peaked; she was now a net importer. He thought the Romanians might have a hard time in stepping up oil imports to cover the deficit. Problems caused by changes in Iran were one factor, but he had also heard rumours that Libya had told the Romanians to alter their approach to Egypt or risk losing Libyan supplies. The Romanians had introduced a major conservation programme aimed at achieving energy independence again by 1990: this objective was probably too ambitious. But the Romanians were looking to nuclear power to meet some of their needs and this gave an opportunity to Western exporters. In recent years Romania had consistently achieved the highest growth rate in Eastern Europe. Although the energy problem might cause the rate to drop somewhat, it would still probably remain comparatively high. If this were so, imports would also remain at a fairly high level. Mr Holmer felt that radical economic reforms in Romania were unlikely.

33. *Mr Male* said that Czechoslovakia's only energy resource was some poor quality coal. There was also some uranium, which was sent to the Soviet Union: the contract would lapse next year and probably not be extended. The Czechoslovaks were heavy consumers of meat and imported large quantities of animal foodstuffs to maintain this diet. Mr Male said that the once efficient industrial base in the Czech lands was now showing its age; Slovakia had been a primarily agricultural area but was now industrialising fast. Czechoslovakia was heavily dependent on the Soviet Union for energy supplies. The Government were looking into conservation measures, and the possibilities of using nuclear energy. They were also seeking to diversify their sources of oil and had sought good relations with Arab countries, especially Iraq, Libya and latterly Algeria. They would however continue to import technology wherever possible and were preparing to increase spending on imports from the West by 50%. Consumer prices in Czechoslovakia had been held stable for a long time as part of the Government's 'contract' with consumers. Recently however there had been some price rises and there were more to come. The possibilities for extensive economic reform were

inhibited by the events of the Dubček era,[32] although Mr Male felt that the present Government had a will to proceed. There were no problems over credits for Czechoslovakia: the Czechoslovak Government were very conservative about getting into debt.

34. *Mr Foster* said that the East Germans' main problem was shortage of labour. They were pushing through a large investment programme, which should give the West improved opportunities to sell high technology.[33] East Germany was probably the most efficient of the Communist countries, with a high standard of living—probably 70 or 80% that of West Germany.[34] One factor in this was the large number of female workers, another aspect of the shortage of labour. The East Germans had a high rate of borrowing, with a debt ratio of 30%, probably second only to that of Poland in Eastern Europe. There were rumours of large price rises, but the leaders appeared to be optimistic, possibly because the East Germans expected to receive preferential treatment from the Soviet Union. East Germany's only energy resource was brown coal. Oil and gas were imported from the Soviet Union, and other resources came from Eastern Europe and the Third World. This partially explained East Germany's active policy in the Third World.

35. *Mr Farquharson*[35] said that Yugoslavia had a shortage of hard currency. Yugoslavia was not dependent on the Soviet Union for oil supplies: the Yugoslavs produced 25% of their oil requirements and also had some coal. In recent years Yugoslavia had managed to balance its trade through remittances from overseas residents and tourism. A recession in the West would obviously have an impact on this source of finance. Mr Farquharson said that 30% of Yugoslavia's exports went to the Soviet Union. The West should do what it could to help Yugoslavia reduce this dependence. He was not suggesting any form of subsidy but there might for example be some coordination of policy to ensure that bureaucratic detail did not obscure this objective, e.g. in the negotiations between Yugoslavia and the EEC.

36. *Mr Blaker* said that the choice was a difficult one. If we made it easier for the Soviet Union to exploit her oil resources we would in effect be maintaining Eastern Europe's dependence on the Soviet Union. If, on the other hand, we worked towards making it more difficult for the Soviet Union to improve production perhaps the Soviet Union would look abroad thus creating further pressure and problems on the world oil market.

37. *Sir Curtis Keeble* said that the Soviet Union currently produced around 600 million tons of oil. Of this, 80 million tons went to Eastern Europe, 90 million tons to Third World countries, and the remainder was for internal consumption. There had been two projections of future Soviet production. The British view was that in 1985 the Soviet Union would be producing roughly the same amount as at present. The US projection was that production would be considerably lower, between 500 and 550 million tons. If the US projection was correct, there would obviously be serious consequences for Eastern Europe and the world market. On the whole he felt that the British view was nearer the mark. Oil supply was so important to the

[32] Alexander Dubček, General-Secretary of the Czechoslovak Communist Party from 1968 to 1969, introduced a series of reforms named 'socialism with a human face', which aimed at a revitalisation of the country's economy (see *DBPO: Soviet Union, 1968-1972*).

[33] Mr Foster suggested redrafting the first two sentences: 'one of the East Germans' major problems was shortage of Labour. Consequently they were anxious to acquire modern labour saving plant and looked to the West as a source of high technology'.

[34] Mr Foster suggested: 'by perhaps 60 to 70'.

[35] HMA, Belgrade.

Soviet Union that they would go to very great lengths to maintain the existing level of supply. Possibly the Soviet Union would be forced to cut back on exports of oil, but not, he felt, to a grave degree. He was sceptical about the degree of influence we might be able to exert over Soviet production. Certainly the Soviet Union was interested in our technology; the UK, the French and the Americans were busily fighting for contracts. But Western technology was probably not of crucial importance. In any case it was unlikely that the Soviet Union could be forced to alter its basic policies in order to obtain technology from the West: if necessary the Soviet Union would divert internal resources to develop its own technology in slower time. The Soviet internal economy was not doing well. Growth had dropped from 6½% to 4% p.a. and the authorities were busily attempting to improve efficiency.

38. *Mr Morrison*[36] said that DEI's estimate was that Soviet oil production would plateau in the next five years and begin to decline after 1985. It was felt that production could not be increased before 1990 as there would be a considerable lead time in the development of new resources. The demand for oil was of course increasing throughout Eastern Europe and this would mean that during the next ten years the Soviet Union would either have to cut supplies to hard currency buyers or starve the Eastern European countries. The Soviet economy was slowing down and the situation was unlikely to improve markedly in the foreseeable future. This suggested that Eastern Europe was in for a bad time from 1985.

39. *Sir Curtis Keeble* said he wished to clarify one point. The Soviet problem was technological; it was a question of getting at more difficult oil resources. So far their exploitation had concentrated on the easier fields. *Mr Blaker* said that this returned us to the original question: should we help the Soviet Union to improve her oil production? As he understood it, *Sir Curtis Keeble* had said that we probably did not have the ability to influence the situation anyway. Sir Curtis Keeble agreed. He doubted whether the West had an effective lever here.

40. *Mr Morrison* said that we probably could help with offshore supplies in deep waters. The Soviet Union however had been reluctant to come to the West for assistance. Indeed the leisurely way in which they had been dealing with the problem suggested that they saw no difficulties. *Mr Browning*[37] said that in speaking recently with senior Russian technologists he gained the impression that the Soviet Union was not particularly impressed by our ability to provide the necessary technology. The feeling seemed to be that the West could provide no help to the Soviet Union on Permafrost fields and that Britain's work in deep waters was not totally relevant to the situation in Soviet off-shore fields.

41. *Mr Pridham* said that while it was fair to say that the Soviet Union had a strong lever over the Eastern European countries whilst oil supplies were maintained, once the Soviet Union told the Eastern Europeans that they could not have further supplies of oil its economic influence over these countries would decline.[38]

42. *Mr Bull*[39] pointed out that Eastern European countries already had ceilings for energy supplies from the Soviet Union. If a country exceeded the ceiling they had to pay for the balance in hard currency. This meant that the Eastern European

[36] Department of Economic Intelligence, MOD.

[37] Probably Rex Alan Browning, Under-Secretary for the Commercial Relations and Exports Division at the Department of Trade.

[38] Mr Pridham suggested amending the last eight words to read 'this card would lose its force'.

[39] Bank of England.

country concerned would be no worse off buying extra oil supplies on the world market. He felt the basic problem was that of indebtedness. But there was of course the point that if rates of economic growth in Eastern European countries fell, the growth of demand for energy would also fall.

43. *Mr Knighton*[40] said it was his impression that Eastern European countries were as worried as Western countries by the impact of OPEC price rises. A recession in the Western economies would have serious implications for the Eastern countries.

EEC/CMEA relations

44. *Mr Parsons* said that the Hungarians wanted an umbrella EEC/CMEA agreement under which they could then build up bilateral relations with the EEC. They might not say so but this was certainly their real policy. This was now generally understood in the FCO but not always in the Commission. It would, therefore, be helpful if Ministers could lose no opportunity to make the point.

45. *Mr Blaker* asked if any other Eastern European governments took a similar view. *Mr Male* said that Czechoslovakia wished relations to be as bilateral as possible and thought that, the stronger the CMEA/EEC relations were the less chance there was of this. *Mr Holmer* said that the Romanians also wanted bilateral relations with the EEC. To this end they wished to conclude agreement with the Commission covering industrial goods and the establishment of a Joint Commission. *Mr Blaker* asked if this meant that the Romanian and Hungarian views were identical. *Mr Parsons* said that they generally agreed. But the Romanians could conclude an agreement with the EEC before the CMEA did, while the Hungarians could only do so afterwards.[41]

46. *Mr Bullard* said that EEC/CMEA agreement was not essential to East /West trade. The point was to avoid positively harmful steps such as a strengthening of the CMEA.

Trade with Eastern Europe

47. *Mr Knighton* said that the questions raised in correspondence had been:

(i) Why had we fallen behind our competitors in East European trade?
(ii) What could HMG do about it?
(iii) Should export promotion have more staff?
(iv) Did commercial success depend on political relations?
(v) Should Ministers be co-Chairmen of Joint Commissions?
(vi) Were long-term cooperation agreements important?
(vii) Did counter-trade erode the benefits from exports?

In his view the answers to these questions were:

(i) Not all the relevant figures needed were available. But it was undoubtedly true both that we had fallen behind in our world trade generally and that our exporters had concentrated on other markets than Eastern Europe.

(ii) This question assumed that HMG should be doing something about specific markets. The Government clearly needed a world-wide trade strategy. But it was up to companies to have strategies for individual markets.

(iii) As befitted difficult markets, the East European posts' commercial departments were well staffed. Should they be better? That would depend on world-wide staffing policies.

[40] William Knighton, Deputy Secretary, Department of Trade.

[41] Mr Parsons suggested: 'while the Hungarian position was more circumscribed'.

(iv) Not to keep up manifestations of good political relations would certainly count against us. But it was less certain that contracts could actually be won by political gestures. HMG's efforts were marginal in comparison with industry's, except in the field of export credits, where arrangements had to be competitive. Our general policy should remain to oppose a credit race but to match others' terms. For example, we were at the moment pressing the French not to give the USSR below-consensus terms when the present Franco-Soviet agreement expired at the end of this year.
(v) In general, we were sceptical about the value of joint commissions. There was no need for more senior British co-chairmen. There might of course be special cases where the matter of the co-chairmen's seniority was getting mixed up in the politics of trade.
(vi) Long-term cooperation agreements were important but only to the extent that they

(*a*) improved the general atmosphere and

(*b*) gave the authority to East European bureaucrats to pursue specific policies.

(vii) Whether counter trade unduly eroded the advantages of trade was a commercial decision which had to be taken in each case by individual firms. Nor was it clear whether exporting countries who agreed to counter trade on particular deals gained wider advantages by doing so.

48. *Mr Blaker* asked what percentage of the BOTB's[42] budget was devoted to the export effort in Eastern Europe and why other Western exporters' trade had not shifted away from East Europe as ours seemed to have done. *Mr Knighton* replied that about 4.8% of the FCO's staff budget and 10.7% of BOTB's budget was spent in Eastern Europe; but the latter figure perhaps gave an exaggerated impression because it covered participation in many trade fairs, which were important in Eastern Europe. The answer to Mr Blaker's second question was very complicated. The big increase in trade between the EEC's six members had taken place in the 1960s. We had passed through this phase only in the 1970s and the resultant shift had been reinforced by the loss of Commonwealth preference, by the changing trading patterns of newly independent countries keen to diversify away from dependence on Britain, and by the pull of OPEC (which seemed to affect us more than others).

49. *Mr Cloake* asked whether we really wanted to increase trade with Eastern Europe. Some people looked on large capital projects as loss leaders while others thought that the Eastern European markets were vital because elsewhere there were no profitable contracts to be had. If Eastern European trade was worth pursuing, the techniques involved needed great political and commercial commitment. *Mr Male* said that Eastern Europe was susceptible to careful governmental cultivation of a sort unnecessary in a more sophisticated market. We spent more on commercial work than other countries. But there was an analogy with guide dogs for the blind. Our exporters needed to be led. According to OECD figures our share of Czechoslovak imports had not fallen behind in the last nine years, chiefly because a range of small companies had gained a number of small and medium contracts. The political dimension was very important, as was our participation in trade affairs. If we had any money, we should spend it on vernacular magazines with an export message. It would indeed be a waste of Ministerial time to sit as

[42] British Overseas Trade Board.

joint commission co-chairmen. Long-term cooperation agreements were important between major firms and big Ministries.

50. *Mr Bull* said that it was important to be selective and to look most closely at profitable markets. The USSR, for example, had no balance of payments problem and had a huge credit, most of which had still to be drawn down. But we had not done very well in the Soviet market. We had on the other hand done very well in Poland. After the BAC 111 contract,[43] Romania had now reached the limit of her borrowing capacity and there was little room for new business. Czechoslovakia had great potential but the GDR was heavily indebted and the outlook was poor.[44] *Sir Curtis Keeble* said that Embassies' commercial staffs could be smaller if firms were able to make more use of western banks' offices and of the Anglo/Soviet Chamber of Commerce. We fell behind in trade for 2 reasons. Our industry was relatively uncompetitive and was less good than say, German industry at cultivating contacts over a long period. It was important to note that in the state trading economies, trade could not be divorced from the inter-governmental relationship. The Germans had gained some Soviet contracts in the wake of Brezhnev's visit to Bonn and the French were following closely.

51. *Mr Parsons* said that the EETC[45] agreed on the value of Ministerial visits as a sweetener of the atmosphere. Industry should also be encouraged to participate in package deals to make best use of counter[46] trade deals. *Mr Pridham* said that British exporters were not falling behind in Poland. In 1978 exports had increased by 30% at a time when other people's exports were falling. We now stood second only to the Germans. It was noticeable that 2 of the 3 large contracts we had recently landed had come after Ministerial visits. At present Davy were competing against the French for a new project. Gierek[47] had just visited Paris. Whether Davy got this contract would therefore be something of a test case. *Mr Farquharson* said that he would emphasise the need to nurse a market over a long period. Counter trade undoubtedly eroded profits. But since there would be no contracts at all without it, it was a matter for commercial judgment whether or not it was worthwhile in individual cases.[48] *Mr Burges Watson*[49] asked whether strategic export controls handicapped exports. The Eastern demand for Western technology might rise in future and it would be a pity to handicap exports if strategic controls were actually unnecessary. *Sir Curtis Keeble* said that Lucas had recently lost a contract worth £20-30 million in the Soviet Union for this very reason. It was therefore important to ensure that there was no cheating by other countries, which

[43] This jet airliner was launched by the British Aircraft Corporation at the beginning of the 1960s. The last UK-built 111 flew in 1982, by which time production under licence was progressively being transferred to Romania where nine were built as the Rombac 1-11.

[44] Mr Pridham suggested the following addition: 'in the afternoon session Mr Bull said that in view of Poland's indebtedness the correct course would be to suspend credit [not noted in the draft record]. I replied that if the UK did this unilaterally the result would be that other Western countries would take over our business. If the West acted jointly the probable result would be to topple Gierek and push Poland back to the sort of relationship with the USSR of 15 years or so again'.

[45] East European Trade Council.

[46] Mr Parsons suggested substituting 'two-way'.

[47] Edward Gierek, General Secretary of the Polish United Workers' Party from 1970 to 1980.

[48] Mr Foster objected that: 'Paragraphs 49-51 suggest that I was silent on trade promotion. Insert after Mr Farquharson's remarks in paragraph 51: "Mr Foster said he had not intervened earlier on this subject because he had written about it in a recent despatch. He wished however to record his agreement with most of the points made by the East European colleagues, especially the need for a co-ordinated politico-commercial strategy."'

[49] Head of the Trade Relations and Export Department, FCO.

would give us the worst of both worlds—we should have lost contracts and there would have been a technology leak to the East.

52. *Mr Browning* said that Britain was losing many contracts because British businessmen failed to pursue them properly. We were lagging behind some other European counties, e.g. the FRG, on counter trade. There were various ways, bad and less bad, of pursuing it. Straight purchases were bad for domestic producers. Third country collaboration was better, but was possible only after a basis of trust had been established.

53. *Mr Knighton* said that Ministerial visits were essential. We should ensure that we did at least no worse than under the previous government.

54. *Mr Bullard* said that he was impressed by the warmth of the Ambassadors' commitment to trade.[50] He referred back to Mr Cloake's question whether we actually wanted to increase trade with Eastern Europe. Did we have no machinery compared with the system by which the French cabinet identified the sectors of industry best placed to supply export markets? We were falling behind the Germans for 2 reasons. They had an industrial base 2 or 3 times greater than ours. Moreover, the FRG deliberately put more effort into Eastern Europe because of the crucial influence the Eastern European governments would have on the future of Germany which the West Germans believed was still open. Referring back to Mr Parsons's earlier remarks about the need for British delegations to multi-national bodies to keep Eastern European posts informed Mr Bullard then discussed the interaction of bilateral diplomacy with Eastern Europe and multilateral diplomacy in, for example, the UN, EEC, and NATO. Posts in Eastern Europe were perhaps more aware of this than were the various delegations. We would try to remedy this.

55. *Mr Mallaby* said that the Department's current work on potential leverage was not about general levers, such as the consideration that the more contact we had with Eastern Europe the more influence we could bring to bear. Rather it was about specific levers which could persuade other countries to take or not take specific actions. The main levers in the economic field were credits, grain sales, and technology transfers. Credit was a potential lever but was unlikely to be used. It would be difficult to persuade other Western countries to join in using curtailment of credit as a lever. France would never play this game: it was not even clear whether she could be brought to adhere to 'consensus' interest terms in credits to the USSR. Moreover several major Western countries did not have intergovernmental credit agreements with the communist countries. Grain was potentially a very powerful instrument, given the chronic inefficiency of Soviet agriculture. Without grain imports, Soviet meat shortages would be even worse. Moreover this was a lever which one Western power—the USA—could exercise alone. But it had not been used. One reason was the strength of the farmers' and grain exporters' lobby in the United States. It was not necessarily in the West's interests to use technology transfers as a lever against the Soviet Union. For example, to deny the supply of oil exploration and extraction technology could

[50] In a letter to Mr Mallaby on 29 October Mr Bullard noted that Home departments tended to support his view that government support was of subsidiary importance to the efforts of firms. Whereas Ambassadors had endorsed the view of Mr Foster who argued that at the margin the political element could be decisive by promoting a propitious climate for British exports and also swing the balance for specific contracts. Bullard agreed that the commercial argument was one reason for the UK to be more active in Eastern Europe, and thought that the DOT's conclusion reflected the mood of the conference: 'You may not gain many contracts through the political dimension, but you may lose them without it.'

force the USSR on to the world oil market and so force up prices for everyone else. But sales of chemical equipment and advanced machine tools might be areas of industry where we could exercise leverage without unwelcome side-effects on this scale. What would happen if the West could agree to deny the USSR equipment in these fields? There would be a slowdown in modernisation and the USSR would be forced to buy more industrial equipment from Eastern Europe and developed neutrals like Finland. This suggested that the Russians would not suffer enormously and therefore might not react as we wanted to an attempt to apply leverage. It was moreover extremely unlikely that France and perhaps the FRG would agree to participate in the attempt. It thus seemed in general that the prospects for successful use of economic leverage, despite the modestly encouraging history of the Jackson-Vanik amendment,[51] were not great. One thing that was clear was that the UK alone had no significant levers to employ against the USSR.

[51] The US amendment of 1974 denied most favored nation status to certain countries with non-market economies that restricted emigration.

No. 3

Memorandum by Mr Joy[1] on the 'Polish Winter of Discontent? (Spark? Conflagration? Change of Leadership?)': December 1979[2]

Confidential (FCO 28/4137, ENP 014/1)

Introductory

1. The question uppermost in the minds of observers of the Polish scene is whether the coming winter months will bring any serious move to change the existing leadership of the country. This Memorandum examines the possibilities for and against such a change.

For change

2. Factors indicating the possibility of a change of leadership derive principally from the country's current severe economic difficulties. This is not the place to catalogue them; suffice it to say that they are likely to increase with little hope of any early relief: there is no light yet at the end of the present Polish tunnel. The First Secretary of the Party, Edward Gierek, offers no promises of an easy or early solution: only sweat and toil and exhortations to greater effort.

3. More specifically bearing upon the man in the Wilanów[3] omnibus is the probability, not to say certainty, of increasing shortages of goods and, most serious, food and energy. In a word, the 'Gierek socio-economic experiment'[4] of the 70s is in serious trouble.

[1] David Joy, Counsellor and Head of Chancery, Warsaw, 1978-82.

[2] This undated memorandum was sent to Mr Mallaby on 4 January 1980, following his request for an assessment of a paper by Mr Braithwaite—who had just made a visit to Poland in November—reflecting on Poland twenty years after he had first been posted there and concluding that 'Poland is a sadder but wiser place' ('Poland after twenty years', 23 November 1979, FCO 28/3784, ENP 014/3).

[3] Warsaw district.

[4] Mr Gierek, appointed in 1970 to appease popular discontent, adopted a programme of economic reforms and industrial modernisation, rescinded food price increases, introduced higher industrial wages and sought foreign aid and loans.

4. The situation is made more difficult for the Government by the rising sound of dissident voices ever more boldly manifesting intellectual discontent and even proclaiming in the streets that Poland is not free, with the citizens' militia looking on. Unrest on the labour front, occasional, dispersed and sporadic, complicates the situation further. The main industrial centres, including the northern shipyards and the Silesian coal and steel complex, have been affected. In all, a bleak and gloomy—even a black—picture, liable to keep even the most popularly-based of democratic leaders awake at night. Gierek recently confessed to experiencing this problem.

Against it

5. On the other hand, factors pointing in the opposite direction may appear equally potent. The Poles, by and large, enjoy considerable material prosperity in contrast to their situation 10 years ago: many more houses and apartments have been built, cars are very much in evidence, as are a whole range of other consumer durables. Their leader still retains some of his early charisma. He identifies well with the working people and it seems unlikely that his current appeals for both individual and national-wide effort to overcome the country's present difficulties will fall on deaf ears. The leadership may be divided on some internal matters but it is determinedly united on swift action to redress labour grievances and correct local shortages whenever they threaten to interrupt the national effort.

6. The 'Gierek experiment' has certainly been blown off course during the past 5 years. But this is arguably due to many factors beyond the Polish Government's control: higher oil prices, Western recession, contracting world markets, combined with successively bad Polish winters and the consequent poor harvests, have tarnished the dream. Nonetheless, much can be seen by all to have been achieved: all Poles can be, and most are, proud of the progress of the last decade. They have little reason to want a change of leader and, more pointedly, they see no attractive alternative at present.

7. The authorities are handling the few emboldened dissidents who embark on demonstrations and similar activities with kid gloves. Relatively light sentences were passed on the 4 who led demonstrations in Warsaw's main Victory Square on 11 November, the 61st anniversary of Poland's re-birth after over 100 years of partition, during which they alleged that 'Poland is not free'. Even these sentences have been suspended pending appeal, possibly even indefinitely, if the Attorney-General does not pursue the case.

8. The workers are the pampered *élite* of People's Poland—carefully coddled by the leadership to minimise the risk of labour unrest, to meet grievances as soon as they appear and limit the spread of news of these to other centres. In other words, to snuff out at once any spark at its point of origin.

Conclusion

9. The overall picture then is one of a populace with little more than normal disgruntlement and grievances over shortages and similar inconveniences against the Government, but with a greater deal to be thankful for, more to lose materially than ever before and vivid and perpetually-renewed memories of infinitely worse times not too long ago, led by a First Secretary they know, respect and sympathise with; and with no-one better in sight. At the same time, Poland has a leadership very conscious from past errors of the need to tread carefully; determined to defuse any grievances quickly as they arise and to limit their effects; and equipped with the state apparatus to do this effectively.

10. A scenario for sparks? No doubt. But not for conflagrations, nor for an early change of leadership; much less, for a violent change—the only kind so far known in People's Poland.[5]

[5] Mr Pridham commented on 4 January 1980 to Mr Mallaby that there was general agreement between Mr Braithwaite's paper, Mr Joy's memorandum and himself that a violent upheaval was unlikely. However, there were nuances of appreciation. Joy had written to Mallaby on 14 December 1979 that the Embassy would 'modify Mr Braithwaite's "hope abandoned" to "hope diminished and deferred"' (FCO 28/3784, ENP 014/3). Mr Pridham found Mr Joy's analysis possibly too rosy, especially given developments on the dissident front. Both thought that material conditions had improved more than Braithwaite had described. Joy still saw considerable difficulties for the Church from the authorities.

No. 4

Lord Carrington[1] to Mr Pridham (Warsaw), 18 January 1980, 2.30 p.m.
Tel. No. 36 Routine,[2] Confidential (FCO 28/4000, EN 021/1)

Policy towards Eastern Europe

1. Following the Soviet intervention in Afghanistan,[3] we shall draw greater and more demonstrative policy distinction between USSR and the Eastern Europeans, so as to avoid associating the latter with this Soviet act.

2. It seems unlikely that the East Europeans were informed in advance, let alone consulted, about the Soviet intervention. The contrast with their involvement in the invasion of Czechoslovakia[4] is important. Despite their expressions of support, most of which have no doubt resulted from Soviet pressure, many of the East Europeans leaders are likely to be very concerned about the implications of the Soviet intervention for East-West relations and their own future room for manoeuvre. The Romanians, notably by their absence from the UN vote on 14 January,[5] have been the most pointed in showing disapproval. The East Germans, although they must be concerned about possible effects on inner-German relations, and the Czechoslovaks have been the most definite in approving the Soviet act. The Hungarians and the Poles, and even to some extent the Bulgarians, have seemed by delay and reticence to indicate disapproval.

[1] Peter Carington, Secretary of State for Foreign and Commonwealth Affairs, 1979-1982.

[2] Repeated Routine to Budapest, Bucharest, Sofia, Prague, East Berlin, UKDEL NATO, Belgrade; for Information to Moscow; for Information Saving to Ankara, Athens, Bonn, Brussels, Copenhagen, The Hague, Lisbon, Luxembourg, Oslo, Ottawa, Paris, Reykjavik, Rome, Washington, UKREP Brussels, UKMIS New York, UKMIS Geneva, Tokyo, Peking, Stockholm, Helsinki, Vienna, Dublin.

[3] On Christmas Eve 1979 Soviet troops began to move into Afghanistan, and on the evening of 27 December they launched a coup in which Mr Hafizullah Amin was killed and Mr Babrak Karmal, brought from exile in Eastern Europe, was installed as Head of a new Government.

[4] The Soviet Union and her main allies—Poland, the GDR, Bulgaria and Hungary—invaded the Czechoslovak Socialist Republic on the night of 20 August 1968 to halt Alexander Dubček's reform program. The Soviet Union installed Gustav Husák, who led the country until 1989 (see *DBPO: Soviet Union, 1968-1972*).

[5] The UNGA held an Emergency Special Session on Afghanistan over five days from 10 to 14 January 1980. The Assembly adopted the first of a series of 'Situation in Afghanistan' resolutions (resolution ES-6/2), in which it deplored the armed intervention in Afghanistan, called for the withdrawal of all foreign forces and asked States to contribute humanitarian assistance.

3. There is therefore no reason to depart from the policy towards Eastern Europe set out in my despatch of 7 December to Moscow.[6] You should maintain normal contacts and exchanges as a means of encouraging independence and diversity. Budapest, Warsaw, Sofia and especially Bucharest should take opportunities to indicate that we recognise that the countries concerned have not toed the Soviet line. At the same time, Posts should continue to make clear the seriousness with which HMG view the actions of the Soviet Union and to try to foster the East Europeans' concerns about the implications, in the hope of encouraging them to use helpfully any influence they may have in Moscow. Action on the statement of 15 January by the foreign ministers of the Nine (my telno 30 to Moscow[7]) may provide opportunities.[8]

4. East Berlin and Prague should note, for their own information, that we shall be bound to take account of the extent of GDR and Czechoslovak expressions of support for Soviet actions in considering future development of our bilateral relations.[9]

5. We shall boost relations with Yugoslavia, particularly in view of Tito's illness.[10] We are pressing for speed in reaching a satisfactory conclusion in the EEC/Yugoslav negotiations (UKREP telno 233[11]) and are considering other possible moves. Belgrade may wish to make suggestions.

6. Posts may draw on this telegram in answer to questions about our policy from allies and other trusted contacts. UKDEL NATO should use it in response to the US enquiry reported in paragraph 2 of their telno 34.[12]

[6] See *DBPO: Afghanistan*, No. 1. The policy referred to was that of 'differentiation' between countries in the Soviet bloc.

[7] Not printed.

[8] The Foreign Ministers of the Nine at their political cooperation meeting on 15 January reaffirmed their 'grave concern' with regard to the crisis created by the military intervention in Afghanistan (see *DBPO: Afghanistan*, No. 38).

[9] This paragraph provoked reactions, especially from Mr Foster in East Berlin and Mr Male in Prague. On 23 January the latter wrote to Mr Mallaby to argue that: 'there was not a great deal to choose between East Europeans in terms of their public reactions to Afghanistan and that in some respects some of the others, e.g. Hungary, have on individual occasions gone further than Czechoslovakia in support of the USSR'. Mallaby replied on 1 February justifying the concept of differentiation: 'we . . . took into account press coverage and the . . . private concern about the Soviet actions that we had received from some of the other East Europeans, notably Poland, Hungary and of course Romania . . . Our political relations with Czechoslovakia were cool anyway and the practical implications if (repeat if) we decided to differentiate among other Europeans would not be great. Commercial relations would continue unchanged and we do not have a great deal planned in the political field.' Mallaby nuanced his analysis in a post-script: 'we've learned of the cancellation of 2 high level Hungarian contacts with the West. It may well be that the scope for differentiation will be slight, given firm Soviet instructions to the East Europeans to abstain from high level contacts' (FCO 28/4078, ENC 020/1).

[10] Josip Broz Tito, President of the Socialist Federal Republic of Yugoslavia since 1953, had been admitted into hospital on 5 January.

[11] Not printed. The EEC and Yugoslavia were negotiating a new trade and cooperation agreement.

[12] Not printed. Mr Glitman, the US Deputy Chief of Mission to NATO, had made a statement at the Senior Political Committee on 14 January that the US government would continue 'to pursue a differentiated policy designed to encourage signs of independence in Eastern Europe . . . To treat Eastern Europe in the same way as the Soviet Union would play into Soviet hands. The US intended however to react to particularly egregious statements of support for Soviet policy, by cooling relations e.g. by cancelling visits . . . The US hoped that the Allies would support the US view that strong political and economic support was necessary for Yugoslavia' (UKDEL NATO tel. No. 34, 14 January 1980; FCO 28/3998, EN 021/1).

No. 5

Letter from Mr Gladstone[1] to Mr Foster (East Berlin), 23 January 1980
Personal and Confidential (FCO 33/4356, WRE 020/1)

Dear Peter,

Policy towards the GDR

1. I thought I should send you a short note to amplify the instructions in paragraph 4 of FCO telegram no. 36 to Warsaw[2] (which incidentally was watered down at our insistence).

2. It is clear, *inter alia* from reports from Bonn, that the FRG is anxious that the Afghanistan crisis should not undermine what has been achieved in inner-German relations and *Ostpolitik* generally in the last 10 years. We have sympathy for this position. Like us, the FRG appears determined to differentiate between condemnation of the Soviet action and the maintenance of normal relationships with Eastern Europe. Ministers have decided that we must bear in mind, when considering fresh initiatives towards Eastern Europe, the vigour with which individual countries have come out in support of the Russians; but we have managed to get it accepted that there is no point in the UK adopting a line so much tougher than that of our European allies that we would risk damage to our interests without any prospect of significantly affecting Soviet policy. So it is business as usual with the GDR on all subjects already under active consideration, e.g. Mr Parkinson's[3] visit to the Leipzig Fair and Axen's[4] visit to London, and the signing of the Legal Procedures Convention.

3. As far as future business is concerned, we may have to go a little more slowly than we had formerly intended, but I shall do my best to ensure that there are no sharp changes of direction such as would distinguish our policies notably from those of our allies without securing any substantial (or material) return. In other words, trade first and no need (at least as yet) to drop hints to anyone (friend or foe) about possible *Bedenken*[5] in the background.[6]

Yours ever,
D.A.S. GLADSTONE

[1] David Gladstone, Head of Western European Department, FCO, 1979-82.
[2] No. 4.
[3] Cecil Parkinson, Minister for Trade, 1979–81.
[4] Hermann Axen, Member of the Central Committee of the GDR *Sozialistische Einheitspartei Deutschlands* (SED) and Chairman of its Committee for Foreign Affairs (1971-90).
[5] 'Misgivings'.
[6] Mr Foster replied on 28 January expressing concerns about the potential 'differentiation' of the GDR, when 'the Nine share the basic approach of "business as usual", but apparently without the same reservation'. This was especially true of the West Germans 'of whose views we have to take particular account'. He asserted: 'It is therefore difficult to see how on the basis of our individual national instructions (as distinct from the conclusions of the Political Committee) we could agree on a common mandate to explore possibilities of action, which presumably means punitive action, at least as far as the GDR is concerned.' He also thought that a policy of differentiation risked driving the GDR further into Soviet arms. He suggested that the Community should warn the GDR and other Soviet satellites that they should not count upon immunity the next time. The FCO replied on 1 February that UK policy was to condemn the Soviet action and pursue 'business as usual . . . on all subjects already under active consideration . . . to take due account of FRG to preserve the fruits of détente in inner German relations: and to do nothing to raise tension in and around Berlin'.

No. 6

Minute from Mr Mallaby to Mr Fergusson, 24 March 1980
Confidential (FCO 28/4261, ENZ 021/1)

Contacts with dissidents in European communist countries

1. Mr Blaker asked me just before Christmas about our policy on this subject.[1] I have checked the practice of our Embassies. In recent years it has been:

(*a*) *USSR*. Occasional contacts have taken place in flats of third parties such as Western journalists. Embassy favour occasional visits to Moscow synagogue to meet '*refuseniks*'.[2]

(*b*) *Poland*. Frequent contact with free thinkers within or close to the official establishment. Occasional contacts with dissidents in flats of third parties. Ambassador favours taking the initiative to arrange rather more contacts with dissidents.[3]

(*c*) *Hungary*. Wide contacts among free thinkers in or near the establishment. There are very few dissidents.

(*d*) *Czechoslovakia*. Occasional contacts in Embassy flats, at restaurants or at Reuter office.

(*e*) *Romania*. There is very little dissidence. Embassy had contacts with free trade union before it was broken up in mid-79.

(*f*) *GDR*. There is no dissident movement. Contacts with many of the prominent individual dissenters.

(*g*) *Bulgaria*. No dissidence to speak of.

(*h*) *Yugoslavia*. No organised groups of dissidents. Emigration no problem for the disaffected. The few dissenters, of whom Djilas[4] is the most prominent, have contacts with Western correspondents and do not seek out Embassies. Subject to developments post-Tito, the Ambassador intends to maintain a policy of not seeking contact but would not avoid contact if dissidents sought it.

[1] Mr Blaker expressed the view 'that our posts should not go overboard in seeking contacts with such people since an Embassy's main business is to deal with the powers that be; but also that we should not be too cautious about contacts with dissidents'. Mr Mallaby had asked embassies in Eastern Europe to report on their practices (Mr Mallaby to Mr Pridham, 20 December 1979; FCO 33/3930, WRE 400/1).

[2] A Soviet citizen, generally Jewish, who had been refused permission to emigrate.

[3] On 24 May 1979 Mr Gray, Third Secretary in Warsaw, had reported to Miss Elmes, First Secretary in Prague, that the American Embassy in Warsaw had 'recently adopted a policy of relatively frequent discreet contacts with representatives of the main Polish dissident groups . . . as a consequence of a decision by the State Department, horrified by their latest *débâcle* in Iran, that American Embassies everywhere should devote more attention to opposition movements in their parishes'. The embassy in Warsaw now wanted to take a 'fresh look' at its current policy and sought views from Prague before possibly asking EESD to countenance a change of tactics (FCO 28/3786, ENP 015/1). Miss Elmes replied on 1 June that it was a 'premise that HM Embassies have a duty to keep in touch with a broad spectrum of opinion in the countries to which they are accredited'. She argued that if Western Embassies isolated themselves completely from the dissidents, it might intensify the authorities' repression and give rise to critical comment at home as well as not according with basic Western concern for human rights. But she warned against unnecessary provocative conduct. They had few calls from prominent dissidents, whereas the Austrians and FRG were much more involved, especially with applications for visas (FCO 28/3670, EN 015/1).

[4] Milovan Djilas, author and Yugoslav human rights activist, published his autobiography in 1978 and travelled to the West in the early 1980s.

2. In general our practice is in line with that of our major allies, although in Prague the French and West Germans are more active than us: and in Warsaw the Americans are a good deal more active than us.

3. I see the following considerations:

(i) Contact with free thinkers in or near the establishment offers advantage without disadvantage, and should be pursued;

(ii) We cannot accept the idea that contact with dissidents is improper;

(iii) Contact with dissidents is a subject where the judgement of Ambassadors in the field should carry much weight;

(iv) In some posts—e.g. Warsaw and especially Belgrade—we have bilateral interstate interests which could be harmed by going too far in cultivating dissidents;

(v) In Moscow, Warsaw, Belgrade and East Berlin most of the information that can be gleaned from dissidents is available to our Embassy from Western press correspondents; but direct contact can still add opinions about the country concerned and the dissidents which can be a useful ingredient in the Embassy's reporting;

(vi) Contacts can help to deter repression of the individuals concerned;

(vii) Contacts in the flats of third parties are a useful method.

Conclusion

3. [*sic*] In this context the most important capitals—substantive and as regards British public opinion—are Moscow, Warsaw and Prague. We have some contracts there. The post-Afghanistan period is not the time to increase them in Moscow, for the KGB might use such contacts to justify action against individual dissidents. But there is scope for a bit more contact in Warsaw and Prague, and in due course in Moscow. I suggest that I should write accordingly to posts.

4. If asked—e.g. in Parliament—whether our Embassies have contact with dissidents, we are just about in a position to give a satisfactory reply. (It might, depending on the question, be better to speak of 'as broad a range of contacts as possible' than to mention dissidents specifically.)

C. L. G. MALLABY

No. 7

Mr Farquharson (Belgrade) to Lord Carrington, 8 April 1980

Confidential (FCO 28/4235, ENU 014/2)

My Lord,

Yugoslavia—Valedictory

1. With Tito fading away,[1] this is a singularly difficult moment at which to try a conventional valedictory despatch. Moreover his long illness has given rise to a quantity of reflective reporting, much of it by experts in this field. And against this moment successive Ambassadors have reported so fully that no addition is needed, in analysis or prediction.

2. So I can venture only a form of last impressions, with an attempt to spot where Yugoslavia stands at present and which way it is likely to move—East or West; North or South.

[1] See No. 4, note 10.

3. First to spot where it is; apart from its obvious commercial and strategic position. It is a mixture here not of two but of three generations. The eldest is passing—the Partisans, who lived and fought for Stalin, as they thought. Tough people, peasantry and bourgeois drop-outs, who needed Tito to bring them round into a more Yugoslav mould. They remain communist and believe that present Soviet policies are a deviation from the true ideas of Lenin and the Revolution. Tito stays in rather the same mind, with a sentiment for 1917. Next are the middle-class generation of party managers, brought up in the same tradition and under the same labels. They have some of the perquisites and status of the ruling classes in the Soviet bloc. They are an 'in-bloc'. But the economic needs of Yugoslavia since 1948 and the system of self-management have made them more flexible and probably more efficient than their Eastern colleagues. Lastly the younger generation, brought up under the same labels, represent a frankly consumer society whose aspirations, if touched and allowed, would be totally western; in the material sense that they can travel, and see, often buy superior goods in the west: and can see that the technology they admire flourishes better in a freer economy.

4. Officially, very deeply felt among the older and middle generations, defence is the mainspring of Yugoslav foreign policy, and a great part of its domestic policy as well, for it is used to cement the different parts of the country. Officially, it is aimed against any kind of foreign domination, but it is privately admitted that the only conceivable military threat comes from the East—which is one reason why the Bulgarian threat is regularly paraded, with the Soviet bogey behind it. I hope and believe that the country would spring to arms in its defence, as it did by degrees from 1941.[2] It is certainly organised to do so. But the success of the economy, in absolute terms, has led to consumer-mindedness, and the degree of militancy, in the old Partisan sense is something that will need watching. More questionable, in the face of sophisticated arms, is the success of armed resistance. Claims that Yugoslavia could hold down 50-60 Soviet divisions are probably exaggerated. (Though genuinely righteous about the evil of Soviet aggression in Afghanistan, some senior Yugoslavs admit privately that it has a saving grace, not just in rallying world opinion against such adventures, but also, they hope, in showing the Russians the military cost of engaging guerrilla forces, less well organised than they would find here.)

5. It was mainly reasons of defence which led Tito to found the non-aligned movement, as a means of rallying world opinion against Soviet aggression, without compromising Communist principles to the extent of nullifying the Revolution in Yugoslavia in his people's eyes, or his own (for he still believes that present Soviet ideology is perverted rather than basically wrong); or giving the Russians the pretext for anathematising him further. It was a pre-emptive move, and has been moderately successful. But Yugoslav reliance on the movement may not be so great in the long term, when Tito's founding influence is removed, and when economic development in Yugoslavia takes the country rather further away from the mass of the developing world. There were already some signs of disillusionment after the Havana Conference in 1979[3] and a feeling that Yugoslavia was being forced, by competition, to support policies which were more radical than were needed by the country's proper interests—nowhere better illustrated than by the disgraceful attitude of the Yugoslavs during the elections in

[2] In resistance to the invasion of Yugoslavia by Germany on 6 April 1941.

[3] The summit conference of the Non-Aligned took place from 3 to 9 September 1979.

Rhodesia, followed by great relief at the outcome, and, as the Foreign Secretary expressed to me, sheepishness almost to the point of apology. Temporarily the outlook for the movement is better. When Tito was first out of action, a good consensus was achieved over Afghanistan, and the Yugoslavs hopefully believe that Cuban domestic difficulties are lessening that country's influence in the movement. But there must be many here who notice that consensus and debate mostly falls back on 'principles', and they might agree with Mr Bevin's minute—'What the Foreign Secretary must have is less co-ordination and something done'.[4] Be that as it may for the short term, the country's present commitment to the Non-Aligned still has much momentum, and no suggestions of ours stand a first chance without paying it ritual lip-service.

6. East-West movement is much more important and more dangerous. It too is predicated by fear of Russian ambition. Since May 1979 Yugoslav-Soviet relations have been as cold as possible between Communist nations, registering only 'correct' on the Communist scale. We must expect some attempt to improve them, perhaps up to the level of 'normal'; and an invitation is to be issued for a visit to Belgrade by members of the Supreme Soviet. But, though the possibility of direct Soviet intervention is presently discounted, the guard is still up. After some hesitation when Tito was first ill, the Yugoslav press is again giving as good as it gets from the Russian side.

7. But this does not presage any significant move westwards in the foreseeable future. For all its relevant benevolence, Yugoslavia is ruled by a self-styled Communist regime, and the stakes in it are held by a Communist establishment. Even without Tito, his authority and example will maintain this for a long time. The 'collective responsibility' he leaves are quite aware that the younger generation, though trained in the dogma, incline to the success of western practices and the need for management and technology. Pronouncements since he fell ill have contained obvious warning not to veer, let alone stampede west, not just to avoid provoking the Russians. The most dangerous scenario we have heard advanced here lately is that the Russians, if they can be less clumsy than usual, will patiently seek to exploit national difficulties here, probably by economic leverage, in the hope that they might get invited by a minority to intervene, ostensibly to preserve Tito's Communist principles.

8. I suggest that the West must be equally patient, understanding and well-informed. The principle of Yugoslav independence can be firmly supported. But any temptation to offer assistance and anything that verges on condescension, let alone interference should be firmly resisted, as counter-productive. There are healthy and welcome signs here of moves toward greater freedom, politically and economically. But we must not be caught commending them. Nor, conversely, must we react on the intemperate side of firmness to disobliging outbursts here—whether they are congenital, as over Croat activities abroad, or calculated, for reasons concerning the Soviet Bloc or the Non-Aligned Movement. The Yugoslavs themselves gave a good example of such an attitude, in their relations with Albania: support for independence, belief in evolution, cultivation of contacts, and occasional turning of the other cheek.

9. The political scene appears stable, with a built-in reluctance to disturb Tito's legacy. The Yugoslavs will persist in their aptitude for debate and legislation; and for paradox, presently between political decentralisation to the Republics and—a

[4] Ernest Bevin, Secretary of State for Foreign Affairs, 1945-51.

new need and fancy—'concentration of capital' at the Federal level. We need to follow and interpret these contortions, but not so earnestly as if local Kremlinology was all-important.

10. It is the economy which remains the dominant problem, the danger to stability between the Republics, and the over-riding local preoccupation. The proper measures to correct its overheating and fragility are hampered by the structure of the country and its government; and have been delayed by Tito's disinterest in the economy and preference for the grandeur of foreign affairs. Matters are not desperate, but they are serious, and could impinge on East-West relations if allowed to deteriorate further.

11. Signature last week of the Yugoslav-EC Agreement,[5] after two years of expensive negotiation, could be a useful lead. Responsible Yugoslavs recognise that it is not a panacea but a challenge for their productivity and marketing.

12. Bilaterally, Anglo-Yugoslav relations are good. They are based on the Partisan relation of the war. With Tito, this will pass into legend, and remain valuable. But we may have relied on it too much, to mask an occasional, sometimes worried interest in this country. We must find a continuing steady way to express our interest and influence. It is expected and will be valued. The last Permanent Under-Secretary[6] went twice on the record to say that he hoped Britain would regain her confidence and influence. He reminded me of this several times, once adding 'perhaps after Rhodesia?'[7] I know this will not be easy. Tourism is a good connection, but is subject to our own yearly affluence. Culture, scholarship and technology are more important. I deeply hope that further cuts in the British Council budget will not extend to this country, where they would be taken as a definite loss of interest. The economy will be the most important field, though it obviously depends on strictly commercial decisions. But any degree of official help and interest would be well invested—as for instance over the Smederevo contract, and the possibility of extending such co-operation into Third Countries. And interruptions in Yugoslav trade to Britain, in e.g. textiles or consumer goods should be avoided, where possible, and at least kept under the eye of foreign policy.

13. I regret leaving the Yugoslavs, all kinds and nationalities of them. They take time to know. They desperately want to be liked, or at least understood. They are rather thin-skinned about themselves and thick-skinned about other people, and can be obtuse and exasperating. But they have great warmth and hospitality, particularly to individuals who take an interest in them beyond cold foreign relations. Despite great urban drag and sprawl they mainly keep the family virtues of the countryside and are a generation or more away from the jealousies of suburbia. Though they are groping towards techniques of management, Universities are still for them places of learning rather than centres of advantage of conceit. They are still natural and pragmatic, in everything but their professed political dogma.

14. Our dealings are, of course, mostly with [the] Secretariat for Foreign Affairs. It is, in my experience, quite remarkably quick and efficient, except where they have to venture on to reserved fields of defence or security. Their communications are excellent—even before they install their new British

[5] See No. 4, note 11.

[6] Thomas Brimelow, Permanent Under-Secretary, FCO, 1973-75.

[7] A reference to Ian Smith's Unilateral Declaration of Independence in 1965 which was only resolved following the creation of the independent republic of Zimbabwe in April 1980.

equipment. Speed of decision is exemplary, except where they are intentionally sitting on the fence. Access is easy at all levels, except for the Ambassadors who waste time with pleasantries for a full half-hour's protocol. (But protocol, without ceremony, is usefully expected and observed. Woe betide the foreigner who flouts it.) For this efficiency their Foreign Service is rewarded, well-paid abroad and honoured at home, during or after service. Their budget has perennial difficulties in the Parliament, but slight ones, since the Foreign Service is accepted as being in the forefront of defence.

15. Archaic as it may sound, I much regret now leaving the diplomatic family. It is particularly close and important here. The colleagues are an able and distinguished lot. Some have been Foreign Ministers, some promoted here from London, Rome or Moscow. All talk freely, though carefully, with the Eastern Bloc, including Albania. Particularly happy—and useful over Rhodesia—has been a revived Commonwealth association here. It perplexes the Yugoslavs, who think they should have cornered the Third World. But it does not seem to annoy them.

16. It is more than a ritual to express gratitude for more than thirty years in the service, in eight foreign posts; and for friendships made in our and other services, and among many other people abroad. I am particularly struck by the quality of our own younger generation, and I am sure they will find their own framework at home and make their own mark abroad. Even less ritual is a tribute to the wives, especially those whom long service and deprivation abroad have made experts in the field. An instance of their work here may now seem unfashionable—the Embassy wives, without exception and without compulsion, helped organise the diplomatic community to provide aid to Montenegro,[8] raising more than a million dinars, which compares favourably with the contributions of many foreign governments. This was cheerfully and proudly done, and may not suit the new image. But I shall remember it proudly as the right spirit of the service.

17. I am sending copies of this despatch to HMRR in Washington, Moscow, Paris, Bonn, Sofia and the United Kingdom delegation in Brussels.[9]

I am, etc,
R. A. FARQUHARSON

[8] Montenegro had been struck by a massive earthquake on 15 April 1979.

[9] Mr Bullard noted that he found 'a great deal of wisdom in a short space here' and the message in paragraph 8 was well understood in the FCO.

No. 8

Letter from Mr Pridham (Warsaw) to Mr Mallaby, 16 April 1980
Confidential (FCO 28/4154, ENP 090/1)

Dear Christopher,

Poland: Credit

1. With the prospect of credit for Poland again being looked at in Whitehall I thought a note on the political arguments against restriction as we see them from here might be useful. The following seem to us the main points:

(*a*) The principal political argument against refusal of further credit to Poland stems from the policy of encouraging the diversity of Eastern Europe as formulated in the Secretary of State's despatch of 7 December 1979.[1] To refuse or seriously limit credit would be to put at risk the social relaxation that has flourished on the back of the economic expansion fostered by Gierek since 1970. To an outside observer Poland's continued adherence to the Soviet foreign policy line may not seem a very satisfactory result of internal relaxation and a decade of Western co-operation and understanding. It is highly probable, however, that the Polish Government's policy of expansion on credit during the 1970s has done more than anything to encourage the natural tendency of the Polish people to look towards the West as their source of inspiration and values, with social, and perhaps political, consequences that are in the longer term incalculable but hopeful for Western interests. For instance, a young generation of administrators and technicians has now been weaned on the policy of looking to the West for growth and, within the obvious constraints of the closeness of the USSR, is refreshingly pragmatic.

(*b*) These developments have done much for human rights within Poland, despite the continuing power of the Party and security organs.

(*c*) Western credit enables the Poles to resist Soviet pressure for greater integration into the CMEA. Denial of further Western aid would be likely to be followed by an imposed programme of greater involvement in the organs and joint programmes of CMEA. If this led to a strengthening of that organisation it would run counter to Western interests.

(*d*) Because the Polish Government is stable, Moscow can allow a remarkable measure of internal freedom. One cannot predict where this will eventually lead Poland if allowed to continue unchecked. It is likely, however, that a Soviet intervention triggered by Western refusal to continue to help Poland would either involve the imposition of stifling controls or provoke the sort of outbursts which could lead to bloody repression, a major crisis in Europe and regression to the human rights position of 20 years ago. The Gierek régime represents the best available compromise for the interests of Poland, the West and the USSR.[2]

Yours ever,
KENNETH

[1] See No. 4, note 6.
[2] Mr Johnson agreed with the views expressed but doubted whether they would 'cut much ice' with the Treasury. For the views of the Treasury see No. 15.

No. 9

Letter from Mr J. Bullard to Mr Holmer (Bucharest), 21 April 1980
Confidential (FCO 28/4178, ENR 020/5)

My dear Paul,

British/Romanian relations

1. The Secretary of State's visit to Romania last month went well and I know he was grateful for your part in ensuring this. We have thought that you described it all very well in your despatch of 24 March.[1]

[1] Not printed. The Foreign Secretary visited Romania, at the invitation of President Ceauşescu, from 12 to 14 March. A visit was thought worthwhile as the Romanians had made clear their

2. One point in your despatch gave me particular food for thought. In the second part of paragraph 8 you argued that we should continue to devote some time and energy to satisfying the Romanian need for visible links with important Western countries. I agree that the Romanians feel such a need and I see sound reasons, concerned with keeping up the number of their friends and demonstrating their international individualism, for their interest. We should indeed try to meet them.

3. But I wonder a bit about your conclusion that, if we want a constantly improving relationship, we must recognise that it cannot stand still. I doubt that a *constantly* improving relationship is possible and I am not sure that it is particularly desirable. If we were to subscribe to this goal, what would it mean in practice besides more and more frequent visits at higher and higher levels? We must accept that Ministers cannot spare very much time for a country where our concrete interests, though real, are not as important as in many other places; and where the regime, for all its international pluck and inconvenience to the Russians, is not one of the most attractive in Europe. This last point is relevant to the question of a return State Visit. The Queen may one day agree to make one. But I think you are aware that She is known not to be keen on the prospect.

4. The reasons why Romania has received high priority in our policy in Eastern Europe are basically its foreign policy and the rather good performance of our exports coupled with prospects for big orders like the one for turbo-generators which NEI[2] hope to win. I think there are arguments for increasing the frequency of high level British visits to Eastern Europe. But we have done far better in Romania than Poland and I think we should pay more attention to the latter and Yugoslavia. In relations with Romania, I think we should envisage a plateau on the level of 1978-80, comprising a State Visit say every 15-20 years and visits by lesser persons at more frequent intervals, ending up with Deputy Foreign Ministers annually.

5. I think the Romanians know, from our frequent prevarication about high level visits, that we will not agree to too many. But to put this to them explicitly would remove one of their major incentives for developing relations and could dispose them to grant to others the contracts which are one of our incentives. I therefore think it best to go on as before, never hesitating to resist pressure for another early visit but agreeing to such visits when—as after Afghanistan—we positively want high level contacts and a top person can find the time. We should not move for a long time towards a State Visit and, if we decide to receive the Romanian Prime Minister, should make clear in advance that a State Visit is not automatically the next step thereafter. When the departing Romanian Ambassador called on the Prime Minister, the former raised the question of a visit by Verdet[3] and Mrs Thatcher said Verdet should say when he would like to come. This is just the kind of polite lack of haste which we shall often have to use.

6. Your despatch implied that British/Romanian relations were like a bicycle, in that we would fall off if we stood still. I hope that they are more like an aircraft which once up can keep going steadily for a long time. One thing they cannot be for us is a bicycle race with other Western countries: I see that Ceausescu may visit

disapproval of the invasion of Afghanistan and had indicated they would not bow to Soviet pressure to abstain from high-level contacts with the West. The visit was judged a success by Mr Holmer, giving a boost to bilateral relations and encouraging the Romanians to maintain their independent line (FCO 28/4183, ENR 026/1).

[2] Northern Engineering Industries.

[3] Ilie Verdet, Romanian Prime Minister, 1979-82.

Paris this summer, only 16 months after Giscard was in Bucharest—a speed of movement which we cannot emulate.

7. I hope that what I have said will not depress you. There is much that can be done in British/Romanian relations if they remain on the level of the past two years. Apart from the possibility of Verdet coming here, there are prospects for visits by Lord Thomson[4] in June and Mr Parkinson in October, as well as the outstanding invitation to Burtica.[5] The department are also exploring the possibility of visits by Giosan[6] and the Mayor of Bucharest. We may wish to recommend a visit by Mr Blaker in due course. And there will be the second Round Table early next year. Not a bad menu!

Yours ever,
JULIAN

[4] Probably Kenneth Roy Thomson, media magnate, 2nd Baron Thomson of Fleet.
[5] Cornel Burtica, Foreign Trade Minister, 1969-82.
[6] Nicolae Giosan, President of the National Assembly of Romania, 1974-89.

No. 10

Mr Bolland (Belgrade) to Lord Carrington, 9 May 1980, 11.15 a.m.
Tel. No. 185[1] Immediate, Confidential (FCO 28/4231, ENU 010/2)

Tito's funeral

1. Tito was buried yesterday, 8 May,[2] in an impressive and moving ceremony attended by an unusually large number of foreign heads of state and government, together with many leaders of socialist, social-democratic, and communist parties. There were no untoward incidents.

2. The occasion was used to demonstrate Tito's greatness, his role in creating post-war Yugoslavia and in establishing its authority in world affairs, more particularly in the non-aligned movement, and its influence in international communism. Since he died on 4 May, the press, radio and TV have been devoted entirely to this, presenting Tito as a figure of heroic proportions. Hundreds of thousands of people lined the streets and half a million filed past his coffin in lying-in-state to pay their last respects. Some wept openly but the majority stood silently in an atmosphere charged with emotion.

3. The presence of so many foreign leaders was stressed and presented as an acknowledgment not only of Tito's importance but also of Yugoslavia's. The arrival and activities of Brezhnev, Hua Guofeng, and Mrs Gandhi, among other important leaders, were proudly noted. President Carter's absence was obviously apparent, although I suspect made much more of by the foreign press than by the Yugoslavs. The Prince Philip, the Prime Minister and Mr Callaghan[3] appeared

[1] Repeated Routine to Washington, Moscow and UKDEL NATO. Saving to Bonn, Paris, Rome, The Hague, Brussels, Luxembourg, Copenhagen, Dublin, Budapest, Bucharest, Sofia, East Berlin, Warsaw and Prague.
[2] Tito died on 4 May.
[3] Rt. Hon. James Callaghan MP, Prime Minister, 1976-79.

prominently on TV. The British partisan veterans, Fitzroy Maclean and Bill Deakin,[4] were especially acknowledged.

4. The main speeches and countless articles re-stated the basis of what Bakarić,[5] the now remaining 'Grand Old Man' of the party has described Tito's legacy. They reasserted, above all, the right of each country and each communist party to be independent, to be free from all foreign interference and to decide its future for itself. In the principal funeral oration, delivered on the steps of the Federal Assembly by Tito's coffin and in Brezhnev's presence, the presiding member of the party Presidium, Doronjski, recalled Tito's refusal to submit from 1948 onwards. There was no need to say to what or to whom. 'Today', he said, 'our destiny is in our hands.' Tito's contribution to Yugoslavia's system of self-managing socialism and to non-alignment, and his adherence to the principles of brotherhood and unity and equality between peoples, were also re-stated. Yugoslavia's leadership committed itself to following all these main paths. Continuity is the watchword—'after Tito—Tito', said the headline in *Borba*.[6]

5. All that has been spoken and written about Tito this week has underlined very heavily indeed the central, decisive position he held in Yugoslavia from the time of the Partisan War. The question is thus already raised as Yugoslavia enters upon the post-Tito era: how can Tito's policies be carried out, his legacy fulfilled, without Tito? As you said in Washington, the last great service of Tito to his people has been to enable the transfer of power after his death to proceed smoothly. The fact that Tito took some four months to die helped the leadership to get into gear and to gain confidence in ruling without him. The unity the Yugoslav people have experienced in Tito during this highly emotional week will also help. All is at present stable and calm. But beneath the surface inside Yugoslavia there remain deep national feelings and unresolved economic difficulties. And abroad there is no shortage of problems, many originating, as they did for Tito, in Moscow. The collective leadership will now have to decide how to deal with these questions without Tito's decisive word and to try to exert Yugoslavia's influence in, for example, the non-aligned movement without Tito's commanding presence. A friendly, helpful, but not interfering West could help them in this daunting task.[7]

[4] Sir Frederick William Dampier Deakin, a British historian and literary assistant to Winston Churchill, was parachuted in May 1943 into Montenegro and fought with Tito. Lieutenant-colonel Sir Fitzroy Maclean was sent by Churchill in July 1943 as the head of a military mission to Tito.

[5] Vladimir Bakarić, Croatian communist and politician.

[6] A Serbian newspaper, formerly the official newspaper of the League of Communists of Yugoslavia.

[7] The Ambassador reported at greater length in a despatch of 12 May, entitled 'The Death of President Tito: The end of an Era', in which he concluded that, without Tito, serious economic problems, latent national differences and the prosecution of Yugoslavia's foreign policy would test the Yugoslav leadership and they would need the West's 'practical and discreet help' (FCO 28/4229, ENU 010/1). In a reply dated 5 June, Mr Battiscombe agreed with the need for the West to provide discreet practical help. He highlighted the economy as the most pressing problem and stressed the need to encourage the Yugoslav authorities to demonstrate their determination to tackle economic problems and preserve their good financial reputation in order to get the best response from Western banks.

No. 11

Mr Pridham (Warsaw) to Lord Carrington, 23 May 1980
Confidential (FCO 28/4141, ENP 015/1)

Dissidents in Poland

Summary . . . [1]

My Lord,

1. A memorandum sent to the Department on 19 July 1979 by the Chancery of this Embassy summarised the activities and importance of the various dissident groupings in Poland.[2] Both the activities of the dissidents and the authorities' response had then been more or less unchanged for some time. The only ripple after the excitements of June 1976 subsided[3] had been a demonstration in Victory Square in November 1978 marking the 60th anniversary of Polish independence.

2. In the intervening months the picture has changed somewhat. Three public demonstrations and a dissident Mass in Warsaw have induced in the authorities a sharper reaction. Instead of the former 48 hours' detention, dissidents have received sentences of up to 3 months' imprisonment. The aim of this despatch is to assess the nature and strength of the present dissident challenge in Poland and the implications of that challenge for Western and UK policy. It does not discuss the 'dissidents' of the Church except in relation to the secular dissidents, by which is meant those who have formed themselves into particular organisations to challenge aspects of the present régime or the régime itself.

The origins of dissent

3. There is nothing surprising in the existence of a dissident movement in a country governed by an oppressive régime. Since the elimination in the 1940s of Parliamentary opposition and armed resistance there have been outbreaks of serious rioting in 1956, 1970[4] and 1976: 1956 no doubt left its legacy and the 1970 riots led to the formation of the still extant Baltic Free Trades Unions.[5] But much of the present dissident organisation and activity originates from the 1976 riots and the subsequent harassment of the participants, which in particular spawned the now

[1] Not printed.

[2] Not printed. The memorandum entitled 'The Internal Situation in Poland' by Mr Gray advised that the Church appeared better placed to achieve results in social reforms than more aggressive dissident groups. The Pope's visit had reinforced the role of the Church. Gray concluded however that the divided dissident groups had virtually no influence upon public life (FCO 28/3784, ENP 014/3).

[3] Mr Gierek's attempt in June 1976 to strengthen the economy by massive price increases provoked widespread workers' protests. The Government abandoned the price increases overnight. Hundreds of workers were subsequently arrested and thousands dismissed. An extensive civil rights movement of Church, workers, peasants, intellectuals and students developed.

[4] In 1956 political ferment grew in Poland following Mr Khrushchev's speech condemning Stalin's crimes. With a threat of civil war Mr Gomułka became First Secretary of the Polish Communist Party and began a programme of liberalisation, whilst retaining most traditional communist economic and social aims. He fell in 1970, toppled by workers in the Baltic cities and Łódź who went on strike against increases in food prices, and was replaced by Mr Gierek.

[5] Also known as Free Trade Unions of the Coast, they were founded in Gdańsk just before May Day 1978 by Andrzej Gwiazda, Krzysztof Wyszkowski and Antoni Sokołowski as the Initiating Committee of the Free Trading Unions (*Komitet Założycielski Wolnych Związków Zawodowych*). They condemned official, state-subordinated trade unions, which they claimed exploited all social groups and defended the right to create organisations free from state control.

active Committee for Self Defence (KOR).[6] Dissent is in any case a peculiar part of Polish tradition stretching back at least to the time of the Partitions and the uprisings of the 19th century.[7] It was not to be expected that the intelligent, courageous Poles, with their western Catholic tradition and culture, would meekly accept an imposed unrepresentative regime.

4. The nature of the various dissident groups was analysed in the memorandum referred to in paragraph 1 above. The principal organisations are the Committee for Workers' Self Defence (KOR), which includes the best-known dissidents Michnik and Kuron;[8] the Movement for the Defence of Civil and Human Rights (ROPCO); the Baltic Free Trades Unions; and the Confederation of Independent Poles (KPN). This last was founded on 1 September 1979 by members of an ROPCO faction. There are a number of other similar groups, disaffected clerics and individuals who engage in one sort of activity or another, usually involving clandestine meetings and publications. Another organisation, not precisely dissident, is the Flying University. This society, basing itself on precedent from the Partition era, aims to fill the gaps in the official university curricula by arranging private lectures and seminars. Many, if not most, of the dissident bodies circulate illegal literature. The total number of more or less active dissidents has been estimated at 3,000-4,000.

5. The dissidents are mostly intellectuals. They include some distinguished academic figures (such as Professor Lipiński)[9] as well as students, writers, etc. Some, like Michnik and Kuron, have no other job and might be described as full-time professionals. Some undesirables have attached themselves and the probability is that there is considerable infiltration by the Polish Security Service. As mainly middle-class intellectuals they seem to have made little impression on either the urban or the agricultural workers. Nor have they much in common with the Roman Catholic Church. It is said that the KOR recently approached the Church with suggestions for a united democratic opposition, which was firmly rejected. The Church lends the dissidents a degree of support in the sense of speaking out against their arrest and detention, and individual priests go further. But the hierarchy certainly distrusts the Marxist wing and keeps a cool distance from all the dissident bodies, with none of which has it any intention of sharing its role as protector of Polish liberties.

The aims of the dissidents

6. It is not easy to analyse the dissidents' aims; indeed a cynical observer might be pardoned for thinking that the dissidents themselves did not know what they wanted. Their objectives are perhaps of two kinds; to alter the political system to a greater or a lesser degree; and, in the interim, to monitor, publicise and thus lessen the abuses of human rights that go on within the present system, by which they hope to expand the range of an individual's freedom to manage his own life. These may be described as the broad and the narrow aims of the dissidents. Beyond that,

[6] KOR (*Komitet Obrony Robotników*) was set up in 1976 by intellectuals to assist workers arrested by the Communist authorities in Radom, where the Party headquarters had been set on fire. KOR provided lawyers for the charged or dismissed workers.

[7] Three partitions of Poland in the second half of the 18th century eliminated sovereign Poland for 123 years. Uprisings took place in 1830, 1846, 1863 which, although ending in defeat, contributed to maintaining Polish national awareness.

[8] Adam Michnik, Polish historian and co-founder in 1979 of the so-called Flying University, and Jacek Kuroń, Polish historian co-founder of KOR, and later one of the main advisers to Lech Wałęsa and Solidarity (*Solidarność*).

[9] Edward Lipiński, Polish economist, co-founder of KOR and adviser to Solidarity.

it is more helpful to examine the aims of the four groups mentioned above in more detail.

7. The Baltic Free Trade Unions could perhaps state their limited aims most definitely and in greatest detail. They want to establish Trades Unions, on the Western model, on the Baltic Coast (and perhaps elsewhere). They have thought carefully about the organisation and structure of these putative unions and could no doubt implement their programme to-morrow if allowed to. At the other end of the spectrum is the KPN. Its declared aims—a free, independent, democratic and sovereign Poland—lack any more concrete formulation, but the words 'free', 'independent' and 'sovereign' carry anti-Soviet implications. KOR tend to concentrate on the narrower field of monitoring and publicising cases of abuse of human rights. In general, they are a left-wing organisation whose aims might be characterised as to humanise rather than dismantle the Marxist state. ROPCO, on the other hand, are a nationalistic and right-wing movement who would probably wish to see a restoration of the Poland of the inter-war years. They have concentrated on holding demonstrations to mark significant dates in Poland's history.

Dissident activity

8. The activities whereby the dissidents have tried to fulfil those aims over the last few years can be listed as follows:

(i) *Demonstrations*

On 11 November 1978 there occurred in Victory Square in Warsaw the first major public demonstration since the war. This has since been followed by three others—in July, September and November 1979—which have followed the same pattern. A Mass in St John's Cathedral to mark a prominent historical event has been followed by a march to Victory Square and a public meeting there addressed by dissidents. In some cases wreaths have also been laid at the Tomb of the Unknown Soldier. In Gdańsk there have been similar occurrences—in December 1979 to mark the anniversary of the riots that brought down Gomułka and in May 1980 to mark the 3rd of May—formerly Poland's National Day. The numbers taking part in Warsaw have usually been about 3,000-4,000 and in Gdańsk possibly more.

(ii) *Small-scale public meetings*

Public activity on a smaller scale is much more frequent than large-scale demonstrations which are both more difficult to organise and provoke more restriction from the authorities. On at least one occasion a Warsaw Church has been 'hijacked' for dissident purposes and there have been other quasi-religious ceremonies recently to mark the anniversary of the Katyn massacre.[10] Below this there are frequent meetings in private flats, which are sometimes raided by the police.

(iii) *Publications*

[10] In 1943 a mass grave of 8,000 Polish army officers and thousands of police officers and intellectuals was discovered. The massacre committed in 1940 wiped out many potential leaders of Polish society. Most Poles believed that the Soviet Union was responsible, a fact it admitted in 1990, having previously accused Nazi Germany. In the late 1970s KOR and the Flying University defied the censorship of Communist Poland and discussed and publicized the massacre. See FCO History Note 16, *Katyn: British reactions to the Katyn Massacre, 1943-2003* (FCO, 2003).

Nearly all dissident movements involve themselves in *samizdat* publications.[11] These vary in quality and quantity but those produced by KOR and the Baltic Free Trades Unions are perhaps the best.

(iv) *Seminars and discussion groups*

These have tended to be exclusively the preserve of the Flying University, as described in paragraph 4 above.

(v) *Letters to the authorities*

This is regarded by some dissidents as a major way of fulfilling their aims. A notable recent example, reported to the Department, was a letter sent by Wojciechowski,[12] a member of Amnesty International, to the Soviet Embassy about the Katyn massacre.

(vi) *Publicity in the West*

This is regarded by many dissident groups as their most important continuing form of activity. All the dissident groups have good lines to Polish communities in the West, who largely finance them, and the Western press, in particular Radio Free Europe, based in Munich. KOR regard the continuing publication of abuses of human rights as one of their most useful activities, but even organisations such as the Free Trades Unions, whose principal aims lie elsewhere, see this as an important adjunct to what they are trying to achieve.

Dissident chances of success

9. Poland's human rights record is far better than that of East Germany, Czechoslovakia and the Soviet Union. The Polish Government has always treated its dissidents very differently from its Eastern European partners, but lately there have been signs that the gap has narrowed slightly. Until about the autumn of 1979 Polish Government policy seemed to be to allow the dissidents as much freedom as was practicable in a police state, with relatively minor harassment such as 48-hour arrests. Economic difficulties, the nature of the Polish people and Gierek's unpersecuting nature, no doubt contributed to the formation of this policy and perhaps a belief that relative freedom would encourage fissiparous tendencies. At all events the policy seemed to be rewarded by a dissident movement too diverse and unco-ordinated to present any real threat to the authorities. The dissidents looked like justifying the old joke that where there are two Poles there will be three political parties.

10. But latterly the dissidents have grown bolder if not much more united and the Government reaction has grown stronger. Perhaps the Government's leniency, the climate of the times and the fact that establishment mavericks were stealing the dissidents' clothes, all contributed to the growth of more frequent activity directed at more sensitive targets. Whereas before they have protested at particular aspects of the régime, they began, towards the end of 1979, to attack its very existence and its subservience to the USSR. Larger and more frequent public demonstrations were arranged. The authorities' response came in the form of longer sentences of detention and more frequent preventive arrests before sensitive anniversaries. A more sinister development has been a tendency to charge dissidents with criminal offences on which the evidence is certainly sometimes, but not always,

[11] Underground publications throughout the Soviet bloc, *samizdat*—or *bibuła* in Poland—were instrumental in dissident activity and harshly punishable. Following a long tradition in Poland in the nineteenth and twentieth centuries individuals reproduced censored publications by hand and passed the documents from reader to reader. In the 1970s and 1980s, books and newspapers were printed, often exceeding 5,000 copies.

[12] Adam Wojciechowski, Polish lawyer, dissident, member of Amnesty International and of KOR.

manufactured. The authorities, moreover, seem to be concentrating much of their effort on the organisers in the background, particularly of dissident publications. The recent example of the detention for several weeks without charge of Mirosław Chojecki[13] is a case in point.

11. So the contest between the régime and the dissidents has sharpened. The former are torn between the desire to preserve their relatively liberal reputation and the need to maintain their authority and defend themselves from Soviet accusations of laxity. What prospects have the dissidents of humanising the present system, or changing it or of making any significant impact on international relations? On the first point it can be argued that they have had some success: for example, in alleviating the harsh treatment of workers after the 1976 riots, although this was achieved with the powerful assistance of the Church and the workers themselves. More recently, 15 dissidents, arrested after last December's mass in Warsaw and expected to be held for 3 months, were released after an approach by other prominent dissidents to the Prosecutor-General. And the dissidents' publicity campaigns are usually the only way Westerners can learn about individual cases of violation of human rights. Against this it can be said that the style of the present Polish Government is in any case relatively pragmatic and liberal, and that some of the dissidents' success has been to alleviate the punishment of dissidents for dissident activity rather than to relieve the population at large. Nevertheless their contacts with the West and the information they feed to foreign newsmen and such institutions as Radio Free Europe serve as a constant goad to the Polish Government. These, if not pressed too far (in which case they would be counter-productive), can have the effect of lessening those abuses of human rights which are not necessary to preserve the system.

12. I see no prospect of the dissidents changing the system itself. Apart from anything else it is generally agreed that the Soviet Union would prevent by force any attempt to take Poland out of the socialist camp. The dissidents know this too and nearly all of them accept that it would be madness to press dissent too far. Nor do I see them bringing about important shifts of policy. Only as an element in an alliance with the Church and the workers would the dissidents present a threat to the régime which could induce it to change course. The major changes of course in post-war Poland have been brought about by the peasants and the Church, not by dissidents within the meaning of this despatch. Changes will come, but by the effluxion of time, by the growth of new generations and new ideas or by major outside events. In this connection the *samizdat* publications, which circulate widely outside dissident circles, may have an important if slow-burning effect.

13. So, barring miscalculations, the contest between the dissidents and the Government will continue in a more acute form. The Government will be essentially reactive to the dissidents and its severity or leniency is likely to depend on the intensity of their protest. The limits of the régime's tolerance have not yet been reached—but they cannot be too far away.

The UK and dissidents

14. Increased dissident activity and sharper Government reaction cannot but impose strains on Poland's relations with the West. Her Majesty's Government has declared its intention of leaving open the option of taking up with the government concerned cases of abuse of human rights abroad, even where British citizens are

[13] Polish publisher, co-founder of KOR, founder of the Independent Publishing House 'Nowa', arrested several times, member of Solidarity, exiled to France in 1981 where he published *Kontakt*.

not involved. The formation of groups in Britain to monitor dissident activity in Poland can be expected to increase pressure on Her Majesty's Government to intervene, or even to encourage dissident activity.[14] The dilemma is perhaps a pale shadow of that facing citizens of countries occupied by the Nazis when to join the resistance meant reprisals on the innocent population. On the one hand, intervention may help individuals or even modify policy. On the other, it may adversely affect our bilateral interests and make matters worse for the Polish people, who are living under the mildest and most enlightened government they have known for 40 years; and for obvious reasons it may drive the Polish Government, whose independence and individuality is a major objective of our policy, further into the arms of the USSR. A great deal would depend on the manner in which the option was exercised and the occasion of it.

15. I am sending copies of this despatch to Her Majesty's Representatives at Moscow, East Berlin, Prague, Budapest, Bucharest, Sofia, Belgrade and the UK delegation to NATO.[15]

I am Sir, etc,
K. R. C. Pridham

[14] Mr Pattison, Private Secretary to the Prime Minister, wrote to Mrs Thatcher on 8 August to inform her that the Polish Ambassador had come to the Foreign Office on the same day to protest against the activities of Mr Alasdair Hutton MEP, on a recent visit to Poland, where the MEP had made fairly public contact with dissidents and 'claimed he was doing so with your authority and encouragement'. The Prime Minister replied: 'I do not know Mr Hutton personally but would certainly be pleased if he made contact with "dissidents" on his visit. The very word condemns the governments of those countries' (PREM 19/331).

[15] In a reply of 26 June Mr Mallaby, whilst mindful of not 'pushing the Polish authorities further into the arms of the USSR', suggested developing contacts, for example when Embassy members toured the country.

No. 12

Record of conversation between Mr J. Bullard and Vice-Minister Czyrek at the Ministry of Foreign Affairs, Warsaw, 17 June 1980, 4 p.m.

Restricted (FCO 28/4269, ENZ 021/319)

Present:

Mr J.L. Bullard	HE Mr J. Czyrek
Mr K.R.C. Pridham	HE Mr J. Bisztyga
Mr D. Joy	Mr S. Pichla
Mr W.V. Fell	Mr J. Fekecz
Mr R.A. Facey	Mr J. Rabś
Mr W.A. Harrison	Mr Knap, Interpreter

1. *Mr Czyrek* welcomed Mr Bullard and said that the dialogue between Poland and the UK was particularly significant given the present international situation.

2. *Mr Bullard* said that it was now becoming clear to what extent East-West relations had been and still were affected by certain events outside the European continent. These had caused a long casualty list. He was referring not to the physical but to the political casualties. These included the understanding between

the US and USSR crystallised in the 1972 Declaration of Principles;[1] President Carter's original faith in disarmament and a reduction in the arms trade; the theory that the Socialist countries are the natural allies of the non-aligned movement; the 1980 Olympic Games as originally conceived; and the extreme caution with which Western countries had been approaching relations with China. The final casualty list might also include the sort of conference in Madrid[2] that the UK had been looking forward to; the credibility of the non-aligned movement itself; the opportunity for negotiations between East and West on Long Range Theatre Nuclear Forces which had seemed to exist at the end of 1979; and perhaps the whole structure of détente as we had known it in the 1970s.

3. In this situation the UK sought acceptance of the principle that selective détente is not possible. The sooner this message was understood and acted on the better. In the meantime, East and West should aim to limit the damage, whether to the CSCE Review Conference in Madrid, negotiations on arms control, or bilateral relations.[3]

4. *Mr Czyrek*, quoting the first words of the Polish national hymn 'Poland is not dead yet', said that optimism had been a very important weapon to the Polish people and that it would be a good thing for the world to think in the same fashion.

5. Poland did not believe that East-West relations were in such a bad state as Mr Bullard had suggested. Relations between the US and USSR were of the greatest significance, but Poland believed that she was also part of the East-West dialogue and that that dialogue and the whole infra-structure of détente had not been damaged and should continue, especially in bilateral relations between European countries. The thesis that there can be no détente in Europe if détente has been damaged somewhere else was a dangerous one and could lead to the Chinese thesis that war is inevitable. It was in the interests of Europe that events there should influence events in the world outside rather than the other way around.

6. Poland accepted that Afghanistan could be looked at from either a regional or global point of view. But the suggestion that tension somewhere destroys détente everywhere was negative, unjust, unhistorical and unrealistic. There had been tensions in East-West relations throughout the post-war period but, despite that, détente had come about. It did not lie in the interests of Europe to take up the problems of other continents; instead, Europe should develop an autonomous process of détente which would allow the continent to speak in the world forum and to be an agent rather than an instrument in international affairs.

7. *Mr Bullard* replied that optimism had a lot on its conscience. In 1975, the high-water mark of optimism, some had believed that the Helsinki Final Act would enforce itself, that it would open a new era in East-West relations, that détente would survive in Europe whatever happened elsewhere and that the arms race would slow down automatically. These had been shown to be illusions. But rather than preparing the funeral of détente, we ought now to reconstruct it on more reliable foundations. This required us first to recognise the seriousness of the situation—as had the United Nations in special session,[4] and more recently the European Council in Venice, which had declared that 'these dramatic developments threaten to jeopardise the climate of international relations for a long

[1] The declaration aimed at restraining hostility and reducing the threat of a nuclear war (see: *Soviet Union, 1968-1972*, pp. 474-77).

[2] See No. 1, note 6.

[3] For further consideration of these issues see *DBPO: Afghanistan*.

[4] See *DBPO: Afghanistan*, No. 31, paragraph 2.

time to come', wording drafted by a French pen.[5] Secondly, it was necessary to work for a solution in Afghanistan, and Britain had ideas on how this should be done.

8. *Mr Czyrek* repeated that Poland wished to restore détente and dialogue as the dominating elements in East-West relations and to separate European détente from events elsewhere. Mr Bullard had been right to mention the US-Soviet Declaration of Principles of 1972. The USSR had regarded it as significant that the US had departed from these principles. The key to improvement in the international situation was for the super-powers to return to those positions of equal partnership and responsibility which they had taken up in 1972. Poland had placed a lot of hope in President Carter's disarmament programme, which, long before Afghanistan, had turned itself into an armament programme under the name of 'modernisation'.[6]

9. Mr Czyrek wondered whether it was the Olympic Games that had been a casualty, or the proposed boycott. Only the FRG and Norway of European nations had completely boycotted the Olympics and even the UK Olympic Committee had decided to go to Moscow.

10. The intensification of relations between Europe and China had started before Afghanistan. The West's use of the China card for anti-Soviet purposes was the cause and the present crisis the effect, not the other way around.

11. There was no reason why Madrid should become a casualty, and if it did, this would be against the interest of both East and West. And the non-aligned movement need not be a casualty because history had shown that states can develop particularly close relations with other states and yet stay non-aligned. Finally, the threat in the Euro-strategic theatre had also already existed before Afghanistan. Poland agreed that it was necessary to limit the negative effects of the present situation and to seek a solution to it. She had never believed in an automatic process of détente, but had always thought that it required a conscious contribution from both sides. The UK had a significant role to play in NATO and with the US, and likewise Poland in the Warsaw Pact and with the USSR.

12. *Mr Bullard* agreed with Mr Czyrek's last point. As to the 1980 Olympics, history would note that 50 countries had boycotted them, representing about a third of the human race and including the countries who had finished second, fourth and fifth in the 1976 medal table.

13. Western policy towards China was not motivated by anti-Soviet sentiments and did not consist of 'playing the China card', an expression which implied that China herself was a passive instrument. But there was clearly a connection between the events of 27 December 1979 and the contacts between the West and China since, especially between the US and China.

14. Mr Bullard reiterated that Afghanistan had spoiled the prospects for the kind of Madrid conference which we had all hoped for—positive, constructive, and imaginative. The conference must now begin with a close review of the implementation of the Helsinki Final Act, including the sentence which did not restrict détente to Europe. The non-aligned movement had done nothing for 5 months because 2 key governments had been rendered impotent by changes in their leadership and the country holding the presidency of the movement had disqualified itself by its line on Afghanistan.

[5] The European Council took place on 13 June 1980.

[6] This refers to TNF modernisation.

15. Mr Bullard said that the East ought to re-examine the NATO communiqué issued last December[7] and consider whether they could not accept the offer it contained. It was also necessary to solve the Afghan crisis. The Poles in particular should recognise the symptoms of a country under foreign military occupation: a Quisling régime, repression, refugees and inevitably a resistance movement. The intervention had been a political and a military disaster and it was time for Moscow to draw this conclusion. The best hope at present lay in the commission set up by the Islamic Conference. This had invited representatives of both the Islamic and the left-wing 'tendencies' in Afghanistan to meet it to find a political solution. The Islamic tendency would accept the invitation and it was desirable for the left-wing tendency to do likewise.

16. *Mr Czyrek* said that the TNF modernisation decision was not a consolidation of European security but rather a threat to it because it introduced the possibility of a regional nuclear confrontation. It also weakened the US guarantee, because the US would now have in Europe the means to reach the territory of the USSR. The West ought to have accepted Brezhnev's proposals made in Berlin in October 1979.[7] How could the USSR benefit from the present NATO offer to negotiate? The USSR had to defend itself in many theatres, the Japanese, Chinese and Middle Eastern, as well as the West European—and the SS-20 was the ideal weapon for this. But it could not reach the territory of the US. Negotiations could only begin if the US stopped the implementation of the TNF modernisation decision.

17. The USSR had recognised that Afghanistan was a problem requiring a political settlement and had said that it would then withdraw its troops; it had also suggested that such a settlement should be jointly guaranteed by the USSR and the US. The withdrawal of troops must be the result of a political settlement and not a pre-condition. *Mr Bullard* saw weaknesses in the proposals put out in Kabul. They allocated to Karmal a role out of proportion to his support in Afghanistan; and they were explicit on Afghanistan's frontiers with Iran and Pakistan but said nothing about her frontier with the Soviet Union or about China. The UK believed that it might be possible to construct a political solution covering all Afghanistan's frontiers, the problem of refugees, the withdrawal of foreign troops, an internal political settlement (which would require a government more broadly based than Karmal's) and Afghanistan's future course in international relations. But a solution was impossible whilst the USSR continued to talk of 'irreversible social changes'; this implied a view of history and of relations between great and small powers which the rest of the world did not accept.

18. Mr Bullard was unhappy with Mr Czyrek's thesis that the West need not worry about the SS-20 because it could only hit Western Europe. He asked if what the West had heard about the characteristics of this weapon was true. *Mr Czyrek* replied that Poland did not possess the SS-20. Their information about it came from Chancellor Schmidt, who had explained its characteristics to them with typical German precision. He had not been trying to say that the SS-20 had no significance for Europe, but to explain the difference in the significance of such weapons for the US and USSR. *Mr Bullard* said that there would of course be a conceptual difference over the word 'strategic' as long as there was an Atlantic Ocean. But if there were already over 100 SS-20s deployed and one more to be deployed each week, then by 1983, when the first Pershing II and Cruise missiles were deployed, there could already be more warheads targetted on Western Europe

[7] See No. 2, note 4.

than there would later be Western warheads targetted on the Soviet Union. The USSR could make use of the interval between now and 1983 for negotiations. *Mr Czyrek* said that Poland wanted to find a more acceptable forum than that proposed in the NATO communiqué and Chancellor Schmidt's one-sided demands for a Soviet freeze. Poland suspected that certain countries in the West were determined to have TNF modernisation and to talk only afterwards, and that the present NATO offer was a tactical smokescreen. *Mr Bullard* did not believe that any Western country was enthusiastically awaiting the arrival of Cruise or Pershing II missiles. He was depressed that the First Deputy Foreign Minister of the Soviet Union's most important ally should know nothing about the SS-20 from the Soviet Union. If the USSR had consulted her allies more closely when she decided to manufacture and deploy the SS-20, Poland would perhaps have pointed out that eventually NATO would be obliged to make an appropriate response.

19. The talks ended at 5.40 pm.

No. 13

Mr Cloake (Sofia) to Lord Carrington, 24 June 1980

Confidential (FCO 28/4093, ENG 014/2)

My Lord,

The two faces of Bulgaria: A Valedictory

A symbol frequently to be seen in Bulgarian churches is the double-headed eagle. Whether this represents Byzantium or imperial Russia is a moot point. But after three and a half years in this country I feel that it would more aptly represent Bulgaria than the rampant lion which still figures on the country's flag and coat of arms.

2. In my first impressions despatch I said that I found many contradictions. I am today not much nearer to resolving them, nor to answering with any confidence the basic question: does the eagle's steady eastward gaze show affection or merely dependence; is the westward look just an envious glance or a real appeal for friendship?

3. Virtually every official pronouncement appears to proclaim the virtues of puppetdom, cosily enjoyed—'I'm so glad I'm a Delta'. But every so often, frequently in apparent joke, there comes a glimmer of something deeper. A national pride? Certainly. A yearning for real independence? Possibly. A longing for the forbidden fruit of the west? Sometimes. A profound boredom with 'eternal friendship'? Often.

4. Are the Bulgarians good communists or frustrated capitalists? Perhaps this begs the questions whether any ruling communist party, even—or especially—the CPSU, can be considered good communists. But in this area it is not just a glimmer of independence that is discernible through the welter of Marxist-Leninist gobbledegook. Day by day the press, especially the Party newspaper, has—thank Heavens—relieved the dreadful monotony of most of its coverage with articles showing only too clearly the persistence despite all obstacles of a spirit of private enterprise, of criticism, of—it is really the only word—bolshiness. As an elderly Bulgarian once whispered to me with a wink, sitting in a village tavern which his family had once owned: 'We Bulgarians are great revolutionaries. Now who have we to rebel against?'

5. Perhaps it is not only the individual, but the system itself, that is beginning to rebel against the system. The 'New Economic Mechanism',[1] if it works, will have borrowed more from capitalism than from *Das Kapital*. The younger economic Ministers, people like Deputy Prime Minister Lukanov and Minister of Foreign Trade Christov, know not only what the West has to offer but how the West thinks and works. And though they are very prompt to point to the shortcomings of capitalism, they are equally aware of the shortcomings of their own system, and are prepared to take what may seem to be ideologically dangerous steps to improve it. Lyudmilla Zhivkova, the President's daughter, dictator of culture (including responsibilities for education and for the media), puts on exhibitions of Bulgarian icons abroad and exhibitions of Bulgarian and Western European religious art at home—in the name of 'humanism' and 'the harmonious development of the personality'. The influence of this new generation of leaders may not yet be decisive, but clearly it is already considerable. They have been advanced rapidly and deliberately, and one day soon they may really rule the country. They will be more open to ideas. They would die in the last ditch in defence of what they conceive to be 'real socialism', but their concept of it will be very different from that of their predecessors.

6. Even if, socially and economically, the gap between East and West is narrowing, the essential difference of approach will remain that of the priority between the rights of the individual and the claims of the State. Is Bulgaria a popular democracy, as it claims, or a police state? Certainly this is no democracy in the western sense, though there may be a small element of truth in the contention that there are some genuine democratic processes within the system, and particularly within the Party. So long as the State can ride roughshod over the individual there can be no real freedom, but the Bulgarians do seem more adept than most (and indeed they have had long experience) at preserving a bit of independence within, or beneath, an oppressive régime. Certainly this current régime has all the machinery of repression available, but it seldom uses it blatantly. The general impression is of a relaxed country, peaceable and friendly, grumbling (as who does not?—but with more cause than most) at shortages, price rises, bureaucratic incompetence, but without serious, let alone organised, dissidence. With an effort a Western diplomat can make friends with some Bulgarians, both official and unofficial. Sometimes such efforts seem even to be favoured. But from time to time the system will raise its ugly head and decree that invitations be not accepted, that contact has reached a dangerous point. And many older Bulgarians, anglophile and yearning for contact, but remembering the bad old days of the late 40s and 50s, will admit openly that they still dare not come to our house. Clearly our contacts are monitored and our front doors, of residence and office, kept under close surveillance, although, [un]like some other western embassies, we have no uniformed policeman at the door. Sofia is a city in which one feels relatively secure from terrorism or other crimes of violence. Despite the massacres (not all one-sided) of a hundred years ago,[2] the violence and assassination in the days of the monarchy and the terrible purges of the 40s and 50s, one does not detect any great propensity to violence lurking under the surface and held in check by an all-powerful and all-knowing state security system. But then one is suddenly

[1] See No. 2, note 31.
[2] A massacre of Bulgarians by Ottoman troops during the Russo-Turkish War (1877-78).

confronted by a Markov case[3]—and the brutality is briefly glimpsed; or by the refusal of a visa to a British born old lady to visit her sister in England—and the full rigour—and spite—of the repressive machinery becomes apparent.

7. So are the Bulgarians sincere at all in their protestations that they want closer contacts with us, and with other western countries? Or are they just out for easy pickings? Once again, at my farewell interviews, President Zhivkov and Foreign Minister Mladenov stressed their desire for high-level visits, their amazement that we almost alone of western countries seemed unwilling to have such exchanges, and their conviction that contacts at this level would lead to improved trade as well as enhanced understanding. Asking in particular that his greetings be conveyed to the Prime Minister, whom he admired, President Zhivkov commented 'We may be far apart politically, but we have a bond—we are both extremists, and we both have the support of our people'.

8. In my despatch 'What Use is Bulgaria?' of 30 July 1979[4] I argued that the urge for recognition was one of the principal motivations of Bulgarian foreign policy. I remain convinced that that is true. I am equally convinced that the Bulgarian leaders are, by their own lights, sincere in their protestations of a desire for friendship. But they are blinkered by the conditioning to which their perceptive faculties have been subjected. I think they really do not see the contradictions between commemoration of the victims of the 1876 massacres and support for the Soviet actions in Afghanistan, between the constantly hostile press treatment of Britain and the desire to be friends, between the denial of exit visas and the demand for more cultural exchanges, between their failure to reply to firms' correspondence or to publish adequate commercial statistics and the complaint that British firms are insufficiently interested in Bulgaria, between a determination to screw the foreigner and the desire to do more foreign business. It is a hard and a long process to get them to appreciate that their practices are often not calculated to achieve their proclaimed goals. But some impression can be made if one sticks at it. I still believe we would do better, when we see the Bulgarian hand stretched out towards us—even palm uppermost—to take the hand and shake it (and perhaps exert a gentle pull) rather than to slap it.

9. Somewhat to my surprise I find I am quite sorry to be leaving Bulgaria and the Bulgarians. To my regret I cannot claim to have done much more in my time here than to keep our relations simmering away, without boiling over too badly and without going stone cold, despite some abrupt changes in temperature. The broth is still sadly thin. I hope that my successor may have more success in adding a little substance.

10. It is no surprise that I have mixed feelings on leaving the Service. In 32 years one grows accustomed to the face—though the face has changed so much. In tasks, in attitudes, in circumstances, the Diplomatic Service of 1980 is not the same Foreign Service that I joined in 1948. It has lost a lot of intimacy, but I think it has gained in humanity. 'Marcus Cheke'[5] now reads like a historical novel. There are, I am sure, no Ambassadors today for whom, as for my first chief, the rudest words in the English language are 'consul' and 'commercial'. The Service has been the repeated target of inspection and reform, much of it justified but some which has

[3] In September 1978 Bulgarian dissident Georgi Markov was assassinated in London, by the Bulgarian secret service, after being jabbed in the leg by an umbrella tip filled with poison.

[4] Not printed.

[5] 'Guidance on the foreign usages and ceremony, and other matters, for a Member of His Majesty's Foreign Service on his first appointment to a Post Abroad' by Marcus Cheke, published in 1949.

seemed change for change's sake alone. It has been the target of largely unjust attack; and, along with the country itself, it has lost a lot of its clout. But not all; and, at least abroad, it still has a lot of influence. It is a dimension too often forgotten that one can seek to influence not only 'the Government to which you are accredited' but also the perception of diplomatic colleagues and thereby that of the Governments which they represent. The reputation of the Service for acumen and accurate analysis remains high among 'the colleagues', and can be of great importance in winning acceptance of our view of events. I am proud to have been a member of a Service against which the criticism was levelled that 'its work is being done to an unjustifiably high standard'. Long may an excess of excellence be our fault. From what I have seen of the two generations of staff in my time at this post it certainly will be. I have been proud of them. My thanks to them all.

11. I am sending copies of this despatch to Her Majesty's Ambassadors at Moscow, Bucharest, Budapest, East Berlin, Prague, Warsaw, Ankara, Athens, Belgrade and Washington and to the UK Permanent Representatives to the North Atlantic Council and to the European Community.

I am Sir, etc,
J. C. CLOAKE

No. 14

Letter from Miss Elmes (Prague) to Mr Facey, 7 July 1980
Confidential (FCO 28/4077, ENC 015/1)

Dear Robert,

Charter 77

1. Thank you for your letter of 27 June.[1] While I am of course pleased that the account of my meeting with Miloš Rejchrt[2] was read with great interest, I am not sure whether you realise that local conditions make such meetings somewhat hazardous to all participants. A few days after the meeting with Rejchrt my car was stolen, and subsequently returned to me slightly damaged, in an incident which was undoubtedly officially inspired. I suggest that you consult Tony Hornyold in Security Department for any further details.

2. Visits to dissident houses in the countryside almost invariably mean that one arrives trailing at least one carload of plainclothes policemen, something which is not always welcomed by the Charter signatory concerned who may have been enjoying a period relatively free of harassment. One of my US colleagues has been

[1] Not printed.

[2] On 20 June Miss Elmes had reported on a conversation with the Czechoslovak Protestant Minister and Charter spokesman, Miloš Rejchrt, on 19 June. He had spoken about the trial of six members of the Vons, the Committee for the Defence of the Unjustly Persecuted. These were: Otta Bednářová, Václav Benda, Jiří Dienstbier, Václav Havel, Dana Němcová, and Petr Uhl. On the same day she reported an interview with the Hungarian philosopher György Bence in a Charter 77 publication, in which he argued that Hungarians had sympathy with the Czechs as they drew some analogies between the Prague Spring in 1968 and events in Hungary in 1956. But he thought that political activity in Hungary was more scattered and irregular that in Czechoslovakia and in Poland. Yet the Chartists were enthusiastic about contacts with the Hungarian democratic opposition—their contacts with the Polish opposition having petered since the arrest of Jaroslav Šabata. The spokesman for Charter 77, who had worked to establish a common platform between Czech and Polish citizens had been arrested at the Czech-Polish border in 1978 (FCO 28/4620, ENZ 015/1).

accompanied on every car journey (even round Prague) for a month since making such a call. Another US colleague (now posted elsewhere) told me his car was bumped several times by one of the following cars, a daunting experience on an unfamiliar road.

3. There are also difficulties in making arrangements to meet since Rejchrt for example, although he gave me his telephone number, urged that we should not ring him except in an emergency since he was surprised still to have the use of a telephone and did not want it cut off. Moreover in general dissidents can see the immediate benefit of talking with Western journalists in the publicity given to their cause, while talking to diplomats from countries whose leaders are unlikely to have any influence with the hierarchy here is less obviously useful to the Charter signatories themselves. I had been trying to see Rejchrt for several months—unsuccessfully until Reuters took a hand because McIntyre[3] was in town.

4. The authorities also tend to take a worse view of diplomatic contacts since in their eyes we are here to deal with the government and not with those they are pleased to regard as criminals or lunatics. However much we condemn this view, cultivating dissidents and not compensating for this with high-level official visits, as e.g. Austria and FRG do, will affect other aspects of our relations, a factor which I assume has been taken into account in London. On a mundane level it affects for example the degree of official cooperation we get from Diplomatic Protocol in trying to meet even official Czechoslovaks, as we discovered during Peter Summerscale's recent visit and as I have experienced in trying unsuccessfully for over a year to get appointments with Slovak officials. Without an OK from the MFA few Czechoslovak officials feel free to meet an Embassy political officer.

5. I am of course aware of the recent correspondence on this subject (Mallaby's letter of 2 April to Pridham, Thomas's letter of 22 May to Battiscombe's and Battiscombe's reply of 30 May),[4] as well as previous exchanges during the past three years, and that it is Mr Blaker's wish that contacts with Czechoslovak dissidents in particular should be stepped up. What I want to point out is that we are not sought out by the dissidents themselves, unlike the Austrians, Germans, Swiss, Swedish, French, Italians and even on occasions the Americans, whose countries are all for one reason or another the first choice of asylum for most prominent signatories and/or whose politicians have some influence here (e.g. the Austrian Chargé told me last night that he never met a dissident outside his Embassy, it was unnecessary because they called regularly at his Consular Section); that the efforts which we have to make to cultivate dissidents meet a mixed response from the dissidents themselves and draw a great deal of unfavourable attention from the authorities; and that we have nothing going for us politically to balance the interest we take in Charter 77, therefore our political relations overall steadily deteriorate. It goes without saying that we shall do our best to further Ministerial wishes in this matter even though when Reuters close down we shall have no suitable third party premises available and no easy intermediaries for setting up appointments. Nevertheless, if I am right in inferring from your letter than you think we can increase the level and frequency of our

[3] Colin McIntyre was Reuters' chief correspondent for Austria and East Europe.
[4] Not printed.

contacts with dissidents without cost to them or ourselves, then I think it only fair to warn you that there will undoubtedly be repercussions.[5]

Yours sincerely,
C. M. T. ELMES

[5] Mr Battiscombe thanked Miss Elmes on 22 July for spelling out the problems of contacts with dissidents. Nevertheless, he wished to see them increasing in countries like Czechoslovakia where dissidents were particularly active. However, he was content to rely on the Embassy's judgement regarding the extent and the practice of contacts and encouraged the Embassy in Prague to learn from other missions there.

No. 15

Submission from Mr Mallaby to Mr Fergusson, 9 July 1980
Confidential (FCO 28/4156, ENP 090/1)

Poland's economic problems

1. I submit the latest JIC paper (JIC(EA) (80)3)[1] on the Polish economy due to issue, subject to any comments you may have, next week (not at the JIC meeting tomorrow).

2. The Polish economy has been in difficulties for many years. It now appears to be reaching a crisis point. On her own best estimates Poland will not achieve a surplus on current account and begin reducing her hard currency debt (now about $22 billion) until 1983 at the earliest. The likelihood is that this will take much longer. At the very least therefore Poland has three or four very difficult years ahead. The signs are that she is already having difficulties in raising the necessary foreign credits to tide her over the 1980 deficit and the paper concludes that her prospects for achieving this are slim. Even if she does she will have to return to the market for further large loans in succeeding years.

3. The paper concludes that if the financing gap over the next few years were relatively small Poland would probably try to muddle through by squeezing the domestic economy still further. It is more likely however that the shortfall will be too large to be bridged in this way, in which case Poland would be faced with two courses:

(*a*) to approach her Western creditors for refinancing; and

(*b*) to request the Soviet Union to bail her out.

The paper also concludes that Western banks would be unlikely to accept the risks of agreeing to refinancing on their own and might therefore propose to Western governments a multilateral rescheduling of all Polish debt. Alternatively such an approach could come from the Poles themselves.

4. A great deal depends on the Soviet attitude. There have been a number of indications that the USSR has already provided hard currency loans this year to prevent Poland defaulting. But the amounts have been fairly small and the paper concludes that, rather than becoming heavily involved, the Soviet Union would probably prefer Poland to continue negotiating for loans with Western lenders and

[1] This paper by the Joint Intelligence Committee's Economic Assessments Sub-Committee is not printed. The paper concluded that Poland would probably fail to raise all the hard-currency financing it needed for 1980.

even perhaps to reach a multilateral refinancing or rescheduling agreement with its Western creditors. In the last resort, however, if the West was unwilling to bail out Poland on acceptable terms the USSR would do so, to avoid the political impact of a default and the consequences for the credit worthiness of all CMEA members.

5. The cost to the UK of a rescheduling of Polish debt would be considerable. On the assumption that there was a moratorium on all repayments over a number of years the UK might have to forego repayments of officially guaranteed credits of up to £150-200 million a year, a not insignificant amount in relation to the Public Service Borrowing Requirements of about £8.8 billion in 1980.

6. Whichever approach they follow the consequences for the Poles are likely to be uncomfortable. Large-scale Soviet help would almost certainly lead to a significant increase in Soviet direction of the Polish economy, with still greater hardship for the Polish consumer and perhaps the increasing diversion of Polish trade from the West towards the CMEA. Poland's room for political manoeuvre would be curtailed. A request to the West for multilateral rescheduling would on the other hand severely undermine Poland's credit-worthiness and international credibility. The Poles will therefore try desperately hard to continue to muddle through and avoid resorting to either course. The recent increases in meat prices are no doubt just the beginning of a further attempt to put their house in order. But the reaction which these moves appear to have provoked, and the memory of public explosions in 1970 and 1976,[2] shows how hard it will be for the Poles to introduce the austerity measures that the situation requires.

7. In this situation the main aims of the Treasury are:

(*a*) to limit the further expansion of UK officially guaranteed credits to Poland (ECGD already has £1,000 million at risk);

(*b*) to ensure that any requests by Poland for refinancing officially backed credits are handled multilaterally.

As regards (*b*) the Treasury informed us last week that Sir K. Couzens[3] had had a meeting with his opposite numbers from the US, Japan, the FRG, and France in the margins of the Venice Summit at which it was agreed that requests for further officially backed credits not tied to specific projects should be considered multilaterally. As regards (*a*) a decision was taken last October to tighten up on the provision of future ECGD credits for Poland. There is likely to be a further meeting of the Export Guarantee Committee shortly at which the question will be considered again. Inevitably in these circumstances and in view of the potential cost to the PSBR there will be a move to tighten up still further. Against this have to be set the political arguments in favour of maintaining at least a certain level of credits for Poland—bilateral relations, value of Poland as an export market in the longer term, Western interest in Poland's stability and the maintenance of a degree of independence from the USSR—and we shall continue to ensure that these are also taken into account.[4]

C. L. G. MALLABY

[2] See No. 11, note 3.

[3] Joint Second Permanent Secretary (Overseas Finance) at HM Treasury.

[4] Mr Bullard thought the JIC paper should be brought to the attention of Ministers because one reason for the Polish Ambassador's zeal in building up the importance of the Secretary of State's forthcoming visit to Poland undoubtedly sprang from financial motives. Mr Blaker also suggested that the Secretary of State see Mr Mallaby's submission. The paper was approved on 10 July by the JIC (EA).

No. 16

Mr Pridham (Warsaw) to Lord Carrington, 15 August 1980, 3.15 p.m.
Tel. No. 236[1] Immediate, Restricted (FCO 28/4160, ENP 212/2)

Labour unrest

1. Yesterday 16,000 workers at the Lenin Shipyard in Gdansk stopped work and presented ten demands to the management. Some of these demands were for pay rises and better allowances and have been met in whole or part by the management. The management also agreed to reinstate two workers at the shipyard who had been sacked[2] and to the principle of a memorial at the shipyard gates to those who died there in 1970.[3] But they declared themselves not competent to grant other demands including the release of all 'political prisoners' in Poland, replacement of the official trade union structure by the Baltic Free Trades Unions,[4] the abolition of commercial meat shops and broadcasting by the media of the workers full demands.

2. This morning workers at the Rosa Luxemburg Wharf at Gdynia also went on strike and it is reported that three or four other less important concerns in the area have done the same. Public transport appears to be affected and there is talk of a general strike throughout the triple city[5] on Monday next.

3. Public transport in Warsaw now appears to be more or less back to normal. But some food delivery drivers have stopped work.

4. Babiuch[6] is to address the nation on television this evening and we will let you have details of his broadcast in due course.

[1] Repeated Immediate to Stockholm (for Private Secretary) and Saving to Moscow, Prague, East Berlin, Sofia, Bucharest, Budapest, Belgrade and UKDEL NATO.

[2] Lech Wałęsa, one of the strike leaders, and Anna Walentynowicz, who had been summarily dismissed from the Gdańsk Shipyard at the beginning of August for their activities as members of the Free Trade Unions of the Coast that had been created in June 1978.

[3] One of the largest shipyards in the world, which served the Soviet Union and other East European countries. In 1970 unrest had spread from Poznan to Gdańsk and led to the formation of an Inter-Factory Strike Committee. On 16 December 1980 the Monument to Fallen Shipyard Workers—48 dead and 1,165 wounded—was unveiled on the spot where the first three victims of the 1970 riots were killed.

[4] See No. 11, note 5 and paragraph 7.

[5] Gdańsk, Gdynia and Sopot, situated along the coast of the Gdańsk Bay on the Baltic Sea.

[6] Edward Babiuch, Prime Minister of Poland.

No. 17

FCO to Mr Lever (Helsinki),[1] 21 August 1980, 4 p.m.

Tel. No. 158 Immediate, Confidential (FCO 28/4269, ENZ 021/319/1)

For Lever from Private Secretary[2]

Poland

1. No. 10 have asked for our assessment of the current situation[3] for the Prime Minister by lunchtime on 22 August. The following is the text of the letter which I propose to send to Mr Pattison. Grateful for any comments by 221100.[4]

1. [*sic*] You asked for an assessment of the current situation in Poland for the Prime Minister. You will by now have seen the report on the situation approved by the JIC yesterday.[5] The following may however help in amplifying this assessment.

2. The labour unrest in Poland, which began in early July as a result of meat price increases, has escalated in the last 10 days with large-scale strikes in the Baltic ports. These have centred on the Lenin Shipyard in Gdansk but have spread to a number of other ports in the area. A large number of enterprises appear to be involved and the strikers have established an inter-factory strike committee to negotiate with the authorities. There have also been rumours of trouble in other areas, including the important mining and industrial area of Silesia and the steel works in Krakow but these remain unconfirmed.

3. The significant feature of the present strikes is that whereas the strikers' demands in July were exclusively economic, the demands now being put forward include many in the political field which it is virtually impossible for the regime to concede. These include the replacement of the official trade union structure by free trade unions, abolition of censorship and the release of political prisoners. Nevertheless by contrast to the situation in 1970,[6] the unrest has so far been largely confined to strikes and there have been virtually no demonstrations and no violence. The Church, always one of the most powerful sources of influence in Poland, has remained on the side lines.

4. The reaction of the authorities has been conciliatory. But they have made it clear that they are unable to concede the political demands now being made and are unwilling to negotiate with the inter-factory strike committee. Speeches on TV by Polish leaders, including one by the party leader Mr Gierek, on 18 August, have warned about the serious economic consequences of the strikes and the hardship they are causing to ordinary Polish people. The main tactic of the authorities is likely to be to attempt to isolate the strikers in the Baltic area and avoid the strikes spreading to other parts of the country and to wear down the resistance and solidarity of the workers and induce them to negotiate on a factory by factory basis. This is no doubt the main reason behind the arrests yesterday of 14 dissident leaders since the dissident movement had been acting as one of the main channels

[1] Lord Carrington was in Finland for a one and a half-day official visit.

[2] Mr Walden was Lord Carrington's Private Secretary and Mr Lever was one of his Assistant Private Secretaries.

[3] See No. 16.

[4] 11 a.m. on 22 August 1980.

[5] Not printed.

[6] See No. 11, note 4.

of information on the strikes. The authorities have very little room for manoeuvre. They will no doubt be prepared to make further economic concessions to reach a settlement and may also be prepared to introduce some reforms in the trade union system. But they cannot give in on the major political demands without undermining their own authority and risking Soviet intervention. The authorities have said that they will not use force and we believe that they will indeed be very reluctant to do so, not least because Mr Gierek himself came to power as a direct result of the use of the force to put down similar unrest in 1970. Nevertheless, the longer the strikes continue, the more the pressures will mount on the authorities to re-assert their authority by taking tougher action. There are no apparent differences yet within the Polish leadership on how the strikes should be handled and Mr Gierek appears so far to have maintained the confidence of the Soviet Union.

5. The USSR must however be seriously concerned, both for the situation in Poland itself and for the risk of the contagion spreading to other East European countries including the USSR itself.[7] Their decision to resume jamming the BBC and Voice of America Russian Services on 20 August for the first time since 1973 (about which we are instructing HM Ambassador in Moscow to make a firm protest) probably reflects the latter fear.[8] We believe however that they would be very reluctant to intervene directly unless the situation gets out of control. Afghanistan and the advent of Madrid will make them still more reluctant. Nevertheless the Polish leadership have made a number of allusions to the threat of Soviet intervention and no doubt hope that this will help in persuading the strikers to exercise moderation.

6. The situation, particularly if it drags on, can only exacerbate Poland's economic problems.[9] Poland's hard currency debts already amount to dollars 20 billion and they had been hoping for a significant turnaround in their hard currency balance of payments this year, not least to revive the flagging banking confidence in the West. They have recently succeeded in obtaining a further loan of dollars 325 million from West German banks. The direct economic effects of the strikes coupled with the inflationary effects of the wage increases the authorities are having to concede and the prospects of another bad harvest can only make the economic outlook extremely gloomy. This will increase the likelihood of further labour unrest, as the authorities try to tackle the problems of the economy, even if they are successful in settling the present difficulties.

7. There has been virtually no official international comment from any quarter on the situation in Poland so far and Lord Carrington, who has approved the above assessment, considers that so long as the Polish authorities are trying to settle the matter peacefully and there is no outside intervention we should continue to keep a low profile. As you may have seen, in answer to a question about what the West should do, following a lecture to the Swedish Institute of International Affairs in Stockholm on 19 August,[10] Lord Carrington took the line that there was nothing

[7] Shortly afterwards, on 1 September Mr Johnson, Assistant Head of EESD, drew Mr Fergusson's attention to a minute of 29 August by Mr Beel of the Soviet section of the Research Department who thought that if the position of the Polish Party leadership became untenable and the monopoly of Party rule were renounced, as a last resort the Soviet leaders would undoubtedly intervene to install a leadership prepared to restore order and Party control (FCO 28/4037, EN 021/31).

[8] At the UNGA in New York Lord Carrington met Mr Gromyko on 23 September and asked him to stop jamming the BBC (see *DBPO*: *Afghanistan*, No. 77).

[9] See No. 31.

[10] Dr Åke Sparring had asked at the lecture—in the context of Polish troops reportedly moving against strike workers in Gdańsk—what the position of Western diplomacy was regarding human

which we could do except to express our disapproval of the use of force if this happened. In our view this was an internal affair of the Polish people and he hoped that the countries in the surrounding area would take the same view.[11]

rights and potential action. Lord Carrington sympathised with the question, but warned: 'There is an increasing tendency in some quarters in my country, and I daresay in yours too, to behave like the proverbial English nanny and to think that the whole world is your business and you have got to put it right', and this was not 'altogether sensible' (Stockholm tel. No. 148, 19 August 1980; FCO 28/4160, ENP 212/2).

[11] On 22 August Mr Bisztyga, the Polish Ambassador to the United Kingdom met Mr Bullard and expressed his thanks for Lord Carrington's remarks in Stockholm and warned the West to avoid actions which 'could make the Soviet Union fear for its own safety or strengthen the hand of Soviet hardliners demanding a tough line in Poland'. At the same time he said that 'the Polish Government would never use force against the strikes' (FCO tel. No. 370; FCO 28/4160, ENP 212/2).

No. 18

Mr Pridham (Warsaw) to Lord Carrington, 3 September 1980, 12 p.m.
Tel. No. 277[1] Immediate, Confidential (FCO 28/4161, ENP 212/2)

My Telno 272.[2]

1. A first study of the agreements concluded at Szczecin and Gdansk shows that although they cover the same basic ground the former is a much shorter and less contentious document than the latter. This suggests that the Gdansk men were the hardcore of strikers.

2. On trade unions, the Szczecin document simply says that self-governing unions, socialist in character and in keeping with the Polish constitution, will be possible and the necessary laws should be prepared, to a timetable, to accord with article 3 of ILO Convention no 87.[3]

3. The Gdansk document is fuller. It says that the new unions accept collective ownership of the means of production, and are not going to form a second political party: they accept the leading role of the PZPR[4] and the existing system of international alliances. The Government guarantees the new unions, which will be separate from the existing council of trade unions, full respect for their freedom and self-government both as regards organisational structure and functioning. The strike committees can act as workers' representative committees pending elections for the new unions which it seems they will organise. The new unions will

[1] Repeated for Information Routine to Moscow, Prague, Sofia, Budapest, Bucharest, East Berlin, Belgrade, UKDEL NATO, Washington, Paris, Bonn, MODUK.

[2] In this telegram of 1 September, Mr Pridham reported that agreements between the Government and the strikers at Gdańsk and Szczecin had been signed on 31 August 'at ceremonies like those for international treaties', which was an extraordinary humiliation for the Polish Government. This resulted for the people in a 'prevailing mood . . . of relief and satisfaction, predominantly the former'. He foresaw austerity and in the short term 'a difficult period of putting the agreement into effect, of getting the economy moving again and adapting to the cost'. He concluded: 'We have so far seen only the end of act 1 of the drama.' The protocol signed in Gdańsk on 31 August was sent by Mr Harrison to Mr Facey on 3 September.

[3] Convention 87—Freedom of Association and Protection of the Right to Organise Convention—guaranteed that workers and employers should have the right to establish and to join organisations of their own choosing without previous authorisation.

[4] The Polish United Workers' Party had governed the People's Republic of Poland since 1948.

participate in decisions about living standards, division of the national income, wages, investment and prices. The new Trade Union Law will provide a right to strike, defining the conditions under which a strike can take place. This still leaves much unclear in particular whether unions more in the British or the Germany style are contemplated.

4. Religious denominations will have access to the media according to agreements to be worked out between the Government and religious groups. Radio and TV should express differing opinions. But censorship is accepted as necessary for the security of the state and its vital economic and other interests. Believers and non-believers should be protected and immoral publications banned. A new law will enshrine these principles.

5. The 3 prisoners specifically mentioned will be released pending an investigation by the Minister of Justice. Dismissals after the strikes of 1970 and 1976 to be considered with a view to reinstatement. Detention without trial is to be limited, but the details have not been published (perhaps significantly). Promotion will be by merit rather than party affiliation. Freedom of belief and political activity not harmful to the socialist structure and basic interests of the state will be permitted.

6. On the economic side.

Despite concessions including the following:

(i) Payment in full of wages for the strike period, in return for which workers will try to improve productivity and reduce the use of materials and energy resources:

(ii) Pay increases to all workers introduced gradually;

(iii) Improvements in meat supplies by making production more profitable, cutting back exports to 'the necessary minimum' and increasing imports;

(iv) Withdrawal from hard currency shops of Polish-made items in short supply domestically;

(v) Raising retirement pensions to a mutually agreed 'social minimum'; and

(vi) Improving the health services by importing more raw materials to increase pharmaceutical supplies, increasing investment in this sector and improving pay and conditions in the medical sector.

7. In addition, the government has committed itself to bringing forward proposals by the end of 1980 to achieve:

(*a*) Economic reform, based on greater independence of enterprises and participation by workers' bodies in achieving this;

(*b*) A binding programme of forward pay increases for the lower paid;

(*c*) A programme for compensating the population for rising prices (in the interim measures will be introduced to hold prices of over 150 basic items representing 55 per cent of total expenditure and 80 per cent of expenditure on foodstuffs). The longer-term programme envisages a uniform pricing system 'governed by economic laws'. It seems that private sellers will be deprived of the power to set their own prices);

(*d*) A programme to ensure better market supplies in future, including rationing if appropriate;

(*e*) A reduction in retirement age for those involved in heavy manual labour and possibly other measures in this field;

(*f*) Regular increases in retirement pensions;

(*g*) Better maternity allowances and maternity leave arrangements;

(*h*) Improvements in the overall housing situation; and

(*i*) Improvements in shift allowances, working hours, staff gradings and sickness benefits.

8. The strikers pressed in addition for an expansion of private agriculture and rural self-government, the liquidations of 'commercial' shops, and lowering of the retirement age to 50 for women and 55 for men. No doubt these points will form the basis of further pressure on the government in the future.

9. For comment see MIFT.[5]

[5] No. 19.

No. 19

Mr Pridham (Warsaw) to Lord Carrington, 3 September 1980, 12.20 p.m.

Tel. No. 278[1] Immediate, Confidential (FCO 28/4161, ENP 212/2)

MIPT: Polish crisis[2]

1. As important as the concessions themselves is the fact that they have been wrung from the Government in the glare of radio and TV publicity and have been enshrined in formal written agreements. This means that the issues have been publicly discussed, the regime's inadequacy confessed, genuine collective bargaining has been visible, and the agreements, unlike those of 1956 and 1970,[3] are on record. To return to the *status quo ante* will, short of Soviet intervention, be almost impossible. The 1956 spring could be clawed back but the world (and the workers' sophistication) has moved on since then.

2. The government has successfully defended the leading role of the party, the collectivist ethic and the country's international alliances. Probably only the former was at all difficult. The signature ceremonies took place under a banner reading 'Workers of the world unite', and right-wing dissidents seemed entirely out of the picture. But to yield at all in such circumstances was of course a shattering defeat for the regime. Just how the new trade unions will develop is uncertain but they can hardly fail to become a force in the country parallel to the Party/Government and the Church. Most ominous of all for the regime is the discovery by organised workers of the power of the strike weapon. When they find (see below) that things will have to get worse before they get better, they may use it again and in a less restrained manner. There is plenty of scope also for argument on implementation of the agreements.

3. Many of the strikers' demands covered comparatively minor matters concerning conditions of work, shifts, health arrangements, leave, pensions, etc. This suggests that had the government been sufficiently in touch with the feelings of the workers and dealt with such grievances a few months ago (i.e. if the party congress in February had fulfilled its proper function), things might not have come to boil as they did. There has certainly been a massive failure of communication. The regime's best hope now is to learn to accept the situation, to offer some genuine power-sharing and, most of all, to establish a proper dialogue with the people. Only in this way might the party revivify itself and stand any chance of

[1] Repeated for Information Routine to Moscow, Prague, Sofia, Budapest, Bucharest, East Berlin, Belgrade, UKDEL NATO, Washington, Paris, Bonn, MODUK.

[2] No. 18.

[3] See No. 11, note 4.

capturing the new unions, which may be its ultimate aim. Meanwhile there are a lot of economic and social grievances which the unions could occupy themselves with for some time without impinging further on politics.

4. A major difficulty however is that so many of the strikers' demands, e.g. for higher pay, lower prices, shorter hours and more meat, will in the short run exacerbate economic difficulties. And new union power will make it harder to reduce over-manning and increase the mobility of labour. Without an economic miracle or large new borrowing, the Government's promises of more food and more flats cannot be made good. Disappointments in these fields may lead to new strikes with less responsible leaders making impossible political demands and perhaps thinking Soviet intervention a paper tiger.

5. The logic of all this is that the West needs to help to keep Poland afloat rather as we kept Tito afloat in the 1950s for different reasons.

6. MIFT[4] discusses more fully the economic implications.

[4] No. 20.

No. 20

Mr Pridham (Warsaw) to Lord Carrington, 3 September 1980, 12.35 p.m.
Tel. No. 279[1] Immediate, Confidential (FCO 28/4161, ENP 212/2)

MIPT: Polish crisis.[2]

The firm concessions made to strikers by the authorities will represent a substantial additional burden to this hard-pressed economy, and a marked switch in policy away from that announced earlier this year by Babiuch will be needed to meet them. Furthermore, undertakings to introduce measures in the fields of housing, health services, pensions, and allowances, retirement age, market supplies etc will be hard to claw back given the new-found power of the workers and the means of channelling it.

2. The first effects of the concessions are likely to be seen on prices, which will be stabilised at enormous additional cost in subsidies: on supplies to the market, especially of foodstuffs, which will involve massive additional imports (a figure of up to dollars 300 million to the end of 1980 has been mentioned privately) and a reduction in Polish exports of goods required internally: and a surge in the nation's wage bill. In the longer-term, fulfilment of other pledges in the social field will require either major new import programmes, e.g. of housing materials and raw materials for medical supplies, or a massive diversion of resources from the export to the domestic market.

3. To the cost of these concessions must be added those of the strikes themselves. If the workers achieve higher production levels as promised, some of the lost ground may be made up but some costs, e.g. demurrage charges on ships left idle for several weeks or more, are probably non-recoverable.

4. The Government has virtually no room for manoeuvre in this bleak situation. Unless it meets its pledges it faces repetition of strike action: but it is difficult to see where the resources will come from to meet its commitments. It may be

[1] Repeated for Information Routine to Moscow, Prague, Sofia, Budapest, Bucharest, East Berlin, Belgrade, UKDEL NATO, Washington, Paris, Bonn, MODUK.
[2] No. 19.

possible to reduce investment-orientated imports still further, although the scope for this must be severely limited in view of the cutbacks made already and demands by workers to be given the means for production. Plans for future new projects will be shelved, but these seemed likely to be few in number anyway. And the expansion in the population's spending power engendered by the new measures will have to be met somehow if the frustration leading to the recent crisis are [*sic* is] to be avoided.

5. Poland's only hope must be for massive outside assistance. Whether her CMEA partners will help must be doubtful in the circumstances. But she is already deeply in debt to the West and there was little likelihood of this debt being reduced before the crisis began. Somehow Poland's leaders must persuade the West to help further, but experience of her recent only partly-successful attempts to raise new finance are drying up. We can therefore expect further very heavy pressure on governments for assistance over the coming months.

No. 21

Lord Carrington to Certain Missions and Dependent Territories, 3 September 1980, 5 p.m.

Guidance Tel. No. 92 Confidential (FCO 28/4161, ENP 212/2)

Poland

1. The strikes in the Baltic ports in Poland ended on 31 August with agreements between the Polish government and the inter-factory strike committees in Gdansk and Szczecin.[1] Strikes in the mining areas of Silesia now seem to have been settled on a similar basis. The agreements reached include the right to establish free trade unions in factories which want them, in parallel with the present official trade union structure; recognition of the right to strike; relaxation of censorship; the release of political detainees, and better access to the media for the church. There have also been a number of concessions in the economic field.

Line to take

2. We wish to restrict comment on the situation in Poland to a minimum, both to avoid appearing to substantiate the Soviet allegation that Western support for the strikers is aimed at subverting the socialist order in Poland and to avoid making more difficult the task of the Polish authorities in implementing the reforms agreed. If asked you may confirm our belief that it is in the general interest that the disputes should have been resolved peacefully between the two sides. You should however emphasise that we continue to regard events in Poland as a strictly internal Polish matter to be settled by the Polish authorities and people themselves.

3. You may draw freely on paras 1 and 4 and on para 5 in talking to trusted contacts.

[1] See No. 18, note 2.

Background

4. The wave of strikes in Poland in the last two months was triggered by the raising of meat prices on 1 July. The strikers' demands were at first largely economic and were met by the wages rises averaging 10 per cent. With the spread of the strikes in early August to the Baltic ports, the demands became increasingly political, finally concentrating on the right to establish a free trade union movement. 14 dissidents who had been active particularly in disseminating information about the strikes were arrested on 20 August, and a number of others subsequently. Most of these were held until the end of the dispute. A number of changes in the leadership were announced, including the dismissal of the Prime Minister, Mr Babiuch, the removal of some notable hardliners in the Politburo and their replacement by men with a reputation for more liberal economic policies. The strikers however continued to hold out and succeeded finally in reaching a settlement in which the authorities conceded the majority of their demands.

5. Although the agreements reached with the Polish workers represent a watershed in the development of the situation, it is premature to forecast the likely course of events over the next few months, or the precise nature of the Soviet response (though what has happened in Poland can only be seen by them as a significant threat to the maintenance of Communist orthodoxy in an area of vital Soviet interest). The phase now beginning during which the Polish government have to set about trying to implement what has been agreed with the strikers is likely to be extremely difficult. On the one hand they will face pressures both from hardliners within their own ranks and from the USSR (which has criticised the strike movement and by implication the Polish authorities themselves) to claw back or in other ways neutralise many of the concessions granted, particularly over the question of free trade unions. On the other hand the workers will clearly be on the watch for any such signs of backsliding. The government's freedom of manoeuvre will be further restricted by the critical economic situation which will have been further aggravated by the effects of the strikes and the concessions granted.[2]

[2] On 4 September Mr Pridham in a long despatch ('The Polish Crisis') described the two phases of the crisis, with the first centred on economic demands by strikers in about 100 places and the second centred on a series of political strikes in the Lenin Shipyard in Gdańsk. He highlighted the key role of Gdańsk Shipyard in the politicisation of the second phase, especially in their demands for free trade unions. After changes in the Government, the Politburo and the official trade unions, the Government conceded independent trade unions. He noted Mr Wałęsa's 'superb' organisation. He agreed with Mr Garton Ash's 'perceptive' article in *The Spectator* of 30 August, which suggested that the dissenting intelligentsia supplied the 'Fabian yeast' for the coastal strikes to take off. He found it encouraging that there had been no bloodshed. Pridham concluded: 'Poland will never be the same again . . . boundaries which Gierek said were uncrossable have been crossed'.

No. 22

Sir C. Keeble (Moscow) to Lord Carrington, 3 September 1980[1]

Confidential (FCO 28/4037, EN 021/31)

My Lord,

The Soviet Union, Poland and Eastern Europe

1. Your despatch of 7 December 1979 on British Policy in East-West Relations[2] stated: 'A major purpose is to do what we can to undermine Soviet power by encouraging the existing tendencies towards diversity within the Warsaw Pact'. You continued: 'We have no interest in provoking a crisis in the area, which would again be ended by invasion if the Russians thought it necessary.' The Polish crisis may, despite strong and growing Soviet allegations to the contrary, have owed little to Western influence, but it illustrates well the matching problems which the Soviet Union and the Western powers face in Eastern Europe. I have reported separately on Soviet reactions as the crisis has proceeded, but in this despatch, for which I am largely indebted to Mr Andrew Wood,[3] I venture to set the question in its wider context. In doing so, I hope I may be excused for trespassing on other people's territory and also for the many generalisations I have been forced to make.

2. Poland has always been a special case. Soviet dominance of the country is an essential element in Soviet defence policy and a pre-requisite for dominance of Eastern Europe as a whole. At the same time the nation is particularly intractable. The Russians have continually to take account of this, of the power of the Roman Catholic Church, of the strong national feelings in Poland and its long history of anti-Russian (and subsequently anti-Soviet) sentiment. The Polish Party, too, had its share of blows at Stalin's hands and since then has perhaps had more experience of authority independent of Moscow than any of the others, except Romania, at present in power. It is, moreover, a Party which has four times suffered the unnerving experience of having its rule severely shaken: in 1956, 1970, 1976 and now 1980.[4]

3. It is obvious enough that the present situation in Poland is a cause of deep concern to the Soviet leadership. The role of the Party in a socialist system is the key element in determining whether or not that system conforms to Soviet standards. The Polish Party's role has now been further called into question by the Polish working class, in particular by the proposal to set up independent Trades Unions. The Soviet leadership must wonder whether they can in future place total reliance on the Party as the directing force in Polish society, and how far those now in charge of it are willing and able to implement those policies which would best meet Soviet interests. The concessions made by the Polish leaders to strikers and dissidents are evidently hard for the Russians to understand. Their sensitivity to the way an Eastern European party approaches its own people fluctuates, but in general the tighter the control of the CPSU in the USSR the greater the need Moscow is likely to see for a firm party hand in Eastern Europe. The mood here is

[1] The despatch was copied to HM Ambassadors at Warsaw, Prague, Budapest, Bucharest, Sofia, East Berlin, Belgrade, UKDEL NATO, Washington, Paris and Bonn.

[2] See No. 4, note 6.

[3] Counsellor and Head of Chancery, Moscow.

[4] See No. 11, notes 3 and 4.

set against experiments within the Soviet Union. *Pravda*[5] has recently reprinted US Communist criticism of Gierek for weakness. I am inclined to believe reports that Brezhnev berated Gierek at the end of July in the Crimea for his failure to demonstrate sufficient energy and resolution in tackling the strikers and Poland's economic problems: I do not know how Gierek replied, but he may well have had a hard time convincing his host his policies were right.

4. It would be presumptuous of me to predict from Moscow what effects the concessions Gierek has made to the Polish working class—if they last—will have elsewhere in the Socialist Commonwealth. What is certain is that the Russians believe that what happens in one Eastern European country will affect the others, and that this awareness heightens their anxiety about Poland's future. The Soviet leadership are fond of describing changes they choose to see as 'revolutionary' and 'irreversible'. For them the Communist regimes in Eastern Europe come into that category. But they know that the regimes they have sponsored are, despite the ideological claptrap, in fact vulnerable. It is not just Poland but also Hungary, Czechoslovakia, the GDR and Romania that have demonstrated that truth in their different ways over the years, and even if Bulgaria has so far shown itself admirably quiescent, who knows what might not happen one day even in Sofia. Poland may be a special case, but it is not an isolated one.

5. One could go further and include the USSR in the argument. The tolerance of the Soviet Union for economic and political mismanagement is of course greater than Poland's or that of any other Eastern European country. The Soviet economy dwarfs the others and there is a better fit between national feelings and aspirations and the structure of Soviet authority than exists in any of the other countries in the Socialist 'Commonwealth'. The Soviet Union, however, shares with its partners the major problem that its political and economic system is no longer geared to the demands of what is now becoming an increasingly sophisticated economy. In Marxist terms the super-structure no longer fits the base. There is no identifiable reform party within the CPSU, and hence the prospects for political change are for the time being limited. I do not believe the USSR is invulnerable to some of the heresies and problems which have troubled the lives of the Eastern European ruling parties but as the stronghold of orthodoxy, the repository of Marxist-Leninist doctrine it has the least incentive to experiment. It is presumably fear of contamination which has led to the jamming of Western broadcasts. There is, moreover, a direct link between the internal security situation in the USSR and the maintenance of ideologically acceptable regimes in Eastern Europe, because the legitimacy of the Soviet regime depends in the end on the ideology it proclaims. This is a weak enough reed as it is. If the march of history were reversed in Poland or Czechoslovakia more people without the Soviet Union and some within it might wonder whether the CPSU might not be wrong in its claim to represent the inevitable future. It is in the logic of the Soviet system that there should be no genuine public exchange of views within the Soviet Union and hence no real tolerance for different approaches from the countries of Eastern Europe which are proclaimed also to be benefitting from the fruits of 'real socialism'.

6. The party-to-party link has so far been a major instrument of Soviet control over the nations of Eastern Europe. Local parties are, however, subject to local pressures and much though they may wish to follow Soviet designs, they may find themselves being driven by such forces. Given Soviet problems in adapting to

[5] The newspaper of the Communist Party of the Soviet Union.

diversity it is inevitable that a degree of tension will result, even when differences in approach between an Eastern European party and the Soviet Union are minimised. The Russians have given a green light to Hungary's economic experiments and it was once assumed that the Soviet regime under Brezhnev and Kosygin regarded Hungary as something of a test bed for the Soviet Union itself. It has not worked out that way in practice and I am inclined to doubt whether it ever will. What indications we have tend to show the Russians looking on the Hungarian model as a slightly suspect aberration. Romania is an example of a country which has been careful to keep its communism acceptably orthodox, but as a *quid pro quo* for turning itself into one of the most nationalistic of the area. In both Romania and Hungary the ruling parties are moreover dealing with a comparatively stable situation. If a local party is to react to a more dynamic set of problems the result can all too easily and all too quickly turn into a direct confrontation with the Soviet Union, as it did in Hungary in 1956, Czechoslovakia in 1968 and could still do in Poland today. A party faced with a volatile and interacting set of problems can quickly be reduced to the choice of confrontation with Moscow or of acting as Moscow's stooge and being seen to do so by its own population. Ulbricht chose the latter course in East Germany in 1953.[6]

7. Anti-Russian feelings in Eastern Europe are historically endemic, though balanced in the past by Slavophilic sentiments. The establishment of oppressive regimes, more or less subservient to the Soviet will, has developed such prejudices into wide-spread anti-Sovietism. Soviet consciousness of it increases their concern about anything which smacks of experiment, blocks local parties in and weakens their value over the long term as instruments of Soviet policies. But the Russians cannot and do not expect Eastern European parties to ignore the wishes of their populations altogether, and, as seen from here, there would appear to be an increasing need for change in Eastern Europe, especially in the search for a more effective way of managing a state-run economy. The result of this contradiction between Soviet conservatism and pressures for reform is a constantly shifting and sometimes precarious balance.

8. The second major instrument of Soviet control over Eastern Europe is of course Soviet armed might. Though delusions may persist in some circles, in particular among the younger generation, and it is arguable that fear of the Soviet Union may have been weakened by the Russian failure so far to produce a definitive solution in Afghanistan, there can be few who would seriously doubt Soviet readiness to use force in Eastern Europe again should the leadership decide that to be necessary or who would question the Soviet capacity to overwhelm any military opposition. There are substantial forces amounting in practice to Soviet garrisons in all the countries of Eastern Europe except Bulgaria, where there has never been any need for them, and Romania, which has resisted their introduction. These forces have their effect on the population and on the leadership's estimate of what they can get away with. One could perhaps indeed argue that they are more effective as a political threat than as an instrument to be used. It is not just a matter of the Russians knowing there to be immediate penalties for using force but of their also knowing that although force can sustain political control, it cannot solve

[6] On 16 June 1953 construction workers went on strike in East Berlin against an effective reduction in salary and then demanded free elections and economic reform. Full-scale riots followed in several East German cities. Walter Ulbricht, General Secretary of the Central Committee of the Socialist Unity Party of Germany, appealed to the USSR for help in putting down the uprising.

and may indeed exacerbate the problems which first threatened that control. The Soviet invasion did nothing to improve Czechoslovakia's economic performance—a serious consideration when one bears in mind that it was economic problems which originally provoked the growth of reform-minded politicians in the country. It goes almost without saying that Soviet use of force exacerbates local nationalism and further develops that anti-Sovietism which is already a considerable force for instability.

9. The Russians would naturally prefer to avoid using their armed forces and to manage their relations with Eastern Europe by developing an interlocking series of mutual obligations and interests. In an ideal world, Soviet defence interests would be protected if the Warsaw Pact could be preserved while allowing Eastern Europe to move into a looser economic and political relationship with the USSR. But in a totalitarian political system claiming world-wide doctrinal loyalty, that will not do. The inter-connections between the USSR and the position in Eastern Europe are now such as to make the Russians see any threat to an Eastern European Communist establishment as coming very close to a direct attack on the USSR itself and to see as a threat anything which dilutes the degree to which communist regimes are answerable to Moscow. The tendency of Soviet policy is therefore to move in the opposite direction, deepening the integration of the economies of Eastern Europe and increasing their dependence on the Soviet Union.

10. The USSR has had a considerable degree of success in developing the CMEA. There are plans to promote its further integration which even the Romanians may not be able entirely to frustrate. The dependence of the Eastern European economies on the USSR is already great and may grow further, particularly in so far as the Soviet Union is a relatively easy market for their products and an important supplier of raw materials and energy resources. But there are penalties which may also increase. The Soviet economy has lost a great deal of its dynamism and will probably stagnate further, with consequent effects on the Soviet ability to cope with East European economic problems. If the Russians now prove reluctant to help bail out the Poles, this may be because they need their money themselves as much as because they want to use economic levers to discipline Poland. The Soviet Union has told its partners it will only be able to supply oil over the next several years at 1980 levels, and at an increasing price. It follows that the Eastern Europeans will have to import oil from elsewhere and to earn the hard currency to enable them to do so. Their need for Western technology, which is already great enough, will be further increased. Their economies are however uncompetitive in important respects and their dependence on the undemanding Soviet and CMEA markets has helped to exacerbate the process as Mr Male's despatch of 17 December 1979 tellingly illustrated in examining the Czechoslovak case.[7] It is hard to imagine the overall situation improving for Eastern Europe without far-reaching reforms which the Russians would regard as politically risky and ideologically unacceptable. From Moscow, it seems, on the contrary, that the area's economic problems, and hence the pressures on the USSR, may well get worse over the coming decade.

11. Soviet attempts to impose uniformity in foreign and defence policies have also enjoyed a measure of success, tempered by economic and political realities. Poland's leaders, for example, are no doubt fully aware of their importance to Moscow within the Eastern European scheme of things. They must know there can

[7] Not printed.

be little chance of their moving towards a more neutral position in East/West affairs and they, like other East European states, share the Soviet interest in keeping Germany divided. The reality of Soviet power in the region is in any case so great that foreign policy issues on the broader front, as opposed to intra Eastern European/Soviet problems, are usually (the Romanians apart) not worth quarrelling over. It is significant that so far as I am aware Polish foreign policy has not been subjected to radical criticism during the past several weeks despite apparently widespread anti-Soviet feeling. This is not to say that East European and Soviet foreign policy interests and concerns coincide. The USSR is a world power with increasing commitments which do not always agree with the more local aims of the East Europeans. Détente policies are tactically useful to the Soviet Union, but mean much more to the Eastern Europeans who see in them the only chance to develop relations with Western Europe and sustain even a semblance of national identity. At the same time, however, they know they must tack to the wind when things go wrong and when the Soviet Union takes some unilateral action which cuts directly across their interest in a better East/West relationship, as she did in Afghanistan.

12. Individually the problems I have sketched out in the preceding paragraphs might be difficult for the Soviet leadership to adjust to. Collectively, and I believe it may be in battalions that they come, they could take on an insistence which might prove deeply troubling. It is in any case hard to avoid the conclusion that, more or less whatever the Russians do about Poland, the growing difficulty of maintaining control over Eastern Europe is likely to be a constant Soviet preoccupation in the 1980s. The economic and political pressures there are such as to continue to create periodic crises, in which Soviet options tend to be limited, and disagreeable. The Soviet aim must be to isolate the sources of dissent and to sustain or reassert control by political pressure in order to avoid an eventual recourse to force which would aggravate the underlying tensions within Eastern Europe as well as doing further damage to the international standing of the Soviet Union.

13. It follows that the Soviet leadership will continue to regard their best option as being that of stopping the rot before it begins. That is, after all, what they try to do in the USSR. I believe they are unlikely to alter their view that any experiment in Eastern Europe is dangerous. In Poland they must hope it will prove possible to claw back the concessions of substance already made by the Polish leadership. We are likely over the next few months to be in for a period of rough politics between Moscow and Warsaw in which Soviet threats, intrigue and persuasion will be directed to limiting the damage, probably trying to bring back harder liners to the Polish politburo, with or without Gierek and frustrating Western influence throughout Eastern Europe. It is an unattractive prospect which is likely to make the Western relationship with this country even more uncomfortable and augurs ill for the CSCE Review Conference.[8] Such essentially negative policies will not work in the longer run. The problem they pose for us meanwhile is that of pursuing policies which will facilitate the decay of Soviet power in Eastern Europe at a rate slow enough not to reach the point of explosion.

I am, etc,
CURTIS KEEBLE

[8] See No. 1, note 6.

No. 23

Letter from Mrs Thatcher to President Carter, 3 September 1980[1]

T169/80 Secret (PREM 19/331)

Dear Mr President,

Thank you for your message of 27 August about the situation in Poland.[2] I have read it with very great interest.

In the few days since you wrote, events have continued to move rapidly and agreement has now, of course, been reached between the strikers in the north and south of the country and the Polish Government. The concessions which have been won by the shipyard workers and the coal miners, and the way in which they have been won, are of enormous potential consequence, not only for Poland itself but for Eastern Europe as a whole. They also have far reaching implications for Western interests and policies in the area.[3]

Further time will be needed to assess the significance of what has happened. Much is yet to play for. I myself doubt whether the situation has yet reached the point of stability. I suspect that the process now launched will either be carried further or go into reverse. The attitude of the Soviet Government will, inevitably, be crucial. The immediate indications are not encouraging. The Russians clearly do not like the extent of the concessions made. They will be watching carefully how the agreement is implemented and will, no doubt, be urging the Polish leaders to try to recover some of the lost ground.

I share your view about the importance of the economic aspect. We here have been concerned for some time about the deteriorating situation in Poland and about Poland's growing indebtedness to the West. The overall effect of the recent stoppages can only have been to exacerbate Poland's difficulties. Like you, I am sure the Poles will soon be asking the West for further assistance. I note what you say about the objectives of the West's aid, and look forward to hearing what you have in mind. I would welcome any proposal for ensuring that our help goes to benefit the Polish people rather than to the shoring up of an unreformed system. But we must take care to avoid accusations of interference.

[1] This letter was despatched at 9.50 a.m. on 4 September. The final letter differed from the original FCO draft, which had been more cautious over the attitude to adopt towards the Polish Government, suggesting that HMG should 'continue to avoid any comments on the situation which might make their task [that of the Polish authorities] more difficult'. The final version excluded several references to the need to reflect on the situation 'over the next few weeks'. The Prime Minister had seen key telegrams from Warsaw before finalising the text to President Carter. The message was also sent to British Embassies in Washington, Paris and Bonn on 5 September (FCO tel. No. 1460 to Washington; FCO 28/4161, ENP 212/2).

[2] President Carter thought events in Poland could 'precipitate far-reaching consequences for East-West relations and even for the future of the Soviet bloc itself'. He thought that the West had been right to express sympathy for Polish efforts to reform and to urge restraint, and also to stress that the matter was for the Poles to decide without foreign interference. He considered the best outcome would be accommodation between the authorities and the Polish people leading to a more liberal and democratic system. He believed that aid from the West should be designed to encourage the Poles to undertake a more fundamental and systematic reform of their economy.

[3] Mr Barrass of the Planning Staff sent Mr Bullard a long report of a visit in Poland between 13 and 21 September, which described cross currents in Polish politics (FCO 28/4138, ENP 014/1). He said that new groupings, with a complex interplay, made it difficult to assess developments in the months ahead. There was a consensus with all those he spoke to that Poland could never be the same again and the perception was that the Soviet Union simply did not understand what was happening in Poland.

These are all matters on which it will be vital for our two Governments to remain in the closest touch. We shall want to consider together, and with those of our allies most directly involved, how we react to the developing situation. I hope that we can also continue to exchange information about our contacts with the Poles. Apart from the usual exchanges on the diplomatic net, Peter Carrington hopes to see the new Polish Foreign Minister, Mr Czyrek, during the UN General Assembly[4] in New York later this month, and will be visiting Warsaw on 30 and 31 October.[5] I will ensure that you are kept fully in the picture about what transpires.

Meanwhile, we here intend to continue to take a careful and restrained attitude in public to events in Poland. We have stressed our view that this is a strictly internal matter to be settled by the Polish people themselves, peacefully and without interference. The Polish Government have told us, as they have told you, that they appreciate this attitude.[6]

Yours sincerely,
MARGARET THATCHER

[4] See No. 27.
[5] See Nos. 33 and 34.
[6] On 7 October President Carter urged the Prime Minister to make clear to the Soviets the consequences of an invasion 'in whatever way and whenever you deem it most appropriate and effective'. The Prime Minister raised the issue of Poland in her key-note address to the Conservative Party Conference in Brighton on 10 October: 'The workers of Poland in their millions have signalled their determination to participate in the shaping of their destiny. We salute them. Marxists claim that the capitalist system is in crisis. But the Polish workers have shown that it is the Communist system that is in crisis. The Polish people should be left to work out their own future without external interference.' A copy of the speech can be found on the Margaret Thatcher Foundation website (www.margaretthatcher.org).

No. 24

Letter from Mr Foster (East Berlin) to Mr Goodall (Bonn), 4 September 1980
Confidential (FCO 33/4354, WRE 014/1)

Dear David,

How Orwellian is the GDR?

1. I found your letter of 19 August awaiting my return from leave and am glad to hear that you found the despatch of 25 June interesting.[1]

2. I think the short answer to your question about whether a 'distasteful but fundamentally stable balance between oppression and discontent' has been

[1] In this despatch (FCO 33/4353, WRE 014/1), Mr Foster had observed that totalitarianism had not disappeared but that life for the ordinary East German was not intolerable and 'though Big Brother is neither as omniscient nor as omnipresent as Orwell had him, his shadow is a fact of life'. He concluded that 'the system is, by democratic standards, nasty, fundamentally hostile to Western interests and externally the more dangerous in not needing to rely on naked terror'. Mr Gladstone, in submitting the despatch to Mr Bullard on 14 August, identified Orwellian features in the GDR: indoctrination from an early age; children spying on their parents; society divided in three classes—inner Party, outer Party and 'proles'; the Stasi's constant presence; population insulated from the outside world. However there were differences: no equivalent to the 'thought police'; 'proles' treated as a valuable commodity; torture seemingly rare and replaced by more subtle means (for example, withdrawing smallish perks or denying equal educational and job opportunities). The big ideological failure was that the East Germans saw the FRG as a model more than their own state.

established would be 'yes'. Although I have not been back long enough to get fully into the swim of things, it is pretty apparent, for example, that the Polish strikes did not prove contagious here. If they gave some people ideas (as they probably did), they remained private thoughts and produced, at least so far as any outsider has yet detected, no physical reaction. Probably the regime was somewhat more worried than they allowed to show. But there was no obvious prophylactic tightening up and the official line seems to be one of bland confidence that such a thing could not happen here, at any rate in present circumstances—1953 being now a long way off both in time and in circumstances.[2]

3. The President of the Foreign Trade Bank, a highly intelligent and likeable man not given to facile propaganda, put it to me this way at the Leipzig Fair. The GDR was not in the same economic mess as Poland. Not only were living standards a good deal higher; economic policy had been conducted with more restraint and good sense. The Germans were disciplined by nature. The average worker, though no doubt less than fully satisfied with his lot, realised that any attempt to push up consumption too fast could only be at the expense of investment and hence of future living standards. I am not saying that I necessarily accept all this as a fair reflection of the feelings of ordinary East Germans. But it may well sum up pretty accurately the view of the ruling elite, who probably believe with some justification (*pace* the long stream of pronouncements by West German economic experts about the dismal outlook for the GDR economy) that, for all their problems over rising import prices and so forth, they have the situation reasonably well in hand.

4. The average East German is not only disciplined by nature. He is also a realist. He knows perfectly well that the grip of the Stasi,[3] underpinned by the massive Soviet military presence, is strong enough to frustrate any organised resistance to the regime and to contain any isolated outbreaks of dissatisfaction, which have occurred on a small scale from time to time.

5. Nor do I see much immediate likelihood of the 'pervading nastiness' becoming intolerable. It is at present well below this threshold—I hope my despatch was not misleading on this point—and it must be the policy of the regime (with Soviet backing) to ensure that living standards do not fall or security and ideological harassment rise to a level likely to produce exasperation.

6. This picture could theoretically be upset if the GDR suffered the kind of economic debacle often prophesied by West German critics or if, perhaps for reasons external to the GDR, the regime were obliged to embark on a drastic clamp-down, or in the event of a major crisis or change of course within the Soviet Union such as to encourage euphoric aspirations in the orbit as a whole. But in that case, of course, we should all be in a completely new ball game.

Yours ever,
P. M. FOSTER

[2] See No. 22, note 6.
[3] The Ministry for State Security.

No. 25

Letter from Mr Hardie (Bucharest) to Mr Cummins, 8 September 1980
Restricted (FCO 28/4185, ENR 090/1)

Dear Rodney,

Ceausescu goes to market

1. Ceausescu paid a working visit to some fourteen food markets in Bucharest on 7 September. He has made similar visits in the past, but this one is clearly a part of the government programme designed to show official receptivity, concern for living standards and for the wishes and convenience of the people in the wake of Poland.

2. With only two exceptions, the reports of the visits indicate that the markets were well provisioned with meat, fruit and vegetables and dairy products. One was inadequate because it had not grown to meet the needs of an enlarged housing estate; and several were criticised by Ceausescu on organisational grounds, but not for availability of food. It goes without saying that the markets will have been stocked specially, and the *Scinteia*[1] piece reports, without apparent conscious humour, that 'this morning, Obor market received large quantities of meat, meat products, milk, cheeses, fruit and vegetables'.

3. The reports stress the contact between Ceausescu and ordinary people, the favourable remarks he heard on the quantity and quality of market provisioning, the spontaneous marks of esteem shown by members of the public of all ages and classes and the thanks he received for the 'care which he invariably has for working men . . . for civilised conditions of life and work created for all citizens of the country'. Those who could press through the throng of well wishers and thankers were able to speak to Ceausescu about the 'continually improving conditions of provisioning' and, for this is democracy at work, 'about certain failures in the work of commercial units'.

4. Some of this will appear crude and farcical to many families, particularly those on single incomes, who cannot afford, or simply cannot obtain, meat. Meat on only two days a week is standard here, and even then it may be inferior stuff (sometimes imported specially). We have been assured that some working families exist on a diet of potatoes and beans—though it is not clear whether this may be partly due to ignorance, laziness or simple failure in housekeeping. As to Ceausescu's concern, and his 'permanent working dialogue with working men' there is a widespread feeling amongst ordinary people that he is so shielded from real life as to have no idea what conditions are now actually like; and no one is prepared to tell him the true facts; in his dialogue with the people he hears what he is meant to hear, and his misconceptions are reinforced. The present public relations exercise is likely to be greeted with some cynicism.

Yours ever,
SANDY

[1] Newspaper of the Romanian Communist Party.

No. 26

Submission from Mr Mallaby to Mr Fergusson, 23 September 1980
Confidential (FCO 28/4037, EN 021/31)

The Soviet Union, Poland and Eastern Europe

1. I submit Sir Curtis Keeble's despatch of 3 September from Moscow.[1] I have written to thank him.

2. There are important ways in which Poland is different from the other Eastern European countries. But the alienation between the regime and the workers, which with consumer shortages has been at the base of the Polish crisis, exists in all Warsaw Pact countries. It is less strong in Hungary, where the consumer is relatively well provided for; but it may nevertheless be more likely to be expressed in Hungary because political repression is relatively less severe there than in the other Warsaw Pact countries except Poland.

3. It is not surprising, against this background, that Poland's allies have displayed concern about the recent events there. The Soviet resumption of jamming of Western broadcasts in Russian should be seen in this light, as should the Romanian regime's announcement that 16% of the overt defence budget will be switched to improve living standards.

4. The existence of reasons for Polish-style troubles in the other Warsaw Pact countries does not mean, however, that such troubles will necessarily spread, at least in the near term. That will depend in part on whether the democratic changes in Poland are successfully consolidated, a matter on which I have elsewhere expressed some pessimism. What one can say at present is that the Polish events will have been profoundly disturbing to the other members of the Warsaw Pact; it is not yet clear whether they will be profoundly influential.

5. Prospects in Eastern Europe are anyway not good. The falling economic growth rates point to the need for economic reform to inject more initiative and momentum into the economies. But Soviet misgivings about economic as well as political decentralisation, will I think, have been reinforced by the Polish Communist Party's failure to maintain full, continuous control over events. The fact that since the crisis the Polish Party has speeded up moves towards economic reform and decentralisation has not been reported in the Soviet media. Sir C. Keeble is no doubt right that Soviet policy will be to try to tie the East European economies to the Soviet Union by means of accelerated integration. In any case new energy infrastructure (gas pipe-lines, electricity grid) will inevitability bind them increasingly closely. Greater integration will tend to slow down the growth of Eastern Europe's economic links with the West. The diversion of hard currency from Western imports to purchases of OPEC oil will add to this trend. In these circumstances, no great improvement in the standard of living is to be expected in Eastern Europe (or, for rather different reasons, in the Soviet Union) in the next few years. This, in turn, will tend to increase public dissatisfaction and foster mutual resentment. The East Europeans may increasingly attribute their stagnating living standards to the economic and political system imposed upon them and the constraints of CMEA integration. And ordinary Russians may increasingly resent Soviet supplies of cheap energy and raw materials and other assistance in order to maintain higher living standards in Eastern Europe that they themselves enjoy.

[1] No. 22.

6. A Soviet invasion of Poland would increase anti-Soviet feelings in Eastern Europe and do nothing to improve economic prospects (indeed, it could well cost the Soviet Union a good deal in the short term, through the loss of additional Western credits which otherwise might have been granted to Poland).[2]

7. The prospects in Eastern Europe are thus bad, and they may prove explosive. I agree with Sir C. Keeble that the growing difficulty of maintaining control over the area is likely to be of constant Soviet pre-occupation in the 1980s.

C. L. G. MALLABY

[2] In a minute of 17 September Mr Mallaby concluded that a Soviet invasion was very much a possibility but, given Poland's history, an invasion by Russian forces from the east and German forces from the West would be highly symbolic and likely to increase resistance by the Polish people.

No. 27

Sir A. Parsons (UKMIS New York) to FCO, 25 September 1980, 11.41 a.m.
Tel. No. 2357[1] Immediate, Confidential (FCO 28/4157, ENP 020/1)

Following from Private Secretary

Secretary of State's meeting with Polish Foreign Minister in New York: 24 September[2]

1. Czyrek said that the danger of an internal confrontation in Poland seemed to have passed. The troubles still occurring were only splinter activities or publicity-seeking. The difficulties had been solved in the framework of Poland's political system and a social consensus established. All sides, including the Church, had shown great maturity and responsibility. Poland had emerged with the sense of national unity strengthened, despite differences of opinion as to what had happened and why.

2. But she now faced long-term problems of great difficulty. The Government wished to fulfil all their commitments to the workers, not only in the social and economic fields but also in the political sphere towards the trade unions. There was a need for confidence and for confidence-building measures. Specific reforms would be required in Poland's economy, whose fundamental soundness had been spoiled mainly by subjective mistakes, e.g. overinvestment in heavy industry. The investment ratio must be lowered and emphasis on consumer goods and agriculture increased.

3. Poland counted on help from socialist states, but also on the understanding of her Western partners, especially the bigger traditional partners including the UK. The main problem was that three-quarters of all Poland's foreign debt was due to be repaid in the three years 1981-83. In the new and worse economic situation Poland would need either to borrow more in order to repay the amounts due, or, where this would be more suitable for her partners, to request a prolongation of these repayments for two years beyond 1983, or both.

4. Poland did not want a moratorium. She would like to solve the problem by bilateral economic and financial agreements. She would not ask for any

[1] Repeated for Information Immediate to Warsaw; Priority to Moscow, Washington, Bucharest, Paris, Sofia, Prague, Bonn, Budapest, UKDEL NATO East Berlin; Info Saving to Belgrade.
[2] Lord Carrington was in New York for the 35th meeting of the UNGA.

prolongation of repayments of private loans, but she would seek this for credits guaranteed by governments. Czyrek did not wish to mention any figures: he was simply asking the British and other Western governments for their understanding. He could assure them that Poland would remain a stable partner and repay all her debts in good time without narrowing her present trade and economic relations. Czyrek trusted that taking these steps would not jeopardise Poland's position on the financial markets. She wanted a solution favourable to her and to her partners.

5. Poland's policies abroad would not change. Even more than previously she needed peace, détente and cooperation. Polish-British relations were good and stable. Czyrek looked forward to the Secretary of State's visit in late October.[3]

6. Lord Carrington said that the Poles would find considerable understanding from the British and other Western friends of the problems they faced. We would look sympathetically at what could be done. He particularly looked forward to his forthcoming visit to Poland. We had followed events closely, but had some difficulty in understanding the reasons for the events of Poland, and the solutions reached. In his experience, when somebody got some cake they wanted another slice. Would the settlement be a final solution? Or would its implementation be made difficult by the effects of the strikes.

7. Czyrek said that the new role of the trade unions would be linked to a bill which was under preparation to regulate self-management in factories. The management too must have a role, and trade unions must accept a balance between rights and duties. The Gdansk agreements gave the impression that the new trade unions were making all the demands and others had to do the giving. No society could survive that way. The workers must have the right of association, but the legitimate interests of the working class must also be defended. Trade unions must accept obligations, in the interest of the national economy. A commission, on which the new trade unions were represented, was preparing the bill.

8. Lord Carrington wondered whether free trade unions were compatible with the form of government practised in Poland. Czyrek said that changes were needed in the relationship between the trade unions and the Government, and between the trade unions and the Party. The latter was the more difficult. The system of party directives would have to go, to be replaced by a democratic process of explaining and convincing the trade unions. This would not be easy. The Poles had scoured legislation on trade unions and strikes in both Eastern and Western countries. Lord Carrington observed that our experience showed that no legislation was effective in this area unless it had the consent of those to whom it applied. Workers in nationalised industries did not think that the industry belonged to them, but that the Government could not let them down. No country had resolved this problem yet.

9. Czyrek said that he was an economist and did not believe in magic. Poland's socialist partners had also drawn certain lessons from her experiences: the Hungarians were expediting a bill amending trade union legislation; the Romanians were conducting a survey of the economy; and price rises due in other socialist countries had been dropped. He himself remained an inveterate optimist. History showed that without optimism there would be no Poland.

10. Lord Carrington said that he would like to see a little of the history of Poland as well as of its modern achievements during his stay.

[3] See No. 33.

No. 28

Mr Bolland (Belgrade) to Lord Carrington, 25 September 1980, 10.30 p.m.
Tel. No. 274[1] Priority, Confidential (FCO 28/4249, ENU 026/1)

Prime Minister's visit to Belgrade

The Prime Minister left this afternoon for the concluding stage of her visit to Yugoslavia in Skopje and Dubrovnik.[2] During her day and a half in Belgrade she was able to have a running dialogue with the Yugoslav Prime Minister,[3] President Mijatovic, other Party and state leaders. The Yugoslavs were clearly determined, both in their preparation and wide publicity, to make it a success.

Bilateral Questions

The Yugoslavs gave priority to bilateral questions, especially the imbalance of trade. Both sides agreed that the principal problem lay with the Yugoslavs themselves in identifying ways of increasing their exports to the United Kingdom, particularly to exploit the opportunities from the recent EC/Yugoslav agreement. The Prime Minister pointed out that, with an open market such as the UK provided and with exchange rates in the Yugoslav favour, it was up to the Yugoslavs to make the principal effort. They accepted this.

There was a brief discussion of the Yugoslav need for credit from western banks. While they clearly looked to the Prime Minister's visit to help over the atmosphere, they accepted the need to work within the western banking system, and did not ask for further help.

Djuranovic raised the issue of Croatian dissident activity in the United Kingdom. The Prime Minister explained the constraints on government action in the UK but her references to the importance of Yugoslav unity, in her main speech and in the discussions, were taken on the Yugoslav side as going some way to give them the reassurance which they sought.

During an informal breakfast discussion the Minister of Defence raised a number of specific difficulties in defence sales (e.g. Rolls Royce Viper engines). The Prime Minister promised that she would look into these on her return before the visit of the Chief of the Defence Staff (6 October). The RB199 engine was not raised, the Yugoslavs clearly having heard of the impediments on the German side.[4]

The Prime Minister invited Mr Djuranovic to visit the United Kingdom and he accepted.

A joint statement, which had been largely negotiated before the visit, was agreed without difficulty (text by bag).

International

[1] Repeated for Information Priority to UKMIS New York (for Private Secretary), Washington, Paris, Bonn, UKDEL NATO, Eastern European Posts and Athens.

[2] Mrs Thatcher visited Yugoslavia from 24 to 26 September, following a visit to Greece. It was the first official visit by a British Prime Minister since the Second World War.

[3] Veselin Djuranović.

[4] A jet engine designed and built by Turbo-Union—a joint venture between Rolls-Royce, the German company MTU Aero Engines and the Italian company FiatAvio—which the UK hoped to sell to Yugoslavia. However the Germans had raised objections to the idea of selling the engine.

The Yugoslavs expressed their concern about the current state of international economic relations, following the unsatisfactory end to the UN special session.[5] They were particularly keen that the West should understand the political implications for the developed world of the frustrations in the developing countries from 'Western inflexibilities'. They suggested that developing countries might be forced to turn for help to the Soviet Union though they admitted that, in discussion, the Soviet Union and Eastern Europeans had shown even greater inflexibility. Mrs Thatcher was able to set out that what the Yugoslavs have said was a convincing rationale of UK policies and of the constraints on them, in the context of the wider difficulties experienced by the international economic system.

On the Iraq/Iran dispute[6] the Yugoslavs said that they had sent messages to both sides, expressing their anxieties and calling on them to reach a solution by political means. They saw the hostilities as a further crisis for the non-aligned movement, but were very uncertain about what further steps should be taken.

Predictably the disagreement was most apparent on East/West relations generally, including the CSCE. The Prime Minister set out her view of the serious consequences of the Afghanistan intervention on the prospects for Madrid. The Yugoslavs in turn believed that in the present international situation it was essential to preserve and build up on the CSCE progress.

The Yugoslavs were clearly worried by the developments in Poland which they saw as a major crisis for the communist system with incalculable repercussions elsewhere in Eastern Europe. They believed that the Soviet Union, while no doubt having considered the use of force, had decided not to do so at present. At no stage did they suggest that they feared contamination from the Polish virus. Indeed President Mijatovic went out of his way to stress the stability and durability of Yugoslavia post-Tito.

On the Middle East the Prime Minister explained the latest state of play over the Venice Declaration[7] and the Thorn mission.[8]

[5] The 11th special General Assembly session of 25 August to 15 September had agreed on the need to improve the position of developing nations in the 1980s but had broken up without achieving anything on global economic negotiations for raw materials, trade, money and energy.

[6] War had broken out between Iran and Iraq on 22 September 1980.

[7] At the Venice Summit of 12 to 13 June 1980 the EEC launched a peace initiative on the Middle East. The Venice Declaration recognised *inter alia* the legitimate rights of the Palestinian people to self-determination, accepted that the PLO would need to be involved in future negotiations and considered that Israeli settlements in the West Bank and Gaza constituted a serious problem to the peace process. In August and September the chairman of the EEC's Council of Foreign Ministers, M. Gaston Thorn, led a fact-finding mission in the region.

[8] Mr Bolland wrote to Lord Carrington on 30 September hailing the visit a 'resounding success', which gave a new impetus to bilateral relations. He had particular praise for Mrs Thatcher who was 'tireless, fresh in appearance, informed and persuasive in speech' and who 'clearly won the hearts of the people, especially the women, she greeted in the streets'.

No. 29

Mr Pridham (Warsaw) to Lord Carrington, 16 October 1980

Confidential (FCO 28/4165, ENP 212/2)

The Polish Crisis: Should We Help? (October 1980)

My Lord,

1. The idealism, independence and indomitable spirit of the Polish people need no emphasising for a British reader. Memories of Polish action during the Second World War are common coin in Britain even to-day. But not even the closest observers of the current Polish scene forecast the convulsions which have shaken the Polish People's Republic during the past few months. The governing party and the Government have had troubles before—in 1956, 1970, 1976[1]—but they have never before had to deal with such a powerful force as has emerged from the Gdańsk shipyards—of workers, intellectuals and Catholics—which, in the form of a free trades union, has, for the time being at least, wrested from the Polish United Workers' Party, its self-awarded leading role in Peoples' Poland. The Party has had to face a revolution of part of the proletariat against its own dictatorship of the proletariat. And, as this is not possible—nor even conceivable under Marxist-Leninist doctrine, the new Party leaders have had to try to explain that the workers' protest was not against Socialism but against 'errors of socialism' perpetrated by the previous leadership, with which most of them subsequently collaborated, and which is currently being purged from the Party. Small wonder that any residual confidence either Party or non-Party members might have retained in the Party has been shattered, and that Party workers to-day unanimously acknowledge their first task is to rebuild the Party's confidence in itself and the people's confidence in the Party.

2. But, even as Party leaders and activists set about this formidable undertaking, their problems continue to grow. The initiative still lies plainly with the free trade unions, the ultimate objectives of whose leaders are not at all clear. Wałęsa, their spokesman, has insisted they are not spearheading a political revolution but are merely striving for a better deal for the workers. Yet, whether they wish it or not, their successful strike pressures against the régime in August have added a new dimension to the existing pluralism of communist Poland and have set the country upon a path from which there is no turning back.

3. The dust raised by these deep-seated tremors in the body politic and in Polish society will not settle for some time. The key sector of this non-violent revolution is at the moment in the registration of the free trade unions by the Warsaw *Voivodship*[2] Court. The battle is being waged with words between the free trade union lawyers and officials of the registration court, as Government and Party on the one hand and the independent workers' movement on the other strive to extract maximum advantage from the somewhat ambiguous phraseology of the Gdańsk, Szczecin and Jastrzębie agreements they signed barely 6 weeks ago.[3] The present battle centres on the statutes submitted by the principal free trade union '*Solidarność*', with its application for registration. The Registration Court has

[1] See No. 11, notes 3 and 4.

[2] Administrative subdivision in Poland. Between 1979 and 1998 there were 49 *Voivodships*.

[3] See No. 18. These three key agreements were signed on 30 and 31 August in the Baltic towns of Gdańsk and Szczecin and on 3 September in the Silesian town of Jastrzębie. Known as the 'social accords', they established in effect the independent *Solidarność* or Solidarity trade union.

objected *inter alia* that the statutes do not explicitly recognise the leading role of the Party, as agreed in the accords; and that they claim to be applicable throughout the country whereas the union is regionally based in Gdańsk.

4. Such debates will continue and will multiply during the coming months, as the authorities and workers adjust to the more liberal atmosphere created by the strikers' success, and in particular, as the new laws on censorship and free trades unions, promised under the agreements, are debated and introduced. Meanwhile, with the Party in disarray, there is no guiding hand at the helm and the Polish ship of state is drifting. It is with this current situation in mind that I venture to offer some thoughts on the attitude Her Majesty's Government might take, on the eve of your forthcoming visit to Poland—the first undertaken by any Western Minister since the present Polish crisis began.[4]

5. Our current policy towards Poland, in its simplest terms, is part of our overall strategy to encourage the diversity we see developing amongst the states of Eastern Europe. The present Polish crisis presents us with a golden opportunity for furthering this policy. Poland is already far gone along the path of greater diversity within the Soviet monolith. To her existing anomalies, for a communist country, of a thriving religious community and a preponderantly private agricultural sector, she has in the past few months added a militant and highly organised independent trade union movement already reputedly as large, at over 3 million, as the Party itself. Indeed, so diverse and pluralistic has she become that Western observers, though very few Poles as yet, are already counting the days to Soviet armed intervention to stop the rot. I do not yet share their pessimism; but I am sure it will be justified if the Polish authorities lose control of the situation because they are unable, for lack of hard currency, to provide basic essentials for their people and thus to avoid fresh explosions of discontent.

6. The vicious circle for the Government posed by the Gdańsk agreements is that, if they carry out their side of the bargain, they are moving the country further down the path to economic disaster but, if they go back on their pledges, they risk further industrial strife which could lead to ideological and political disaster. A dramatic rise in productivity (which on present form seems most unlikely) might help to soften the obvious incompatibility between the economic imperatives of the current situation and the Government's pledges; but it cannot be achieved overnight. Meanwhile Poland's economic situation is moving from the disastrous to the indescribable.

7. The Party and Government need time to work out a more liberal *modus vivendi* with this powerful new force in Polish society. They need time to work out new economic plans and reforms. There is no question of renouncing socialism, or the Soviet alliance; geopolitical and historical realities rule that out. But within the Soviet orbit, and within the Warsaw Pact, there may be room to-day for something that could not exist in Czechoslovakia barely 12 years ago: a movement towards establishing 'socialism with a more human face': and in Poland, based on workers' power, it might just come off without provoking Soviet intervention with all that that implies for European and world stability.

8. We know the sort of aid the Poles are likely to ask us for: more and softer export credits and our agreement either to re-finance capital repayments to Britain in 1981 and 1982 or to stretch the period of their repayment into the late 1980s. The commercial case for agreeing to a larger and better credit package has already

[4] See No. 33.

been made strongly and consistently by this Post to the Department of Trade and Export Credits Guarantee Department over the past few months and I shall not repeat the arguments here.[5] To them is added the political case in the foregoing paragraphs. Moreover, if we fail now to set an example to our Western partners by providing generous financial help to Poland, we shall have lost much of our status for complaint and protest when the Soviet Union steps in with its 'fraternal' help, whether purely financial or of a more sinister kind. There is, of course, no guarantee that this flowering of liberalism in Poland will not be nipped in the bud by the Soviets, as were those of the Hungarians and Czechs, even if the Soviet Government can point to no general breakdown of Party or Government control in the country. Additional Western financial help over the coming difficult years would, however, be a major factor in minimising the risk.

9. On the political side I recommend that we should firmly eschew any temptation there may be to offer encouragement to those few elements in Polish society whose objective is the revolutionary overthrow of the communist system. That would be to encourage useless violence and bloodshed. Our current declared policy of non-interference in Polish internal affairs (by ourselves and others) is clearly right.

10. To sum up I recommend Western financial aid as the best hope of encouraging a more liberal Polish régime and society, of avoiding Soviet intervention and of maintaining stability in the world. I hope, Sir, that during your visit, you will be prepared to offer the right kind of help and encouragement to your Polish hosts and that, after your visit, you will be willing to influence your Western colleagues in the same direction.

11. I am sending copies of this despatch to Her Majesty's Representatives at Moscow, East Berlin, Belgrade, Budapest, Bucharest, Prague, Sofia, Helsinki, Bonn, Paris, Washington and the United Kingdom Delegation to NATO. I am also sending copies to the Secretary of State for Trade, the Chancellor of the Exchequer and the Governor of the Bank of England.[6]

I am, etc,
K. R. C. PRIDHAM

[5] See No. 31.

[6] On 23 October Mr Fall, on Mr Fergusson's instructions, thanked Mr Pridham for his despatch (FCO 28/4165, ENP 212/2). He attached a minute sent by the Lord Privy Seal to the Prime Minister (No. 31), adding: 'you will see that this is the message FCO ministers are putting across to their Whitehall colleagues. As you will appreciate, however, the decision is a very difficult one and there will need to be a good deal of discussion here in Whitehall and consultation with our allies before we are able to hammer out a line' (FCO 28/4157, ENP 090/1).

No. 30

Letter from Mrs Thatcher to President Carter, 20 October 1980[1]
Secret (PREM 19/331)

Thank you for your further message of 7 October about Poland.[2] I agree that it is essential for us to remain in close touch over this.

The situation in Poland is obviously still precarious and the Party leadership in disarray. The Russians seem prepared for the moment to leave it to the Polish authorities to try to reassert control. But they are clearly not confident that the Government will be able to implement the agreements reached last month in a way that both avoids further trouble with the workers and safeguards the supremacy of the Party. I share your view that the Russians would intervene if they believed that communist control was in jeopardy.[3]

Like you, we have been watching closely the military activity in the Western military districts of the Soviet Union together with certain evidence from the communications field. Our assessment at the moment is that these are contingency moves and do not in themselves presage an early invasion. But they have the character of precautionary steps in case an armed intervention should appear necessary.

While we should have some warning of an impending invasion, this might not amount to more than a few days. It is therefore important that we should be ready to react quickly if an intervention seemed imminent. I know that our officials, together with those from France and Germany, have been discussing the steps we might take in such a situation.

I have no doubt that the Russians know very well that an invasion would have very serious consequences for East/West relations, but I agree that the point is one which can usefully be underlined. I have made it clear publicly, most recently during the Conservative Party Conference,[4] that Polish affairs are for the Poles alone to resolve; and we shall be putting that message across also in private.

[1] Copied to HM Ambassadors in Washington, Paris and Bonn for their personal background information. Opening and concluding salutations omitted from the filed copy.
[2] See No. 23, note 6.
[3] Western and Polish fears were raised further following a speech made by the East German communist leader, Herr Honecker, on 12 October, when he declared: 'Poland is and will remain a socialist country. It belongs inseparably to the socialist world. The wheel of history cannot be turned backwards—we'll see to that, together with our friends.'
[4] See No. 23, note 6.

No. 31

Minute from Sir I. Gilmour (Lord Privy Seal) to Mrs Thatcher, 20 October 1980

Confidential (CAB148/189)

Prime Minister,

Possible economic assistance for Poland

You will recall that in his message to you of 27 August[1] President Carter referred to Poland's likely need for further economic and financial assistance from the West and suggested that our aid should be designed to encourage the Poles to undertake a more fundamental and systematic reform of their economic system. In reply, you said that you looked forward to hearing what the President had in mind (we have had no response), that you would welcome any proposal for ensuring that our help went to benefit the Polish people rather than to the shoring up of an unreformed system, but that we would have to take care to avoid accusations of interference.

2. The Polish Ambassador[2] called on me last week to put forward, on the instructions of his Prime Minister, a number of specific requests for economic assistance from the UK. The details are attached at Annex A.[3] The Ambassador made it clear that, while the subject would not be formally on the Agenda, the Poles would want to pursue it during the Foreign Secretary's visit from 29-31 October. We shall therefore need a line before then. Officials from a number of Departments have now looked at this.

3. The Poles have told us that they are making similar approaches to the US, France, FRG and Italy, and they seem to have been in touch also with Austria, Belgium, Norway and Sweden. The Americans have already given us details of the informal requests they have received (which include one for $3 billion in further credits on favourable terms), but they have not indicated how they intend to respond. We shall be following this up with them and comparing notes also with other countries involved. We should coordinate our response closely. It may suit the Poles to try to handle the matter by separate bilateral contacts, but there is no reason for us to go along with this provided we are discreet.

4. None of us will find the question easy. The Polish economy is in serious difficulty and the authorities have had to make concessions to consumers and wage earners which will make things worse at least in the short term. Poland needs external credits to stay afloat until the economy can be restored to health. That will take several years at best, and Poland will have difficulties in servicing her debts. It seems quite possible, as indicated in the press, that Poland's hard currency debt may rise from $22 billion at present to $30 billion or even more in the next 3-5 years—assuming lenders are found. We do not have the same means of ensuring that Poland will adopt sensible, and, if needed, painful policies of adjustment as we

[1] See No. 23, note 2.

[2] Jan Bisztyga.

[3] Not printed. The requests included the postponement of the repayment of ECGD guaranteed debt in 1981 and 1982, further credit from the ECGD for certain commodities with five year repayment periods, the lowering of the minimum size of contract which could be covered by ECGD guarantees, the liberalisation of British quotas for imports of Polish leather goods and small television sets, and British support in GATT for the suspension until the end of 1982 of the Poles' minimum import growth quotas.

do when the IMF is involved, and it is generally accepted that the Russians would not tolerate a Polish move to join the IMF in the present circumstances. Furthermore the political situation in Poland remains precarious, and it is impossible to say at this stage whether the significant move towards democracy represented by the event of the last few weeks can or will be maintained.

5. Yet what is happening in Poland is of major political importance not only for that country but for Europe. The West has a substantial interest in any loosening of the Soviet system. To achieve this the reforms already agreed will have to be consolidated. The Poles cannot do this without financial assistance. We can safely assume that the Russians will not provide the requisite economic aid without setting very harsh conditions. If we refuse to help therefore the implication will be that we are indifferent to events there, which is not the case. Without outside assistance the Poles will be forced to crack down economically. This would provoke more strikes and probably Russian intervention, with all the dangers that that would entail. The end result would be the opposite of what we and other Western countries have been trying to encourage in our policy towards Eastern Europe.

6. There are other considerations to bear in mind. There will be financial limits to what individual countries can do. And there are a number of dangers which each will wish to avoid: in particular that of committing money over a long period without the possibility of withdrawing if economic or political conditions should change for the worse; and of making concessions to the Poles which have been refused, or could not be offered, to countries who might consider they had a better claim and whose cases could not plausibly be distinguished. We should watch carefully the use to be made of any British money provided, given the glaring facts about the nature of the Polish economy and our wish to avoid shoring up an unreformed system. We could also look for ways of helping Poland in ways which do not involve government guarantees or spending public money for example by helping them with their marketing in hard currency areas. Any assistance we do make would have to be in instalments, so that it can be withdrawn if the Poles or the Russians crack down. And of course even with Western financial aid there can be no guarantee that the Russians will not intervene.

7. The balance is not easy to strike. But, at the end of the day, I believe that at least the Americans, the French and the Germans will conclude (as President Carter and Herr Schmidt have already indicated) that something should be done to help the Poles and to provide concrete evidence of Western interest in their future. All three have recently provided some extra finance for Poland, either new money, guarantees or refinancing. We shall be expected to play our part, and I think on balance we should.

8. If you and other colleagues agree [with] this general conclusion, neither the Foreign Secretary during his visit to Warsaw nor the Minister of State for Trade (who will be leading our team at the Annual Anglo-Polish Joint Commission in Warsaw on 10-14 November) need to be drawn into too much detail on what we may be able to do. But they will need to have guidance on the points on which they could indicate our willingness to enter into more detailed discussion with the Poles. I would suggest the line at Annex B.[4] I am sorry that the Polish approach has not given us much time before the Foreign Secretary sets off on 27 October.

[4] Not printed.

9. I am sending copies of this minute to Geoffrey Howe, Keith Joseph, John Nott, Peter Walker and Sir Robert Armstong.[5]

I[AN] H[EDWORTH] G[ILMOUR]

[5] The Chancellor responded on 22 October that he was very cautious about increasing UK exposure to Polish debt at a time when it might be more prudent to look for a reduction. However he accepted that, politically, help may have to be given to the Poles, but did not want to see the UK getting ahead of the other major countries involved. Writing on the same day, the Secretary of State for Trade noted that he was not enthusiastic about increased cover but was prepared to agree with plans for a refinancing package. At a meeting of OD on 23 October (OD(80)60) there was general agreement that it was in the UK's interest to assist Poland 'but only to the extent justified by our own economic circumstances' and in line with what was being done by other Western countries.

No. 32

Mr Cartledge (Budapest) to Lord Carrington, 29 October 1980, 6.15 p.m.

Tel. No. 595[1] Immediate, Confidential (FCO 28/4129, ENH 026/4)

Secretary of State's meeting with Mr Kadar[2]

1. Mr Kadar said that 1980 had been a difficult year internationally. Hungary had used her influence, such as it was, to maintain the international dialogue, however acute the issues. There were some recent signs of improvements, e.g. the meetings between Brezhnev, Giscard and Schmidt, the continuation of the MBFR talks in Vienna and Soviet/American contacts on TNF. Lord Carrington's visit also reflected a desire on both sides to maintain contacts. He understood that talks with Mr Puja had been cordial, even though full identity of views was not to be expected.[3]

2. He was glad that Lord Carrington had said that relations between Britain and Hungary were undisturbed and had agreed that bilateral relations should be further developed. There had also been an agreement that political solutions should be sought in areas of tension. History showed that even complex problems could be solved by a responsible and sober attitude. In its absence, there was a risk that we might all go into a long dark tunnel without knowing what was at the end, with every country grasping for national advantage. This risk had once been a fantasy, but was now a reality.

3. Hungary was very interested in international cooperation, and had the intellectual and other resources for this. She needed international contacts for her

[1] Repeated for Information Immediate to Warsaw, Washington, Paris, Bonn and UKDEL NATO; Priority to Luxembourg, East Berlin, Moscow, Bucharest, Prague, Sofia, Belgrade and Madrid.

[2] Lord Carrington paid an official visit to Hungary from 27 to 29 October to discuss international issues and give fresh momentum to bilateral relations, in particular to show sympathetic interest in Hungary's economic reform. In addition to talks with Mr Kádár, General Secretary of the Hungarian Communist Party, Lord Carrington also had talks with Mr Puja, the Foreign Secretary, and met both the Prime Minister and the President. He also paid a brief trip to a state farm at Agárd, where the General Manager was surprised to learn that Lord Carrington was also a farmer and pleased with the Foreign Secretary's offer to cut short the oral briefing and look at the pigs instead.

[3] In a despatch of 3 November Mr Cartledge recalled that Mr Puja, 'delivered a ritual and tedious catalogue of Hungarian positions on most issues and areas of the world', in which he blamed the US and NATO for the decline in East-West relations. He concluded: 'The only merit of this 90-minute recital was to underline the contrast between Hungary's orthodox foreign policy and relatively liberal domestic policy.'

economic construction plans. Without wishing to drive wedges between western countries, he noted that the West Germans had long been Hungary's biggest trading partner, even in politically difficult periods when they had called each other everything under the sun. He had told the French that they should increase their interest in Eastern Europe, as well as their traditional ties in e.g. Africa. This went for Britain too. There was a kind of inertia in this field. It was unthinkable that East and West Europe should not develop closer links. Hungary's possibilities were not unlimited, but 'a small fish was a good fish' as the German proverb had it. He saw no ideological obstacles to closer economic contacts.

4. Lord Carrington said he would not dissent from anything Mr Kadar had said. There was too little real content in our relations: we needed to put flesh on the bones. (Kadar agreed, and said that this included culture. Hungary particularly welcomed tourists.) Even when he and Mr Puja had disagreed, they wanted the same results, e.g. on détente and arms limitation. Britain too was a European country and agreed wholeheartedly on the importance of détente. However, détente needed to be seen in the round. The search for détente in Europe should not be abandoned, but the lack of trust which events outside Europe had caused inevitably affected the atmosphere in Europe itself. Afghanistan worried the West deeply. Maybe our fears were groundless, and we had misinterpreted Soviet motives. But if Afghanistan could be settled in a way which satisfied the fears and doubts of the Soviet Union, which was acceptable to Pakistan and Iraq, and which reassured the West, the greatest single factor of tension would be removed. He did not know what would happen to the Soviet or American leadership in the next year. Smaller countries had a role in keeping the super powers on the right course.

5. Kadar said that there was an inter-reaction between events inside and outside Europe. The Helsinki Agreements had been a positive beginning, and had exercised a positive effect outside Europe at the time of their conclusion. We should try to ensure that Madrid continued what had been begun in Helsinki. We could argue there, but something, however small, should come out of it. There had also been some small results on MBFRs but we were bogged down on data questions. Europe was even now one of the more peaceful regions, but the main front line was still here and the situation in Europe affected everything else. He accepted Lord Carrington's expression of concern over Afghanistan: this was therefore a subject of concern to the Hungarians too. A political solution must be found, especially at a time when the Middle East dispute had not been resolved, and when the Iranian revolution (which was not the East's creation) was continuing. The revolution had however created a fundamentally different situation in the region, which had been further complicated by the Iran/Iraq War. He did not know whether the West had had a hand in this war, though he had seen no sign of it so far. The war was a common headache to East and West.

6. Hungary accepted the Soviet view that Afghanistan affected her security. If we were nervous about the new Soviet leadership, we should cross our fingers for the health of Brezhnev who was a man of peace. Speaking responsibly and with agreement of the Soviet leadership, Brezhnev had recognised in an interview in *Pravda* in January this year that the West's nervousness over Gulf oil was understandable. He had, however, gone on to ask why in that case the West itself was undermining the security of the oil routes. The implication was that the Soviet Union understood the West's vital interests, but did not want the West to complicate the situation in the region. There were now uncomfortably large forces there, with American bases in Egypt and Saudi Arabia and Soviet troops in

Afghanistan. We should remember that the Russians reflected and calculated like other people, and did not simply look for targets to attack.

7. Lord Carrington reverted to the need for trust. Brezhnev recognised western concerns, but did nothing to remove them.

8. In a brief discussion of the situation in Poland Kadar stressed and Lord Carrington strongly agreed, that the Poles should be left to resolve their own problems: domestic changes other than to the basic structure were necessary and inevitable but this was a matter for them.[4] (At his subsequent press conference Lord Carrington said that the Poles should be allowed to settle their internal problems without interference and expressed the hope that all other countries took the same view.)

[4] In Budapest tel. No. 596, of the same date, Mr Cartledge added that the Hungarians were worried about Poland as an international question but not the domestic implications, as they had been through 1956 and drawn 'all the necessary conclusions'.

No. 33

Mr Pridham (Warsaw) to FCO,[1] 3 November 1980, 1 p.m.

Tel. No. 420[2] Immediate, Confidential (FCO 28/4151, ENP 026/4)

Your visit to Poland: 29-31 October

1. Your visit would always have been important but its timing made it exceptionally important for the Polish Government and people.

2. This was shown first by the determination of Kania and Pinkowski[3] not to miss you. The result being that you were rushed on arrival in the evening of 29 October into hour-long talks with both of them prior to their surprise departure for Moscow early the next morning, the first but not the last sudden change of programme. It is not just that the Polish Government hope for economic aid from us, or even that they wanted to display the normality of their foreign relations, but that at this critical time, they saw your visit in a way which they might themselves find hard to define, as something of a reassuring window to the West. It can only be a guess but Kania may have found his talk with you, with its clear exposition of our position on the Polish crisis (and perhaps on other matters), a help in what must have been painfully difficult discussions with Brezhnev.

3. Both Kania and Pinkowski were relatively optimistic that a political solution to Poland's troubles would be found (as they had to be in conversation with you). These are both men who have only recently emerged from the shadows, but I think you detected in Kania qualities of realism, flexibility and a surprising sense of humour: and in Pinkowski an underlying toughness which belied his very quiet exterior. The message of both men seemed to be that they were determined on change and would yield a great deal to the strikers but that on the fundamental

[1] Lord Carrington was in Luxembourg on 4 November 1980 to sign an agreement marking the accession of Zimbabwe to the second ACP-EEC Convention between the African, Caribbean and Pacific States and the European Economic Community.

[2] Repeated Information Routine to Luxembourg, Moscow, Prague, Sofia, Budapest, Bucharest, East Berlin, Belgrade, UKDEL NATO, Washington, Paris, Bonn, Helsinki, MODUK.

[3] Stanisław Kania succeeded Edward Gierek as First Secretary of the Polish United Workers' Party on 6 September 1980. Józef Pińkowski, succeeded Edward Babiuch as Prime Minister of Poland on 24 August 1980.

socialist character of the state and of its alliances they would not give way come what may. I believe that they and indeed all Poles were pleased (and relieved) by your clear statements that the Polish troubles were entirely a matter for Poles. These were given wide publicity.[4]

4. There was very great satisfaction also at your necessarily guarded statement that we were considering with sympathy Polish requests for economic and financial help. Pinkowski said that things would become very difficult in the payments field by the turn of the year and I earnestly hope that even if we can offer nothing concrete for Mr Parkinson's visit[5] we can produce something by December. If we delay too long it may be too late and the effect of your visit will be dissipated. If we can come up with something soon we shall reinforce it and our commercial and political position here.

5. The official talks which you had with the Polish Minister for Foreign Affairs produced few surprises except an admission that the SS20s did threaten Europe.[6] On foreign affairs the Poles gave an impression of unhappiness and embarrassment over Afghanistan, of genuine worry about TNF[7] and great relief that negotiations have started, and of slightly desperate hope for Madrid.

6. A major achievement of the visit is that the two main leaders of the Polish regime have for the first time been exposed to the Western point of view put by a Western minister. No amount of reading briefs or newspapers is a substitute for this.

7. I regret that the visit was so rushed but this was inevitable once the Krakow section was included. I hope and believe that you found this added a dimension to your understanding of the Polish character, a facet of which was illustrated by their determination that you should live in a Polish house and travel in a Polish aircraft and a Polish car.

8. This tel. delayed by mechanical fault in Hanslope.[8]

[4] There was also wide publicity in Britain. For example, Lord Carrington was interviewed in Warsaw by the BBC Eastern Europe correspondent, during which he stated that current difficulties were the Poles' business and that he did not want to interfere in their internal affairs.
[5] Planned for 10 to 14 November 1980.
[6] The SS-20 was an intermediate-range ballistic missile with a nuclear warhead deployed by the Soviet Union in Europe from 1976. In response to this threat NATO took the decision, in December 1979, to modernise its Theatre Nuclear Forces in Western Europe by deploying Pershing II rockets and cruise missiles. However deployment was to be linked to the offer of arms control talks with the USSR—the 'twin-track' approach.
[7] See No. 2, note 4.
[8] The FCO Central Receiving Station at Hanslope Park, which dealt with telegram messages.

No. 34

Minute from Mr Walden to Mr Fall, 12 November 1980

Confidential (FCO 28/4151, ENP 026/4)

Secretary of State's visits to Poland and Hungary

This minute, which has been compiled in discussion with you and Mr Bullard, has been approved by the Secretary of State, and reflects conclusions drawn by him after his first visits to Eastern Europe.

The essence of our policy towards Eastern Europe and the Soviet Union is that it should be discriminating. To some extent, it already is. We have been careful not to apply to Eastern Europe the measures we have taken to bring home to the Soviet Union the costs of their invasion of Afghanistan. And the fact that the Secretary of State has recently visited Romania, Hungary and Poland and has at present no plans to visit Bulgaria, Czechoslovakia or the GDR reflects a justifiable discrimination between the countries of Eastern Europe.

Afghanistan provides a clear example of the need for a discriminating policy but it is not the only reason for it. We should maintain this view also in the longer term, and give thought to how such a policy might be taken further. The following are among the points which should be considered:

(i) Afghanistan is a reason to discriminate against the Soviet Union. But in the longer term the overwhelming importance of the Soviet Union is a reason for paying it more rather than less attention. It would be wrong at present to revert to 'business as usual' when the Russians are showing no signs of looking for a political solution in Afghanistan and are being particularly obdurate at Madrid. But no business at all is equally wrong. We recognise this in the commercial field and have agreed that preparations for the next meeting of the Joint Commission should be put in hand. On the political side, we are looking for ways to resume the dialogue at official level. We should also seek to ensure that unofficial visitors to Moscow are not only those likely to tell the Russians what they want to hear.

(ii) It is not enough in Eastern Europe to discriminate between countries. Hungary, for example, will repay a degree of special attention, but there is a very obvious limit to what can be achieved by talking to Mr Puja.[1] We must try to pick the right people too. Exchanges tend to get institutionalised. We cannot change the system over-night and we should make the best of visits which are inevitable. But we should be more ready to pick our horses and to make a special effort where the circumstances and personalities are right. Ambassadors should be encouraged to make proposals going outside the existing pattern of visits where it makes sense to do so. The Secretary of State will be ready to give his support where appropriate.

A more discriminating and more active relationship with the East will require more sophisticated handling of the traditional subject matter. It is a question of differentiating not only between one country and interlocutor and another, but between different kinds of meetings. Arguments that may be quite sufficient for a single session of official talks in the Foreign Ministry in Sofia may not stand up to 48 hours of personal contact between Foreign Ministers in Warsaw.

Examples of subjects where some fresh thinking is required are:

(*a*) *Afghanistan*: the Resolution of the UN General Assembly[2] speaks for itself, but we need to answer the Hungarian question: what is the difference between the Soviet invasion of Afghanistan and what the French did in Chad and the Central African Republic?[3]

(*b*) *CDE*[4]: we need to show why the definition of Europe as Atlantic to the Urals[5] is the right one; to reconcile this with our insistence on arms control as a field for small practical steps rather than grand gestures; and to answer the

[1] See No. 32, note 3.

[2] Adopted on 14 January by 104 votes to 18, the Resolution called for the immediate withdrawal of foreign troops, recognition of Afghanistan's territorial integrity, non alignment and right to determine its own form of government.

[3] French troops had intervened in the ongoing civil war in Chad and in September 1979 had removed the ruler of the Central African Republic, Jean-Bedel Bokassa, from power.

[4] Conference on Disarmament in Europe.

[5] The expression, 'Europe, from the Atlantic to the Urals', was coined by President de Gaulle during a speech he made on 23 November 1959 in Strasbourg.

question what the West proposes to do if the Russians, as seems inevitable, reject our starting point.

(*c*) *TNF*: the need here is for arguments not only to rebut Soviet accusations that it was NATO who made the escalating move last December, but also to make an impression on East Europeans who were no more consulted than we were about the Soviet decision to manufacture and deploy the SS20,[6] and who simply feel helpless between two power blocs.

(*d*) *Détente*: in arguing the case for the indivisibility of *détente* we need to answer Dobrosielski's[7] question whether this does not lead to the indivisibility of tension. Here too we need to reach the audience in Eastern Europe which feels concerned but helpless.

Finally, our whole approach to the East must of course be related to what is happening in Madrid. The CSCE process has bred a group of arcane issues and a generation of specialist officials who understand them better than does the general public. Part of the process of recapturing credibility for this process is to ensure that our CSCE policy is organically linked with the rest of the government's policies towards the Soviet Union and Eastern Europe. The multilateral context limits the extent to which we can discriminate in Madrid between individual East European countries and between them and the Soviet Union, and it is inevitable that the Warsaw Pact countries will feel constrained to follow the Soviet lead. We need not take at full value everything they tell us about the limits of Soviet tolerance, but we should keep it in mind that the Final Act gives to those most concerned to develop their bilateral links with the West a degree of authority to do so which will be reduced if the Soviet Union dissociates itself from the CSCE process or if for any other reason the process collapses.

I should be grateful if your department could assume responsibility for ensuing that these general guidelines are followed, and that follow-up action with other departments is pursued as necessary.[8]

G. G. H. WALDEN

[6] See No. 33, note 6.

[7] Marian Dobrosielski, Polish Deputy Foreign Minister.

[8] The minute was circulated by Mr Fall to HMAs in Moscow, Belgrade, Bucharest, Budapest, Prague, Sofia, Warsaw and East Berlin for their views. He commented that the policy of discrimination they were aiming for was not static but an 'active policy of differentiating between the countries concerned in terms of what makes sense in particular circumstance at a particular moment'. Sir C. Keeble, in a letter of 27 November, thought the Soviets saw little incentive to improve relations, apart from the possible public relations benefit, and were content tactically to place Britain in the Atlantic rather than the European sphere. Mr Holmer, in a letter of 12 December, wondered whether the exercise of discriminating between one Eastern European country and another could be reflected through the issue of entry visas to the UK (FCO 28/4011, EN 021/2).

No. 35

Record of a conversation between Lord Carrington and Mr Lukanov (Deputy Prime Minister of Bulgaria), 14 November 1980
Confidential (FCO 28/4107, ENG 026/1)

Present:	
Secretary of State	Mr Lukanov
Mr Bullard	Mr Shterev[1]
Mr Fall	Mme Popova[2]
Mr Lever	
Mr Campbell	

East-West Relations

1. *Lord Carrington* asked Mr Lukanov how he saw the prospects for East-West relations. *Mr Lukanov* replied that it was difficult to evaluate the situation until it became clear what difference the election of Reagan would make.[3] There were two schools of thought. The first looked at the people who might advise President Reagan, noted their professional qualifications and remembered the experience of the last Republican Administration. The second school merely took note of the public speeches by Mr Reagan.

2. *Mr Lukanov* felt that practical policies were necessary to secure peace in the aftermath of Helsinki. He felt there was no real sense in talking about human rights if there was no peace. Peace was the basic human right. Logic, not subterfuge lay behind the Eastern group's tactics at Madrid. Peace must come first in order to preserve the quality of life whether a country was governed by a socialist or capitalist system. The historic controversy between the two systems was a controversy about the quality of life.

3. *Lord Carrington* said that Reagan had surrounded himself with well-informed and capable people. Schulz or Haig were tipped for the job of Secretary of State.[4] There was no doubt an element of campaign rhetoric in the public statements of the last few months. *Mr Lukanov* agreed with this but said that he felt that détente could not endure further strains. *Lord Carrington* spoke of his recent visits to Hungary and Poland. Both countries wished détente to continue. They had all agreed that the dialogue must be kept going. The Hungarians had expressed their concern about what would happen if the situation in Poland became internationalised.

4. On the CSCE *Lord Carrington* wondered whether the Soviet Union still considered the process to be worthwhile. Or were they coming to the conclusion that the disadvantages for them outweighed the advantages? The usual assessment was that the Soviet Union would wrangle for a long time in negotiations but would eventually reach a compromise. This did not seem to be the case on this occasion. *Mr Lukanov* replied that everyone should be concerned about European security. It was wrong to concentrate on the human rights principles of the Final Act. One should not ignore the implementation of the Final Act, but neither should one

[1] Bulgarian Ambassador, London.

[2] UK desk officer at the Bulgarian MFA.

[3] On 4 November Ronald Reagan was elected US President. During the election campaign he had made tough statements about the Soviet Union and the dangers of communism.

[4] Alexander Haig became US Secretary of State.

concentrate merely on this one aspect. Discussion of military détente was very important. *Lord Carrington* replied that it would be wrong to sweep disagreeable facts under the carpet. Relations would then develop on shaky foundations. He preferred to have things out in the open. He also disliked sweeping generalised resolutions. There was a need to look more at specifics. On disarmament the most constructive path was through discussion of arms limitation. There was a need for a gradual build up of trust during which neither side should be disadvantaged.

5. *Mr Lukanov* said he felt that we were now at a crossroads. The West was creating a situation of danger in the updating of its nuclear weapons. *Lord Carrington* replied that over the last few years the West had suffered under the threat of Soviet SS20 missiles being pointed in their direction. We had merely tried to catch up with the Russians. NATO took the decision to deploy Cruise missiles and it was only on this basis that the two super-powers had been able to agree to discuss limitation. Before the introduction of Cruise missiles we were at a disadvantage. *Mr Lukanov* said that it was impossible for the Warsaw Pact countries to consider three systems of security, i.e. in relations to Europe, the USA and China. He felt that there must be an overall global system of security. The arms race would make a catastrophe 'technically inevitable'. It was possible that we had already reached this situation and that the fate of the world could be decided in a few minutes. *Lord Carrington* questioned the idea of technical inevitability. We should, of course, prevent a disaster now occurring, but we would not be able to do this with general concepts. We needed practical measures to reduce danger.

Bulgarian economy

6. *Lord Carrington* asked how the economic recession in the West would affect Bulgaria. *Mr Lukanov* replied that next year would be more difficult for Bulgaria, but they were not in recession. They were planning for 5.5 per cent growth in production next year, and had achieved balance of payments surpluses in 1979 and again this year. They were dependent on the West and the Third World for only some 27-28% of their total trade. They were now selling to the Soviet Union more machinery, including electronics, than they bought. The investment programme for the next 5 year plan would amount to $40 billion.

Bilateral relations

7. (i) *Visit by Secretary of State*

Mr Lukanov said that in over 100 years of Anglo-Bulgarian relations there had never been a visit by a British Secretary of State to Bulgaria. *Lord Carrington* replied that he would like to visit Bulgaria and that we would see what could be done. 1300 years of history was indeed a long time. *Mr Lukanov* said he hoped that the visit could take place in the anniversary year.[5]

8. (ii) *Trade/GSP*[6]

Mr Lukanov said that he was not displeased with the overall state of bilateral relations but he regretted the opportunities which had been lost in the field of trade. There had been very few significant economic successes for various reasons. On GSP, he had explained the Bulgarian position to Mr Blaker[7] and Mr Eyre. If the EC decided to raise the threshold, that would be one thing, but discrimination was inequitable. Bulgaria could not have normal relations with States who

[5] The 1300th anniversary of the Bulgarian State in 1981.

[6] Generalised Scheme of Preferences. These were EC rules to ensure that exporters from developing countries paid lower duties on some or all of what they sold to the EC.

[7] Mr Blaker had visited Bulgaria from 30 September to 3 October.

discriminated against her. The only argument put forward by the Commission had been that Bulgaria was too rich to qualify. This judgement was apparently based on World Bank figures. The Bulgarians had discussed them with the Bank, and considered that the figures were based on wrong methodology and were too approximate to allow conclusions to be drawn. The Bulgarians were also talking to the Commission.

9. The meeting ended at 9.50.

No. 36

Mr Pridham (Warsaw) to Lord Carrington, 19 November 1980
Restricted (FCO 28/4165, ENP 212/2)

The Polish Crisis: Act Two

Summary . . . [1]

My Lord,

In my despatch of 4 September[2] I analysed the First Act of the Polish crisis—from Babiuch's raising of the price of meat on 1 July to the conclusion of the Gdańsk agreements on 31 August. The Second act may be said to have lasted from 1 September to 10 November, the day on which the Supreme Court agreed to the registration of *Solidarność* on more or less the terms demanded by its founders. The object of this despatch is to recount and to analyse the events of that period and to try to draw from them some conclusions about the likely course of events in Poland in the near future. Such predictions ought, it seems to me, to centre on four inter-related questions: the prospects for further change in the Party hierarchy; the chances of implementation of the outstanding promises in the Gdańsk agreements; the likely situation in the markets during the winter; and the likelihood of Soviet intervention. In this analysis I take it as read that the political and economic crisis in Poland is not at an end, and that the present calm brought about by the Supreme Court's decision is no more than a lull in the storm.

Course of the Crisis

2. Detailed accounts of the events of the period under discussion have been sent to the Department—as they occurred.[3] I attach a chronology. Three strands are worth emphasising here. Firstly, the Sixth Plenum, which took place on 5-6 September and 4-5 October. During its two sessions the Party made further far-reaching changes in personnel (of which Gierek's replacement by Kania was, of course, the most important), which have been supplemented by the dismissal of a number of local Party bosses, of which Grudzień[4] and Karkoszka[5] were the most powerful. The Plenum expelled Babiuch and others of his stamp from the Central Committee and began the process of calling past leaders to account. The wide interval between the two sessions probably reflects the time needed by Kania to

[1] Not printed.

[2] See No. 21, note 2.

[3] Nos. 16-21.

[4] Zdzislaw Grudzień was First Party Secretary in Katowice and member of the Politburo of the Polish United Workers' Party.

[5] Alojzy Karkoszka was First Party Secretary in Gdańsk during the riots in December 1970; Deputy Premier of Poland (1975–76); Secretary of the Central Committee of the Polish United Workers' Party; and member of Politburo until 1980.

establish himself. The Party also announced its decision to call the IXth Party Congress, but without fixing a date. Secondly, despite the Gdańsk agreements, and those of Szczecin which preceded them, strikes continued throughout Poland, albeit at a trickle. A third series of agreements was signed at Jastrzębie[6] on 3 September. But disputes continued, and are still continuing, among sectors as diverse as postal workers, hotel waiters and workers in health and education. Poznań,[7] Wrocław, and Gdańsk itself were among areas particularly hit.[8] Thirdly, the months of September and October were marked by a growing sense of identity, purpose and strength in the embryonic independent trades unions. At a meeting in Gdańsk in early September it was decided to set up a national umbrella organisation rather than a series of regional ones. Suggestions that the authorities intended to try to draw back some of the concessions won at Gdańsk caused strong statements from *Solidarność's* leaders and an impressively organised one hour warning strike on 3 October. Meanwhile, Wałęsa embarked on a nation-wide tour, following in part the route taken by the Pope more than a year earlier—but visiting also the Silesian coalfields. He was watched (and listened to) by large crowds. By this time, no one in authority can have had much doubt that the new trades unions would be a force to reckon with.

3. It was against this background that *Solidarność's* application for registration came to court. The Warsaw *Voivodship* Court was opened for registration applications on 13 September. *Solidarność* made their application on 24 September. After some discussions the Court registered *Solidarność* on 24 October, gratuitously adding to its statutes a clause acknowledging the leading role of the Party—the major issue between the Court and the union. *Solidarność* filed an appeal to the Supreme Court. Meanwhile, on 30 October (shortly after receiving you, Sir) Kania and Pińkowski had flown to Moscow. On 31 October talks between the Government (led by Pińkowski) and *Solidarność* (led by Wałęsa) broke down without agreement on a *communiqué*. Then, on 10 November, the Supreme Court announced that *Solidarność's* appeal had been in large measure successful: acknowledgement of the Party's leading role was relegated to an annex (as the Union's leaders had offered some weeks before); the annex was also to include sections of the ILO Charter;[9] the troublesome passages defining the

[6] See No. 29, note 3.

[7] Situated in west-central Poland, Poznań had been a centre of protests and strikes in the locomotive industry in 1956 considered as an early expression of resistance to communist rule. In June of that year, a protest march against the Communist Party and the secret police headquarters was repressed by the army resulting in 67 people killed according to official figures.

[8] From 9 to 11 November, Mr Joy visited Gdańsk, Gdynia and Malbork to lay the annual wreath at the Malbork Commonwealth cemetery. On 14 November he reported in a letter to Mr Fall 'the widespread extent of the support for Solidarity in that area, the determination and even recklessness of some of the Solidarity supporters and the frankness and sincerity of local government and Party officials in recognising the legitimacy of popular protest and seeking to guide it into constructive channels'. He met 'idealistic' students belonging to the Solidarity branch of their university, who wanted a radical change of the Polish society and political system and thought that the Party was discredited: 'they were determined that Poland would never be the same again'. Joy concluded: 'The average man (or woman) in the Gdansk omnibus certainly sees Solidarity as a panacea for accumulated woes and frustrations. It seems at least doubtful whether even Russian tanks could reverse this'. His report generated interest at home, Mr Fergusson annotating: 'Useful to have the flavour. This, like much of the press reporting, suggests both inexperience and a certain recklessness in the younger supporters of Solidarity' (FCO 28/4164, ENP 212/2).

[9] The International Labour Organisation, established in 1919 by the Paris Peace Conference, included a charter protecting labour unions and workers' rights, in particular freedom of association.

circumstances in which the Union would call a strike were to be omitted altogether—the question to be resolved in the new trade-union legislation.

4. During the critical period of 30 October to 10 November, however, a great deal more happened than the bare outline above reveals. The public mood passed through three fairly discernible phases. Kania's visit to Moscow and Pińkowski's meeting with Wałęsa were accompanied by a mood of quiet optimism. As the next week progressed and the date of the hearing approached this mood was replaced by one of disquiet and then sheer despair. The happy outcome of 10 November naturally produced a mood of great relief. The earlier, mounting despair and tension was caused by sabre rattling on both sides. Wałęsa and company said repeatedly that, if the Court did not register on their terms, they would stage a general strike from 12 November. Plans for this strike (which envisaged a steady escalation from the planned starting-points of Warsaw and Gdańsk) were drawn up and freely available. Meanwhile, on the Government side, major statements by Kania, Grabski, Olszowski and Klasa[10] (Party press spokesman) attacked the unions for not giving way, indicating their own determination to make a stand and preparations to do so. The worrying conclusion being drawn by almost everyone at this stage was that both sides were ready and willing for a fight. Whilst the events that made that fight unnecessary are largely obscure, analysis of this latest crisis may have a bearing on the future prospects for Poland.

Analysis of the Crisis

5. There are two schools of thought. One school assumes that the Government was indeed ready for a fight right up to Sunday, 9 November, and then, at the last moment, changed its collective mind. The second school assumes that a compromise of the specific question of the statute was actually reached between the Government and *Solidarność* at a much earlier stage (at, or soon after, the Pińkowski/Wałęsa meeting on 31 October) but that both sides decided, out of mutual suspicion and because agreement on all points under discussion at that meeting had not been reached, to make a show of strength before the Supreme Court's ruling made the compromise public. This school answers the objection that the Supreme Court's ruling was not a compromise but a further retreat by the authorities, by assuming that *Solidarność* on its side has conceded more than has yet been announced.

6. The first school base their argument partly on the many rumours (some of them contradicting others) that on the evening of Sunday, 9 November, there were informal consultations among the Politburo, in smoked-filled rooms, possibly involving lawyers. It is also rumoured that Pińkowski visited Moscow that day, presumably to clear the change of mind with Moscow. These rumours are supported by two pieces of more tangible evidence: (i) During Sunday, 9 November, and Monday 10 November, all Western journalists in Poland, save those accredited here permanently, were told to leave. The decision was rescinded at 3 p.m. on 10 November after the Supreme Court's ruling. The obvious conclusion is that the Ministry of Internal Affairs was preparing for a rather different ruling; (ii) On 10 November the *Voivoda* of Częstochowa, one Mirosław Wierzbicki, told his factory managers that they were to expect trouble from *Solidarność* but that the expected strikes had been declared illegal. If strikes did

[10] Stefan Olszowski, member of the Politburo of the Polish United Workers' Party, 1970–85 and Central Committee's secretary for ideology and media, August 1980–July 1982; Tadeusz Grabski, Deputy Prime Minister of Poland from August to October 1980; Jósef Klasa, Central Committee's Information and Media Secretary.

occur the leaders were to be arrested and troops were available to break them. He was somewhat nonplussed when one of the managers told him of the Court ruling. Clearly he was acting on the basis of plans drawn up against a different outcome. (He has since been forced by *Solidarność* pressures, to offer his resignation!)

7. The second school adduced an additional piece of evidence about the Pińkowski/Wałęsa meeting on 31 October, which indicates that this meeting was on the point of signing a long *communiqué* listing the points which had been agreed which included the 'compromise' over the transferral of the statute amendments to an annex. One of the advisers to *Solidarność* present at the meeting has indicated privately to visiting Canadian/Polish professor Adam Bromke[11] that Pińkowski was summoned from the room at that moment and later returned (after consulting Kania) to say that only a short *communiqué* would be signed that night. It may be argued that such a compromise was later worked out between the Government and *Solidarność*, but at a later date and in a less formal setting, since the meetings were resumed the following week, albeit without publicity. The first school assume that this additional evidence indicates that a compromise on the statute itself was reached at that point, but that mutual doubts about good faith persisted and led both sides to prepare for the worst outcome, whilst continuing to negotiate during the following week. This left the issue in doubt until the last moment before the Supreme Court judgement and encouraged hard-liners in the Politburo to make a last ditch attempt to prevent the Government and Party taking a further step in retreat and suffering a further humiliation at the hands of the workers.

8. The two theories are not of course incompatible, and it is possible that both versions actually took place, or of course that Moscow intervened with varying instructions. I myself favour the first explanation. The fact remains, however, that to state a position very strongly and then to retreat from it is a demonstration of indecision and/or weakness.

Future prospects

9. If this analysis is correct, what bearing does it have on the four questions listed above? I turn first to the one least affected by the events of last week, the prospects for the market during the winter. Poland's economic situation is parlous. Because of a disastrous summer, the Government cannot hope to supply the needs and aspirations of its people with enough food unless it is prepared to import vast amounts. Whilst to do so would need credit better diverted elsewhere, all the recent pronouncements, both in public and at the Anglo-Polish Joint Commission,[12] indicate that the Government will import food for 'socio-political' reasons in the short term, and in the long term will hope to produce more food at home. In the coming winter the hardship slaughter of animals could marginally help the supply position. Both importing and slaughter will bring very short-term benefit while adding to Poland's long-term troubles. So, the prospects for the market are not optimistic. And there is no reason to suppose that major local difficulties will not occur, given the difficulties of transport in this country, the endemic inefficiency of everything and the possibilities of sporadic strikes. Food riots are possible if not probable.

10. In assessing the prospects for implementation of the outstanding parts of the Gdańsk agreement it is worth making a distinction between those (such as the

[11] A prominent Polish-born political scientist and editor of newsletters on behalf of the Free Europe Committee.

[12] See No. 31, paragraph 8.

housing problem) on which the unions are unlikely to bring early pressure and those which they expect to see implemented quickly. Of these latter, it is possible to pick out two on which there may be confrontation: censorship (especially *Solidarność*'s access to the media and right to publish); new trade union laws. On censorship, a draft bill is soon to be published. But an alternative draft, prepared by the Writers' Union also exists; the two are said to differ sharply. The draft union law, when it appears (and the Government must publish it by 31 December) will reopen at least one major issue (the strike question) which the Supreme Court merely shelved. And as *Solidarność's* statutes are subsumed in Polish law, the Government may use this opportunity to try once again to claw back the lost ground. The last week has surely had one certain consequence: the extremist and militant elements in *Solidarność* have strengthened their position. For they can argue that now that the Government has twice caved in after threatening to make a stand, they can expect to win all future battles. So they face the next confrontation with confidence. The Government, on the other hand, is still very much on the defensive. I doubt if either censorship or the union law will be a rallying-point for them.

11. In assessing the prospects of further change in the Party leadership it is necessary to return to my analysis of the events preceding the Court ruling. If the Government and Party hierarchy did indeed change their minds at the last minute this implies a high degree of confusion, uncertainty and division in their ranks. This time the pragmatists seem to have won yet again. But apart from signs of division the Government and Party are faced with a disturbing tendency in their ranks (led perhaps by Moczar,[13] who is too old to return to power but not too old to settle old scores) to brood on the past rather than plan for the future. They are no nearer to producing a coherent programme in answer to the unions than they were in August. The leadership lacks the political confidence in itself and in its future to name a date for the IXth Party Congress (although the Seventh Plenum is now reported to be planned for later in November). Add to this the continuous and credible rumours of splits in the leadership and it seems fair to assume continued instability at the least, and almost certainly further changes in personnel.

12. Finally, the most important question is whether the Soviet Union will decide to intervene militarily in Poland to stop the rot. I must of course leave Moscow to comment in detail on the thinking of the Soviet leadership. But seen from here the arguments run as follows: there are two sets of circumstances under which Moscow would interfere: if the reforms taking place here caused Poland to cross a line unacceptable to Moscow; or if the Polish Government was no longer able to govern effectively. Given that Moscow has not intervened so far, the uncrossable line has obviously been drawn fairly generously. It may be that the Soviet Government is merely waiting to see whether the present trends are really irreversible. But it seems likely, given the distance the Poles have already travelled in the few short months of their *odnowa* (renewal) that Moscow is unwilling to intervene because of the further burdens this would impose on her at a time when her resources are already extended. However, whilst, in the first case, Moscow is more or less a free agent in deciding whether to intervene, she would have little or

[13] Mieczysław Moczar was a member of the Central Committee of the Polish United Workers Party (1965–81) and of its Politburo (1980–81). In the March 1968 students' protests he led the faction of hardliners inside the Communist Party favouring harsh repression. He was eliminated from power by Gierek, but returned briefly in 1980 as a possible replacement for Kania, before being eased out by General Jaruzelski.

no choice in the second, i.e. if the Polish Government were unable to continue to govern effectively and if she wished to secure her westward lines of communication. Such a situation could arise if, say, martial law were declared in Poland and the Polish army were unable or unwilling to enforce it. I suspect that that very nearly happened last week (though it is most unlikely, of course, that the Polish Government would declare martial law unless it was pretty certain it could enforce it). A more insidious danger is of a gradual political breakdown on the part of the Government—a drift into bloodless anarchy which would leave the country drifting every which way. A decision in Moscow that enough is enough; a breakdown in law and order; or a political collapse: any of these things would produce intervention. Any of a multitude of events—a food riot, another legal dispute, Kania's resignation—could provoke them. Or, at Moscow's will, they could be provoked by turning off the oil or gas taps! Whilst I see the present lull continuing for at least a few weeks and maybe through Christmas, I think the chances of confrontation building up in the New Year are quite high.

13. Of the arguments deployed by those who believe the Soviets are unlikely to intervene, the most compelling at first sight is that the Soviets have long tolerated certain idiosyncrasies in Poland—especially her largely private agriculture and her Church. But on closer examination this argument is not so compelling. No one would want to copy Poland's agriculture and no one can copy her Church. The idiosyncrasies that have emerged of late on the other hand are of the infectious type. Of course the Russians must know that intervention would be resisted and would have to be supported by massive economic aid—which, if they play their cards right, might be obtainable by Poland from the West. These arguments will persuade them to be more cautious, to explore most carefully every other avenue, before intervening. So they will have given Kania more latitude on 30 October than they gave Dubcek. Meanwhile many Poles seem oblivious to the limits within which they should be working. A high proportion of activists seem not to believe in the possibility of intervention; or, if they do, not to care enough about it to modify appreciably their demands.

14. There are two vital factors at this stage. First the extent to which the Government can ensure essential supplies of food, heating and other necessaries of life. If these break down, so will the Government. This of course is relevant to Western aid.

15. Secondly the extent to which Wałęsa and his supporters can control the extremists. Wałęsa himself is not among the Poles referred to in the preceding paragraph. He does see the need for caution. So on the other side does Kania. If these two and their supporters can maintain power in their respective fields, Poland may just pull through. I say nothing of the third power in Poland, the Church, except that I believe that the hierarchy and most priests will, in most circumstances, throw their weight behind the moderates of both other powers.

16. I am sending copies of this despatch to the Secretary of State for Defence, to Her Majesty's Ambassadors at Bucharest, Budapest, Belgrade, East Berlin, Moscow, Prague, Sofia, Bonn, Paris and Washington, and to the UK Permanent Representatives to the North Atlantic Council and the European Communities.[14]

I am, etc,
K. R. C. PRIDHAM

ENCLOSURE IN NO. 36

Chronology of events in Poland: 1 September – 14 November, 1980

Throughout September: A trickle of strikes continues throughout the country.
1 September: Polish goods removed from Pewex[15] in accordance with Gdańsk agreements.
3 September: Agreement signed in Jastrzebie
5 September: Gierek taken ill. Kania becomes First Secretary.
8 September: Kania and Jagielski visit Party activists in Gdańsk.
9 September: Kania, Grudzień and Żabiński visit Party activists in Katowice.
10 September: Mixed committee set up to monitor implementation of strike agreements.
11 September: Jagielski[16] meets Brezhnev in Moscow.
13 September: Council of State decrees that all unions are to be registered in Warsaw *Voivodship* Court.
16 September: Union from Huta Katowice[17] applies for registration at *Voivodship* Court.
17-18 September: Meetings of unionists in Gdańsk to consider registration of new unions.
24 September: *Solidarność* presents registration to Court.
1 October: Jagielski meets *Solidarność* in Gdańsk.
3 October: Warning strike by unions lasting one hour.
8 October: Ministerial changes announced by Pińkowski.
22 October: Kania meets Cardinal Wyszyński.[18]
24 October: *Voivodship* Court registers *Solidarność* with altered statutes. *Solidarność* decides to appeal.
27 October: *Solidarność* Committee holds a meeting in Gdańsk.
30 October: Kania and Pińkowski meet Brezhnev in Moscow.
31 October: Pińkowski holds long meeting with leaders of *Solidarność*.[19]

[14] In a letter of 19 December, Mr Fall believed that the internal situation had relatively improved, with the Gdańsk commemorations of 16 December passing without serious repercussions, but long-term threats and a serious social and economic crisis remained. An annotation by Mr Fergusson testified of the seriousness of the situation: 'Happy Christmas in what I fear will still be rather tense circumstances. I shall be on call if needed throughout the holiday period.' (FCO 28/4165, ENP 212/2).

[15] Short for *Przedsiębiorstwo Eksportu Wewnętrznego - Internal Export Company*, a chain of shops which sold products—otherwise unavailable to the Polish population—in foreign hard currencies.

[16] Mieczysław Jagielski was Deputy Prime Minister of the People's Republic of Poland, 1970-July 1981; member of the Politburo of the Polish United Workers' Party, 1971-81; and of its Central Committee, 1959-July 1981.

[17] Katowice Steelworks situated in Dąbrowa Gónicza, east of Katowice, where the Katowice Agreement was signed. This was the fourth and final agreement between the newly created free trade union and the Communist Government.

[18] Primate of Poland, 1948-81; Cardinal Archbishop of Gniezno and Warsaw, 1953-81.

5 November: Party press announces *Solidarność* decision to appeal.
10 November: *Solidarność* registered by Supreme Court with original statutes plus an annex incorporating an acknowledgement of the leading role of the Party. Strike planned for 12 November called off.
14 November: Kania meets Wałęsa.

[19] Mr Pridham had reported quite optimistically on this twelve-hour meeting, foreseeing a possible compromise acceptable by moderates on both sides. The Government had indicated that the Supreme Court would give their verdict on Solidarity's registration no later than 10 November, Mr Wałęsa still threatening a general strike on 12 November (Warsaw tel. No. 419, 1 November; FCO 28/4163, ENP 212/2). The compromise reached on 10 November, thus avoiding a general strike, 'represents a much more significant climb-down on the Government side than the Union's. The reference to the leading role of the Party was diluted by the inclusion of six points from the ILO charter (Warsaw tel. No. 446, 10 November; FCO 28/4163, ENP 212/2).

No. 37

Minutes by Messrs Fergusson, Mallaby, J. Bullard and Manning on possible Soviet intervention in Poland, 20-26 November 1980

Confidential (FCO 28/4038, EN 021/31)

What attitude should we take to Soviet intervention in Poland?

At yesterday's East/West Heads of Mission Conference[1] it struck me that no-one asked the fundamental question whether there were not circumstances in which Soviet intervention which brought an imposed stability to Poland might not be more in our interest than chaos. Here are some thoughts.

2. The Western interest is not to change the system of government in Eastern Europe but to create conditions in which the Eastern Europeans themselves can slowly create the elasticity of their relationship with the Soviet Union to give them greater freedom of action both at the State and at individual level.

3. This applies as much to Poland as to the others. The immediate risk in Poland is that internal forces will provoke change in such a way as to de-stabilise the system. This is not in the Soviet interest. But it is not in ours either. The West therefore shares an important common interest with the Soviet Union. This leads to the question how we should act (tacitly in alliance with the Soviet Union) in such a way as to reinforce these elements in Poland tending to stability. The immediate answer is, of course, by the provision of economic aid.

4. If, however, Polish stability breaks down in such a way that the Eastern European system could be seriously affected the Soviet Union—despite all the obvious disadvantages—will intervene to re-establish that stability which is, in practice, both in the East's and the West's interest.

5. We do not have the power to prevent the Soviet Union. They know this, so do the Poles (that is why Poles of many different opinions are so cautious).

6. Western sanctions after Soviet intervention in Poland are therefore largely cosmetic. They may impose penalties but we should not in fact want them to be so effective that they achieved their apparent object of Soviet withdrawal if the alternative were chaos. That is why, for instance, the French and the Germans will be reluctant to do more than the minimum required by their own public opinion and by the attitudes of their allies etc.

[1] For a record of the conference see *DBPO: Afghanistan*, No. 80.

7. Threats beforehand might delay Soviet action. It is not certain, however, that delay might not, in some circumstances, lead to a worse situation later, worse in the sense that the trouble would be more widespread, the Soviet intervention on a more massive scale, consequences more disruptive and the risk of spread to other countries greater. With the Soviet Union's first interest that the Poles should settle things themselves, they will not want to intervene unless they deem it necessary and their judgment on timing will be better informed than ours.

8. Nevertheless, Soviet intervention in Poland might justify the withdrawal of certain economic concessions which the West had decided that it had been wrong to concede before (technology, credit, etc). But even if such were called sanctions, they would not be intended as such in practice.

9. At present Western aid to Poland could well merely defer Poland's default, with the consequences for the Western banking/credit system which that would involve. It is also possible nevertheless that the Soviet Union, because of the ramifications elsewhere, would continue to protect Poland, and thereby the West, from the worst consequences of default. It is an interesting question what attitude the Soviet Union would take to Poland's debts to the West if they had intervened militarily? It is possible (I have discussed this with Sir Curtis Keeble) that because they would want to assert the legitimacy of the 'new Polish state' they would accept the obligations, at least partially. How far they would do so might well depend on the intensity of Western response to intervention.

10. Poland does not adjoin NATO. Would the military consequences of tying down 40 divisions in Poland necessarily be to our disadvantage?

11. Finally, our response to an intervention in Poland will of course have to take account of our assessment of the effects on those friends elsewhere (not only friends) whose confidence in the West's willingness to stand up against Soviet activity could be eroded by acquiescence over Soviet intervention in Poland.

12. Having made these points, I should say that I do not over-look the impossibility, granted likely public attitudes, of our not taking a stern declaratory line. But that should not necessarily deter us from Sonnenfeltism in practice.[2]

E. A. J. FERGUSSON
20 NOVEMBER 1980

Poland and the possibility of Soviet intervention

1. With reference to your thought-provoking minute of yesterday, I suppose that the possible future courses of events can be divided into three types:

(*a*) The provisional endures, i.e. the Russians keep on trying non-military tactics for reducing the significance of the independent trades unions for so long that, perhaps because some other event like Brezhnev's death intervenes, the possible time for intervention passes and they miss the bus.

[2] Helmut Sonnenfeldt, an expert on Soviet and European affairs, was a senior advisor to Dr Henry Kissinger during the Nixon and Ford Presidencies and a prime architect of the Nixon era policy of détente. In January 1976 he gave a private talk to American Ambassadors to Eastern and Western Europe in which he said: 'it must be our policy to strive for an evolution that makes the relationship between the Eastern Europeans and the Soviet Union an organic one . . . [O]ur policy must be a policy of responding to the clearly visible aspirations in Eastern Europe for a more autonomous existence within the context of a strong Soviet geopolitical influence' (*New York Times*, 6 April 1976). His remarks, dubbed the 'Sonnenfeldt doctrine,' were characterised by critics as conceding that Eastern Europe naturally fell within the Soviet sphere of influence, a point which Sonnenfeldt denied.

(*b*) The Russians intervene.
(*c*) The situation gets out of hand to the point where European security is endangered.

2. I agree that (*b*) is better for us than (*c*). Apart from preventing the Polish crisis from causing East-West hostilities, it would probably have the by-product, unlike Afghanistan, of increasing cohesion among the Western powers. But I think the fundamental consideration is that the Russians will intervene before things get badly out of hand, in other words that (*c*) above is extremely unlikely. If this is correct, there is little or no disadvantage in warning the Russians publicly and privately against intervention. The effect of such warnings would not be, and would not be designed to be, to make intervention impossible and thus to make (*c*) more likely. It would rather be to make the Russians hesitate for a little longer about intervening, i.e. to make (*a*) more likely. The possible effect of our warnings can only be to make the Russians delay in a situation where public order and the party in Poland have not crumbled. Once either of those things happens, intervention, I suggest is inevitable.

3. The purpose of economic aid to Poland would be to make (*a*) more likely; in other words, to help to prevent an economic crisis in Poland in which the gains of democracy would be more likely to be swept away than if economic disaster is avoided. I agree that in principle it would be useful to act tacitly in parallel with the Russians to reinforce the elements in Poland tending to stability. To take one example, the best thing in many ways would be if it was the Polish regime which won the next confrontation with the workers. That would be the best way of reassuring the Russians and gaining time for the gains of democracy to become established and cause (*a*) to ensue. But it is one thing for the Vatican to urge restraint on the workers and quite another for the West. It is questionable, since everyone knows we cannot intervene militarily whatever happens, whether advice to the workers would influence them. It would no doubt be resented. And Western contacts with the workers' leaders could well be misrepresented by the Russians as having the opposite purpose: to interfere in order to make the Polish crisis worse.

4. So far as I know, the regime and the workers in Poland are content with our public stance of emphatic non-intervention. Both, I imagine, will be even happier if, as I very much hope, we manage to provide some economic help. On the whole I think that a policy based on these two planks, coupled with more warnings to the Russians, is the right course for us. We cannot ensure that (*a*) above will happen but this policy at least does not make it less likely. If (*a*) does happen—and I fear that (*b*) is on balance more likely—it will be very greatly in our interests because of the undermining of the Soviet monolith in Eastern Europe.

5. I suggest that the question of the Soviet attitude, after an intervention, to Poland's debts needs some careful analysis. The entire Soviet record in this field suggests that the Russians care very much about being seen by Western bankers to be utterly reliable. That has also seemed to be the Soviet wish for the other members of the Warsaw Pact. It would cost the Russians a lot to service Poland's debts entirely for two or three highly expensive years and perhaps partially thereafter. But failure to pay would be seen as a vicarious Soviet default on Poland's behalf. That would surely destroy the possibility of the Soviet Union or Poland borrowing from Western banks for a long time. The revelation that the Soviet Union would not in the last resort pay its allies' debts would, moreover, severely prejudice the future borrowing of other members of the Warsaw Pact. Although the Russians are flush with foreign exchange at present, they cannot rely

on being able to do without Western credits in future. My own feeling, like yours, is that the Russians would service Poland's debts. But the experts in Whitehall and the Bank of England might be able to produce additional arguments either way.

C. L. G. MALLABY
21 NOVEMBER 1980

Poland and the possibility of Soviet intervention

1. I have some comments on your minute of 20 November. It raises interesting questions, not all of which I can answer.

2. I think it *is* in the interests of the West that 'socialism' should be seen to fail and to be rejected by those who have tried it. This helps to block the advance of the socialist doctrine in the Third World. A renunciation of it by Cuba would be even better than by Poland.

3. I am doubtful whether the West and the Soviet Union have a real common interest in Polish stability. It would in my opinion be worth accepting a bit of instability in Poland for the sake of progress towards the objective in paragraph 2 above. The instability would in any case be at the expense of Moscow and the Warsaw Pact. Even what you call chaos in Poland could have certain attractions, provided the West keeps its nerve. As you say, tying down large numbers of Soviet divisions in Poland would help NATO. On the other side, the kind of 'stability' which the Soviet Union would impose after a forceable intervention in Poland would not, I think, be any more in the interests of the West than what they have imposed in Czechoslovakia, although in 20 or 30 years it could develop into something much more acceptable, as has happened in Hungary.

4. I do not share your faith in the Soviet ability to judge the best timing for an intervention. In an operation of such gravity there would be factors of many kinds, not all of them rational: you heard what Mr Mackintosh[3] said the other day about the possibility of a 'nationalist' consensus in Moscow for a move against Poland. If it is in the Western interest that the Soviet Union should not intervene, every day is a day gained. It is true that an intervention later could have to be more massive, but here we run into the points which I have already covered.

5. If all we were concerned about was repayment of Poland's debts to the West, we might contemplate a deal with the Soviet Union by which Moscow got a free hand in Poland in return for promising that the debts would be faithfully repaid. Even to state this possibility is to make it clear how unthinkable it is.

6. As you know, I have always seen a good deal in Mr Sonnenfeldt's doctrine provided it is correctly stated. I am going to a lunch in his honour early next month.

J. L. BULLARD
24 NOVEMBER 1980

What attitude should we take to Soviet intervention in Poland?

1. You invited comments on Mr Fergusson's minute of 20 November.

2. I would not accept Mr Fergusson's contention that we have an interest in stability in Eastern Europe which is a shared 'common interest' with the Soviet Union. On the contrary, I would suggest our interests and those of the Russians are sharply divergent: we want to see the most rapid and dynamic political evolution

[3] Malcolm Mackintosh, Soviet adviser at the Cabinet Office.

of Eastern Europe that is compatible with Soviet restraint (a very difficult line to draw); the Soviet Union wants to see as little change to the status quo as possible. The only point where the interests of East and West converge is that neither would wish there to be a political/military upheaval in Eastern Europe (or Western) which would put at risk European stability in a way that threatened an East/West confrontation. (I do not believe this is a probable outcome of the current Polish crisis however it works itself out.)

3. It remains true for the moment that the Soviet Union will not allow any East European country to establish political pluralism, or to leave the Warsaw Pact. But it is just possible that the Polish situation will develop in such a way that the Communist system is incrementally and progressively eroded. To a powerful church and a private agriculture, this year's events have already added free unions, a diluted censorship, a Catholic Deputy Premier (the United Front in reverse?) and stirrings in the Sejm,[4] e.g. real voting and PQs. More is possible e.g. a bridled Secret Police. In other words, if the Poles can avoid sharp confrontations that degenerate to the point where the Russians feel obliged to intervene, Polish Communism may become little more than a façade, and Poland might evolve into something midway between Hungary and Finland.

4. The odds against this may be long (though much shorter than appeared plausible six months ago), but if this did happen it would be an immense improvement for the Poles themselves and a significant gain for the West. Meanwhile, however unsettling the Polish crisis may be for the tempo of East/West relations (already upset by Afghanistan), the longer it continues, and the more concessions the Polish workers can extract from the system, short of provoking Soviet intervention, the better. In the long term the present Polish experience is likely to hasten change elsewhere in Eastern Europe (Mr Fergusson's para 2); while in both the short and longer term, events in Poland provide a welcome diversion of Soviet time, energy and resources. As far as the West is concerned therefore, I think the tension surrounding the Polish events should be seen as creative, in that for the Russians it is disruptive. We want to see the pot continue to bubble but not boil over.

5. I would also disagree with Mr Fergusson's view that a destabilised Poland (i.e. a de-communised Poland) would lead to chaos. This is to underrate the sophistication and political culture of the Poles. If the Communist system disintegrated in Poland, which it would if the threat of the Red Army disappeared, I have little doubt that the Poles would be quite capable of establishing a democracy of a recognisably West European kind, with strong Catholic, Peasant and Socialist parties. It would be a democracy that sought to rejoin the Western mainstream from which the Poles feel they have been unnaturally separated by their barbarian neighbours to the East.

D. G. MANNING
26 NOVEMBER 1980

[4] The lower house of the Polish Parliament.

No. 38

Lord Carrington to Sir N. Henderson (Washington), 29 November 1980, 6.29 p.m.

Tel. No. 1852[1] Immediate, Secret (FCO 28/4040, EN021/31)

From Bullard for Ambassador (or if unavailable Minister)

Poland[2]

1. We have been considering very tentatively whether there is anything more that the West might do either to arrest what appears to be a gradual drift towards crisis point inside Poland, or at least to minimise the international consequences if this point should be reached.[3]

2. At the moment Western policy on Poland appears to consist of not much more than waiting upon events and hoping for the best. We are looking at the Polish request for economic assistance, but we know that it may be a case of throwing good money after bad and we frankly have little idea what effect even massive economic support would have on the political situation. Both public and private warnings against intervention have been conveyed to Moscow, but these do not become more effective with repetition and probably add little to what the Russians have already worked out for themselves. We have a contingency planning check list, but it does not happily fit the case (which seems to me increasingly likely) of a very limited and restrained Soviet intervention in response to a genuine, repeat genuine, request by the Polish leadership and in cooperation with at least part of the Polish security forces.[4] In all this we are in the position of reacting to events, not guiding them.

3. We do not know what may have been said recently between the United States and the Soviet Union, whether by the present administration or privately by Mr Reagan and his team. But one thought which naturally occurs to us, against the background of past events, is that there might perhaps be value at this time in the kind of private exchanges of an exceptionally intimate and confidential character

[1] Repeated to Moscow, Bonn and Paris.

[2] On 9 November the US Secretary of State, Mr Muskie, had written to Lord Carrington stressing that the primary aim of the current situation should be to deter Soviet intervention in Poland. The US had already warned the Soviets of the 'incalculable consequences' for East-West relations of intervention but Muskie believed it essential that this be made unmistakably clear if tensions continued to build. In his reply of 24 November, Lord Carrington wondered if 'press leaks or messages through unofficial channels' could be used to emphasise the extent of the reaction the Soviets could expect (FCO tel. Nos. 1824 and 1825 to Washington, 24 November; FCO 28/4164, ENP 212/2). In a minute to Mr Fergusson of 27 November, Mr Bullard recorded that Lord Carrington had asked for more imaginative thinking to be done over Poland to see whether there was any alternative to the present policy. Mr Walden pointed out that the Americans could not be expected to take a lead as they were between Presidents, so the European allies might have to think up a role for the US to play and sell it to Washington (FCO 28/4165, ENP 212/2).

[3] A draft of this telegram was sent for approval on 28 November to the Prime Minister who was 'very unhappy' about the idea, which she thought could be interpreted as 'the West backing up the Soviets in turn backing up the Polish Government' against the activities of the trade unions (PREM 13/331). The final telegram is more speculative than the draft, inserting phrases like 'very tentatively' into paragraph 1.

[4] Mr Mallaby, in a minute of 2 December, voiced his doubts about this scenario. Any limited intervention by Soviet troops in support of Polish security forces would risk provoking more extreme popular opposition without being strong enough to ensure success. Mr Fall, replying on 4 December, thought the scale of any Soviet military intervention would depend on how much they trusted the loyalty of the Polish army.

with which the 'back channel' is associated. It would of course be essential to avoid doing anything which could give the impression that the superpowers were ganging up against the interests of Poland.

4. Some preliminary thoughts on points which might be included in a message to the Russians are in MIFT.[5] I would stress that we have not yet formed a definitive view on whether anything should be said, and if so what, but we are considering asking the Americans whether they do not agree that an exchange would be appropriate, if it is not happening already. We may also wish to sound out the French and Germans very privately in the margin of the European Council meeting in Luxembourg on 1-2 December.

5. We would therefore be grateful for your comments by immediate telegram, repeated to Luxembourg to arrive there by 1200z on 1 December. Telegrams should be marked DEDIP[6] and Personal for Private Secretary or Bullard. At this stage we are only seeking your general thoughts on whether the West ought to be looking for a more active means of forestalling an intervention in Poland. Please do not limit yourselves to the points in these telegrams: any other ideas would be welcome. It may well be your view that our present attitude is the correct one in the circumstances, and that the UK should leave matters as they stand between the United States and the USSR.[7]

6. You should of course not, repeat not, consult the Government to which you are accredited at this stage.

[5] Not printed. Points included: (*a*) the US and USSR identifying common ground in pursuit of a peaceful outcome; (*b*) the US confirming it was not the West's intention to detach Poland from the Warsaw Pact or CMEA; (*c*) the US making clear any foreign intervention in Poland would provoke a 'world crisis of extreme gravity'; (*d*) the US and USSR issuing complementary statements to ensure their respective attitudes were fully understood; (*e*) the US and USSR collaborating in the interest of Poland, for instance in the economic field; and (*f*) arranging for the 'hot line' to be immediately activated if the situation deteriorated in order that each government had advance notice of the others intentions.

[6] 'To be deciphered by a member of the diplomatic staff'. The marking DEDIP was given to telegrams of exceptional delicacy.

[7] Sir N. Henderson replied, in Washington tel. No. 4738 of 30 November, suggesting that the first step was to establish what messages the US had given to the Soviets over Poland. He went on to point out that the idea of any joint management of the crisis envisaged by the FCO would not be acceptable to the Americans 'if it means condoning the suppression of liberal tendencies in Poland', or to the Russians, if it meant 'allowing the dissolution of the Party's supremacy to continue.' For both the Carter and future Reagan administrations the issue had moved 'beyond words' and they were likely to want to know what commercial and economic sacrifices, affecting the whole realm of détente, the Europeans were willing to make and to what extent they were prepared to make their intentions known to the Soviets in advance.

Sir R. Hibbert, in Paris tel. No. 978 of 30 November, thought it unlikely that the French Government would want to involve itself in encouraging the activation of any US-Soviet back-channel but they might agree to a general definition of what all the Western Powers should try to say to the USSR when the opportunity arose.

Sir O. Wright, in Bonn tel. No. 886 of 1 December, reported that the Germans attached great importance to the US making it abundantly clear that Polish problems were for the Poles to settle without outside interference. They had the greatest interest in preventing a Soviet intervention which would spell the end of *Ostpolitik* and *Deutschlandpolitik* with very real political and practical problems. He thought the course of action proposed was a good one and worth floating as discussion might validate the ideas proposed or spark off different ones. It might even produce a bonus confirmation or denial as to whether the US had activated the 'back channel'.

No. 39

Letter from Mrs Thatcher to President Carter, 8 December 1980

T238/80 Secret (PREM 19/559)

Dear Mr President,

I was on the point of replying to your message of 1 December about Poland when I received your further message of 7 December[1] on the same subject, in which you refer to evidence indicating that the Soviet Union has made the decision to intervene. This goes further than our own judgement, but I have asked our experts to compare notes urgently with yours.[2] It is more than ever important that we should keep in very close touch on these assessments.

As far as messages to the Soviet Union are concerned, we have as you know made our position very clear both nationally and in the statement issued after the meeting of the European Council on 1 and 2 December.[3] Peter Carrington summoned the Soviet Chargé d'Affaires on 3 December to reinforce this message and to seek assurances from the Soviet Government that they would respect their international obligations. The *communiqué* of the Warsaw Pact Summit clearly does not fore-close the option of intervention and we shall bring out in our comments on it the need for the principle of the non-use or threat of force, referred to in the *communiqué*, to be strictly applied in relation to Poland.

The question of giving SACEUR[4] pre-delegated authority to take five specific measures immediately if an invasion takes place has already been discussed in the North Atlantic Council. I understand that the Council today discussed the possibility of giving SACEUR discretion to take these measures when he considers necessary, even in advance of an invasion. I am instructing the United Kingdom Representative on the Council to approve this latest proposal on the understanding that at this stage only covert action is involved.

Yours sincerely,

MICHAEL ALEXANDER[5]

[for Mrs Thatcher]

[1] In his first message President Carter had expressed his increasing concern about the possibility of intervention in Poland by Warsaw Pact forces. In the second he stated his belief that preparations for Soviet intervention in Poland were largely complete and urged Western nations to take whatever steps they could to affect Soviet decision-making (FCO 28/4041, EN 21/31).

[2] A meeting of Warsaw Pact countries was held in Moscow on 5 December and the conclusion drawn by Sir C. Keeble, in Moscow tel. No. 772 of 6 December, was that the Soviet Union had decided, for now, to try to resolve the Polish problem by exerting maximum political pressure rather than by military intervention and hoped to limit the damage to its relations with the West (FCO 28/4063, EN 062/1).

[3] The communiqué issued by the European Council after the Luxembourg Summit reminded those States signatory to the Helsinki Final Act that they had agreed to recognise the right of all people to pursue their own political, economic, social and cultural developments as they saw fit and without external interference. It called upon signatory States to abide by these principles with regard to Poland and warned that any other attitude 'would have very serious consequences for the future of international relations in Europe and throughout the world' (www.consilium.europa.eu).

[4] Supreme Allied Commander Europe.

[5] The Prime Minister's Private Secretary for Overseas Affairs.

No. 40

Letter from Sir C. Keeble (Moscow) to Mr Fall, 8 December 1980
Restricted (FCO 28/4039, EN 021/31)

Dear Brian,

1. There is little enough opportunity to learn what happens when leaders of the Socialist countries visit Moscow, so I pass on to you without comment the following story told me by the Tunisian Ambassador. He said that a Soviet official whom he knew well, who worked in one of the Institutes and who, in that well worn phrase, was 'close to the Central Committee' had told him that when Gierek had come to Moscow, Brezhnev had told him that the Polish army must be used to bring the situation under control. Gierek had one of his Generals with him and when this was put to him the General said the army could (or would) not do it. The Ambassador's friend had ended the tale by telling the story of the three Soviet tank drivers who met: 'Bloody awful business this in Afghanistan' said the first, 'Ah, you should have been in Czechoslovakia—the girls there were quite something' said the second, 'Watch it, or I won't take you with me to Poland' said the third.

I don't know what to think of the first part of the story, but the second part at least illustrates the current sense of humour among Soviet officialdom.

Yours ever,
CURTIS

No. 41

Record of a conversation between the Prime Minister and the Deputy Prime Minister of Poland, Mr Henryk Kisiel, at 10 Downing Street, 9 December 1980, 12.30 p.m.
Confidential (PREM 19/559)

Present: Prime Minister	H.E. Mr Bisztyga
Mr M.O'D.B. Alexander	Mr Kisiel
	Mr Kucharski

The Situation in Poland

After an exchange of courtesies, during which Mr Kisiel conveyed to the Prime Minister his own Prime Minister's warmest regards, *Mr Kisiel* said that Poland was living through difficult times. He himself had been a member of the Polish Government for a long time and had been aware for a considerable period that the situation in the country was bad politically as well as economically. The previous leadership had ignored the development of a new spirit among the workers. Last summer's rebellion had been carried out by a new generation whose mentality was quite different from their predecessors. They believed that they owned the means of production and they wanted a say in how they were to be used. The technocratic and bureaucratic methods of the past would work no longer. The new generation could not simply be told what to do.

Unfortunately no serious effort had been made to prepare the ground for the take-over of power by this new generation. It was not the first time that a Polish Government had been faced with a crisis from which they had to draw conclusions.

The methods used in 1956 and 1970 could not be used again. They had been too painful. Too much blood had been spilled. This time the problem had to be solved by argument and persuasion. Authoritarianism was out. Democratisation was not a gesture it was the right of the people. The discussions in August had led to the conclusion that this was the only path. The previous leadership had been too conscious of their own past experience and had therefore had to be changed. Of the fifteen members of the Politburo in August, only four now remained. This was the first step towards a restoration of trust between the Government and the population. Without that trust nothing could be done.

The workers, for their part, had set up Solidarity. It was not easy for the Government to find a way from their former methods to new methods in which the workers would have confidence. Hence the various changes of course in recent months. But for the moment the situation, though tense, was characterised by stability, quietness and a 'tendency to order'. There was also considerable anxiety about possible unpleasant developments. The population were tired and worried about 'what might happen tomorrow'. Some of those involved in recent developments had unrealistic hopes. These could, if not controlled, lead to unpleasant confrontations. The Government were very patient. They had enough patience to calm down the hotheads of the younger generation. It was not excluded that there were some forces who might not have a positive attitude to recent changes. There were some 'cold political players' who did not realise the dangers to which their activities could lead. They were steering young people into dangerous situations. They could not be treated as 'good Poles'.

It was to try to contain this situation that more and more open discussions were taking place between the Government and Solidarity. The hope was to create confidence that the Government would not try to revert to the previous situation. The fact was that there was no way back for the Government. They had burnt the bridges joining them to the past. Admitting this frankly had made it easier for the two sides to get on. In Walesa's words: 'a Pole with a Pole will always find a solution'. Failure to do so in this instance would lead to grave dangers for the future of the country.

The Polish Government were aware of Poland's special place in Europe. Their friends to the East and to the West wished Poland well but were uneasy about the future. The Polish Government understood this. But they needed a little more time and patience from their friends. They had to have time for the new way to be developed. They had to give proper weight to the role and influence of the church. They had to give room for a new generation who wished to create their own future.

The *Prime Minister* said that, as someone looking at the situation from the outside, she was conscious of having witnessed a change of a kind that had not occurred in a socialist state in the last 60 years. This was not a case of the traditional replacement of the old generation by the new within the same system. A new group of people were asking for power on their own terms. They wanted to exercise it independently of the Government. New centres of power and influence were being formed. The task of the Government was to be to regulate democratically other centres of power. This, for a Communist Government, was, of course, an absolutely fundamental change. The new situation imposed tremendous responsibilities both on the Government and on the emerging centre of power. The price of power was responsibility. It would require time for the new leaders to acquire the wisdom to exercise their power properly.

The Prime Minister said that the present developments were very exciting for someone who believed, as she did, in liberty. The socialist system had succeeded in suppressing the human spirit for a surprisingly long time. But she had always been confident that eventually there would be a break through. Of course others were aware of the significance of what was happening and were wondering whether they could allow it to go on. Afghanistan had at least served to alert the rest of the world to the willingness of the Soviet Union to impose a system on people who did not wish it. The British people were watching events with close attention and great goodwill. Their interest in Poland was qualitatively different from their interest in other countries. There was a large Polish minority here and we had, after all, gone to war over Poland in 1939. Everyone here knew what was at stake.

Mr Kisiel said that he agreed with the Prime Minister's analysis of the situation in Poland. The fundamental desire was the desire to govern one's own future. The greatest fault of leadership in Poland in recent years had been to concentrate on centralising rather than de-centralising authority. The leadership had lost its feel for the wishes of the Polish people.

The *Prime Minister* said that she wished the Poles well and hoped they would find a way through the present crisis. If they did so, the whole world would benefit. Western governments, strongly though they felt, had been careful to be restrained in their reaction. But they were also being vigilant. *Mr Kisiel* said that the Polish Government had been conscious of the wisdom and patience of Western governments. They knew that the West wished them well.

As regards the attitudes of the Soviet Government, Mr Kisiel said he thought there had been a development in recent months. When he had visited Moscow in September he had thought that there was not a full understanding. But he believed that Soviet visitors to Poland such as Mr Baibakov,[1] whom he had himself entertained, had learnt a lot. So had President Brezhnev from his discussions with Mr Kania. The Polish leadership had returned from their visit to Moscow last week in a more relaxed frame of mind. *The Prime Minister* urged Mr Kisiel not to relax and to remember Czechoslovakia. *Mr Kiesel* said that the Polish Government was indeed alert. He exampled the speed with which they had rebutted the *Tass communiqué* the previous day. The Poles felt that they were a little different from the other Eastern European states and had the right to create their own path to socialism. He hoped that when Mr Brezhnev returned from Delhi, it would be possible to make further progress towards resolving the outstanding problems.

At the end of the discussion, *The Prime Minister* said that she hoped Mr Kiesel would feel free to come to see her whenever he was in London. The discussion ended at 13.10.

[1] Nicolai Baibakov, Chairman of the State Planning Committee, 1965-85.

No. 42

Minute from Lord Carrington to Mrs Thatcher, 16 December 1980

PM/80/85 Secret (PREM 19/559)

Prime Minister,

Poland: Contingency Planning

1. The meeting of NATO Foreign Ministers in Brussels last week was dominated by the question of Poland. There was a very strong feeling, reflected in the *communiqué*, that a Soviet military intervention would be a development of the utmost gravity, striking at the root of détente and creating an entirely new situation in East/West and international relations.[1]

2. It was recognised that, although there was little more that we could do to deter an intervention, the early provision of aid to Poland would make it less likely that economic difficulties this winter would provoke a breakdown of law and order and thus a pretext for intervention.[2] The point is an important one. Food aid from the Community will help to meet it, but I am concerned that the Paris meeting of Western creditors is taking too leisurely an approach to the urgent problems in the short term. We should aim to make it clear to the Poles at the meetings on 22 and 23 December[3] that, although what we may be able to do to help the Poles in the longer term will require careful consideration, we are prepared to offer them some new credit and refinancing to tide them over the next six months. The sooner we are able to give them figures on this, the better.[4]

3. Discussions in Brussels then turned to what action Western countries should take in response to an intervention. Permanent Representatives in Brussels were instructed to keep the situation under close review and to work out proposals for the kind of response which, it was agreed, the West would need to make.

4. In subsequent discussions with our closest allies, officials have worked out a catalogue of the economic measures which could be considered by Governments in the event of outright Soviet invasion of Poland, recognising that they would of course need to be accompanied by a full range of political measures; that actual decisions would be reserved to Governments to take at the time; and that a Soviet intervention in a form falling short of outright invasion would call for a proportionately lesser response. I enclose a copy of the catalogue.[5] The seven

[1] The North Atlantic Council met in Brussels on 11 and 12 December.

[2] Mr Pridham in Warsaw reported that the economy was in a very bad way. In a dispatch of 11 December entitled 'The Polish Economy: Why has it gone so seriously wrong; and can it recover?' he blamed an inefficient agricultural sector, ill-judged investment policies in the 1970s, an unrealistic pricing system, excessive external indebtedness, bad luck and the dead hand of a cumbersome socialist system for bringing the country to its knees. He rated Poland's chances of staging an economic recovery at 'rather less than 50:50'. In a reply, of 23 December, Mr Fall noted that the Bank of England and the Treasury were likely to draw more pessimistic conclusions than 50:50. The Bank in particular had fought hard against economic assistance to Poland on the grounds that it would be throwing good money after bad (FCO 28/4159, ENP 090/1).

[3] A meeting of Western creditors scheduled to take place in Paris.

[4] At a meeting of OD on 10 December Ministers had agreed to seek with fellow creditors at Paris an assistance package for Poland covering the first half of 1981, which would include both debt relief through refinancing and also new credit. If possible, the package would only commit the UK to two-thirds of what (on a pro rata basis) the Poles had asked for under those two headings; but the remaining third would be provided if this was necessary to keep in line with her main partners (OD(80) 26th meeting, CAB 148/183).

[5] Not printed.

headings in it constitute a text we have agreed with our closest partners as a basis for further discussion. The sub-headings are items which we and they have agreed informally to study in capitals.

5. I think we now need to reach an agreed inter–Departmental view on the various items in this catalogue in preparation for the next round of discussions both in the same small group of close allies and in the Nine/Ten and NATO. (Other institutions, such as OECD and COCOM, would need to be brought into the process once the Allies had agreed to take action.) If you agree, I suggest that the Cabinet Office should arrange the necessary coordination.

6. The situation in Poland is such that Soviet intervention might occur at any time and with very little warning. I am therefore obliged to ask that this exercise be got under way and completed as soon as possible.

7. I am copying this minute to the members of OD and to Sir Robert Armstrong and to the Departments of Energy and Industry.[6]

[6] The Prime Minister noted her agreement to the Cabinet Office coordinating an agreed interdepartmental view as soon as possible. In a letter of 17 December, the Chancellor picked up on points in paragraph 2, and expressed a reluctance to give figures to the Poles and instead recommended giving only 'generalised statements of intent'. He did not want to get out in front of other countries. Sir R. Armstrong, in a minute of 18 December to the Prime Minister, thought confusion stemmed from the fact that OD, in their meeting on 10 December, only decided on a line to take with fellow creditors and not what should be said to the Poles. The Chancellor was under pressure from the Bank of England not to be too generous to the Poles and the Governor was under pressure from British banks, who had unsecured loans to the Poles as well as Government-guaranteed loans.

No. 43

Minute from Mr Mallaby (Planning Staff) to Mr Fall, 22 December 1980
Confidential (FCO 28/4039, EN 021/31)

Eastern Europe

1. I attach a lively minute by Gloria Franklin[1] on some of the wider questions about Eastern Europe which the Polish crisis provokes. The minute points clearly towards the conclusion that a major East/West crisis is rather unlikely to be caused by developments in Eastern Europe. But there are other interesting questions, e.g.:

(*a*) Are the economic crisis and the loss of production in Poland causing, or likely to cause, severe problems in Eastern Europe?

(*b*) Can the GDR survive indefinitely in its present form if the gains of democracy endure (by a miracle) in Poland?

(*c*) What are the prospects that other Eastern European countries will change radically, for instance by contagion from Poland? Is Hungary really less prone to this because of its greater prosperity and relatively relaxed atmosphere? Is Ceausescu's dictatorship in Romania more brittle because of its very inflexibility? Are we right in assuming that Bulgaria and Czechoslovakia are steady for now?

(*d*) Will relationships among the Warsaw Pact countries change in nature?

2. I suggest that a short paper on this subject is needed. You and others will wish to suggest further questions.

[1] Planning Staff.

3. On question (*a*) above, one could spend ages comparing the various five-year plans in order to calculate the effects on Eastern Europe and the USSR of the loss of coal and other Polish supplies and manufactures. But perhaps a not too elaborate estimate can be made relatively easily by taking Poland's main exports and calculating the proportion of total supplies that each product represents for each of the other East European countries. It may also be possible to estimate the effect of stoppages in Polish ports and less than full use of road and rail transportation across Poland.

4. Question (*b*) above is military, political and psychological, as well as economic. I should have thought that Honecker would feel extremely uneasy if his lines of communication across Poland remained at risk because [of] the altered political situation. He would also be very worried that the GDR, sandwiched between a liberalised Poland and the West, would be bound one day to move away from dictatorship. He might therefore resort to greater internal repression and a go-slow in relations with the Federal Republic. He might even want more Soviet troops, to enable him to sleep at night.

5. The questions at (*c*) and (*d*) above should each be considered on the separate hypotheses of Soviet intervention in Poland and of something like the present situation continuing. Question (*d*) can be answered simply, by saying that changes within an Eastern European country create tensions with the USSR and the other Warsaw Pact countries. That preoccupies the Russians and tends to weaken them. But the changes in relationships will be more complex than this. The obvious example is that the GDR's need for Soviet protection is redoubled by trouble in Poland. As for the Warsaw Pact itself, it is, in organisational terms, an institutionalisation of Soviet hegemony rather than a forum for joint decision making. So it might not need to adapt greatly in the face of greater diversity among its members. CMEA may be another matter. It is genuinely multilateral. The answer to question (*a*) will help to answer the one about the effects on CMEA.

6. When we have made progress on these and similar questions we should consider the most interesting one: what Western policies will best serve our interest in promoting peaceful change in Eastern Europe? Another, subsequent paper might consider whether the Soviet Union, given *all* its problems, has passed its zenith before ever becoming fully established as a super-power; whether it will become more nationalistic in foreign policy; and whether the prospect is a slow decline, a cataclysm or a renaissance.

7. I suggest that we proceed as follows:

(*a*) Minutes from departments commenting on this one. EESD's could perhaps attach copies of useful and relevant letters from posts. I hope that RD's[2] could make a stab at question (*a*).

(*b*) A letter from Planning Staff to posts, pulling together the material from the minutes and seeking comments.

C. L. G. MALLABY

[2] Research Department.

ENCLOSURE IN NO. 43

Crisis in Eastern Europe[3]

1. You asked me to think about the implications for the West if a Polish crisis turned into a wider East European crisis, in the sense of countries like the GDR or Romania becoming 'infected'. The following are a few quick, not particularly novel, thoughts.

2. I have not attempted to assess seriously the likelihood of the Polish situation's leading to major instability in the rest of Eastern Europe, since I presume this is already being done by people with greater knowledge than mine. But I am rather doubtful about the likelihood of serious disturbances, at least in the short term (see Annex).[4]

3. If we start from the assumption that such disturbances *are* possible the main question that concerns us is: would they spill over into the West? There are two obvious dangers:

(*a*) Defections from East to West, perhaps on a large-scale; and

(*b*) In the other direction, East European *émigrés* or sympathisers in the West trying to smuggle in literature, arms and even themselves.

4. Possibility (*a*) opens the greatest risk of actual fighting between East and West, because of the chances of hot pursuit (particularly if the defectors were military). If, for example, Warsaw Pact fighters were to attack fleeing Polish aircraft in NATO airspace, SACEUR's Rules of Engagement (as you know) allow for them to be fired upon. Large-scale outbreaks across the East German border or in Berlin could also result in shooting. And the possibilities in the Baltic are endless.

5. Possibility (*b*) could lead to plenty of protests by the Soviet Union, but is unlikely in my mind to lead directly to a situation in which shooting breaks out between East and West.

6. Faced with the prospect of public disorder in two or more countries of Eastern Europe, how would the Russians behave? Two possibilities can, I think, immediately be ruled out:

(*a*) They would 'press the button'; and

(*b*) They would launch a conventional attack on Western Europe.

7. It is sometimes suggested, vaguely, that in order to deflect attention from its internal problems, the Soviet Union would embark on some kind of adventurism abroad (i.e. in Western Europe). Although I find it hard to believe that they would go directly for options (*a*) or (*b*) above in *any* circumstances, it seems to me even more unlikely that they would undertake them in a period of crisis in Eastern Europe. Despite scare-talk about 'windows of opportunity' the Russians know that (even in the next few years) an attempted first strike on the West would invite massive retaliation, if not from ICBMs, then from SLBMs. One has to presume a complete lunatic in charge to make this a credible scenario. History doesn't help: after all, Hitler launched his attacks only when he had clear superiority, and before the Bomb had been invented. He took the pill only when Germany had already been reduced to rubble and all hope had gone. Even the Caligula proposition does not hold water; for Caligula, besides being mad, was also a coward.

[3] Minute of 18 December 1980 from Miss Franklin to Mr Mallaby.
[4] Not printed.

8. A conventional attack on Western Europe must similarly be ruled out as suicidal, not only because of the retaliation from the West, but because Eastern European and even Soviet troops themselves might not be counted on. This would apply particularly if they had just seen their own people, or the peoples of other East European countries, put down by Warsaw pact (or Soviet) forces.

9. A third possibility which I suppose should not be ruled out, though I also think it unlikely if they were tied up elsewhere, is that the Russians would try to grab another country on their borders, both to divert attention and to make up for other losses. Yugoslavia is an obvious possibility. Iran and Pakistan rather less so. Or Yugoslavia could be indirectly involved if troubles in or with Romania made the Russians invade her.

10. With the establishment of the RDF the Americans are indicating that Iran (and much less certainly Pakistan) would be a *casus belli*. But the West's interest in Yugoslavia is more ambiguous. *Would* we go to war over 'faraway'[5] Yugoslavia if the Russians attacked?

11. This leaves the possibility that localised problems, such as those mentioned in para. 4, might break out into more general war, as it were by accident. Call me an incurable optimist, but I doubt this. For both sides would be doing their utmost to ensure that such problems *remained* localised, since it would be in neither's interest to escalate. The moral for us, however, is that we should take steps to ensure that if we do fire on Warsaw Pact forces, they understand fully the reasons for, and limits, to our actions.

12. In the longer term I foresee (indeed, look forward to) the 'infection' spreading. This will happen more quickly if Poland gets away with its experiment in peaceful evolution. But it will happen anyway eventually. Events like Czechoslovakia and (if it happens) Poland, are set-backs; but they can only hold up the process, not prevent it. Our aim should remain to encourage the East Europeans to move slowly and quietly, and preferably in harness with one another. The quickest way out for them is for the Russians to be beleaguered on so many fronts that they simply give up and go home. That I believe will happen soon, but they will go with a whimper rather than a bang.

[5] A reference to Prime Minister Neville Chamberlain's remark, made in a radio broadcast on 27 September 1938, on the possibility of war over Czechoslovakia: 'How horrible, fantastic, incredible it is, that we should be digging trenches and trying on gas-masks here, because of a quarrel in a faraway country between people of whom we know nothing.'

No. 44

Lord Carrington to HM Representatives Overseas, 23 December 1980, 4 p.m.

Guidance Tel. No. 134[1] Priority, Confidential (FCO 28/4165, ENP 212/2)

Poland

1. The following is primarily for your own information, but you have discretion to draw on it as appropriate in discussion with official contacts.

[1] This telegram was sent to all posts in Central and Eastern Europe and major posts.

Current position

2. Soviet forces are at a high state of readiness in Central Europe, and in the Western USSR, and could move into Poland quickly and with very little warning. The Russians clearly recognise that an invasion would bring many costs, and will use that option only as a last resort. Meanwhile, they may hope that the implied threat of intervention will strengthen the hand of those in Poland who are working to reassert the authority of the Party.

Poland political

3. The situation in the last few weeks has been characterised by an uneasy calm with Solidarity's leader, Walesa, the Church and the Polish Government all appealing for calm and order, and a return to work. These appeals appear to have been heeded and Poland is currently free from serious strike action. The ceremonies in the northern ports of Gdansk and Gdynia, on 16 and 17 December, in memory of those workers killed by the security forces during the 1970 troubles, passed off peacefully, with the stress on the need for national reconciliation rather than recrimination.

4. However the situation is precarious and there are many issues which could easily provoke renewed confrontation between workers and the Government in the weeks ahead, e.g. arrest of workers/dissidents, food shortages, forthcoming legislation on censorship and on trades unions, and the review at the end of the year of some aspects of the Gdansk agreement, signed in August between Solidarity and the Government.

Poland economic

5. Poland's economic difficulties are acute. Polish indebtedness to the West is in the order of 24,000 million dollars, food and fuel are in short supply (limited food rationing is being introduced) and the strikes seriously disrupted production and the overall level of economic activity. The Poles have approached East and West for help. The Russians are reportedly providing a hard currency credit of over 1 billion pounds, while both the US and the EC are providing food on special terms. It is likely that further Western aid will be forthcoming, at least to help the Poles with their debt service burden over the next few months while more detailed consideration is given to the problems of the longer term. We shall be prepared to play our part in such interim measures in conjunction with other major western creditors of Poland.

Warsaw Pact (WP) reaction

6. Soviet leaders have for the most part avoided commenting publicly on Polish events but have signalled their concern by replaying in the Soviet press some of the hard-line articles that have appeared in the Czechoslovak and East German Party papers. The GDR and Czechoslovakia have displayed the greatest nervousness at Polish developments with the Romanians (privately) also showing signs of acute concern.

7. A disturbing element in some Soviet and other Warsaw Pact commentaries is the attempt to blame the West for fostering difficulties in Poland. This, together with emphasis on Poland remaining part of the socialist community, must be seen either as a threat of intervention or as a step towards providing justification for one should 'fraternal assistance' be thought necessary. At a more authoritative level, the WP Summit in Moscow on 5 December[2] will have brought home to the Polish leadership the depth of concern felt by the other WP leaders. Poland is on

[2] See *DBPO*: *Afghanistan*, No. 90, paragraph 6.

probation, and the Polish leadership under Kania may have been given a last chance to reassert the authority of the Party.

Western reaction

8. Western reaction has been to insist that the crisis is a matter for the Poles alone to resolve and that there should be no interference from any quarter. Western Governments have been scrupulous in avoiding interference. They have, however, done what they can by way of public and private warnings to make a Soviet intervention less likely. The menacing Soviet military preparations detected in November led the European Council on 2 December[3] and the NATO Summit on 12 December to issue strong warnings that the invasion of Poland would have 'very serious consequences for the future of international relations in Europe and throughout the world' (EC) and that detente 'could not survive if the Soviet Union were again to violate the basic rights of any state to territorial integrity and independence' (NATO).

9. The main Western concern remains to make a Soviet intervention less likely. Warnings, and a strict policy of non-interference on our part, contribute to this end. Economic assistance in response to requests from the Polish authorities will also contribute, as the possibility of food shortages over the winter is one of the factors which might lead to a breakdown of authority in Poland and thus provide a pretext for Soviet intervention. Western countries are also, however, considering what they would do if an intervention took place, and consideration is being given on a highly confidential basis within NATO to the political and economic measures which would be appropriate.

UK reaction

10. Our reaction has been in line with paragraphs 8 and 9 above. We are playing our full part in the work in NATO and we have also issued public and private warnings to the Russians of the consequences of an invasion.

Prospects

11. It is very difficult to predict developments. The Russians will be weighing not only the costs of intervening but the costs, as they see them, of not doing so in circumstances where they may fear that the situation is slipping out of control. Among the factors they will be considering are:

(*a*) Political developments in Poland, including the cohesion of the Polish Party, the future actions and attitudes of the new unions, and the prospects for the Polish economy.

(*b*) The effect of Polish events on the rest of Eastern Europe (both the risk of political infection if the Polish Party is unable to keep events under control, and the economic costs to CMEA partners of a breakdown of the Polish economy).

(*c*) The cost in terms of their economic and political relations with the West if they do invade, including the loss of the trade, credits and arms control agreements they see as the benefits of detente.

(*d*) The effect on world opinion, and on their relations with a new US president, of yet another Soviet invasion.

Poland is crucial to the Russians' perceptions of their security interests. While invasion may be the measure of last resort they will use it if they judge the situation has become intolerable. But it is unclear just when they would reach such a judgement, and it may still be so to the Russians themselves. Intervention is not inevitable (and it is important that the West should not give the impression that

[3] See No. 39, note 4.

they regard it as such), but the danger remains and may do so for some time. The period over the winter and up to the Polish Party Congress (expected to meet in extraordinary session in March/April) will be particularly difficult.[4]

[4] Mr Pridham, in his Annual Review for 1980 dated 1 January 1981, agreed that the situation at this point was dominated by the Soviet Union convening the Warsaw Pact Summit on 5 December and concentrating forces around Poland, which brought home the reality of the Soviet threat. Observing the continuing instability and at the same time a sobering up of the population, he forecast better political than economic prospects. He assessed that moderates in the three main institutions—the Party, the Unions and the Church—would have to control the 'extremists and obstructionists' in their ranks (FCO 28/4493, ENP 14/2).

No. 45

Minute from Mr Fall to Mr Mallaby, 7 January 1981

Confidential (FCO 49/970, RS 021/10)

Eastern Europe

1. I minuted on 23 December about the work in hand on question (*a*) in your minute of 22 December.[1] You will have seen Mr Vereker's minute of 2 January on question (*b*).[2] We shall be letting you have separately some copies of letters from posts. The following are some thoughts on questions (*c*) and (*d*).

Hypotheses

2. You suggest that we should look at two hypotheses: Soviet intervention, and 'something like the present situation continuing'. I agree that we should avoid a confusing multiplicity of scenarios, but I think that we shall need a slightly more complex structure to take into account the appalling economic problems which Poland now faces. As I see it there are two scenarios which would offer Poland the prospect of stability for a period of years. They could be called in shorthand the Czechoslovak and the reformed.

(i) The *Czech scenario* would involve a successful clamp down on Polish dissidents and on the unions on a scale which would almost certainly involve Soviet military intervention followed by continuing close supervision. There would be no prospect of Western economic assistance in such circumstances; the Polish economy would be run—for better or worse—on Soviet lines; and future Western economic dealings with Poland would depend essentially on decisions taken in Moscow: whether or not to lend the Poles the money to service their debts to the West, and how large an extra-CMEA trade sector to allow.

(ii) The *reformed scenario* assumes that the Poles achieve a political consensus which allows them to tackle their economic problems in a way which attracts continuing Western support. The path to economic recovery will be a long one; and success will require substantial innovation in the political and economic fields (including aspects of the relationship between a Warsaw Pact country and the West).

3. The idea of 'something like the present system continuing' falls between these two stools. If one looks at the political situation alone, it is conceivable that

[1] No. 43.
[2] Not printed.

Poland might muddle along like that for some time. But the Russians won't like it, and the pressures to do something about the economy will I think be too strong: I do not see how the West can agree in the longer term to lend money to Poland without requiring—as it would from any other debtor—evidence of policies leading to economic recovery; and the CMEA countries have their own reasons for wanting this (your question (*a*)). Somebody will have to take a grip. Meanwhile, we might call a continuation of the present situation the *marking time* scenario.

4. There is another position between the stools which may be worth considering: that of an unsuccessful clampdown. One might envisage a Soviet military intervention which provoked active resistance by the Poles (including at least some units of the Polish forces) in the short term, followed by a longer campaign of passive resistance and/or continuing acts of sabotage. The result, at least in the short to medium term, would not be a Czech solution, but something more like the war-time occupation of a hostile country. This might be called, for want of a better title, the *Afghan scenario*.

Implications for Eastern Europe

5. These four scenarios are I think sufficiently distinct for it to be worth looking separately at the implications for Eastern Europe. Perceptions may vary from country to country; and, while not all such differences will be equally important it will be interesting to see what posts come up with. We could perhaps have a word about whether we should ask them to give substantive answers to questions or to comment on a rough draft of a paper. If we decide on the latter, the following may be helpful.

6. *Marking time scenario*. Such risk of infection as there is in the present situation does not derive from any particular attractiveness of the carrier. Poland is virtually bankrupt; it faces a winter of food and fuel shortages; and it may be invaded by the Russians and subjected to the rigours of fraternal assistance. If there is a consensus between rulers and ruled in Eastern Europe, it must surely rest on the proposition that these are things which all should work together to avoid.

7. The reason that East Europeans are worried about the marking time scenario (leaving aside the economic problems covered by question (*a*)) is that they recognise it to be unstable and likely to be succeeded by one of the others. Conservatives, who don't like uncertainty anyway, may feel that things have already been allowed to go too far; that the boundaries of the permissible have been dangerously extended; and that the reform or Afghan scenarios seem increasingly more likely than a Czech solution. Liberals may agree, though for different reasons, that the stakes have grown dangerously high. The people in between—proletarian nationalists—do not like proletarian internationalism, either from the aid-giving or from the aid-receiving point of view.

8. *Czech scenario*. There are precedents (I have begged the question), and I think that precedent would be followed. With individual differences which posts will analyse, I would expect the reaction to be:

(i) Comrade Reactionary and his faction are not very clever (and they certainly have no idea about how to run our economy in the present difficult circumstances), but they have powerful friends;

(ii) this does not mean that we must conform in every way to the Soviet model—it is remarkable how far the Poles were allowed to go before the clamp-down—but we cannot ignore what has happened;

(iii) Comrade Smooth's recommendation that we react by '*reculer pour mieux sauter*' is superficially attractive but misguided: jumping is always dangerous in

Eastern Europe, and both the retreat and a subsequent controlled advance could prove difficult to operate;

(iv) the better course is to try to maintain the ground we have won over the years, with a minimum of public display where our practice differs from that of the Soviet Union and with much demonstration of loyalty where it does not: our more sophisticated Western interlocutors will understand.

In short, the East Europeans will expect another spring; and they will be unpleasantly surprised if the winter proves very much harder or very much longer than last time.

9. The *reform scenario*. This is where the real risk of infection resides. If there is no intervention, and if Poland recovers economically with some Western and some Eastern help while maintaining the national consensus which carried her through the Gdansk anniversary, there will be an important new feature on the political landscape of Eastern Europe. The room for manoeuvre open to individual countries and to groups within them will be seen to have been enlarged. Some in Eastern Europe, and perhaps also in the Soviet Union, will see this as a tide and swim with it. Others, in the Soviet Union and perhaps also in Eastern Europe, may look for an opportunity to effect a dramatic reversal, either in Poland or by clamping down hard on the beginnings of a reform movement elsewhere.

10. In practice, both tendencies may co-exist for a while; and Eastern Europe will be less predictable and less stable as a result. New circumstances may produce new options. The prospects for radical change in Eastern Europe are at their greatest under this scenario, and the implications for the inner-German relationship will be of particular concern.

11. The *Afghan scenario* may be fairly generally recognised as the nightmare. The conservatives won't like it, because it will expose the limits to their power and encourage challenge to do it elsewhere. The liberals won't like it, because of the conservative reaction which it is bound to provoke. The effect would be quantitatively different to the Czech scenario, in that the winter would be both colder and longer than expected. The longer the Polish resistance were sustained, the greater the probability of qualitative change in the relations between individual East European countries and Poland, with implications for the relationship between the Soviet Union and Eastern Europe. An East European policy of waiting for the thaw to revert to détente as usual would be difficult to maintain; and the West for its part would have few obvious and no very attractive policy options. The West Germans in particular would face an acute dilemma over the maintenance of the inner-German relationship, and some might argue for a German way out of an overall East/West stalemate.

12. I do not think it probable that an Afghan scenario would persist for long enough to produce results very different from the Czech, but the possibility cannot be excluded. It may in particular be sufficient to encourage a 't'were better t'were done quickly' attitude on the part of some in Eastern Europe who would not naturally be counted as proponents of intervention.

Western policies and Soviet problems

13. I agree that these are subjects for a subsequent stage. In particular, I am not sure how much advantage there would be in taking a fresh look at the question of what the West can do to promote peaceful change in Eastern Europe until we know whether the changes which have taken and are taking place in Poland are likely to be peacefully consolidated. The answer to that question will also be relevant to an

assessment of developments in Soviet foreign policy over the next few years, as it is likely to be a major determinant of the East/West relationship in that period.

14. The changes which have taken place in Poland can obviously not be attributed solely to Western policy, nor even to 'détente' seen as a policy which has been conducted by East and West over the last decade. But, as a policy for promoting change in Eastern Europe, détente seventies-style has not done too badly. It has helped to create the conditions in which changes have taken place and have some chance of being maintained. The West German *Ostpolitik* (or, to look at the matter from the other side, the Soviet decision to conduct a European policy without a bogeyman in Bonn) was perhaps the most important single factor. SALT, Helsinki and extensive bilateral contacts between governments of East and West also played their part in creating a world where Poles travel extensively in the West, where a Pole becomes Pope and returns to visit his country and where freedom of information, while not absolute, is sufficient to nurture a politically-conscious generation.[3]

B. J. P. FALL

[3] On 8 January Mr Hurd reported to the Cabinet that the situation was very tense and that if the Polish Government continued to give way to Solidarity on each issue which arose, its position would grow progressively weaker (CC(81)1, CAB 128/170). Matters had not improved by the end of the month. On 30 January Mr Bullard minuted to the Secretary of State's office: 'The free trade unions are maintaining their demands, some of them highly political; the Government are talking as if they regarded a confrontation as inevitable and perhaps even desirable; and the Russians and Czechs are supplying background music of a threatening kind' (FCO 28/4337, EN 021/5/81).

No. 46

Letter from Mr Loehnis (Bank of England) to Mr Fall, 15 January 1981

Personal and Confidential (FCO 28/4516, ENP 090/1/81)

Dear Brian,

Thank you for your response dated 8th January to my letter of 17th December to Ken Couzens, which we found very helpful.[1] It is certainly encouraging that you see common ground between us.

Part of the cause of the creative tension may be that we approach the common ground, naturally enough, along the different paths of our own basic professional preoccupations. You see the Polish situation as one where, for all the dangers, there may be a perhaps unique chance to make a decisive thrust against the Soviet hegemony in Eastern Europe. But this depends on the West providing enough assistance to keep the Polish economy afloat to make the cost/benefit analysis of

[1] Neither letter is printed. There had been an ongoing correspondence between the FCO, the Bank of England and H.M. Treasury over the Polish economy's chances of recovery and the degree of assistance the West should provide. At a meeting of OD on 12 February the Committee accepted the principle of concerted debt relief but called for further study over whether refinancing or rescheduling was the best method. The UK was to take its lead from other major Western Governments on the question of new credit to Poland. The proposed debt resettlement would initially not run beyond the end of 1982 and British negotiators were to aim at a settlement providing no more than 85 per cent debt relief, and with their initial proposals lower still. The 85 per cent ceiling might be lowered further if new credit was also offered, or raised if other Western Governments pressed strongly for it (CAB 148/197).

the consequences of Soviet intervention sufficiently uncertain to keep the Russians out, while the forces unleashed by the Solidarity movement work their effect on the socio/economic fabric of Poland. This, at least, is what I take you to have in mind as the 'good political reasons' for the West to provide financial help.

We approach the Polish situation from the point of view that the economy is in a disastrous mess; that the socio-economic forces unleashed by the Solidarity movement are likely to worsen rather than improve the economy; that in such circumstances it must remain unlikely that western assistance will succeed in bringing it round, anyway within a reasonable time frame; that the Soviet Union is unlikely to feel it can afford to wait so long for recovery; and that the political aim of avoiding Soviet intervention will probably not therefore be achieved, but meanwhile the West may have poured more money down the drain and achieved nothing in political terms. Furthermore, very dangerous precedents for dealing with other bankrupt countries may have been created by the terms of assistance we feel obliged to afford Poland—and those bankrupt countries may include military allies or other countries with greater moral claim on our benevolence than Poland. Thus our preference is for an approach which starts from the basic stance that Poland is a profligate country now bankrupt, which must face up to its moment of truth and go on to deal with its external indebtedness to the West on the same tried and tested principles which have been used with other bankrupt countries. You cannot in the last analysis finance or borrow your way out of bankruptcy: you must adjust to it, and those who lend you money in such circumstances are almost bound to lose it.

We accept of course that in all situations of national bankruptcy important political considerations intrude, and that the manner in which each case is actually dealt with will represent some form of compromise between the financial and political realities. Our aim is simply to bring home to those who have to forge that compromise the severity of the financial realities. So let us indeed keep closely in touch.

I have of course grossly oversimplified, and for this reason propose, like you, not to copy this letter to the recipients of my original one.

Yours ever,

ANTHONY A. D. LOEHNIS

A tense situation developed in January 1981 between the Government and Solidarity, with the threat of widespread strikes concerning the implementation of the Gdańsk agreements. Andrew Wood, Counsellor and Head of Chancery at the British Embassy in Moscow, who visited Poland for two days at the beginning of January, sent his impressions to Mr Montgomery on 9 January 1981. He met a number of the Embassy's contacts, the 'range' of which he envied. He found the Party in worse shape than he had previously understood, being divided and lacking in a sense of direction: 'The average Soviet observer might well conclude that the counter-revolution had already succeeded' and if the Russians invaded they would have to reconstruct the party. It would be very difficult for them to reverse the situation. He observed that 'an uncomfortable number of Poles seem to regard the possibility of Soviet intervention without much concern'. He concluded: 'From the Kremlin's point of view it is a considerable risk to allow a genuinely reformist Extraordinary Congress in March. The Russians will no doubt be looking for tangible evidence before then that the PZPR is making progress towards overcoming its difficulties'. Mr Wood's analysis was widely commented on throughout the FCO. On 19 January Mr Fergusson noted: 'a vivid addition to the number of increasingly gloomy portrayals of the growing anarchy on the Polish scene' (FCO 28/4542, ENP 212/2).

The Cabinet—made aware of ongoing developments—discussed the situation on several occasions in January and February. Thus, on 15 January, the Lord Privy Seal reported the tense situation with further strikes, Solidarity's demand for a five-day week and a sharpening in the tone of Soviet comments. On 29 January, Lord Carrington reported on the 'increasingly serious situation' in Poland, noting the split in Solidarity between those who demanded more gains, a cautious wing, and an intermediate group led by Mr Wałęsa, who had just come back from Rome where on 15 July the Pope embraced him and counselled 'courage and moderation' (2nd and 4th conclusions of meetings on 15 and 29 January 1981, CAB 128/70). On 31 January, Mr Pridham reported that a general strike had been averted by a compromise on two of the three issues in dispute, namely: a forty-hour working week with one Saturday in four worked; a weekly television programme for Solidarity; coverage of their National Committee's decision in the national press; and a right to reply to criticism. The third issue—registration of rural Solidarity—had not been agreed (Warsaw tel. No. 73, FCO 28/4538, ENP 212/1). On 5 February Lord Carrington reported this compromise to the Cabinet, noting that it was 'once again' in Solidarity's favour and that it was unclear how long the Government could continue to give way especially given the worsening economic crisis. He also remarked that a hard-liner such as Mr Olszowski might succeed Mr Kania (CC(81)5, 5 February 1981, CAB 128/70).

On 9 February, Mr Pinkowski resigned as Premier, and the Defence Minister, General Jaruzelski, replaced him on 11 February. On 12 February, Mr Fall noted the extent to which the situation had further deteriorated in six weeks, as demonstrated by Pridham's comprehensive reporting. It showed that 'neither the regime nor the union leadership are fully in control of events, and that unless both sides can succeed in putting their houses in order the prospects for Poland must be bleak indeed'. He was disturbed by the fact that both sides stood on their positions not seeing the common good, but hoped that 'the appointment of Jaruzelski is put to good use'(FCO 28/4493, ENP 14/2).

No. 47

Mr Pridham (Warsaw) to Lord Carrington, 6 February 1981, 10.15 a.m.
Tel. No. 92[1] Immediate, Confidential (FCO 28/4542, ENP 212/2)

Moscow Telno 65: *Poland.*[2]

1. I fully agree that the slide to anarchy in Poland is reaching such a point that the Soviet Union may find it impossible not to intervene.

2. At the same time we must recognise that if invasion and its consequences for the world are to be avoided Solidarity has a part to play too. There is an increasing section of Polish opinion which, encouraged by President Reagan's recent

[1] Repeated for Information Immediate to Washington, Paris, Bonn, UKDEL NATO and Moscow.
[2] Not printed.

statements[3] (which are carefully reproduced in the Solidarity newspaper), wants to press on and damn the consequences, hoping for World War III to rescue Poland, rather as many Poles between 1815 and 1914 longed and worked for a European war. A further public warning might be salutary for the Russians but it would encourage those Poles at precisely the time when moderation on their part is needed.

3. I therefore recommend that any such warning should be accompanied by an indication from the West, which means effectively the Americans, that while we have the greatest sympathy with the aspirations of the Polish people, if Poland is to be saved they must have regard to political reality and not seek to do everything at once.

[3] At a press conference on 29 January President Reagan said that détente had been 'a one-way street' that the Soviet Union had used to pursue its own aims and the goal of the Soviet leadership was to promote world revolution and a 'one-world Socialist or Communist state'. He went on: 'Now, as long as they do that and as long as they, at the same time, have openly and publicly declared that the only morality they recognize is what will further their cause, meaning they reserve unto themselves the right to commit any crime, to lie, to cheat, in order to attain that, and that is moral, not immoral, and we operate on a different set of standards, I think when you do business with them, even at a détente, you keep that in mind.' *Public Papers: Reagan (1981)*, p. 57.

No. 48

Letter from Mr Fall to Mr G. Bullard (Sofia), 6 February 1981
Confidential (FCO 28/4451, ENG 026/4)

Dear Giles,

Visit by Madame Zhivkova

1. Ministers have now agreed that Mme Zhivkova be officially invited to visit the UK in 1981 in conjunction with Bulgaria's 1300th Anniversary celebrations.[1] Mr Blaker, as the Minister in the FCO responsible for cultural relations with other countries, would be the host.

2. In my more cheerful moments, I look on this as a difficulty overcome. In my gloomier ones, I wonder whether it is not the start of many more. Ministers are clearly not enthusiastic about the idea, to which they agreed only after a careful sounding of opinion in the Conservative Party in Parliament. They are firmly of the view that the visit should be played in a low key, which I think that we should take to mean: (i) that it will not be easy to arrange a call on a more senior Minister, although I accept that there is a protocol case to be made for this; and (ii) that it would be a very brave man who sought to persuade the Prime Minister that she should receive Mme Zhivkova, and that he would be more unlikely to succeed. Finally, Ministers are decidedly not keen on the idea of a programme which has the stamp of Robert Maxwell too firmly upon it.[2]

[1] The Bulgarians had been pressing since 1971 for an official invitation for Madame Zhivkova to visit Britain. In July 1979 and September 1980 the Government had rejected a recommendation that she should be invited on the grounds that a visit would arouse strong feelings in Parliament resulting from the murder of the dissident Georgi Markov in 1978. The 1300th Anniversary celebrations offered an opportunity to remove what Mr Fall called 'this minor irritant in our relations'.

[2] Originally from Czechoslovakia, Maxwell built an extensive publishing and media empire in the UK. He cultivated political contacts in Eastern Europe and published sycophantic biographies of

3. Against this background, the hand will clearly have to be played with some care and I am very much open to your advice. All of us here take and are sympathetic to the point in paragraph 6 of your Despatch of 10 November[3] (to which John Macrae is replying by this bag) about the desirability of giving the Bulgarians some concrete evidence that we regard 1981 as something of a landmark in Bulgarian history. The 1300th Anniversary celebrations coupled with a visit by Mme Zhivoka ought to go a long way towards producing this result, provided we can put the ingredients together in the right way. And if the visit could coincide with the signature of a Cultural Agreement so much the better. The trouble is that at the moment it is not clear that the Bulgarians are thinking along those lines or indeed that the negotiations for the Agreement will not throw up snags.

4. Whatever happens about the Agreement it is clear that a Zhivkova visit must be firmly tied to the cultural scene and the 1300th Anniversary celebrations. Accordingly, you might like to say to the Foreign Ministry that we are glad now to have received the list of events which the Bulgarians have it in mind to stage in Britain to mark the 1300th Anniversary; that we hope that these will be successful and that we wonder whether Mme Zhivkova might be interested in opening or attending one of these events; that, if so, we would be glad to extend to her a formal invitation from Mr Blaker to visit the UK as a guest of HMG; and, finally, that we envisage the visit as being a cultural event linked to the 1300th Anniversary and would make the arrangements accordingly. If you wanted to introduce the possibility of signing a cultural agreement too we should have no objection. If you think that this would be likely to work please go ahead on these lines. If not, let us think again.[4]

Yours ever,
B. J. P. FALL

Communist leaders such as Todor Zhivkov, Erich Honecker and Nicolae Ceausescu. Mr Blaker noted that Mr Maxwell will 'no doubt insist on getting in on the act' but they should not appear to be 'in cahoots' with him.

[3] Not printed.

[4] In a reply of 12 February Mr Bullard advised that Bulgarian sensitivities were such that an invitation might not be well received unless it was at a higher level. Mme Zhivkova was a member of the Politburo and First Lady used to being received at Foreign Minister or Head of State level, having called on President Giscard d'Estaing in Paris in 1978 and Chancellor Schmidt in Bonn in 1979. In response the Secretary of State agreed to make her visit the centrepiece of the UK contribution to mark the 1300th anniversary. She would be invited in the name of the Lord Privy Seal, who would also host a lunch in her honour, and the visit would include a call on the Secretary of State. The invitation was accepted but the Bulgarians suggested that Mme Zhivkova should meet Mrs Thatcher for a discussion on political and economic questions, and also pay a courtesy call on H.M. The Queen. In a meeting with the Lord Privy Seal the Bulgarian Ambassador was prepared to concede the meeting with The Queen but declared that his country 'would feel humiliated' if Mme Zhivkova could not see the Prime Minister. Nevertheless the FCO held firm, offering instead that Mme Zhivkova might discuss political issues when she met the Secretary of State. However all the hand-wringing was in vain as Mme Zhivkova died on 21 July.

No. 49

Lord Carrington to Mr Pridham (Warsaw), 18 February 1981, 4 p.m.
Tel. No. 83[1] Immediate, Confidential (FCO 28/4499, ENP 20/1)

Your Tel. nos 130, 131 and 133: Call on Polish Prime Minister[2]

1. You should draw as appropriate on the material below when you call on Jaruzelski tomorrow.

HMG's attitude to Poland's problems[3]

2. British Ministers have repeatedly made it clear that we regard Poland's problems as a matter to be settled by the Poles themselves. We are resolved to adhere strictly to the policy of non-intervention which we have followed throughout. We consider it essential both for Poland and for Europe and the world that all other countries should do the same.

3. We do, of course, follow with great interest what is happening in Poland. We are members of the same European family, and our bilateral ties are close and valued. Poland occupies a position of great geo-political importance in Europe, and the outcome of the current period of stress has implications for all the peoples of our continent. The responsibility is one [of] which Jaruzelski himself must be deeply conscious. This is the context in which the Prime Minister's message to him should be seen (para 9 below).

4. We noted with care the published proceedings of the 8th Plenum of the Central Committee[4] and the speech of Prime Minister Jaruzelski to the Sejm.[5] It appears to us that the Polish leaders continue to emphasise moderation, that they remain committed to the renewal (*odnowa*) and that they are determined to tackle now, and in due course to overcome, the very serious economic problems which face the country.

5. This line commands our sympathy and understanding. We do not underestimate the difficulties, but we hope that they can be overcome by peaceful means in such a way as to mobilise the efforts and talents of the Polish people as a whole.

[1] Information Priority to Bonn, Paris, Washington, UKDEL NATO, Moscow and Saving to Prague, Budapest, Bucharest, Sofia, Belgrade and East Berlin.

[2] Not printed.

[3] The FCO had briefed the Cabinet on 12 February, noting that neither the Polish authorities nor the Solidarity leadership seemed in control. The appointment of General Jaruzelski could 'buy some time' and reassure the party faithful and the Soviets, while his reputation of opposing the use of force could help with Solidarity (brief for Cabinet, FCO 28/4504, ENP 021/4). At the meeting Lord Carrington noted that the situation continued to deteriorate and that the outcome was unpredictable (CC(81)6, CAB 128/70).

[4] On 11 February Mr Pridham reported the main points of the Plenum, which insisted on the need for the country to go back to normal and make the *odnowa* work at a time when it was threatened by extremists and by 'forces hostile to socialism'. Party members were requested not to take part in political strikes and to prevent trade unions from abusing the right to strike. It asked journalists to report 'responsibly' (Warsaw tel. No. 105; FCO 28/4480, ENP 14/1).

[5] On 13 February Mr Pridham reported General Jaruzelski's speech the day before as 'well balanced between firmness and assurance of continuation and acceleration of the renewal, though he stated unequivocally that there could not be two authorities in one state'. He recommended that the Prime Minister should send a message of congratulation (Warsaw tel. No. 119; FCO 28/4480, ENP 14/1). In his speech General Jaruzelski had called for a three-month moratorium on strikes to allow for 'the introduction of a program of economic stabilization' and 'a sweeping reform of the economy'.

6. (If necessary). As regards the Ambassador's message of 12 February (FCO Tel. No. 72)[6] you should not assume that HMG would tacitly support any action which the Polish Government might take, particularly not of a kind which could bring a chain reaction. The British attitude would depend on that of Polish public opinion.

British/Polish relations

7. We value our bilateral relations with Poland and we want to develop them. We think that this is in the interests of both our countries and that it reflects the close links between the British and the Polish people. I was particularly pleased to be able to pay a visit to Warsaw myself last October, at a time when high-level contact between the Polish leadership and their Western counterparts was of special value. I hope that Mr Czyrek will be able to pay a return visit to Britain shortly, and we have suggested some dates before the UK takes over the burden of the presidency of the EC. Contacts are developing also at other levels. The Anglo/Polish Joint Commission last November was attended for the first time by a British Minister, Mr Parkinson. The Marshal of the Sejm will be visiting Britain soon, and the British/Polish round table will take place in Oxford in March. We value also the very many private contacts between our people, which give substance to our official relations.

Economic assistance to Poland

8. We have, as you know, responded to the Polish Government's requests for assistance in the economic field by making credits available for purchases of goods (including food at special prices under the EC decision) and for debt relief during the first quarter of this year. The emphasis should now be on the longer term. We shall be participating in next week's Paris talks[7] in a positive spirit. There seems to be common ground between Western creditors and Polish financial experts that there will have to be a multilateral debt relief operation in which we shall be prepared to play our part. The exact terms and conditions of such an operation will clearly have to be related to the kind of assurances which the Polish Government is able to provide with regard to the long-term economic outlook.

Message from the Prime Minister

9. The Prime Minister has approved the following message: 'Please accept my warm congratulations and best wishes on your appointment as Chairman of the Council of Ministers. I look forward to cooperating with you in developing further the good relations between our two countries'.[8]

[6] Not printed.

[7] See No. 42, note 3.

[8] On 19 February Mr Pridham reported that General Jaruzelski had expressed appreciation of Mrs Thatcher's message and had said that Polish foreign policy would remain unchanged, stressing the importance of relations with Britain. Pridham reiterated the principle of non-intervention. General Jaruzelski confirmed the Government's wish for dialogue and to establish trust with the people, firmly reasserting that the Poles alone should solve their problems. He regretted that some groups were enemies of stabilisation and received assistance and encouragement from certain Western circles. Western governments should make clear they disapproved, as the destabilisation of Poland could only lead to the destabilisation of Europe (Warsaw tel. No. 136).

On the same day Pridham added that the meeting had not altered his previous assessment that dialogue would be tried once more but that if it failed greater firmness would be applied, but 'he does not want, just because he is a soldier, to be dubbed a man of force'. He did not believe that General Jaruzelski, 'a rather intellectual type of soldier', was willing to call in the Soviets (Warsaw tel. No. 137). The Lord Privy Seal reported to the Cabinet on 19 February—which met in the morning before Pridham sent the two telegrams—that General Jaruzelski 'appeared for the moment to have achieved the double feat of reassuring the Soviet Union and at the same time reducing the pressure of strikes inside Poland. But potentially dangerous issues remained unsettled e.g. in relation to censorship and to trades union legislation'. He concluded that the threat of Soviet intervention seemed to have receded (CC(81)7, CAB 128/70).

No. 50

Minute from Mr Gladstone to Mr Fergusson, 19 February 1981

Confidential (FCO 33/4702, WRE 020/4)

German reunification

1. As reported in East Berlin telegrams nos. 31 and 32,[1] Herr Honecker raised the subject of German reunification in a speech in Berlin on 15 February.[2] This speech was the subject of an editorial in *The Times*[3] on 18 February, written by Mr Richard Davy with whom I conversed the day before.

2. I have little to add to the editorial, which seems to me to get the balance just about right. It is hard to know how much significance to read into the speech, but I think it is more interesting than the analysts in the Federal Government appear willing to allow. There is nothing essentially new in the message itself: Herr Ulbricht frequently mentioned the possibility of reunification under Communism and Herr Honecker himself did so last in a West German newspaper interview in 1978. Nevertheless:

(*a*) official GDR policy remains *Abgrenzung*: the erection of as many formal barriers as possible between the two German states. The GDR Constitution was amended in the late 1960s precisely in order to remove all references to ultimate reunification. Only the current Head of the Party seems to be allowed to air the heresy from time to time.

(*b*) Herr Honecker must have a reason for reviving the issue now. One can only speculate about his motives; but I suggest that they might be (in descending order of importance):

(i) to boost morale among the party faithful (whom he was after all addressing directly);

[1] Not printed.

[2] The speech was to SED provincial delegates in East Berlin. Addressing those in the FRG who continued to speak about the union of two Germanies, he said: 'if the day comes when the workers in the Federal Republic turn to a socialist system, then the question of the two Germanies will present itself again. There should be no doubt as to how we would then decide'. It was the first time that Herr Honecker had spoken in such clear terms about reunification (the GDR using the term 'unification') (East Berlin tel. No. 31, 16 February 1980). Honecker's speech was mentioned at the meeting of the Ten on 16 February at which Mr Bölling, the new FRG representative in the GDR and Helmut Schmidt's former spokesman, gave three possible explanations for Honecker's declaration: to reassure East Germans; to have some impact on public opinion in the FRG, which Bölling dismissed; to frighten the Poles. Mr Foster favoured the second as Honecker 'may have calculated that it was tactically unwise to disabuse too completely hopes in the Federal Republic for the ultimate unity of the German nation', as it might encourage more accommodating responses over 'military détente' or less resolute reactions if Western unity were challenged by an invasion of Poland. This might be part of a peace offensive 'to drive a wedge between America and the West Europeans' (East Berlin tel. No. 32, 16 February 1981).

[3] Mr Davy, correspondent for *The Times* in Eastern Europe, saw the speech as potentially opening a new phase, with Herr Honecker aiming to improve morale in the GDR by reducing its feeling of isolation.

(ii) to throw an apple of discord into the Bonn political arena in the hope of driving wedges not only between the warring wings of the SPD but also between the Federal Government and the (already possibly suspicious) Reagan Administration; (iii) to make Polish flesh creep.[4]

3. In support of (*b*) (ii) above, the recent controversy occasioned in the FRG by Herr Gaus's[5] recent interview with 'Die Zeit', in which he advocated a more flexible approach to the GDR generally and to the nationality question in particular,[6] can hardly have escaped Herr Honecker's notice. It may also not be entirely coincidental that, during the first call by Herr Boelling, the new FRG Representative in East Berlin, the GDR Prime Minister (Stoph) emphasized the 'special role' which the two German states can play within their respective alliances. Beguiling music to many an SPD ear.

4. But whatever Herr Honecker's immediate intentions, one implication of his remarks seems clear: since according to good Marxist theory the FRG is historically bound to follow the GDR along the road to Socialism one day, German reunification is likewise, in the long term, inevitable.

5. I am sending these papers to Bonn for further comment.

D. A. S. GLADSTONE

[4] On 5 March Mr Foster replying to a letter of 25 February from Mr Pridham, agreed that more emphasis should be given to the Polish angle and less perhaps to the internal GDR one: 'At least among "ordinary" East Germans, Honecker's remarks do not seem to have evoked much interest . . . reunification is a very distant and nebulous concept and few would, in any case, have a clear idea of what it would mean in practice. More actual and central in their dreams are greater personal freedoms, particularly to travel' (FCO 33/4702, WRE 020/4).

[5] Günter Gaus was the FRG representative in the GDR from 1973 to 1981 and a career journalist. After 1981 he focused on the process of German unification, interviewing politicians, artists and dissidents from the GDR.

[6] Published in *Die Zeit* on 30 January 1981. The article fuelled a debate in the FRG as Herr Gaus asked his countrymen to rethink their attitude towards East Germany in the light of German history.

No. 51

Minute from Lord Carrington to Mrs Thatcher, 10 March 1981

PM/81/10 Secret (FCO 28/4607, ENS 091/2)

Contingency Planning about Poland

1. I should like to comment on the Trade Secretary's minute of 4 March.[1]

2. The purpose of the contingency planning now taking place in NATO, about which officials in the Department of Trade and other interested departments have

[1] In this minute Mr Biffen argued that in drafting measures due consideration needed to be given to the implications for UK commercial interests and the economy. He shared a concern expressed by the Chancellor (in a minute to Lord Carrington of 19 February) over the vulnerability of the UK as a major world financial centre, and added that trade measures had greater general implications for the UK than for most of her allies. He considered trade sanctions 'a fairly empty gesture' and an ineffectual way to deal with international political problems.

Both the Secretary of State for Trade and the Chancellor were responding to a report of 13 February entitled 'Economic Sanctions in the Polish Context', circulated as OD(81)10 (CAB 148/197). The report had been prepared at the Foreign Secretary's suggestion that inter-Departmental agreement needed to be reached on economic sanctions in the event of a major act of repression in Poland to provide the basis for discussion with other Western Governments (see No. 42).

been consulted, is to identify a range of possible measures against the Soviet Union. NATO Ministers would meet shortly after any Soviet intervention in Poland, to decide which of the measures to implement in the light of the actual nature of such an intervention and all other relevant circumstances. I should obviously wish to consult colleagues collectively before departing for the NATO meeting.

3. A Soviet intervention in Poland would be an extremely serious matter, and greatly against the interests of the West. You have said in public that it would mean the end of détente. We must be ready with our Allies to take concrete steps going well beyond those taken after the invasion of Afghanistan. Yet there is only a limited range of possible measures for demonstrating Western disapproval and trying to make the costs to the Soviet Union as high as possible. The list being drawn up in NATO consists of diplomatic moves (public statements, suspension of some arms control negotiations, action in the UN Security Council, avoidance of high level contacts and publicly visible bilateral events, temporary withdrawal of Ambassadors) and also economic measures. The most important of the latter is an embargo on exports to the Soviet Union. Exports under existing legally enforceable contracts, but not under framework agreements, would be exempted. We have been resisting pressure for a reference to the possibility of considering the inclusion of services under an embargo, but others may insist on a very general sentence about this in the NATO paper.

4. There is no doubt that an embargo on exports of goods under new contracts would hurt the Soviet Union considerably. In 1979, Soviet imports from the OECD countries were $14 billion or 24.4% of all Soviet imports. The new Five Year Plan (1981-85) suggests that there is no intention of changing this general pattern. Some of the Soviet imports from the West, notably foodstuffs and certain types of technology, are of particular importance to the USSR. We calculate that British exports to the Soviet Union would fall by two thirds in the first six months of an embargo on new contracts and that the great majority of the remainder would cease within two years. French officials think that this would also apply approximately to their exports to the Soviet Union. The United States and Germany calculate that their exports would decline by two thirds within a year. Although I recognise that there would be a problem in choosing the time for lifting trade sanctions, there is probably no other measure which could have such a significant effect on Soviet interests.

5. While I note the Trade Secretary's point about the particular British dependence on overseas trade, I do not think that this applies in the case of trade with the Soviet Union. British exports in 1979 were $694 million (0.17% of our GDP), in contrast to French exports of $2007 million (0.35%) and German exports of $3619 million (0.47%). (These are OECD figures: the British figure for UK exports was $883 million or 0.22% of GDP, still well below the French and German figures.)

6. I quite agree with the Trade Secretary that action in this field should be undertaken in close cooperation with our allies. There are strong signs that the French and Germans accept on this occasion that serious measures against the USSR would be needed. Indeed, it was the French who introduced the proposal for an export embargo into the NATO discussion.

7. In the case of a lesser event in Poland, such as the use of force by the Polish authorities, I am inclined to think that economic measures against the Soviet Union would be an inappropriate Western response. The emphasis of our actions *vis-à-vis*

the USSR would probably be to warn against outside intervention. But this too would be for decision at the time.

8. I am copying this minute to members of OD, other recipients of OD(81)10, to the Chief Whip and Sir R. Armstrong.[2]

CARRINGTON

[2] There followed an exchange of correspondence between the Department of Trade and the FCO over contingency measures agreed by NATO. In letters of 17 and 27 March the Secretary of State for Trade pushed for measures sympathetic to British trading interests and did not feel that his Department had been adequately consulted; in particular he wanted exclusions from any trade embargo not only for legally enforceable contracts but also for on-going business relationships. He refused to accept the assertion by the Foreign Secretary that NATO had now reached agreement on contingency planning and it was too late to change it.

No. 52

Letter from Mr Birch (Budapest) to Mr Facey, 12 March 1981
Confidential (FCO 28/4519, ENP 090/1)

Dear Robert,

Hungarian aid to Poland

1. A current joke in Budapest goes as follows:

Kania: We can hold things in Poland provided you let us have three million tons of potatoes.

Brezhnev: OK.

Kania: And two hundred thousand tons of beef.

Brezhnev: I think we can manage that too.

Kania: And five hundred thousand bananas.

Brezhnev: Oh dear, I am not sure whether Kadar has got them.

2. This type of joke underlines Hungarian apprehension that they may have to join an economic rescue operation in Poland. This fear has replaced their earlier tendency to gloat over the failure of the Poles and the comparative prosperity of Hungary. The official line is that Hungary is giving Poland full political and ideological support but no mention is made of economic help.

3. We have now had a report from the French Ambassador, who has heard from 'a reliable source', that Hungary has agreed to give fts 2000m (about £30m) in financial assistance to Poland. He took advantage of a recent call at the Foreign Ministry to mention, deadpan, this help and to ask why the Hungarians were being so secretive about it. The Deputy Foreign Minister to whom he spoke replied simply that the Government preferred to say nothing publicly. This suggests that the French information is accurate and that the lack of publicity is designed to avoid irritating Hungarian workers who might think it odd that their Government was making a substantial gift to the Poles for not working, at a time when they were being told to work harder. Indeed, the major criticism here amongst ordinary people appears to be not that the Polish complaints are unjustified, but that people ought to improve their lot by working harder.

Yours ever,
J. A. BIRCH

No. 53

Mr Pridham (Warsaw) to Lord Carrington, 23 March 1981, 11.15 p.m.
Tel. No. 204[1] Immediate, Restricted (FCO 28/4538, ENP 212/1)

My Telno 199: Events in Bydgoszcz.[2]

1. The main developments over the weekend have been the establishment of a higher-powered commission chaired by the Minister of Justice:[3] a meeting between Walesa and Rakowski followed by Solidarity's decision to call off today's planned strike action; a tough statement by the Politburo; and a statement by Cardinal Wyszynski. The principal victim's state of health is improving and the other two hospital cases should be released in a week or so. A new *voivod* has been appointed in Bydgoszcz.

2. The commission headed by Bafia contains representatives of other Government departments as well as Professor Zawadzki, a Znak[4] Catholic Member of Parliament. No findings have yet been published but the commission has made preliminary overtures to the local branch of Solidarity, which has not yet agreed to cooperate with it.[5] Solidarity itself has called off today's strike action and its Presidium is meeting in Bydgoszcz at 1600 hours today. The national strike alert remains in force and today's meeting will decide whether to hold a two-hour strike later this week. Talks between Walesa and Rakowski are due to resume on Wednesday.[6]

3. While the Central Government has issued no statement of what happened, the general tenor of the local authorities' version of the events in Bydgoszcz is to suggest that they were only part of a series of incidents which have occurred there in the last month. A detailed chronology published in today's press says that there were previous incidents of harassment by rural Solidarity of the police and security functionaries in Bydgoszcz. It goes on to explain that the Solidarity members were several times asked to leave the *Voivodship* premises peacefully but refused, when the police were called. The local authorities' statement further says that no one was beaten by the police, whose operation ended at 7 p.m. It adds that one of the victims was at Solidarity HQ having his injuries photographed at 8 p.m. and that

[1] Repeated for Information Immediate Maastricht (for Private Secretary); Information Routine to Moscow, East Berlin, Prague, Paris, Bonn, Washington, UKDEL, NATO, The Hague, MODUK; Saving to Sofia, Budapest, Bucharest, Belgrade, Helsinki, Stockholm, UKMIS New York, UKREP Brussels.

[2] Rural Solidarity members attending a local council meeting were evicted and beaten-up by police leading to the threat of further strike action. Pridham reported: 'What exactly happened in Bydgoszcz is still not clear . . . But it could spark off something dangerous' (Warsaw tel. No. 199).

[3] Professor Jerzy Bafia.

[4] Znak was an association of lay Catholics in Poland, active between 1956 and 1976. It was the only Catholic organisation that was tolerated by the communist Polish United Workers' Party and supported by the Catholic hierarchy. It was disbanded in 1976 after its only representative in the Sejm had not approved the amendment to the Polish constitution that underlined the leading role of the Communist Party and 'eternal friendship' with the USSR. A remainder of the group—officially renamed *Polski Związek Katolicko-Społeczny* and known as neo-Znak movement—existed until 1980. It had representatives in the Sejm.

[5] Mr Pridham reported on 21 March on the commission's preliminary findings that the police had acted in a determined but not brutal fashion. Jaruzelski had issued a statement calling for dialogue, welcomed by Solidarity's national Presidium which met in an emergency session in Bydgoszcz. They also demanded a full and open enquiry and punishment of those responsible and guarantees that this would not recur.

[6] 25 March 1981.

the worst injured victim was admitted to hospital at midnight. On the official side it is claimed that the authorities had every right to remove trespassers from government offices but even the local party (and the Warsaw Party) concede that what happened after the offices were cleared must be explained.

4. Local and other Solidarity members appear to be making the most of the affair and posters suggesting assaults with knuckle-dusters by the police have gone up. Walesa is clearly trying to calm matters and may be working for acceptable terms of reference for Solidarity to take part in the work of the Government Commission.

5. Meanwhile the Politburo probably has not helped by publishing on 22 March a strong statement (text in MIFT not to all).[7] The statement refers to an attempt to occupy the *Voivodship* headquarters and says there are forces in the country trying to overthrow the political system and that any strike by Solidarity at this time would create a state of anarchy. The statement also attacks Solidarity for propagating a tendentious version of events in Bydgoszcz. The police in Warsaw have been removing such publicity from trams and public places. Cardinal Wyszynski for his part has issued a fairly even-handed statement calling for calm and patience but saying that the authorities must act responsibly (text in second IFT,[7] not to all). This statement is perhaps the furthest that Wyszynski has gone in criticising the actions of the authorities and is indicative of the seriousness with which he must view the latest developments. Archbishop Macharski[8] has cancelled his visit to Rome in view of the seriousness of the situation.

6. The Politburo, which now contains only 2 members of the Government, may have been influenced by Moscow or by its own hard-liners or by some aggressive Solidarity propaganda. But its strong statement may cut across what Jaruzelski is trying to do. His early attempts at consultation and fast action seem to have impressed at least the leadership of Solidarity and to have gone some way towards defusing the situation. What happened after the police had cleared the government offices is now a crucial point and the Government Commission must clear this up, in conjunction with Solidarity.

It will be no good for both sides to issue their own versions. Evidently tempers were running high in Bydgoszcz (where militant farmers are still occupying the Peasant Party premises) and perhaps there was some private settling of score by police or others. But inevitably the incident has awakened memories of police violence in 1970 and 1976. There is a situation ripe for exploitation by extremists on both sides. It is important that outsiders should not interfere and if we are asked for comment I suggest we refer simply to the Government Commission.

FCO please pass saving addresses.

[7] Not printed.
[8] Franciszek Macharski was Archbishop of Kraków. Pope John Paul II had been his predecessor.

The situation did not calm down. On 24 March, Mr Pridham reported that Trybuna Ludu, *the official newspaper of the Polish United Workers' Party and the largest in Communist Poland, considered Poland to be in its most serious crisis since August 1980: 'This assessment seems to be shared by most Western observers and I am inclined to think that this is correct'. The Solidarity National Commission in a stormy meeting in Bydgoszcz warned that if a state of emergency were declared or enforced there would be a general strike throughout Poland*

(Warsaw tel. No. 208). Pridham also expected that Jaruzelski would act quickly on the findings of the Commission but would limit himself to taking disciplinary steps against individual policemen if relevant rather than 'throw to the wolves the officials who called the police'. He emphasized the potential of the extremists in Solidarity, although the fact that Wałęsa still had some support may have offered a ray of hope for the Government (Warsaw tel. No. 211).

No. 54

Letter from Mr Pridham (Warsaw) to Mr J. Bullard, 23 March 1981
Confidential (FCO 28/4497, ENP 014/6)

Dear Julian,

1. I am not a great one for trying to hammer out policies for all conceivable eventualities and last December I resisted a suggestion from within the Embassy that we should stimulate the Foreign Office to re-think and re-state British policy towards Poland. It seemed to me that, given the constantly moving picture, we had as good an indication of HMG's policy as it was reasonable to expect. In my Annual Report for 1980 I summarised our objectives as to keep the Polish economy going and to foster the preservation of Polish independence, leaving just how this should be done in a fluid situation to the decisions of the moment.

2. After the passage of a further 3 months, however, the existing policy document, FCO despatch of 7 December 1979,[1] reveals increasing gaps so far as Poland is concerned. For instance, it argues that we should seek to encourage diversity within the bloc, exemplified by Romania's foreign policy, Hungary's New Economic Mechanism and Poland's brand of pluralism. Poland's brand of pluralism has greatly changed since then: the country is awash with diversity and it now needs a period of calm and relative unity. The 1979 despatch says that we have no interest in provoking a crisis which would be ended by invasion by the Russians if they thought it necessary. This remains broadly true but I suggest that we could define more closely the balance in our policy between sympathy with the newly-emerged forces in Poland and the need for them to act with restraint. To what extent can we or should we counsel caution without unduly encouraging the forces of reaction internal and external or seeming to interfere in matters which we have said are for Poles alone? To what extent can we warn the Russians against intervention or the Polish Government against repression without stimulating the wilder elements of Solidarity and thus defeating our object? Probably none of these questions are capable of clear answer but there would be value in injecting them into a fresh assessment.

3. There is then the totally new factor of economic aid and its objectives and limitations to be fitted in, together with the extent to which we can and should impose economic and political conditions: the weight now attached to our commercial position here (very little judging by the current DOT attitude); how British public opinion may enter into the argument; and how what is going on in Poland fits in with our overall concept of East-West relations in the Reagan era. I understand that much work is going on about policy after a Soviet intervention; but

[1] *DBPO: Afghanistan*, No. 1.

let us hope that what we shall actually have to carry out is a policy towards a still independent Poland.

4. I do not have in mind a massive paper but something more in the nature of a guidance telegram. The question remains when would be a suitable time to consider a draft. It is arguable that we should wait for the next Party Congress. On the other hand, that may be to defer for several more months. If you agree that something new is needed, we should be glad to assist in the drafting.[2]

Yours ever,
KENNETH

[2] Mr Fall, in a reply of 2 April, agreed that Poland needed a period of calm and stability. The aim, in so far as Britain had any influence, was to promote the consolidation of gains already won rather than encouraging further gambles. To this end Britain was attempting to stabilise the situation by providing emergency food aid through the EC, working for long-term debt rescheduling and calling for restraint and negotiated solutions in the press.

No. 55

Paper by East European and Soviet Department on the 'Umbrella Theory': Soviet reaction to the possibility of a Polish default, 26 March 1981[1]
Confidential (FCO 28/4519, ENP 090/1)

1. The traditional assumption ('the umbrella theory') has been that the Russians will act as lenders of last resort in order to prevent a default by one of their allies: for as long as they continued to assess that they would demonstrably stand to lose by a major default in terms of access to Western financial markets they would take steps to ensure that their allies met their debts. The primary motivation would be the perceived necessity to maintain the credit-worthiness of the CMEA countries as a whole. It is clear that had it not been generally relied upon by Western leaders, the hard-currency indebtedness of several CMEA countries would not have been allowed to reach present levels. The theory is predicated upon the assumption that the Soviet Union has sufficient hard currency to meets its clients' hard-currency debts without undue strain.

2. The traditional assumption needs looking at again in the light of the Polish economic crisis.

3. Poland is by far the largest CMEA borrower (see Annex C).[2] In 1979 Polish debt amounted to over a quarter of all CMEA hard currency debt and by 1981 its total liabilities were estimated to be about $24 million. So far the Soviet Union has been prepared to offer some additional financial help to Poland. In the autumn of 1980 the figure of £1.1 billion was mentioned although the Poles insisted that this

[1] This paper was drafted to examine the argument put forward by the Bank of England that the Soviet Union would, in the last resort, do whatever was required to keep Poland solvent and this meant the West could do less. The paper was drafted after consultation with HM Ambassadors at Warsaw and Moscow. The paper was circulated to HM Treasury, The Bank of England, the Department of Trade, and the Ministry of Agriculture, Fisheries and Food. In his covering letter of 26 March, Mr Montgomery noted: 'As long as the Western debt relief operation remains a subject for active consideration the questions of how much we can realistically expect the Russians to pay and how best to ensure that they do so will remain pertinent to our deliberations.'
[2] Not printed.

figure was exaggerated and represented a consolidation of large numbers of short term debts and a relatively small amount of untied cash available for settling the West's debts. At the same time both the Soviet Union and other CMEA partners (some under pressure from the Russians) assisted Poland's balance of payments in various ways including the postponement or cancellation of contracts for vital raw materials, notably coal. Poland's ability to meet Western debts during the last quarter of 1981 reflected this assistance although the Poles probably received help from some Western creditors as well. On 24 February the Poles announced the deferment of repayment of credits drawn from the Soviet Union from 1976-80 until 1985.

4. These gestures reflect the Soviet Union's anxiety to keep Poland afloat financially but they fall far short of a complete umbrella. A note at Annex A sets out a number of variations which an umbrella operation might take. They may give the Russians some leverage on Poland but more importantly they seem designed to facilitate an arrangement with Western creditors. The Poles told their creditors in Paris on 25 February that their reserves were sufficient for only two weeks imports. They maintain that without interim assistance from Western creditors both in the form of debt relief and new credit they would have no choice but to default. Obviously the Russians who have a strong incentive to avoid a situation developing where its Allies are able indirectly to pledge its credit to the West, have an interest in ensuring that the Poles play this record for all it is worth. There is reason to believe that a certain amount of disinformation is being spread to the effect that the Russians' generosity has been exhausted. But the theory that the Russians will stump up in the last resort cannot be put to the test without the risk of precipitating a disastrous default should it transpire that the Russians are not bluffing. But if the Russians were resigned to the idea that in the last resort they must step in and meet Poland's debts no matter what, they might be less willing than they appear to be to allow the Polish government to be drawn into a Western style debt-relief exercise with its implied conditionality.

5. The principal argument against the assumption that the USSR will extend the umbrella is that it cannot afford to do so. Though the costs of the most expensive option could average out at around $6 billion per annum, the costs in earlier years would be higher—perhaps $10 billion in 1981 and $7.5 billion in 1982. It is difficult to estimate the Soviet potential to earn a convertible currency surplus. However, it is possible to argue that the $4.1 billion current account surplus achieved in 1979 could be sustained and that, probably, higher energy prices will offset export volume reductions, thereby adding $1.2 billion to current account earnings. A current account surplus of $5.3 billion could be supplemented with increased gold sales (up to a further $1.8 billion could probably be earned without drawing on reserves). Soviet payments [of] about $7.1 billion would involve some change of policy on the part of the Soviet leadership. The shortfall in 1981-82 could be met by drawing on gold or foreign exchange reserves, diverting resources from other uses (e.g. less aid to Cuba and Vietnam) or enlisting additional economic support from East European allies. Some combination of these policies could enable the USSR to meet the maximum cost of the umbrella in 1981-82. However, the USSR is unlikely to be willing to adopt all these measures and may prefer to limit the umbrella to the least expensive options, i.e. coverage of either debt service due to 'business as usual' creditors or, at a minimum, financing Poland's trade deficit in the early 1980s.

6. It would be natural for the Soviet Union to use its financial leverage to exert political pressure on Poland. Some pressure has undoubtedly been brought to bear. But to date the Polish government has neither suppressed the Trade Unions, clawed back the concessions given last year nor crushed the dissidents. Instead it has reaffirmed its intention of honouring the Gdansk and other agreements, of implementing radical economic reforms and of maintaining its contacts with the West. Soviet leverage would be stronger if it enjoyed a monopoly of potential help, but the Soviet government is clearly aware of Polish contacts with the West and seems prepared to acquiesce in order to avoid shouldering the entire burden of Poland insolvency.

7. In the event of a sharp crack-down by the Polish government upon Trade Unions and dissidents an interesting situation would arise. The Russians would undoubtedly welcome the reassertion of party authority and the elimination of dangerous 'subversive' tendencies and could be expected to support such moves. But they would watch anxiously to see whether the West was prepared to continue to help Poland. If the West decided to withhold further assistance a major constraint upon Russian interference would be removed (although others i.e. the destruction of détente) would remain. The Soviet Union might consider that the credit-worthiness of the CMEA group was at stake and accordingly be prepared to provide massive economic assistance to the Poles. But it is equally arguable that the Soviet Union would not be willing to envisage a drain on its resources on the scale envisaged in paragraphs 3 and 4 above and would take the view that the Poles had only themselves to blame for their misfortune. If the West tried to make further assistance conditional upon some internal relaxation the Russians might be prepared to leave it to the Polish authorities themselves to determine what they could concede, reckoning that there could be no return to the *status quo ante*. They might rely too upon the Poles convincing their Western creditors that a restoration of 'law and order' was an essential prerequisite for the economic reform upon which Poland's recovery and her ability to eventually repay her debts must depend. They would no doubt be prepared to provide a continuing minimum level of help, both as a 'reward' to the Polish regime and as an incentive to the West to help also.

8. In the event of a Soviet intervention we have to assume that the Russians would have weighed all the consequences, and accepted the costs. They would nevertheless seek to minimise their political and economic losses as far as possible. Some additional Russian support would be forthcoming but there would be strong incentives for urging a puppet Polish government to maintain its contacts with the West and pursue business as usual as far as possible. The Soviet Union might even be ready to permit a firmly subjugated Polish regime to make some significant gestures calculated to win continued Western economic support e.g. application for IMF membership. The Russians would have to assume however that all Western economic assistance to Poland would be at an end for the foreseeable future. In such circumstances it could be argued that the Russians would provide the Poles with the necessary finances to avoid a default at the same time using this to increase their leverage by imposing political conditions (e.g. payment only to countries prepared to carry on business as usual). But in such circumstances the Russians would already have all the leverage they needed *vis-a-vis* the Poles. Moreover, the Banks themselves would probably consider it to be in their best interests to call a default. It seems more likely that the Russians would put away their umbrella. If the West reacted to an invasion with a cut-off in economic assistance to Poland as well as economic sanctions against the Soviet Union (and

any other CMEA country participating in an invasion) the Russians might well decide that all bets were off and that they were in a new ball game. They might argue that the debts had been contracted by a Polish regime subsequently denounced as anti-Socialist. But the pretext would be immaterial. The decision would reflect the Russians' assessment that the severity of the Western reaction offered no incentive for meeting the costs of avoiding a default. We might then see a concerted effort to lock Polish and other CMEA economies yet more closely to the Soviet Union. The Russians might provide some help to enable the Poles to make essential imports particularly oil from Third World countries. The default upon Western debts would be presented as removing the yoke of Western capitalism thus enabling the Poles to put their economy to rights within a truly socialist framework. Economic reform would proceed—but upon drastically different lines form those at present.

9. *To sum up*. The Russian interest in maintaining Polish credit-worthiness is balanced by the economic and political cost to themselves. The economic cost of shouldering the present Polish debt liability is such that the Russians have shown themselves ready to pay a considerable political premium as the price of involving the West in shouldering the major burden of Polish debt. They have been prepared to help, but there has been no suggestion that they could or would take on the whole burden. The umbrella is by no means waterproof, and it cannot be relied upon in strong political winds. In the event of repression or invasion the Soviet Union might be prepared to maintain a certain level of assistance and even make political concessions in return for continued Western assistance in Poland. But if the Soviet Union envisages a total cut-off of Western help it would have little reason to maintain the umbrella for its own sake and considerable incentive to cut its losses. It might well calculate that it need only sit the 'cold phase' out until the Western political reaction faded. Once the economic interests of Western exporters began to reassert themselves, business circles and bankers could be expected to convince themselves that the circumstances were unique, the Poles had brought their problems on themselves, the Soviet Union had provided some help and that a total freeze in East-West commercial/financial relations was an absurdity. The FRG would be under strong pressure to revive the inner-German relationship (particularly if the East Germans had played little part in an intervention). In a number of other cases there might appear special circumstances i.e. the need to safeguard existing investments to justify a restoration of business. East European credit ratings might not be as good as in the seventies, but before long selective lending would be resumed, the attractions of the huge Soviet market with its valuable commodity exports would reassert itself, and even Poland might become a candidate for a 'new ideal' if only in an attempt to recoup some of the astronomical losses occasioned by the default.

ANNEX A

The umbrella could take various forms:

(i) full financial backing for Poland, to the effect that the USSR guarantees debt service payments and meets Poland's requirements for new credits;

(ii) the Soviet guarantee extends to all Polish debt service obligations, but exclude any new convertible currency credits;

(iii) the guarantee covers only debt service obligations to countries which maintain 'business as usual' following domestic political repression or invasion;

(iv) the USSR provides sufficient convertible currency or guarantees loans to meet Poland's trade balance requirements, but no Soviet guarantee is extended to any debt service.

These options are arranged in descending order of costs to the USSR. Taking Polish figures to illustrate the potential costs (see table attached at B,[3] for want of better information), we calculate that the minimum costs of the four options in 1981-86 could be as follows:

(i) $29.5 billion plus/cumulative trade deficit (surplus);

(ii) $29.5 billion;

(iii) $0-29.5 billion, depending on number of 'business as usual' creditors;

(iv) Poles project a trade surplus over the period as a whole, so cost to USSR would be zero.

Estimates (i) and (iv), which depend on the cumulative trade account position, are likely to be underestimates of the actual cost to the USSR. In the event of an invasion the Polish economy would be disrupted and it could take several years before convertible current trade surpluses were attained.

[3] Not printed.

No. 56

Sir C. Keeble (Moscow) to Lord Carrington, 1 April 1981, 2.40 p.m.
Tel. No. 182[1] Routine, Confidential (FCO 28/4539, ENP 212/1)

Soviet Policy towards Poland

1. The events which followed the Bydgoszcz incident[2] marked, for the Soviet Union, a serious failure of the attempt to restore authority in Poland. It may be helpful if I try to set out the way things could now look to the Soviet leadership:

(*a*) At the meeting on 4 March, Kania and Jaruzelski were told with the full force of the senior members of the Soviet Politburo that the course of events must be turned back. At that point the Soviet leadership had clearly concluded that a failure to re-establish the Polish Party's authority would prejudice their own aim of maintaining the degree of control over Polish policy which they believed necessary to safeguard essential Soviet security interests.

(*b*) The Polish leadership were therefore expected to take firm action in the event of any further trial of strength with Solidarity. The Russians may not have expected them to precipitate a clash at Bydgoszcz or elsewhere, but when it occurred, they must have seen it as a test case, in which authority had to be re-asserted.

(*c*) The warning strike on 27 March and the threat of an indefinite general strike from 31 March[3] constituted a challenge which, from the Soviet point of view, publicly demonstrated that Solidarity was a counter-revolutionary political organisation. Tass statements made plain that the Soviet Union saw Solidarity as

[1] Repeated Washington, Paris, Bonn, NATO, Warsaw, Peking (for Private Secretary).

[2] See No. 53.

[3] On 27 March the national coordinating committee of Solidarity called for a four-hour warning strike and for a general strike on 31 March if the Government did not punish the culprits. On 28 March Wałęsa accompanied by a delegation of Solidarity met Cardinal Wyszyński, who appealed for moderation. A day before the scheduled general strike the Government admitted its error, and the strike was cancelled.

challenging the power of the state, seeking to discredit the existing authorities and usurping some of their functions in matters related to internal security.

(*d*) From then on there was in Soviet terms an irreconcilable conflict; either the Party had to control the state, assert its authority and break Solidarity as a political force, or an essential element of Soviet power, not only in Poland but throughout Eastern Europe would be prejudiced. In Leninist terms '*kto-kovo*' (only one can be the master).

2. Up to this point the analysis of Soviet policy rests on public statements and requires little by way of inference. The next stages are more speculative. We do not yet have a public reaction to the Polish Central Committee plenum, but I do not see how the Soviet assessment can be other than pessimistic. At a time when it had been made abundantly clear that compromise had gone too far, the Party seems to have compromised again, leaving Solidarity with the best of the argument so far as the Bydgoszcz incident is concerned and with its wider demands still extant. Worst of all from the Soviet position is that a timetable for the Party congress has been set before the Party has restored its internal cohesion, with the hazard the greater if delegates are to be elected by secret ballot from an unlimited number of candidates. The assessment here must be that the present Polish leadership has lost the initiative, that it has little prospect of regaining control and that July could see Poland controlled by a widely based political reform movement, operating both outside the Party and within it—a prospect similar to but worse than Czechoslovakia in 1968. How then to restore control? The options must seem equally unattractive:

(*a*) Another attempt to stiffen the present leadership in the hope that it will at least prevent the extension of Solidarity's influence in the political field.

(*b*) A new hardline leadership ready to break KOS/KOR,[4] to use force against any new challenge by Solidarity and to ask for fraternal help if need be.

(*c*) Soviet military intervention.

I think the first Soviet priority will be to assert control over the Polish Party, at the least by firmly establishing a Moscow-orientated group within it, which will seek by pressure on Kania and Jaruzelski to hold them in line and to dictate suitable arrangements for the Party congress. My impression from reading Warsaw telno 231,[5] however, is that it may already be too late for this: the pressures for proceeding with the '*odnowa*' appear to have been considerable at the plenum, the alternative of looking to a harder-line leadership must be tempting, even if that in effect means bringing about a coup against Kania. The need to act before the Congress preparations are too far advanced may become increasingly pressing. Externally another Soviet-Polish or Warsaw Pact Summit may well be necessary as a means of pressure. The avoidance of recourse to the use of Soviet force has appeared to be a primary Soviet objective up to now and it probably still is—if only because force will be no solution. But I suspect that there is now a growing feeling here that no political pressure, whether internal or external, will tame Solidarity and that at some point force will be needed, probably including fraternal help. It may be that the political game can be played until July, but intervention could come at any point during this period. Whether and when it comes will depend primarily on the Poles. I do not think that six months ago the Soviet leadership would have contemplated that they could let things slide as far as they

[4] The Workers' Defence Committee.

[5] Not printed.

now have. There may yet be a possibility that, if the Poles stay just short of the brink (general strike or public disorder) the Russians will week by week come to accept an even more unacceptable degree of liberalisation. From the Eastern and Western point of view the stakes are now very high indeed. There cannot be much doubt in Moscow about the Western reaction to intervention. This will not be a decisive deterrent, but (see para 3 of mytel 749 of 30 Nov 1980)[5] the threat of it may be the more effective if it is balanced by a positive alternative. Economic aid to Poland will be part of this, but there is also a need for a clear signal, in reply to Brezhnev's messages, that, in the absence of an intervention in Poland, there can be a serious dialogue with the Soviet Union on strategic issues.[6]

[6] The Lord Privy Seal gave an update on the situation in Poland to the Cabinet on 2 April. He thought the decision to call off the proposed general strike had brought the country back from the brink of a major crisis (CAB 128/70).

No. 57

Meeting of the Cabinet Defence and Oversea Policy Committee, 15 April 1981, 11.30 a.m.[1]

OD(81) 8th Meeting Confidential (CAB 148/197)

Polish debt

The Committee had before them a letter from the Chancellor of the Exchequer's private secretary to the Prime Minister's private secretary covering a note by Treasury and Foreign and Commonwealth Office officials which described the existing position as regards current international negotiations on Polish debt and related matters and listed six questions for Ministerial decision.[2]

THE CHANCELLOR OF THE EXCHEQUER said that an acceptable Polish debt settlement appeared to be taking shape. Only one of the six questions for decision presented any real difficulty. This concerned the provision of new credit for Poland. Britain had already agreed to provide a total of £40 million in 1981, all but £8 million of which was already committed. This was not ungenerous, given the

[1] Those present included: William Whitelaw (Chair), Lord Carrington, Sir G. Howe, Francis Pym, Sir Ian Gilmour, John Biffen, Sir Keith Joseph, Peter Walker and Sir Robert Armstrong. Mrs Thatcher was not present at the meeting but she had already indicated that she was content with the Chancellor's approach to the issue in response to a minute from him of 3 April updating her on the situation (PREM 19/560).

[2] The note explained how a task force of five countries (US, FRG, France, Austria and the UK) representing the 15 largest Western creditor Governments had prepared a draft debt settlement agreement with Poland. The main features were: relief of a high percentage (80%); agreement in principle to consider extending this treatment to maturities in 1982 and 1983; a grace period of four years with repayment spread over a further four years; commercial rates of interest during the period of postponement; provision for regular review; comparable treatment to be given to other creditors; a break clause to suspend the agreement if the USSR invaded or the Polish Government resorted to force (though these events were not specifically stated); creditors to choose whether to reschedule or refinance debts.

The questions for decision were: 'Should the UK sign the debt relief agreement as it now stands; should we then reschedule or refinance; should the UK attend any meeting about the provision of new credit; if so, are Ministers prepared to increase the £40 million already approved for the rest of 1981, and by how much; do Ministers wish to maintain short-term cover of approximately £10 million at any one time; should any statement be made to Parliament?'

state of the Polish economy and the poor prospects for repayment. Poland was overborrowed already. Some of Britain's fellow creditors, such as France, had their own reasons for offering more extensive credit and would no doubt press Britain to go further. In general such pressure should be resisted, although there might be a case for assisting further food exports and for some limited concessions of a pump-priming nature to help the Poles re-establish their export industries and thus improve the prospects for eventual debt repayment.

In discussion there was support for the view that Poland's economic situation made it unwise to contemplate further new credit on the scale the Poles themselves were currently seeking. But on political grounds, and because of the close interaction between Poland's political and economic prospects, it was strongly argued that some additional British credit should be provided as a contribution to the overall Western effort. Britain's economic stake in Poland was not much less than that of France or other major creditors; and she had made a major political interest in working to avert Soviet repression there, on which a strong British line had rightly been taken in public. Poland's request for over £80 million more from Britain in 1981 was clearly too high. But there was a good case for providing a further £35-40 million.

THE HOME SECRETARY, summing up the discussion, said the Committee agreed that Britain should sign the proposed debt relief agreement; and that the British technique for providing debt relief should be to reschedule rather than refinance. On balance it was further agreed that British representatives should attend any international meeting about the provision of new credit and should agree to provide a further £35 million in 1981. The Export Credits Guarantee Department should be directed by the Secretary of State for Trade to provide this under the trade encouragement provisions of the Export Guarantee Act. The new credit should not be limited to agricultural exports, on the extent of which the Ministry of Agriculture, Fisheries and Food should consult further with the Treasury; and where non-agricultural exports were concerned further consideration should be given to the possibility of tying the credit to items of particular importance to British industry. The ECGD should also continue short-term cover for Poland of approximately £10 million at any one time. Parliament should at an appropriate stage be informed of the arrangements for further new credit; but there should be no undue publicity, because many countries in the Third World might resent the special treatment being given to Poland.

The Committee:

1. Invited the Chancellor of the Exchequer, in consultation with the Foreign and Commonwealth Secretary to arrange for the United Kingdom to sign the proposed multilateral debt relief agreement with Poland; and, in consultation with the Secretary of State for Trade, to arrange for Polish debts to be rescheduled accordingly.

2. Invited the Chancellor of the Exchequer, in consultation with the Foreign and Commonwealth Secretary and the Secretary of State for Trade, to arrange for the United Kingdom to participate in any further international meetings on the provision of additional new credit for Poland in 1981 and to offer £35 million under that head.

3. Invited the Secretary of State for Trade, in consultation with the Chancellor of the Exchequer, to instruct the Export Credits Guarantee Department as necessary that further new credit for Poland should be provided under the trade encouragement provisions of the Export Guarantee Act and that short-term cover

should continue to be provided for Poland on the existing basis; and, in consultation with the Chancellor of the Exchequer and the Chancellor of the Duchy of Lancaster, to arrange for Parliament to be informed.

4. Invited the Secretary of State for Trade to consult the Chancellor of the Exchequer and the Minister of Agriculture about the extent to which the agreed new credit should be applied to agricultural exports; and to consult the Chancellor of the Exchequer and the Secretary of State for Industry about the extent to which it might be tied to items of particular importance to British industry.[3]

[3] A Debt Relief Settlement was concluded with Poland on 27 April. The agreement provided for debt relief of 90%, rather than the 80% agreed in OD, until the end of 1981 in order to maintain a common front with other Western creditors. This added an additional £8m to the PSBR and as a result the Chancellor wanted to reduce the figure available for new credits from £35m to £25m. In a minute to the Prime Minister of 11 May Lord Carrington argued for the higher figure which was already substantially less than Poland's other major Western trading partners were making available. He maintained that the Polish economy could not be turned around without further imports from the West, which required further hard currency credits, and there was already difficulty in deciding how the £35m should be allocated between agricultural and industrial exports (FCO 28/4521, ENP 090/1). However, the Prime Minister sided with the Treasury. At the 9th meeting of OD on 20 May it was decided that allocating the additional £10m to Poland 'would not represent the best use of the United Kingdom's limited credit resources' and any pressure to go beyond £25m should be resisted (CAB 148/137).

No. 58

Letter from Mr Foster (East Berlin) to Mr Mallaby (Planning Staff), 15 April 1981[1]

Confidential (FCO 28/4364, EN 021/27)

Dear Christopher,

1. Thank you for sending me a copy of your letter of 3 April to Kenneth Pridham with your draft paper on Crisis in Eastern Europe.[2] I did not find much in the text to disagree with, though I am annexing some marginal comments. The obvious difficulty in deciding on the scope of the paper is, as you recognise, that of considering long-term trends in the specific context of a fast-moving and particularised situation. This is especially the case when it is necessary with your present terms of reference to examine the implications of such radically different situations as on the one hand Soviet intervention in Poland and on the other hand what you call reform or renewal in that country. Since a good deal has already been written about the consequences of intervention, I wonder whether it might be more useful to focus on the reformist alternative.

2. Forgive me therefore if I philosophise about change in Eastern Europe beyond my rightful province. The starting point would be that Soviet domination since the War and the 'revolutions' forced upon the East European countries produced an entirely unnatural situation, which was bound to change over time, more or less irrespective of what we in the West might do about it. As your paper recognises our scope for influencing events has always been pretty limited.

[1] The letter was circulated to Warsaw, Prague, Sofia, Budapest, Bucharest, Moscow, Belgrade, Bonn, Paris, Washington and UKDEL NATO, as well as to Mr Fall, Mr Fergusson and Mr Murrell.
[2] Not printed. For a final version of the paper see No. 102.

3. In the early post-War years it looked as if, however unnatural the situation was, the Soviet Government could prevent change by sheer brute force. This idea seemed quite plausible under Stalin but has looked less and less plausible ever since. It is true that by and large there was and is no chance (the present situation in Poland being a possible exception) of rapid and dramatic change. But events over the years have shown that Soviet domination is not a completely irremovable object whereas the pressure for change is an irresistible force.

4. One might use the geological analogy of the tensions which build up along seismic zone or fault line until there is an earthquake or a volcano eruption. Two points about this analogy seem worth noting. The first is that the dramatic events do not take place simultaneously all along a fault line and it is hard to predict precisely when and where an earthquake or volcanic eruption will occur. This has its parallel in Eastern Europe, where the build-up of tensions in different countries has never synchronised: 1953 East Berlin, 1956 Hungary, 1968 Czechoslovakia, 1980/81 Poland and so on. Nor have serious eruptions, from which I exclude the rumblings of Poznan in 1956 and Gdansk in 1970, been so far repeated in any one country. It is an interesting speculation what the possible cycle might be. The second point of the analogy is that the violent release of tension does not stop the gradual but irresistible force of change. Given enough time the landscape is transformed.

5. Human affairs move a lot faster than geological time and on any objective analysis things in Eastern Europe have changed a great deal since the War, even in the Soviet Union. The most striking change is that although Communist régimes have succeeded, sometimes only with the help of Soviet intervention, in maintaining their monopoly of power, they have found it necessary or expedient to use it less ruthlessly to impose uniformity and discipline on their peoples. However objectively nasty the internal situations are in the East European countries, ordinary people have achieved over the years considerable success in freeing themselves from thought control and in generally bucking the system. The moral, and to some extent even the physical authority of Communist régimes has declined visibly. Not only, as the paper says, is there widespread cynicism throughout Eastern Europe about Communist theory and practice. Increasingly people even inside the Party have been feeling emboldened to express it—in extreme cases like Poland openly, but in all cases, I imagine, privately to close friends and as occasion offers to foreign observers. At any rate that is the case in the GDR.

6. All this may seem pretty obvious. But it needs to be borne in mind when considering the present situation in Poland. Dramatic as it has been and still is, it should, I suggest, be seen as an episode in the inexorable crustal movements which are bound in time to change the face of the land. In other words the Marxist model of the inexorable march of history put into reverse.

7. Putting aside geological analogies and turning to another trend of long-term importance, both East and West are suffering from a common disease: the breakdown of idealism and the exposure of materialism as a hopelessly inadequate substitute. In the West unparalleled advances in physical comfort for the masses have left them more discontented, more selfish, less disciplined, more difficult to govern. Welfare advances through technology and legislation, though brilliantly successful in purely material terms, have miserably failed to produce the human satisfaction and social harmony foreseen by the early Socialists and reforming Liberals. We have long been familiar with this syndrome in our own society and have more recently become aware of its East European counter-part. There the

easing of the more brutal forms of repression and compulsion and higher priorities for consumer goods have made life objectively more tolerable, but encouraged a parallel increase in cynicism, skiving and corruption. Without work ethic or community spirit, the frenzied efforts of the party agit-prop machine remains [*sic*] largely irrelevant background noise. Thus both East and West have faced a growing problem of motivation, made worse in the East by the positive discouragement of private initiative. It is not surprising that Communist regimes have felt obliged to seek the help of the Churches as a force of social discipline and motivation, while continuing as far as possible to restrict their political influence. But they cannot square the circle. The more brutal traditional mechanisms of social and industrial discipline are losing credibility and the political system is viewed with deepening cynicism even by members of the Party.

8. Walesa's revolt against monolithic authority seems to have high-lighted the internal contradictions of Communism in an almost ideal way. Instead of questioning the country's strategic alliance as happened in Hungary or preaching political pluralism like Dubcek, he emerged as an ostensibly non-political champion of workers' rights bolstered by fervent religious faith. He has not so much challenged the leading role of the Communist Party as exposed its total lack of democratic mandate even in the Marxist context of class interest. He has, whether sincerely or tactically, expressed contempt for Western political institutions (e.g. in his interview with Oriana Fallaci)[3] and has not pressed for changes in Poland's basic constitutional system. He has 'simply' founded a free trade union and bargained for worker's rights and social reforms. But that is enough to make the country ungovernable, or at least governable only with the consent of Solidarity, as Britain was governed under Mr Callaghan[4] with the consent of the TUC.

9. If this description of Solidarity's position is anywhere near correct, it puts the Polish Government and Party in a nigh intolerable position. Even if they were able, without going bankrupt, to meet the workers' present expectations, for how long will the latter remain content? All Western experience suggests inevitable escalation within a year or two at most, unless there continues to be very strong outside pressure like the Soviet, Czech and GDR sabre-rattling we have witnessed in recent weeks, the effectiveness of which would be gradually eroded by familiarity. If one discounts early intervention, the logic seems to point to a prolonged period of internal tension interspersed with episodes of external pressure and hence international tension. For how long could either side live with this? Within the parameters of the Polish Government's presumed aim to claw back concessions already made and Solidarity's presumed determination to consolidate its gains, the only alternative to tragedy is a compromise producing a more stable situation.

10. What it might be I do not profess to know. Kenneth Pridham, on whose patch I have already trespassed far enough, may say that no such compromise is conceivable, which would not either lose Solidarity its hard-won independence or take the government still further down the road of power-sharing. The Poles would in effect be trying to solve a problem which has so far defeated most Western Governments operating in far more favourable circumstances and with only partially nationalised economies. The most hopeful model which springs to mind is

[3] Italian journalist.

[4] Rt Hon James Callaghan MP, Prime Minister, 1976-79.

the West German miracle, to achieve which employers and trade unions worked together to rebuild a shattered economy through parallel advances in productivity and living standards. But this was under the aegis of Erhard's[5] free economy. Is anything analogous conceivable between governments and trade unions in any society, Eastern or Western?

11. It is on the answer to this question that everything would seem to depend: by which I mean not only the immediate future of Poland, but the influence of her experience on other countries. For if the nature of a possible compromise is so difficult for us to discern—and what is at stake is not just the purity of Communist doctrine but the practical management of an economy—it is a small wonder that the instincts of ordinary people in countries like the GDR, not to speak of their rulers, have prompted extreme caution and scepticism over the Polish case, and not only out of healthy respect for the secret police. If on the other hand something workable and durable emerged from the present dust and confusion in Poland, it might prove highly infectious, with all the attractions of a genuine historic compromise. It could lead to a rebirth of Marxism, with effects extending beyond the Communist orbit.

12. The thought is a bit fantastic. It is probably in irreconcilable contradiction with all experience of Marxism in practice (even in Yugoslavia?) and with most of the laws of human nature. Even more fantastic might seem the question whether it has occurred to the Soviet leaders. But there is a kind of precedent. For somewhat different reasons, but basically because the cost was presumably accounted too high, they allowed Tito to get away with it in 1948, the Romanians less blatantly in the 1970s and so far the Poles. The results of these examples of tolerance have not been wholly unfavourable to Kremlin strategy. An independent Yugoslavia has proved a useful asset in promoting in the Third World a form of non-alignment by no means unhelpful to Soviet interests. To some extent the same may be true of Romania. I do not suggest the Kremlin planned it this way. But it has found compensations for having accepted these unpalatable situations. It might likewise, find compensations in tolerating, within limits of course, the development of a Poland 'road to socialism', if such a road could be built without sinking into the marshes of anarchy or outright revisionism.

13. I would not pretend to have detected so far any evidence that the Kremlin has accepted the Polish situation beyond the fact that it has restricted itself to huffing and puffing. But the Soviet dinosaur has always reacted slowly. How long was it before there was a formal reconciliation with Tito? For how long has the West worried about a possible intervention to discipline Ceausescu? Has it not also been the case that after each challenge to its authority, even challenges successfully repressed, the Kremlin has modified its tactics in an apparently 'liberal' direction, e.g. détente Mk I following the invasion of Czechoslovakia and, it appears, détente Mk II following Afghanistan and Poland? In the past the West has tended foolishly to interpret such changes as positive overtures towards itself, relaxations of basic hostility, rather than tactical adjustments to pressures within the Soviet orbit or the exploitation of perceived opportunities for expansion in the outside world. But this does not alter the reality of the changes. It would not therefore be entirely surprising if the Soviet planners, in spite of current huffings and puffings, are considering how the situation in Poland could be exploited to their advantage, as distinct from liquidated by a *coup de main*.

[5] Ludwig Erhard, Minister for Economics 1949-63 and Chancellor of the FRG, 1963-66.

14. Most obviously they might hope to gain credit by refraining from the use of force, thereby weakening Western solidarity and resistance to their blandishments in the Third World engendered by the invasion of Afghanistan. Beyond that, Poland could be used as a test-bed of a new 'road to socialism' with, if successful, an especially disarming appeal—and the rider that, if Solidarity patently 'abused' the tolerance shown it, intervention remains as a last resort and might in many quarters be accepted as the logical end of a misguided experiment. This could be what GDR Ministers and officials have in mind when they profess optimism, as they have been doing for several months, over Poland's future. Either way, they might hope, the head of indignant steam over Afghanistan *et seq.* would have been largely dispersed and another cycle of confusion over the real nature and intentions of the Soviet system would be inaugurated, as the suppression of the Prague spring.

15. Or is all this over-sophisticated and beside the point? Is Soviet 'moderation' looking no further ahead than the French election and the need to avoid prejudicing Mitterrand's chances?

Yours ever,
P. M. FOSTER

No. 59

Mr Bolland (Belgrade) to Lord Carrington, 24 April 1981
Confidential (FCO 28/4645, ENU 015/3)

My Lord,

Kosovo

1. The recent demonstrations and disorder in Kosovo, Serbia's southern Province, have once again highlighted the apparently intractable problems of this part of Yugoslavia's multi-national society. In my telegram No. 45 of 7 April,[1] I gave an initial assessment of the events. In this despatch I offer, on the basis of the information now available, a more considered account of what happened, why and what the consequences might be.

The events

2. The demonstrations began at about 7 p.m. on 11 March after several days of complaints by students at Priština University about their bad catering arrangements. A student threw down a tray of food in disgust, but this did not spark off the ensuing violence. That was apparently caused by a group of about 30 students, who burst into the refectory, shouting and throwing chairs and tables through the windows and at the cashier's desk. They then emerged onto the streets, forming a crowd of about 400, and headed for the town centre, where they clashed with the militia, injuring about ten. The militia eventually drove the students back to their hostels, though some stayed outside until about 2 a.m. shouting political slogans. The next day, the rector and some of the teaching staff met the students and discussed ways of improving their living and studying conditions. It looked then as if the trouble were over, though a mysterious fire at the Serbian Orthodox Patriachate in Peć during the early hours of 16 March might have been the work of

[1] Not printed.

Albanian nationalists, despite official denials, which were unenthusiastically endorsed by the Church.

3. However, on 26 March a group of about 40 students went into action again at about 6 a.m. locking the doors of the three student hostels, so that the other students could not get out. They then persuaded the latter to gather in the University precincts, where they formed a crowd of several hundred, soon to be met by the rector and a number of the teaching staff. The student leaders began to negotiate with the rector about their rights but he broke off when they started making political demands. The political demonstrations seem to have begun at this point, when the demonstrators pulled out ready-prepared banners and shouted hostile slogans. By about 4 p.m. they began throwing stones at the militia, who had formed a cordon around them, in an attempt to break out of the campus and into the town, where some 40,000 people were gathered to greed the arrival of the Tito baton on its journey across Kosovo in the annual round-Yugoslavia youth relay run. The militia responded vigorously, some say brutally, and 23 demonstrators were injured and 22 of their leaders were arrested, while 14 militiamen also suffered injuries. Over the next few days, there were further acts of violence, e.g. broken shop windows and smashed cars, particularly in the communes surrounding Priština but also as far away as Prizren.

4. The trouble was renewed in Priština on 1 April with a boycott of classes by some secondary school pupils and students. Around 1 p.m. three groups of demonstrators moved in towards the town centre, gathering on their way school-children and some workers. According to a British eye-witness, the violence started when the workers joined in and the demonstrators went on the rampage, smashing shop windows and setting cars and a house on fire as they marched towards the Provincial Committee building. The groups, each numbering 6-800 people, gathered at about 3 p.m. in front of the building, where they waved banners and shouted slogans, which were being passed around on slips of paper, such as: 'Kosovo a Republic', 'We are Albanians, not Yugoslavs', 'We don't want capitalism, we want socialism', 'Down with revisionism' and 'We want a united Albania'. Around 6.30 p.m. two of the demonstrators went up to the militia on the doors and said they were waiting to begin negotiating with someone. But the crowd then started to press forward and the militia reacted by releasing smoke bombs and tear-gas to disperse the demonstrators. The latter seemed prepared for this: they had ready wet towels to reduce the effects of the tear-gas and kept re-grouping as if, some said, they were directed by walkie-talkies. At no stage in Priština did the militia open fire though two demonstrators were found shot, but they were obliged to return fire in other places. Units of the Armed Forces then moved into Priština from various parts of the country to secure strategic points there and elsewhere in the surrounding area, where demonstrations were reported on 2 April and, sporadically, over the next two days.

5. Since then no further disturbances have been reported. The curfew imposed on 2 April was lifted on 8 April, but other restrictive measures remain in force, including the prohibition of any unofficial public gatherings, even football matches, rigorous physical checks on all travellers to the area and a ban on visits by foreigners. After being closed for a fortnight, primary schools reopened on 13 April, to be followed a week later by secondary schools and the University.

6. Speaking to an invited group of foreign journalists in Priština on 17 April, the President of Kosovo's Provincial Committee admitted that all the organisers and supporters belonged to the Albanian community, that workers as well as students

were among them, and that they also included some members of the League of Communists. He gave revised statistics to show that only 75 civilians were injured and eight killed, while 131 members of the security forces were injured, four seriously and one killed, all of them Albanians. 28 people were in prison on charges of being the organisers of the demonstrations, while 194 people were sentenced for having taken part in the demonstrations and other hostile acts.

The causes

7. All the evidence suggests that the demonstrations were deliberately organised and led by politically-motivated Albanians, mainly students. The slogans and banners were clearly Albanian nationalist and irredentist in character. Other elements from the left and right of the political spectrum, as various official spokesmen claimed, may have been involved, but we must look to Albanian nationalism for the main cause. Indeed, a leading member of the Slovene Central Committee said recently in connexion with Kosovo that 'the basic causes of all Yugoslavia's serious crises to date might be found in nationalism and not so much in social problems'.

8. Kosovo has erupted in violent outbursts of nationalism on several occasions since the Second World War. From the outset, the Kosovars were reluctant to join Yugoslavia and an uprising in 1944-45 was ruthlessly suppressed, though limited resistance continued for some time afterwards. In 1955, a state of emergency was declared to quell disturbances apparently instigated by terrorists from Albania. Ranković[2] and his Serb-dominated security police (UDBA) were particularly associated with the brutal suppression of the Albanian majority in Kosovo. After his downfall in 1966 and changes in the UDBA, the Albanians in Kosovo and in Macedonia felt encouraged in June 1967 to demand a separate Republic within the Federation and organised large-scale demonstrations in November 1968, which were eventually put down by the Armed Forces. Nationalist disturbances continued however throughout the '70s: members of the 'Albanian Nationalist Liberation Movement' were imprisoned in 1975; 31 students were imprisoned in 1976 for belonging to the Movement; there were further arrests in 1979 and Tito himself visited Kosovo to calm the situation; and in 1980, eight of those previously arrested were sentenced to terms of imprisonment of three to eight years. The Kosovo nationalists' demands have fluctuated between fusion with Albania and independence from Serbia as a Republic within Yugoslavia, though the latter might also be only a stage towards the former. With each outburst and subsequent changes in the Province's constitutional status, Kosovo has moved a step nearer self-determination in Yugoslavia, but it is clear that the nationalists are still not satisfied with Serbia's nominal tutelage, although they have won equality in almost every other respect with the Republics of Yugoslavia.

9. The events also have an international dimension. I have no evidence of Soviet involvement and Grličkov,[3] a member of the Presidium of the League of Communists, expressly ruled it out in a conversation with me on 6 April. Albanian involvement, though denied officially in Tirana and not admitted openly in Belgrade, is possible. Certainly the temptation to meddle must be strong, when across the border live half as many ethnic Albanians as in Albania itself. And Tirana made it clear in a strongly worded article in *Zeri i Popullit*[4] on 8 April,

[2] Aleksandar Ranković, once considered a successor to Tito, was expelled from the Party and Government in 1966 after bugging Tito's sleeping quarters.

[3] Aleksandar Grličkov.

[4] '*Voice of the People*'—the official newspaper of Albania.

much to Yugoslavia's embarrassment, that Albania had the same right as Yugoslavia or any other country to defend its national minorities. Moreover, the Albanian Ambassador here makes no secret of his country's dissatisfaction with the present borders with Yugoslavia. But, as various Yugoslav leaders have pointed out in renewed critical exchanges with Tirana, stability in Kosovo is just as much in Albania's interests as in Yugoslavia's. They might have added that this applied particularly as Enver Hoxha[5] approaches the end of his reign, when a struggle for power could develop. Indeed, there is much speculation that among the demonstrators were elements who had the latter situation in mind as a motive for agitating now. There is some evidence of involvement in the demonstrations of Kosovars returning from working abroad who might have been in touch with the various Albanian émigré organisations seeking a change of regime in Albania itself. Reports of émigré protests in various parts of Europe and the United States indicate at least moral support for the Kosovo demonstrators.

10. It seems likely that these political causes were accentuated by economic and social grievances. Despite the considerable efforts to develop Kosovo with aid from the Federal Fund for the under-developed regions and more recently with direct investment by the Republic and individual enterprises, the Province still lags far behind in every respect (apart from its phenomenal birth-rate!). Prospects for employment have not kept pace with the aspirations of the excessively large number of young people leaving school and university, who, having been educated mainly in Albanian, do not have the same mobility to find work elsewhere in Yugoslavia. Thus, the population jumped from 733,000 in 1948 to 1,566,000 in 1979 of whom 382,000 were at school and 47,497 at university, while only 168,000 were employed in the social sector. The lack of work has not prevented people, mainly poorly educated peasants, from flooding into Priština and other towns, which are bursting at the seams and hardly able to cope with the enormous social problems.

11. Another factor, which is coming to light, was the failure of the local leadership to listen to warnings about growing discontent amongst the students and, certainly after the first outburst on 11 March, to take adequate remedial measures. My German colleague has told me that senior Party leaders spoke about this to Mr Willy Brandt during a recent visit to Belgrade, implying that Bakali[6] himself, the Communist League President in Kosovo, was ill-informed and complacent.

The consequences

12. Although it will probably take some time for the internal political consequences to emerge, it is therefore already likely that there will be changes in the Kosovo leadership for their poor handling of the events. It is clearly accepted by the Party leadership that the causes lay not in the external threat, but 'in our own weaknesses, the insufficiently developed socialist self-management system'. The Communist League and other socio-political organisations are analysing how it was possible for them to have been taken by surprise and to have miscalculated the first indications of political trouble. But, whatever the results of these enquiries, the inescapable conclusion is that once again the Kosovo leadership have shown their inability to resolve the old dilemma of representing the national

[5] Socialist leader of Albania, 1944-85.
[6] Mahmut Bakali, President of the League of Communists of Kosovo, 1971-81.

aspirations of their Province while adhering to the Party line which admits of no basic change in Kosovo's status.

13. By any logical criteria, Kosovo, within its present borders, ought to have equal status in Yugoslavia with the Republics of Montenegro, Slovenia and Macedonia, since its population is as large and as ethnically homogenous as any one of them. But the Yugoslav leadership has resolutely refused to yield to such logic for internal political and security reasons. Immediately after the War, the Party did not want to antagonise the Serbs further by hiving off Kosovo, since the latter had already 'lost' Macedonia and Bosnia and Herzegovina from pre-War Greater Serbia. Kosovo, as the heart of the medieval Serbian kingdom destroyed by the Turks in 1389, was then, as now, capable of stirring up intense feelings among Serbs. Moreover, after 1948 Albania was a hostile country and Yugoslavia could not risk a separate Albanian Republic in Kosovo which might become disaffected. Having adopted such a policy, the Party has been obliged to prosecute it uncompromisingly ever since, because to change it now would be to open a Pandora's box of requests: first, from the significant Albanian communities in Macedonia and Montenegro to join the Kosovo Republic; then from the Autonomous Province of Vojvodina for parity, which would upset the Serbs both there and in Serbia proper; and, finally, for readjustments of other Republican borders to take account of minorities' wishes. As Dolanc[7] a member of the Party Presidium, put it: 'The creation of a Republic would mean absolutely certainly an attack on the integrity of Yugoslavia.' And the Party Secretary, Dragosavac,[8] said unequivocally: 'The question of Kosovo is resolved, it is an integral part of Serbia and the Yugoslav Federation.'

14. Thus it would seem we are witnessing, once again, the classic situation of the irresistible force of nationalism meeting the immovable object of official policy. Something, somewhere has to give: Yugoslavia's problem is to decide what. In the past, it has succeeded after each outburst of nationalism in Kosovo in calming the situation by offering constitutional concessions which cumulatively have given Kosovo virtually Republican status. It is difficult to see—as senior Party leaders themselves admit privately—how much further they can go short of granting total Republican status itself. But I have no doubt that Yugoslavia's ingenious constitutional experts will be re-examining the problem.

15. Meanwhile, another part of the Communist League's apparatus is examining the faults which the events revealed in the system of public information. The press, led by some caustic leaders in *Politika*,[9] is full of criticism about the delays in providing information on what really happened. Although by the press standards of other communist countries the events have been remarkably well documented the Kosovo, and indeed the central authorities, were at first very reluctant to tell anything like the whole story. For example, after a day of rioting on 1 April in Priština, the press carried the next day only the briefest of reports. No live television coverage was permitted. As many people remarked: 'We were better informed on Brixton than on Kosovo!'[10] *Politika* complained that the initial blackout and subsequent restraints were not of the media's own choosing. Questions are now being asked in political circles about the role of the media and

[7] Stane Dolanc, a member of the Federal Council for Protection of the Constitutional Order.

[8] Dr Dusan Dragosavac, Secretary of the Presidium of the Central Committee of the League of Communists of Yugoslavia, 1979-81.

[9] Serbian newspaper published in Belgrade.

[10] From 10 to 12 April serious rioting had broken out on the streets of Brixton, south London.

the obligation to inform the public at once on matters of legitimate interest which could be of considerable significance for Yugoslavia's further development.

16. Externally, the main political consequence was the deterioration in Yugoslavia's relations with Albania after a steady improvement over the last two years. The Yugoslav leadership were careful in their public statements to avoid implicating Albania. This attitude changed following the leader in *Zeri i Popullit* of 8 April, which was immediately condemned as interference in Yugoslavia's internal affairs for offering support to the nationalists and inciting them to open rebellion. It is clear however that Yugoslavia has no wish to over-react. It obviously could not pass over the Albanians' cleverly worded commentary on the events but sought to give the lie to the charges of neglect and backwardness in Kosovo and to show its resoluteness in dealing with any pretentions to its territorial integrity. This has not put a stop to the flourishing trade and cultural links between the two countries, which were maintained throughout the events, but political relations are likely to remain in cold storage for a long while to come.

17. In the meantime, the authorities have been grappling with the immediate problems of restoring the situation. A start has been made on improving conditions for students at Priština University and other short-term measures have been introduced such as reducing the price of certain basic foodstuffs. Political leaders are now concentrating on longer-term measures. Communist League members have been firmly called to order and the other social and political organisations are taking action to reassert the official line. During the next five years Kosovo will receive about £20 billion for the development of the economy and social services from the Federal Fund, where its share has been increased from 30-43%. Under the new 5-year Plan Kosovo will also receive other funds on a greater scale than ever before which will enable a big expansion in education, culture and public health, the erection of 40,000 new flats and the construction or expansion of industrial plants, particularly to exploit Kosovo's mineral wealth and energy resources, thus providing more jobs and a growth rate 60% above the Yugoslav average.

To sum up

18. The events in Kosovo came as a rude awakening to the Yugoslav leadership as it completed its first year without Tito. They revealed, however, not a new but rather an endemic problem which, with all his authority and charisma, even Tito had not been able to solve. Nor, as they accept, can the present leaders. But they did show on this occasion, after their initial surprise, a welcome maturity in the restrained and positive way in which they handled the situation. With a minimum use of force, they quickly brought the disorders under control and prevented them from involving the people of Kosovo at large. This attitude together with their refusal to accept calls for the use of the 'firm hand' and instead to continue along their chosen path towards greater democratisation provide reasonable grounds for believing that the leadership will be able to keep the Federation together.

19. Are the Kosovo events likely to affect us? They are to the extent that the Yugoslav authorities can be expected to show an increased concern for their unity and territorial integrity, and consequently a sharper sensitivity towards nationalism as a disruptive force, more particularly as expressed in the activities of their emigrants or neighbours. There is little we can do to meet Yugoslav demands to restrain their hostile emigrants and we do not intend to become involved in local Balkan disputes. But, with her firm statement last year of the value we place in their countries' territorial integrity and independence, the Prime Minister gave

much satisfaction to the Yugoslavs.[11] The forthcoming visit of the Foreign Secretary, Mr Vrhovec, to London in June will give us yet another opportunity to reaffirm this support.

20. I am copying this despatch to HM Representatives at Washington, Moscow, Athens, Sofia, Bucharest, Budapest, Rome, Bonn, Paris, the United Kingdom Permanent Representatives to the North Atlantic Council and HM Consul-General at Zagreb.[12]

I am, etc,
E. BOLLAND

[11] See No. 28.
[12] Tensions in Kosovo remained throughout the year. On 7 December Mr Bolland reported that the Yugoslav authorities had endorsed self-management, rather than an independent Republic, as the solution to the Kosovan national question. He also thought that the frankness of the debate around the question had marked a step forward in Yugoslavia's democratic evolution. But although order had been restored the underlying problem of Albanian nationalism in Kosovo remained and it was still unclear whether it could be contained and diverted (FCO 28/4646, ENU 015/3).

No. 60

Letter from Lord Carrington to Mr Biffen (Department of Trade), 1 May 1981

Secret (FCO 28/4608, ENS 091/2)

Dear John,

Poland: Contingency planning

Thank you for your letter of 28 April.[1] I had assumed that Geoffrey Howe's letter of 3 April[2] crossed Ian Gilmour's letter of 2 April[3] and that there was no need for further correspondence. Your letter makes it clear that this is not the case.

I have no doubt that our Allies would endorse Geoffrey Howe's point that it is generally important not to interfere with normal trade and that, if special circumstances require otherwise, our action should not be such as to harm ourselves more than our adversaries. They would also agree with your point that sanctions have wide implications and need to be carefully thought out before a crisis hits. That is why we have been working on this subject in NATO since December, and why agreement on the contingency paper was reached only in March after careful consideration in capitals and through debate in the Alliance.

It is, however, the general view of our Allies that the precise Western response to a Soviet intervention can only be decided by Ministers when the nature and extent of the Soviet action is known. I am sure this is right. One could draw up endless intervention scenarios, but I cannot see governments committing themselves in advance to a particular response to each. Our line on Poland can, therefore, only be defined in advance in general terms. We must recognise that we are dealing with a question of fundamental political and strategic importance. If

[1] Not printed. In this letter Mr Biffen indicated that he remained unhappy about some of the trade aspects of the contingency planning paper agreed in NATO (see No. 51).
[2] The Chancellor wrote to sympathise with the Secretary of State for Trade. He thought a more selective approach to trade sanctions was needed than the one advocated in the paper which the NATO Council had agreed.
[3] See No. 51, note 2.

there is a Soviet invasion of Poland, and if the Western reaction falls short of the quick, effective and appropriate response which the Prime Minister foresaw in her speech to the Diplomatic Writers on 8 April,[4] we shall do lasting damage to the creditability of the West in the eyes of the Soviet Union and of third countries who weigh in their own interest what they see as the balance of power between East and West.

The fact that the Soviet Union is evidently reluctant to deal with Poland as it did with Czechoslovakia must owe something to the clear signals which have come from the West that the costs of such an intervention would be much higher than they were in the case of Afghanistan. The Prime Minister made this point in the same speech on 8 April. If the worst comes to the worst, we shall have to take steps to show that we mean what we said if we are to have any hope of influencing Soviet behaviour in the future. The particular measures to be taken will be a matter for decision when we can see the exact nature of a Soviet intervention. But Western Governments have said publicly that economic as well as political measures will be used, and we have very few instruments at our disposal. We must recognise that effective action in the trade field will be an essential part of the Western response. On this basis there is a good chance that not only the NATO countries but also Japan, Australia, New Zealand, Spain and Ireland will join in. But this will not happen unless we show that we are prepared to go considerably further over Poland than we were over Iran or Afghanistan. Personally, I feel that, in the event of large-scale Soviet intervention in Poland, we should have little alternative to the proposed ban on new commercial contracts—not least because this will satisfy the requirement that all countries should be seen to be playing their part.

The subject of contingency planning is bound to come up in general terms at the NATO Ministerial meeting next week and I propose to make clear the importance we continue to attach to a quick and effective Western response should the Soviet Union intervene in Poland. At the same time, I should be quite content for officials to examine the feasibility, cost and potential impact of the four options which your officials have now put to the Cabinet Office, and which they in turn plan to include in a revised version of their paper. Indeed, my officials wrote to the Cabinet Office on 23 April to propose this.

I am sending copies of this letter to the Prime Minister, other members of OD, the Chief Whip and Sir Robert Armstrong.[5]

CARRINGTON

[4] In the speech, given at New Zealand House in London, Mrs Thatcher said that in the face of the developing situation in Eastern Europe the free world must stand together. If called on to react, she believed the NAC would do so 'far more quickly, effectively and appropriately than after Afghanistan'. The Polish crisis affected the European Community more immediately than any group of nations apart from the Warsaw Pact: 'It demands that we really do co-ordinate our foreign policy—in deeds and in words. We must both be resolute and be seen to be resolute.' A copy of the speech can be found on the Thatcher Foundation website (www.margaretthatcher.org).

[5] Mr Biffen, whilst not changing his position, agreed that the continuing correspondence was producing little agreement and acceded to the suggestion that officials look at how best to meet his concerns without causing unnecessary difficulty for the British position in NATO (Mr Pownall (DoT) to Mr Burges Watson (FCO), 7 May 1981). A report was prepared by officials and circulated as OD(81)26. The issue was discussed by OD on 1 June where it was agreed to defer a decision until a likely contingency arose (PREM 19/560).

No. 61

Mr Pridham (Warsaw) to Lord Carrington, 11 May 1981
Confidential (FCO 28/4480, ENP 014/1)

Valedictory Despatch

Summary . . .[1]

My Lord,

1. With so much in Poland uncertain this is not an easy time to write a valedictory despatch. At the pace things have been moving in the past 9 months some of what I write may be out of date by the time it reaches the Department. I shall, nevertheless, attempt some reflections on the causes, course and possible future development of the Polish revolt.

2. The People's Republic of Poland did not arrive from nowhere in 1945. Poland has a long and in some spheres distinguished history. But it has not been well governed, by the standards of the times, since the 16th century, and for the past 200 years or more there has been an explosion against misgovernment roughly every 30 years.

3. If the explosion of 1980 should be seen in this context it arose most immediately from the coincidence of 3 things, none of which alone would have sufficed: the shortage of food and other consumer goods, the incompetence and insensitivity of the Gierek régime and the relative freedom granted nonetheless to dissident and other critical activity and literature. The last was a product of détente and to that extent détente has been a cause of the Polish revolt. Détente has no doubt also been a factor in the failure of the Soviet Union so far to suppress it.

4. The past 9 months have seen the extraordinary rise of a new independent power—the Solidarity union—accompanied by an unprecedented decline in authority of the Party. So that now, against all communist orthodoxy, there are 3 overlapping powers in Poland: the Party, the Church and Solidarity. And they are soon to be joined by a fourth, the peasants' Solidarity, whose influence and effect on the others it is too early to assess.[2] Yet the struggle during these months has been in one sense muted and unreal. Each party has deliberately refrained from exerting its full strength from unspoken fear of the great outside factor, the Soviet Union. Had it not been for this factor the Polish régime would by now have gone the way of the Shah of Iran. As it is, the Government administers the country but for much of the past 9 months it has hardly governed in the accepted sense of the word. The Government's policy under Prime Minister Pińkowski—if one can call it a policy—of resisting Solidarity's demands until the pressure became too strong lost it prestige and gained it ridicule and odium, as well perhaps as time. Yet to say that it was always wrong to do so would be to follow too easily the Whig

[1] Not printed.

[2] Rural Solidarity, a trade union of Polish farmers, was established at the end of 1980 and claimed to represent over one-and-a-half million smallholders. The Polish Government signed an agreement with the striking farmers in February 1981, making limited concessions regarding legal protection of inheritance of land, permission to build more churches in the countryside and a promise of equal treatment of individual farmers. But the Government refused to register the organisation arguing that the farmers were not wage earners. It was officially recognized on 12 May 1981 after the farmers' strike in Bydgoszcz (see No. 53).

interpretation of history which sees life as an eternal struggle between virtuous progressive Whigs and obstructive reactionary Tories.

5. The 3 immediate questions now, all of which are interconnected, are whether the economy will collapse, whether the régime will keep control of the situation and whether the USSR will intervene militarily.

6. The economy is in an appalling state. The country cannot pay its debts nor afford food and other imports to keep going: nor can it grow enough to feed the people. Things were on a long-term downward slope under Gierek but the present crisis is due to the collapse of work discipline. It follows that that must be restored before things can get better, which in turn depends on a *modus vivendi* between Government and Unions. Next agriculture must be got right. The Government have made a major concession in recognising Rural Solidarity and it may be that this, with other concessions about land purchase and security of tenure, will be sufficient to reverse the decline in agricultural production, always provided enough fertilisers can be imported. With a good harvest, supplies of dairy products might increase later this year, though the meat situation could not noticeably improve for a year or two, and to modernise the country's partly medieval methods of agriculture will take much longer.

7. The industrial outlook, which of course impinges on agriculture, is much more uncertain. The structure is wrong; the system ossified; the burden of debt difficult to break out from. There may be a collapse this year. On the other hand, the country is rich in raw materials; and the people are capable of excellent industrial organisation (the big steel works at Katowice was a model of efficiency and productivity). The 'renewal' ought in theory to generate economic, political and administrative reform to a degree that will inspire new life, energy and the will to work in Polish industry. Alas, so far its results in this field have been strikes, absenteeism and a catastrophic fall in production. It is reasonable to believe that this phase may now be on the wane and that, with fresh Government concessions and a realisation by Solidarity of the seriousness of the situation, things will begin to improve. But on the most optimistic estimates results cannot be expected for 2 or 3 years. And meanwhile the Polish people will have to go short. The most important thing is for agriculture to be turned around. If that is done the food import bill will sink, shops will be fuller and at once there will be hope.

8. The economic situation can only improve if a measure of political and social peace returns and if motivation to work and more confidence in the Government are established. Solidarity's leadership seem prepared to accept the leading role of the Party and Poland's international alliances. But their very demands in the social, economic and sometimes political field greatly erode the Party's role. The Party indeed seems of necessity to welcome this. In the first place the Party has largely lost confidence in its right to rule. Throughout the ages the right of the ruler has been sought from God, the social contract, the ballot-box or some kind of historical determinism. The Polish Party can claim none of these and has almost openly fallen back on the truth that it was imposed by the Red Army and has to stay lest worse befell. Furthermore, partly with a view to taming Solidarity, partly because there is no other way the state can be run, the Party is striving to bring the union into a share of responsibility for Government decisions of major importance.

9. One could see this process developing so far that, as some sociologists have suggested, the Party might ultimately become like a sort of constitutional monarchy, the real power passing elsewhere. Another possibility is that the Party, under grass-roots pressure, will move so far away from orthodox Marxism-

Leninism that there will develop something not very unlike social or Christian democracy. Few Poles believe deeply in communism and such things are possible in the long term, provided that neither Solidarity nor the régime respectively press too hard and for and against change. There are those in Solidarity who would like to sweep away the régime and there are those in the régime who would like to return to the Gierek era or worse. If catastrophe is to be avoided these people must be controlled by the moderates. Had the Bydgoszcz incident been followed by a general strike, the Government would have proclaimed a state of emergency or martial law and used the army to run essential services. Clashes and even civil war could then have resulted. The greatest threat lies in the eruption of a comparable incident. Barring that, there is a reasonable hope that there will be a sufficient meeting of minds between a greatly but not impossibly liberalised régime and a sobered Solidarity to keep the country from falling over the edge.

10. The likelihood of Soviet intervention, in the light of the now almost universal Polish determination to reform the State, is endlessly debated. My own feeling is that there is more give in the Soviet ideological position than we have tended to believe. The situation is quite different from that obtaining in Czechoslovakia in 1968. Czechoslovakia had no Solidarity, the West had no unified position. Moreover, the Russians may reflect that if the end result of the Polish revolt is communism with a human face that may not be wholly in the interests of the West or wholly against those of the Soviet Union. The Russians would intervene militarily, I believe, to prevent the régime from being overthrown, to remove a threat to their military communications and to suppress anarchy and chaos in the country. While they could not accept erosion of the Party's leading role beyond a certain point, that point is now very much further away than anyone would have believed possible in July 1980.

11. The unpleasant and unsatisfactory option of military intervention is not, however, the only Russian weapon. Poland is heavily dependent on Soviet raw materials. Then there is what one might call the German card. Poles have grown used to occupying large chunks of former German territory, but the Polish Government is quietly reminding Solidarity of some of the background. The Russians have it in their power to stir up, to put it no higher, the whole question of German unity and the German frontiers. Some Poles in 1945 opposed the annexation of this German territory precisely because they believed it would tie Poland to Russia for all time. The likelihood (provided that there are no major changes in the international situation or in the Soviet Union itself) is that Poland will keep just this side of the brink, that the Russians will not send their tanks in, but that the country will go on lurching from crisis to crisis for some time to come.

12. The Polish character is in many ways a noble and attractive one. Courage, loyalty and a fierce patriotism are among their outstanding virtues. The romantic devil-may-care image that also attaches to the Poles is, however, one which some of them (notably Foreign Minister Czyrek) rather dislike. They would like to see it replaced by more prosaic Germanic characteristics. (In fact there must be a strong admixture of German blood in the Polish nation and *vice versa*: Poles do not like to recall that the SS General who suppressed the Warsaw rising was named von dem Bach-Zelewski.)

13. Unfortunately, Polish virtues are offset by one major vice which surprised me when I arrived here, my only other experience of a communist state being a Yugoslavia with still some remnants of the partisan morality. This is the almost universal petty corruption which permeates such bodies as the police, the customs

and any other office with power over people's daily lives. Few things get done without some kind of a bribe. Corruption at the higher level also exists: but I think it will be found that even under the Gierek régime it was not very extensive if one takes, as I do, the various perquisites which senior officials and others allowed themselves not as corruption but as something which they considered their due, as an 18th century politician would accept a sinecure. At least something is being done about corruption in high places but I have not noticed the slightest attempt to check it in low places, where it affects people much more.

14. Corruption or not, life in Poland has greatly improved in the non-material sense since July 1980. People can speak and write much more freely: it is obvious from the expression on the average Polish face that a great deal of the fear and constraint which surrounded daily life has disappeared. Materially people are much worse off and there is a possibility that the bulk of the population may ultimately prefer shorter queues and more bread to political freedom.

15. Our own policy of helping to keep the Polish economy afloat and of otherwise promoting Polish independence seems to me absolutely right. I trust we should never take the view (sometimes expressed in the United States) that Soviet intervention might be rather a good thing since everyone would then wake up to the Soviet danger. I would, however, agree with the United States Secretary of State that too many public warnings to the Soviet Union to keep out may defeat their purpose. They begin to look more like a challenge than a warning. I also think we should recognise that Solidarity must exercise moderation as well as the Government and beware lest any public statements of ours might encourage their wilder spirits to the contrary.[3] What they have achieved in the last 9 months is almost miraculous. With cool heads, vigilance and steady but flexible pressure they could bring Poland at least to that measure of liberty it enjoyed before the Stalinist guillotine came down in 1947,[4] and possibly much further. Immoderate or violent action by Solidarity may well, however, lead to the sort of catastrophe from which Poles will look back on the Gierek era as a golden age.

16. In the course of my diplomatic career I have lived in one right-wing and two left-wing dictatorships. There is no doubt that to those, like foreign diplomats insulated from their more unpleasant side, they present certain agreeable features. For instance, freedom from terrorism and casual street violence, freedom from all-pervading moronic advertising and from the nastier offshoots of the permissive society. Yet not so long ago Western democratic countries were also free of these things. What a pity that in this respect they have taken such a wrong turning.

17. And how comic or tragic to see the British far-left parading and demonstrating in favour of the sort of system which Polish workers are hoping to get rid of. Some of our exchange visits should bring the two together. It is already

[3] At his farewell party on 27 April, Mr Pridham had been approached by Professor Romuald Kukulowicz, Cardinal Wyszynski's representative with Solidarity, to ask whether if Mr Wałęsa paid a visit to London he could be received by Lord Carrington. The FCO were anxious to avoid giving the Russians a pretext for claiming that HMG were encouraging such a visit and the Ambassador was asked not to raise the matter with Mr Czyyrek, or with the Cardinal (FCO 28/4539, ENP 212/1).

[4] In the general elections the Communist-controlled bloc was awarded 382 seats out of 444 in parliament, claiming 90% of the vote. Great Britain protested that the elections had not been conducted freely or fairly, and infringed what had been agreed to at Yalta in February 1945 (see *DBPO: Western Security*).

instructive to see the guru of British unilateral nuclear disarmament, Mr E.P. Thompson,[5] painfully defending himself against the criticisms of Czech dissidents.

18. In the past 9 months we have at various times half-expected to see Soviet tanks in the streets or hear sounds of civil war. Throughout these alarms the staff of the Embassy have remained admirably calm. I should not wish to end without paying tribute to the devoted work done at all levels in this Embassy to promote Britain's interests.

19. I am sending copies of this despatch to Her Majesty's Ambassadors at Moscow, East Berlin, Budapest, Bucharest, Sofia, Prague, Belgrade, Washington, Paris, Bonn, Helsinki and Stockholm, and to the UK Permanent Representative to the North Atlantic Council.[6]

I am, etc,
K. R. C. PRIDHAM

[5] Edward Palmer Thompson, a British historian, writer and socialist, and a prominent intellectual of the Campaign for Nuclear Disarmament. In 1980, he co-authored the pamphlet *Protest and Survive*, which revived interest in the peace movement and an *Appeal for European Nuclear Disarmament*, which called for a nuclear-free Europe from Poland to Portugal. The *Appeal* opened contacts between East and West, associating the campaign for peace with the movement for democracy in Eastern Europe.

[6] Commenting on the despatch on 9 July, Mr Broomfield was less sanguine than Mr Pridham noting that 'the continuing failure of the Polish leadership to take a firm grip on the economy has been one of the most depressing aspects of the otherwise exhilarating developments of the past ten months. Without progress on the economic front, the *Odnowa* is probably doomed with or without an intervention.' He agreed that there was a reasonable hope of averting a catastrophe but although both sides had showed some moderation, the danger of a 'lunatic fringe' in Solidarity could not be discounted. Broomfield thought that the Poles would still put up with a surprising amount of material suffering in order not to jeopardise their hard-won gains. Finally he agreed that public statements on Poland should be carefully considered, concluding: 'Certainly the Poles can best pursue their internal policies over the next few months in an atmosphere of international calm' (FCO 28/4482, ENP 014/1).

No. 62

Minute from Mr Broomfield to Mr Fergusson, 8 June 1981

Secret (FCO 28/4340, EN 021/5)

Poland

1. This minute draws together current reporting on Poland's internal and economic situation. It is based on reporting from the Post and other sources. It sets out the options facing the Russians. It outlines action in hand.

Political

2. It is clear that the elections of delegates to the Party Congress (14-18 July) will result in an over-whelmingly reformist congress. Up to 70% of the delegates may be new. Wojna, a member of the Polish Central Committee has predicted that only about 15% of the members of the Central Committee will be re-elected and possibly only three or four of the current Politburo. Many of the delegates will also be members of Solidarity.

3. The election of delegates is supposed to be completed by 20 June. But this deadline may well be extended. Concurrently with the election of the delegates there is discussion of the programme to be adopted at the Party Congress. This is based on the theses circulating now. It is not yet clear, however, what will be in the

draft programme put to the Congress but it is very likely that it will be a reformist document.

4. One of the effects of the tense internal debate is that neither the Government nor the Party leadership has time for much else, in particular economic management. Mr James has commented on the lack of leadership and general sense of drift.

5. Relations between Solidarity and the Government are currently under renewed strain. The Bydgoszcz Solidarity Committee together with three others have recommended a two-hour warning strike on 11 June to be followed, if necessary, by a complete national strike on 15 June if the Government does not fulfil its commitment to bring those involved in the assault on Solidarity members in Bydgoszcz in March to justice.[1] Vice Premier Rakowski is currently engaged in negotiations with Solidarity who want more concessions. In Rakowski's view the Government are not in a position to make any.

Economic

6. The Polish economy is in a bad way. Production, especially coal, is falling. Exports are also falling. Industrial unrest has exacerbated the situation. According to Wojna, Poland is 'the first European industrial nation in the twentieth century to be on the verge of famine'.

7. Western action so far has been to roll over Polish debts falling due from 28 March onwards. On 27 April Western governments agreed to provide 95% debt relief until the end of 1981. Western banks have proved more difficult but it is likely at their next meeting on 24 June that they will agree to a 95% debt relief (principal only, not interest) until the end of 1981. According to Polish figures the fifteen Western creditors countries have given $2 ½ billion new commercial credits to far of which $1 billion has been utilised up to 1 April.

8. At the last round of meetings on 1/2 June between the Poles and the Western governments the Polish case for further commercial credits failed to convince the fifteen creditors who urged the Poles to make a greater effort to ensure that the stabilisation programme worked; to get their priorities right and where necessary trim their requirements; to utilise export revenues more efficiently; and to insist on more help from their CMEA partners.

9. Attitudes in the CMEA are hardening. The Soviet Union is almost certainly annoyed at the use of their hard currency credits to the Poles to pay off the West. This probably accounts for the reported cut-off of Soviet credits at the end of March. The Poles have, however, assured us that the Soviet Union and others have agreed to run deficit trade balances. But there are Polish press reports claiming that their CMEA partners have threatened to withhold raw materials if Poland does not fulfil its coal deliveries. A CMEA meeting to consider the impact of the Polish shortfalls on the five years plans and programme of CMEA as a whole has been reported as likely to take place very soon.

10. Food rationing and EC assistance seemed to have staved off, for the time being, a disaster over food. The harvest prospects look good. It will not be clear for some months whether Wojna's gloomy predictions about famine are likely to be borne out.

11. The basic problem would appear to lie with the Poles themselves. Although attention to the economy may be as important as resolving the political crisis the Government does not have time to devote to it.

[1] See No. 53, note 2.

Military indications

12. The latest CIA report talks of a 14-day warning period before a full-scale invasion can be mounted. We think this may be over-optimistic. Much would depend on whether the Russians intervened with over-whelming force—i.e. 30 or 40 divisions—or whether they invaded initially with a smaller force—perhaps 20-25 divisions. In the latter case we would almost certainly get less than 14 days warning since most of these divisions would come from the GDR and Czechoslovakia and are already in a high state of readiness. In the case of a 30-40 division invasion we could probably expect a warning time of about ten days. An invasion of this scale would require the mobilisation of divisions in the Western Military Districts and we would expect to detect signs of this well before it was completed. In addition we should expect to pick up communications indicators at an early stage, whichever scenario the Russians chose. Communications activity is currently at a low level but the networks set up before Easter could quickly be reactivated.

Soviet views and options

13. From the outset the Soviet Union has had three main options:

(*a*) intervention

(*b*) restoration of the situation by the Poles themselves; and

(*c*) wait and see

14. The Soviet preference would clearly be for the Poles to put their own house in order. They obtained assurances from Kania and Jaruzelski in March when they visited Moscow that this would indeed happen. Suslov's visit to Warsaw was no doubt intended to check on progress and remind the Polish leaders of their commitments. Nevertheless the Russians must now be very sceptical of the ability, or even the desire of the Polish Party leadership to exert the sort of control that the Russians would wish to see.

15. The Soviet Central Committee has sent a letter to the Polish Central Committee calling for a change of course within the Polish Party and for firm measures to be taken against counter-revolutionary tendencies in the Party. The message apparently also said that if necessary, the Soviet Central Committee would be prepared to help. On receipt of this letter the Polish Politburo went into urgent session and is continuing to meet. A meeting of the Party Plenum is due to take place on 9 June. On past form it could prove stormy.

16. If this latest Soviet move fails, and it seems likely that it will, the Russians will be facing an acute dilemma. If the Party Congress goes ahead it will almost certainly be attended by a reformist majority and pass a reformist programme. From the Soviet point of view the Party will have become an unreliable instrument for re-establishing control. They may urge that the Party Congress be postponed or indeed the Poles may themselves decide to postpone the Congress as the lesser of the many evils they face. But such a decision will not be easy given the over-whelming enthusiasm for the holding of a Congress. A postponement could therefore spark off a further round of tension between the Party, Solidarity and the Government.

Work-in-hand

17. Soviet intervention will mainly be decided by their assessment of the internal Polish situation. But at a time when the balance between intervening and not must become increasingly problematical to them, external factors take on a disproportionate importance.

18. A short paper is in preparation with the Planning Staff setting out some of the possibilities open to the West, visits etc which may act as additional inhibitions on the Russians.[2] Mr Bullard may draw on the ideas in this paper in the limited consultations he is to have on 15 June to see if our suggestions recommend themselves to the Americans and others.

19. On the economic side we are preparing a telegram of questions to be put to our main Western partners to check their assessment of the state of Poland's economy. Mr Bullard will be comparing notes on 15 June. Mr Czyrek will no doubt raise the economic problems during his visit from 18 to 19 June. Although it will probably be undesirable to indicate this to him we have in fact an additional £25 million credit for the second half of 1981 up our sleeves which we have not yet disclosed to the Poles.

20. We will continue to keep a close watch on the economic situation. It is possible that the Russians may themselves be hoping for or even trying to engineer an economic collapse in Poland to discredit Solidarity. The present timetable for multilateral activity is as follows. The US will be producing a questionnaire for agreement by the other Western creditors to be put to the Poles in July. The Poles will be asked to reply to it in August. The Western creditors will meet the Poles in Warsaw in September to discuss their response and to elicit any further information necessary. This will be followed by a further meeting of the Western creditor nations in October to assess the effects of Western debt relief and to decide on what ought to be done for 1982. This timetable will give us a number of opportunities for feeding in ideas if our own assessments, or the Poles themselves, indicate that an unavoidable economic crisis is imminent.

N. H. R. A. BROOMFIELD

[2] See No. 63.

No. 63

Minute from Mr Broomfield to Mr J. Bullard, 9 June 1981

Confidential (FCO 28/4340, EN 021/5)

Poland: Constraints on the Soviet Union

1. The situation in Poland is again becoming critical. The political and economic crisis in the country is acute, and there have been indications recently of increasing Soviet disenchantment with international developments generally and with Polish developments in particular. Mr Manning explores both these questions in his minutes to me of 2 and 3 June.[1] The Soviet debate as to whether or not to intervene may now be very finely balanced. The main restraints on Soviet intervention are still the risk of considerable resistance, and the cost of reviving Poland in the aftermath of an intervention. But as the calculation of advantage and disadvantage becomes more difficult for the Russians, international factors may take on a decisive importance.

2. We have, therefore, discussed with Planning Staff what further measures the West might take to try to deter Soviet intervention in Poland. Some of the

[1] Not printed. These two minutes were dated 2 and 4 June (not 3 June).

following possibilities might be tried out on the Americans in restricted consultations on 15 June:

(i) *US/Soviet Summit*: The Russians have made it clear ever since President Reagan came to office that they are keen to resume the superpower dialogue (reach an understanding on matters of strategic importance) interrupted by Afghanistan. But, in their present mood, the Americans are unsympathetic to the idea, and in recent weeks there have been signs that the Russians have become irritated and increasingly discouraged. Soviet press attacks on the Reagan Administration have become much sharper and have cast doubt on the prospect for US/Soviet relations. Until now the Russians' desire to establish a working relationship with the Reagan team has acted as a constraint on their handling of the Polish crisis. If they are now coming to believe that dialogue with the new US Administration is going to prove impossibly difficult, this will weaken that constraint. In the circumstances, agreement by President Reagan to a summit meeting late this year (November or December) would be far and away the best 'carrot' the West could offer the Russians with a view to reinforcing the constraints against intervention. A summit at that stage would be almost a year into the Reagan Presidency and need not arouse too many false hopes if it is presented as exploratory. It need not actually achieve anything: it will be enough that summit level contact has been resumed. As far as Poland is concerned, it will have served its purpose if it buys more time for the results of the Party Congress to be assimilated and (hopefully) put into effect.

Secretary of State's visit to Moscow[2]

(ii) The Secretary of State's planned visit to Moscow early next month may also provide opportunities for exerting some pressure on the Russians. It might be possible to construct an indirect link between our Polish and Afghan objectives. We might consider asking the Americans to remind the Russians before a visit by Lord Carrington to Moscow, of President Reagan's remark about looking more favourably on negotiations if there were movement on Afghanistan. We might ask the Americans to add that they particularly hoped that the Soviet reaction to Lord Carrington's proposals about Afghanistan during the visit would be positive. This formula (much less definite than that proposed in Mr Manning's minute of 2 June)[3] would not doom the US/Soviet summit idea to sink or swim with movement on Afghanistan, but would lend power to Lord Carrington's elbow. In due course we should ask our closest friends whether they have any plans for visits to Moscow at a similar level. (Mr Bullard will wish to check on the state of play and consultations before mentioning on 15 June, the possibility of a visit to Moscow.)

The CDE

(iii) There is little specific action that the West could, or should, take over the CDE proposal to help deter Soviet intervention in Poland. The only such action that we can envisage would be to make some concession on the CDE designed to make it more attractive to the Russians. But we would not wish to offer anything of this kind which would undermine the principal elements of the French proposal and thus diminish the security benefits which a CDE offered to the West. This would in any case run counter to our general policy on arms control and disarmament, which is to pursue only those negotiations which are in our security interests. At the same time, some kind of conference on European disarmament has been a Soviet objective for a long time. We do not discount the possibility that the

[2] For more on this visit see *DBPO: Afghanistan* No. 98ff.

[3] Not printed.

Russians may be prepared to agree to a conference which would include the basic elements of the French proposal. For the Russians agreement on a CDE would be an addition to the *acquis* of detente. Hence it would increase the price which they would have to pay for an invasion. This suggests that the West should continue with its present line at Madrid—to express strong interest in holding a CDE, as long as it is on the right terms.

TNF

(iv) Contacts between the Americans and the Russians have begun and Mr Haig and Mr Gromyko are to meet in September. But there are unresolved differences in the US Administration about the Western negotiating approach and the Russians must expect progress to be slow. The Americans could make it clear to the Russians that they are anxious for progress in these talks. But, as in the case of the CDE, this would mean that the basic aim of securing an agreement clearly in our security interests would be set at risk by subordinating these to separate political considerations.

(v) *Security Council Summit*: One of the proposals put forward by Brezhnev at the 26th Party Congress in February was that there should be a UN Security Council Summit. Like other Western countries we have dismissed this as a typically propagandist 'peace proposal' of no value. Perhaps we should reconsider our view. There are certainly drawbacks to the proposal; the agenda would offer openings to the Russians as well as the West. But we might mention the idea of a Security Council Summit to the Americans in the context of a discussion about ways of restraining the USSR, perhaps with a view to goading them to think more positively about a bilateral US/Soviet summit.

3. In addition to these 'carrots' we should consider the possibility of using visitors as a further inhibition on the Russians:

(i) *A visit by the Prime Minister to Poland*: There is an invitation outstanding for Mrs Thatcher to go to Poland (in return for the Jaroszewicz visit here in 1976). This could prove useful as a complicating factor in any Soviet timetable for intervention. Mr Czyrek's imminent visit here offers an opportunity to pursue this.[4]

(ii) *Other visitors*: Visits to Poland by other Western leaders e.g. Schmidt, Mitterrand or Haig would also complicate things for the Russians.

4. The range of options is not great. A definite commitment to a US/Soviet summit would be incomparably the best move the West could make. But in a situation as delicately posed at the Polish crisis now is, the other measures might all help, albeit on a much more modest scale, to give the Russians pause.

5. This minute does not go into what might be done to help Poland over its growing economic crisis. It is difficult to assess whether the Russians would regard this as a 'stick' or a 'carrot'. It is a 'carrot' to the extent that the West's contribution means a lesser burden on Poland's CMEA associates. It is a 'stick' if the Soviet hope is that economic collapse will discredit the renewal movement.[5]

N. H. R. A. BROOMFIELD

[4] See No. 71.

[5] Mr Fergusson read the minute 'with interest' but disagreed with the idea of holding a summit which, he thought, should confirm agreements carefully worked out in advance. Mr Bullard commented on 31 July: 'As things have fallen out, it is economic collapse rather than a Soviet invasion that Poland needs to fear.'

No. 64

Mr Bolland (Belgrade) to Lord Carrington, 10 June 1981, 1.30 p.m.
Tel. No. 85 Immediate, Confidential (FCO 28/4652, ENU 026/1)

My Telno: *Vrhovec.*[1]

1. On the eve of Vrhovec's visit, Yugoslavia remains politically and economically stable, still set on its non-aligned course, but beset by some potentially destabilising forces.

2. Politically, the collective and rotatory leadership designed by Tito is being consolidated: no one has yet challenged it. Efforts continue to perfect the system of socialist self-management which embraces political and social as well as economic life, the 3rd self-managers congress, taking place during Vrhovec's visit, promises no surprises.

3. There are, however, some strong contradictory influences just below the surface. The most immediate is the demand of Albanians in Kosovo to change its status from that of an autonomous province within Serbia to a republic. After some violent demonstrations in March and April, the authorities seem to have the situation under control.[2] But they admit it remains very serious and there is no easy or early solution. It is clear many local Albanians are sympathetic to the demonstrator's demands and are still stubbornly refusing to co-operate in the current purge. The Prime Minister of the Interior gave more details on 10 June on the extent and destructiveness of the demonstrations and on their careful organisation. He expressed fears of possible future hostile activities, including terrorism. The security forces in Kosovo he said are being further strengthened (see my Telno 86).[3] Yugoslav authorities state they do not intend to grant republican status as it would threaten the territorial integrity of Yugoslavia i.e. by leading eventually to Kosovo joining Albania.

4. There are also persistent claims by the Roman Catholic hierarchy in Croatia for more religious freedom and some minor dissident stirrings for more political freedom. The authorities have reacted firmly to all such attempts to undermine the unity of the Federation or the rule of the League of Communists. They have tended to put the blame for internal opposition on Yugoslav émigrés, especially Croats and now Albanians, about whose activities they remain extremely sensitive.

4. [*sic*] Economically, the authorities are wrestling with some intractable problems which worsened earlier this year. Inflation continues unabated at some 50%, exports have not increased sufficiently and the economy remains over-dependent on costly imports, industrial production is well below target, unemployment continues to grow. There is widespread reluctance to tighten the belt. The authorities, however, indicate with their new five year plan that they are determined to set their house in order. It seems they will need more foreign financial help: in 1980 they borrowed some $1.6 billion; they are I understand intending to look for a similar amount this year. London banks will probably again be asked to help organise a consortium loan.

6. Internationally, it is clear that Tito's commanding presence is missed: Yugoslavia no longer exercises its former influence in the non-aligned movement or elsewhere. But it remains highly active in NAM, the UN, CSCE and with

[1] Josip Vrhovec, Yugoslav Minister of Foreign Affairs. He paid a visit to the UK in June.
[2] See No. 59.
[3] Not printed.

individual countries, to some effect. This year it has devoted much attention to Africa, where it considers the NAM has a firm hold. Namibia is to the fore. Yugoslavia's political relations with the Soviet Union are lukewarm but this year they have sharply increased their trade. On Poland, Yugoslavia remains firmly opposed to any outside intervention. A joint meeting of the State and Party presidencies reiterated this stand on 10 June. It maintains good relations with Romania, Hungary and East Germany, satisfactory with Czechoslovakia and fratchy with Bulgaria. It sides naturally with the South against the North and with the disarmers against those who intend to balance arms control with security. Some Yugoslavs see merit in Brezhnev's disarmament proposals. There is growing dissatisfaction with the working of the EC/Yugoslav treatment.[4]

7. Britain has no serious problems with Yugoslavia. On the contrary, we stand high in its esteem. Vrhovec's visit will, I hope, give the Prime Minister again and now you, Sir, opportunities to show understanding for Yugoslavia's underlying difficulties and to renew our assurances that we value highly its unity, territorial integrity and independence. Vrhovec may raise the émigré question: although fortunately no Albanians or Croats have been noted here as demonstrating in Britain over Kosovo, the Croats in Britain are very active in their propaganda campaign against the regime. Vrhovec may also repeat the requests made to Mr Parkinson[5] for help in increasing exports to Britain (this is a Yugoslav responsibility but we are doing what we can to help) and open the campaign for more financial support (where again I hope we can show sympathy but, thinking of Poland, caution). But above all, the visit will enable you to explain to Vrhovec our views on international issues. He is alert and frank and has travelled much (most recently to Japan, North Korea and China). His year as a journalist in London in the late fifties has left him with a real affection for Britain as well as a reasonable knowledge of English.

[4] See No. 4, note 11.
[5] Cecil Parkinson, Minister for Trade.

No. 65

Minute from Mr Wright (Cabinet Office) to Mr Alexander (No. 10), 24 June 1981
Confidential (PREM 19/560)

Aid to Poland

It seems likely that the Foreign and Commonwealth Secretary may wish the Prime Minister to resolve the difference between himself and the Chancellor of the Exchequer which is set out in his minute to the Chancellor of the Exchequer dated 22nd June and the latter's reply on 23rd June.[1] The problem, which is likely to

[1] Not printed. Lord Carrington argued that events had reached a critical phase in the run-up to the Polish Party Congress which he thought represented 'the first and last opportunity for the supporters of a more liberal and popularly supported administration in Poland to establish their position and obtain the mandate they need to offer the country firm leadership, on which both economic and political stability will ultimately rest.' He added: 'I believe that it is in the broadest Western interest that they should be given this chance'.

However the Chancellor made it clear that any Bank of England participation in a loan would need to be secured using Polish gold reserves or, in the likely event this was unavailable, the

come up at next Monday's European Community Heads of Government meeting, arises from the Polish request to ourselves and our principal European partners (including the Swiss Central Bank) for $500 million in additional financial assistance to enable Poland to make use of existing lines of credit. Mr Czyrek explained to the Prime Minister on 19th June how lack of liquidity was preventing Poland from drawing on these. The proposal is formally set out in the attached translation of a letter from the French Finance Minister, Monsieur Delors, to the Chancellor of the Exchequer: the British share amounts to $100 million in short-term financial credits for six months.[2] The Foreign and Commonwealth Secretary recognises that the economic case for giving yet more help to Poland is weak, but believes that the Government should make a favourable response in the particular circumstances prevailing at present. In his view if each of the creditor countries were to contribute $30 million, the total figure would come close to that for which the Poles have asked.

2. The Chancellor of the Exchequer considers that the proposal should be rejected. He believes that a number of other creditor countries, including West Germany and the Italians, are unlikely to be enthusiastic and that if this country shows an interest, we may be asked for considerably more than $30 million. Secondly he is doubtful if even $500 million will turn the Polish economy round. It would be more likely to go to finance the Polish deficit for the rest of the year, and simply become an addition to the already large total Polish debt. Thirdly he knows that the Bank of England would be very reluctant to join in such a venture. It is the Bank's view that the Polish economy is already in a disastrous state and that the socio-economic forces at work in that country are likely to worsen rather than improve it. Massive economic assistance has already been given to Poland by the West. There must be real doubt whether the debt relief operations will survive in their present form. The Bank does not believe that additional Western assistance on the scale this country is likely to be willing or able to afford, can make much contribution towards bringing the Polish economy round within a reasonable time, or that any such assistance will make the repayment of existing loans more likely. The Bank is also concerned that what is done for Poland will create precedents for dealing with other bankrupt countries some of which may be military allies or countries with greater claim on British benevolence than Poland.

3. The difficulty about this problem is that the Chancellor of the Exchequer is presenting arguments on the financial and economic level which are unanswerable in those terms. But the case which the Foreign and Commonwealth Secretary is putting forward is entirely political.

4. It is a relevant factor that part of the reason for the immediate problem is the breakaway move by 11 American banks at the end of last week. If American financial institutions can take this hard-nosed attitude despite the presence of a very substantial Polish community in the United States, there do not seem to be strong reasons for the United Kingdom to adopt a more benevolent attitude towards Poland, particularly if the Poles used any extra assistance from this

guarantee would have to be given by the FCO and the contingent liabilities regarded as a potential charge against the FCO public expenditure programmes. He added: 'The risk that the guarantee would be called is so great that I do not believe you would want to take it on these terms' (FCO 28/4522, ENP 090/1).

[2] Not printed. The letter of 22 June asked the UK to join in a loan to Poland to be syndicated by the Bank for International Settlements.

country to ease their problems with their more pressing creditors, which would probably include the American banks.

5. The initial reactions of the West Germans and Canadians seem to bear out the Chancellor of the Exchequer's scepticism. There appears to be a clear possibility that the whole proposal may collapse for lack of support. In these circumstances this country might be awkwardly placed if we had come forward too soon with a clear offer of more assistance. But if the matter cannot be resolved like this and a specific reply has to be given at or very soon after the meeting next Monday, the Foreign and Commonwealth Secretary might be invited to take the necessary decision in relation to his own suggested offer of $30 million. It would however be a condition that the necessary guarantee would be attached to the unallocated margin of the aid budget rather than the contingency reserve, and it would be the aid budget which would bear the brunt of a Polish default next December.[3]

D. J. WRIGHT

[3] The Foreign Secretary wanted to avoid giving a negative response to the Polish request for a loan before the Party Congress. As a tactical move he persuaded the reluctant Chancellor to postpone a final decision until the immediate outcome of the Polish Congress had become clear by allowing the Governor of the Bank of England to join an exploratory discussion of the problem with other central bank governors, without commitment.

No. 66

Minute from Lord Carrington to Mr Whitelaw (Home Secretary), 25 June 1981[1]

Confidential (FCO 28/4549, ENP 227/1)

Home Secretary,

1. I am grateful to you for giving me the opportunity to comment on your proposed decision not to grant the request of the Polish Government that the remains of General Sikorski[2] should be repatriated to Poland next week. We discussed this on 12 June.[3]

2. Since our meeting, I have met Mr Czyrek, the Polish Foreign Minister, who emphasised the importance which the Polish Government attach to this request. There was no doubt from the way he spoke that the view that the General's remains should be placed in Wawel Cathedral at Krakow[4] was shared by the Government, the Church and the people of Poland as a whole. There is also no

[1] The minute is not dated, but the date of 25 June is referred to in a submission by Mr Broomfield to Mr Fergusson dated 26 June.

[2] The Premier and War Minister of the Polish Government-in-Exile during the Second World War died in an aeroplane crash in Gibraltar on 4 July 1943. He was buried in Newark cemetery.

[3] The question had been discussed by HMG for some time, first on the occasion of the centenary of the General's birth, in May 1981. Mr James in a telegram of 26 May had explained that the Polish Government was keen to play on the theme of national unity and Polish independence in the country's current dark hours and had popular support including from the Church and Solidarity. The Home Office was aware of the evolution in the Polish Government's position but wanted to take into account opposition from Polish émigrés, including Count Raczynski, regarded as the head of the émigré Polish community. After some discussion Mr Whitelaw accepted Lord Carrington's advice that they should agree to the request, but wanted to think further (Mr Fall to Mr Broomfield, 12 June 1981).

[4] The place of coronation and mausoleum of the kings of Poland.

doubt in my mind that a decision on our part to refuse this request for the foreseeable future would not be understood in Poland and would adversely affect our bilateral relations.

3. Mr Czyrek also told me, and you were not aware of this when you approved the draft announcement of your decision, that the Poles are no longer committed to the 4 July deadline.[5] Mr Czyrek made it clear that, if we needed more time to consider the issue, the Polish Government would understand, and indeed would prefer, that the remains be transferred at a later date. They are anxious to avoid the risk that the return of the remains might trigger off a wave of uncontrolled nationalist (i.e. anti-Soviet) fervour just before the Party Congress on 14 July. They now feel that a slightly later date (linked, for example, to the anniversary of the outbreak of the Second World War on 1 September) would have positive advantage in allowing the transfer of the remains to be placed firmly in an Anglo-Polish context. This gives us the option to postpone a decision and give further consideration to the problem of how to handle the domestic political questions.

4. I continue to believe that we should agree to the Polish request. When we discussed this problem on 12 June we agreed that the normal Home Office criteria in such cases had been satisfied and that foreign policy considerations also supported the return of the remains. Whatever decision we take must be one which we can defend both to our own people and to the Polish Government. I can see no publicly defensible position which does not rest squarely on our normal practice. Political considerations such as the wishes of the émigré community would be difficult to defend in arguments which we will certainly have with the Polish Government. Nor can we, in the face of the arrangements they have proposed, argue convincingly that the remains would not be handled with 'due decency or propriety' either here or at Wawel Cathedral.

5. I hope therefore that you will agree that we should take advantage of the change of deadline to suspend a decision while you take account of recent developments and the points made above. I would hope that you might come to a favourable decision in principle but not announce it until nearer September which will give us a chance to see how the situation in and around Poland looks then.

6. I should be very glad to have another word with you if you still see difficulty in this. But in any event I hope you will at least agree not to make any public announcement which ruled out any transfer of the remains for the near future now. In the present highly-charged atmosphere in Poland, this would be seen as an unnecessary and brutal snub from a quarter to which the Poles have been accustomed to look for sympathy and help. I appreciate that you need to say something in response to enquiries about whether we intend to hand the remains back before the 4 July deadline originally given by the Poles. But I see no reason why you should not simply say that the Polish request remains under consideration, while making it clear that no reply can be expected before 4 July. If you agree, perhaps our officials could be in touch to work out a suitable formula.[6]

CARRINGTON

[5] The date of General Sikoski's death in 1943.

[6] On 30 June in an answer to Mr Churchill, Conservative MP for Stretford (1970–83), the Home Secretary replied that he had received an application for a licence authorising the removal of the remains of the late General Sikorski to be returned to Poland by 4 July and that after careful consideration he was unconvinced 'at the present time that the relevant criteria for meeting the application have yet been satisfied'. He had not therefore proposed to grant the licence (*Parl. Debs., 5th ser., H. of C.*, 30 June 1981, vol. 7, col. 340W).

No. 67

Minute from Mr Montgomery to Mr Broomfield, 30 June 1981
Confidential (FCO 28/4398, EN 101/1)

External financing prospects for Eastern Europe and Yugoslavia to 1985

1. You suggested that in view of the far reaching implications of the Polish debt problem and the possibility of default that we should take note of the situation in other East European countries and consider whether there was a prospect of any of these following the Polish example.

2. Mr Williamson[1] has now produced a very useful note (attached). The two countries which give cause for serious concern are Yugoslavia and Romania. The largest debtor is Yugoslavia ($20 billion). However, in Mr Williamson's view the Yugoslavs' problems are essentially those of short term liquidity and are capable of being surmounted. Admittedly, the Government are having difficulty in getting to grips with the situation but they recognise the nature of their difficulties and the Federal authorities at least appear to be making a more determined and coherent effort to ratify matters than their counterparts in Poland. Romania's difficulties bear a somewhat closer similarity to those of Poland. The size of the debt is much smaller ($9 billion) but the symptoms, over-investment, unrealistic targets and uncompetitive exports, are much the same. The Polish crisis has undoubtedly given Romania's leaders a shock and there are some signs that they are trying to take remedial action. Unlike the Poles they enjoy the benefits of IMF membership although their request for help suggests they are placing undue reliance upon their ability to raise very large additional sums in the West. In the wake of the Polish crisis it seems unlikely that they will be able to obtain all they are seeking but if this leads them to draw in their horns and modify their policies before they become completely overextended this will be no bad thing. None of the other East European countries appears to be at risk in the immediate future.

3. It appears to me that the conclusion we should draw from Mr Williamson's survey is that when asked for our views on the credit-worthiness of projects or export orders in Romania and Yugoslavia we must be careful to avoid automatically endorsing these either on the recommendation of the Post or with a view to boosting trade within our own parish. There is a real danger of countries like Romania and Yugoslavia getting out of their depth as Poland has done and we should certainly not encourage them to take on responsibilities which they cannot meet. Fortunately, both Western banks and ECGD have been given a shock in the case of Poland and I believe that neither will be so ready to extend loans or underwrite credit as readily as they have been in the past. A greater degree of caution seems to me to be in the interests both of the present customers and of the UK.

4. I am asking Mr Williamson to copy his note to Posts for comments.

A.E. MONTGOMERY

[1] Martin Williamson, FCO Economic Service (International Division).

ENCLOSURE IN NO. 67

External financing prospects for Eastern Europe and Yugoslavia to 1985

1. The external financing problems now confronting Poland, and Western creditors' rejection of the 'Soviet umbrella' theory, raise the question as to whether or not other East European countries will run into debt problems. This note assesses these countries' prospects on the basis of their present position and their intentions (as shown in their Five Year Plans). The conclusion is that Romania is the most likely to follow Poland's example, and Yugoslavia may run into temporary problems. Though the GDR needs watching, the others are relatively safe.

2. The accumulation of debt does not necessarily lead to debt problems. In most cases the loans which give rise to the debts are used prudently in ways which strengthen the borrower's debt service capacity. International borrowing allows the debtor to adjust the economy's structure to changed circumstances at a level of activity which is higher than would otherwise have been possible. But, as Poland shows, not all loans are used prudently and debt problems can arise. Where problems do occur it is important to distinguish between two types of debt problems:

(i) a *liquidity crisis*. This is an essentially temporary debt problem, usually caused by unanticipated fluctuations in foreign exchange payments or earnings. This type of problem can be cured by allowing the country to borrow its way out of difficulty, but a radical change of economic policy is not required;

(ii) *over-indebtedness*. This is a more fundamental problem than a liquidity crisis. Poland is a classic example of this case. The problem arises because the debtor takes on substantial debt service obligations but fails to raise the efficiency of investment, or increase domestic savings to levels which cover debt service obligations, or fails to promote the foreign currency earning/saving sectors. The solution to the over-indebtedness problem is not more borrowing in the absence of policy changes, rather creditors should insist on policy changes to raise the efficiency of investment, savings and foreign currency earning/saving sectors.

3. There may be some confusion at the onset of an over-indebtedness problem, for the first signs of difficulty are a shortage of liquidity. But the fundamental causes are different, as are the appropriate solutions. It is important not to confuse all East European debt problems with Polish-type over-indebtedness.

4. *Romania* is the East European state most likely to run into over-indebtedness. Her problems include the legacy of an over-ambitious and inefficient investment policy; an apparent inability to raise adequate levels of saving (not least because the leadership are aware of the need to boost living standards); and an export sector becoming increasingly uncompetitive in Western markets as a result of over-valued exchange rates and an insistence on counter-trade. Moreover, Romania is consistently in danger of a liquidity shortage—foreign exchange reserves are low, short term debt accounts for a substantial proportion of her total $9bn debts and payments delays and even arrears have occurred. Plans to borrow $3.7bn (gross) in 1981, mainly from commercial banks, may be unrealisable and financing problems in 1982 are almost inevitable unless Romania takes steps to improve her performance within the framework of a more realistic IMF programme than that introduced in 1981.

5. *Yugoslavia*, with debts approaching $20bn this year, is also in danger of running into a debt problem but in her case it will be a liquidity crisis. The plans

introduced for 1981 within the framework of a three-year IMF standby are proving over-optimistic. The Federal authorities are having little success in damping down economic activity; inflation and domestic demand are running above targets. Yugoslavia's convertible currency problem is exacerbated by her exporters' shift toward CMEA markets, leaving Yugoslavia dangerously vulnerable to a convertible currency liquidity crisis. A liquidity problem could be overcome if the Federal authorities take more effective steps to deflate domestic demand and give more incentives to promote exports to convertible currency markets. One worrying point is that the 1981 IMF programme exhausted Yugoslavia's access to international overdraft facilities, but not all the money has been drawn and there still may be time to avert a request for debt relief from her Western creditors. As in Romania's case, much will depend on the willingness of the IMF to impose tougher conditions in the second year of the present standby agreement.

6. Other East Europeans are unlikely to run into debt problems, though the *GDR's* performance should be monitored closely. Her debts are high by international standards (around $9bn, net of reserves) but the economy is adapting to the deterioration in the terms of trade and the need to import larger volumes of oil at world market prices. The GDR is running a tight ship and will be vulnerable to a liquidity problem but her adjustment strategy is sound so she should not become over-indebted.

7. *Hungary* and *Czechoslovakia* are also coming to terms with higher energy prices—the former somewhat faster than the latter—and are considered good risks by most creditors. Hungary's debts are quite large $7bn (net) in 1979, but her Five Year Plan shows a bias in favour of exporting to Western markets and a willingness to accept two years of austerity during the adjustment phase. Czech progress is slower than Hungary's but growth plans have been scaled down and she is reluctant to go for higher growth at the expense of more debt to the West (her debts now are only slightly over $3bn). Both Hungary and Czechoslovakia are introducing more flexibility in their planning—a move which should help them to avoid the inefficiencies and rigidities apparent in Poland.

8. *Bulgaria's* performance is a success story. She has maintained relatively high growth rates whilst adjusting to the changed external environment. She is running a convertible currency trade surplus and her planners are confident that debts (about $3.5bn) are under control. Similarly, the *USSR* is in no danger of either a liquidity crisis or over-indebtedness. Problems may occur in the mid-1980's as oil export earnings decline by more than the increase in gas exports, but creditors will continue to focus their attention on the USSR's underlying economic strength and the large natural resources at her disposal in the 1980s.

No. 68

Brief by the Foreign and Commonwealth Office on East-West Trade, 9 July 1981[1]

PMVL(81)6 Confidential (FCO 28/4394, EN 091/2)

Points to make

1. Agree that consistent and careful approach to East-West trade is needed, reflecting Western political and security as well as economic interests.

2. Development of East-West economic relations can help to encourage Soviet interest in less antagonistic relationship with the West.

3. Our trade with East should be on basis of mutual advantage. Where Soviet Union seems to be deriving excessive benefit, Western countries should look again at the ground rules.

4. Agree with Americans that any measures to tighten control of East-West trade must be taken on as broad a basis as possible. Must avoid measures which are divisive among us—or impose unfair burdens on some. Poland contingency planning shows what can be done and serves as useful precedent.

5. Agree Soviet Union should not be allowed to extract undue commercial/economic advantage by obtaining unreasonably cheap credit. OECD credit rules due for revision this year.

6. Must recognise that there are varying degrees of Western involvement in trade with East, particularly differences between US on one hand and Western Europe on the other. If trade is to be more strictly controlled, the burdens must be shared fairly.

7. Should not over-estimate possibilities for governmental control over trade.

8. Do not think current Western purchases of Soviet energy, which will decline gradually over coming decade despite increased gas imports, involves unacceptable risks. Soviet Union will still need hard currency earnings from energy exports.

9. [If raised] Considerable technical and cost problems in providing surge capacity from UK continental shelf.

10. Ideas in US paper[2] deserve further detailed consideration. Some we can support now, e.g. idea of more intensive consultation on strategic imports. Earlier US proposal for high-level COCOM forum worth examining. Others pose problems we would need to look at carefully.

Background (Can be drawn on freely)

11. The Americans have distributed a revised version of their paper on East-West trade, the main points of which are:

(*a*) that strategic controls of sensitive exports to the Soviet Union should be strengthened by widening lists of items to be monitored;

[1] The brief was prepared for the (G7) Ottawa Economic Summit which met from 20 to 21 July. It was cleared with all interested FCO Departments, the Treasury and the Department of Trade.

[2] In May the Americans circulated the first draft of a paper entitled 'East-West Economic Relations: A Prudent Approach' which they wanted discussed by Heads of Government at Ottawa (FCO 28/4393, EN 91/2). The UK view was that some of the paper's assumptions and arguments were contentious and likely to be disputed. They thought the paper had far reaching policy implications (covering issues such as the export of sensitive items to the USSR, export credits, energy security and food exports) and had the potential to lead to political strains if not handled carefully.

(*b*) that contingency planning for threats arising from potential Soviet actions should be extended;

(*c*) that Western countries should guard against vulnerability caused by dependence on trade with the East;

(*d*) that Western commercial interests should not override wider economic and political objectives; and that we should try to exert economic influence on the political behaviour of Soviet Union and Eastern Europe.

12. We agree on need for careful control of sensitive exports to the Soviet Union. But control on technology affects Western Europe more than the US, and the Americans need to support by argument the case for extending the category of goods contributing substantively to Soviet military potential. The Americans' suggestion that the present no general exceptions policy in COCOM should be extended indefinitely ignores the problem of equitable burden sharing.

13. We agree with the American aim of giving serious thought to improvement of contingency planning. What has been achieved in relation to a possible Soviet intervention in Poland has been valuable. But this was undertaken as a matter of urgency, and set against a specific scenario with agreed implications for East-West relations. To broaden planning to take in possible Soviet actions in the indefinite future in other theatres would be more difficult to manage.

14. The American implication that the present levels of East-West trade entail Western vulnerability is open to question. The Americans have only a small stake in trade in industrial goods with the Soviet Union. Their trade is mainly in agricultural exports and they have met the interests of their domestic farm lobby by lifting the partial grain embargo imposed after Afghanistan, which the EC had acted to support. The Canadians have also recently negotiated a long-term grain agreement with the Soviet Union. The American paper also over-states Western dependence on Soviet energy exports and under-estimates the Soviet need to maintain hard currency earnings from energy exports. The Americans have expressed particular concern at the implications for certain Western European countries (FRG, France, Belgium, Netherlands, Italy) of gas imports under the major West Siberian gas pipeline due to be constructed in the first half of this decade. However, gas imports will increasingly take over from Soviet oil, and overall Western dependence, at present only 5%, will decline gradually over the coming decade. Furthermore the Germans and French maintain that diversification of sources of supply, particularly away from the Middle East, spreads the political and economic risk. The US have in the past suggested informally that one way in which we could contribute to greater energy security would be to provide surge oil and gas capacity against a possible Soviet cut-off. This would be exceedingly expensive and pose considerable technical problems.

15. We are in favour of increasing consensus rates for export credits. We allowed the 1975 Anglo-Soviet Credit Agreement to lapse after Afghanistan: Proposals are now considered on a case-by-case basis. US Eximbank[3] do not support export credits for the USSR, and, like ourselves, the Italians have allowed their bilateral agreement to lapse. However, interest rates under the Franco-Soviet Credit Agreement are at present around 1% below consensus and the Soviet Union are making use of this in negotiations on the West Siberian gas pipeline project by encouraging Western firms to offer credit at the preferential French level. There

[3] The Export-Import Bank of the United States—the official export credit agency of the United States.

are signs that the new French Government may be more willing than its predecessor to cooperate over consensus rates.

16. There are limits to the economic influence Western countries can bring to bear on the political behaviour of Eastern Europe and the Soviet Union. Governments in Western Europe do not have complete control of the activities of private firms engaged in East-West trade. Furthermore recent Western coordination over economic involvement in Eastern Europe, e.g. the Polish debt agreement, was not exploited to exert political influence on Eastern European actions. Finally, while we see advantage in increased Eastern European participation in international financial institutions and hence in the international monetary system, we do not want, given Soviet reservations, to press for this. Soviet membership would have greater impact, not necessarily of advantage to the West, but seems most unlikely in the foreseeable future.

17. If the Americans wish to pursue the ideas in their paper, the best forum for further discussion would probably be in NATO—with some special arrangement to associate the Japanese with the work. There is no convenient way of doing the work in the Economic Summit Group which does not further bureaucratize the process.

No. 69

Mr Holmer (Bucharest) to Lord Carrington, 16 July 1981
Confidential (FCO 28/4554, ENR 014/1)

Could it happen here?

My Lord,

1. The vulnerability of Ceausescu's regime has been frequently debated over the years. Eight years ago one of my predecessors, Sir Derick Ashe[1] (in his letter of 13 February 1973 to Mr Bullard) predicted, with remarkable accuracy, that Ceausescu might run into some political danger in a few years' time when the Romanians eventually discovered that they had over-invested in certain sectors of the economy, that they had attempted too broad and too swift an industrial advance, that the economy was under serious strain, and that targets would need to be revamped. That economic situation can now be said to have arrived. It is exacerbated by a sharply increased total of convertible currency indebtedness and, more immediately, by prolonged and widespread food shortages. It has arrived, moreover, at a time when the *débâcle* in Poland casts its shadow over the entire 'socialist' bloc. Most Western observers speculating about the next Eastern European country which might go the way of Poland seem to consider Romania to be the most likely candidate. But Romania is not Poland and Romanians are not Poles; their characters, history and tribal memories are quite different. Could it happen here? In this despatch I propose first to touch on the major problems currently facing the Romanian leadership, and then to consider the prospects for domestic unrest and the relevance of the Polish experience. Finally, I shall attempt to assess the implications for Ceausescu himself.

2. The problems which afflict the average Romanian are well known and are chronic. Poor housing and food shortages are the greatest material irritants. The ambitious programme for constructing apartments is behind schedule (20% below

[1] HMA Bucharest, 1972-75.

Plan in 1976-80), and Trade Union officials are under constant pressure from their members to get something done about it. Food has never been plentiful for the citizens of the Socialist Republic of Romania. The relative neglect of agriculture, increasing diversions of food to the hard currency export market, bad distribution and frequent spells of bad weather have combined to make the problem more acute. Over the past year the shortages are widely regarded as being the worst since the War. The effect of pay rises has been eroded by price rises for fuel and foodstuffs. Although standards of living have undoubtedly risen since Ceausescu came to power in 1965, progress is slow, and getting slower. Romanians are aware that they are generally regarded as having the lowest standard of living in Eastern Europe.

3. Industrial workers in Romania work long hours in factories which, more often than not, were built hastily and with limited regard for safety or comfort. The problem is evident to factory visitors; it can be discerned in the trade union newspaper *Munca* and in published reports on serious industrial accidents. As for working hours, most are still on a 48-hour, six-day week. The modest reduction programme (to 46 hours by the end of this year, and to 44 hours by the end of 1985) is itself conditional on Plan fulfilment, and has been repeated postponed in the past. Pay, too, is related to monthly norm-fulfilment; fines of up to 20% of wages may be imposed for under-fulfilment. Thus a potential source of industrial friction exists in every factory every month.

4. Romanian trade unions take a legalistic view of their industrial relations role: they are there to see fair play according to the rules. In practice, a senior trade union official is essentially a production assistant and a dispenser of patronage and favours. These people look tough and confident and some are of high calibre, but they have not thrown off their reputation as the Party's stooges. For most workers the key figure is the *maistru* or foreman, who cracks the whip but works with his men and will take up their grievances; quality varies from the very good to the idle and corrupt.

5. The industrial relations situation is one which calls for the sympathetic attention of a receptive political system. It does not get it. Theoretical study is given to sociological questions in Bucharest and the trade unions filter their findings upwards; behind all this lies the information-gathering activities of the Party's watchdog and seeker-out of its potential enemies, the *Securitate*.[2] In the name of socialist democracy, Party units are urged to mix with the masses and to draw people into discussion of current issues: in practice these attempts to stimulate democratic participation usually end up as an institutionalised caricature, requiring only passivity of its audiences. To the Westerner brought up in the liberal tradition, the regime's disregard for the comforts, or indeed the rights, of its citizens is astonishing. In this respect, however, the Party falls heir to a long Romanian tradition of autocratic rule carried out by corrupt and arbitrary functionaries. This helps to explain why there seems to be relatively little popular resentment of official privileges; they are accepted as part of a natural order of things. Nor should we underrate the stability which Ceausescu's iron rule has brought to Romanian affairs; and a Balkan people of Latin stock are perhaps less disturbed than we would be by the perennial gap between rhetoric and practical action which is a feature of Socialist Romania.

[2] The Department of State Security.

6. Serious distortions in the Romanian economy are becoming evident; over-investment in certain sectors (oil-refining, petro-chemicals and energy-intensive industries) and a general imbalance between industry and agriculture have been publicly admitted. The growth in the National Income in 1980 was a mere 2.5% (as against a planned increase of 8.8%) and some important Plan targets were seriously under-fulfilled while agricultural production actually fell. Energy imports are costing too much. Convertible currency indebtedness has grown steeply in recent years and stood, at the end of 1980, at over 9 billion dollars, of which over 2 billion dollars represented short-term debt. Without more stringent measures, involving a further increase in retail prices, the situation seems likely to get worse. At all events it seems clear that the consumer is going to have to wait a very long time for any improvement in his standard of living.

7. Deteriorating economic conditions have also obliged the Romanians to seek a closer relationship and expanded trade with their CMEA partners. But this puts Ceausescu in something of a quandary. If as a *demandeur vis-à-vis* CMEA he is compelled to trim his independent foreign policy too obviously, he may find his nationalist appeal—which underpins popular acquiescence in his domestic policies—seriously diminished. At the same time it seems unlikely that CMEA partners, especially the Soviet Union, will be ready to accord generous terms to Romania so long as Ceausescu is at the helm with his policies substantially unchanged.

8. These, in brief outline, are Romania's most pressing problems. There is no denying that individual frustration, tension and discontent are widespread. But will this discontent ever be expressed collectively and effectively? It is remarkable how often in the past decade Romania has appeared to be on the verge of a popular explosion. But then the sun begins to shine, eggs reappear on the market, a grievance is palliated, one or two trouble-makers are removed, and one or two official heads roll. Ceausescu, the trouble-shooter, drives into town, makes a big speech and promises another new deal. The 'crisis' subsides. This has tended to be the pattern; but could it be different this time? It may be that we should take current tensions, food shortages, work stoppages and cynical jokes about Ceausescu more seriously than before, particularly if, as may be the case, these should be seen as belated manifestations of a developing working-class consciousness already evident elsewhere in Eastern Europe.

9. It is true that the Romanians, stemming from generations of oppressed and landless peasants, are on the whole a passive and patient people, if somewhat world-weary and cynical in their outlook. Faced with an arbitrary imposition, the Romanian, unlike, perhaps, the Pole, does not instinctively link hands with his neighbours to resist; he reacts as an individual and looks for ways round the immediate problem, using personal contacts, money or his native ingenuity. If these are insufficient, his instinct is to put up with the problem (and hope it will go away). Above all, Romanians are horrified by the prospect of confrontation with a stronger force; they would tend to regard an uncompromising or principled stand in the face of even an admitted injustice as pointless if injustice has superior force on its side. Such fools deserve what they get, which may be imprisonment or a beating at the police station. It is not that Romanians do not complain: they can boil up rapidly and vociferously. This has on occasion led to spontaneous disturbances of brief duration. But bad tempers tend to be short-lived and to be sublimated in other ways (even in wife-beating!). Moreover, Romanians have learnt to be cautious about coming to the notice of the *Securitate*. In Romania, unlike some Slav

countries, there is no strong revolutionary or conspiratorial tradition, and there appear now to be no underground or conspiratorial groups. Even the short-lived dissident movement of 1979, the so-called Free Trade Union of Romanian Working Men (SLOMR), did not take itself very seriously. (The toughest dissidents, small in number, are probably to be found in the ranks of the neo-Protestant sects.)

10. But things might be changing. In one generation, a new working class has been created, living and working in close proximity. In 1950, 23% of the population lived in cities and 19% worked in industry. By 1980, the figures were 48% and 55% respectively. Such changes must, in Romania as elsewhere, bring in their wake changes in attitudes; a new 'class consciousness' is likely to emerge, leading to a growing perception of collective strength *vis-à-vis* management and government. In 1977, immediately after the strike of 35,000 miners in the Jiu Valley, Ceausescu seemed to be acknowledging this phenomenon when he spoke of 'the growth of the ranks of the working classes, the raising of the consciousness of the masses, becoming ever more conscious of the strength they represent'. The miners, a relatively mature work-force, had been militant throughout the 1970s, striking over meat price increases, pension law changes and working conditions. In 1972, there were isolated work stoppages in other industries over housing legislation. In 1979 SLOMR articulated what seemed to be widespread resentments among the working population. In 1979-81 some militancy has been reported in Bucharest, Constanța, Târgoviște, Maramureș and elsewhere over pay, conditions and food. It seems to have been directed as much against the Government as against management. Militant action has not always taken the form of strikes or disturbances; other forms have included brief work stoppages, 'dumb insolence' and group petitions. Ironically, official publicity given to successful group protests or petitions which bypass the Trade Union machinery may well have served as an encouragement to collective action.

11. Collective action is however still an isolated phenomenon. The discontented worker normally resolves his problems individually, by changing jobs. Turnover, the classic symptom of labour instability, is high, especially among the under-30s seeking more money, better facilities and food, or a job closer to home. The familiar problems of industrial indiscipline (lateness, absenteeism, bad workmanship and drunkenness) are growing and are beginning to assume fairly serious proportions at such major factories as the '23 August' heavy engineering works (18,000 workers) in Bucharest. Other problems stem from the feelings of anonymity and alienation engendered by mass habitation in the new housing areas. Urban hooliganism has begun. Attitudes change in cities, and the habitual deference and tolerance of the peasant disappear. The first generation of industrial workers in post-war Romania had a hard time. But they could look back to still harder times on the land in the recent past. The more mature second generation still has a hard enough time, but doubtless has higher expectations. A large and growing number of Romanians would like to emigrate to the West, but are denied passports; these people, who were criticised by Ceausescu in a recent speech as selfish and unpatriotic, are a further source of discontent. All these factors provide ground in which the seeds of collective militancy might sprout.

12. The leadership's tactics must take account of this situation. If they are too permissive, the workers may start pushing for more; if they are repressive, they may stoke up resentment. The main existing deterrent to industrial militancy is undoubtedly intimidation: the *Securitate*, it is widely believed, would sniff out

conspiracy and the Militia would use tough methods. Nobody seriously doubts Ceausescu's willingness to use force if necessary. He threatened to 'crush' the Jiu Valley miners in 1977 (when two engineers were widely believed to have been shot), and last autumn he was privately critical of the Polish authorities' reluctance to use force against their strikers. Repression in the Jiu Valley was, however, accompanied by some real and lasting improvements in conditions. This combination of repression and palliative measures characterises the leadership's general approach, which is reactive and defensive. Force has not been used in recent, lesser strikes in Romania; instead, managers have been sacked. Perceptive workers, comparing Government reactions now and at the time of earlier periods of stress in the 1970s, might conclude that their goodwill is being cultivated. There are other pointers. Industrial centres are being given priority in food supply; price incentives to food producers have not yet been passed on to consumers; a storm of mainly working-class protest (some of it reflected in the press) forced the amendment of some draconian housing legislation last October. It is clear that industrial and social relations and a correct balance between use of the stick and the palliative will require sensitive handling in the period ahead.

13. The improved terms and conditions (e.g. the 5-day week) which Polish workers are seeking or have gained, will have become known by way of Western broadcasts to the Romanians, who cannot be kept wholly isolated from major shifts in the industrial climate elsewhere in Eastern Europe. Comparison with conditions in Hungary, for example, has long been a sensitive subject. The general introduction of a 5-day week in Eastern Europe (with Hungary moving to 42 hours by mid-1982) could create a focus of resentment and an abiding irritant in industrial relations here.

14. But although any 'bread and butter' gains achieved by Polish workers will be observed here with envy, and could encourage emulation, there is as yet no evidence to suggest that the wider implications of what is happening in Poland have been properly appreciated by Romanian workers or are even considered by them to be really relevant to their own situation. Conditions here are indeed very different. Workers here could not expect to receive help with organisation or communications from any dissident network since no such network exists. Although there are a few increasingly vociferous writers, the intelligentsia as a whole are a timid lot, demoralised by the aggressive leading role of the Party and the anti-intellectualism of the leadership; many of the brighter young people have left. Nor could the Romanian Orthodox Church, with its long tradition of playing along with the secular authorities, begin to represent an alternative focus to the Party in the way that the Roman Catholic Church does in Poland. Thus many of the crucial conditions which have sustained the Polish 'renewal' do not exist here.

15. The regime has nevertheless shown itself highly sensitive to events in Poland and has been quick to react. Legislation was brought in quickly to deal with certain abuses (notably enrichment of Party officials) which had attracted criticism in Poland. The leadership of the official trade union movement was formally separated from the Minister of Labour; hitherto, both functions had been performed by one man. Ceausescu publicly admitted that agriculture had been neglected in favour of industrial growth, and announced greater efforts to improve agricultural production.

16. Some Romanian officials claim privately that political events in Poland are being watched by the regime here in a positive and hopeful spirit, with a view to eventually adapting to Romanian conditions any real advances made towards

greater democracy and greater freedom from Soviet influence. Ceausescu's main reaction in this field has been to enlarge and nominally to strengthen the powers of the nation-wide organisation of 'Working Men's Councils'. This move (which to a Western observer is of a blatantly cosmetic character) is presented as a further important step towards securing participation by the workers in decision-making. In an important speech to the Second Congress of Working Men's Councils on 24 June, Ceausescu also called for a flexible approach which would foster the constant evolution of new forms of democratic participation. Here indeed is 'renewal', Ceausescu-style. In this effort to capture and contain any potential movement for renewal, and indeed to steal its vocabulary, Ceausescu showed that he is now reacting to this aspect of the Polish phenomenon with all his customary political skill, which he appears to have regained after an initial period of confusion and over-reaction when he had seemed almost excessively intent on maintaining confidence in his regime both at home and abroad by measures designed to demonstrate that 'it couldn't happen here'. His line on Poland is now clear: the Polish Party and people must be left to solve their problems without interference, and they must be given plenty of time; it is a process which could take years. Meanwhile Ceausescu will continue to watch events in Poland warily, and will continue to react appropriately to head off any dangerous infection here.

17. It is in the economic rather than the political field that Ceausescu is most vulnerable. He is most unlikely to be unseated by widespread, well-organised strikes in favour of a genuine measure of workers' autonomy, as in Poland. What is much more likely to make his position less secure—or even ultimately untenable—would be an indefinite prolongation of the deterioration in the Romanian economy or a further very sharp decline, especially if food supplies were allowed to become so exiguous as to lead to rioting in the streets or prolonged stoppages in the factories, rather than mere grumbling, or if a breakdown in his efforts to curb unrequited imports from the West should produce an acute liquidity crisis or severe over-indebtedness. In such circumstances, we might begin to envisage the emergence of new leaders from the shadows. But, for the reasons adduced above, economic conditions in Romania would have to be a great deal worse than they were in Poland last year, to being about changes in the leadership. It is not possible at this stage to make any reasonable guess as to who might form an eventual new leadership in these conditions. The new leaders might be men prepared to toe the Soviet line in exchange for massive Soviet and CMEA assistance. They might be men prepared to take rigorous economic measures in order to attract and retain the support of Western banking institutions. Or they might attempt to combine improved economic performance with the sort of balancing act in which Ceausescu himself has always been so adept. In any event, the geo-political realities of Romania's situation would be bound to ensure continued membership of CMEA and the Warsaw Pact.

18. I am sending copies of this despatch to HM representatives in Moscow, Warsaw, Sofia, Budapest, Prague, East Berlin, Belgrade, Washington and on the North Atlantic Council.[3]

I am, etc,
PAUL HOLMER

[3] In a reply of 6 August Mr Broomfield agreed with Mr Holmer's analysis, in particular that economic factors were likely to play an increasingly important role in the way Romania developed in the 1980s. If the West, cautious because of economic exposure in Poland, proved difficult over credit and investment then the attitude of the USSR would become increasingly important. Of particular importance would be how they decided to play Romania's growing dependence on intra-CMEA trade and Soviet energy, and what this might mean for Ceauşescu. The view from London was that, on balance, the Soviets had a greater interest in sustaining in power a weakened and more compliant Ceauşescu. Writing from the Moscow Embassy on 20 August, Mr Brooke Turner thought that although the Soviets were not always happy about his foreign policies they liked the rigidly controlled system that Ceauşescu operated but preferred to deal with him when he was feeling 'more cautions than cocky'.

No. 70

Note for the record by Mr Foster (East Berlin), 16 July 1981[1]
Restricted (FCO 33/4745, WRE 400/1)

1. According to colleagues, my speech (in German translated by myself into English) in reply to Abrassimov[2] at my leave-taking from the local Diplomatic Corps was something of a sensation and is still being talked about. Compliment or shocked disapproval? At any rate I decided not to repeat the customary platitudes. Since these things grow in the telling, it may be as well to record what I actually said.

2. After the obligatory politenesses and acknowledgement of the ghastly pompous present, a huge inscribed Meissen vase, which Abrassimov inflicts, at great expense to all one's colleagues, on departing Ambassadors—I had tried unsuccessfully to persuade him to give us something smaller and more *salonfähig*[3]—I mentioned a few of our impressions of the GDR, which had caused us to modify perceptions:

(*a*) German punctuality: nonsense, guests normally arrived ten minutes at least before the appointed time;

(*b*) The classless society: nonsense, lorries knew no restraint and obstructed traffic at their pleasure, while private motorists were hounded for the slightest peccadillo;

(*c*) The will to work: nonsense, because Germans spent every other week on holiday or *Kur*.[4] Harvey, by discovering the circulation of the blood (*Kreislauf*) was one of the greatest saboteurs of all time, causing more working days to be lost on *Kur* than in other countries on strikes.

[1] In a covering letter dated 17 July to Mr Gladstone, Mr Foster explained that this stood in lieu of a traditional valedictory despatch.
[2] Soviet Ambassador in East Berlin (1962-71 and 1975-83).
[3] 'Socially-acceptable'.
[4] Health cure.

3. I acknowledged these remarks to be typical of British frivolity and addressed myself contritely to the more serious subjects of peace, détente, disarmament and democracy. The only problem was the semantic one of definition.

4. Peace had posed such difficulties as far back as 2000 years ago, when Tacitus had remarked in excusable puzzlement that 'they make a desert and call it peace.'

5. People had now started to distinguish between 'détente' and 'real détente'. Détente (*Entspannung*—relaxation) might perhaps vary in its effects, as with the Sekt we were drinking, with the strength of the dose. Two glasses—relaxation; four glasses—real relaxation; six glasses—you no longer knew the difference; eight glasses—it might come to blows.

6. Disarmament. The difference between tactical and strategic weapons being between those that can hit you and those that can hit me. The German saying 'Wer rastet, rostet' (who rests, rusts) adapted as 'Wer rüstet, röstet' (who arms, roasts) or 'Wer rastet und nicht rüstet, wird geröstet' (who rests and does not arm, gets roasted).

7. Democracy: we all professed it, but the only country which directly consulted its citizens by plebiscites on important questions (Switzerland) had as a consequence no Summer Time.

8. Ending with a toast to our profession: relatively easy if you only try to understand your own point of view and difficult if you try to reconcile it with that of others.

9. All rather flippant I suppose. But at least it proved controversial and thought-provoking. Abrassimov and Nier, Deputy Foreign Minister, clearly didn't know what to make of it and showed as much on their faces. My less wet colleagues liked it: Bölling even said he had reported approvingly to Bonn![5]

P. M. FOSTER

[5] Mr Gladstone noted to Mr Bullard on 24 July that he thought that relations between Britain and the GDR were now normal and could indeed in some ways be described as 'friendly'. Both sides had made clear that they wanted to develop a productive relationship but Gladstone thought that 'this must depend in the first place on a real expansion of trade'. Bullard, on 26 July, noted that he agreed (FCO 33/4700, WRE 020/1).

No. 71

Mr James (Warsaw) to Lord Carrington, 23 July 1981
Confidential (FCO 28/4494, ENP 014/3)

The IX Extraordinary Congress of the Polish United Workers Party

Summary . . . [1]

My Lord,

'In a way beset with those that contend on one
side for too great Liberty and on the other
side for too much Authority, 'tis hard to passe
between the points of both unwounded'.
(Thomas Hobbes)

[1] Not printed.

1. I have the honour to report that the IX Congress of the Polish United Workers Party took place from 14 to 20 July in Warsaw. In this despatch I shall try to chart briefly the course of the Congress and to assess its implications for the future of the Party and of the country.

2. In many respects, this was Kania's Congress. It legitimised him and his policies. It took an occasional twist here and there which he might have wished otherwise. But it came to rest on a moderate, central position, promising limited reform while avoiding extremes which would have been impossible for the Soviet Union to swallow. This balancing-act, performed in the uncharted space of democratic procedures, required coolness and good judgment. Kania and his collaborators showed both, as well as great determination. Yet at one time it looked as if either the Congress would not take place or that Kania would not preside over it.

3. When Kania replaced Gierek as First Secretary early in September 1980, he proposed an early Extraordinary Congress to re-establish the morale, confidence and unity of a Party whose self-adjudicated leading role in Polish society had been undermined, if not replaced, by a genuine, popular and successful workers' protest movement. Reformists within the Party demanded an early Congress: reactionaries insisted on delay in the hope of moderating reform. The leadership's interest came to lie in postponement for the same reason, although the Politburo was itself divided. Initially there was talk of a Congress before the close of 1980; later, a date at the end of March was announced, but the leaders were still not ready by then. They feared a reformist Congress, bringing a landslide change of leadership and with it the increased danger of Soviet military intervention. It was thus only in April that the IX Plenum decided on the dates 14-18 July.

4. Soviet and internal hard-line pressures for postponement or even abandonment of the Congress continued. The letter from the Soviet Central Committee to the Central Committee of the Polish Party in early June may have been intended to topple Kania and put off the Congress. That was certainly the interpretation of several well-placed Polish officials. In the event it did neither. But it had its impact: it brought home to the Party the restraints which the Congress should observe and strengthened the hands of those who were in a moderate or conservative position.[2] I think Kania showed courage and cunning in the way he stayed on course against Soviet pressure. He succeeded in rallying support within the Party for his leadership while multiplying protestations of loyalty to the Soviet camp. The visit of Gromyko in early July suggested that the Soviet Union had accepted the inevitability of the Congress and were prepared to put their best face

[2] The Soviet Central Committee had sent a letter before the majority of delegate conferences at *Voivodship* level had taken place thus hoping to influence the elections. Mr Broomfield had explained to Mr Bullard that the letter 'set out in unmistakable terms Soviet views of the "mortal danger" facing the country, the failure of Kania and Jaruzelski personally to fulfil the promises given in Moscow . . . The letter's main thrust, however, is towards the Party Congress and the danger to "Marxist/Leninist forces" coupled with the more general danger to "socialism" and the existence of an independent Polish State'. The letter was discussed in a plenary session of the Polish Central Committee, which took place on 9 and 10 June. Mr Kania had made a tough speech about the dangers facing the country but had given little indication of measures to deal with them. 'More importantly, however, he confirmed that the Congress would go ahead as planned and he reaffirmed his commitment to the renewal process' (Broomfield to Bullard, 12 June 1981). On the same day Mr James had assessed that there was a 'good deal of evidence to suggest that the Soviet Union wished to displace Kania and put in his place a hard-line faction. They have failed and the Party has rallied round Kania—at least for the time being' (Warsaw tel. No. 439; FCO 28/4481, ENP 014/1).

on.[3] This was certainly my impression when talking to Mr Aristov, the Soviet Ambassador here, who is a member of the Soviet Central Committee and was a delegate to the Congress. He said that he expected the Congress to be moderate and to help Poland take a step forward. But whatever the convolutions of Soviet pressure, it was clearly a relief when Kania was able to stand up on the opening day of the Congress, in the presence of a Soviet delegation, and say 'our Congress is an irretrievable fact'.

5. The Congress lasted a full week, two days longer than scheduled but rather shorter than at one time seemed likely. A great deal of it was conducted under the cameras of the television. It was also fully reported in the press and radio, and it undoubtedly stirred deep public interest throughout Poland. The main event of the first day was the wrangle in closed session over electoral procedures and the decision to postpone the election of the First Secretary until after that of the new Central Committee. I have heard a suggestion from a good source that Kania and his collaborators tried too hard to manipulate the Congress at the beginning and were rebuffed by the delegates. It is certainly a fact that Kania had to wait until nearly the end of the Congress before he was endorsed as First Secretary, and it may well be that the delegates were determined not to be taken for granted. Kania's keynote speech followed previous patterns and was an astute mixture which had something for everyone. The Soviet delegate's opening speech was awaited with tense expectation and, though firm, was not so chilling as many expected. The second day brought a powerful and enthusiastically-applauded speech by Rakowski, the Editor of *Polityka*[4] and now Vice-Premier in charge of negotiations with unions. His stock rose high and there were some who thought he might be bidding for the leadership. But, on further reflection, the judgment of the Congress seemed to turn against him and he fell back into the shadows. There were numerous speeches from the floor, some critical and outspoken but tending towards the parochial. On the third and fourth days the election to the Central Committee was greatly delayed by manual counting by inexperienced operators, and the schedule began to slip. The election of Kania as First Secretary took place on the fifth day and that of the new Politburo and Secretariat on the sixth. The other main feature of the Congress was the success and popularity of Prime Minister Jaruzelski, a stiff, buttoned-up but respected figure, who is becoming the guardian of Poland's national spirit. The Congress faded away with a closing speech by Kania, simple and effective for once, remitting to various working groups the task of producing detailed resolutions.

6. It is difficult to judge how far the composition of the Congress reflected the grass-roots of the Party. One reputable Polish analyst has said that the grass-roots wanted a much more radical and reformist Congress and that there will be

[3] See *DBPO*: *Afghanistan,* No. 108. Lord Carrington who had visited Moscow on 5 and 6 July reported to the Cabinet that he had found Mr Gromyko 'surprisingly' relaxed and communicative. Having just returned from a visit to Warsaw, Gromyko was clear that the economic prospects for Poland were extremely serious, but he gave the impression that he did not regard the political situation as too critical and that the forthcoming Congress of the Polish Communist Party was unlikely to lead to circumstances in which the Soviet Union would feel compelled to intervene' (CC(81)27, 9 July 1981, CAB 128/71).

[4] The well-known journalist, Mr Rakowski, had been appointed Deputy Prime Minister in charge of relations with trade unions at the Party Plenum on 9 February at the same time as General Jaruzelski had been appointed. The magazine *Polityka*, established in 1957, was reputed for a moderately critical journalism, although always remaining within the communist-imposed boundaries.

disappointment at the way things have developed. Against this, the new Central Committee has more working men and peasants on it than the old one and is more representative of the country as a whole. It is true that there was no great surge of reform in the Congress and that all the speakers were careful to couch their contributions in terms which took account of the underlying political restraints imposed on Poland by her history and geography. It is too early to say whether the gap between the desire for reform from the grass-roots and moderation at the centre will cause difficulties for the Party. But this is certainly an area which we shall have to watch.

7. The new Politburo and Central Committee seem predominantly centrist, like Kania, but with a reformist fringe. Forty of the 200 members of the Central Committee belong to Solidarity, as does one member of the Politburo, Mrs Grzyb. She is not a known Solidarity activist, however, and it is unlikely that Solidarity's leadership will have much direct influence on the Party, either through her or through the Central Committee. The Politburo also contains three hard-liners in Milewski, Siwak and Olszowski. Siwak was something of a surprise. His speech was almost Stalinist in its tone, but he seemed to have a way with the delegates—a sort of Polish Enoch Powell. Personalities were important at the Congress— more so than ideology or the economic problems. The elimination of Grabski and Żabiński was not altogether unexpected. They had over-played their hands and had been out-manoeuvred by Kania. There are no radicals except possibly Łabęcki from the Lenin shipyard in Gdańsk. I have the impression that Olszowski has moved closer in the last few weeks to the position of Kania and that there may now be some understanding between them. The Party probably emerges from the Congress stronger and more united. Kania now has a popular mandate and should, therefore, be able to exercise greater authority. But there is no certainty that this stronger and more united Party will be able to take over the popular protest which produced Solidarity. I think there is a danger that the Polish people will be disappointed that reforms have not gone far enough. Reformists outside the Party and Government are already beginning to voice disillusion. The very prudent nature of the middle line, Kania's quality as a manager rather than an inspirer may make the Party incapable of touching the imagination of the nation. The appeal issued at the end of the Congress is good, solid stuff, but it is not likely to trump Solidarity's cards. Future relations with Solidarity will be uncertain, at least until Solidarity's own congress is complete in early October. Much more therefore depends on the ability of men such as Łabęcki from Gdańsk to maintain Solidarity's trust and to impart to his colleagues a deeper understanding of the way Solidarity operates.

8. Where does this Congress leave Poland? Has it been something of a charade, despite the secret ballot, with Kania still in control and the extremists on both sides cunningly eliminated? Have exaggerated hopes been placed on it? How will it affect future relations between Poland and the Soviet Union? The sceptics may feel that a great deal of blather has produced a mouse. I do not agree with this view. The Congress, for the first time in Eastern Europe, showed a measure of open and frank public debate within a communist party. It was not the House of Commons. It made up procedures as it went along. Nearly 40 years of a communist system leave their mark on a people, even if they are a people with a great thirst for personal liberty like the Poles. But, as one senior Polish official said to me: 'You cannot imagine how important it is to us Poles to see a debate like this, imperfect though it may be, carried out in public. It helps to make up for some of our

hardships.' The expert on the Soviet Union used to canvass two main theories of change inside the Soviet system. The first was the theory of *embourgeoisement*. As people got better off, so would they want more freedom. That theory has been discredited, particularly where the Party hold is firm and the aspiration towards freedom—as in the Soviet Union—is limited. The other view was that the communist parties would slowly begin to democratise themselves, starting at the edges of the Soviet *bloc*. Under the slogan of the *Odnowa*, the Polish Party has embarked on a path of limited democratisation. The debate is still cast in many of the nauseating clichés of entrenched communist power. But there have been flashes of genuine freedom. Poland may prove to be unique within the bloc but I doubt whether the poisons which this Congress has secreted can be entirely contained. The Congress has solved none of the problems of the Polish economy, so dependent still on the Soviet Union; nor has it alleviated the plight of the ordinary people who may yet spark into protest. It has probably failed to satisfy the radicals. But the Polish Party was never forgetful that it was required to hold its first experiment in democracy under the watchful and malevolent eyes of its allies.

9. As far as I can judge from Warsaw, the Soviet Union seem to have accepted the Congress—or at least they have not yet set out to discredit it. The presence of their delegation throughout the proceedings and the comparatively restrained tone of their comment suggest that they are prepared to wait and see how things develop. They are probably relieved that there are some familiar faces in the Politburo and that most of the statements made by the Polish leadership were moderate and avoided ideological heresy. It is arguable that at the present time the Congress did as much as could be reasonably expected in the direction of reform and that it pushed to the limits of permitted freedom, which are already further than we or probably the Soviet Union thought, without quite going over the edge. Quite a feat even for the Poles.[5]

10. Now that the leadership has been elected and legitimised, the real tests begin. The Party and Government will have to find a way to come to terms with Solidarity, and Solidarity will have to demonstrate enough responsibility to reach agreements. It is still not possible to say whether the Government will be able to show the necessary energy and sense of urgency. Nor do we know whether the economic situation will in the end undo this process of democratisation and plunge Poland again into a yet greater crisis. Another fundamental problem is whether the Party can begin to close the gap between it and the mass of the Polish population who view the Party with a mixture of cynicism and scepticism. These are questions for the future and outside the scope of this despatch. I am sure, however, that it was necessary for this Congress to have taken place before the Polish Party or Government could begin to address them. Kania's role could be crucial. It is still uncertain how this Hobbesian Pole will emerge but he seems to be about as good a leader as the Party can find for the time being.

[5] Sir C. Keeble, in a despatch written on the same day entitled 'The Soviet Union and Poland', saw the period between 1980 and 1981 as 'the most serious and still undecided challenge to Soviet power in Europe'. For the Soviet Union, he wrote that things had gone from bad to worse over the past year; but although the Polish leadership had not fulfilled their promises to recover lost ground, the Soviet Union had not used force. In a note of 5 August, Mr Fergusson found the despatches 'important, clear and reasonable' providing useful background for the current political and economic assessments. At the same time he noted: 'The crucial question, not addressed in these papers but to which they contrive, is whether economic collapse can be avoided, at any payable price, and if not what the consequences will be' (FCO 28/4495, ENP 014/3).

11. I am sending copies of this despatch to her Majesty's Ambassadors at Belgrade, Bonn, Bucharest, East Berlin, Helsinki, Moscow, Paris, Prague, Sofia, Stockholm, Washington, Hanoi, Havana and Ulan Bator, to the UK Permanent Representatives to NATO, the European Community and the United Nations, and to the Secretaries of State for Defence and Trade.[6]

I am, etc,
CYNLAIS JAMES

[6] Mr Broomfield responded to Mr James on 30 July agreeing that this was in many respects Kania's Congress, 'though as he surveys the economic scene he may feel a little like a man who has safely navigated the rapids only to find the river opening out into a whirlpool'. Marking a clear break with orthodoxy 'it was a remarkable event and may prove of long term political significance', although he predicted that if the *Odnowa* collapsed, it seemed fair that the Congress would be deleted from history. He insisted that the economic crisis needed to be solved, in which Solidarity would have a crucial role to play. Now the Congress had taken place there was no excuse for not tackling it: 'as you say, the real tests must now be confronted. Kania will need all his courage and cunning; Walesa all the persuasive authority he can muster. Reason suggests the outlook is pretty bleak' (FCO 28/4495, ENP 14/3).

No. 72

Mr Cox (Mexico City) to FCO,[1] 3 August 1981, 9 a.m.

Tel. No. 312 Secret (PREM 19/560)

Info immediate from Private Secretary.

Poland

1. Secretary of State discussed question of economic assistance with his American, French and German colleagues in the margins of the meeting at Cancun.[2] He said that, even if it were met, the present Polish request for an additional dollars 500 million would be followed by others and that it was not possible for us to take decisions on a hand to mouth basis. What was needed was an overall political and economic assessment, covering both what the West might be able to do to put the Polish economy back on the right track and the consequences of doing or not doing so.

2. There was general agreement that an assessment on these lines was needed as a matter of urgency. Genscher argued in particular that the position of Poland should be seen in a wider historical and political context. The question at stake was whether Poland would once again be 'dismissed into the eastern hemisphere' as it had been after the war. There must not be another disappointment now. This was seen by other Eastern European countries as well as by Poland as a test case of Western readiness to help. Haig emphasised the difficulties he faced domestically in continuing economic assistance to Poland and thought that a general assessment

[1] Lord Carrington was attending preparatory discussions for the International Meeting on Cooperation and Development (the Cancun Summit) held in October.

[2] Mr Broomfield hoped these conversations would provide the 'political impetus to break through the financial barriers in Whitehall which, for good, if parochial reasons, are manned more vigorously every day.' He asked for a view on when the economy might seize up. The FCO feared a moratorium on debt repayment, followed by a run-down of industrial output, and civil disorder, the final stages of which might be Soviet intervention to assist the Polish authorities (FCO tel. No. 420 to Warsaw of 2 August). Mr James replied (in Warsaw tel. No. 547 of 3 August) that it was impossible to predict. He added that short-term financial credit might not be enough to help them get through the next few months, and stave off default, 'but without it their chances of doing so are worsened' (FCO 28/4524, ENP 090/1).

(which he might wish to supplement by sending an American team to Poland to make a first-hand economic assessment) would be helpful. Cheysson, while agreeing on the need for assessment, was more concerned about the short term financial problems. He explained that the French had now worked out between government and banks an arrangement which would in effect provide the Poles with export credit without any down-payment.

3. There was general agreement that it would be desirable if the Poles were to join the IMF, and Cheysson in particular argued that we should urge them to do so. The Secretary of State said we should not reach decisions on this before we had seen the overall assessment he had suggested. It was however agreed that individual countries might meanwhile usefully explore the question of IMF membership with the Poles in their bilateral contacts.

4. It was agreed that the assessment work should be undertaken as a matter of urgency, and that there should be meetings in Paris (probably at the end of the week beginning 3 August) involving political directors and economic directors and Poland task force representatives. The note for the record in MIFT[3] incorporates comments by the US (Hormats) and Germans (Lautenschlager), and has been favourably received by the French (Camdessus).[4]

[3] Not printed.

[4] The Chancellor was not happy about this initiative. His Private Secretary wrote to Mr Fall on 4 August warning that the UK should not be manoeuvred into the lead over the provision of further economic assistance to Poland. The meeting should not be used to start negotiations over 'the size, apportionment, or method' of any further assistance. He also thought the Foreign Secretary should have brought any fresh proposals of this kind before OD for discussion. Fall replied, the same day, saying Ministerial decisions could not usefully be taken without an overall assessment of both the political and economic considerations, and it was better that any such assessment was formed jointly with the UK's principal allies.

Meetings took place in Paris on 7 and 8 August and discussion was conducted in two groups, one political and the other economic. Mr Arthur, Private Secretary to the Lord Privy Seal, reported the outcome in a letter to No. 10 of 12 August. Both groups had produced agreed assessments. The political paper drew attention to the importance of doing everything possible to sustain the Polish renewal, both for strategic, moral and humanitarian reasons. The economic paper made clear the scale of the economic crisis confronting the Poles, the size of the hard currency gap in 1981 and their need for additional short term credit.

No. 73

Mr James (Warsaw) to Lord Carrington, 7 August 1981, 2.25 p.m.

Tel. No. 562[1] Priority, Restricted (FCO 28/4483, ENP 014/1)

Polish situation

1. The Government's talks with Solidarity broke up after midnight this morning.[2] Yesterday there were strikes and protest actions throughout Poland, and today there is a four-hour strike in Silesia.

[1] Repeated for Information Priority to Moscow and Saving to East Berlin, Prague, Budapest, Paris, Bonn, Washington, MODUK, UKDEL NATO, Sofia, Bucharest, Belgrade, Helsinki, Stockholm, UKMIS New York, and UKREP Brussels.

[2] In a deteriorating economic situation, a general strike had been declared on 5 August in response to food prices and shortages. Throughout July and August there had been 'hunger marches' in several cities on this issue.

2. The Government's version is that Solidarity broke off the talks unilaterally after attempts to draft a communiqué had failed. Solidarity, according to the press behaved with unprecedented arrogance and with no regard for the principles that ought to govern such talks. This morning the radio continued to attack Solidarity, suggesting that it was press-ganging hunger-marchers and that future troubles should be laid at its door. Rakowski said that he was waiting for an answer to questions he had asked Solidarity on Monday about some of their activities which went beyond their statutes.

3. At a press conference today, Solidarity said that there was little agreement of substance at the talks, and that the sticking-point had come when the Government had tried to add to the draft communiqué a preamble about the general situation in the country in language unacceptable to Solidarity. Solidarity have invited the Government to resume talks in Gdansk on Monday 10 August, but there is no indication yet whether this will be accepted.

4. The CC plenum scheduled for tomorrow has now been postponed to next Tuesday (11 August). There are rumours that Kania has received a letter from the Soviet Party and that he may have gone to the Crimea to see Brezhnev for the usual annual consultations.[3]

There are also rumours that he is not well.

5. The Government has its back to the wall. It has at last shown some determination in tackling the country's problems, through the various commissions it has set up. It has made an effort to communicate with the people, in particular by televising more of the proceedings of government. But it has failed to carry Solidarity with it. The latter's intransigent attitude, exemplified by the unusually hardline stance of Walesa, may be a reaction to pressure from the grass-roots, or due to fatigue after a tiring year. Whatever the reasons, it is a bad omen when the govt, and Solidarity fall out in this way, even if on this occasion the govt have a good case.[4] We must hope that the forces of moderation (like the Church) work on both to resume a dialogue.[5]

FCO please pass all saving addressees.

[3] From 1971, Mr Brezhnev held annual bilateral summits with each of the Eastern European leaders in the Crimea. Brezhnev did hold a meeting with Kania and General Jaruzelski on 14 August and instructed Kania to change the course of events in Poland.

[4] In July the Government drafted an economic reform. It limited central planning to outlining strategic goals and establishing independent, self-governing and self-financing enterprise as the basic economic unit.

[5] On 10 August the EC counsellors in Warsaw met to discuss why the talks had collapsed. It was thought that the extremists within Solidarity—who wanted to exercise continuing political pressure—had won the day by making sure that the joint communiqué would be rejected. Solidarity's political demands were growing, for example to release political prisoners, and to undertake electoral reform and profound economic restructuring. For the first time the Government exploited this radical turn to its advantage, presenting it as mere tactics. But the counsellors thought that this advantage would be short lived as such polarised positions would jeopardize the necessary national consensus. Mr Joy thought that 'the effect of the Government's tactical advantage had paradoxically been to weaken the Solidarity moderates' position and was likely to enhance radical demands and make a compromise more difficult'. But he thought that commonsense would prevail, especially within Solidarity's National Coordinating Commission, which would undoubtedly agree on a compromise with the Government (Joy to Mr James, 10 August 1981; FCO 28/4506, ENP 021/5).

No. 74

Mr G. Bullard (Sofia) to Mr Montgomery, 24 August 1981
Restricted (FCO 33/4710, WRE 021/4)

Dear Alan,

The Bulgarian Wall

1. Peter Longworth[1] and I were talking to the FRG chargé, Klaus Bosch, recently about the anniversary of the building of the Berlin Wall. He said that his Embassy has had even more DDR callers than usual this summer, asking for advice on how to escape to the West. Most of them have been young people in their teens or early twenties. All are told that the Embassy cannot help them. This is apparently just the tip of the iceberg. Bosch said he did not have the exact numbers, but he knew that there were many would-be escapers in prison in Bulgaria and he had it on good authority that a planeload, that is to say about 120, were sent back to the DDR each week from Bulgaria during the summer tourist season. Only about 5% managed to get out of Bulgaria mainly to Greece and Turkey, but also to Yugoslavia. The percentage of successful escapes was he thought falling because of the strengthening of the border defences and the way in which Bulgarians living near the border cooperated with the authorities in reporting and even apprehending suspicious characters. He said he knew of one case where a successful escaper had been chased into Greece by what he described as the entire population of one border village.

2. Bosch also suggested that Bulgaria was used by would-be escapers as a place in which they could make contact with organisations specializing in bringing families out of the DDR, escape plans being discussed here though often put into effect elsewhere.

Yours ever,
GILES BULLARD

[1] Head of Chancery and Consul.

No. 75

Record of a meeting between Lord Carrington and officials to discuss economic assistance to Poland, 27 August 1981, 10 a.m.[1]
Secret (FCO 28/4525, ENP 090/1)

1. *Mr Fergusson* outlined the political and economic arguments for providing further economic assistance to Poland but emphasised that whatever Western aid was provided there could be no guarantee that the Polish economy would not collapse.[2] Until the Polish Government had worked out a stable relationship with

[1] Those present were the Secretary of State, Sir M. Palliser, Mr Fall, Mr Fergusson, Mr Richards, Mr Mallaby, Miss Harvey, Mr Montgomery, Mr Green and Ms Brown.

[2] In a despatch dated 17 August entitled 'The Polish Economy: The Chances of Recovery' Mr James reported that all economic courses open to Poland were 'wretched'. The Government had produced a plan to stabilise and reform the economy, and had probably gone as far as it dared, but there would be little recovery in the short term. Solidarity might have no option but to accept large parts of the stabilisation plan because there was little alternative. Mr James warned that if the West withdrew its support 'the edifice would almost certainly collapse, and with it any hope of Poland's

Solidarity it would be impossible to predict how successful the Polish government's plans for economic and political stabilisation would be. Solidarity's National Congress, the first part of which began on 5 September, would be a crucial indication of how its relationship with the Government would develop.

2. *Lord Carrington* asked how much Western economic assistance to Poland in the medium term would cost.

3. *Mr Green* said this was estimated to be in the order of $2-3 billion per annum for a period of five years. Western agreement to go to 100 per cent rescheduling of Polish debt over this period would reduce the amount but the Poles would still require substantial assistance to implement a plan of economic recovery. The cost to the UK of rescheduling debts falling due in 1981 was estimated to be approximately £75 million. The Treasury expected to cover this sum out of ECGD's overall profits in the financial year but it was doubtful whether further rescheduling costs could be similarly financed over a longer period.

4. *Sir M. Palliser* pointed out the similarity of the Polish situation now to that of Turkey four years ago. The West had decided then to step in and help Turkey. Now under the present military rulers, stringent economic measures had been introduced with immediate and beneficial economic effects. *Mr Fergusson* said that the situation in Turkey however had not been so serious and the economy had had greater strengths.

5. *Lord Carrington* asked what was the present position on the proposal of M. Delors that the Western creditors should participate in underwriting a syndicated BIS loan to Poland to cover the request for $500 million short term finance. *Mr Montgomery* said that the Treasury remained adamantly opposed to UK participation in the proposal. The Chancellor had suggested that if the FCO wished to press the case the matter should be considered in OD and guarantees for the loan given by the FCO using a PESC[3] transfer from the ODA vote.

6. The French had promised to contribute $125 million to this scheme and the Italians and the Swiss had said they would participate (amounts not specified). The Germans hoped to be able to contribute and the German Cabinet would discuss this on 2 September. It was not certain that the Germans would arrive at a favourable decision. Several of the smaller creditor nations e.g. the Norwegians had indicated they would also contribute if we and the other major creditors were favourably disposed.

7. The *Secretary of State* said that he was worried that all of our major partners would be seen to be helping the Poles except the UK and that this would look extremely bad for our foreign policy. Equally, however, he recognised that the argument that contributing $30-50 million now would be merely throwing good money after bad was convincing and would command the support of the majority of the Cabinet. He rejected the idea that money for Poland should come off the aid budget especially in the run-up to the Cancun summit.[4]

8. *Mr Mallaby* said that short-term financial help would now of course only buy the Poles a little time but it was time in which they could consolidate further the political gains which the West supported and postpone a *débacle* which could lead

economic recovery, and of our seeing any of our money back.' In a reply of 27 August, Mr Montgomery did not demur from the view that the UK should continue to provide what economic assistance it could, albeit on a piecemeal basis, and the FCO was very conscious 'of the need to avoid a situation where the UK could be accused of 'pulling the plug' on Poland'.

[3] Public Expenditure Survey Committee.

[4] See No. 72, note 1.

to a Soviet intervention. To refuse the Poles this would look bad with public opinion in the UK who would draw the conclusion that the Government was prepared to show sympathy but not provide any real help in time of need.

9. The *Secretary of State* said that this argument was the most telling but he could not ask the Government simply to throw money down the drain. We would need a better argument. He imagined that the Banks also would reach a stage at which it was no longer feasible to pour in further money to recover their investment. At what stage would this process stop? He was opposed to piecemeal assistance and for this reason had suggested at Cancun that officials should consider the longer term prospects and the overall cost of helping Poland. But the economic meeting in Paris had failed to identify these issues, presumably because of the gigantic nature of the sums involved.[5] It would be important for the Poles to join the IMF since this would give some finality to the issue and introduce an element of monitoring and discipline. Mr Fergusson said that entry into the IMF would not however provide immediate financial benefits and some Western assistance would still be required.

10. *Mr Green* said that it might be possible to find the money for Poland by linking this with the extra funds wanted for the Cancun summit. We might for example be able to persuade the Treasury to allocate an extra £40 million over three years to the aid budget if the FCO agreed to meet the $30-50 million required now for Poland from the ODA Vote. It was agreed that Mr Green would submit separately on this idea.

11. In conclusion, the *Secretary of State* indicated that he was not in favour of bringing the question of the UK response to Delors to OD on 8 September where a slot had tentatively been reserved. He preferred to wait and see what the Germans decided on 2 September. It was also considered sensible to delay a decision until after the meeting of the Creditors 'Task Force' with the Poles in Paris on 9-11 September, when we could get the latest Polish assessment of their economic situation and prospects and when a further secret meeting of Economic Directors would probably be held to revise the economic paper.

[5] See No. 72, note 4.

No. 76

Letter from Mr Joy to Mr Montgomery, 28 August 1981
Confidential (FCO 28/4545, ENP 226/1)

Dear Alan,

The Polish Church

1. Thank you for your letter of 14 August to the Ambassador who is on leave.[1] It came at an opportune time, as we were considering sending you something about

[1] Not printed. In this letter Mr Montgomery commented that although Archbishop Glemp might not achieve a stature comparable with that of Cardinal Wyszyński, if he proved more flexible it might not necessarily be a bad thing due to the current very different situation. Regarding the division within the Church hierarchy, he thought that much would depend on the new Archbishop's ability to win the loyalty of the episcopate and also on political developments—especially if a major difference developed between Solidarity and the Government, which would force the Church to make unenviable choices. This would severely strain relations between 'collaborationists' and

the Church in an attempt to assess how Glemp, the new primate,[2] is shaping up to his task. With the caveat that the Ambassador may want to reply more fully to your letter, this letter attempts to make this assessment and to comment on some of the points you make.

2. When the Ambassador wrote his despatch of 10 June[3] he was able to set out the problems that face the Polish Church. But he did not know the identity of Wyszynski's successor and so was only able to make a limited assessment of the church's ability to overcome them. Now that Glemp has been appointed, I think that we might usefully begin by considering the differences between him and Wyszynski. We have not much to go on as yet. Glemp has yet to chair a full Council of the Episcopate (which meets roughly every two months, apart from a long summer break). The main impressions we have of him are based on the Ambassador's call (our telno 572)[3], his first meeting of the Central Council of the Episcopate (our telno 484)[3], his sermon at Czestochowa[4] (our telno 601)[3] and one or two other scraps. Firstly, it is clear that Glemp is much more accessible than his predecessor. He readily agreed to our request that the Ambassador should call on him and seemed keen to see him again from time to time. He has had visits from all sections of Polish society in his first few weeks as primate. (For example, he recently met a delegation of Polish teachers.) He has already met with both Kania and Jaruzelski. A consequence of this will be that, although Wyszynski's personal relationship with Wałesa has gone, Glemp should be able to replace it by building up relationships with Solidarity, the Government and other important sections of Polish society. He should be able to exercise influence over a much wider range of Polish society if he is ready to talk to more of its members. A second difference is that Glemp is much more diffident than Wyszynski. It would be hard for anyone to emulate Wyszynski's strength of character. But Glemp appears to be quiet, even shy, and laconic in his pronouncements. This may not be a bad thing. Wyszynski's autocratic methods of running his Church caused some resentment among his bishops and may well have helped widen the splits in it. Glemp's style may help conciliation. Thirdly, although Glemp is undoubtedly following the middle line of Wyszynski and not identifying himself with either wing of the Church, it is clear that he weights the balance more in favour of Solidarity than his predecessor did. The communiqué of the recent meeting of the Central Council of the Episcopate was much the most pro-worker pronouncement that the Church has yet made. Similarly, the Czestochowa sermon, of which I enclose a text,[5] is balanced towards Solidarity's viewpoint. This may well reflect Glemp's recent experience in a largely rural diocese where he had reasonable contacts with Solidarity without being too closely identified with them.

3. How well is Glemp coping with the problems outlined in the Ambassador's despatch? Perhaps it would be fairer to ask how well he will cope with them, since

'liberals', in which case Pope John-Paul II might have a crucial role to play—a Pope who had 'made his positions on human rights and freedom very clear'.

[2] He succeeded Cardinal Wyszyński, who died on 28 May.

[3] Not printed.

[4] Częstochowa situated in southern Poland on the Warta River is famous for the Black Madonna in the Pauline monastery, which is a shrine to the Virgin Mary. Pope John Paul II prayed before the Madonna during his historic visit in 1979.

[5] Not printed. Archbishop Glemp said that both the Polish Government and Solidarity should cease their reciprocal recriminations and realise that their constant bickering would only serve to magnify tensions while 'poverty is knocking at our door.' He nevertheless made clear that the Church supported Solidarity's demands for access to the news media.

he has only had a few weeks to deal with problems which are in many cases long term. He should be able, firstly, to overcome the legacy of Wyszynski's primacy. He is already emerging as a very different man, who is no less worthy of respect. He is unlikely to continue the autocratic methods of his predecessor. This in itself will make a major contribution to solving the second problem—the split within the Church hierarchy. It is unlikely that Wyszynski could have countenanced anything like an agreement to differ within the Church, or indeed that he would have understood it. His approach to subjects like ecumenicism was doctrinaire (to say the least) and he probably had a similar approach to Church politics. Glemp seems to be far less rigid on both theological and political matters. He should be well placed also to help the Church find a new role within the emerging pluralism in Poland. Unlike Wyszynski he has grown up in an era of dissidence and emerging pluralism and he will have seen Solidarity's early growth in Olsztyn.[6] Flexibility is likely to be a key factor in solving this problem, and he appears to have plenty of it. It is still too early to say how he will handle the fourth problem outlined by the Ambassador, how the Church should react to the benefits brought by the *odnowa*. Time will tell.

4. Finally, there are the deeper implications of the *odnowa* and the irony that a triumph of liberalism might pave the way for the Church's decline. You touched on this in para 6 of your letter. I am inclined to agree with you that a decay of religious life in Poland would not be as rapid nor as complete as elsewhere. Certainly, while the external threat to complete Polish independence persists, the Church is always likely to be seen as one of the guardians of Poland's integrity. And the Church has never in its history been identified with the oppressor in Poland, even if it has not always been identified with the struggle to overcome him. Everyone in Poland agrees that the roots of Solidarity lie as much in the papal election and visit as in the worker riots of 1970 and 1976. Personally, I do not think that this generation will forget that. The next generation will not be Glemp's charge.

5. Glemp has shown courage in putting his reputation on the line [at] an early stage by calling for a peaceful September. This will be a crucial test of his approach. Will Solidarity respond to his support for some of their aims by heeding his appeal? Or will they only listen to the parts of his sermon that suit them, and ignore the rest?

Yours ever,
DAVID JOY

[6] From 1979 to 1981, he was Bishop of Warmia-Olsztyn, where Solidarity was strong, especially among printers who had organised strikes.

No. 77

Mr Joy (Warsaw) to Lord Carrington, 10 September 1981, 2.05 p.m.
Tel. No. 633[1] Immediate (FCO 28/4540, ENP 212/1)

Solidarity Congress[2]

1. The Solidarity Congress yesterday adopted a message to working people in Eastern Europe. Text is as follows:
'The delegates assembled in Gdansk at the first Congress of Solidarity send greetings and support to the workers of Albania, Bulgaria, Czechoslovakia, the German Democratic Republic, Romania, Hungary and all the nations of the USSR.[3] As the first independent trade union in our post-war history, we deeply feel the linking of our fates. Despite the lies being spread in your countries, we assure you that we are a genuine ten million strong representation of the workers founded as a result of strikes by workers. Our aim is the struggle to improve the living conditions of all working people. We support those of you who have decided to embark on the difficult road of struggle for a free trade union movement. We believe that it will not be long before your representatives and ours are able to meet to exchange experiences about trades unions'.

2. For comments and other notes of Solidarity Congress see MIFT.[4]

[1] Repeated Routine to Washington, Moscow, Budapest, Bucharest, Prague, Sofia and East Berlin. For Information Saving to Paris, Bonn, UKDEL NATO, MODUK, UKREP Brussels, UKMIS New York, Belgrade, Stockholm and Helsinki.

[2] The first round of the first Solidarity congress took place from 5 to 10 September. Its aim was to agree a two-year programme and consider Solidarity's internal organisation and statutory amendments. A second round was planned from 26 September to 3 October.

[3] On 22 September Mr Jenkins informed Miss Brown and Mr Manning in the EESD that, prior to the Solidarity Congress, the Founding Committee of Free Trade Unions in the USSR had sent greetings by telex to the Mazowsze (Warsaw) branch of Solidarity dated 18 August. It ended with a message of hope: 'The day will come, we firmly believe, that Polish and Russian workers will go arm in arm to meet democracy and progress. Today Solidarity is a signpost to us. At the cost of persecutions, blood and sufferings the Polish workers have broken the shackles of the regime trade unions'.

[4] Not printed. In this telegram Mr Joy noted that the message was reported to have been 'watered down from a more extreme draft'. Although the most radical proposals had not been discussed by the Congress—including deleting the preamble of the Union's statutes, which acknowledged the leading role of the PZPR—it did pass some important amendments such as promising that the Union would protect its members' civil rights as well as their rights as employees. Joy considered that the statement about free trade unions in other Eastern European countries would have serious implications and that such radical initiatives at least momentarily diminished the chances of a moderate Congress result. Joy commented: 'Seen from here, the statement is likely to arouse Moscow's deepest fears that the workers' revolution in Poland will spread.'

No. 78

Mr Joy (Warsaw) to Lord Carrington, 11 September 1981, 1.50 p.m.
Tel. No. 638[1] Immediate (FCO 28/4540, ENP 212/1)

Solidarity's message to the workers in Eastern Europe

1. The MFA have issued a statement on Solidarity's message to the working people of Eastern Europe.[2] Text is as follows. Begins.

The first Congress of Solidarity sent a message to the working people of Eastern Europe. This was done in the name of a movement which is several million strong. It was an act which is harmful to the national interest of Poland.

Recently the MFA had talks with representatives of Solidarity and explained the principles of Poland's foreign policy. Solidarity assured the MFA that it would observe these constitutional principles, to which it is also obliged by its statutes.

Solidarity's message constitutes outright interference in the internal affairs of other socialist states. Is this the way in which Solidarity wishes to make clear that it belongs to another world? Those who inspired the message violated the overriding principles of Poland's foreign policy and damaged Poland's *raison d'État*.

Poland's independent existence and the inviolability of her frontiers are based on friendship and alliance with the Soviet Union and other socialist states. This constitutes the cornerstone of the structures of security in Europe. The Polish Republic knows the value of relations with her neighbours. For the first time in modern history we have only friends as neighbours. The socialist Polish state will not allow this historic gain to be lost.

The MFA states that the initiators of this message have shown their potentially dangerous misunderstanding of the fundamental interests of the nation and state in the modern world and a misunderstanding of the balance of forces and the system of alliances which guarantee stability and a peaceful future in Europe. They have thus become, whether consciously or not, an instrument of the forces of confrontation.

The MFA feels obliged to state that the message sent by the first Solidarity Congress is also harmful to the millions of union members whose fate is bound up with Poland's international position and interests.

Ends.

2. In a statement to the Sejm Foreign Relations Committee, Czyrek reiterated some of the above themes and said that the playing of the 'Polish card' (presumably by the West) would hamper détente.

3. For the comments of the Warsaw Tass correspondent on the above message, see MIFT.[3]

FCO please pass saving to all saving addressees.

[1] Repeated for Information Priority to Moscow and Washington. Routine to Budapest, Bucharest, Prague, Sofia and East Berlin. For Information Saving to Bonn, Paris, UKDEL NATO, Helsinki, Stockholm, UKMIS New York, UKREP Brussels and MODUK.
[2] See No. 77.
[3] Not printed.

No. 79

Mr Joy (Warsaw) to Lord Carrington, 11 September 1981, 2.50 p.m.
Tel. No. 641[1] Immediate, Restricted (FCO 28/4540, ENP 212/1)

MIPT: Solidarity Congress[2]

1. The series of uncompromising statements and resolutions with which the first stage has ended would seem, as of now, virtually to preclude a moderate outcome to the congress as a whole. Solidarity has made it brutally clear that it is fighting a political battle and has drawn up the lines for future conflict. The closing declaration reads not unlike the outline manifesto of a political party.[3] The implications and repercussions of what has been resolved and done will not be forgotten or forgiven and the adoption of formal resolutions of this tenor goes beyond a mere letting-off of steam. We can only hope for a cooling-off period and the resurgence of moderate views and methods during the second phase. But this hope must now be considerably dimmer.

2. There has been a disturbance at Konin[4] involving gypsies and arising from a quarrel over cigarettes. Crowds took to the streets and threw stones at the local police station. They were brought under control with the aid of police mobile units and an army squad. Possibly merely an example of pent up local frustrations surfacing, but a bad omen.

3. The voting figures have been announced at the referendum at Huta Katowice. 9,851 workers voted for the resignation of the director and 1,594 voted against. Just over 3,000 workers did not vote. The Minister of Heavy Industry has already said that the referendum is illegal and that he will ignore it. This conflict situation, too, could escalate.

FCO please pass saving to all saving addressees.[5]

[1] Repeated Priority to Moscow and Washington. For Information Saving to Paris, Bonn, UKDEL NATO, UKREP Brussels, UKMIS New York, Helsinki, Stockholm, East Berlin, Sofia, Belgrade, Bucharest, Budapest, Prague and MODUK.

[2] Not printed.

[3] The main objectives were: the elimination of poverty, exploitation, fear and lies; improvement of food supplies by controlling the production, distribution and prices in cooperation with rural Solidarity; economic reform with the setting up of genuine workers self-management and the end of the party influence on the manning of top jobs and economic mechanisms; public control over the media; teaching of true facts in schools and at cultural events; free elections to the Sejm and peoples' councils; equality of all before the law; freedom for political prisoners; defence for those victimised for publishing activities and the trades unions; protection of the natural environment; proper living and working conditions for the miners. The declaration ended by saying that the creation of an external threat would not deprive Solidarity of the will to struggle for the ideals of the August 1980 agreement and its implementation (Warsaw tel. No. 640).

[4] City in central Poland on the Warta River.

[5] On the same day Miss Collett, Information Officer at the Embassy, sent a report on Congress atmospherics to Miss Brown. After the first press conference, she had attended a concert of banned songs—very reminiscent, she thought, of a 1960s Dylan concert. The Congress started with the hymn 'God Who Protects Poland', for which there are two endings—'Keep Poland free' and 'make Poland free'—, the latter having been sung at the Congress. Although East European delegations had been invited, only the Yugoslavs appeared.

On 14 September Mr Montgomery wrote a brief for the Cabinet on the outcome of the Congress highlighting the success of the extremist elements, the threat to the Polish Communist Party and Government, and the challenge to the Soviet Union. At the same time he had explained that the Congress could serve as a safety valve for rank and file frustration. The room for manoeuvre to restore the balance in favour of moderates in the second round had been narrowed by overtly political statements and resolutions. With the hardening of the Government's attitude the scope for compromise was reduced. The Soviet Union and her Allies had been alarmed and launched a media counter-attack.

Poland was discussed by the Cabinet on 15 September during which Lord Carrington reported that Solidarity appeared to have gone 'considerably further than previously'. He also reported that the Polish Government had asked for further food aid and that decisions might be needed shortly on further credits (CC(81)31, 15 September 1981, CAB 128/71).

No. 80

Minute from Miss Brown to Mr Broomfield, 16 September 1981

Confidential (FCO 28/4540, ENP 212/1)

Solidarity National Congress

1. You asked for an assessment of the outcome of the first round of Solidarity's National Congress (5-10 September).

2. Mr Jenkins's minute of 15 September (copy attached)[1] gives the background and summarises the main resolutions and measures adopted by the Congress.

3. Any assessment of the meeting must remain tentative at this stage and the final outcome of the Congress will not become clear until the conclusion of its second phase, planned for 26-29 September. Most, if not all of the resolutions and Congress documents must now be debated at regional and local level and the final details of the proposed changes to Solidarity's organisation and Statutes have still to be formally adopted by the Union. Equally it remains unclear, as Mr Jenkins indicates, to what extent the leadership of Solidarity will be constrained in the future by Congress decisions and how far it will continue as in the past largely to exercise its own discretion and initiative as it saw fit.

4. Despite the reservations however the following conclusions may be drawn:

(i) The Congress demonstrated the strength of radical feeling in Solidarity and the degree of frustration of the rank and file at increasing economic hardship and political stalemate in Poland.

(ii) It also revealed the inability of the more moderate leadership (bound by ultra-democratic procedures) to control the disparate groups assembled at the Congress. Walesa appears to have kept a low profile and only came to the forefront when a radical victory over organisational changes appeared imminent.

(iii) Congress statements and actions will have dispelled any lingering doubts of Solidarity's political ambitions. Delegates unanimously passed a series of resolutions which effectively challenged the bases of Party and Government authority in Poland, and set forth an alternative programme of demands for far reaching social, economic and political reform.

(iv) The hard-line resolutions passed at the Congress and the generally militant tone, while these may be modified in the interim period, have nevertheless, for the time being at least, raised the level of tension in Poland and significantly reduced the scope for compromise in negotiations with the Government.

(v) Although the moderates may be able to restore the balance in the second phase of the Congress, the movement appears committed to a tougher line and will be

[1] Not printed. Mr Jenkins noted that the Congress's style was 'completely alien to East European political culture' and therefore left much room for misinterpretation from the Polish Party and Poland's allies (FCO 28/4540, ENP 212/1).

unable to resist pressure from the grass roots unless it can produce greater results. There seem to be few limits on Solidarity's ambitions at the present moment and it appears undaunted by Soviet threats.

5. Immediate official reaction has been sharp and uncompromising. The leadership has said it will resist any claims put forward by Solidarity to political power and it has been announced that a Central Committee Plenum will be held soon to determine the Party's response. The Party has taken an increasingly firm line with Solidarity since its own Party Congress in July, and Kania has warned that the authorities would be prepared to contemplate the introduction of a state of emergency if anarchy threatened. But the Party faces a dilemma. The adoption of a tougher line risks producing an equally uncompromising response from Solidarity (as appears to have occurred on the eve of the Congress when failure to agree on official press coverage of the Congress ended in deadlock). A more restrained approach however will only increase criticism and pressure on the leadership from the Soviet Union and its allies and increase tension still further.

6. The outlook for political stability, industrial peace and economic recovery looks therefore, at this stage, difficult and uncertain. Control of the media, workers' self-management, prices and rationing are all issues on which there may be confrontation in the near future. Solidarity has made it clear that workers control of factories as they understand this, is crucial to their vision of necessary economic and political reform. Equally the Party has emphasised its position: that it alone retains the right to control key appointments and overall policy. Prospects for compromise on this issue look slight and may be diminished if Solidarity consolidates its position on this platform in the run up to the next round of the Congress.

7. The Russians have reacted angrily to the Congress and in particular to Solidarity's message to workers in Eastern Europe encouraging the latter to form their own trade unions.[2] A fierce propaganda campaign has been launched which is likely to increase in the run-up to the concluding phase of the Congress. The final adoption by Solidarity of policies which strike at the roots of socialist authority in Poland would greatly increase the likelihood of eventual Soviet intervention. But for the time being the Russians are not apparently exerting military or other pressures on the Polish leadership and will wait and see how events develop.[3]

[2] See No. 77.

[3] On 18 September the Polish authorities published the text of a Soviet statement they had received complaining about the growing unchecked anti-Sovietism in Poland and demanding 'determined and radical steps' to 'cut short the malicious anti-Soviet propaganda and actions hostile to the Soviet Union' (Warsaw tel. No. 653). Commenting on the statement in Warsaw tel. No. 654, Mr Melhuish called it 'unprecedentedly blunt and threatening' and the strongest indication yet that Soviet patience over developments in Poland was nearly exhausted. But he thought the statement unlikely to force the Government into taking decisive action against Solidarity or deter Solidarity from further confrontational activities. The vast majority of Poles no longer seemed bothered by the threat of Soviet intervention: 'They have convinced themselves that, since it has not happened up till now, it will probably not happen at all, and, if it does, Poland will be acting out its historic destiny.' He did not think that a Soviet intervention was imminent but if the statement made no impact on the local situation 'the Soviet Union is left with very few cards to play short of direct action'.

Sir C. Keeble, in Moscow tel. No. 587 of 19 September, thought that Soviets hopes of an acceptable compromise solution being found, without their intervention, must be dwindling: 'Their patience must be near its limit but there is no reliable evidence on which to base a guess as to precisely when it might snap.'

On 16 September, Mr Melhuish at the Embassy in Warsaw sent a despatch to Lord Carrington entitled 'Solidarity between Congresses' (FCO 28/4540, ENP 212/1). It confirmed the complex compromise—qualified as 'hideous'—reached between the more moderate centralists and the more extreme federalists. He thought that this would generate continued differences between the regions and Gdańsk and between central authorities and the unions. He also thought that the appeal to workers in Eastern Europe—which had gone further than any previous Solidarity statement on foreign affairs—would have confirmed the 'worst fears of the Russians about Polish heresy'. This also 'laid bare a contradiction at the heart of the Communist bloc . . . : if Solidarity can get away with it in Poland, why should there not be free trade unions elsewhere?' This was bound to have worried the Polish Government more than anything else at the Congress. Melhuish concluded that Solidarity was ready to challenge the Government in all spheres and indeed that the protection of members' civil rights and the call for free elections presented an undisguised threat to the socialist system in Poland. From past experience he could not really hope that the moderate element would be strengthened before the second stage of the congress. He thought that it must have been obvious to everyone that Solidarity was now actively campaigning as an alternative power in Poland.

On 25 September, Mr Broomfield thanked Mr Melhuish for his despatch and sincerely hoped that 'jaw-jaw would not lead to war-war' and that the critical economic problems would soon receive the degree of attention they deserved from both Solidarity and Government.

No. 81

Lord Carrington to Sir N. Henderson (Washington), 18 September 1981, 3.15 p.m.

Tel. No. 1390[1] Immediate, Secret (FCO 28/4484, ENP 14/1)

Following for Bullard.

Poland

1. Secret source material on recent events has been sent separately. You may, however, wish to have the following assessment of present state against background of the Polish Politburo statement (Warsaw telno. 652)[2] and the Soviet Central Committee letter (Warsaw telno. 653).[3]

General

2. Political situation in Poland appears, in the last few days, to have become increasingly tense. The Polish Politburo statement and Soviet letter represent reactions to resolutions and declarations at the first part of Solidarity's Congress which touched on fundamental questions of power and control in Poland.

3. Points of interest in the two statements are that although Polish Politburo accused Solidarity of breaking earlier agreements and seeking confrontation and

[1] Repeated for Information Priority to Warsaw, Moscow and UKDEL NATO.

[2] Not printed. The statement dated 17 September accused Solidarity of breaking earlier agreements and of seeking confrontation and bloodshed. The Politburo requested the Sejm (due to meet on 24 and 25 September) to finalise legislation on workers' self-management and economic stabilisation measures.

[3] Not printed.

bloodshed it nevertheless affirmed the party's readiness to continue a dialogue and 'work with those who were not against socialism and the interests of the motherland.' Passages in the Politburo statement reaffirming socialist renewal and readiness to build an alliance of all were significantly omitted in the Tass version (Moscow telno. 582).[4]

4. Soviet statement harps incessantly on the anti-Soviet theme but does not refer explicitly or implicitly to the Brezhnev doctrine.[5] The onus is laid squarely on the party leadership and the Polish Government to take steps to cut short 'malicious anti-Soviet propaganda and actions towards the Soviet Union.'

Soviet intention

5. Soviet intention must be to put pressure on the party to live up to its numerous previous assurances and specifically to put a stop to the anti-Soviet theme in Solidarity's campaign which is not only offensive in itself but clearly feared as a strongly unifying factor to Solidarity's advantage.

6. By addressing their message to the Central Committee the Russians indicate a lack of confidence in the Polish leadership. They appear to be following the same tactic as before the Party Congress, hoping that a public shot across the party's bows will have the dual effect of stiffening their resolve while at the same time moderating discussion at the second round of the Congress.

7. We do not think that the Soviet intention is to force the Polish leadership into fulfilling Kania's earlier hint before the Solidarity Congress first round that a state of emergency might need to be proclaimed. The Russians probably consider that to prevent the second round taking place would provoke a major confrontation between Solidarity and the Government for which neither the Government nor (according to sources) are the Russians making requisite military or other preparations. Although the Russians may hope that later in the winter hardship and hunger may lead to disillusion with Solidarity this stage has not yet been reached.

Effects

8. It remains to be seen what effects the two statements have on Solidarity. They have certainly narrowed both sides' room for manoeuvre and agreement on compromises after the Congress. The balance of advantage is fine. While the moderate element in Solidarity will probably take heed of the need to respect some limits *vis-à-vis* their own and the Soviet leadership the more radical elements in Solidarity may react strongly against a public Soviet attempt to bring them to heel.

Western action

9. We have considered whether Western warnings to Solidarity to exercise moderation would be desirable or possible. Options appear limited. Western leaders could continue to emphasise in public statements the need for moderation and restraint 'from all the parties concerned.' But perhaps the only figure capable of really influencing the situation within Poland is the Pope. He could do this through reference to his recent encyclical which, *inter alia*, gave support to social and political rights of workers.[6] If the situation deteriorates further an approach to

[4] Not printed.

[5] See *DBPO: Soviet Union, 1968-1972*, No. 22.

[6] The encyclical '*Laborem Exercens*' ('On Human Work') was delivered at Castel Gandolfo on 14 September 1981. Pope John Paul II re-asserted the importance of workers forming unions, which should aim at social justice and 'defending the vital interests of those employed in the various professions', including farming unions. He also declared that 'union activity undoubtedly enters the field of politics, understood as prudent concern for the common good'. He affirmed the right of unions to strike—'an extreme means that should rarely be used'.

the Pope might be advisable.[7] It would obviously come better from others than UK though we could participate in joint approach.

Conclusion

10. It will not be possible until after second phase of Solidarity Congress to know how the pieces will lie between the Party and Solidarity as they meet to grapple with the urgent economic problems. If moderation prevails at the Congress then there will be some hope of dialogue on political and cooperation on economic, problems. But if the second phase is a repeat of the first it is difficult to see how confrontation can be avoided.

[7] On 29 September Sir M. Heath sent a telegram to London to report a meeting with Monsignor Proggi, who since 1974 had been Head of the Holy See Delegation in Poland. He said that the Church's attitude was unchanged and that it wished to avoid a military Soviet intervention. The Church advised caution, moderation and compromise by all concerned. When the Polish Government, at a meeting at the end of September, summoned the Polish hierarchy to discuss a Soviet note which contained an unpublished sentence saying that the second phase of the Solidarity Congress must not be allowed to proceed, the bishops declared their inability to stop it (Warsaw tel. No. 19; FCO 28/4546, ENP 226/1).

No. 82

Extract from the minutes of a meeting of the Cabinet Defence and Oversea Committee, 18 September 1981, 10 a.m.[1]

OD (81) 16th Meeting Secret (CAB 148/197)

3. *Economic aid for Poland*

The Committee considered a minute to the Prime Minister from the Foreign and Commonwealth Secretary dated 16 September and a letter of the same date from the Minister of Agriculture to the Chancellor of the Exchequer, proposing that the United Kingdom should take part in a third operation to provide European Community (EC) food supplies to Poland at reduced prices and on special credit terms.[2]

THE FOREIGN AND COMMONWEALTH SECRETARY said that the current Polish request for food aid came at a bad time. Latest indications suggested that under Soviet pressure the Polish Government were contemplating a major clamp down on the Solidarity free trades union movement. Looking further ahead, it was now clear that even if a political crisis were averted the Poles' economic situation in 1982 would be even more serious than earlier foreseen and might lead them to seek Western economic aid on a larger scale than it would be possible to meet. The longer-term problem might be eased if Poland joined the International Monetary Fund; but it seemed unlikely that she would feel able to do so, at least in the foreseeable future. Meanwhile the political case for helping the Poles economically, and in particular with the present food aid package, was very strong. Political liberalisation in Poland was one of the most significant international developments since the Second World War, and its success or failure could have a major effect on the future of the world. It would be highly damaging if British

[1] Those present included: Margaret Thatcher, Lord Hailsham, Sir G. Howe, Lord Carrington, Francis Pym, Humphrey Atkins, Patrick Jenkin, Nigel Lawson, Peter Rees, Leon Brittan, Neil Martin, Alick Buchanan-Smith, Anthony Berry and Sir R. Armstrong.

[2] Not printed.

policy were thought to have done anything to weaken the liberalisation movement. In the present case the EC budget was in a position to finance the proposed 15 per cent discount on world prices. Britain would need to provide £15 million worth of credit if the package included 150,000 tons of British barley as proposed. It could not be argued that such a sum would by itself be crucial to Poland's future; but, since it would be small by comparison with the contributions of Britain's major European partners, and with what the United States were doing under their separate food aid programme, a British refusal to participate would be extremely invidious.

THE MINISTER OF STATE, MINISTRY OF AGRICULTURE (Mr Buchanan-Smith) said that Britain had the barley available and by providing it would save perhaps £1.2 million in intervention storage costs. Shipments would begin in the near future and probably continue into the first quarter of 1982. Other barley producers would certainly seize the opening to step in if Britain declined to help.

In discussion the following points were made:

(*a*) Contrary to earlier indications there was enough credit for Poland left, out of what the Committee had already authorised, to enable the Export Credits Guarantee Department (ECGD) to cover the full £15 million which the proposed export of barley would require. This residue had hitherto been earmarked for the support of industrial rather than agricultural exports to Poland, and the British chemical industry in particular was known to be interested in the prospects. But it was not clear how much of the credit would in fact be taken up if the previous earmarking were maintained, and it was therefore difficult to argue that the present agricultural opportunity should be foregone.[3]

(*b*) It was arguable that Poland's food problem could be overcome by better distribution rather than by more imports, and that industrial equipment would provide more lasting economic benefits than barley. But conditions were now so chaotic that such judgements could not be made with any confidence; and it was clear that food was what the Poles themselves saw as their most urgent need from the West.

(*c*) Very difficult decisions would be required later in the autumn when the Committee came to consider Poland's economic needs in 1982. It was not at all clear how these could be met. Among Britain's partners, the French seemed ready to contemplate the provision of almost unlimited assistance; but the Germans were likely to take a more balanced and realistic view.

THE PRIME MINISTER, summing up the discussion, said that in the Committee's view the proposed export of barley should go forward. No further ECGD credit could be provided beyond what had already been authorised. Credit previously earmarked for industrial exports would therefore have to be used. The shipment of barley and the provision of credit should of course be urgently reviewed if serious internal repression were to develop in Poland.

The Committee:

1. Invited the Foreign and Commonwealth Secretary, in consultation with the Minister of Agriculture, to arrange for Britain to contribute 150,000 tons of barley to the proposed package of European Community food aid for Poland.

[3] At their 9th meeting on 20 May, OD had decided that new credit for Poland should be limited to £25m in 1981 and divided equally between agricultural and industrial exports.

2. Invited the Secretary of State for Trade to arrange for the Export Credits Guarantee Department to provide export credit cover for this contribution from within their existing authorities for credit for Poland.

No. 83

Sir A. Parsons (UKMIS New York) to FCO, 22 September 1981, 4.22 a.m.
Tel. No. 878[1] Priority, Confidential (FCO 28/4484, ENP 014/1)

Following from Private Secretary

Secretary of State's meeting with Polish Foreign Minister: 21 September

Summary

1. 45 minute conversation was entirely taken up with discussion of situation in Poland. Czyrek, while speaking frankly about political and economic difficulties, said that he was not a pessimist. Solutions to problems would take time and the process (which had to take into account both the domestic and international situation) might be difficult for others to understand. If the West helped Poland, both economically and by encouraging political moderation, they should find the results would be as they would wish.

Political

2. Czyrek said that Solidarity had gone too far at the first stage of their Congress. The message to workers in Eastern Europe was silly and provocative ('as we say exporting counter-revolution').[2] Another danger was Solidarity's failure to respond positively or even tactfully to the Government's attempts to persuade them to share economic responsibility. Solidarity's attitude on the appointment of managers was not the key point[3] (both Solidarity's and the Government's proposals would require consensus) but their position on elections to parliament was a political challenge. If one partner would not cooperate and share responsibility and instead threw down the gauntlet and strove for power, it was not surprising that the Polish politburo had made the statement it had, to try to bring people to their senses.[4] But the Polish authorities had not closed the door, and hoped that Solidarity would make use of the remaining gap before and during the second half of the Congress. The Government were doing all they could to this end.

3. Czyrek added that no-one should be surprised that the Soviet Ambassador had made the approach he did. Asked by the Secretary of State whether the Polish authorities had found the Soviet statement helpful, he answered that they would not have published it if they had not.

4. The Secretary of State said that we wanted to do what we could to help but:

(i) Indications of the economic help which might be needed in the longer term were more and more alarming. If things went on in that way the West might not

[1] Repeated for Information Priority to Warsaw. Information to Bonn, Paris, Washington, UKDEL NATO, Moscow, Budapest, Bucharest, Prague, Sofia, East Berlin, UKREP Brussels. Information Saving to other NATO Posts. Lord Carrington was in New York for the 35th meeting of the UNGA. He also met Mr Gromyko (see *DBPO*: *Afghanistan,* No. 111).

[2] See No. 77.

[3] See No. 79, note 3.

[4] See No. 81, note 2.

have the capacity to help. We would rather take an overall look than face new decisions every three months.

(ii) If after the second part of the Solidarity Congress the Polish authorities found themselves having to take measures they would have wished to avoid, things would be made very difficult for the West.

5. Czyrek responded to the first point by saying that this was exactly what the Polish Government were trying to explain to Solidarity, and to the second by saying that the Government would not resort to extreme measures unless their attempts to ensure respect for law and order by normal means were ignored and the country appeared to be heading for anarchy.

6. Czyrek saw some grounds for optimism in the position of the Church, which he believed would work in the same direction as the Party and the Government.[5] He argued also that elements in Solidarity had dropped their mask during the first stage of the Congress and that there was now more criticism of the organisation and some 50,000 resignations. People were afraid of where Solidarity was leading both politically and economically, and even those who did not agree with the Government were beginning not to agree with Solidarity. 800,000 members of Solidarity were also members of the Party. A third force was emerging though it was still passive. These were positive developments which might have a beneficial influence on the second stage of the Congress. He hoped also that Solidarity's reply to the Soviet statement would show evidence of goodwill (he seemed more concerned about form than substance).

Economic

7. Czyrek said that the West had so far not helped as much as the Poles had expected, especially as regards deposits and in the industrial sector (he acknowledged the help which had been given over food and the Secretary of State said that we were ready to play our part in the third tranche of EC food). Czyrek expressed particular concern about down payments for credits and asked also whether the community would be prepared to offer temporary preferential treatment for Polish exports.

8. The Secretary of State said that these were questions which it would be much easier to consider as part of a firm overall plan to get to grips with Poland's economic difficulties. He asked about IMF membership. Czyrek said that there were differences of system which made the question a hard one for Poland, but implied that the Poles might apply if it could be demonstrated that IMF membership would contribute to the stabilisation of the economy and provide tangible results: so far, they had only been asked questions. He accepted the Secretary of State's argument from British experience[6] that IMF conditions could be helpful to the Government concerned.

[5] See No. 81, note 7.

[6] In 1976, Britain had asked the IMF for its biggest ever loan.

9. Czyrek confirmed good indications of the Polish harvest. Poland would have no need to import sugar next year and the potato harvest was estimated at 50 million tons. The Government intended to give priority to the agricultural sector, but this would require imports of equipment, fertilisers and pesticides.[7]

[7] The FCO briefed the Cabinet on Poland for its meeting on 24 September, attaching a copy of this telegram. The brief warned of the acute tension ahead and that the risk of confrontation had increased with the hardening of both the Government's and Solidarity's positions. It summarised the results of the first round of the Solidarity Congress, and predicted poor prospects for the moderates in the second round, which would determine the future nature of Solidarity (CAB 128/71).

No. 84

Letter from Mr Maxey (East Berlin)[1] to Mr Fergusson, 23 September 1981
Confidential (FCO 33/4700, WRE 020/1)

Dear Ewen,

UK/GDR relations

1. Following my presentation of credentials I have called on, among others, Willi Stoph and senior members of the Ministry of Foreign Affairs: Krolikowski, Nier (Deputy Foreign Ministers) and Plaschke (Head of West European Department). I have also attended the Leipzig Fair and had a chance of talking to businessmen about trade prospects.

2. Needless to say the consistent feature of all encounters with senior East Germans these days is a lecture about peace, the threat to stability posed by NATO's TNF plans and the US decision to produce neutron weapons, and the pressing need for negotiations to control the arms race and if possible reverse the trend. The presentations varied in length, intensity and sophistication, but the tone is always one more of sorrow than anger. Although the East Germans are doing everything possible through propaganda and direct contact to promote the Soviet aim of disuniting NATO and forcing the Americans into arms control negotiations with the Soviet Union in a disadvantageous position, there is no reason to doubt the genuineness of their concern at the present situation. It seems clear that meanwhile the East Germans do not want East/West tensions to do lasting damage to their relations with West European countries. This has been most evident lately of course in inner German relations, where the GDR leadership are anxious to keep the dialogue open. The message to me in my recent interviews has been that our already good relationship can and should be developed further and that the GDR Government stands ready to cooperate fully with us in bringing about an improvement on all fronts: political, economic and cultural.

3. The line that I have been fed shows every sign of being well prepared and carefully coordinated. Although there is every reason to believe that the East German aim for the next stage remains to secure a visit by the Secretary of State, the idea has not been specifically mentioned by any of my interlocutors from Honecker down to Plaschke. This may indicate a wish on the part of the East Germans themselves not to seem too eager and to place themselves in the position of *demandeurs*. Indeed in order no doubt to counteract any such impression

[1] Mr Maxey succeeded Mr Foster as Ambassador to the GDR in September 1981.

Krolikowski at one point indicated that the rate of progress in developing relations was very much up to us: if we wanted to delay the East Germans would not object. Fischer, the Minister of Foreign Affairs, on whom I paid a short call before presenting my credentials, was inclined to be reproachful: it did not seem to him that we perhaps placed as much weight on our relations with the GDR as they could and should bear. Since the GDR authorities are fully aware of the connection we make between a further development of political relations and an expansion of GDR imports from the UK, Krolikowski launched into an effort to undermine our case when I called on him. The GDR, he said emphatically and at length, had every interest in doing business with us on a practical commercial footing, but all too often our firms were not competitive, flexible and rapid enough in their operations and our credit arrangements also fell short sometimes of those offered by our competitors.

4. The East Germans have indicated in the course of this softening up process that I would be welcome to call at the MFA once I have settled in to review our relations and to see how they might be carried forward. I have responded positively; but I have not committed myself to any particular timing and propose to make no early move. The MFA's tactics seem to me, as I have said, to be designed in part at any rate to prevent the GDR getting in the position of *demandeur* and to put pressure on us. Our purpose on the other hand is to keep the pressure on the GDR to be more forthcoming over trade if it wants a further development of political relations. This purpose is well served by the present situation. The East Germans understood our position before I came here and I have, starting with my talk with Honecker, reiterated HMG's view that economic relations have lagged behind political relations and that we are looking for an expansion of trade to restore the balance. I will continue to make this point when appropriate in my calls on GDR Ministers and senior officials. We should sit back and let this medicine work.

5. I am confident that this is the right tactic for pursuing our present policy in bilateral relations with the GDR. It is a separate question, but one which I think needs to be examined, whether that policy itself is fully valid in current circumstances. We are insisting that political and economic relations between the two countries must go hand in hand, that economic relations have lagged badly and become unbalanced and that a further development of our relations (notably a visit by the Secretary of State) is not feasible until GDR imports from the UK have shown a substantial increase. Our emphasis in this context has been very much on the sort of larger contracts which British industry needs and of which we have won all too few. The Secretary of State himself told me before I left London that he would not come until we had got some big orders. The trouble about this line now is that, as everybody appears to be agreed, the scope for the GDR to place large orders in other countries has been sharply reduced as a result of the curtailment of this country's plans for industrial expansion. Certainly there are no big projects on the horizon for which British firms appear likely to be asked to bid. If any large projects of interest to us came into view, it could, as we know from experience, be a couple of years before a deal was likely to be concluded. We seem therefore to be in a position of pressing for a significant boost in GDR imports from the UK before the Secretary of State will come here, while having to recognise that such a boost is unlikely for some considerable time. As a consequence of our pressure the East Germans may now intend to step up their purchases from the UK to the extent that they can. But even if there was an effort on their part to show goodwill the

effect would probably be modest and slow to appear. If we continued in these circumstances to refuse a visit by the Secretary of State, the East Germans could well turn nasty and exclude us completely when their economy turns up and large-scale investment is resumed. (I am leaving out of account the extent to which the East German contention that British firms are just not competitive enough may be justified. To some extent it certainly is.)

6. It is hard to avoid the conclusion that as things stand the policy of withholding a visit by the Secretary of State in an effort to persuade the East Germans to give us more business can hardly bring significant benefit in the short term and could do us damage in the long term. As far as our commercial interests are concerned, a visit by the Secretary of State during the course of next year, provided there were clear signs meanwhile of an East German readiness to expand trade (even if only modestly), could prove to be the most prudent and productive move (unless of course there was a crisis over Poland).

7. There are of course other factors than the commercial ones which have to be taken into account in deciding on a visit by the Secretary of State. But it is the commercial considerations which were emphasised during my briefing in London and I think they need to be looked at again.[2] The question is not so much whether the principle on which we are proceeding is right as whether the criteria are. Nor am I advocating—at least not yet—a decision in favour of a visit by the Secretary of State next year. It is too soon to reach a firm conclusion about that. But presumably we should be sorting our ideas out around the end of the year: and by that time we should have a much clearer idea whether some improvement in trade is in prospect.[3]

Yours ever,
P. M. MAXEY

[2] Mr Gladstone wrote to Mr Maxey, on the same day, acknowledging that relations with the GDR had improved but noting that it would be even better if this translated into commercial substance. He thought that it was becoming increasingly important to get an accurate understanding of the effect on the GDR of developments in Poland. The understanding in London was that the GDR was irritated with what they considered as unrealistic demands by the Poles and old German-Polish antagonisms had been revived (FCO 33/4746, WRE 400/1).

[3] Mr Bullard noted: 'Mr Fergusson will wish to sign a considered reply, with a paragraph setting out our general philosophy on contacts with the East as background.' He suggested reiterating the principle of discrimination between countries in Eastern Europe, which had been approved by the Secretary of State (No. 34).

No. 85

Mr James (Warsaw) to Lord Carrington, 25 September 1981, 12.05 a.m.
Tel. No. 669[1] Priority Confidential (FCO 28/4540, ENP 212/1)

The forthcoming Solidarity Congress

1. I thought you might like to have some thoughts, inevitably speculative, on the way the Congress and the present Polish situation might develop.

[1] Repeated Priority to Wellington (for Private Secretary). Information Routine to Moscow, East Berlin, Budapest, Prague, Paris, Bonn, Washington, UKDEL NATO and MODUK. Information Saving to Sofia, Bucharest, Belgrade, Helsinki, Stockholm, UKMIS New York and UKREP Brussels.

2. There are various pressures on Solidarity to behave moderately at the next Congress: the Soviet messages, the moderation of the Polish leadership, the Church (including possibly some intervention by the Pope), a part of its own membership. Underlying the present crisis, a dialogue still continues between the Sejm and Solidarity and it was this that produced the compromise on worker self-management. But already elements in Solidarity are denouncing the compromise, and it is by no means certain that if Solidarity's leadership were to seek endorsement for their moderate position on the floor of the Congress, they would win the day. The social forces which now march under the banner of Solidarity stretch from those who wish to overthrow the system and its alliances to those who wish to effect deep changes in the economic and social fabric of Poland. But even if the moderates like Walesa are more or less acceptable to the Polish Government in its present state of weakness, they remain anathema to the Soviet Union. It is thus surprising that General Jaruzelski should have yesterday made a speech in which he fully recognised the strength of 'this great movement' while condemning extremists like KOR. This type of studiously moderate language must make the Russians livid.

3. Can the Polish Government act against Solidarity or elements of Solidarity? Would they be able, for example, to round up KOR and put them behind bars? When this question was raised yesterday among the NATO ambassadors, the general conclusion was that Solidarity would come out on a general strike. Even if Solidarity behaves moderately and produces resolutions which are not totally unacceptable to the Government, how long can a dialogue continue? I cannot give any clear answer to this but I would agree with the assessment of the JIC that another crisis would seem inevitable before long—the social forces involved are too disparate and volatile to permit any situation of stability in the foreseeable future. And the leadership of Solidarity know that their movement can only remain united so long as it advances.

4. Yet I am drawn to the conclusion that the Government must do something more to satisfy the Soviet Union. So far they have really done very little. Jaruzelski's statement yesterday that the army would be used to protect order in the country and the more visible presence of armed soldiers on the main streets of the central part of Warsaw, with helmets on their heads and carrying guns (but not in combat uniform), may be intended as a low-key show of determination. But I doubt whether it will make much impression on the militants in Solidarity. I think therefore that some further action by the Party is probably necessary, and the only room for manoeuvre that it seems to have is to change its leadership. Yet Kania and Jaruzelski undoubtedly enjoy some degree of grudging popular support. If a harder-line leadership take over, can they hope to achieve any better results with Solidarity? I can only see an aggravation of the present situation with presumably a greater pressure for an appeal for outside assistance. We simply do not know if that is the scenario which the Russians are now beginning to engineer; or whether they wish to give the appearance of such a scenario in order to put the wind up the Poles.

5. Each time a Polish crisis has reached a peak in the past, it has subsided into some messy form of compromise. We must hope that the same will happen again after the Solidarity Congress. But the pitch of criticism has now grown to a point where it is difficult to see how the Soviet Union can live with the political pretensions of Solidarity even if a weak Polish Government can. They are using every pressure to make the Polish Government and Party do their repressive work

for them and I am sure this is their preferred solution. Their appalling dilemma is that no Polish Government is or will be strong enough to do so by itself and has no other course but that of accommodation. Changes in the leadership may therefore buy time but not much else.[2]

[2] On 19 September the FCO had received news that the US had warned the Polish authorities of the very negative effect on US public opinion of any crack down on Solidarity resulting from Soviet pressure. In FCO tel. No. 526 to UKMIS New York of 21 September (copied to Washington, Warsaw, Moscow, UKDEL NATO), it was made clear that a démarche along American lines risked being misinterpreted and leaked, with the result that the Soviets could claim Western interference in Polish affairs. It could also act as encouragement to extremist elements in Solidarity. The UK did not see any need to go beyond the current line—that the Poles should be allowed to solve their problems without any outside interference (FCO 28/4484, ENP 014/1).

No. 86

Letter from Mr Thomas (Prague) to Mr Montgomery, 1 October 1981
Confidential (FCO 28/4422, ENC 015/1)

Dear Alan,

Trials of Czechoslovaks for 'illegal' religious activities

1. We have already reported by telegram[1] the progress of the three trials which started on 25 September in Bratislava and on 28 September in Olomouc and Louny. This letter is intended to give you, and posts to which it is copied, a fuller account of the events and their background.[2]

2. There has been no official publicity so far about any of these religious trials. We have had to rely for news about them largely on the excellent AFP[3] correspondent here, Bertrand Bollenbach.[4] Since many of his sources are semi-clandestine, we sometimes wonder how long it will be before he is asked to leave (he is constantly tailed by security men).

3. The first trial to start, in Bratislava, was of the Salesian father Günther Matej Romf, who was accused of conducting religious ceremonies (catechising two gypsies), when not licensed by the state to do so.[5] For this offence Romf faced a sentence of between six months' and three years' imprisonment. Although we believe that the trial was concluded on 25 or 26 September there is still no information available as to the sentence imposed. You may recall that it was at Bratislava that seminarists went on hunger strike last October in protest against 'Pacem in Terris' (an association of Party stooge priests). It is possible that Romf may have had some connection with this protest.

[1] Not printed.
[2] Mr Rich in his telegram of 28 September (Prague tel. No. 239) advised that the trials at this stage could not be influenced by bilateral action and recommended against issuing a public statement on behalf of the Ten after sentences had been passed unless they were unexpectedly severe. But he did not rule out a confidential démarche once the trials were over if there was a consensus within the European Community. He also recommended that the planning for Lord Trefgarne's visit should continue but that he would be in a better position to give a recommendation after the sentences were passed. A démarche was indeed carried out on 7 October (No. 88).
[3] *Agence France Presse.*
[4] See articles in *Le Monde* by AFP: 'Un prêtre est condamné pour avoir célébré "illégalement" la messe' (30 September 1981) and 'Six personnes, dont deux prêtres, condamnées à des peines allant de dix mois à trois ans de prison' (1 October 1981).
[5] The State retained the right to licence all priests and pastors—and approve their placements.

4. The trial in Louny, Bohemia, of Josef Kordík, a former 'licensed' priest, who had his licence revoked when he signed Charter 77 in October 1978, was for the same category of offence. Cardinal Tomášek was able to intervene officially on his behalf, by writing to the President of the Court, on the technical grounds that the State had suspended Kordík from his religious functions directly, rather than informing the Cardinal that this should be done. Perhaps because of this intervention, Kordík received the comparatively light sentence of one year's imprisonment suspended for three years. It is understood that the Cardinal had also made unofficial representations on behalf of the other defendants, but, at least in the case of those on trial at Olomouc, he has no technical grounds for an official approach to the court.

5. The largest trial, at Olomouc, Moravia, was of six defendants, five of whom, Jan Krumpholc (aged 54), Frantisek Lizna (40), Rudolf Smahel (30), Jozef Adamek (67) and Jozef Vlcek (61) were accused of the unauthorised production and sale of literature and the sixth, Jan Odstrcil (57), of theft of socialist property (the paper on which some of the literature was printed, which was taken from the offices of the archdiocese of Olomouc, the vicar-general of which, Dr Veselý, is a prominent 'peace priest'). Krumpholc was additionally accused of making a profit from the illegal sale of literature,[6] whereas Smahel and Lízna were also accused of currency offences arising from allegedly accepting the sum of DM 5000 from a West German monk, Joachim Witt, in July 1979. Lízna is also believed to have been the contact of two West Germans Englisch and Grill, expelled from Czechoslovakia in July of this year.[7] Charges are reportedly being prepared against another Czechoslovak, Dominik Duka, in connection with this case. Technically they were therefore all charged will civil offences, although the literature concerned was certainly religious.

6. Of the six, two are signatories of Charter 77, Lízna and Adamek, and two are priests, Lízna and Smahel. The offences to which the trial relates were committed as early as May 1979 and all the defendants were detained at that time, but released later in the year, or early in 1980. Thus, at the time of the trial, only one was being held in custody, Lízna, and that for a separate political charge for which he was detained in July 1981 (presumably the Englisch/Grill affair) and for which he is yet to stand trial. Two of the defendants, Krumpholc and Adamek, had been imprisoned on almost identical charges (of disseminating religious literature) for periods of ten and eleven years respectively in the 1950s.

7. The heaviest sentence was three years imprisonment for Krumpholc. Smahel was given two years, Lízna, Adamek and Vlcek 20 months and Odstrcil 10 months. At first sight these variations make little sense, especially as Lízna is generally regarded as having been one of the two 'organisers' (the other being Smahel). However, Krumpholc's maximum sentence may result from the earlier conviction and the fact that his house was apparently used for the printing, whereas in Adamek's case age may have been a mitigating factor. It remains surprising that Odstrcil, who risked a higher maximum sentence than the others (five years imprisonment as against three) should have received the lightest sentence.

[6] Under Czechoslovak law private trading was prohibited.

[7] The West German priests, Rudolf Englisch and Rudolf Grill, were stopped at the border with East Germany by Czech police and accused of collecting information of anti-socialist character. They were imprisoned for twelve days until their expulsion from the country on 5 August.

8. Two Frenchmen (one of them a priest) representing the Vatican's Justice and Peace Commission[8] as well as the Human Rights Federation and the Association of Christians for the Abolition of Torture[9] were outside the courtroom at Olomouc, but were refused entry to the proceedings.

9. There is no doubt that some of those sentenced (particularly the three Charter signatories) were engaged in political as well as religious activities, but it seems that these proceedings were solely concerned with the religious offences; this is, I think, borne out by the relatively light sentences on Lízna, Adamek and Kordík. It remains to be seen whether the authorities will treat Lízna more harshly when he is brought to trial for his 1981 'political' offence.

10. It is also clear that some, at least, of these cases had been pending for some time, and that the authorities had only recently agreed to bring to court a group of people, who, in some cases, may have been persistent 'offenders'. There is probably little connection between this crack-down on 'illegal' religious activity and the expected trial of Chartists.[10] It is still not known here when, or even if, this is to take place. If there is an 'underground church' on a scale which the press inside and outside Czechoslovakia has sometimes alleged, the accused in the Olomouc case may only be the fringe of it, if they are part of it at all. The real 'underground church', if it exists, is unlikely to get caught with this level of offence and is likely to be at its strongest in Slovakia.

11. The Ambassador had the opportunity to discuss the trials briefly with Cardinal Tomášek. As we have already reported, the Cardinal requested that any démarche we might make on this subject should be a private one, so as to avoid a delicate situation becoming even more complicated. I enclose a copy (for FCO and HOLY SEE only) of the Ambassador's minute of the conversation,[11] as you may consider it advisable to ensure that Cardinal Hume is briefed before he meets Cardinal Tomášek in Rome on 12 October (Canon Hamond Moore's letter of 23 September to the Ambassador here, copied to you and Mark Heath.)[11]

Yours ever,
RICHARD THOMAS

[8] Pope Paul VI established the Pontifical Commission '*Justitia et Pax*' in 1967 and gave its definitive status in 1976.

[9] Action by Christians for the Abolition of Torture was set up in Paris in 1974.

[10] See No. 2, note 17. The human rights situation had deteriorated in May 1981 with Chartists detained in Prague, Bratislava and Brno.

[11] Not printed.

No. 87

Mr James (Warsaw) to Lord Carrington, 5 October 1981, 4.05 p.m.
Tel. No. 689[1] Immediate, Restricted (FCO 28/4484, ENP 014/1)

My Telno 688: Solidarity Congress: Confrontation with the Government.[2]

1. Walesa's election encouraged hopes that the Congress would pursue a more moderate path. These hopes have been dashed by the handling of the compromise on workers' self-management and by the Government's proposal to raise the price on cigarettes.

2. The vote on workers' self-management undoes the compromise achieved between Solidarity and the Sejm.[3] The Congress resolution states that the Sejm has ignored the views expressed in the first round of the Solidarity meeting on 8 September.[4] The Congress has therefore voted to hold a referendum on this issue and so seek changes on important aspects of the compromise relating to the election of directors and the right of the state to define the enterprises' tasks. *Trybuna Ludu*, the Government paper, criticised the Congress for the way in which the resolution was passed. It seems that there was a great deal of confusion in the hall at the time and there may have been irregularities. Nevertheless some of the delegates were deeply dissatisfied with the compromise and with what they regarded as the undemocratic and high-handed way in which the leadership had reached agreement with the authorities.

3. Given the combustible atmosphere of the Congress, it is astonishing that the Government should have decided to embark on a price rise in cigarettes without any apparent preparation of public opinion. As recently as 1 October the State Price Commission had announced that there was a draft scheme to increase prices for fuels, electricity, gas, sugar, jams, starch, salt and matches. No mention was made of cigarettes. The Minister responsible for prices commented that all price changes would be subject to consultation with Solidarity and the trade unions. He now claims that he did consult Solidarity about cigarette price rises and that Rulewski and Lis had agreed in the summer not to challenge rises in cigarette prices. Solidarity claim however that, although consulted on the principle, they were not consulted as they expected to be on the timing or the details.

[1] Repeated for Information Immediate to Melbourne (for Private Secretary), Washington and UKDEL NATO. Repeated for Information Saving to Moscow, East Berlin, Prague, Budapest, Paris. Bonn, Sofia, Bucharest, Belgrade, Helsinki, Stockholm, UKMIS New York, UKREP Brussels, and MODUK.

[2] Not printed.

[3] There were two significant events on the third day of the Solidarity Congress on 29 September. First, Professor Lipiński, one of the leaders of KOR, proclaimed its dissolution, on the grounds that 'Solidarity had now achieved the aims set for itself and KOR at its foundation'. He also launched a fierce attack on the Government, describing its brand of socialism as 'anti-socialist' and criticising the 'fascist' appearance of some official press organisations. Second, a 34-point draft programme was circulated for discussion. The programme mainly reflected Solidarity's trade union concerns, but also political calls for pluralism, for a second parliamentary chamber, and for freedom of conscience and the press. Its first point was to 'demand the introduction of . . . democratic reform at all levels of administration, a new socio-economic order which will link the plan, self-government and the market'. And it closed: 'Solidarity demands a new social agreement'. The Warsaw embassy thought that nevertheless 'the bulk of the programme' did hold out 'the possibility of Government/Solidarity cooperation if the Government wish to seize it' (Warsaw tel. No. 676 of 29 September 1981; FCO 28/4540, ENP 212/1).

[4] For the first round of the Solidarity meeting, see Nos. 77 to 80 and 85.

4. The Government seem to have added to their own blunders by despatching the Chairman of the State Price Commission and the Minister of Finance, to explain themselves to an angry Solidarity Congress. They were given a rough time and told to go away and seek an annulment of the rises from the Prime Minister. According to journalists who were there, the mood of the Congress at that moment became very ugly and seems to have compelled Walesa to adopt an uncompromising negotiating stance. The row has now acquired the proportions of a test of strength for both sides. If the Government backs down, it will show how very weak it has become and that it cannot do anything without Solidarity's approval. It may be possible to fudge some sort of compromise but once again this incident reveals the disintegration of authority in the country and the reality of power which now rests with Solidarity.[5] Whatever the merits of the case, the Government was inept to engage in a trial of strength on ground which was not essential to its economic plans and where public opinion was so easily inflamed. Smoking is one of the rare comforts left to a Pole.

[5] The Congress, which ended late on 7 October, adopted the Union's draft programme which called for a just and self-governing Poland. It demanded the abolition of centralised economic management to be replaced by a 'communally-owned enterprise managed by its work force' and a 'Social Council for the National Economy' which would be empowered to oversee the Government's economic policy. It also demanded pluralism as a basis for democracy and the implementation of political, economic and social programmes, with genuine and freely-elected bodies at factory, regional and national levels to supervise implementation. The State should guarantee basic civil liberties, equality before the law and the beliefs of minorities. Market forces should be reconciled with socialised planning and public institutions should be democratised. But it also stated a desire to avoid bloodshed by implementing demands gradually (Warsaw tel. No. 701 of 9 October 1981). In a letter to Lord Bridges on 9 October, Mr Montgomery wrote that the Party leadership must now be aware that Solidarity had become 'a *de facto* opposition' in all but name. Mr Broomfield wrote to Mr Fergusson on 12 October emphasising the strong challenge to Wałęsa from radical candidates and the importance of the future balance of power in Solidarity's 20-man Presidium. But he thought that if the Central Committee Plenum reaffirmed *Odnowa*, and Wałęsa retained sufficient room for manoeuvre within the Union to ensure a moderate approach, it was likely that dialogue would resume between Solidarity and the Government (FCO 28/4541, ENP 212/1).

The UK, as President of the EC, had planned a protest declaration in case of trials of Chartists in Czechoslovakia but it was religious leaders who had been tried at the end of September. Instead the Presidency proposed to its EC partners that it should speak to the Czechoslovak authorities on behalf of the Ten, if possible before the conclusion of the trials but, if not, after sentencing. The British, who had taken a strong position on dissidents at the CSCE meeting in Madrid in November 1980, wanted to be consistent and they also thought that not protesting would give the wrong signal to the Czechoslovak authorities and be prejudicial to potential future trials (FCO tel. No. 166 to Prague of 29 September 1981). When the sentences in two of the trials became known on 1 October, the Presidency suggested a confidential démarche should be made. The line agreed was to deplore the recent trials for religious activities, as they violated commitments to religious liberties in the Helsinki Final Act and the terms of the UN covenant on civil and political rights, and to emphasize the negative impact on public opinion (COREU Tel. No. CPE/MUL/ETR 3171).

No. 88

London COREU to all COREU, 7 October 1981, 6.28 p.m.
CPE/MUL/ETR 3297 Priority, Confidential (FCO 28/4422, ENC 015/1)

Czechoslovak trials

1. The Presidency[1] spoke today on lines agreed to the Czechoslovak Ambassador in London. Similar action is being taken in Prague.[2]

2. The Ambassador argued that there was no discrimination on grounds of religion in Czechoslovakia. He also maintained that the démarche amounted to interference in Czechoslovak internal affairs. The Presidency said that the charges preferred against those recently sentenced hardly bore out his first point and that the CSCE and UN commitments undertaken did indeed permit the member states to raise such issues with co-signatories.

3. The Presidency also took the opportunity to connect the demarche explicitly with possible trials of Charter 77 signatories. In this context the presidency referred to the statement which the Irish Foreign Minister made on behalf of the ten on 26 October 1979.[3]

Fin de texte

[1] Mr Broomfield represented the Presidency.
[2] Mr Rich made a démarche to the Foreign Ministry on 8 October. The Deputy Foreign Minister argued that the EC should stick to economic and trade affairs; and interference in internal matters was contrary to the Final Act. He also expressed surprise that the UK should act as a spokesman of human rights, making an implicit reference to Northern Ireland. The Ambassador referred to governmental accountability on freedom of religion in Principle VII of the Final Act and argued that the Czechoslovak media were ill-informed about Northern Ireland (FCO 28/4423, ENC 015/1).
[3] This had established the Western official position on dissidents.

No. 89

Letter from Mr Fergusson to Sir C. Keeble (Moscow), 13 October 1981
Confidential (FCO 28/4484, ENP 014/1)

Dear Curtis,

Poland

1. Many thanks for your letter of 24 September.[1] I was in Stockholm and Helsinki the week before last and just missed last Wednesday's bag—fortunately, because Kenneth James has now had time to comment (his letter of 8 October).[2]

[1] Not printed. In his letter written before the second stage of the Congress, Sir C. Keeble thought the Soviets must be preparing for the eventuality that the Congress did not pass off quietly and swift action would be necessary. Moscow would try to exploit the same techniques of pressure they used successfully in 1968 which had left the Czech leadership 'fatigued, disorientated and bewildered' in order to minimise the risk of serious opposition. He added that 'military indicators may be as important as the political from now on'.
[2] Mr James commented that the Soviets faced 'appalling difficulties' if they were to intervene now that Solidarity had become a national political force. Mr James thought the whole country would come to a standstill if Soviet leaders managed to persuade the hard-liners in the Polish Party to stage a show of force against Solidarity or its leaders. Mr Fergusson, in a marginal comment, doubted whether any Polish leader could impose a crackdown now with any degree of success. Mr James also thought that whilst there were few signs at present that hardships and privations would turn Poles against Solidarity but this might not necessarily last, especially as winter progressed.

2. I agree that we ought from time to time stand back from the constantly shifting pattern in Poland to see if we can detect any general trends. Incidentally, we have much appreciated your full and prompt reporting of Soviet reactions to developments in Poland.

3. Writing with the benefit of 3 more weeks hindsight than you, but at a time when the Soviet attitude to Solidarity appears to have taken another dive (Moscow telno 625)[3] we are still continuing to watch the political indicators as closely as the military. Perhaps the most remarkable feature of developments in Poland since August 1980 has been the number of crises, in which it seemed reasonable to suppose that Soviet patience had finally been tried beyond endurance, but which were nevertheless defused by one means or another.

4. Our view is that the Russians remain highly reluctant to intervene in Poland. It is very likely that they did not want the second phase of Solidarity's Congress to take place. The intensity of the present propaganda campaign is no doubt a measure of their anger and frustration, both at what is going on as well as the failure of the Polish Party to take resolute action. That said, however, we still have no evidence that the Russians have urged the Polish leadership to use force against Solidarity which, as they must realise, would probably lead to a situation where Soviet intervention could not be avoided. The Soviet message, sharp as it was, in a sense evaded the issue by calling for decisive action only against anti-Soviet manifestations. Although, therefore, I agree that the Soviet assessment of the Party's chances of re-establishing control must be fairly pessimistic, we do not have grounds yet to say that the Russians have decided that their previous policy is hopeless.

5. I think all of us agree on the 'internal' restraints on Soviet action: a bloody fight; devastated economy; no likelihood of general acceptance of an imposed leader; down-grading of Poland's contribution to the Warsaw Pact etc. But neither of the two critical points, withdrawal from the Warsaw Pact or real threat to strategic East/West lines of communication, have yet been triggered. The Solidarity programme (Warsaw telno 701)[3] has a carefully constructed passage about 'International Alliances'. Externally, however, the arguments in favour of not intervening have been strengthened (as you recognise in Moscow telno 620)[3]. The dialogue with the Americans has resumed, and not just on TNF. Agreement has been reached with the Americans on grain and finally the gas pipeline negotiations appear near conclusion with a probable signature during Brezhnev's visit to Bonn in November.[4]

6. Against that background we believe that the outcome to Solidarity's Congress is important, not least Walesa's election, however qualified by the elections to Solidarity's National Commission. And today's news of the Government's offer to Solidarity of a Joint Commission is, with luck, a sign of greater skill, on the part of the Party and Government, in dealing with Solidarity. If now Solidarity can show some disposition to work with the Government on economic issues we would have thought that the Russians would be content to wait and see how matters develop. They may hope that there are developments within Solidarity itself, in the attitude of the Polish people to Solidarity and also possible regroupings within the Party which could improve the outlook from their point of view.

[3] Not printed.
[4] President Brezhnev visited Bonn from 22 to 25 November.

7. In this respect, I very much share the views expressed by Kenneth James in the second paragraph of his letter. Recognising the profound reluctance which the Soviet authorities must feel for taking a final decision over intervention at the present time, I think that they may well be looking to a time when growing 'economic misery and despair may make a 'strong' solution more possible'. My view is, however, that true though that may be, the longer the delay the more difficult it will be for them. Whether at the last resort the Russians could live any length of time with an outwardly conformist but inwardly revisionist Poland (paragraph 3 of Kenneth James' letter) will in my view depend to a large extent on the reactions of the other Eastern Europeans. At present the risk of contagion seems small. But with time and above all a little economic success the Polish heresy might exert a powerful attraction for its neighbours.

8. That said we have no doubt that immediate Soviet pressure will be maintained on such important issues as censorship, worker/management etc. There could still be recourse to the escalatory political measures you refer to in paragraph 4 of your letter, and indeed, we would expect the Soviet Union to exhaust its various political options before deciding that the condition of Poland was only susceptible to radical surgery. But finally I would hedge my bets in the sense that misjudgement, miscalculation or deliberate provocation could result in a very rapid confrontation between Solidarity and the Government in which neither side had the time or the control to look for compromises. If another 'Bydgoszcz'[5] took place we might indeed find the whole process telescoped and the problems of military intervention confronting us at very short notice. We are all very much on the look-out—in short, even if the criteria for intervention have not been fulfilled, none of us discounts the possibility that they may be. And we all know how quickly things could move.

Yours ever,
EWEN

[5] See No. 53, note 2.

No. 90

Letter from Mr Fergusson to Mr Maxey (East Berlin), 14 October 1981
Confidential (FCO 28/4384, EN 026/3)

Dear Peter,

UK/GDR relations

1. Many thanks for your letters of 23 September[1] and 1 October,[2] which have been read with considerable interest.

2. Our general philosophy over discriminating between the Soviet Union and Eastern European countries was set out in George Walden's minute of 12 November 1980[3] (a copy of which was sent under a covering minute of 19 November from Brian Fall to Peter Foster). Brian Fall's minute put a gloss on this and made it clear that the discrimination should not be static, but flexible and evolutionary, taking into account changing circumstances in the respective countries concerned. If I may say so, your letter reflects very well the requirement

[1] No. 84.
[2] Not printed.
[3] No. 34.

to keep our bilateral relations with East European countries under constructive review.

3. The GDR has hitherto fallen into the category of those countries that have, in comparison with others, been discriminated against. Berlin considerations and the GDR's policy of rigidly toeing the Soviet line have been the determining factors, and the conjunction of GDR membership of the Security Council with the Soviet invasion of Afghanistan exposed the GDR to the need to stand very conspicuously by the Soviet Union. That had its effect on our attitude. Furthermore, apart from Axen, we have been unable to identify particular personalities in the GDR leadership who might warrant special attention from us. Our policy has therefore been to insist on expansion in parallel of our political and economic relations, that is to demand a price in terms of commercial contracts for meeting the GDR's wishes on the political front. We have so far openly linked the question of Ministerial visits, including a visit by the Secretary of State, to our being offered substantial commercial plums.

4. We agree with you that circumstances now call for some reappraisal of this policy. Despite the GDR's relative economic strength, we have had to recognise that, like its Eastern European neighbours, the GDR is now retrenching on Western trade, partly because of the recession but also because of the lessons of the Polish economic crisis. The prospects of our obtaining major contracts are obviously much reduced; moreover, ECGD is adopting a very much more cautious approach towards the expansion of Government credit to Eastern Europe as a whole. We also have to accept that the GDR's confidence in their own international stature has grown; as your experience seems to demonstrate, they are no longer so ready to put themselves in the position of demandeurs. And although it is only a year since the GDR aggravated the deteriorating situation in inner German relations by increasing the Minimum Exchange Requirement, since then it has been clear that the GDR have shared the general wish to avoid the tension over Poland spreading to Berlin. And I believe that it would be difficult to impose a more stringent conditionality in respect of commercial contracts upon the GDR than for example upon Czechoslovakia, which has—at the least—a no more enviable record on human rights.

5. All this has led us to conclude that there may be a case for a visit by the Secretary of State to the GDR in 1982. The Secretary of State visited Poland, Romania and Hungary in 1980. Of the remaining members of the Soviet empire the GDR is undoubtedly the most significant both in its own right and because of the current situation in Poland. Moreover, Lord Carrington, during Axen's visit in June, accepted an invitation in principle and said he hoped to make the visit as soon as possible after the UK Presidency. We should not expect objections for 'quadripartite' reasons; although East Berlin is unlikely to be visited by a US Foreign Secretary in the foreseeable future, a French Foreign Minister has already been there (M. François-Poncet in 1979 i.e. before Afghanistan), but David Goodall may like to comment.[4] Assuming continuing tension over Poland, a visit by the Secretary of State could be turned to advantage to remind the GDR of the need for strict non-interference in Poland's affairs (while if an invasion were to

[4] On 21 October Mr Goodall, HM Minister in Bonn, advised waiting until at least the end of the year before speaking to the GDR to take into account wider considerations, notably the impending visits of Brezhnev and Honecker to the FRG (Mr Goodall to Mr Fergusson, 21 October 1981; FCO 33/4700, WRE 020/1).

take place with active GDR support, cancellation of the visit would be one more way of indicating our disapproval).

6. We accordingly recommend to the Secretary of State that we should plan quietly on the basis of a visit to take place some time in 1982, but that tactically it would be unwise for us to declare our hand to the GDR yet. He has agreed that we should keep open the option of a visit. The most fruitful course of action might now be to continue to stall *vis à vis* the GDR for the time being (say until the end of year/UK Presidency), still hinting strongly at the need for substantial improvement in our commercial relations to balance improvements on the political side. We would aim to reach a final decision on a visit at the turn of the year.

7. All this is I think in accord with your own thinking. I should be grateful for any further comments and in particular for your recommendations on the timing and procedure that we might now follow.

8. In the aftermath of Axen's visit, the further development of our political relations with the GDR depends crucially on if and when the Secretary of State pays his visit. But we have not forgotten the side issues: we have noted that your interlocutors are still plugging a Science and Technology Agreement and the Department will be looking at the possibilities again.

9. I am not, at present, giving the correspondence a wider circulation, but we may want to do so—and shall let you know—in the context of letting other Eastern European posts know how the visits programme for 1982 is shaping up.

Yours ever,
E. A. J. FERGUSSON

No. 91

Mr James (Warsaw) to Lord Carrington, 15 October 1981

Confidential (FCO 28/4541, ENP 212/1)

Summary. . .[1]

Some Thoughts on the Solidarity Congress and the Future of the Union

My Lord,

1. I should like in this despatch to look at the Solidarity Congress taken as a whole and at the direction and shape which Solidarity is now taking. The picture is not clear since Solidarity is an enormous mass movement which stretches into every part of Polish life and which has a dynamic of its own, part evolutionary, part revolutionary.

2. The second Congress, however, led to some consolidation of the organisation of Solidarity. It gave it an elected leader, a presidium of 18 members and a National Co-ordinating Commission—organisationally, a sort of mirror image of the Party, the only kind of political organisation most Solidarity members know. Wałęsa was elected President, as expected, with 55% of the vote. There are those who think that he expected to get much more and that the vote could be seen as a limitation on his position—a Giscardian 'Oui, mais . . . '[2] If he

[1] Not printed.

[2] This referred to Monsieur Valéry Giscard d'Estaing's positioning before the French parliamentary elections of 1967, in which he launched his new party the *Fédération Nationale des Républicains*

were a Western trade unionist or political leader who took on 3 opponents of differing complexions and defeated them decisively on the first round, he would undoubtedly be regarded as having won an overwhelming victory. But he is not a leader who has come up by some normal institutional path. He is (not to mince words) a living legend. To the majority of its 9-10 million members, Wałęsa is Solidarity. I think it is, therefore, fair to conclude that the vote did dent his standing somewhat. His election address was a disappointing one and there are some signs that he took things too much for granted. He was subject to considerable criticism in the margins of the Congress for being too high-handed, too big for his boots. His remarks after the election suggest that he does not intend to change his style or let the critical voices inhibit him. I think he would remain 'a powerful and charismatic leader'.

3. For the immediate future, we can therefore expect Solidarity to remain in the Wałęsa mould—a moderate but tough movement, close to the people but advised by intellectuals and experts, and linked in dialogue to the Church. How important is the Presidium? How much is it likely to count in the next year? Mr Rakowski, the Vice-Premier who has had long negotiations with Solidarity, told me shortly after the Congress that he thought the new Presidium was more radical than the old and Wałęsa would not always be able to have his own way. He inferred that his wings had been clipped. I asked him why he thought the Presidium was more radical and it was clear that he did not know most of the people. He based his assessment on the fact that the members of the Presidium came from regions where there was a high radical tradition. Against this, it has been argued by some observers that since Wałęsa put up the list of candidates for the 12 elected members and 11 of these were elected, the list is Wałęsa's list. I think this is probably too simple a conclusion. The two most prominent of the 11 elected members are Onyszkiewicz and Palka and they are far from moderate. I think it is more likely that Wałęsa put together a slate which he knew reflected the composition of the National Co-ordinating Commission and which was as close to his line as he could reasonably hope to achieve. It will take time before we know how the new Presidium works out in practice and a final assessment must wait a while. But it is already clear that Wałęsa is not faced with a group of yes-men and he could have a rough ride at times. The Church see Wałęsa's victory as immensely important. They believe it is a guarantee that Solidarity will stay on a moderate course and not be over-political. They tend rather to dismiss the other members of the leadership. But from what we know of such regional firebrands as Słowik and Bujak, this may prove to be wishful thinking. But the Church is probably right in essence. Wałęsa is the man who will count for the next two crucial years provided he has got the character and stamina to stay on target and not to be deflected by fame. I judge he may be a sufficiently remarkable man to do this. We must hope that his visits abroad will not take him away from his roots or for too long away from Poland.

4. Solidarity is not a trade union. It is a political and social force on a national scale. Some of Solidarity's resolutions passed at the Congress, notably the demand for free elections to the regional councils, can by no stretch of the imagination be regarded as anything other than purely political. The programme produced by Solidarity confirms the union's political pretensions. It says at one

Indépendants. Although still supporting the right-wing majority, he aired reservations about de Gaulle's economic, social and European policies and campaigned for a more 'liberal' approach, using the symbolic phrase 'yes, but . . .'

point that the only way to save Poland from destruction is to restructure the state and the economy. It says at another point that pluralism should be the basis of democracy and that the union will try to carry out political programmes as well as social and economic ones. The demand for a social council to oversee the Government's economic policy, in which Solidarity would have a part, would—if fulfilled—make Solidarity into a partner in government. From a Soviet point of view, there can be no question that the programme of Solidarity is a 'counter-revolutionary document'.

5. It is clear that the Government and Party have in effect recognised that Solidarity is now a political force. Wałęsa himself no longer tries to keep a fig-leaf over the organisation by claiming that it is confined to the Gdańsk agreements. He said at one point recently that life has moved on and Solidarity with it. It is true that Solidarity has no clear political objectives and that its programme is a hotchpotch of points—some vague, some precise, some realistic and some an illusion. The moderates in Solidarity recognise that they must not question the socialist nature of the state or Poland's alliances; but there are some extremists who would like to go as far as advocating a change of system.

6. Another important question which emerges from the two Congresses of Solidarity is whether the central organisation will now be able to control the regions, in particular those regions which are radical. The first indications are that control may, at times, be uncertain and intermittent. The National Co-ordinating Commission called for a suspension of all strikes and protest actions until talks with the Government had taken place and the results been assessed. Even as I write, two regions have already disobeyed that call and others seem likely to follow. Although the central Solidarity authorities now enjoy elected status and should thus be better able to control the regional 'barons', and although some of the most powerful regional barons have now been brought formally into the central authorities, it is likely that this trend will continue. In the first place, the regional barons are more beholden to their membership, who can depose them, than to Wałęsa *et al*, who cannot. In the second place, experience suggests that when local feelings are running high in, say, Silesia, there is little that can be done about it in Gdańsk. Nevertheless, the organisation of Solidarity is impressive and it has a remarkable capacity for communication at the regional level. Its hidden strength is the determination of the people to accept sacrifices in order eventually to get a better way of life.

7. I was told recently by someone who knows the Solidarity leadership and advisers well that Solidarity recognised that in practice it would have to prop up the Government and Party, that it could not go too far and that it must at all costs not try to remove the fiction that the Party was the most important pillar of the state. But the question is whether Solidarity can put its policies into effect (e.g. self-management, freedom of access to the media and, much more controversial, free regional elections) whilst bolstering the Government. Much of Solidarity's programme runs counter to Government policy. So if Wałęsa is to have a dialogue with the Government and to accept a certain degree of power-sharing, he will have to ignore or fudge part of his union's programme. He has said that he would be prepared to do this. But he will have to be careful because he cannot be sure that if he departs too far from the programme he will be able to contain all the forces within the movement. The Government must look to Solidarity, and Wałęsa in particular, to negotiate constructively (which they will probably try to do) and to put certain delicate issues on to the back burner (which they also

probably will). But if economic conditions get worse and regional industrial unrest grows, Solidarity's room for manoeuvre may be narrowed and it will not wish to be tainted by the inadequate policies of the Government. The best hope for the Government would be to establish some form of institutionalised co-operation with Solidarity. There are signs that they are trying to do this by setting up a Joint Commission to examine certain economic problems, though the first reaction of Solidarity has been to reject the idea of a Joint Commission while agreeing to hold bilateral talks. The Government realise that they need Solidarity's co-operation to get the workers back to work and to raise productivity. They have not yet, however, recognised that they may have to share power in order to do this, and they are likely to refuse to do so for some time. Solidarity's dilemma is that by co-operating too closely with the Government it may weaken its original impulse which was anti-governmental. It will not want to be drawn into National Fronts where it would be one of a number of organisations and where the Government would be able to hold the ring. Distrust of the Government's intentions is deeply implanted in the Polish people.

8. There is still a great deal of resistance to Solidarity in the Party, especially among the hard-liners who believe that it must be disciplined, though no-one can tell me how the Party or the Government think they are strong enough to do this. There is, however, a growing feeling that the Polish situation is now so desperate economically that exceptional solutions must be sought and that these solutions may require a convergence of moderate forces on to some common ground. It remains to be seen whether some institutional form can be found to express such a convergence. So far, there is still too much suspicion between Solidarity and the Government and too much hostility towards the Party and its works by the people.

9. Before this despatch reaches London, the Party Central Committee will have met and probably fought a fierce, if at times concealed, battle over the leadership. We do not know whether the present so-called moderates, Kania and Jaruzelski, will maintain their positions or whether new men, who will try to take a firmer stand against Solidarity and come up with a more successful approach to the economic crisis, will move towards a take-over. But whether the present leadership remains as before, as seems most likely at present, or whether a new group of Party leaders take their place, there is no hope that the Polish economy can be got moving again, that the process of mobilising the productive forces of this country can be really started, without accommodation and negotiation with Solidarity. The leaders of Solidarity will also bear a very heavy responsibility if they press the Government and Party too hard and refuse to reach reasonable agreements. For the moment they have the massive support of the Polish people. But this may change if conditions get very bad, as they may well do this winter (we have already had our first power cuts). The gleam of light is that more people are beginning to see that a national consensus and effort is necessary. I think Mr Len Murray's message to the Solidarity Congress was the right one: protect your interests but deal with the Government of the day.[3] For its part, the Government

[3] After attending the Solidarity Congress, Mr Murray spoke with Mr James, and commented that the leadership had been criticised for reaching a compromise with the Government without properly consulting the rank and file at the regional level. He was positive about Mr Wałęsa and thought he would probably win Solidarity's leadership election, because of his position and personality, and because there was no obvious rival. For Murray the most serious problem was reconciling those in the leadership who favoured dialogue with the Government with those who refused. Murray put his hopes in the more moderate elements although he recognised that splinter groups might 'fray'

must recognise that it is speaking from a position of weakness and find means of maintaining a regular and constructive dialogue with Solidarity if the Polish economy is ever to get back on its feet. I think there are even some faint signs that the Soviet Union is beginning to accept this reality. Unless they wish to intervene militarily and massively in Poland, they and the Polish authorities must accept (whatever they may say) that for a long time Solidarity is likely to be a major part of the political and economic landscape of Poland and that business must be done with it. The Polish people still have plenty of courage and (strange though it may seem to a West which has never known real economic hardship) plenty of hope that the country will come out of the present morass better than it went into it.[4]

10. I am sending copies of this despatch to Her Majesty's Representatives at Belgrade, Bonn, Bucharest, Budapest, East Berlin, Helsinki, Moscow, Paris, Prague, Sofia, Stockholm, Washington, NATO, the European Community and the United Nations, and to the Secretary of State for Defence.

I am, etc,
C. M. JAMES

Solidarity at the edges. James had the impression that Murray was 'agreeably surprised by the seriousness and organisational strength of Solidarity' (Warsaw tel. No. 673 of 28 September; FCO 28/4540, ENP 212/1).

[4] On 15 October Mr Joy reported on an EC Counsellors' meeting in Warsaw that took place that day and especially considered the Solidarity Congress. The Counsellors thought that: the Congress had institutionalised Solidarity; Mr Wałęsa's position had been strengthened; internal schism had been avoided; the 'Wałęsa Praesidium' would be moderate; Wałęsa would not feel bound by the programme; but it had high significance for Solidarity's international image and was a convenient target for the Soviets (FCO 28/4506, ENP 021/5).

No. 92

Points made during a seminar on 16 October on the medium term prospects for Eastern Europe[1]

(FCO 28/4365, EN 021/28)

The Polish Crisis and its implications for the rest of Eastern Europe

1. (*a*) *The Polish 'Renewal'* had brought about immense economic dislocation. Worker self-management, if conceded, could add to the chaos, though if it led to

[1] The seminar was organised Mr Mallaby to discuss a draft paper with a small group of leading academics and journalists who specialised in East European affairs, along with representatives from Whitehall Departments. These included: Philip Windsor, London School of Economics; Philip Hanson, University of Birmingham; George Schopflin, London School of Economics; Richard Davy, *The Times*; Mark Frankland, *Observer*; Martin McCauley, University of London; Alex Pravda, University of Reading; Dr Wlodzimierz Brus, Wolfson College, Oxford; Professor D. Mario Nuti, University of Birmingham; Professor Alex Nove, University of Glasgow; Professor Peter Wiles, London School of Economics; David Watt, Chatham House; Ewen Fergusson, Assistant Under-Secretary, FCO (Chairman); Christopher Mallaby, Shaun St John, Planning Staff, FCO; Nigel Broomfield, David Manning, Charles Gray, Judith Brown, East European and Soviet Department, FCO; Keith Manning, Trade Relations and Export Department, FCO; Patsy Harvey, Martin Williamson, Economic Service (International Division), FCO; Patrick Laver, Geoffrey Murrell, Joe Banks, Dick Jenkins, Research Department, FCO; Malcolm Mackintosh, Cabinet Office; Michael Hawtin, HM Treasury; John Pownall, Department of Trade; Moray Stewart, Ministry of Defence; Peter Bull, Bank of England; Gloria Franklin, Ministry of Defence.

the end of the *nomenclatura* system[2] there was the chance of more competent managers being appointed. It was still possible that Poland would emerge with a form of 'socialist corporatism', involving cooperation between the party and other forces, which could offer a new political stability in Eastern Europe. Meanwhile the Polish Renewal seemed to have widened the scope of feasible political change in Eastern Europe.

(*b*) There seemed to be a pattern in the *Soviet Union's reactions to crises in its empire*. The USSR tended first to mobilise its armed forces, then to embark on intensive bilateral discussions with the client state, and to intervene only when discussions had failed to resolve the crisis. The Czechoslovak and Afghan crises had both developed in this way, and Poland had already gone through the first two stages.

(*c*) But the USSR had so far shied away from any attempt to turn the tide of events in Poland by military means. Two of the factors mentioned were a lingering guilt about Tsarist Russia's treatment of Poland: and that an intervention would mean the USSR having to take on full responsibility for the Polish economy. Besides, the Kremlin knew full well, as it had known in 1956, that the Poles would resist. The Russians might try to exert *economic pressure* on the Poles, especially during the winter months, by refusing to run a trade imbalance. This would relieve the USSR of the immense cost of subsidising the Polish economy. It would also allow them to apply gradual pressure in a way which was impossible by military means. But the effect of economic sanctions would merely be to unite the country against them and to risk precipitating disorder on a scale that would compel the USSR to intervene with troops.

(*d*) *Eastern Europe as a whole* faced considerable difficulties, brought about by the world recession, increased prices for Soviet raw materials and inflation, and there were pressures for both investment and growth to be cut back. The economic prospects for the region already hinged on continued access to Western capital. The East Europeans wanted to balance the current account by the end of the decade. This required sustained growth and the annual increase of exports by 6% and imports by 3%. To achieve this they would need to increase their indebtedness by a factor of 2.5 above present levels. If this was impossible their present plans were unrealistic. This could have dire consequences for stability in Eastern Europe.

(*e*) *If reform endured in Poland* the risk of political infection had to be taken seriously. The East Germans, who had begun by prophesying intervention, now spoke in terms of Poland going 'bourgeois'. There had already been a *de facto* cessation of democratic centralism in the Polish Party. The East German Manifesto Group, which comprised perhaps 50 middle-ranking officials, seemed pledged to rethink democratic centralism in the GDR as well, though it could be argued that theirs was no more than a tactical ploy to gain preferment. The Polish Renewal must also have slowed down progress towards economic integration in COMECON.

(*f*) This might make the USSR hesitant about allowing others, such as Hungary, to continue down their present mildly reformist paths. The USSR might be tempted to encourage the emergence of more authoritarian regimes in Eastern Europe as it had done in Poland. But this could in itself prove both politically and economically destabilising.

[2] The system of appointments to key administrative positions, made by the ruling Communist party, which allowed the regime to exercise strict control over all aspects of state and party activity.

(*g*) It might be possible to reduce this problem if future authoritarian governments were able to carry out relatively reformist economic policies. Kadar's Hungary and the reforms in Soviet agriculture now in prospect showed what might be possible. Hungarian economic reform had, however, taken place gradually, over a long period of time, in a country with a particular tradition and work ethic. It was very possible moreover that as time went on the Hungarian party's lack of involvement in economic management would lead to a dilution of party authority. And one reason for Hungary's stability was that a whole generation had been traumatised by the events of 1956. The success of the Hungarian experiment was also heavily dependent on Kadar's personality and prestige. The results of the Soviet experiments were yet to be seen.

(*h*) *If against the odds the USSR intervened in Poland* there would be a massive rift in East/West relations. A key question in forecasting what might then happen would be the reaction in the Federal Republic. The extent of the GDR's participation in an invasion would help determine this. If there was no invasion of Poland there could well be a major increase in anti-nuclear and unilateralist sentiment in the FRG, leading to pressure for appeasement of the USSR and even for FRG withdrawal from NATO. If Poland was invaded opinion in the FRG would become more convinced of the need for strong defences and agree to put such projects as the gas pipeline on ice, but might later revert to a more scared kind of pacifism.

Western policies towards Poland and the remainder of Eastern Europe

2. (*a*) The Warsaw Pact constituted an immediate military threat to the West. Anything which lessened that threat increased our military security and offered the possibility of reducing the burden of defence spending. There was moreover an equal Western interest in the long term transformation of the Soviet empire into a freer, more open society which would be content with a non-adversary relationship with the West.

(*b*) Economic assistance to Poland might serve both these ends, and avoid the international tension which a Soviet intervention would give rise to. Western refusal to help the Poles by contrast would be seen both in Moscow and in Eastern Europe as washing our hands of all interest in internal change in the Soviet empire. It was even arguable that both our long and short term commercial interests lay in promoting the Renewal; a descent into chaos or a Soviet intervention would reduce our chances of recouping our existing investment, and make it subsequently harder for us to regain a foothold in Polish markets. But there was another side to the coin—if the USSR had to find the resources to support Poland unaided, this could weaken the Soviet economy and constrain Soviet military growth.

(*c*) Further assistance to Poland would have to take the form of aid. Public opinion in the West would therefore need to be convinced that Poland was as deserving a recipient as those poorest countries on whom the aid programme was now concentrated. In fact aid given to Poland would be far more productive economically than aid given to Third World countries. £1 of aid might generate £10 of output by mobilising unused capacity. This would have a further multiplier effect. Poland was suffering badly from short term credit withdrawal; and, because of the stimulus this would give British exports, the opportunity cost to the West of £1 aid might be not more than 25-50p.

(*d*) But for further aid to be effective it was essential to have some central authority in Poland capable of taking and implementing decisions—otherwise resources would be squandered. This in turn raised the question of the Western role in promoting a consensus between the authorities and Solidarity. There was a risk that Western banks in particular had already become over-identified with the more cautious elements in the Polish administration. But it would be impractical and undesirable for the West to go as far as acting as an intermediary between the Government and Solidarity, not least because of the reaction this might provoke in Moscow. It should be possible to devise ways in which agreement between the two could be made a precondition of continued Western assistance.

(*e*) There had been real difficulties in getting the central banks and finance ministries of the 16 principal creditor countries to agree on the refinancing of Polish debt. It would be far preferable if there were only a single Western representative negotiating with the Poles. This was where, if Poland were to rejoin the Fund, the IMF could make a real contribution. But Poland would almost certainly find IMF conditions totally unacceptable.

(*f*) The West should consider whether it might not capitalise on present and future crises within the Warsaw Pact by making Western assistance conditional on some relaxation of the Soviet grip on the states concerned. This 'Finlandization'[3] of Poland for instance might give it a military status in the Warsaw Pact similar to that of France's in NATO.

[3] The term refers to the influence the Soviet Union had over Finland's policies during the Cold War.

No. 93

Letter from Mr James (Warsaw) to Mr Broomfield, 22 October 1981
Confidential (FCO 28/4485, ENP 014/1)

Dear Nigel,

General Jaruzelski: First Secretary, Prime Minister, Minister of Defence and commander-in-chief of the armed forces

1. You have all the details of General Jaruzelski's career and I will not bother you by repeating them. But I think it might be of interest to have a few impressions since I have had one long session with Jaruzelski when he was Prime Minister and have seen him socially on a couple of other occasions. I have also discussed him with Poles and others who know him.

2. The idea that he is a soldier's soldier is misleading. He has been a Party man for 20 years and his career in the army has been primarily due to his position in the Party. He is however very much a soldier in his deportment, carrying himself stiffly and with a certain dignity. He is always well dressed and dapper in his appearance. I think he wears dark glasses because he had trouble with strong artificial lights. I am fairly sure that he also wears a small hearing aid. He has the faculty of impassivity. I have watched him sitting in the long dreary sessions at the *Sejm* expressionless and still while Kania and Jabłonski[1] shift around or fidget.

3. When I met him I was impressed by his clear and careful powers of exposition. Again one was reminded of a very good briefing by an articulate General. I was told by Dobrosielski that he is very quick to master his brief and has a meticulous memory. Those who know him speak of him with a certain affection as well as respect. Dobrosielski implied that he was thoughtful of his

[1] Henryk Jabłonski, chairman of the Council of State of the People's Republic of Poland from 1972-85.

staff and liked by them—though I am sure that he can be glacial. No-one seems to doubt that he is essentially a moderate man who wishes to avoid the use of force in Poland and believes in accommodation and compromise. At the same time, I have heard it said that he would not shirk use of force if he felt that the authority of the army was in any way threatened. I am sure that behind his stiff and formal manners there is a man with strong views and feelings. But he is shy and reserved. I have also the impression that, like Kania, he is a counter-puncher rather than an attacker. An example of this was his failure to appear on television immediately after he was elected First Secretary. The occasion cried out for someone to give a lead and make an appeal to the Polish people. He may be inhibited by the fact that he is not a very charismatic figure, and that he has no special talents for the television. But then none of the other Polish leaders has either. They all read through their texts in a bumbling and boring way (I am sure it is one of the strengths of Wałęsa that he has the self-confidence to speak naturally and without notes).

4. There is a feeling among some of the Poles to whom I have talked that Jaruzelski will not last, that he is a stop-gap, that he is not essentially a strong man and that as Prime Minister, before he became First Secretary,[2] he failed to get to grips with the situation. This theory assumes that Jaruzelski is the last resort before the installation of a hardliner like Olszowski, with the risks this contains of an appeal to the Soviet Union.

5. I am not sure. It depends whether he will rise more to the occasion as First Secretary than he did as Prime Minister. I was interested that when the US Ambassador here saw him the other day, in company with a group of visiting US businessmen of very high calibre, Jaruzelski appeared much more relaxed and at his ease than he was as Prime Minister. He made a strong impression on the Americans as he did on Cheysson, the French Foreign Minister, as a man with a crisp and hidden reserve of determination. We shall see.[3]

Yours ever,
C. M. James

[2] He became Prime Minister on 11 February 1981 and First Secretary on 18 October 1981.
[3] Mr Broomfield replied on 28 October (No. 96). The information found its way to the Cabinet, with the Foreign Secretary reporting on 20 October: 'The change of leadership in Poland was probably for the better, and might lead to a Government which was more dynamic and better able to take decisions. The new Party leader General Jaruzelski was essentially a moderate. The leader of the Solidarity trade union movement, Mr Wałęsa, had welcomed his appointment' (CC(81)33, 20 October 1981, CAB 128/71).

No. 94

Mr James (Warsaw) to Lord Carrington, 27 October 1981, 8.30 a.m.
Tel. No. 736[1] Immediate, Confidential (FCO 28/4485, ENP 014/1)

Call on Mr Czyrek

1. Mr Czyrek asked me to call late yesterday evening and said that he wanted to speak to me as a follow-up to the conversation that he had with you in New York in September.[2] You had said that the *Odnowa* had now lasted for some time and it

[1] Repeated Immediate to Luxembourg (for Private Secretary) and Information Routine to Moscow, Paris, Washington and Bonn.
[2] See No. 83.

was perhaps the moment for consolidation. He had replied that you were quite right but that this was something that needed to be said to Solidarity more than to the Government.

2. He wanted me to know and to convey to you that since he had spoken the situation in Poland had seriously deteriorated, on the economic, social and political fronts. The Government had struggled to find answers and had offered to create a wider national consensus. They had suggested a broad national front in which independent forces would be represented. They had offered to set up a joint commission with Solidarity and other unions. They had tried to engage in constructive negotiations with Solidarity. But the last Solidarity declaration which had put the entire responsibility for everything that had gone wrong on the Government showed that Solidarity were only prepared to react very negatively. They had made demands which they knew the Government had not the economic resources or the foreign currency to satisfy.

3. The Polish Government were not helped by the attitude of certain western Governments, and he mentioned the United States and the FRG, which had said they would react adversely on the economic and political fronts if any actions were taken to counter the policies of Solidarity. He wanted me to know that the situation now was very serious and that the Government had no more field for manoeuvre. If Solidarity did not show some greater sense of realism and patriotism, the risks of confrontation were high and the consequences of such confrontation would be felt inside and outside the frontiers of Poland.

4. I said that I was glad to see that he had not had to criticise statements by HMG. As he knew, the British Government were sympathetic to the difficulties which Poland was experiencing and their attitude throughout had been helpful and responsible. Mr Czyrek said that he knew that Britain had every interest in the stability of Poland.

5. I said that I understood it was the intention of the Polish Government to broaden its base to bring in new elements, and this would be done at the end of the week. Would this process still not be helpful? It would surely be right for the Government to persist obstinately with its search for national consensus. Mr Czyrek said that the plenum would meet on Wednesday and the Sejm on Friday, and changes would then be made in the Government but these would be no use if Solidarity maintained its present negative stance. This was leading to anarchy and to disintegration. He repeated that there was no room for manoeuvre and that the Government had its back to the wall.

6. I asked whether the new operational task forces would help. He said they might do something but that they did not affect the main issue, which was the attitude of Solidarity. I said that I was concerned by what he had said and would of course report it to you. Did he think that there was a possibility of a State of Emergency being declared? He said that this would depend on the sense of realism of Solidarity. I said that I thought Mr Walesa had shown a positive attitude to the announcement of General Jaruzelski's appointment. He said he agreed that it had been fairly positive but it had been followed by Solidarity's declaration which had been negative.

7. We talked a little about the Solidarity Congress and I said to him that I hoped he had noted that when Mr Len Murray, the General Secretary of the TUC, had been in Gdansk, he had stated that the TUC had always been ready to talk to whatever Government was in power. Mr Czyrek said that this was the sort of

statement which was helpful and he inferred that he had no complaint about the British attitude.

8. Mr Czyrek had seen the French Chargé d'Affaires immediately before me and the Swedish Ambassador was waiting to see him after me. I assume that he was saying much the same thing to them.

9. Mr Czyrek's tone was friendly but sombre. By his manner and words he clearly intended to impress on me the gravity of the situation and possibly to give advance warning that stronger action against Solidarity would not be excluded. His last remark was that the next few days would be decisive for the history of the country.

No. 95

Mr James (Warsaw) to Lord Carrington, 28 October 1981
Restricted (FCO 28/4485, ENP 014/1)

Poland: Autumn 81

Summary . . .[1]

My Lord,

1. Roman Polanski, the distinguished Polish-American film director who is currently playing the title role in Peter Shaffer's 'Amadeus' in Warsaw, said to me recently that even in Stalin's time life in Poland was not as dreary as it is now. The object of this despatch is essentially to examine whether there is any truth in this observation. Polanski is an intelligent if eccentric man who understands Poland well and has visited Warsaw regularly for many years. I take his observation seriously. What follows is therefore an attempt to give a few snapshots of life in Poland today.

The failure of an economy

2. A visitor from the West to Poland is struck first by the evidence of economic decay. The government claims that every 1,000 złoties in people's pockets is covered by only about 700 złoty-worth of goods. This has created shortages of almost all foodstuffs (except fruit and vegetables in their very short season) and many essentials of daily life. Meat has long been a problem, and was the first item to be rationed last summer. The average monthly ration (3½ kg: but the system is, needless to say, a highly complicated one by which some get more and some less) seems reasonable if not exactly generous by Western standards. But the Poles are great meat eaters. Like the dinosaur, they have found it impossible to adapt in order to survive. The Pole desires roast beef and pork of the highest quality and looks down on poultry (even duck and goose), fish (save at Christmas) and sausages. A second problem is that the government has found it impossible to cover the meat ration cards. In some areas, the shortfall has been as high as 48% (the average fortunately is not so high). So meat queues have become squalid affairs, their members squabbling and the elementary courtesies neglected. Sadly it is not only meat that is rationed or in short supply. Huge supermarkets have great spaces on their shelves and carry only a limited range of items. Cigarettes, sugar, bread, washing powders, and soaps are all scarce. So is alcohol: so there are now marginally fewer drunks littering the streets. Luxury goods are difficult to obtain.

[1] Not printed.

A bar of soap has to last the average Pole a month, so a ride on a Polish tram (or even a visit to the waiting room of our visa office) can be a daunting experience. Petrol too is in short supply which has caused lengthening queues at garages. In some areas (mainly the south) it is virtually impossible to obtain petrol due to the poor distribution system. A member of my staff who visited Wrocław, a city in the south west, saw one queue of 370 taxis and another of 480 private cars. Strangely, this does not seem to have dented the Poles' addiction to the use of the car. On the contrary, the average Pole these days has to spend more time driving around the country searching for food which is sometimes on sale at local markets and private farms. Another way in which the Poles have tried to overcome the food shortage is by greater use of their allotments to grow vegetables in place of flowers.

3. The decline in the supply of consumer goods has been matched by a fall in the quality of public services. Public transport has been worst hit. At any time, around a quarter of the buses and trams are off the road. Broken down buses are a common sight in Warsaw. Water, electricity and gas supplies are becoming increasingly erratic. The roads, which have never been in good condition, take longer to repair and roadworks, once started, upset the traffic system for long periods. In places, the street lighting is virtually non-existent. All this combines to give Warsaw at night something of the appearance of a wartime city. The fly-blown shop windows never change their displays, the nightlife stops early and the streets after around ten are deserted save for a (dwindling) population of drunks.

Social Problems

4. Poland's underlying social problems have existed much longer than her immediate political or economic ones. Most Poles live in extremely bad housing conditions. The waiting list for a residence (usually a two room flat) of one's own is about 13 years and getting longer. It is not uncommon for 6 adults to be sharing a tiny flat whilst the younger couples wait for a place of their own. The flats themselves are unattractive, in large blocks with inadequate facilities. Centralised heating often breaks down which turns the blocks into ice boxes during the winter. Public amenities are also inadequate. Town planning is not well coordinated and it is common for a new estate to be in existence for up to 5 years before such things as shops are built. So travelling time must be added to the queuing time when considering the problems of the Polish housewife. Seas of mud and piles of builders' debris remain for years. For those Poles who can afford to go to restaurants, the menus are very limited and the food is often not very good. Many restaurants have closed. There are very few public eating places outside the centres of the large towns.

5. Life in Polish villages is in some ways harsher than in the towns. But whilst the towns saw considerable improvements during the 70s the countryside on the whole did not. So the recent decline in living standards has probably changed the countryside less. The main features of Polish country life are horses and carts, a predominantly peasant agriculture and an absence of young people, particularly young men. Throughout the countryside, and up to the fringes of the towns, it is normal for the houses to have no running water. The roads in the villages themselves are filthy. Country villagers are probably not hungry. There are plenty of chickens, geese and ducks running around in every Polish village and farms are able to hoard food for themselves and their close families. The countryside is attractive, particularly in spring and autumn. It has a sense of space, an almost 19th Century atmosphere of tranquility and quiet. One can walk for miles by great rivers, without seeing a soul and without any human or mechanical sound. The

lack of pesticides may have had a bad effect on Polish agriculture, but it has meant that butterflies still abound.

6. Hospitals have not improved since before the war. Whilst some Polish doctors are among the best in the world, nursing standards are quite appalling. Basic hygiene is ignored and the food given to patients is inadequate. Nursing has to be done by visiting relatives who in some cases may have to bribe their way in to see the patients. Everyday drugs are in short supply. The handicapped are not well cared for in Poland, and the remnants of the laws safeguarding a socialist society makes it difficult for private charities to assist them. The old and mentally ill seem to be no better off. Those who are old and ill obviously suffer more from the frustrations of queuing.

Cultural Life

7. In Warsaw and some other major cities there is a thriving cultural life. A good example is the 'Warsaw autumn': a festival of contemporary music which is equalled nowhere else in the world. Throughout the festival, programmes of purely contemporary music play to packed houses. Poland rejoices in two world class contemporary composers, Penderecki and Lutosławski.[2] Warsaw also has a first-rate symphony orchestra which still attracts a fair number of international guest artists. However, it is rumoured that plans for the future are being affected by the shortage of hard currency. The opera is below international standards but it is something for a keen opera goer to be able to buy the best seat in the house for less than a pound and see magnificent sets, good stage management and vast choruses. It is reminiscent of Covent Garden before the war when Sir Thomas Beecham had to make do with British singers only. There are about 30 theatres in Warsaw—the same number as in London. But London has more than three times the population and a very large number of tourists. And the repertory is of a much higher standard than in London. The productions are well put together and acted with considerable vitality. Warsaw also has good art galleries. Polish film making is world famous and there has always been a cultural tolerance for western films.

8. In the large provincial cities such as Krakow, Łodz, Wroclaw and Poznan there are strong cultural traditions though on a smaller scale than in Warsaw. For example there is the world famous Tomaszewski mime theatre in Wrocław. Outside these larger centres there is little or no cultural life.

9. More generally, the nation's cultural life is being hampered by shortages of hard currency to buy foreign books and of paper. There is also, perhaps more seriously, a cultural brain drain born of the frustrations of life here. Many academics are actively looking for appointments abroad. Even if they disclaim any intention of permanent emigration, Poland cannot afford to lose them.

A life in the day of a Pole

10. It is perhaps worth re-constructing the daily life of an 'average' Pole. It is impossible to generalise of course, so I am taking the example of a young married woman with a child who works in a factory. She will get up very early by British standards. The factory's shift starts at about 6 a.m. and lasts until 2 p.m. Our Pole thus rises at 5 a.m. and has a first breakfast of coffee and bread. She travels to work by tram or bus from the flat she shares with her parents and husband after depositing her child in a crêche. Work is not desperately hard. To begin with, the shortage of raw materials means that there is often little or no work to do. Then,

[2] Krzysztof Eugeniusz Penderecki (1933-), composer and conductor. Witold Roman Lutosławski (1913-94).

the local branch of Solidarity will take up much of the working day in the preparation or conduct of an industrial dispute either local or national. Further, if news reaches the work-force that a consignment of some desirable commodity (such as meat or cigarettes) has come in to the local shop, the entire crew will down tools for an hour or so to go to queue. Around 11 am our lady worker will eat her second breakfast which in principle consists of bread, cold meats, Polish sausages etc. At 2 p.m. the factory shift will be over. In theory, the average Pole would now eat *obiad* which corresponds roughly to lunch. It is the main meal of the day but can be eaten any time between 2 and 5 in the afternoon. In practice however, our lady worker will now collect her child from the crêche and begin her main work of the day—queuing. Shops in Poland open from 11 in the morning until 7 in the evening so that people who work can use them. This has been useful for the Poles in the recent crisis since shopping takes 4 or 5 hours of each day. The strain on shop assistants is considerable. Our Pole will arrive home around about 7 in the evening completely exhausted and probably demoralised. She and her husband and her parents will have *kolacja*, or dinner. They will watch television. Programmes are dull, but the standard is improving. The *dziennik* (or Evening News) tells the Poles more and more about what is really going on in their country, even though it is slanted to the government's point of view. There are some western serials of the 'Charlie's Angels' variety, but they are likely to get fewer and further between for the usual reasons of hard currency shortage (I do so wish we could get some good British television on the Polish screen). The television ends its programmes early and the couple then go to bed on a sofa in either the dining or sitting room of the two-room flat.

11. The average Polish weekend will probably be spent driving into the country to look for food. Solidarity has won the Poles more leisure time in the shape of increased free Saturdays. Some western leisure pastimes are available to the Poles. Drink is in shorter supply than it was. Football of a high standard can be watched in the big towns.

General Atmosphere

12. It is not surprising that there is a degree of social disintegration in Poland at the moment coupled with pessimism about the future. Given the economic circumstances, no-one can blame the Poles for this. But against that, the Poles are unusually sustained by their nationalism and their religion. The Poles are quite simply enormously proud of the fact that they are Poles. A senior Polish official recently told my colleague from Prague that despite all the difficulties the Poles had to face at the moment he would 100,000 times rather be a Pole than a Czech. The Poles regard themselves as different both from the other Slavic nations and from the Germans, whom they cordially hate. Polish nationalism is linked to the Catholic Church. The Church is the undying symbol of Poland, past and future. The churches are full. Any visitor to Poland notices this immediately he goes for a walk on a Sunday morning. What perhaps is not so immediately obvious to him is that the church he saw full for mass at 11 was also jammed to the doors for hourly masses from 6 onwards. An agnostic Irish novelist told me recently how impressed she had been by the sight of so many young men at prayer in the churches, even on weekdays. She said that this would not be seen in Ireland.

13. Underlying everything there is then a certain spirituality which makes the Poles prepared to put up with great privations. Nor is everything here all gloom and doom. The Poles have a sense of humour, often macabre and black. The large number of good Polish jokes about meat queues and Russian intervention testify to

an ability to laugh at themselves. Political humour is also good. It ranges from the sophisticated to the utterly revolting. The Poles also have style and are well, if gaudily, dressed. The women have maintained a sense of chic which has been helped by their interest in fashion and by their traditional links with France and Italy. The people in general have courtly manners which are now under strain. They have no great addiction to work but they are addicted to discussion (no Pole seems able to stand up without speaking for at least thirty minutes) and to all forms of intellectual activity. I am not sure whether their inability to make things work in practice is due to some patrician distaste for practical accomplishment; but they do love ingenious theories. No Pole will make things difficult when with a little skill and effort he can make them impossible. One final and most important point about the Polish character is worth mentioning here. Poland looks to the West. Its people are western orientated. They travel to West Germany, France, Britain, America and elsewhere, they read western books and magazines and watch western films.

Conclusion

14. I am not in a personal position to assess Polanski's comparison of Poland today with Poland at the time of Stalin. As a general judgment, I should say that life has deteriorated dramatically from a material point of view in the last year, but still remains, in Warsaw at least, stimulating intellectually. What is sad now is that it is becoming increasingly difficult for people to amuse themselves. The restaurants are closed or have little food, the cinemas are getting fewer foreign films; life consists of queuing and hanging around after a day's work. We cannot judge the strains that the present hardships inflict on Polish families, on personal relationships and on marriage, but they must be considerable. However, the Poles seem to be survivors, and given a chance their optimism wells up. They will be tested this winter as at no time since the immediate post-war years.

15. I am sending copies of this despatch to Her Majesty's Representatives at Belgrade, Bonn, Bucharest, Budapest, East Berlin, Helsinki, Moscow, Paris, Prague, Sofia, Stockholm, Washington, NATO, the European Community and the United Nations, and to the Secretary of State for Defence.

I am, etc,
C. K. JAMES

No. 96

Letter from Mr Broomfield to Mr James (Warsaw), 28 October 1981

Confidential (FCO 28/4485, ENP 014/1)

Dear Kenneth,

General Jaruzelski

1. Thank you for your interesting letter of 22 October on Jaruzelski.[1] He is very much at the eye of the storm at the moment. The strengths and weaknesses in his character could prove to be a decisive element in the way in which the situation develops.

2. I am aware that I have not written for some time. I hope Ramsay Melhuish will have reassured you, if that was necessary, that relative silence from this end betokens neither lack of interest or activity. We are now entering, at the Whitehall end at least, a very active phase of the battle over rescheduling and new credits for

[1] No. 93.

1982. Peter Mountfield will no doubt have given you his view which, I regret to say, is becoming more and more pessimistic, about the wisdom of further assistance above and beyond what we would in any case do to protect our economic interests. I will try and let you know when a view from Warsaw on both the economic situation as well as the effects of giving/not giving new credits will be helpful in terms of Ministerial decisions. I am aware that medium term forecasting in Poland at the moment usually means not much farther ahead than next week. But we will have to do the best we can on the day however hedged about with qualifications our advice to Ministers may be.

3. I also enclose a short note summarising points made at a meeting chaired by Julian Bullard on 27 October.[2] Nothing said was particularly new. I enclose it merely as a check list of points which are under review here. We have all had a go at producing imaginative 'solutions' to the Polish problem, in particular to the problem of Western assistance. I am afraid to say that even such long shots as tapping the Saudis have been explored without much success. At the political level the difficulty of getting across an appeal for moderation and negotiation to all the parties also runs into the problems which you know better than I. It would seem that both Walesa and Jaruzelski are prepared to take the path of compromise and negotiation. But both have had their room for manoeuvre considerably curtailed by their respective programmes/resolutions. The sort of spokesmen like Len Murray[3] who can talk directly to Solidarity without risking the charge of official external intervention in Poland's affairs are unfortunately few and far between. As far as influence with ordinary people is concerned which includes rank and Solidarity members, I suppose the Church wields the greatest influence. Your contacts with Glemp[4] are thus of considerable influence.

Yours,
NIGEL

[2] Not printed.
[3] See No. 91, note 3 and Nos. 94, 103, 105 and 108.
[4] See Nos. 76, 109 and 155.

No. 97

Minute from Mr Broomfield to Mr Fergusson, 30 October 1981
Confidential (FCO 28/4413, ENA 020/1)

Albania

1. Lord Trefgarne has asked for a note on where we stand in our efforts to solve the financial problems which have so far prevented a resumption of relations with Albania.

2. Britain has had no diplomatic relations with Albania since before the war although we recognise the People's Republic of Albania. There are two main problems.

3. The Albanians have not so far been prepared to discuss the resumption of relations before the delivery to them 'with interest' of the gold provisionally allocated to them by the Tripartite Commission for the Restitution of Monetary Gold in partial compensation for the much larger sum looted from the National Bank of Albania by the Germans during the war. The gold, which at 28 January 1981, was worth $26.5 million, is held by the Bank of England on behalf of the

Commission. There are two other members of the Commission (the United States and France), two claims against Albania (British and American) and on the gold itself (Italy).[1]

4. Until 1980 a second obstacle was that the Albanians had not paid the compensation of £0.8 million awarded to Britain in 1949 by the International Court of Justice in respect of the Corfu Channel incident in 1946 when two Royal Navy ships were mined and 44 British seamen died.[2] But last year Ministers decided that we should no longer regard the Corfu issue as an obstacle and that an attempt should be made to restore relations. Accordingly, HM Ambassador at Belgrade formally made clear to the Albanian Ambassador that for our part we were now ready to resume relations without preconditions and without waiting for a resolution of the financial problems: but we would at the same time continue to work towards a settlement of the latter. The Albanians turned down this offer. We are therefore continuing to pursue a settlement of the financial questions with the other countries concerned.

5. In practice this has meant that we put to the Americans two suggestions. These were:

(*a*) that the Tripartite Commission should deliver all the gold to Albania in exchange for an undertaking to comply with the Corfu Channel judgement;

(*b*) alternatively, that we should give new thought to a solution first discussed in 1966 that the gold should be split four ways between the UK, US, Italy and Albania. We pointed out that the increased value of the gold might make it possible to satisfy the British, American and Italian claims and yet leave enough to return to the Albanians the original value of their allocation of the gold plus a reasonable rate of interest.

5 [*sic*]. The Americans rejected both these proposals. They turned down (*a*) on the grounds that their own 1974 Trade Act, which rules out the return of the Czechoslovak gold before American claims have been satisfied, would clearly apply similarly to the Albanian gold. They could not therefore consent to its release until provision is made for American claims. These claims are still unadjudicated and even when this process has been completed the chances of the Albanians agreeing to meet the American claims are very remote.

6. The Americans rejected our second proposal on the grounds that it would be illegal for the Tripartite Commission in effect to seize Albanian gold to pay claims which had not been established by an international tribunal (i.e. at least the Italian and probably their own) pointing out the dangerous parallel between this proposal and the Congressional proposals (which we and the French are resisting) to seize Czechoslovak gold.

7. The Americans did, however, suggest that they might be prepared to allow the Tripartite Commission to release the gold if the Albanians would place in escrow,[3] say $10 million, against a possible eventual settlement of American claims. We think it most unlikely that the Albanians would be ready to do this which could subsequently be held to imply that they recognised the justice of the American claim. The Department is therefore working on a derivative of this idea, namely that the Commission might deliver part of the gold to Albania while retaining, say $15 million, as it were in escrow. This would comprise the $10

[1] See FCO History Notes 11 and 12, *Nazi Gold: Information from the British Archives*, Parts I and II (FCO, 1996 and 1997, www.issuu.com/fcohistorians).

[2] This issue is covered in more detail in Chapter 5 of *DBPO: Western Security*.

[3] A financial instrument held by a third party on behalf of the other two parties in a transaction.

million which the Americans have mentioned and a sum (for illustrative purposes say $5 million) to cover our own claim of £843,947 plus an element of interest. We would not actually seize this sum, but would leave it in the custody of the Tripartite Commission against the day when a more generally satisfactory solution would be reached.

8. This idea has not yet been put to other departments in Whitehall; but it seems likely that most of the departments with an interest (principally the Treasury but also MOD and perhaps the Bank of England) will be unenthusiastic. And even if Whitehall and the Americans agree there would, however, be some chance that the French would veto this suggestion. At present their relations with Albania are improving. They might therefore be reluctant to prejudice those relations by giving their formal approval to a manoeuvre which would continue to deprive the Albanians of approximately $15 million worth of gold. We might however be able to persuade the French to take on the task of trying to convince the Albanians that half a loaf was better than no bread at all. We shall also have to face the question of the Italian claim: Research Department are at the moment looking into its legal standing.

9. I will be submitting separately on the related question of whether we should now release to the Public Records Office some of the pre-1957 Foreign Office papers which have been retained in the FCO under the Public Records Acts.[4]

N. H. R. A. BROOMFIELD

[4] Diplomatic relations with Albania were not restored until 1991. A settlement of the Corfu Channel Incident was reached in 1992 when Albania agreed to pay $2 million in compensation. The Commission finally returned the gold to Albania in 1996.

No. 98

Mr James (Warsaw) to Lord Carrington, 5 November 1981, 3.40 p.m.
Tel. No. 769[1] Immediate, Restricted (FCO 28/4485, ENP 014/1)

Meeting between Jaruzelski, Glemp and Walesa.

1. Jaruzelski, Glemp and Walesa met yesterday for 2 [hours]. Only very sparse details have been published in the Polish press indicating that the 3 men discussed the possibilities of creating a front of national understanding. It was also agreed that the meeting should serve as a preparation for further consultations, although it is not clear whether this would be at the same high level.

2. This was obviously a very important meeting. It shows that the Government has recognised some of the important political realities in Poland and it may represent the first step to some convergence of the principal forces in the country in the form of a loose coalition. However, each of the three parties is under certain constraints. Walesa went to Warsaw after facing severe criticism from some elements in Solidarity's National Commission who are meeting in Gdansk (my tel No. 761).[2] Whilst some of the Commission were reportedly prepared to give him a

[1] Repeated Immediate to FCO; Information Routine to Washington, Moscow and UKDEL NATO; Information Saving to East Berlin, Prague, Budapest, Paris, Bonn, MODUK, Sofia, Bucharest, Belgrade, Helsinki, Stockholm, UKMIS New York and UKREP Brussels.
[2] Not printed.

free hand in his negotiations with Jaruzelski, others wished to limit drastically his freedom of manoeuvre, presumably because they did not trust him. He will have to give an account of the talks to the National Commission today and this may give us a clue as to what went on at them. Certainly there are elements in Solidarity who would not wish to see any form of loose coalition with the Government and would resist what they saw as a further attempt to entrench the Party's leading role.

3. There must also be elements within the Government and Party who will wish at least to dilute the coalition in a manner which is unacceptable to Solidarity. They may, for example, work through the branch unions who will not wish to be left out of a coalition. Jaruzelski will have to try to steer a course which is acceptable to these elements. But it is important to recognise that any coalition is unlikely to have much significance unless it is effectively limited to the three parties who met yesterday with perhaps a small additional independent element.

4. The attitude of the Church will also be crucial. Glemp is unlikely to want members of the episcopate to sit formally on a new national front. But the Church may be able to contemplate the inclusion of prominent lay-Catholics in whatever institution is set up.

5. It must be distasteful to the Soviet Union to see the three main social and political forces in Poland sitting around the same table. But if Jaruzelski can persuade the Soviet leadership that the meeting has opened up the possibilities for improving the internal situation here, they may be prepared to live even with this degree of power-sharing for a time.

FCO please pass saving to all saving addressees.

No. 99

Memorandum by Lord Carrington for the Cabinet Defence and Oversea Policy Committee on Poland, 9 November 1981

OD(81)52 Confidential (CAB 148/198)

The Western Strategic Interest

1. The United Kingdom and the West in general have a long-term interest in the ending of the artificial alliance between Moscow and the states of Eastern Europe. The achievement of this aim would transform the political and strategic balance in Europe and have far-reaching effects outside it.

The Polish Renewal

2. The Polish Renewal represents the most serious challenge the Russians have yet had to face in their East European empire. Developments in Poland stem from widely based and deeply held dissatisfaction with the material conditions of life created by the political and economic system which has been imposed on Poland. The aspirations of the majority are for political accountability of the leadership to the people and a more flexible decentralized economic system. The first of these goals, and probably the second too, is incompatible with Soviet control as it has existed since 1945.

Public Opinion

3. Western governments must also take account of popular pressure to assist the Poles on moral and humanitarian grounds. Western public opinion expects their governments to show support for Polish efforts and aspirations.

Effects of the Renewal

4. The positive effects of the Polish Renewal have so far been:

(*a*) to weaken Soviet control over its largest and most important East European ally;

(*b*) to challenge the socialist system which has been shown to be economically unsuccessful and politically bankrupt.

5. If the Renewal is consolidated and successful, its effects could be:

(*a*) to weaken the political, economic and military cohesion of the Eastern European states and to provide an alternative model of 'reformed' Communism; and eventually

(*b*) to influence political developments in the Soviet Union itself.

6. If the Renewal collapses the result will be a major ideological and propaganda victory for the Russians, particularly if there has been a demonstrable lack of Western will to support it.

7. If the Renewal is crushed by a Soviet invasion, with or without preceding internal collapse in Poland, there will be economic consequences for the West:

(*a*) Polish commitment to repay outstanding debts in the long term will be in doubt;

(*b*) The Western allies will consider and may implement economic sanctions against the Soviet Union (contingency planning has been agreed); and

(*c*) The Western Europeans (those members of NATO) will come under heavy US pressure to increase defence spending.

The Ideal Solution to the Polish Crisis

8. The ideal solution to the Polish crisis for us and our allies:

(*a*) should avoid both Soviet intervention and a major clampdown by the Polish authorities;

(*b*) should preserve the gains extracted by Solidarity from the Polish regime over the past 15 months;

(*c*) should set the Polish economy on the road towards recovery and repayment of Poland's debts to the West;

(*d*) should allow for further development of Poland on lines which reflect the wishes of its people and may, in due course, have an effect elsewhere in Eastern Europe.

But the prospects for such a solution are placed at risk by the increasingly desperate state of the Polish economy (See Annex A).

Conclusion

9. The stakes are high. Economic arguments might suggest doing no more than is needed to recover the existing investment of public and private funds in Poland. But Poland offers a unique opportunity to influence the direction in which events in Europe evolve. If the Renewal degenerates into chaos leading to intervention, the effects on East/West relations will be profound and costly; probable economic sanctions and increased military expenditure. If the Renewal survives and ultimately succeeds in establishing a new, pluralistic model in the biggest Eastern European state in the Soviet glacis, the effects could be of historic significance. By helping Poland at this juncture we shall be doing what lies in our power to secure a political shift in Europe of lasting benefit to ourselves and to the West.

The British Contribution

10. We have been doing all we can politically, both bilaterally and multilaterally to help Poland. But it is essential to provide practical assistance as well.

11. I therefore invite my colleagues to agree that we should:

(i) reschedule official debts in 1982 and consider how the terms could be eased;

(ii) provide a minimum of £90 million new credits to Poland in 1982 under the four headings outlined in the Chairman's Note:

(a) *URSUS*[1]

We should honour our commitment undertaken in 1974 and renewed in 1980 to proceed with the URSUS project. ECGD should continue to guarantee loans under the existing line of credit (estimated draw down approximately £30 million in 1982).

(*b*) *Food Aid*

We should allocate £20 million extra of public expenditure in 1982 for loans to finance food purchase.

(*c*) *Industrial Credit*

We should provide a minimum of £40 million extra of public expenditure as loans to finance purchase of industrial products,

(*d*) The necessary funds cannot be found from existing FCO programmes, and must therefore be treated as a net addition to the overall budgetary provision for 1982/3 and provided from the Central Contingency Reserve.[2]

CARRINGTON

ANNEX A

The Polish Economy

1. The paper prepared by officials to provide an agreed consensus on the prospects for the Polish economy (and attached to OD(81)51), makes gloomy reading. The Poles believe that in 1982 they will need external loans totalling $4.3 billion in addition to a debt rescheduling requirement on the same scale as this year's.

The Domestic Consequences

2. The domestic consequences of the economic situation are worsening shortages of essential foodstuffs, rationing, price rises, unemployment and, with the onset of cold weather, serious power shortages. These factors have constantly aggravated the political situation in Poland, sharpened political attitudes and reduced the chances of obtaining the vitally needed agreement between Government and Solidarity on measures to bring the economy under control. A further rapid deterioration in the economy could make the political dialogue inside Poland untenable and civil unrest could ensue.

3. There is a persistent risk of confrontation between the authorities and the population which could well lead to the re-emergence of a hardline Polish regime or to the breakdown of law and order and Soviet intervention. In either case the gains of the Renewal would be lost.

Further Assistance

4. The solution to Poland's economic problems must lie primarily with the Poles themselves. In any event, they face a long period of austerity and painful adjustment to the structure of their economy. Their financial position will remain very precarious. Western assistance cannot be on a scale which protects the Poles

[1] The Ursus tractor factory took large loans from the West in the 1970s in order to modernise but inefficient investment left the company with unfinished projects and heavily indebted.

[2] At OD (81) 17th meeting, the Committee agreed to reschedule Polish official debt for 1982 and underwrite loans required for the URSUS project up to a total of £30 million, but not provide other medium or long term industrial credit or food aid. The Foreign Secretary was to report back if circumstances changed (CAB 148/197).

from these painful changes, nor should it be. We and other Western allies have made this clear to them. Nevertheless, it is the West's fundamental interest to help the Poles find time to achieve this adjustment and to stave off the economic collapse which could be fatal to the Renewal. We also need to demonstrate both to our own public opinion and to the Poles themselves that we are ready to help and are not withdrawing our support at the time of their greatest difficulty.

Other Measures

5. Poland should not depend on its Western creditors alone for outside help. We shall continue to make it clear to the Russians that we expect them to go on helping the Poles, particularly with supplies of energy and raw materials. The Poles have also indicated that they intend to join the IMF. Although unlikely to provide significant early relief it could establish a framework for further assistance and international monitoring of the economy. Our current information on assistance likely to be provided by our major allies is in Annex B.

ANNEX B

Assistance to Poland by Western Allies

1. At present we believe that our allies' position on new credits is as follows:

(*a*) *France*

The French have said that if by mid-December no final decision on new credit has been taken by all Western creditors, France will provide a total of $200 million for cereal purchases to include a new credit of Francs 300 million for industrial purposes.

(*b*) *US*

The Poles have asked the Americans for credit to purchase $740 million worth of agricultural commodities. They would prefer another zloty sale or they have asked for a more generous repayment period (5-7 years after a grace period of 2-3 years).

(*c*) *FRG*

The Germans have said no figure for new credits to Poland in 1982 can be given until the budget as a whole is approved. The provisional allocation in the budget is $200 million.

(*d*) *Italy*

The Italians agreed in October to a bilateral grant of food aid worth $25 million separate from the EC programme. The Italians have also agreed to an additional credit ($52 million) to enable the Poles to take up $345 million of existing credit which the Poles have not been able to do because of 15% down payment requirement. The Italian Government has also agreed that Italy's share of a BIS loan should be $20-25 million, if others agree to participate in this loan.

No. 100

Letter from Mr Clark (Belgrade) to Mr Montgomery, 10 November 1981
Confidential (FCO 28/4642, ENU 014/1)

Dear Alan,

The Domestic Political Scene

1. Reading through our recent reporting, one might have the impression that the problems in the economy dominate to the exclusion of all else. It is true that, for good reasons, the economy occupies the foreground, but all around it a wider political debate goes on with an intensity and a degree of frankness rare in socialist countries and at times even surprising for the Yugoslavs themselves. There are three discernible catalysts for this debate: Kosovo, the economy itself, and the 12th Congress next June: they are all interconnected.

Kosovo

2. Among the many catchwords circulating at the moment is 'responsibility'. It cropped up first in the aftermath of the events in Kosovo. Who was responsible for what happened? And later, when those held immediately responsible were dismissed from their functions, the press, whose burgeoning role in the political debate is of outstanding importance, began asking questions about responsibility for allowing Kosovo's leaders to act as they did. The whole question of Kosovo's relationship to Serbia has been under review and was recently the subject of a round-table discussion by political scientists on the political system in Serbia (from which, significantly representatives from Vojvodina and Kosovo appear to have deliberately absented themselves). From this discussion, which the press reported at length, one idea emerged that perhaps the solution was for Serbia to become a federation of Serbia and the two Autonomous Provinces. Ingenious and certainly food for thought. Kosovo is to be discussed again by the Central Committee on 17 November when a new platform for its further development is promised.

The economy

3. The economic mess has also given rise to questions in the press about responsibility for it. Should Ministers be held responsible? Should Ministers resign? These are daring questions, indeed, which have so far been met with bland answers about responsibility being collective and resignations not being unknown (but rarely practised) in this society. This is not to say action is not being taken at all, for the press frequently reports whole bodies at various other levels resigning, or being compelled to resign, for incompetence or misdemeanours. And we are promised a debate in the Federal Assembly about ministerial responsibility for public pronouncements, the first of its kind in the 7½ years of the delegate Assembly. This arose after a dissatisfied Slovene delegate failed to obtain an answer to a question posed three months earlier about differing public statements made two weeks apart in July by Finance Secretary Kostić ('a collapse in our current account, a metastasis which threatens liquidity in payments abroad, a bad assessment given by the IMF') and National Bank Governor Bogoev ('our credit/monetary policy is in the best order, liquidity in payments abroad is also in order and the IMF assessed our stabilisation efforts favourably'). According to extracts quoted in the press, the official answer was that the two statements were equal and that they described the situation when they were made and not the present trend. After some sharp exchanges, including with Kostić himself, a debate

on the whole question of responsibility for official statements appeared to have been proposed as a way out of an awkward situation.

4. Kostić has also been under attack in the Slovene press for making twice unwise statements about re-introducing the proposed so-called travel tax (ND. 1,500 per person on each journey abroad), which led to people streaming over the border to buy up goods in short supply before the tax was introduced (if it ever should be, as the Slovenes are resolutely against it because of the effects it would have on their cross-border trade). In a TV interview, Dolanc[1] agreed that Kostić was responsible for making the statements, but also put responsibility on the people who had panicked and had forgotten the interests of the nation. The forthcoming debate could be interesting.

5. This kind of public fireworks is not confined to Belgrade. In a discussion on the economy in the Croatian Central Committee last week, one member indirectly accused another (in fact Stipe Suvar, the so-called *enfant terrible* of education and culture in the Croatian Government),[2] of leading a Jacobin revolution campaign against the 'leftist forces' in the Party. Suvar, who is never short of a word, riposted vigorously, if somewhat obliquely, that the 'new left' in question was in fact an expression of a particular extreme right and did not follow the line of the Party. This 'dialogue' is forecast to be resumed at the next session of the CC LCC.[3]

12th Congress

6. The debate in the Party about the preparations for the 12th Congress has been progressing in a more dignified but nonetheless intensive manner. As forecast earlier, democratic centralism is proving a lively topic. Every few days someone manages to find a forum in which to define what democratic centralism means for him. The Marxist Centre in Belgrade has even published a 250-page book on the subject, quoting every authority on the subject in the LCY[4] since the 10th Congress. Everyone of any standing seems to agree that the principle is immutable but differences arise over how it is observed in practice. What most people appear to be saying (and thereby begging the question) is that democratic centralism needs to be applied more democratically, i.e. the Party membership needs to be more involved in the discussion before the policy is reached, and more effectively, i.e. once a decision is agreed it has to be observed consistently. At the same time, the Party is determined not to let any wild ideas about admitting the principles of self-management to be introduced in the Party. As *Komunist*[5] said recently, there is a proposal under discussion that members of the CC LCY should be responsible to those who elected them and should be obliged to consult them before taking decisions. This was assessed as 'introducing the principle of delegate decision-making which is not in harmony with the principle of democratic centralism, from which the LCY does not intend to turn'.

7. The CC's Statutory Committee has also been beavering away on the consequential amendments to the Party's Statutes following Tito's death. Various proposals are also under public discussion to introduce secret voting at elections at all levels (not just those listed at present in the Statutes), to put up alternative candidates at elections at all levels, to democratise the election of members of the

[1] Stane Dolanc, a member of the Federal Council for Protection of the Constitutional Order.
[2] Croatian minister for culture and education, 1974-82.
[3] Central Committee of the League of Communists of Croatia.
[4] League of Communists of Yugoslavia.
[5] Newspaper of the League of Communists of Yugoslavia.

CC LCY by secret vote instead of acclaim at the Congress, and whether to elect a President and Secretary of the LCY or, as at present, of the Presidium. The discussion on secret voting and alternative candidates is evidently necessary because as one commentator in *Politika* put it wryly, already the 'town is full of stories about who is going to get what job at the Spring re-shuffle'.

Comment

8. As I have indicated, the striking feature of this political ferment is that so much of it is in public. In a way, it reminds me of the liberal wind which was blowing through the press in 1969-71. Then, as now, even the most hardened critics were talking enthusiastically of the role of the press in opening up taboo subjects. Kosovo has clearly been the key to opening up the locked doors to sources of information. The public demand to be fully and timely informed about the events in Kosovo has since been extended to other areas and the press is full of revelations on political and economic abuses. The press is not allowed to publish everything—as indeed it sometimes tells its readers. But it is clear that the press is being admitted to important political fora and, although still subject to certain guidance and a measure of self-censorship, is becoming increasingly frank in its criticisms.

9. None of this freedom would have developed if it had not had the political backing of some leading figures in the Party. When Grličkov[6] says, as he did in an interview with *Politika* last month, that no one has a monopoly of the truth and that political forces should speak openly about their problems, it is not surprising that people are doing just that. The question is how far people will be allowed to go. In the early '70s, first in Croatia and later in Serbia, a line was drawn and those who were beyond it suffered the consequences. Apart from the basic tenets of Yugoslav policy the line to-day appears not yet to have been drawn. For example, some people are even daring to lay the blame for the economic difficulties on 'the Kardeljisation[7] of the system' and, as NIN[8] pointed out this week, 'Kardeljisation' means 'Titoisation'. So, where will the limit of criticism lie? Probably we shall not know definitely before the Republican Party Congresses in May and the 12th Congress itself. It is possible that the leadership will show itself a good deal more restrictive then than the present liberal trend would suggest. But, unlike ten years ago, this time there is no Tito to put the genie back into the bottle.

Yours ever,
JOSEPH

[6] See No. 59, paragraph 9.

[7] Edvard Kardelj (1910-79) was second only to Tito as the most prominent political figure in Socialist Yugoslavia. He was the chief theoretician of Yugoslav Marxism and helped create the Yugoslav system of workers' self-management.

[8] '*Nedeljne informativne novine*—Weekly Informational Newspaper'. One of the oldest Serbian political newspapers.

No. 101

Record of talks between Mr J. Bullard and Dr Berecz[1] at the FCO, 16 November 1981, 11.30 a.m.

Confidential (FCO 28/4468, ENH 026/1)

Present:	
Mr Bullard	Dr Berecz
Mr Barrass, Planning Staff	Dr Banyasz, Hungarian Ambassador
Miss Brown, EESD	Mr Demus, Counsellor, Hungarian Embassy
	Dr Butykay, Interpreter

Introductory

1. Mr Bullard said he was glad Dr Berecz had been able to take up the invitation which he had extended during his visit to Budapest in December 1980.[2] He welcomed the opportunity to continue their discussions and invited Dr Berecz to decide what they should now discuss.

2. *Dr Berecz* thanked Mr Bullard. The invitation to visit the UK had been accepted by him on behalf of the Central Committee of the HSWP. He had had a briefing meeting with Mr Kadar on the eve of his visit to London in preparation for his talks. He thought these should range over any subject that occurred, but recognised that Europe continued to be of prime interest to both Britain and Hungary. He would be happy to answer any questions on developments in Hungary.

East/West Economic Relations

3. *Mr Bullard* said that Lord Trefgarne had asked him to concentrate on the economic aspects of East/West relations. Discussion at a series of meetings of British Heads of Mission the previous week had identified several negative factors on the East/West economic scene. He had drawn the personal conclusion that the 1980s would be a decade in which reality would be sharply distinguished from illusions. This had occurred in the political arena at the end of the '70s and was now happening in the economic sphere. We had identified events in Poland as a cause of economic instability and had noticed a ring of subsidiary effects around Poland. Hungary however seemed better placed than most countries to withstand these effects. How did Dr Berecz see these developments and what were the prospects?

4. *Dr Berecz* said that there would have been economic difficulty in Eastern Europe even without an international recession. The three decades since the War had witnessed a period of intensive economic and especially industrial development in Eastern Europe, with an average annual growth rate of 8-9%. It was inevitable that sooner or later a stage would have been reached when these resources would have been exhausted and a switch to different policies required. Such a switch was inevitably accompanied by a degree of trauma. The question was at what stage this necessity was recognised and what conclusions were drawn. Some socialist countries had striven to achieve autarky and by doing so had not

[1] Head of the International Department of the Hungarian Socialist Workers' Party.

[2] In addition he had meetings with the Foreign Secretary and Lord Trefgarne, discussions at Chatham House and the International Institute for Strategic Studies, as well as talks with leading members of the Labour Party.

made the best use of their economic systems, in particular seriously weakening their agricultural sectors.

5. Hungary had reached this stage of recognition in the mid '60s and had attempted to solve it by a reform of economic management. Despite some 'stops and starts' this system had been consistently pursued. The second major stage in Hungary's economic development had occurred in 1974 when it was recognised that Hungary's industrial and agricultural production was out of tune with international realities. The authorities had accordingly taken steps to readjust Hungary's capabilities to the international market. Sometimes decisions taken by Hungarians came as a shock to outsiders but they were in fact all part of the same logical process.

6. The first stage of this recognition process had occurred in most East European countries, although the latter had generally failed to take as consistent measures to deal with the problems as the Hungarian authorities. The Hungarians felt sympathy for the Polish people. The latter had given clear warnings in 1970 and 1976 of the strains on their system but their leaders had apparently been unable to draw the right conclusions. Hungary now felt sympathy for Romania. Despite many warnings, the leadership was going ahead with a heavy investment programme although they had exhausted their resources for intensive development. The Hungarians were taking what defensive measures they could to mitigate the burdens being imposed on the CMEA. They believed it was vital for those countries to join forces to ensure that there were e.g. sufficient supplies of energy. This was logical. Within the bloc there were plentiful supplies of energy and other vital raw materials.

Economic Effects of Poland

7. *Dr Berecz* said that the Polish economic situation had had a serious effect. But for the moment it was not a major economic problem for CMEA countries with the exception of the Soviet Union. The Polish economic crisis had not affected Hungary particularly, although it was a warning that Hungary should continue with its present economic policies. As a general comment, he believed that the necessity of a change in economic policy should be recognised in all socialist countries. The more courageous the recognition the better the prospects for further successful development. All Hungary could do was recommend a course of action; it could do no more.

8. *Mr Bullard* said he had drawn up a list of five 'illusions' that had been held in the 1970s about the development of East/West trade:

(i) the belief that economic growth in Western and Eastern Europe would always continue;

(ii) that Western banks would always be willing to lend money to finance East/West trade;

(iii) that Western governments/tax payers would always be willing to subsidise credit for East/West trade;

(iv) that Governments in Eastern Europe could be trusted to judge what was a safe level of borrowing;

(v) that if ever they miscalculated, the Soviet Union would put up an umbrella to minimise the consequences.

9. Mr Bullard said that all of these illusions had now been exploded. He would propose to replace them with a list of 'realities'. These were:

(i) that country would survive best that could guarantee its food supplies;

(ii) that provided its own energy and/or was able to pay for this;

(iii) that kept its foreign debt under control;
(iv) that had the necessary instruments to manipulate the economy;
(v) whose political and economic systems commanded the allegiance of its people.

Mr Bullard said he would pay Hungary the compliment of passing all five of these tests.

Poland

10. If however, the same question was asked about Poland, the answer supplied itself. Nevertheless he believed that in Poland one could see some signs of reality breaking in. For example, the introduction of the military into the Government and Party administration. This seemed an acknowledgement that a military uniform still commanded a certain degree of respect and that the military chain of command at least could be relied upon to carry out orders. The recent meeting between Solidarity, the Party and the Church had formalised the *de facto* cooperation that exists between the three main centres of power. This was a hopeful sign. But an unfortunate disparity remained between the pace at which the political scene was evolving and that of economic developments which were heading fast downhill. Dr Berecz and he had agreed a year ago on British and Hungarian objectives in relation to Poland: that Poland should solve its own problems and that these should not be internationalised. But who should pay for the time for the political process to work itself out?

11. *Dr Berecz* said that so far both East and West had had to carry the burden. He estimated this cost at $9 billion, shared roughly on a 50-50 basis. He agreed there were certain hopeful signs. The time of illusion was over. But the Polish problem was difficult to handle, being partly a spontaneous one and also of an historical nature. Of the three pillars of society mentioned he observed that not one commanded the interests and loyalty of all the Polish people. This was a fundamental weakness. Cardinal Wyzsynski had given his best sermon in August 1980 when he had counselled the Polish people to return to work. But the people had not obeyed. The Church was able to tell people to pray but its exhortations to work were in vain. Walesa last week had attempted to stop local strikes but people had refused to listen. There was a lack of organisation within Polish society which made economic and political consolidation extremely difficult. The best possible outcome would be if the three pillars could agree on the need for quiet and for work. On the basis of this they could then decide what further steps would be necessary.

12. Dr Berecz said he was aware of the value of the Polish coal supply. The Polish people would be cold this winter. There was no reason why they should be cold but the fact was that they had not stockpiled sufficient supplies. He was afraid that if the Poles could not reach a settlement reasonably soon the nation would drift to the point of political suicide. He agreed that the Poles should settle their own problems and that there should be no international involvement, except economic. But he could not predict what would happen if there were spontaneous disturbances in Poland. This was not a question of confrontation between the Party and Solidarity but rather of other centres developing within the country, aided and abetted by extremist elements.

13. *Mr Bullard* said that Lord Carrington would no doubt confirm to him that it was the policy of the British Government that the Poles should solve their problems by themselves. The British Government had had a lot of contact with Polish representatives, particularly with Mr Czyrek who was a factor of continuity

in the Polish scene. He agreed that the heart of the matter was that the Polish people should return to work. How could this result be achieved? Only by a combination of exhortation, persuasion and incentive. Given the nature of Polish society, the incentives would need to be political as well as economic. The Polish people would work more fervently for a different kind of political/economic system than they possessed. This could not be a capitalist system; this was excluded by Poland's geographical position and history. Nor would the existing military alliances be challenged. But there could nevertheless be large scale changes within the framework of a socialist system. Would the Warsaw Pact or the CMEA be capable of absorbing a member of this character?

14. *Dr Berecz* said he did not know exactly what would emerge in Poland, but he was sure that the situation could not be as it had been before 1 June 1980. He could give two examples of what the Eastern Community could withstand. Although Yugoslavia was not within the community it was acknowledged to be as it was. The Hungarian example was also accepted. The system had therefore shown that it was capable of development and of toleration. How Poland would develop we would see. The main question was what was happening today and whether this would lead to confrontation which would have incalculable consequences. *Mr Bullard* said it was important that Poland's allies should continue to show patience. We also believed it was vital that these allies should continue to provide assistance to Poland as they had during the last 18 months. *Dr Berecz* assented.

CSCE

15. *Mr Bullard* said that present reports from Madrid were not encouraging. The leader of the UK delegation had reported that the gap between East and West delegations was growing wider.[3] The UK was still working on the assumption that it would be possible to produce a comprehensive and balanced document by Christmas. If it were possible to find a solution to the question of the limits of the zone of application of the CDE, the other elements would fall into place. Our preferred solution to that problem would be that the proposals made by the West should be adopted, subject to the slight changes in wording made at the beginning of November. The definition of the geographical zone embracing the sky and the sea beyond Europe's shores should be a functional and not a geographical one. The West had made some careful studies and believed this would not damage the interests of either the Soviet Union or the US. What did the Hungarians believe was the reason for the lack of agreement?

16. *Dr Berecz* said the Hungarians had received more optimistic accounts from Madrid. He believed that the Conference would go on at least until Christmas and that there was scope for further initiatives. The difficulties over the CDE could be traced to two things: firstly, the Soviet Union felt that the proposed extension of the zone as far as the Urals was not balanced by an appropriate counterweight. Negotiations should continue until the opposing positions were reconciled. Secondly, although he did not wish to enter into detail, he deplored the inflexibility

[3] The European security review conference in Madrid was dominated by disagreements over rival proposals for a European disarmament conference (CDE). A Soviet-backed Polish proposal called for a conference on military détente and disarmament, but lacked the guarantees for verification of security measures demanded by the West. A rival French initiative proposed new confidence-building measures in Europe, extending from the Atlantic to the Urals, which would be militarily significant, binding and verifiable, but the Soviet bloc wanted US territory included in any security zone.

of some delegations on the question of human rights, which had made the atmosphere more difficult and blocked co-operation. In addition, there were a number of external factors bearing on the discussions in Madrid. Firstly, the forthcoming TNF negotiations;[4] secondly the Polish situation, which was itself a destabilising influence; and thirdly the uncertainty whether an agreement on gas supplies would be signed between the Soviet Union and the West. He was not sure that agreement could be reached by Christmas but considered that it was better to go on talking than not.

17. *Mr Bullard* said the UK was not happy about the Madrid Conference becoming a permanent feature of the European landscape. If this happened it could discredit the Helsinki Final Act. On balance we would prefer an adjournment to indefinite continuation. We had hoped it would be possible to conclude this by Christmas. We would be interested to see whether Mr Brezhnev would have any proposals on this when he arrived in Bonn next week. On the question of the zone the position was simple: we regarded the European part of the Soviet Union as a part of Europe and therefore the question of compensation did not arise, although we recognised there should be an element of balance: hence our proposals for the functional approach on the use of the sea and air. The question of human rights was an integral part of the Final Act and it was natural that there should be discussion of this at Madrid. It was unfortunate in the year since Madrid had begun that some countries had taken actions in this respect which were difficult to reconcile with the wording of the Final Act. He noted in particular the shocking treatment which had been applied to academics in a certain Eastern European country of which he happened to have particular knowledge.

18. Discussion ended at 12.45 p.m.

[4] The US and the USSR were due to resume negotiations on reducing the level of European theatre nuclear forces (TNF) in Geneva on 30 November.

No. 102

Paper by the Planning Staff on Crisis in Eastern Europe, 17 November 1981[1]

Confidential (FCO 28/4364, EN 021/27)

I. *Introduction*

1. This paper has two aims:

(i) to assess how developments in Poland may affect other East European countries[2] in the next five years or so; and

(ii) to consider the implications for our relationships with those countries and for Western policies towards the region.

[1] Drafting for this paper began in the spring and was sent to a number of non-governmental experts on Eastern Europe, who were brought together for a one-day seminar on 16 October to discuss the paper (No. 92). The attached draft took account of this seminar with academics and of the Heads of Mission Conference on East-West relations held on 12 November. In a covering note to the PUS, Mr Mallaby suggested that the paper should be discussed at the regular meeting of DUSs and then, given the topicality and importance of the subject, distributed to a wide range of posts and some government departments.

[2] A footnote to the original document read: 'Defined as: Bulgaria, Czechoslovakia, the GDR, Hungary and Romania.'

In order to keep the paper within manageable length, we have focused on the implications of the Polish Renewal for Eastern Europe, rather than trying to deal directly with its effect on the Soviet Union and the latter's relations with the West. This should be the subject of a separate paper. Nor have we dwelt on the way in which simultaneous but independent developments in the USSR, such as a change in the Soviet leadership, might influence the outcome of events in Eastern Europe. But because of the Soviet Union's enormous importance for Eastern Europe and for the latter's relations with the West it has not been possible or desirable to exclude the Soviet dimension entirely.

II. *The Tensions*

2. Soviet policy in Eastern Europe since the war has been to maintain a group of buffer states, each with a political system broadly similar to the Soviet one in which the Communist Party is supreme. Various instruments help to maintain this state of affairs, from the Warsaw Pact and the Council for Mutual Economic Assistance (CMEA) through a series of interlocking bilateral treaties, to consultations on numerous subjects at various levels. But the ultimate guarantor of the status quo is the Soviet Army.

3. Increasingly in recent years various regimes in East European countries have tried to assert their individuality in response to persistent domestic tensions, which caused major outbursts of popular resentment in the GDR in 1953, in Poland and Hungary in 1956, and in Czechoslovakia in 1968. The tensions may be classed under two main headings: political and economic.

A. *Political*

4. The present system in Eastern Europe was established as a result of subversive action by national Communist Parties backed up (except in the case of Czechoslovakia) by threats of (rather than actual) Soviet military intervention. Soviet domination seemed after the war to have the merit of providing protection against Germany. But with time that has come to be seen to be much less relevant. Though the USSR can continue to rely on a wide spread of official vested interests, Soviet power today has no more than the passive acceptance of the populations. It has not suppressed the individual characters of the East European peoples. Most of the regimes are unpopular because of their association with Soviet Russia and their oppressive policies. Marxism-Leninism has not taken root. The general attitude to it ranges from apathy through scepticism to contempt, and people, even inside the Party, have increasingly felt emboldened to express such sentiments. Nationalism, in some cases accompanied by a traditional anti-Russian feeling, is a powerful and growing force, frequently connived at by the regimes themselves in an attempt to win legitimacy. And the West continues to exert a strong attraction.

B. *Economic*

5. Because of their ideological weakness, East European regimes must retain public tolerance primarily by satisfactory economic performance, the main goal in any case of the philosophy to which they purport to adhere. Living standards, which were generally low, have risen significantly over the last two decades and, although they have not caught up with those in the West, the governments have been able to claim a relatively good economic performance. The system has nevertheless failed conspicuously to meet consumers' aspirations: and, with growth rates slowing throughout Eastern Europe, and expected to deteriorate still more, this situation is likely to become even worse. The decline in growth rates is in part a result of the world recession, in some cases exacerbated by a poor endowment of natural resources. But the fundamental cause has been the many

weaknesses endemic in centrally planned economies: inefficiency, low productivity and poor management. In all East European countries, State and Party assume direct responsibility for economic shortcomings, especially the failure to satisfy the demands of consumers. The expected lower growth rates in future years may therefore make for considerable unrest.

6. The Soviet Union, itself suffering a slow-down in economic growth which is likely to continue in the next five years, is limiting the subsidies on its supplies of energy and raw materials to Eastern Europe. Moreover, although total Soviet energy production will continue to increase, Soviet oil production is approaching its peak and will shortly be in decline, so that the Russians have for some time been making it clear that they will not be able to meet all East European oil requirements in future. While this may to some extent be off-set by increased supplies of Soviet gas, the probability is that the cost of energy to the East Europeans will go on rising, and that they will be forced to look increasingly to world markets to make good their requirements. Even if they can achieve somewhat greater energy efficiency—for which there is plenty of scope—their ability to boost growth, as in the seventies, by importing Western goods and technology will decrease because of the greater amounts of convertible currency being spent on energy imports. And any severe restrictions on energy consumption would further impair the already poor prospects for economic growth and thus for improvement in living standards.

7. Some organisational reforms to increase efficiency have been tried, most successfully in Hungary, with lesser experiments taking place in Czechoslovakia and even Bulgaria. This may continue, with Soviet blessing, and may succeed in mitigating the economic difficulties. But there may be risks: even if reforms to date have not provoked calls for political change, this may not always be the case.

C. *The Prospects*

8. The importance attached by the Soviet authorities to the preservation of the East European glacis, which serves to isolate the USSR from the West in military, ideological, political and to some extent economic terms, will not diminish in the near future. The Russians see Eastern Europe as their rightful sphere of influence, the natural extension of the Socialist heartland, where their system ought to prevail; and not merely as an area to be controlled for military reasons. Moscow will therefore be determined to maintain control over the internal and foreign policy orientation of the East European countries.

9. On the other hand, the most striking recent change before the Polish crisis was that, although the Communist regimes succeeded in maintaining their monopoly of power (sometimes only with the help of Soviet intervention), most of them found it necessary or expedient to use it in normal times with decreasing ruthlessness. Moreover the Soviet Union was clearly prepared to allow individual countries to begin to assert their national identities, but to an extent neither unlimited nor known. Pressures for change will persist in Eastern Europe and economic difficulties will get worse; crises are therefore very possible.

III. *The Polish Renewal*

10. We must view current developments in Poland against this background. Although the crisis arose out of a variety of political, social, national and historical factors, it was triggered by economic discontent at home. There has so far been little interest in the international political aspirations which were voiced in Hungary in 1956 and which made Soviet intervention—in retrospect—inevitable:

notably demands that Soviet forces be removed and calls for withdrawal from the Warsaw Pact.

11. Nonetheless, the existence of independent trades unions in Poland and a major erosion of the leading role of the party are in fundamental contradiction to the Marxist-Leninist state system. Although Poland already had a kind of pluralism because of the independent role of the Church and the existence of private agriculture, the establishment of new independent organisations in the very political area of workers and farmers' representation is a change of the utmost potential significance.

12. The Russians presumably tolerated the initial concessions in August 1980 because they hoped that minimal implementation of the agreements (as occurred after the setting up in 1956 of Workers' Councils)[3] would defuse the initial crisis and permit subsequent claw-back of what had been implemented. This was no doubt seen in Moscow as preferable to a military intervention which would bring bloodshed, an international crisis and heavy economic penalties for the Soviet Union and other East European countries. But since then the Polish Party has given way in a series of confrontations with Solidarity. Change has spread into the Party itself. It may well be weaker now than Solidarity. Pluralism may possibly be institutionalised in some form of coalition involving Solidarity, the Church and the Government. The economy has gone from crisis to the brink of collapse. So the 'internal route' to ending the Renewal is looking increasingly hopeless.

13. There now appear to be at least five possible outcomes to the crisis. One is a thoroughgoing internal clampdown by the Polish authorities, perhaps in the form of martial law. But this would be likely either to leave much of the Renewal in place or to cause disorder on a scale which would precipitate Soviet intervention. A second possibility would be a long drawn-out trial of strength between reformers and conservatives in which neither gained the whip hand. This would amount to something like a continuation of the present situation in Poland. It is very possibly what will happen for some time. But it would remain inherently unstable, and would be unlikely to endure in the long term; and if it implied continued economic dislocation it could not persist without risking the collapse of the economy and, with it, a breakdown in order very probably leading to Soviet intervention. Some people have suggested that economic pressure by the Soviet Union might be an alternative to military intervention. Economic measures have apparently been threatened. But the implementation of major ones would be likely to cause major unrest in Poland; the latter could precipitate a breakdown in public order and make military intervention essential. Such implementation would therefore be likely only if Moscow had decided on intervention. The two remaining scenarios might be termed 'reform' and 'intervention'.

A. *Reform*

14. In this case, the Poles would achieve a political consensus which suspended the struggle between reformers and conservatives while satisfying the Soviet Union that public order, membership of the Warsaw Pact and the nominal leading role of the Party could be maintained. There might then be sufficient goodwill both to secure the cooperation of the workforce in repairing the economy, and to attract continuing external economic support. All this would demand a determined but

[3] Worker councils spread across Poland during uprisings in 1956 seeking better standards of living and they became powerful centres of revolutionary debate. The Party agreed to give them full legal recognition in November 1956 but by 1958 they had been watered down into Conferences of Workers Self-Government.

respected leadership and a public weary of the constant upheavals and in favour of cooperation between all moderate elements. It seems at present that it could conceivably take the form of an 'historic compromise' in which the Party, Solidarity and the Church were involved in some power-sharing arrangement.

15. Yet such a consensus might prove to be only a truce. It would be unlikely to exorcise the underlying tensions. In particular, the USSR might well press the Polish Party to begin to claw back concessions once the crisis had subsided, and the success of the Renewal to date might well spur ambitious reformers to try to nudge Poland further away from the Soviet model. The position of the Party might grow increasingly tenuous. It is doubtful that periodic crises with the Soviet Union could be avoided. Important landmarks could be the local elections due in 1982 and the Parliamentary elections due in 1984.

B. *Intervention*

16. The Soviet forces involved in an intervention would be large enough to ensure success in overrunning Poland. Other Warsaw Pact countries could very probably be involved either on a token or significant scale. Popular resistance is probable, not only from civilians, but also from members and perhaps units of the Polish armed forces. This might be followed by a longer campaign, perhaps lasting several months, of passive resistance and sabotage, such as destruction of industry and flooding of mines, and the sabotage of the Druzhba pipeline[4] and other infrastructure and communications. Following an intervention there would be little prospect of Western economic assistance, other than possible rescheduling of debts to protect Western creditors. The Polish economy would be restarted by the USSR.

17. It seems plausible to take these two very different scenarios as the basis for our examination of the implications of the Polish crisis for the remainder of Eastern Europe, for its relations with the West, and for Western policies. This approach should make up in relative clarity for what it loses through simplification. It is used in full consciousness that in each of the two scenarios there are a number of gradations rather than a single model contrasting starkly with its opposite: and that evolution towards one outcome or another may be an erratic process.

IV. *Consequences for the rest of Eastern Europe*

18. Poland is in many respects the leading CMEA country in Eastern Europe, accounting for a third of the total population, a quarter of the overall gross national product and a third of energy production. It is an important part of the regional transport network. It participates in numerous CMEA specialisation programmes as a supplier of components to Soviet and East European industry.

19. The economic impact of recent Polish developments on the rest of the CMEA has varied from country to country, the GDR being most affected not least by the slow-down in economic integration in COMECON which Honecker so prizes. Probably the most damaging impact has come from the short-fall in Polish coal deliveries. Worse disruption would have a ripple effect on the rest of Poland's CMEA partners. Should the transport network and the port facilities be disrupted for a considerable period, whether through strikes or sabotage, alternative routes avoiding Poland would become very congested. Their use would also involve longer transit times and higher costs.

20. So far there has been little observable political spill-over from Poland to the other East European populations. The unenviable economic state of Poland may be

[4] The pipeline carried oil from the Soviet Union to countries in Eastern Europe.

partly responsible. In Romania there have been a few signs of discontent with the recently intensified economic problems. But the regime has reacted with concern and taken steps to head off any suggestion that independent trades unions are needed. There have been few manifestations of sympathy for Solidarity in the GDR (where there is considerable anti-Polish feeling) or Czechoslovakia although the authorities in both countries have shown distinct nervousness. In Hungary, sympathy for Poland's assertion of independence has been tempered with impatience at the Poles' failure to resolve their own problems without imposing a burden on their neighbours, coupled with a lively fear of the effects on Hungary of a deterioration in East/West relations such as would follow an intervention.

21. The reactions of the different regimes do not necessarily reflect the real vulnerability of the countries concerned. Although the more advanced East European countries all have strong syndicalist traditions and other institutions capable of developing into alternative power centres, Poland has a uniquely strong combination of potentially pluralist elements. But few of the other East European regimes can afford to be entirely confident about the future. The most vulnerable country is probably Romania, where the Polish events have coincided with an indigenous economic crisis and where a repressive regime has engendered increasing resentment over the years. In Hungary, there is perhaps some possibility that liberalising trends could lead to increased popular demand for change. And although the GDR is comparatively well managed and its people apparently resigned, it is very difficult for the regime to appeal to nationalism and the attractions of West German life make the authorities anxious. In Czechoslovakia, with its strong syndicalist tradition and widespread corruption, a responsive chord could be struck by Solidarity's success in defending the interests of the workers and removing corrupt officials. And memories of the Prague spring still linger. Bulgaria seems relatively quiescent.

22. In the next five years there could be succession struggles in any of the East European countries. New leaders might handle problems less adroitly than their predecessors. This applies particularly to Hungary, where Kadar's regime has succeeded in performing a remarkable balancing act and younger generations are more interested in change than their seniors; and to Romania where, when Ceausescu goes, the Stalinist grip may have either to relax or cause significant internal tensions.

23. The history of the Polish Renewal so far shows that the Soviet Union may be willing to allow more change in Eastern Europe than had previously been thought. It is, of course, arguable that Poland is a special case: the costs of invasion—notably the probability of armed resistance—no doubt weigh heavily with an ageing Soviet leadership already burdened with a war in Afghanistan. But as long as political methods for countering a threat in Eastern Europe remain possible, the Soviet Union, even under new leadership and in different circumstances, may prefer them to military measures. On the other hand, the dangers of hesitation or procrastination will have been highlighted by the Polish experience, and on a future occasion decisive action could be swiftly taken. One big consideration would be the nature of the changes that were taking place in the other East European country (or countries) concerned. Another would be which country or countries were involved. Changes which the Russians might try to combat by political means in Hungary might provoke speedy military suppression in the GDR.

A. *Reform*

24. The possibility of future political change in the rest of the area would increase greatly if the Polish Renewal were to endure. While Poland is far from being an attractive example economically, a consensus where free trade unions and the Church continued to exert an influence on the Polish government would be an extremely important new feature on the political landscape of Eastern Europe. The room for manoeuvre open to other governments and groups would appear to have been enlarged.

25. Perhaps the most likely result would be a period of tension and uncertainty in Eastern Europe. The USSR might henceforth nip all political reform in the bud. Most regimes might tighten security and suppress dissidents, while trying to seem keen to satisfy consumers' expectations and to animate the official trades unions (a reaction already noted in Czechoslovakia and Romania). One or two (e.g. Hungary) might seek first to modify their institutions and practice so as to diffuse discontent, only cracking down as a last resort. The success or otherwise of a hard-line political approach would depend in part on the extent—disputed among Western experts—to which it could be reconciled with the economic liberalisation which may be needed to stave off mounting economic difficulties. But, whatever the outcome, in due course certain groups and tendencies in the area could be expected to try to copy at least some aspects of the Polish Renewal in asserting their own interests. If such groups then attempted to win concessions beyond, or even as great as, those conceded to the Poles, a crisis might well ensue in which not only the new reform movement but also the Polish one might be at risk.

26. Politically and militarily it would be very difficult for the Soviet Union to invade both Poland *and* another country, particularly if the situation in Poland had stabilised and presented no obvious excuse for intervention. But, given the acute risks to Soviet power in the area as a whole, intervention at least in the additional country would be likely and perhaps in Poland as well.

B. *Intervention*

27. A massive intervention in Poland and the restoration of order within a matter of weeks would confirm that the Soviet Union will not allow major changes in the Marxist-Leninist state system. The Brezhnev doctrine would be seen once more to be a cardinal principle of Soviet policy. Neighbouring regimes would clamp down on dissent and expressions of popular opinion.

28. The chance of sympathetic unrest in other East European countries if Poland were quickly quelled would be slight. But if Polish resistance dragged on, it would represent a highly visible example of a dissent which obviously had popular roots. Moreover, the economic effects of a Polish armageddon, particularly on the GDR and Czechoslovakia, could add to popular feeling. It is not inconceivable that the combined effects of controlling armed resistance in Poland and Afghanistan could exacerbate problems in the Soviet Union itself.

29. Nevertheless intervention would be a major blow to the development of diversity in the region. The Polish system might regress even further than Czechoslovakia under Husak: alternatively a more enlightened Soviet leadership might come to regard Kadar's Hungarian model as the more appropriate and ultimately less troublesome one in this case. Although economic reform would not be likely to be interrupted in Eastern Europe, internal political liberalisation would be halted and might not be a factor again within five years.

30. Soviet intervention in Poland and a skilful Western response to it could carry significantly further the process of destroying the international appeal of

Soviet communism by once again exposing its hegemonial character. This could encourage the kind of questioning of policies within the Soviet Union which apparently happened after Afghanistan. Such questioning might not last. But one result of an invasion of Poland might be to make the Soviet leaders even keener to avoid such intervention when eventually the next crisis occurred in Eastern Europe.

V. *Consequences for relations between Eastern Europe and the West*

31. One of the things that people in the West hoped to achieve by means of 'détente' was a gradual breaking down of barriers to the spread of Western ideas in Eastern Europe and the Soviet Union and the encouragement of indigenous trends towards diversity among these countries.

32. It has been claimed by Chancellor Schmidt, among others, that the Soviet restraint in not invading Poland so far is an achievement of 'détente'. That is an oversimplification. Other reasons—military and economic—are likely to have been more important. But it is true that Brezhnev's personal investment in détente may have been one factor. More important, Soviet efforts to keep alive the German bogey in Eastern Europe used to be a potent factor in making Soviet hegemony acceptable: and the *Ostpolitik* and CSCE have made it much more difficult for the Russians to play this card effectively. So the advances in East/West relations since 1968 have created a climate in which change has been made easier in Eastern Europe, and conversely have made the price to be paid for an invasion that much higher.

33. The way in which the Polish crisis develops will have significant implications for East/West relations in the next few years. In the case of the Reform scenario, people in the West would be encouraged to take a more positive view of the prospects for change in Eastern Europe. But intervention would cause major doubts to be raised (as they were after the invasion of Czechoslovakia) about whether it is worth trying to influence conditions in Eastern Europe and whether lasting change is even possible.

A. *Reform*

34. It would be an exaggeration to say that, if the Polish Renewal endures and succeeds in establishing a political system that is notably different from the Soviet model, the end of the Warsaw Pact or Marxism-Leninism as a whole will only be a matter of time. But Soviet hegemony in Eastern Europe and the monolithic nature of the East European landscape would be called into question, and the durability of the status quo challenged. The Soviet Union's power and prestige for dominating the Warsaw Pact and CMEA would be undermined. Empires decay not only as a result of military defeat, but also because of a decline in political will at the centre and in the application of authority on the periphery. Soviet policy towards Poland may prove to be an example of both.

35. The highly visible erosion of Soviet power represented by a continued Polish Renewal would make the Soviet leaders feel even more on the defensive in international affairs than is already likely because of other factors, including their economic difficulties and demographic change and ideological sterility in the USSR. A Soviet Union which saw its empire declining, and which remained very strong militarily but not in other ways, would need exceptionally careful handling by the West. East-West relations, although under this scenario they would be spared the dramatic shock of a Soviet intervention in Poland, might not be better than in recent years. Given the risks of reform spreading in Eastern Europe, the Soviet Union might decide that the pace of contacts between East and West should

be deliberately slowed down. Trade would be hampered by caution on both sides about allowing East European indebtedness to grow too much.

36. The continuation of the Renewal would have one unwelcome effect for Western governments. Those in the younger generations in Western Europe, especially the FRG, who deny the existence of a Soviet threat and oppose nuclear weapons would be reinforced in their views and might gain more support. It would become harder for governments to counter such opinions.

B. *Intervention*

37. The immediate consequences of a Soviet intervention in Poland would include an East-West crisis greater than in 1968. More particularly there could be:

(*a*) Increased tension in the Baltic as a result of Polish defections and possible Soviet hot pursuit. The USSR might bring pressure to bear on Berlin either unilaterally or as a reaction to political and economic sanctions imposed by NATO. There might well be increased military readiness on the Central Front for a time. This would be most unlikely, however, to escalate into East/West conflict provided that the West did nothing to suggest that it intended to interfere in Poland militarily, or politically on a major scale.

(*b*) A permanent increase in the Warsaw Pact forces facing NATO; but because policing Poland would henceforth preoccupy large numbers of Soviet troops and because the Polish forces would be a largely broken reed, the overall military effectiveness of the Warsaw Pact would be reduced.

(*c*) An immediate stiffening of Western governmental and public attitudes towards the Soviet Union, particularly in the larger countries, leading to support for increased defence spending which could paradoxically be followed by,

(*d*) an increase in pacifist tendencies in Western European public opinion, caused by concern at the heightening East/West tension. This would be particularly likely if, as seems probable, arms control negotiations were suspended. The USSR would do what it could to exploit this factor and might in particular dangle the prospect of a neutral united Germany before German eyes to woo them away from the Alliance.

(*e*) A serious, possibly catastrophic, effect on relations between Western and Eastern European communist parties. But, given their internal difficulties and divergent trends, the Western European parties would be unlikely to adopt a unified position in opposition to the Soviet Union.

(*f*) A serious blow to Inner-German relations. If East German troops were involved in an invasion of Poland, the damage to Inner-German relations would be much greater. The Federal government would face pressure from its own public opinion and its allies to take concrete steps to demonstrate disapproval of such involvement. The East German regime, too, would probably find it expedient to put up further barriers to East-West movement. But the Federal government and public opinion would not wish to set back too severely the development of Inner-German relations, and, even if the East Germans participated in an invasion, economic links might not be affected greatly or for long.

(g) A serious reduction in the level of personal contacts between East and West. The goodwill built up by exchanges under the umbrella of the official bilateral Cultural Exchange Programmes would suffer. This might cause Western governments to divert funds set aside for contacts with Eastern Europe to other, less contentious areas.

38. The resulting crisis in East-West relations generally would probably be intensified by the West cutting back sharply on contacts and trade with the Soviet

Union. Because the West is now more conscious of the case for treating each Warsaw Pact country differently, Western counter-measures might be directed above all against the Soviet Union, even if some East European countries participated in an intervention. But Western Governments would not seek actively for some time to make new progress in relations with any East European countries involved in an invasion. And the Soviet Union, as after the invasion of Afghanistan, would no doubt require that all East Europe's relations with the West should be frozen.

39. Yet the underlying East European and Western motives for resuming the development of their relations would still exist. The East Europeans would want in due course cautiously to resume the attempt to express their individuality in limited fields, through commercial, technical and even cultural exchanges. The Soviet Union, knowing that economic difficulty could precipitate popular discontent in Eastern Europe and not wishing to finance these countries more than it must, would probably not be averse to their resuming the development of economic contacts with the West, though it and Western governments could be expected to resist any repetition of indebtedness on the Polish scale. The Russians themselves would still have an interest in détente (avoidance of crises; acquisition of technology and grain; limited arms control; international respectability). Moscow would probably come eventually to see the cautious resumption of East European relations with the West as a way of re-creating an impression of business-as-usual, which would help the USSR itself to emerge thereafter from the international dog-house.

40. The West would however have to approach the subject of relations with the East European countries with a new realism. Western public attitudes would inevitably be coloured by a deeply negative view of the USSR itself. But would the Western attitude towards Eastern Europe be fundamentally different from before? We would know that the Soviet Union is liable to intervene to reverse change in Eastern Europe when it reaches a certain point. We would know that 'détente' could not prevent such intervention—only make it more difficult. Yet we know these things already. And we would be even more conscious of the importance of change in Eastern Europe being gradual.

VI. *Policies for the West*

41. The latitude available to Western planners when devising policies for relations with Eastern Europe is limited by the overriding need to avoid provoking confrontation between East and West which could escalate into a military clash. This rules out any direct military action in response to internal events in Eastern Europe. But there are other instruments with which we can seek to influence those events, even if these are insufficiently powerful or finely tuned to allow us to control the pace of developments.

A. *Reform*

42. If the Polish Renewal survives, the case for Western governments continuing to encourage individuality among the East European countries will have been confirmed. Indeed there will be a temptation, fuelled perhaps by domestic political opinion, to step up our relations with the countries concerned. Yet it would not be in Western interests to encourage hasty change, which would be far less likely to last than gradual reform. Moreover, Western proposals for major advances would be self-defeating: anxious about the durability of its empire, the Soviet Union would be likely to insist that the East Europeans reject such

overtures, and to take the chance to accuse the West of interfering to foment trouble.

43. Under this scenario, as now, the most difficult aspect of policy towards Poland itself would concern financial support, which would be needed for some years even after a stable political consensus had been reached. To deny support could precipitate the collapse of the Renewal. To provide it cannot guarantee the continuation of the Renewal. The arguments in favour of providing money are political, strategic and moral. Those against are budgetary. It is in our interests that the Renewal should not collapse, notably because it undermines Soviet hegemony in Eastern Europe and preoccupies the Kremlin in a way which may reduce the likelihood of its meddling in other parts of the world. It weakens the military position of the Warsaw Pact facing NATO. For the West to terminate financial support would be incompatible with our beliefs and statements about freedom and would undermine our credibility in Eastern Europe and elsewhere. But the difficulties of finding the large funds that may be required, and of rating Poland versus other recipients (Turkey, Zimbabwe), are enormous. The IMF may have a useful role to play, once Poland has rejoined.

44. The considerations in para 42 point towards a carefully balanced and gradual Western policy. We should take note of the East Europeans' own views. We may be able to move further with them if, as far as possible, we offer similar advances in relations to the Soviet Union, thus reducing any appearance of splitting tactics. British policy in Eastern Europe might be:

(*a*) steadily to build up relations with Poland, without ostentation;

(*b*) to try to increase Ministerial contacts with the other countries, with roughly annual visits of Foreign Ministers and occasional top level contacts with Hungary and Romania at least;

(*c*) to maintain the present effort of the BBC in the region;

(*d*) to increase contact in the academic, scientific and cultural fields by means of exchanges and symposia under the agreed Cultural Exchange Programmes implemented by the British Council; and to encourage the development of direct exchanges between academic institutions outside the strict provisions of these Programmes.

45. There would be times when the West would have an interest in trying to influence reformists in Eastern Europe not to move too fast. The West could emphasise that political *evolution* was a major contribution to stability in Europe. When the risk of Soviet intervention loomed, the West should try to follow the broad mixture of policies which has worked so far in respect of Poland, including emphatic warnings to the Russians, and contingency planning, which the USSR should be made partially aware of, about reactions to any Soviet intervention.

46. One casualty of Soviet nervousness about further change in its empire could be the CSCE. The Final Act is still trumpeted as a success of Brezhnev's détente policy. As long as he is party leader the Russians are likely to want to keep the process in being. They will not attribute the Polish crisis to CSCE alone; but, like us, they may consider the Final Act to be part of the backdrop against which the Renewal was able to take place. So Brezhnev's successors might not be keen on continuing the process. A possible Western policy in these circumstances might be discreetly to encourage the neutrals to lobby the East Europeans, a number of whom regard the Final Act as a useful charter for the contacts which they seek with the West. The Russians might see enough arguments in favour of the process to acquiesce, although they might well try to impose conditions on how it should

be conducted. There would be dangers in any such negotiation, but the West, by standing on the text of the Final Act, should be able to preserve an acceptable balance. The best guidelines for the West, assuming the process were continued, might be to press not for human rights *per se* but for a multiplicity of contacts and exchanges tending to undermine the monopoly of power which East European regimes seek to preserve.

47. There are also economic questions concerning Eastern Europe as a whole. It has been suggested by some American commentators[5] that Western economic links with Eastern Europe (and the USSR) merely help to put off the day when these societies must radically reform their inefficient system in order to survive. While this is an exaggeration, it is indisputable that Western technology has helped East European governments to reduce the effects of some of the weaknesses in their systems. In the coming years of greater economic difficulty they will probably be particularly interested in Western assistance to satisfy consumer expectations. Even so, a denial of most Western goods and technology might not encourage reform. It is equally likely that East European regimes would batten down the hatches and draw closer to the Soviet Union. Even if the result were occasional violence, this would probably be containable for many years to come.

48. It would, moreover, hardly be feasible or in accordance with Western values for Western governments in normal times to forbid economic links with Eastern Europe. East-West trade is in any case in the West's economic interests besides being a force for political stability. It also brings East European exposure to the West. And other kinds of Western contacts with Eastern Europe which bring such exposure would hardly be conceivable if economic links were cut off.

49. Events in Poland have shown, however, that East-West economic links can go too far. It is arguable that Western banks, in their anxiety to find outlets for OPEC deposits, and Western governments, acting both as original lenders and as guarantors of private loans, encouraged an over-ambitious expansion of the Polish economy; and that the credits to Poland only postponed the economic crisis and ensured that it was more serious when it came. Now that Poland's debt has had to be rescheduled, Western banks and governments will presumably be more prudent in future about extending credit to Eastern Europe, and the East Europeans in turn will be more circumspect in accepting credit on an excessive scale. Trade will go on, but will be constrained by the economic difficulties of the region, and credit for it will still be available, albeit perhaps at higher rates. The risks of over-extension will be less.

B. *Intervention*

50. We have suggested that the West would still have an interest, even after a Soviet intervention in Poland, in seeking to encourage diversity in Eastern Europe. After an interval, perhaps up to a couple of years, we should seek to resume the development of our relations.

51. Two particular purposes for the West in East-West relations would be suggested by an intervention in Poland. One—the need to moderate the speed of political change when crisis looms in Eastern Europe—has been discussed above. The conclusion as to the West's ability to influence events must be pessimistic. The other would be to devise specific policies for making Soviet intervention harder on future occasions. Can such policies be devised? The answer is: no

[5] A footnote to the original document read: 'cf Professor Richard Pipes, A Round-Table Discussion, International Herald Tribune, 29 January 1980.'

absolutely effective ones. Threats of Western military action if the USSR invaded a Warsaw Pact country would not be credible and could create a risk of world war. Experience suggests that an attempt to enmesh the Soviet Union in a multitude of interests in East-West relations can add somewhat to the constraints on aggression, but will not deter action when Moscow sees an imperative need. (Such a policy can also create 'reverse linkage' as shown by the Federal Republic's reluctance to contemplate damage to its trading relationship).

52. It has been suggested by Philip Windsor[6] that a more elaborate system of Confidence Building Measures (CBMs) by 'creating a code of behaviour for the application and movement of military force', could do 'much to meet the . . . objective . . . making it less likely that the USSR would intervene with force in the affairs of Eastern Europe'. The French proposal for a CDE has this kind of aim very much in mind. The West should pursue the idea, if only to put the USSR on the defensive. But the latter, especially given the Polish experience, may not accept the sort of CBMs which it would have to violate directly in order to invade an East European country. CBMs might, however, possibly be devised which would make it harder for the Russians to *threaten* the use of force by deploying troops, as they have done during the Polish crisis.

53. After an intervention in Poland there would be even fewer illusions in the West about the ability of CSCE to promote political change in Warsaw Pact countries. But it could remain a potentially valuable multilateral framework for developing relations, and, since the argument for encouraging individuality in Eastern Europe would still hold, there would be a case for trying to revive the process after an interval—perhaps a couple of years.

54. The future of major East-West negotiations on arms control after a Soviet invasion would be very uncertain. In the short run they would very likely be suspended. Their later resumption would be favoured by the West Europeans but perhaps less readily by the Reagan Administration.[7] The subject may later require a major separate study.

55. Even if economic sanctions following an intervention in Poland were directed primarily against the Soviet Union, trade between Eastern Europe and the West would be inhibited by the enormous setback to overall East-West relations.

56. Given that Western governments have agreed to reschedule maturities due on the Polish debt in 1981, the USSR would be unlikely after an invasion to take over and meet Polish maturities on schedule in subsequent years. Poland, at Soviet prompting, might declare a moratorium and would no doubt seek a further rescheduling negotiation. Western governments would face a nasty dilemma: whether to have dealings with, and be seen to make financial concessions to, a puppet Polish regime; or to refuse to negotiate and continue to insist that intergovernmental debts be repaid before there was any question of further official Western credits for Poland. The Russians, realising that our financial self-interest as creditors pointed to the former course, would be inflexible in negotiation. We

[6] A footnote to the original document read: 'Change in Eastern Europe'. Chatham House Papers London 1980.'

[7] At the Heads of Mission conference Sir N. Henderson, HM Ambassador in Washington, noted that there had been no thought-out overall approach to East-West relations in Washington apart from taking a tough line with the Soviet Union, both in substance and rhetoric, and making life difficult for Cuba. This line had been somewhat modified because of relations with the European Allies, so the US now had an interest in dialogue with the USSR, on strategic as well as theatre nuclear arms (FCO 28/4408, EN 400/2).

might try threatening to deny all CMEA countries further access to official Western credit. But if most economic cooperation with the East had been severed in the wake of a Soviet intervention this might be a weak card.

No. 103

Sir R. Hibbert (Paris) to Lord Carrington, 20 November 1981, 5.30 p.m.
Tel. No. 1009[1] Routine, Confidential (FCO 28/4529, ENP 090/1)

Poland: economic assistance
From Mountfield.[2]

1. The Joint Commission of Poland and 16 creditor governments met in Paris on 19 and 20 November, preceded by a meeting of the Creditors' Task Force on 18 November. Spain attended the commission for the first time and the IMF sent observers. The creditors agreed to recommend that Polish debt to these governments maturing in 1982 should be rescheduled on terms broadly similar to the 1981 operation. The Joint Commission will meet again in Paris on 14 and 15 January to finalise and sign the agreement, provided that a banking agreement has been signed by then, and unless overtaken by a polish default.

2. The Task Force presented an agreed report on Polish economic performance in 1981 and prospects for 1982 and later years. Although all the figures are dubious, the financing gap for the remainder of 1981 appears to be around 0.7 billion dollars, and in 1982, even allowing for rescheduling, about 4 billion dollars. Performance in 1981 fell far short of the targets agreed in April as a condition of the 1981 rescheduling. The Task Force recommended tighter conditionality on IMF-type lines in 1982. It made no written recommendations to the Joint Commission on the terms of the new rescheduling. However, agreed proposals emerged following an informal Task Force meeting on 19 November, and were put by Haberer to the group and with their approval to the Poles on 20 November.

3. The likely terms of the 1982 operation, if approved by governments, would be much as before. 90% of principal and interest on maturing medium and long-term debts would be rescheduled over eight years including a four-year grace period, at commercial rates of interest. Interest on previously rescheduled debt would not be rescheduled. Conditionality would be limited to the targets laid down by Poland and incorporated in its economic report which would be annexed to the agreed minute. The debts to be rescheduled would be split into two consecutive lists. The second, covering debts due in the last six months of 1982, would only be rescheduled upon approval by the Joint Commission of Polish economic performance in the first half-year. This staging reflects US insistence (with support from Belgium and Japan) on making rescheduling for the second half of 1982 subject to review. There was no disposition on the part of any of the creditors to soften the terms of rescheduling. This would, it was felt, set undesirable precedents. Poland sought unsuccessfully to make rescheduling conditional upon promises of new credit. But most creditors opposed the inclusion of any commitment to new credit in the agreement.

[1] Repeated for Information Routine to Warsaw, Washington, Bonn, UKREP Brussels, UKDEL IMF/BRD Washington; Information Saving to Stockholm, Brussels, Madrid, Oslo, Copenhagen, Rome, Tokyo, Ottawa, Helsinki, Berne, Vienna.
[2] Peter Mountfield, HM Treasury.

4. Italy disassociated itself from the report of the Task Force (of which it was not a member) and deplored its reference to conditionality, which it described as an interference in Poland's domestic affairs.

5. Poland argued that rescheduling was not enough to bridge the gap. The French chairman (Haberer) therefore made a formal 'Chairman's statement' drawing attention to the need for new credit in 1982. He then arranged a short separate meeting in the afternoon of 20 November to consider new credits for 1982. As expected there were few signs of generosity. The US had nothing to offer apart from emergency food aid. FRG said its budgetary problems made any further assistance in 1982 unlikely. France, with an early visit by Prime Minister Mauroy to Poland in prospect, is keeping its powder dry. As agreed by our ministers, we said that our main effort in 1982 would be continued support for URSUS.[3] France stole the US's discarded clothing and suggested that any new credits in 1982 should be short-term and closely tied to imports generating a high export multiplier. The proceeds of such exports should be segregated in a separate account and repayment of the special credits would be a prior charge on this account. It was agreed that all countries would reflect further on this idea. There will be further discussion of new credits at the meeting in January.

6. Poland warned of the risks of a moratorium if sufficient new funds were not made available to meet the down payments due to private banks after signature of their rescheduling agreement on 10 December. No-one was impressed by this threat. The US and France expect the banking talks to drag on into January (hence the provisional nature of the timetable in para 1). US, France, Austria and UK all said that they did not expect any banking failures as a result of a Polish moratorium or an externally imposed default. FRG thought one or two German banks might fail and admitted to considerable worries. But no country saw this as a reason for a major rescue operation at this stage. IMF pointed out the risks of a cumulative collapse of banking confidence in Eastern Europe generally. France said a rescue operation might be necessary at the last moment and undertook to call an early meeting if the situation deteriorated further.

7. The US representative (Meissner) told us privately that the administration is still considering the political case for a major rescue. In his view it would have to amount to at least 3 billion dollars for 1981 and 1982 combined, including a contribution from the banks, to be worth doing at all. He did not rate the chance of presidential approval very highly.

8. Tyler (IMF) said that now the Polish application had been received it would be processed in the normal way.[4] He did not expect a decision before August 1982 and thought it most unlikely that any money could be drawn during calendar 1982.

9. The general impression is one of unenthusiastic fatalism. Budgetary problems are outweighing political pressures. Apart from rescheduling, assistance in 1982 seems likely to be much lower than in 1981 and the chances of default now seem very high. France agreed that if this happened it would summon an immediate meeting of at least the principal (i.e. Task Force) creditors to consider Western reactions. But no contingency plans were considered.

FCO please pass saving to all.

[3] See No. 99, paragraph 11.

[4] Poland formally applied for IMF membership on 10 November.

No. 104

Lord Carrington to Mr James (Warsaw), 21 November 1981, 11.24 a.m.
Tel. No. 616[1] Immediate, Confidential (FCO 28/4534, ENP 101/1)

Visit of Polish Foreign Minister: 20 November.[2]
Following is text of COREU we have sent out today.
Begins.
Visit to the UK by Polish Foreign Minister. CPE/MUL/ETR 3726.

1. Lord Carrington and M. Czyrek had a session of talks followed by a working lunch on 20 November.

2. M. Czyrek gave the following assessment of the international situation and of the political and economic situation in Poland.

International

3. The policy of dialogue and detente was of importance to Poland. Only in this context could Poland hope to live through the difficult period ahead. It was necessary to find a 'common denominator'[3] which would be sufficiently strong and lasting to bring this about.

4. In Czyrek's view superpower relations were still characterised by a lack of mutual confidence. Even though disagreeing with certain Soviet policies, the US should acknowledge the principle of equal security. Despite the talks starting in Geneva on 30 November,[4] he saw no change in the US doctrinal and strategic approach. Poland took very seriously 'voices' about the possibility of limited nuclear war in Europe. The possibility for superpower conflict existed in the Middle East and potentially in Iran. The world economic situation was becoming increasingly complex and difficult.

5. In Europe the Poles were observing closely the Soviet Union's dialogue with its principal partners. They hoped this would evolve in the direction of detente. They also hoped it would be possible to conclude the Madrid conference by December. The CSCE process should not be left chiefly to the superpowers now treated in an 'instrumental' way.

6. Lord Carrington disagreed with M. Czyrek's assessment of the US position. US views had evolved during the last year. The sincerity of the US commitment to arms reduction, most recently spelled out in the President's speech of 18 November, should not be doubted.[5]

Poland

[1] Repeated Information Priority to Washington, Paris, Bonn, UKDEL NATO, Moscow and Information Saving to other EC posts, Bucharest, Budapest, Sofia, Prague, Belgrade, Helsinki, East Berlin.

[2] Mr Czyrek had asked to visit Lord Carrington in his capacity as President of the European Council.

[3] On 19 November Mr Broomfield in a minute to Lord Carrington referred to a report from secret sources, which claimed that Mr Czyrek would '(albeit obliquely)' suggest that the Polish crisis must be divorced from the East-West context and a 'Pan-European' solution found for Poland's problems'.

[4] See No. 12, note 4.

[5] In his speech to the National Press Club, Reagan offered to cancel the US deployment of Pershing II and ground-launch cruise missiles if the Soviets dismantled their SS-20, SS-4 and SS-5 missiles. He also offered to open negotiations on strategic arms as soon as possible, to achieve equality at lower levels of conventional forces in Europe, and proposed a conference to develop effective measures to reduce the chance of war arising out of uncertainty or miscalculation. *Public Papers: Reagan (1981)*, pp. 1062-7.

7. Czyrek said that the Government was determined to resolve Poland's problems, not by reversion to centralism and dictatorship, but by greater decentralisation and democracy. The Government would not however tolerate two or three independent centres of power. The question was whether, in the face of obstruction and 'blockade' by Solidarity, the Government would be able to carry this policy forward. The position was critical. A collapse would have unpredictable consequences.

8. Poland was dependent on her Western and Eastern partners. Notwithstanding its own agricultural problems the Soviet Union would be supplying 30,000 tonnes of meat and also 50,000 tonnes of fish. But the Western position had hardened. Did this indicate a change of policy? Was it really true that the sixteen major Western creditor countries could not raise dollars 500 million [*sic*] between them? Difficulties were also emerging in the rescheduling talks in Paris. The Americans appeared to be pressing for a rescheduling agreement for only six months, not a year. It even seemed that consideration of the Polish application to join the IMF[6] would be deferred until after Hungary's. This might mean membership only in the 1983 [*sic*].

9. Lord Carrington said that the UK did not approach the Polish difficulties from a doctrinal but from a practical point of view. Czyrek interjected that this was most important. Lord Carrington explained the economic pressures on the UK budget. The same pressures existed in other countries. We had to weigh our priorities against our means. Within those means Poland would have a high priority.

10. In answer to questions M. Czyrek gave an imprecise answer about what might happen on 10 December if the Poles were unable to find funds to pay the banks.

11. Lord Carrington informed M. Czyrek that he would give an account of these talks to his colleagues at the European Council on 26/27 November.[7]

Ends.

We will be briefing the US embassy here on 23 November.[8]

[6] Lord Trefgarne, who met Mr Czyrek after lunch, asked him what the Poles hoped to obtain from their membership of the IMF. Apart from direct credits, Czyrek replied that the Government hoped that it would help the population to understand the necessity for difficult decisions.

[7] See No. 108, note 2. The Poles had specifically asked that the visit should take place before this European Council meeting hoping that it would consider economic assistance. The FCO informed European partners of the visit and explained that Lord Carrington intended to listen to Czyrek but give no specific commitment apart from continuing to support efforts by the Polish Government to solve its political and economic problems (Mr Broomfield to Mr Fall, 19 November 1981).

[8] Also on that day Mr James reported to London a meeting with Mr Czyrek on his return from London. He found him in good spirits but disappointed about the $500 million credit. In a press conference, Czyrek recalled that it was his third meeting with British Foreign Secretary—which was evidence of 'intensive Anglo-Polish dialogue'—and said that the talks had concentrated on Anglo-Polish economic relations (Warsaw tel. No. 808).

No. 105

Letter from Mr Murray (TUC)[1] to Mrs Thatcher, 23 November 1981
(PREM 19/56)

Dear Prime Minister,

Poland: European Council

You will be aware that Solidarity in Poland has made a public appeal to Governments, and in particular those in the European Community, to undertake extraordinary and immediate assistance to Poland.[2] Solidarity has also approached national trade union centres including the TUC with a request that they should do all in their power to obtain from Government and intergovernmental institutions assistance to overcome the grave economic and social difficulties confronting Poland.

The most serious immediate problem in Poland is the acute shortage of most kinds of basic food, which can only become worse in the coming winter months, and could increase political instability and civil and industrial unrest. Our Finance and General Purposes Committee have today discussed the position, and consider that it would clearly be in the interests of the United Kingdom and of all other European countries for Poland to receive all possible assistance in meeting its basic food needs. I believe that that view is shared by all our colleagues in the Western European trade union Movement.

The forthcoming meeting in London of the European Council, and your chairmanship of it, provides an opportunity for the UK to give a lead to the European Community in providing assistance to Poland in the form of food aid. That would help Poland to avoid massive unrest, the consequences of which might be extremely dangerous for Europe as a whole and for Poland in particular. We would hope that, if additional food aid is made available, means could be found by arrangement with the Polish authorities to enable Solidarity to assist with its distribution inside Poland. The involvement of Solidarity would, I am sure, help it to play the constructive, practical role its leadership seeks.

[1] See No. 91, note 3.

[2] The 'Appeal to Workers and Trade Unions of Western Europe' which had been issued on 19 November stated that Solidarity enjoyed the support of workers all over the world. In the face of economic and social difficulties in Poland they had put forward a programme to pull the country out of the crisis. The appeal requested help as it would take time to improve the situation, acknowledging that Solidarity was 'well aware that the future of Poland lies in the hands of the workers whose efforts are the major element in leading the country out of the crisis'. Solidarity would make sure that aid would be properly distributed. Solidarity concluded: 'Solidarity knows neither frontiers nor limits'.

On 1 December the Secretary of the International Department of the TUC had also informed Mr Toms, the FCO Labour Adviser, that the TUC had received a letter from the International Confederation of Free Trade Unions concerning the Solidarity appeal. He drew his attention to the fact that the letter had specified that Mr Wałęsa had indicated that the appeal was not limited to European trade union organisations. Solidarity had also asked to be kept fully informed of the action taken by the governments so as to be able to inform the Polish workers and to be able to monitor the use of such assistance to Poland.

I hope that you will agree that the issue of food aid for Poland should be included in the agenda of the Council meeting; and that the Government will strongly support the requests for assistance which have been made recently.

Yours sincerely,
LIONEL MURRAY

No. 106

Minute from Mr Broomfield to Mr J. Bullard, 27 November 1981
Confidential (FCO 28/4485, ENP 014/1)

Poland

1. Mr Bisztyga called at 0900 hours this morning. He had a personal message to transmit from Mr Czyrek to Lord Carrington. He was at pains to stress the personal nature of the message. It was not a formal communication from the Polish to the British Government

2. Mr Bisztyga read out the message. I attach our note of it.

3. In explanation Mr Bisztyga made the following comments;

(*a*) the message followed an analysis of the economic and political situation by the leadership on 26 November (presumably in preparation for the VI Party Plenum);

(*b*) the leadership's analysis had taken account both of the debt rescheduling talks in Paris as well as Mr Czyrek's own talks with the Secretary of State.

4. I asked Mr Bisztyga which of the economic problems facing the Polish Government was considered to be the most acute: paying the banks on 10 December; getting enough credit for 1982; or food supplies.

5. Mr Bisztyga said that the first priority was sufficient credit in 1982. Without it Polish industry would seize up because it would not be possible to import raw materials and semi-finished products. The second priority was the $500 million for the banks and the third was food. He did not think that the Poles would be able to pay the banks. But food supplies although difficult were not yet critical.

6. I asked whether the political situation had deteriorated further since Mr Czyrek's meeting with Lord Carrington. Mr Bisztyga said that the spread of disorder into clearly political fields like the students—'on the basis of clear planning'—and the opposition of extreme elements in Solidarity to Walesa's moderate line, were highly disturbing.

7. I told Mr Bisztyga that as far as I knew Poland had already been discussed at the Council. He repeated that he hoped the political importance of the issues would be taken into consideration when arriving at economic decisions.

8. My assessment of the message is that it is an emotional response to the growing realisation of the intractable nature of the problem they are now facing.

9. Mr Bisztyga admitted that he had known Mr Czyrek for many years but had never received an emotional message of this sort.

10. I would recommend that when the Secretary of State sees Mr Bisztyga on 30 November for his farewell call, he should ask him to take back to Warsaw on 1 December a personal acknowledgement of the message together with a brief account of discussion at the European Council. Lord Carrington might add that he hoped the Poles were making their views equally clear to their other main Western

partners, and above all, to the Americans. We could develop this in the briefing that we will in any case be submitting for the call.

11. Thereafter any economic decisions taken at the Plenum can be considered at the Economic Directors' Meeting in Paris on 2 December. Political developments, including any views expressed to Lord Trefgarne in Warsaw[1] (30 November-2 December) can be taken account of in the Political Directors' Meeting preceding the Quadripartite Ministerial Dinner in Brussels on 9 December.

N. H. R. A. BROOMFIELD

ENCLOSURE IN NO. 106

Note of oral message passed by the Polish Ambassador from the Polish Foreign Minister to the Secretary of State

1. Mr Czyrek asked for a more flexible approach to be taken by the West. The difficulty of maintaining the economic situation to secure the process of reform and 'renewal' was becoming acute. If the economic problems could not be alleviated this would have dangers for the 'normalisation' and 'stabilisation' programmes in Poland. This assessment was the result of an analysis by the leadership concerning the foreign trade balance and likely supply of raw materials to Poland in 1982. Mr Czyrek concluded by saying that time was running out—the situation was becoming dramatic.[2]

[1] See No. 109.

[2] The Secretary of State gave Mr Bisztyga a personal reply to pass to Mr Czyrek which stated that he understood the problems Poland was facing and the difficulties for the Polish leadership. The UK would, within its limits, continue to do what it could to help but found, like others, that there were constraints upon what they could do (FCO tel. No. 628 to Warsaw of 30 November; FCO 28/4529, ENP 090/1).

No. 107

Note by the Joint Intelligence Committee, 3 December 1981
UK Confidential, Cabinet Office, JIC (81)(N) 64

Implications of developments in Poland for other East European Countries

1. In this Note we examine the reaction so far of other East European Warsaw Pact countries to developments in Poland and the longer-term political and economic implications for them (other than for repayment of their debts to the West) both if the Soviet Union intervenes militarily in Poland and if it does not. Developments within these countries are of course determined principally by domestic issues and, to a lesser extent, by the state of international relations, but both of these will be influenced by what happens in Poland. The military implications for the Warsaw Pact were examined in a separate Note, JIC(81)(N) 52.[1]

Background

2. The East European countries have been suffering from steadily increasing economic difficulties since the mid-1970s. The rigidities of their planning systems

[1] Not printed.

and the inefficiencies of their production arising out of insufficient incentives, inflexible price-formation systems and low quality products, have made it difficult for them to adjust to the energy crisis and the recession in the West. Misdirected investment and over-eagerness to borrow from the West compounded these problems. By the end of the decade there was a general slowing down in economic growth, virtual stagnation in living standards and a growing hard currency debt burden. While all East European countries shared these problems to a greater or lesser extent and even Hungary, with its pragmatic approach, has not been able to avoid them altogether, Poland was a particularly bad case. Indeed, living standards in Poland were declining in real terms and the debt burden was by far the worst in Eastern Europe.

3. The Polish crisis was sparked off by sudden price increases imposed in an attempt to deal with some of these problems. But the way in which the crisis developed in Poland was determined by political circumstances which are markedly different from those of any other East European country. Among Poland's most striking deviations from the Soviet model are its strong Church and largely private agriculture. In addition the workforce has a history of sporadic revolts under communist rule, mostly sparked off by sudden increases in prices though fuelled by wide ranging distrust of a series of Party leaders who were felt to have betrayed earlier promises. Under Gierek a broad range of underground dissident activities was tolerated. The Polish situation in August 1980 was thus very different from that of any of its allies.

Impact of Poland so far

4. In spite of the dissimilarities between Poland and their own countries, East European leaders reacted with varying degrees of alarm to the wave of strikes in Poland in the summer of 1980, the establishment of an independent trade union and its subsequent legalisation, and the mass revolt against the way the country had been governed. Czechoslovakia and the GDR for various reasons displayed the greatest anxiety; Hungarian leaders took a more relaxed view. In the event the short term impact of Polish developments has been relatively slight, particularly in the political sphere. The demand for new and more representative trade unions, for Party reform and for greater freedom of speech has not spread to other countries; the economic repercussions for the rest of the area from the dislocation of the Polish economy, though serious, have not been intolerable; and some of the economic effects—for instance, the need to divert additional exports of foodstuffs and consumer goods to Poland—have only served to reduce further the level of sympathy for Polish workers and exacerbate historical antipathies where these exist.

5. Western attitudes to the provision of credit to East European countries have become more cautious since Poland got into difficulties, partly because of a loss of faith in the Soviet 'umbrella' which had previously been expected to avert the risk of a major default. Hungary's application on 4 November to join the International Monetary Fund (IMF) was probably motivated by a long-standing desire to strengthen Hungary's economic independence as well as by practical considerations such as a desire to participate in World Bank projects and to move towards convertibility of the forint; but its precise timing was probably the result of a lifting of Soviet objections to IMF membership brought about by Poland's desperate need for additional Western finance.

6. East European leaders are concerned about the longer-term implications of developments in Poland and, together with their Soviet mentors, they have been

examining what caused the Polish crisis and how such developments might be avoided in other countries. Despite the propaganda about Western subversion it is generally agreed that the blame rests on the policies of the Gierek regime. (To blame the fundamentals of the system is of course unthinkable.) The Soviet view of the lessons to be drawn was set out in a politburo statement of 22 August on Brezhnev's series of meetings with East European leaders in the Crimea. This referred to the need to strengthen links with the masses, perfect socialist democracy, pursue a realistic economic policy without running into excessive debt to the capitalist states, educate working people to the spirit of internationalism, display revolutionary vigilance, and give a timely and resolute rebuff to anti-socialist forces. In other words, it recommended a mixture of propaganda, economic measures and repression. Individual East European countries have singled out particular areas for attention. The more developed countries have dwelt on the need to protect consumer supplies, adopt sound investment policies and avoid excessive foreign debt. The Hungarians accept that an independent trade union could in principle play a positive role in economic development, though they have joined the Czechoslovaks and East Germans in criticism of Solidarity as it has taken on an overtly political role.

7. So far there have been few changes in policy in Eastern Europe to implement this analysis. The granting of a 5-day week to the Polish strikers last autumn clearly influenced the Hungarians to speed up the gradual introduction of a 5-day week for their own workers. Ceausescu has criticised the relative neglect of agriculture in Romania, but there has been little sign so far of a significant change in the direction of his economic policy. There are also signs of a slight strengthening of the hardline element in the Czechoslovak Party Presidium: changes in the party and Government in June suggest that, although the Party intends to persevere with the modest improvements in the economic system, it is determined to ensure that these limited reforms are supervised by people who will keep the process under strict control. In the latter part of 1980 there was some anxiety of Czechoslovakia, Hungary and elsewhere to prove that the trade unions in those countries were by and large doing their job properly, although mild hints were given that they could do even better. No changes in the legal standing, mode of operation or even in the leaderships of the unions were made except in Romania, where the changes were purely cosmetic.

8. Polish developments do not appear to have given any particular stimulus to dissident intellectual activities in Eastern Europe nor to have affected the handling by regimes of the dissident problem. Those regimes which already had such a problem, notably the GDR and Czechoslovakia, had dealt firmly with it. It has proved less tractable in Czechoslovakia than in the GDR, where it is a less important factor. In Czechoslovakia there may not be an increase in the frequency of trials, but the sentences will probably be more severe. The Hungarians also appear to be anxious about their smaller but growing dissident groups, but there have been no trials so far.

The Future Alternatives

9. Any attempt to look at what will happen in Eastern Europe in the next decade must be highly speculative. A number of domestic and international factors will influence developments in the region. But these will in turn be affected by what happens in Poland. Whether the Soviet Union intervenes militarily will of course be crucial. But even without Soviet intervention much will depend on whether Poland continues indefinitely in its depressed economic state, or can turn the

corner and achieve at least a modest prosperity; and whether Solidarity remains a powerful force in Poland or survives, if at all, only in emasculated form. We look at four possible scenarios, but a very wide range of situations is of course possible.

(*a*) *Intervention*

10. Whatever the circumstances of Soviet intervention it would almost certainly be followed by a period of social, political and economic chaos in Poland, with widespread strikes and dislocation, active or passive resistance by the population, and possible economic sabotage. In the short term any disruption of the transport and pipeline systems and interruption in Polish exports would affect all the economies of Eastern Europe, although those of Bulgaria and Romania to a lesser extent. If Western economic sanctions were imposed against countries involved in joint Warsaw Pact action, as they all fear, this would increase the strains. Hungary in particular currently does 47 per cent of its foreign trade with non-CMEA countries. Although Western sanctions would be unlikely to last more than a few years, their consequences could persist for much longer. The Soviet Union's ability to provide economic support would also be impaired by the cost of intervention and occupation, and the effects of Western sanctions on the Soviet Union itself. In addition, Western financial institutions would be likely to take an even less favourable view of the economic prospects of most East European countries and hence of their creditworthiness, whatever the policies of Western governments. The East European countries are already facing the prospect of very low growth over the next few years, after a period of which rising living standards have helped to buy the acquiescence of the population but also increased expectations. Any deterioration in living standards following Soviet intervention in Poland would lead to increased consumer dissatisfaction and possible unrest, necessitating more repressive internal policies.

11. Intervention would probably be accompanied by Soviet attempts to impose tighter control over its East European allies, as happened after the invasion of Czechoslovakia in 1968. The Soviet Union would probably insist on a return to more orthodox policies internally, though economic reform programmes would probably not be affected in view of the overwhelming need not to harm the already hard-pressed economies even further. In the hostile East-West climate created by intervention there would be Soviet pressure for even greater foreign policy co-ordination, and the East European countries would be forced to adopt a harsh propaganda line which would further exacerbate relations with Western countries. This effect would be increased if the West imposed a political freeze on the whole of Eastern Europe. All this could mean a general turning in upon themselves among the Warsaw Pact countries, a fact with [*sic*] would be accepted as inevitable but could still lead to a resentment against the Soviet Union among at least more liberal East European allies—at the popular level if not that of regimes. All Soviet pressure on Eastern Europe to increase its defence efforts could also sour relations. A strong build-up of resentments in Eastern Europe against either the Soviet Union or repressive domestic regimes could lead to a further explosion in a few years' time.

(*b*) *Continued Stalemate*

12. Poland could carry on for some time in a position slightly better than the present stalemate, without achieving real economic recovery but managing to avoid a slide into chaos and consequent Soviet intervention. This would not be without certain advantages for other East European regimes. Economic disruption would cause them some damage, but a readjustment of trading patterns and co-

operation agreements could get over much of this in the longer run, though at some cost. The East European regimes would seek to blame Solidarity for Poland's depressed economy and poor living standards. Other East European workers would not be encouraged to challenge Party authority and embark on a road which would set at risk their own living standards in the uncertain hope of broader freedoms and a greater say in the running of their country. Such a situation in Poland would however be inherently unstable. Prolonged economic stagnation would probably lead to a weakening of Solidarity and resumption of Party control, or to a further and more serious challenge to Party authority leading to intervention.

(*c*) *Resumption of Party control*

13. This is the option clearly favoured by the Soviet Union and other East European countries. What they would like to see is a Poland in which Party authority was restored, Solidarity, if it survived, did so only as a strictly trade union organisation shorn of its radical wing and its political ambitions, and the country again became a reliable Warsaw Pact and CMEA partner. We find it difficult to envisage how this situation could be brought about quickly without provoking a general breakdown in law and order leading to intervention, but it could perhaps be achieved by a long slow process of attrition. In any event this scenario would have the least serious implications for East European regimes in terms of political infection. Independent trade unions would not have survived as a permanent and powerful factor in society, and the spectre of successful challenge to Party authority would be removed. The economic spillover effects would depend on whether the Polish authorities could get the economy moving again—a difficult task in the face of a probably sullen and unco-operative workforce. A resumption of Party control in Poland would not significantly affect Western bankers' attitudes to credit for East European countries, which would depend on the economic prospects for individual countries.

(*d*) *Recovery in Poland*

14. The most unwelcome outcome for the other East European regimes (and the Soviet Union) would be the emergence of a pluralist and economically successful system in Poland, one in which Solidarity would remain a strong but positive force, able to defend the rights and freedom already won but not pushing for changes which would trigger off Soviet intervention (and paying lip-service to the leading role of the Party), and at the same time making a powerful contribution to economic reconstruction. With sustained determination and immense effort on all sides this might lead to the beginnings of an economic revival within 2-3 years, if a solution can also be found to Poland's external debt problem. Debt servicing and repayment will put a substantial brake on economic recovery. While default would remove the immediate problem of heavy debt servicing, it would limit Poland's ability to import raw materials and spare parts needed to get the economy going again. On the other hand even massive Western financial help would not guarantee economic recovery unless an overall political settlement is reached in Poland.

15. If Poland could regain a reasonable level of prosperity while preserving its political gains, the Polish model would become highly attractive to the peoples of Eastern Europe, though the essential historical and social differences would make direct emulation unlikely. If they were faced with a broadly-based demand for a more open and genuinely democratic society, the regimes would have to decide whether to attempt to suppress such aspirations (a policy which would certainly be urged on them by Moscow), thereby creating dangerous internal tensions; to permit just sufficient change to act as a safety-valve—though, as the Poles have

discovered, such a process is difficult to stop once it is set in motion; or to undertake radical changes which they would hope would give a firmer basis of legitimacy to the Communist regimes—though this, too, is a process that could easily get out of hand. We discount the possibility that any East European regime would contemplate, or the Soviet Union permit, any change that would lead the country to abandon Communism or the Warsaw Pact. How regimes would actually react to popular pressure for change would depend on a combination of circumstances which we cannot foresee—the current state of internal and international relations, the composition of the leadership, the economic position and other factors. Their creditworthiness would depend again on the actual economic prospects for each country, so long as domestic policies fell short of outright repression.

Outlook

16. Soviet intervention would create the greatest immediate problems for the whole region, with severe economic disruption, a tightening up in internal policies, and a closing of ranks in the Warsaw Pact and CMEA in the face of a hostile external environment. A continuation of the present dislocation short of total breakdown in Poland or a resumption of Party control would probably have the least impact on the rest of Eastern Europe; the economic effects could be limited over the longer term and the risk of the spread of Polish ideas would be minimised. The emergence of a prosperous pluralist Poland would present the greatest dangers to its allies. We cannot judge at this stage how the regimes might respond to pressures for change. In all probability the response would vary greatly from country to country. But, whatever the outcome in Poland, at least short of intervention, other regimes will have been encouraged in the view that Moscow's requirements in terms of political orthodoxy are not so strict as they might have thought, and could be encouraged to adopt limited reforms which would ease internal problems without endangering the key levers of Party control.

17. Before the Polish crisis we assessed[2] that the economic problems of Eastern Europe would worsen during the eighties, that economic policies might have to be adopted that could lead to unrest, and that differences between the Soviet Union and its East European allies over how to deal with these problems could cause strains in bilateral relations. The socio-political background in each of these countries is very different and the regimes can be expected to deal in different ways with their problems, many of which are similar to those of Poland. A precise repetition of Polish events in other countries is therefore unlikely. But the underlying economic weaknesses which lie beneath what has happened in Poland are common to all the countries of Eastern Europe; and their common systems of government and their relationship with the Soviet Union limit their ability to respond to challenges and change. Moreover, whatever happens in Poland the crisis there has exacerbated and will continue to exacerbate the economic problems of its allies.

18. The Polish crisis has highlighted some of the fundamental defects, both political and economic, of the East European systems, the limited extent to which the Soviet Union can control developments short of the use of overwhelming force, and the divisions existing behind the facade of socialist unity. None of these features in new, but all are likely to be strengthened by recent developments.

[2] A footnote to the original text read: 'JIC(80)7 dated 7 February 1980 "The relationship between the East European countries and the Soviet Union".'

Strains and stresses within and between the members of the Warsaw Pact are likely to increase in the eighties. A period of social and political ferment in one or other of the East European countries is more likely within the next decade, but we cannot at present foresee what form this will take or what the Soviet reaction to it will be.[3]

[3] The note was approved by the Committee at its meeting on 3 December.

No. 108

Letter from Mrs Thatcher to Mr Murray (TUC), 4 December 1981
(FCO 28/4543, ENP 212/3)

Dear Mr Murray,

Thank you for your letter of 23 November[1] about economic assistance to Poland. As foreseen in our discussions on 25 November, the Council did indeed discuss the situation in Poland. You may be interested to see the enclosed copy of the Council's conclusions on Poland,[2] about which you will have seen press reports.

The Government is very conscious of the potential dangers of the situation and of the food shortages which Poland faces. Thus, together with our partners in the European Community, we have over the past year played a substantial role in supplying food and agricultural products to Poland. The Community budget has borne the cost of the special discount, while individual Member States have made available the necessary credit to cover the products they have supplied. Under decisions taken in December 1980 and in April and May this year the Community has responded to specific Polish requests by making available large amounts of food from Community stocks at special prices (an average 15 per cent discount from normal world prices). These offers have so far included 452,500 tonnes of barley (all from the United Kingdom), 272,500 tonnes of wheat, 100,000 tonnes of meat (including 3,000 tonnes of beef from the United Kingdom), 40,000 tonnes of butter (including 10,000 tonnes from the united Kingdom) and 100,000 tonnes of sugar.

On 7 October the Community approved a further offer of food and agricultural products to be made available to Poland in the last quarter of 1981 on the same special terms as the earlier offers. The United Kingdom will supply the 25,000 tonnes of barley included in that offer. At the same time the Community agreed to consider proposals by the European Commission for further deliveries to Poland in

[1] No. 105.

[2] Not printed. On 30 November Lord Carrington sent to all European posts the statement issued by the European Council on 27 November following its meeting at which Lord Carrington reported the Polish Foreign Minister's visit to London on 20 November (No. 104). The statement referred to the Council's recent acceptance of the European Parliament's initiative to release additional sums to Poland for food at special prices through Community programmes. The Council had reaffirmed willingness—'within the limits of the means of the Community and its Member States and in collaboration with others'— to respond to the Polish Government's requests for continued support in the recovery of their economy. It believed rescheduling the Polish debt and new credit would make an important contribution. (London COREU CPE/MUL/ETR 3916; FCO 28/4505, ENP 021/4).

the first quarter of 1982. These proposals are likely to come forward in the near future. Meanwhile, on 24 November, the Budget Council agreed, in response to a proposal made by the European Parliament, that an additional sum of 10 mecu (about £5.8m) should be made available to the Commission to assist the supply of food from the Community to Poland. And in August a resolution was adopted by the Council making it possible for Member States to deliver to Poland, free of charge, fruit and vegetables withdrawn from the Community market in accordance with the provisions of the Common Agriculture Policy.

The Community's contribution therefore has been substantial, and the UK has played a full part in that contribution. As the European Council statement makes clear, the Community and its Member States will continue to assist Poland's economic recovery within the limits of the resources at their disposal and in collaboration with the efforts of others. At the same time, as I explained to you and other representatives of the European Trade Union Conference at our meeting on 25 November, there is clearly no easy solution to Poland's economic problems. Food supplies are only part of the answer. And there are limits to what any of Poland's Western creditors can do in the face of their own economic problems.

I note that you hope that the Polish Government and Solidarity can join together to make arrangements for the distribution of necessary foodstuffs throughout Poland. This is something of course for the Poles themselves to decide. It is encouraging that the Government and Solidarity are now jointly discussing economic issues, including action to end the economic crisis and to alleviate the consequences of winter. As I am sure you will agree, no amount of external aid will by itself solve the economic problems which Poland faces. The only people who can finally overcome these problems are the Poles themselves, by agreeing on solutions and putting them into effect as quickly as possible.

Yours sincerely,
MARGARET THATCHER

No 109

Minute from Lord Trefgarne to Lord Carrington, 4 December 1981
Confidential (Trefgarne Papers, FCO)

Poland

1. You may like to have my impressions of the visit I paid to Warsaw from 20 November - 2 December. Mr James' telegram summarises the main points and events. Because of the importance and topicality of this subject, I am giving you a fuller account than is normal.

2. Our flight out was delayed by the first serious fall of snow in Poland. An inch of snow makes the city of Warsaw look less grey than it really is; but the change of season also heralded the formal opening of the winter campaign between Solidarity and the Government.

3. The programme organised by the Ambassador was excellent. I was able to get, at first hand, views from all the main participants in the political struggle which is now under way. I also paid a brief visit to the URSUS tractor factory.

4. Not surprisingly two main subjects dominated the discussions: how to institutionalise the actual division of power in Poland today and the imminence, or otherwise, of economic collapse.

5. The economic question was uppermost in *Dobrosielski's* mind. He devoted practically the whole of the first restricted session of talks to it. I took him through the European Council Statement stressing the financial constraints on what the West could do. Dobrosielski expressed clear disappointment when I told him of the UK's contribution. He was, however, relieved when I clarified our position on rescheduling. He appeared to have been misinformed about the results of the last Creditors' Meeting with the Poles in Paris and thought that terms for rescheduling in 1982 would be worse than in 1981. Dobrosielski ended by giving me a lengthy dissertation on the acuteness of the economic situation and the political consequences of an economic collapse on much the same lines as that given to you by Czyrek on 20 November. I am sure that we are far from hearing the Poles' last word on this. They will be back for additional commercial credits in 1982 which they maintain are vital for their industrial recovery (and political stability) and thus ultimately to their ability, one day, to repay their Western creditors.

6. I got no clear answer to my question: what will happen on 10 December with the banks? I was left with the impression that the Poles will either somehow find the money (possibly by completely emptying their coffers) or the banks will agree to defer payment yet again while some other arrangements are made.

7. *Olszowski* struck me as a powerful and intelligent figure. It was clear to me why he is regarded as the mostly likely successor to Jaruzelski if the latter fails. It was significant that he agreed to see me. I understand that I was the first Western Minister he has seen in the last eighteen months. While he too concentrated on the acuteness of the economic crisis he was more optimistic about the chances of getting agreement to a Front of National Unity. At one point he referred to its establishment 'in the first half of December'. I believe, however, he was deliberately overstating his case, possibly to demonstrate the reasonableness of the Party. He referred throughout to the 'main role' (not 'leading role') of the Party in any Front. The Party would be able to live with the fact that its views were not always accepted.

8. There is clearly a lot of hard bargaining ahead. Olszowski was still talking of Solidarity being one among seven equal members. What, however, was obvious was that Olszowski accepted, as a fact of political life in Poland today, that some new constitutional arrangement which more nearly reflects the division of power, has to be found.

9. With Olszowski I raised one of the central questions. Was political agreement a pre-condition for economic reform (price rises etc) or was economic reform necessary to ease the path of political adjustment. The Government has a vested interest in arguing for continued economic assistance from the West to help their economic reform plans along. My own view is that without agreement on some new power-sharing arrangement, be it the Front of National Unity or some other, there is no real chance of lasting economic reform or revival. Indeed Olszowski admitted that for the Government to introduce price rises without national consent would be a futile and dangerous exercise.

10. *Archbishop Glemp* struck me as a quiet, shrewd man very much involved in the political power struggle. His style is laconic, but unlike most Poles, very much to the point. He considered the Party a spent force. Some new political arrangement was necessary. Solidarity on its own could not fill the bill. At one

point he remarked that if no new political force emerged the Church might have to speak directly to the Russians. He declined to comment further when we asked him exactly what he meant. Glemp's sympathies clearly lay much more on the side of Solidarity than the Party. He admitted that the Church had benefitted from the concessions obtained by Solidarity (access to media etc). We discussed the plans for the Pope's visit to Poland in August next year. This will obviously be a major political, as well as religious, event.

11. I had a long talk with *Mr Lech Walesa* over breakfast. He was open, direct and self-assured. Although our meeting took place during the final phase of the breaking of the fire cadets strike he appeared unperturbed. In his view the revolution, and he stressed that that was what it was, could continue peacefully and slowly or become sudden and violent. The Russians would not invade because they knew the Poles would fight, even though they would lose. The only way to get the economy going was to 'banish ideology from economic management'. Solidarity would not fall for any power-sharing gambit which made them hostages of the Party as had happened in the 1945/46 National Front of Unity. If the political struggle took time, then so be it. The economic problems could wait. Coal production was being increased. The miners would work on Sundays if necessary. But not under the present system. Solidarity was not a political party. After a new political power-sharing structure was agreed and tested, Solidarity might break up into separate unions and some elements might become a political party. But the main priority now was to carry through the peaceful revolution.

12. Walesa is a remarkable man. He appeared confident of the strength of his position and the likelihood that economic failure would be blamed on the Government and not Solidarity. His longer view may stem from his religious conviction. The Madonna worn so prominently on his coat lapel is no empty symbol.

13. Following my meeting with Walesa I was subjected to a 45-minute lecture on Polish economic reform by *Władysław Baka*, the Minister responsible for it. The draft laws which are now under discussion in the Parliament go farther in the direction of decentralisation and market economy than anything which now exists in Eastern Europe. Whether they emerge in that form, and even more problematically, whether they can thereafter be implemented, remains to be seen. I have my doubts. In the short term they will, if anything, add to Poland's difficulties.

14. *URSUS* was impressive. It will eventually be the biggest tractor factory in the world. Several vast factory buildings house a large collection of Western high technology machinery. If it works out, this project will make a major contribution to Polish agriculture and to export earnings. The British technical advisers there who cultivate good relations with the Poles seem to have a thorough plan for both handover and training of locals on the equipment. The prospects are therefore not unpromising even though I am sure it will test the Poles managerial skills to the limit to make full use of everything they have got. For the UK it has become the major flag-carrier of our economic assistance to Poland and I believe we should make the most of it.

15. I regret that I can come up with no clear analysis or simple solution. What, however, is clear to me is that the key question of how genuine power-sharing in a communist state in Eastern Europe is now being decided. All the main participants acknowledge that some form of rearrangement is essential. Two of them want it to be real and irreversible. If they succeed they will have achieved a major and

possibly historic breakthrough. To the extent that we can I therefore believe that we should continue to support what is happening in Poland both politically and economically.

TREFGARNE

No. 110

Letter from Mr Makepeace (Prague) to Mr Wilson, 9 December 1981

Restricted (FCO 28/4423, ENC 015/1)

Dear Fraser,

Dissident Affairs

1. I reported in my letter of 4 December the start of a press campaign against dissidents and émigrés, which set out to demonstrate that they were all in the pay of the CIA.[1] A further radio programme in this series was broadcast yesterday and reported today in *Rudé Právo*[2] under the headline 'Anything for Dollars'. To ensure that no one misses it, the programme will apparently be re-broadcast this evening.

2. The content was much the same as last week. No further evidence of CIA involvement was produced, although last week's inconclusive quote was repeated. The attack centred on the activities of the Palach press[3] and featured extensive recordings of conversation in, and telephone calls from, Tigrid's flat in Paris.[4] The only other point of note was that two dissident contacts in Czechoslovakia were mentioned by name (although the recording was very indistinct at this point). One was Šabatová,[5] the other perhaps Bartoš (not a name known to us, although there are three Chartists named Bartošek).

3. Once again, it is remarkable that the Czechoslovaks are prepared to make such a public display of their clandestine activities abroad. Interestingly, dissident circles now confirm that the voices in the recordings appear to be genuine. It would therefore seem that they are the fruit of a major clandestine operation by the Czechoslovaks in the first half of this year, and that perhaps they are being broadcast at the behest of hard-liners, who wish to force the hand of those who seek to delay the expected show trial for fear of international repercussions.

[1] Mr Makepeace had reported that the authorities had launched a campaign to demonstrate that the Czechoslovaks—arrested after the seizure of material in a French vehicle at the border—were in league with émigré groups and through them with the CIA. On 3 December the radio broadcast what were claimed to be recordings of conversations between leading émigrés—which thus clearly indicated that they bugged their conversations. Makepeace thought that the Czechoslovak authorities' aim to scare the émigrés might have outweighed any offence caused to the governments concerned. It could also have been a warning to Czechoslovaks at home that they could be overheard.

[2] The official newspaper of the Communist Party of Czechoslovakia.

[3] Based in London, the Palach Press was formed in February 1976 to provide the media, libraries and individuals with up-to-date information, in-depth interviews and political documents about the current situation in Czechoslovakia and Poland. It was managed by Jan Kavan, a Czech opponent who spent 20 years in exile in the UK.

[4] Czech author, publicist and essayist, he founded the exile quarterly *Svědectví* ('Testimony'), the main political and cultural review of the Czechoslovak exile. He had been in exile in Paris since 1960.

[5] Anna Šabatová was a Chartist, VONS activist, daughter of Jaroslav Šabata and wife of Petr Uhl. When her husband was imprisoned she edited and produced *Information on Charter 77*, 1979-84.

4. Charter 77 too has been active in recent days. In a letter from the Charter spokesmen to Husák, they called for an amnesty for political prisoners to be announced at Christmas. This, they argued, would show the strength of the authorities, rather than their weakness. In reference to the authorities' increasingly frank accounts of the country's economic problems, they declared that all should work together to solve these, but that this could only be done in freedom.

5. A further letter from the same source, which is expected to cause even greater irritation on the part of the authorities, was addressed to the Soviet Ambassador in Prague, Botvin. Claiming to represent a good body of Czechoslovak thought, they asked the Ambassador to intervene on their behalf in the Sakharov case.[6] On humanitarian grounds they called for action to stop the loss of the life of such a great scientist and former Nobel Prize winner.

6. Whilst there is no news of the trial itself, rumours suggest that Kyncl's position may be deteriorating, both literally and figuratively.[7] It is thought that he may have been returned to the prison hospital because of further serious health problems, and also that he may have been singled out by the authorities as the main target in the expected show trial.

7. A report emanating from Vienna suggests that Hodic, the Czechoslovak informer who returned to Prague amidst a blaze of publicity earlier in the year, but has since dropped from sight, has been admitted to a mental institution. This may serve to confirm rumours prevalent in the summer that he had in fact been pressured by the Czechoslovaks into giving information against émigré circles, perhaps by threats of action against his daughter, still resident in Czechoslovakia.[8]

8. Finally, not exactly a dissident manifestation, but certainly one of which the authorities disapproved, occurred yesterday on the anniversary of the death of John Lennon. Groups of young people gathered to honour his memory at the 'tomb' which has been set up opposite the French Embassy.[9] The police were also there in force, and took down the identities of those concerned. There was no protest of any

[6] On 22 January 1980 Dr Andrei Sakharov, nuclear physicist, Nobel Peace Prize winner and leader of the dissident movement was arrested, charged with anti-Soviet activities, and exiled to the closed city of Gorky.

[7] Karel Kyncl was a Chartist, former journalist, opponent of the regime since 1968 and former prisoner of conscience, who in 1980 decided to emigrate as he had been forced to perform menial jobs. The UK had granted him political asylum, but before he could leave he was arrested on 6 May 1981, together with a number of other Czechoslovak dissidents on charges of subversion 'in collusion with a foreign power' and 'on a large scale'. He faced a prison sentence of up to ten years. His health condition deteriorated seriously during pre-trial detention. He was released in March 1982 and after further criminal proceeding allowed to emigrate at the end of 1982. He arrived in the UK in February 1983.

[8] Josef Hodic was a historian dismissed in 1969 from his post at the Military Academy of Politics. A Chartist, he emigrated to Austria in 1977. At the end of June 1981, he suddenly disappeared from Vienna. Radio Prague announced that a prominent and trustworthy member of the Czech Secret Service identified as 'J.H.' had returned to Czechoslovakia after a successful long mission abroad investigating 'traitors' activities. It is unclear whether he was indeed a Czech agent or the victim of blackmailing by the Czech authorities about his two daughters and five grandchildren living in Czechoslovakia. As a result of his sudden 'disappearance' from Austria, a State visit by President Husák to Austria was postponed indefinitely. Dr Bruno Kreisky, the Austrian Chancellor, told journalists that the initiative to call off the State visit had been taken in Prague (*The Times*, 4 July and 10 September 1981).

[9] After the murder of the Beatle in 1980, the 'Lennon Wall' displayed graffiti and pieces of lyrics from the Beatles' songs, as well as grievances. At the time, Western pop songs were banned.

kind, but it was nonetheless a significant incident in a country where a gathering of more than about ten people is automatically regarded as potentially seditious.[10]

Yours ever,
RICHARD MAKEPEACE

[10] On 18 December after martial law had been declared in Poland, Mr Makepeace reported to Mr Wilson the Czech authorities' determined effort to stop dissidents making statements about events in Poland, as well as increasing surveillance of Western journalists and diplomats.

No. 111

Mr James (Warsaw) to Lord Carrington, 10 December 1981, 10.15 a.m.[1]

Tel. No. 867 Immediate, Restricted (FCO 28/4486, ENP 014/1)

Polish Situation

1. There was a series of important meetings yesterday. Glemp met Walesa and Zablooki,[2] the head of the Catholic Znak faction, in Parliament. Jaruzelski met in turn all three leaders of the Catholic factions in Parliament. The published reports give very little indication of what was discussed, although the report of Jaruzelski's meeting referred to the 'critical' situation in the country. This is an advance on yesterday's reports which only described the situation as 'worsening'.[3]

2. We understand that the meeting between Glemp and Walesa lasted three hours and that attempts were made to arrange a meeting between Walesa and Jaruzelski. As Walesa does not have to return to Gdansk for tomorrow's meeting of the National Commission until this evening—and at a pinch need not return for it at all—it remains a possibility that a meeting with Jaruzelski could still take place. But the continuing spate of meetings is a clear indication of the political tension here, well illustrated by the radical Solidarity Factory Committee at the Paris Commune shipyard in Gdynia, which yesterday decided to call a strike alert because of the 'worsening situation in the country, provocation by the Government and (the Government's) torpedoing of all understanding'. There is no one specific issue that has led to the atmosphere of confrontation, but it is clear that the resolution of the Fire School strike[4] and threats to introduce emergency measures have been key factors.

[1] Repeated for Information Routine to Moscow, Washington, UKDEL NATO and Saving to East Berlin, Prague, Budapest, Bucharest, Sofia, Belgrade, Helsinki, Stockholm, Paris, Bonn, UKREP Brussels and UKMIS New York.

[2] Janusz Zbigniew Zabłocki, a member of ZNAK since 1977 and a member of the Sejm since 1965.

[3] Mr James had reported in a telegram on 9 December that the Central Committee Secretaries, *Voivodship* First Secretaries and Central Committee Heads of Departments had met to discuss the worsening socio-political situation, which indicated the seriousness of the situation. On the other hand, the strikes in universities were dying down, the Primate having sent a message to Polish students unmistakeably endorsing the strike but asking them to end it now. It was also understood that the Primate had sent a letter to the Sejm calling on deputies not to vote for emergency powers. James saw that as a departure on the part of the Primate, who had endorsed the students' strike to an unprecedented degree and given Solidarity the backing of the Church should it decide to protest about emergency measures. James concluded that the atmosphere continued to worsen with both sides strongly reacting to one another (Warsaw tel. No. 864).

[4] This important statement had been issued by Solidarity on 3 December 1981 at the end of a session in Radom. This followed the storming of the Fire Brigade School in Warsaw and the arrest

3. Today's press contains the first firm mention of possible emergency measures. An article reviewing the progress of various legislation through the Sejm mentions plans to give the Government special powers.[5] The article suggests that the Government intends first to introduce the new Trade Union Bill and to assume special powers only if the Bill, when law, was ignored. But the article claims that Solidarity have not followed the rules laid down in the Bill, even though both sides agreed to observe it as if it were law some time ago. The article also alleges that the Sejm's appeal of 30 October, which was made at the time as a substitute for emergency measures has been ignored. Whilst no timescale is given for the introduction of emergency powers, and indeed the Sejm spokesman has accepted that no work is at present being done on such legislation, the fact that they are mentioned at all is likely to raise the political temperature. The suspicion is growing that Jaruzelski, aware of the risks of confronting Solidarity on the emergency powers issue, will try to evade the problem by concentrating on the Trade Union Bill. He might hope to sell the provisions in that Bill for banning strikes as proof of his Government's firmness. This course does on the other hand risk considerable danger of a conflict with the growing band of hard-liners in the Politburo and CC Apparatus.

4. Much will depend now on whether Walesa and Jaruzelski meet and what, if anything, they can agree. The National Commission of Solidarity, which will begin its meeting tomorrow, is likely to reaffirm the hard line taken at Radom.

there of trainees who had been on strike. At the Radom meeting some Presidium members had demanded a strong response, such as setting up a provisional government. For the first time, a Solidarity document contained the demand for democratic elections to People's Councils at all levels and therefore a change of the system (see Solidarity NCC Presidium, 'Position Taken by the Presidium of the National Coordinating Commission and Leaders of the NSZZ', 3 December 1981, in 'Tygodnik *Solidarność*', No. 37, 11 December 1981, p. 3). Radom had been at the forefront of events since 1976, when KOR had been set up there to defend workers arrested by the authorities (see No. 11, note 6).

[5] On 9 December Mr James also noted that meetings in the Sejm were due to take place on 15, 16 and 21 December with two main items for debate: the draft trade union law and the economic reform Bills. There was no mention on the agenda of emergency measures.

CHAPTER II

The imposition of martial law in Poland
13 December 1981 — 23 December 1982

No. 112

Mr James (Warsaw) to Lord Carrington, 13 December 1981, 5.15 a.m.
Tel. No. 873[1] Flash, Confidential (FCO 28/4486, ENP 014/1)

From Melhuish.[2]

Poland: Internal situation

1. Version of tonight's[3] events carried by BBC is accurate. The Mazowsze[4] Solidarity Headquarters building, 2 blocks from the Embassy, was raided about midnight and the road in front of the building is currently cut off by militia vehicles and a small number of *Zomo* (military police) and WOW (internal security) personnel. Sliwinski, Mazowsze's foreign relations chief,[5] has been arrested at home.

2. At first there were few other signs of unusual activity. About 0415 I walked around the streets near the Mazowsze HQ and apart from these two road blocks, only saw early morning buses and pedestrians and the odd snow-plough. There were no lights in Council of Ministers building nor in Party HQ. Our Defence Attaché has however just reported sighting 16 Polish tanks with communications vehicles going north along main dual carriageway road on west side of the Vistula. Army staff cars are also picking up officers from home to take them into Ministry of Defence.

3. All internal and external telephone and telex facilities were cut about 0015 this morning. BBC and agencies are using special Reuters facility which bypassed normal telex. We have no idea what is happening elsewhere in the country but, if the authorities have bothered to arrest Sliwinski, a small fry, I presume they have tried to pick up all the Solidarity top brass, conveniently concentrated in Gdansk for National Council meeting. Or at least to seal off the Lenin Shipyard where they are meeting.

4. I will report further as we get more information. My initial estimate is that this is a carefully planned swoop on the Solidarity leadership known to few and

[1] Repeated for Information Immediate to Moscow, Washington, Paris, Bonn, UKDEL NATO, MODUK, HQ BAOR and HQ RAFG.

[2] At this time Mr James was hospitalised after suffering a heart attack.

[3] Date of 12 December pencilled in.

[4] The region of Mazowsze covered Warsaw and surrounding districts.

[5] Krzystof Sliwinski was the leader of the international section of Solidarity in Warsaw.

carried out efficiently. It is bound to provoke serious and possibly violent reaction from Solidarity and from the country at large. I see it as Jaruzelski's last ditch attempt either on his own initiative or on orders from Moscow to prove his credentials before his rumoured visit to Moscow on Monday.[6]

5. So far there is no threat to the British community in Warsaw but I intend to call in our wardens when it gets light. I will advise community to stay put. I have no way of knowing what is happening to the community elsewhere in Poland.

6. BBC and *Daily Telegraph* correspondents asked earlier whether they could use our communications facilities; fortunately they were able to send copy via Reuters but BBC correspondent has now again requested our assistance if Reuters are cut off. I have said that I could not endanger or clog up our own communications but, if there were no other means of getting information out to the West, I would be prepared to authorise short pooled copy from all British correspondents here. Canadian Embassy have lost their communications link with Ottawa and I have agreed to help out.

[6] In fact General Jaruzelski was to have his first talks with Soviet leaders after the declaration of martial law on 1 and 2 March (see No. 147, note 3).

No. 113

Mr James (Warsaw) to Lord Carrington, 13 December 1981, 9.20 a.m.
Tel. No. 874[1] Immediate, Confidential (FCO 28/4486, ENP 014/1)

From Melhuish.

Our Tel 873[2] Poland: Internal Situation

1. Warsaw Radio has carried at regular intervals since 0600 Jaruzelski's speech to the nation declaring a State of Emergency and the establishment of a Military Council to govern the country.[3] The text of the speech, which was followed by the national anthem and then by some Chopin piano music, will be available to you in London and the BBC has carried a good summary.

2. Three separate teams from Defence Section have been touring Warsaw and its outskirts this morning looking for evidence of what the Polish authorities may next be planning. They had no great difficulty moving around. When stopped at road blocks they produced identity cards and were waved through. They have brought back no clear-cut picture. There are now many soldiers in position on main streets in Warsaw, mostly to the south and with a heavy concentration around a particular housing estate which is known to contain a number of generals. Road blocks are ready to be swung into position on the E8, from the Soviet Union and Lublin, on the E12 from Bialystok[4] and on the T11 from Jablonna[5] at about 10-15 kilometres outside Warsaw. There are no apparent blocks on the Gdansk road nor

[1] Repeated for Information Immediate to Washington, Moscow, Paris, Bonn, UKDEL NATO, MODUK, HQ BAOR and HQ RAFG.

[2] No. 112.

[3] Sir C. Keeble, in Moscow tel. No. 740 of the same day, informed the FCO that General Jaruzelski's broadcast had been reported by *Tass*, the Soviet news agency: 'Martial law had been introduced "in the face of irresponsible actions by Solidarity's extremist forces which openly strain after power"' (FCO 28/4486, ENP 014/1).

[4] North-Eastern Poland.

[5] East-Central Poland.

on the main roads from the West and South. The four Vistula bridges are open to traffic although the US Defence Section said they were closed earlier this morning.

3. It looks as if the authorities are seeking to establish their ability to seal Warsaw off if necessary. This could be useful to them both to maintain Solidarity's current inability to communicate and to prevent any movement of Solidarity or other activists into Warsaw. But this must be a tentative conclusion. The patchy and haphazard arrangements bear the hallmark of Polish inefficiency.

4. We still have no news from the rest of the country. The next important, and perhaps crucial, development must be Solidarity's reaction to last night's events. I do not see how this can be anything other than sharp and nasty.

5. I have been summoned to the MFA along with other Ambassadors at 10.15.[6]

[6] Earlier on 13 December the FCO had contacted all posts in major Western, Eastern European, neutral and non-aligned countries to make them aware of the planned line with the Ten and NATO the following day: close consultation and coordination were essential; clearer facts on the situation were needed before substantive decisions were taken; at this stage public statements should be of a preliminary nature; the main Western interest was that the crisis should be kept under control; Poland should settle its affairs without outside interference; progress in the last sixteen months should not be lost; and Western responses should take account of public opinion in Poland and the reaction of other governments (FCO tel. No. 121, FCO 28/4664, ENZ 021/1).

No. 114

Mr James (Warsaw) to Lord Carrington, 13 December 1981, 7.40 p.m.

Tel. No. 884[1] Immediate, Confidential (FCO 28/4486, ENP 014/1)

From Melhuish.

Poland: The State of Emergency

1. The Polish Government has taken this grave step following a gradual increase in tension during the last few days. It seems likely that it was triggered by yesterday's confirmation by the Solidarity National Commission of the Radom Declaration.[2] Such evidence as we have supports this view, although the Government will obviously have been drawing up contingency plans during the last week. They have enjoyed some luck in that Solidarity's decision was made on Saturday evening, thus enabling the State of Emergency to start on a Sunday.

2. The Government has moved against Solidarity primarily because of its growing frustration with the union. Moscow's attitude will also have been crucial, although it is impossible to say whether the initial impulse for the move came from Moscow or Warsaw. On balance, we think it likely that this attempt to impose a Polish solution without at this stage involving the Soviet Union was Jaruzelski's last-minute answer to his critics at home and within CMEA.

3. As expected, today has been quiet, and there has been no reaction so far to the State of Emergency in Warsaw (it is still impossible to say what is happening elsewhere in Poland). Obviously, no strike can begin before tomorrow morning at the earliest. But there is the danger that public anger might erupt into street demonstrations or even violence today or tonight. The fact that the Army, after initially lifting the cordon round Solidarity's Warsaw Headquarters, has reimposed

[1] Repeated for Information Immediate to Washington, Moscow, Paris, Bonn, UKDEL NATO.

[2] See No. 111, note 4.

it, is an indication of the seriousness with which the authorities view this possibility.

4. The next stage will be to see how Solidarity reacts. Although the Government has detained most of the top Solidarity leadership, and may continue to hold them in custody, the organisation is well structured and others will step into the shoes of those detained. This rump leadership is likely to be younger and more radical than the regular leadership, but just as well organised. They will have several options open to them:

(i) Selective strikes.

(ii) An 'active' strike.

(iii) A general strike.

(iv) Protests in the streets.

(v) Attempts to rush prisons or even the Lenin Shipyard in Gdansk and release the imprisoned Solidarity leaders.

An active strike can be virtually ruled out as it is a weapon for times of social quiet. Selective strikes in the mining industry, the power industry and the railways would probably be the most effective weapon that Solidarity has at hand. But it is more likely that the passions of the membership would in time turn a selective strike into a general strike. Widespread street protests are also likely to burst out spontaneously at some stage and I would not be at all surprised if a few Solidarity hotheads organised raids on the prisons or Milicja headquarters where Solidarity leaders are imprisoned. If, as seems likely, the Lenin Shipyard has been sealed off, then an attempt may well be made to break into it.

5. A further unknown factor is Walesa himself. The Government spokesman has just told Western journalists that Walesa is at liberty and is discussing possible solutions with the Government in the Warsaw region.

6. The Government has given itself the power to indict strike leaders before military courts. It will use that power, but, as soon as it cuts off Solidarity's heads, new ones will sprout. A more important factor is whether the membership and people in general will follow the lead of the rump of the leadership of Solidarity. A British subject who has been active in Solidarity in Gdansk has told us that the mood there yesterday was determined and that Solidarity members are resigned to the possibility of violence.

7. Tomorrow is likely to be a crucial day. The workers will return to their factories, whereupon Solidarity can start organising them. It would be self-defeating of the Government not to let the workers return to work. In the longer term, the attitude of the Church and in particular the Pope will be crucial. It is also not clear how long the Government proposes to continue the state of emergency. But now that they have locked themselves into this situation they can hardly draw back without inflicting a major defeat upon themselves. So it looks as if the emergency will continue for weeks rather than days unless the situation worsens to the point where Soviet intervention is called for.

No. 115

Mr James (Warsaw) to Lord Carrington, 14 December 1981, 10.25 a.m.
Tel. No. 886[1] Immediate, Restricted (FCO 28/4486, ENP 014/1)

Poland: the state of emergency

1. Although the ruling Military Council have now assumed sweeping powers, they do not seem to be enforcing them in any systematic or authoritarian way. There is an air of a Phoney War.[2] Children throw snow-balls at armoured personnel carriers parked at most cross-roads. Troops with armoured vehicles have been posted on routes into Warsaw but seem to be doing nothing to check vehicles in-bound or out-bound. Bridges were last night being patrolled in freezing weather by soldiers who took no notice of the traffic. Yesterday in the streets around the Embassy riot police stood watching crowds watching them but made no attempt to enforce the new ruling on illegal gatherings. The Mazowsze Solidarity HQ is sometimes guarded but often not. The only consistently well-guarded area is Jaruzelski's home and his route to the office.

2. Last night seems to have passed without major incident in Warsaw. The military have adopted a lower profile this morning, moving back their roadblocks and hindering traffic movement rather less than yesterday. Buses and trams are running normally, although they seem to be carrying fewer passengers than usual. Most of our local staff have arrived for work, although early arrivals had some difficulty passing a police/army guard on the Embassy. It seems that no Polish citizens will be allowed into the Embassy today.

3. Glemp's sermon delivered yesterday morning at Czestochowa was broadcast for 3 hours on Warsaw radio in the evening, which indicates that the authorities have been reasonably satisfied with it. Whilst it leaves no doubt about Glemp's desire to avoid violence, it also makes clear Glemp's disapproval of the government's actions and his sadness at the State of Emergency. For full details see MIFT.[3]

4. We plan to check up on some of the major factories in Warsaw today to see if the reported strike call from the Solidarity leadership in Gdansk[4] is being heeded.

[1] Repeated for Information Immediate to Prague (for Private Secretary: Lord Trefgarne), Washington, Moscow, Paris, Bonn, UKDEL NATO, MODUK, HQBAOR and HQRAFG.

[2] The phase of the Second World War from 1 September 1939 to 9 April 1940 when there was no major military action.

[3] Not printed.

[4] On 15 December, Mr Melhuish reported that two Danish journalists had been locked in the Lenin Shipyard in Gdańsk for two days. They had witnessed clashes among the 13,000 to 15,000 workers gathered inside. This resulted from the management, supported by riot police, having asked the workers to leave, causing disagreement among them as to whether or not they should obey.

No. 116

Lord Carrington to Mr James (Warsaw), 17 December 1981, 7.22 p.m.
Tel. No. 701 Priority, Secret (FCO 28/4487, ENP 014/1)

For Melhuish from Broomsfield.

Poland: Present Position

1. I had hoped at close of play this evening to let you have a reasonably clear idea of what we thought and the way ahead. The news in your tel. No. 948[1] which has since been confirmed on Polish radio changes the situation markedly.

2. Our policy so far, which has been reflected in the various public statements, has been to suspend judgement on the commitments by Jaruzelski to continuation of reform and renewal until his actions proved otherwise.[2] We have had to tread the fine line between two dangerous alternatives. 'We cannot be seen to have acquiesced in the repression of Solidarity. On the other hand, we cannot say or do things which can be portrayed after the fact as provocative incitements which lead to breakdown, violence and Soviet intervention' (extract from Haig's message to the Secretary of State).[3]

3. The strains of staying in line on this are now becoming real. The US have been hardening daily and have the Soviet influence very much at the back of their minds.[4] The French, for domestic reasons, are now becoming much tougher[5] and I am sure that at tomorrow's meeting with the Secretary of State we will harden too.

4. We will be considering quadripartitely on 22/23 December what we should do now. The options are limited and the levers mainly economic.

[1] Not printed. Mr Melhuish reported he had meetings with the Deputy Foreign Minister Mr Olechowski and with the Polish Ambassador in London, Mr Staniszewski, on his way to London. Olechowski told Melhuish confidentially that seven deaths had been reported in a Silesian coal mine. Staniszewski acknowledged that there had been arrests. He said that Mr Wałęsa was in discussion with Mr Rakowski and other Minsters in Warsaw. Melhuish protested against the restriction of movements for the Embassy staff, the ban on telecommunications and the police stopping Polish visitors to the Embassy. On the same day Mrs Thatcher's Private Secretary, Mr Coles, in forwarding this telegram to her, annotated: 'Important. The first deaths' (PREM 19/561).

[2] On 17 December the Lord Privy Seal duly informed the Cabinet—which met at 10.30—that the situation in Poland was still confused. He thought that as the Polish army consisted mainly of conscripts—with family ties with Solidarity—they could not be expected to be able to maintain control if there were widespread unrest. The Polish Government might therefore feel obliged to call for Soviet military help. There was also much uncertainty about foreign food aid and rescheduling of official debts, although what had been agreed would not be cancelled (CAB 128/71).

[3] Mr Haig informed Lord Carrington on 15 December that his Government had very sensitive intelligence which convincingly confirmed that the Soviets were intimately involved with the Polish Government from the outset in the planning the operation and that there was also provision for a second phase to bring Soviet forces into Poland if the Government was unable to maintain control. In a reply to Haig on 17 December, Carrington thought the question of whether Jaruzelski had acted in response to Soviet pressure or acted to forestall a Soviet intervention was a false one, as both were true. The important question was what the West were going to do and he recognised that the West was walking a tightrope between acquiescence and provocation (FCO 28/4489, ENP 014/1).

[4] On 17 December Sir N. Henderson reported President Reagan's statement in a press conference on Poland calling for the Polish Government to negotiate and compromise, and threatening to suspend economic aid while martial law was imposed. He added: 'The Polish nation, speaking through Solidarity, has provided one of the brightest, bravest moments of modern history' (Washington tel. No. 3832).

[5] On the same afternoon Mr Hibbert, HM Ambassador in Paris, reported that events in Poland and strong reactions in French trade union and political circles prevented a 'soft' line by the French Government.

Much will depend on an assessment of Jaruzelski's real intentions and room for manoeuvre. Are his statements sincere when he talks of preserving the renewal? And what does he mean by that? Is it possible that he will allow an independent trade union to exist again? And how soon is 'as soon as possible'? ('the basic content of the socialist renewal . . . brought into effect.' Military Council Declaration 16 December).

5. I will try to let you know where we stand at close of play tomorrow night. But you should pay particular attention to the statement I expect to emerge at mid-day on 18 December.[6] It will reflect our reaction to the deterioration you have just reported. Otherwise policy on options should be worked out on 22/23 December. If before then you could give your views on some of the difficult questions in para 4 above, in a 'open' telegram we would find it very helpful.

6. Could you also confirm that there is no jamming of the BBC's Polish Service broadcasts?[7]

[6] See No. 117.
[7] See No. 129.

No. 117

Minute from Lord Carrington to the Cabinet and OD Committee, 18 December 1981[1]

FCS/81/138 Confidential (PREM 19/561)

Poland[2]

My colleagues may welcome a note about Poland before the start of the Christmas holiday.

The action taken so far has been carried out by Polish security forces assisted by some 150,000 Polish troops or half of the Polish Army. The Russians undoubtedly knew what was going to happen and approved of it. I assume that there is a contingency plan for the possibility of the situation getting out of control of the Polish authorities. In that event Soviet forces could not fail to be involved. But there is no sign of this at the moment. Jaruzelski and his colleagues in the Military Council may be at least partly sincere when they talk of Poland returning in due course to the path of reform and Renewal. But I am very doubtful whether events are going to permit this, at least in the next few weeks and possibly months. A more sombre interpretation is that we are witnessing the start of the extinction of the process of Renewal which began in August 1980.[3] We are, and shall stay, closely in touch with allies and partners about the crisis and how to handle it.

All this has required and will continue to require difficult decisions, not least about the line to take in public. The statement issued by the Foreign Ministers of

[1] The document is undated but the draft is dated 18 December and Mrs Thatcher's Private Secretary initialled it as having been read by the Prime Minister on the same date (Mr Broomfield to Private Secretary; FCO 28/4488, ENP 14/1).
[2] Earlier in the day the Secretary of State had decided, in a meeting with ministers and senior staff involved in the Polish situation, on the following: no immediate restrictions on Polish diplomats but objections to be presented to the Polish Ambassador; no pooling of information with the press at the British Embassy for security reasons; no suspension of visas; the Polish Ambassador to be made aware of the importance of re-establishing BA flights to Warsaw and consular access to Gdansk; a public line to follow Lord Carrington's declaration in Strasbourg on 17 December; no formal approach to be made to the Russians.
[3] See No. 16.

the Ten on 15 December[4] was criticised in some quarters here as too weak, and a stronger line is certainly required now, to match the worsening situation and the tone of comment from other Western capitals, especially Washington.[5] I added a stronger piece on Poland to my speech to the European Parliament in Strasbourg on 17 December.[6]

Humphrey Atkins[7] was asked in the House about the possibility of increasing the broadcasting hours of the BBC Polish Service. I find that for an annual cost of £53,000 it would be possible to add an extra 15 minutes three times a day, making five hours a week. More than that would require additional staff. I am not at the moment convinced that a small increase would be worth making.

There is a potential problem about immigration. Our usual practice has been to grant visas to Poles fairly freely. There are 2,000 outstanding applications from before 13 December, but it has not been possible to process these for communication and other reasons. But if the situation degenerates further we could see Britain becoming a country of refuge for Poles, as Austria is already. I have asked my officials to look at this urgently with their colleagues in the Home Office.

There may also be a problem with the voluntary agencies. There has been considerable pressure for the government to play at least a coordinating role. The position should be clearer after a meeting of the various charities on 21 December which the Red Cross has called.

Lastly there are the complicated and difficult economic questions. The position at the moment is that economic assistance from Britain and the rest of the Community already 'in the pipeline' is not being held back (this includes 8,000 tonnes of beef which the Ten Governments agreed to supply to Poland free of charge in time for Christmas). There will shortly be a need to decide, for example, whether to proceed with the second stage of the third tranche of subsidised food from the Community;[8] what policy ECGD should follow from now on; whether the rescheduling operation for 1981 should be suspended, and whether that envisaged

[4] The statement, in profound 'sympathy' for the Polish people, expressed 'concern' at the imposition of martial law and the detention of trade unionists. It asked signatory states of the Helsinki Final Act to refrain from any interference in the internal affairs of the Poles, who should solve their own problems without the use of force so that the process of reform and Renewal could continue (FCO tel. No. 666 to Warsaw; FCO 28/4486, ENP 14/1).

[5] See No. 116, note 4.

[6] He referred to Poland as a 'man-made disaster on a colossal scale' and insisted that there be an 'early resumption of the process of negotiation and conciliation, including the release of those in detention' (*European Political Co-operation*, fourth edition, Press and Information Service, Federal Republic of Germany, Bonn, 1982, pp. 300-301). On the evening of 17 December the European Parliament overwhelmingly adopted a resolution, which: condemned the Polish authorities' measures; called for a repeal of the 'state of war', the immediate liberation of those arrested and the reestablishment of civil and trade union liberties; opposed all external interference; emphasized that 'it is up to the Polish people—and them alone—to freely determine their own future'. The Counsellor at UKREP in Brussels commented on 18 December that Lord Carrington had set the tone for the debate, during which there had been much talk about appeasement and Munich (Strasbourg tel. Nos. 118 and 119; FCO 28/4488, ENP 14/1).

[7] Lord Privy Seal.

[8] Mr Wałęsa had issued an underground appeal to the West for food aid to continue, but to be distributed by the Church, and for financial assistance to cease and be used as a bargaining counter to persuade the authorities to release Solidarity activists and negotiate with them (FCO tel. No. 711 to Warsaw, 18 Dec; FCO 28/4488, ENP 14/1). On the Community's position see No. 119, paragraph 12.

for 1982 can take place as planned;[9] and what to do about the URSUS tractor plant in Warsaw, to which £30 million of credit had been allocated for 1982.[10] None of these matters requires to be decided before Christmas, but officials are meeting to consider issues and set them out in a form which will facilitate decisions in case they are needed urgently.

CARRINGTON

[9] See No. 132, paragraph 13.
[10] See No. 99.

No. 118

Minute from Mr Mallaby to Mr J. Bullard, 20 December 1981
Secret (FCO 28/4488, ENP 014/1)

Poland: action vis-à-vis the Poles and the Russians

1. This minute makes initial suggestions about how we might respond to President Reagan's and Mr Haig's messages of 19 December.[1] The Americans make clear that they want the West to undertake new measures to put pressure on Jaruzelski and steps to make clear to the Russians that we understand their role and to make more credible our efforts to deter their intervention.

Measures towards Poland

2. There are several small steps which could quickly be taken:

(*a*) Announce postponement of the meeting on 14-15 January about 1982 re-scheduling (para 4 of the attached brief on conditional economic support for Poland[2] for your meeting on 22 December).

(*b*) Announce the freezing of industrial credit lines for Poland (paras 5 and 6 of attached brief).

(*c*) Restrict movement of Polish diplomats in UK.

(*d*) EC démarche in Warsaw as suggested by Italians.[3]

3. These are really gestures. If we wanted to put real pressure on Jaruzelski, we would have, I suggest, to put together a large package of Western aid and attach political conditions to it (paras 8-10 of attached brief).

[1] These messages stressed the danger that Soviet military intervention in Poland would have on reform efforts in Eastern Europe and East-West relations generally. Reagan ended his message: 'This may well be a watershed in the political history of mankind—a challenge to tyranny from within. We must not let this moment pass us by without clearly demonstrating that we understood and that we acted.' In a telephone conversation at 10.45 a.m. on 20 December Thatcher and Carrington were not impressed by the 'cataclysmic' sentiments found in the messages. They thought it 'absurd' and 'unwise' to punish the USSR if they had not actually invaded (PREM 19/871). The Prime Minister's reply to the President, sent on 22 December, noted the difficult situation and the need for a clear and united response from the West.

[2] Not printed. This suggested that the meeting could be postponed a month or two as a gesture of disapproval, or the creditors could meet alone without the Poles to exchange views and demonstrate concern and continuing consultation.

[3] An EC démarche from Lord Carrington was delivered by Mr James on 22 December but rejected by Mr Czyrek as interference in Poland's internal affairs. He denied that anything was being done in Poland that was against the law and stated that the Government had acted as it had to safeguard the process of renewal. Czyrek was said to be very angry at the démarche: the points made 'visibly went home' (Warsaw tel. No. 1019 of 22 December).

Measures towards Soviet Union

4. I have looked through the contingency plans for Western actions in the case of Soviet intervention, and have identified certain moves which might be taken *before* such intervention, as the Americans seem to be suggesting:

(i) Coordinated top level Western messages to Brezhnev. These would no doubt warn against Soviet intervention but would also make clear that we held the Soviet Union to be co-responsible for the clamp down in Poland. (A variant of this would be try to send a senior Western emissary, for instance Lord Carrington in his Presidency capacity, to Moscow to make the same point; but the Russians could of course refuse to receive him.)

(ii) A NATO declaration about Poland, with the above points about the Soviet Union as well as other points about Poland itself.

(iii) Cancel forthcoming bilateral events with the Soviet Union that are [not] particularly in Western interests, e.g. any major cultural events. The trouble here is that most of the eye-catching types of event have been suspended since Afghanistan.

(iv) Withdraw ambassadors from Moscow. When this has been suggested in other contexts, Lord Carrington has been reluctant. To withdraw Sir C. Keeble would weaken our capacity for making representations about Poland.

(v) US announces that negotiations with the Soviet Union on a new grain supply agreement, due in the New Year, are postponed *sine die*. This would not affect grain supplies before October 1982, when the old agreement expires.

(vi) Western Governments agree to ask their firms to go slow in negotiations on remaining contracts connected with the gas pipeline project. The utility of this depends on whether any contracts essential to the project are not yet concluded. EESD are investigating the question.

(vii) Western Governments suspend credit cover for the Soviet Union. A big step. Exporting countries with lower domestic interest rates would gain a competitive export advantage. Probably very difficult to get agreement on this.

(viii) Deny over-flying rights and technical stopovers to Soviet aircraft.

5. I have left out the UN because we might encounter majority opposition so long as there is no explicit Soviet intervention in Poland. I have left out arms control negotiations because I do not think it is in Western interests to suspend them so far.

C.L.G. MALLABY

No. 119

Lord Carrington to Sir N. Henderson (Washington), 21 December 1981, 10.30 a.m.

Tel. No. 1974[1] Immediate, Confidential (FCO 28/4489, ENP 014/1)

Poland: declaration of martial law

[1] Repeated to Moscow, Paris, Bonn, Belgrade, Bucharest, Budapest, Prague, Sofia, East Berlin, Rome, The Hague, Luxembourg, Brussels, Copenhagen, Athens, Dublin, Ankara, Lisbon, Oslo, Ottawa, Reykjavik, UKDEL NATO, Stockholm, Helsinki, Vienna, Berne, Madrid, Canberra, Wellington, Peking, Tokyo, New Delhi, Islamabad, Tel Aviv, Cairo, Pretoria/Capetown, Brasilia, Buenos Aires, Mexico City, Strasbourg, UKDEL Madrid, UKMIS New York, UKMIS Geneva, Kathmandu.

1. On the night of 12/13 December the Polish Prime Minister, General Jaruzelski, declared Martial Law and announced that a 'Military Council for National Salvation' had assumed responsibility for governing Poland. Military Officers have been appointed to oversee central and local government: the borders have been sealed: telex and telephone links have been cut: civil liberties suspended: and a ban imposed on strikes.

2. In announcing the measures Jaruzelski stressed that they would be of short duration and would be rescinded when calm and order were restored. He said that the essentials of the Polish Renewal of the past 17 months would be safeguarded and claimed that, in due course, reform would continue.

Explanation to Western governments

3. In explaining these measures to Western governments, the Polish authorities have claimed that the situation had become so serious that they had no alternative, and that a declaration of martial law was the least violent of a number of alternatives. They have reiterated Jaruzelski's claim that the measures will be short-lived, that there will be no return to the policies prevailing before August 1980, and that, as soon as the internal situation has stabilised, martial law will be rescinded and civil liberties restored. They have appealed to Western governments for understanding and have asked them to continue to provide substantial economic assistance.

Soviet attitude

4. The Soviet Union has expressed support for Jaruzelski, but comment has been kept comparatively low key and factual, with considerable stress on the fact that these developments must be seen as Poland's internal affairs. At present, the Russians are clearly trying to suggest that they are not involved and cannot be held accountable. But it must be assumed that they know what Jaruzelski intended to do, and agreed with it. Soviet forces are at a high state of readiness but there are no indications to suggest that Soviet intervention is imminent. However, if the Polish military authorities are unable to control the situation, Soviet intervention is likely.

Polish popular reaction

5. The imposition of martial law was carried out with considerable efficiency and achieved a large measure of surprise. The authorities were able to detain many of Solidarity's leaders, including Lech Walesa, who we believe is under house arrest in a suburb of Warsaw. Shocked by developments and deprived of leadership, Solidarity's reaction has taken time to develop. However, in the last few days there have been reports of widespread strikes and sit-ins (perhaps affecting as many as 200 plants), and the Polish authorities have admitted that 7 people were killed in a clash between miners and security forces at a mine in Katowice in southern Poland.

6. There have undoubtedly been other violent incidents (the authorities have admitted that several hundred people have been injured, many of whom they claim are police), and strikes and sit-ins are continuing. The position in the mining region of Silesia is giving the Polish authorities particular trouble: reports suggest that up to 20 mines are occupied by miners who have taken their families into the mines with them. We also know of a large demonstration in Warsaw on 17 December which police broke up with truncheons and tear gas. The authorities have set up hastily constructed detention camps but we do not know how many, nor the number of people interned in them.

Current position

7. It is difficult to give an overall assessment of the position at the end of the first week of martial law because reliable information is scarce. Western Embassies are restricted to Warsaw and internal communication in Poland remains cut. However, it appears that, while Warsaw is for the most part calm and tightly controlled by the military authorities, active resistance elsewhere in the country, particularly in Silesia and on the coast, is continuing. It also seems likely that there is considerable passive resistance, and that few industrial enterprises are working normally.

The Western position

8. Immediate Western reactions to the crisis, which were closely co-ordinated in the Ten and NATO, were to mark our concern at the suspension of civil liberties and the imprisonment of trade unionists, but to avoid acting in a way which might complicate the situation. Our major interests are that: the crisis should be kept under control; that Poland should solve its own problem without outside interference; and that the democratic gains of the last 17 months should not be permanently lost even if they are temporarily halted or reversed.[2]

9. We remain in close touch with our partners and our attitude will be determined by developments in Poland, including the fate of Solidarity, the degree of popular resistance, the use of force by the authorities, and by our assessment of Jaruzelski's intentions. The latter are not easy to judge. We may be witnessing the start of the extinction of the process of Renewal begun in August 1980, but it is possible that Jaruzelski may be at least partly sincere in his references to returning to the path of reform and Renewal. However, it is doubtful whether events will permit this at least in the next few weeks and months, whatever Jaruzelski may intend. The deaths and casualties of the last few days are likely to leave a bitter legacy and to prejudice still further the prospects for any resumption of a dialogue between the authorities and Solidarity. The gulf between the rulers and ruled, one of the principal causes of the present crisis, is likely to grow even wider.

Line to take

10. Although you may draw on the foregoing in talking to reliable contacts, you should be particularly careful in explaining HMG's policy to stick closely to the public line taken by Ministers.[3] This will be adjusted as necessary to take account of developments. In this connection you should draw on the statement by me in the

[2] This assessment was partly based on a telegram received from Mr Melhuish of 19 December in which he stated: 'We have in fact just witnessed a military take-over of Poland planned well in advance and executed efficiently and ruthlessly. Regarding non-interference he stated: 'We find ourselves emasculated by the logical consequences of our past utterances' and 'we should both recognise dispassionately what kind of regime has been established and try to estimate how long the "temporary" state of emergency will last'(Warsaw tel. No. 974, FCO 28/4488, ENP 14/1). In a telegram three hours later, he recommended a 'vigorous denunciation . . . This would of course be interference in internal Polish politics but, if the concepts of parliamentary democracy, the rule of law and basic human rights really mean anything in the West, I think we have no option but to denounce their deliberate and callous suppression here.' He also suggested reconsidering with EC allies a ban on food aid and all British export credits until martial law was lifted (Warsaw tel. No. 977).

[3] On 21 December Lord Carrington met the new Polish Ambassador, who delivered a message from Mr Czyrek, claiming that martial law had been a lesser evil for the country on the brink of civil war. Renewal would be continued, the Gdańsk agreements respected, civil liberties gradually restored and foreign debt repaid. He implied that Western sanctions would aggravate the situation. Carrington replied that the West could not wait patiently and provide aid, whilst detentions and shootings created an 'extremely unfavourable impression' both on Government and public opinion (FCO tel. No. 769 of 24 December to Warsaw, FCO 28/4490, ENP 14/1/).

Lords and by the LPS in the Commons on 14 December[4] (VS 295/81); on the Statement of the Foreign Ministers of the Ten of 15 December (Retract No 62515): the FCO Press Spokesman of 14, 16, 16, 17 December (not to all): and my speech in Strasbourg on 17 December.[5]

11. On the question of economic assistance to Poland, you should be guided by the Prime Minister's statement to the House of 15 December (Retract No 62515).[6]

12. If you are asked about Community food aid, you may say that Ministers of the Ten have decided that decisions already taken and announced should be implemented. No new decisions fall to be taken for the time being.

[4] Lord Carrington and Mr Atkins both stated that HMG was closely following the developments and remained in consultation with EC and NATO partners. They hoped that problems would be resolved by compromise and consensus and without bloodshed. They would adhere to non-intervention and expected all signatories of the Helsinki Final Act to do the same (*Parl. Debs., 6th ser., H. of L.*, 14 December 1981, vol. 426, col. 8 and *Parl. Debs., 6th ser., H. of C.*, 14 December 1981, vol. 15, col. 19).

[5] See No. 117, note 6.

[6] The Prime Minister had stated: 'it is too early for anyone, either Governments or banks, to make any changes in arrangements for the rescheduling of Polish debt repayments or the provision of new credit. For the moment, therefore, we shall leave things as they are . . . but . . . keep a close watch on what is happening in Poland' (*Parl. Debs., 6th ser., H. of C.*, 15 December 1981, vol. 15, col. 150).

No. 120

Sir A. Parsons (UKMIS New York) to Lord Carrington, 23 December 1981, 12.36 a.m.

Tel. No. 1614[1] Immediate, Confidential (FCO 28/4490, ENP 014/1)

My Tel. No. 1601: *Poland*[2]

1. After some discussion between the US Mission and ourselves through the day, Mrs Kirkpatrick telephoned me from Washington this evening (22 Dec). She said that the Administration had decided that they must initiate urgent action in the Security Council about the human rights situation in Poland. Their line would be that human rights violations there constituted a threat to international peace and security. Their intention was to put in a formal request tomorrow (23 Dec) for a meeting of the Council to take place on 28 Dec. She asked for my advice.

2. I said that the US would encounter serious problems. It would be possible to get to informal consultations of the whole Council. But the Russians and GDR would then strongly oppose a formal meeting on the ground that Poland was entirely an internal matter, falling under Article 2 (7) of the Charter.[3] There would be much reluctance on the part of the non-aligned and even Western non-permanent members (Ireland and Spain). Even if it proved possible to force a

[1] Repeated for Information Immediate UKDEL NATO, Washington, Paris; Info Priority Warsaw, Moscow, Bonn.

[2] Not printed. In this telegram, dated 18 December, Sir A. Parsons reported a conversation with Mrs J. Kirkpatrick, US Ambassador to the UN, in which they first discussed whether anything should be done at the UN about Poland. Parsons put forward the same arguments made in this telegram (FCO 28/4488, ENP 014/1).

[3] The Article states that the UN has no authority to intervene in matters which are within the domestic jurisdiction of any State.

formal meeting of the Council, the Russians would fiercely oppose the adoption of the agenda. I was doubtful whether the Americans would be able to mobilize nine votes to get the agenda adopted, in which case the West would have been defeated at the outset.

3. I went on to make a number of points which she had either not thought of or on which she had got the wrong end of the stick. First I contradicted her view that it would be better to get into the Council before the Russians assumed Presidency on 1 January. She had not realised that, as President, the Russians would be to some extent muzzled. They would not be able to lead the procedural battle either in the informal consultations or in the Council itself. Even their ability to stall would be less than it would be if they could lead the attack from outside the Presidency. Secondly, Poland would become a Member of the Council on 1 January, which opened up interesting possibilities. Thirdly, the non-aligned composition of the Council would be marginally more manageable by the West in January with Togo and Zaire replacing Tunisia and Niger. The other changes made little difference.

4. Mrs Kirkpatrick seemed impressed by these arguments. She said that she was going to consult Leprette (France)[4] and that you and Cheysson[5] would probably be receiving messages from Haig. Finally she said that the NSC would be meeting again at 11 a.m. Washington time on 23 Dec: she would put to them the points I had made and would telephone me in the afternoon.[6]

5. I had already been over the ground with Adelman (Mrs Kirkpatrick's Deputy). It was as a result of his passing my views to her that she telephoned me instead of going straight ahead with the President of the Security Council.

6. In my view, it is most important that the Americans should be persuaded not to make a mess of this question out of their desire to demonstrate instant activity. If they go ahead as planned, the odds are that the Russians will win the procedural battle and the West will look as though they had made a clumsy and unsuccessful attempt to take an East/West propaganda trick. This will make it even more difficult than it will be in any case to mobilise non-aligned support when the right time comes i.e. when evidence of direct outside intervention in Poland is overwhelming, or when the human rights situation has degenerated to a point where there can no longer be serious doubt—even outside Western circles—that international action is imperative.

7. I am not sure how far Eagleburger[7] is in the picture or whether action at the UN will be on the agenda for tomorrow's meeting in Brussels. But I believe that if the Americans are to be dissuaded from falling at the first fence in the UN it may be necessary to intervene at a high level to convince them that our doubts are not due to faint-heartedness but to the way we see the practical possibilities here.

[4] Mr Jacques Leprette was the French Permanent Representative to the UN and President of the Security Council.

[5] French Foreign Minister.

[6] Sir A. Parsons telephoned Mrs Kirkpatrick just before she went into the NSC meeting to say that he could not think of a time when a question of human rights in an individual country had been brought before the Security Council—not even in the case of Idi Amin or Pol Pot. He also warned that it would create a dangerous precedent which others could use against the West in contexts such as Chile, Guatemala, El Salvador and even Northern Ireland. He advised that if the US felt the need for immediate action the General Assembly would be the right forum (UKMIS NY tel. No. 1618 of 23 December). Kirkpatrick argued these points at the NSC meeting and it was agreed to hold potential action at the UN in abeyance for the time being (minutes reproduced at http://www.thereaganfiles.com/).

[7] US Under-Secretary of State for Political Affairs.

No. 121

Lord Carrington to Sir N. Henderson (Washington), 24 December 1981, 1.32 p.m.

Tel. No. 1990[1] Immediate, Secret (FCO 49/916, RS 014/2)

Poland

1. Eagleburger was in London for a few hours on 23/24 December for consultations similar to those which he had earlier in Rome, Bonn, Brussels and Paris. He saw Bullard.

2. Eagleburger saw recent events less in a Polish context than in that of the East-West struggle and the US-Soviet relationship. Strong measures by the West were needed to match the American public mood, to fit the Reagan Administration's international stance and to send the right signal to Moscow. Soviet co-responsibility for the imposition of martial law in Poland should carry penalties, and the West should not hang back from applying particular sanctions simply because they had not been earmarked for the contingency of Soviet military intervention.

3. Bullard said that Britain was ready to look at any measures the United States could suggest. We had contributed to the consultations in NATO (UKDEL NATO Tel Nos 507-509).[2] As I had told Mr Haig by telephone the Foreign Ministers of the Ten were being invited to a special informal meeting on Poland in London next week,[3] and we should want to keep closely in touch with the Americans before and after that. But Bullard did not think it irrelevant, as some American [*sic*] had argued, whether Jaruzelski acted to forestall Soviet intervention or under Soviet pressure, or how far he was an independent agent or a tool of the Soviets, to take two of Mr Haig's phrases. Since we were dealing with Poles and Poland, the truth was more likely to be complex than simple. If we wanted to influence events in Poland we needed to be sure about what Jaruzelski himself was hoping to achieve and how much freedom of action he had. The intelligence available to us in London did not suggest that Jaruzelski had been imposed on Poland by the Russians in October, or that he took power then with the intention of declaring martial law two months later. He had perhaps had no alternative on 13 December and he probably had few options now. The objective of bringing Poland back to the path of renewal was the right one but it was likely to take time to achieve. The broader consultations mentioned by Eagleburger were important, but we should be clear in our own minds whether it was for the sake of these or in the hope of changing conditions in Poland that we were being asked to consider some of the wider-ranging measures which the Americans seemed to envisage.

4. Eagleburger did not argue the point as regards Jaruzelski etc. but he continued to see this aspect as less important for the US than the US-Soviet and domestic consideration. He went on to give some information, now overtaken by events, about President Reagan's speech of 23 December[4] and his letters to

[1] Repeated for Information Priority to UKDEL NATO, Moscow, Warsaw, EC Posts.

[2] Not printed.

[3] See No. 122, note 5.

[4] 'Address to the Nation about Christmas and the Situation in Poland' in which President Reagan claimed that events in Poland had been 'precipitated by public and secret pressure from the Soviet

Jaruzelski and Brezhnev.[5] He said that the US would be asking its allies to consider following the American example but implied that it was likely to proceed down the road he had indicated, whether the allies went along or not.[6] The German Ambassador has since given us an account of Genscher's talk with Eagleburger on 21 December. He reports Genscher as saying that the aims for the West should be (*a*) to prevent Soviet military intervention and (*b*) to make possible a continuation of the Polish renewal. Genscher said that it was not a question of firm attitudes or soft attitudes, but of how to achieve these two goals.

Union' and warned of serious consequences if the 'outrages' in Poland do not cease: 'we cannot and will not conduct "business as usual" with the perpetrators and those who aid and abet them.' He announced the US would take 'immediate action to suspend major elements of our economic relationships with the Polish Government', but that the shipment of food direct to the Polish people through private humanitarian channels would continue. See *Public Papers: Reagan (1981)*, pp. 1185-88.

Lord Carrington had been concerned that the President would announce measures in his speech that had not been discussed with the European allies. Speaking to Mr Haig on the afternoon of the 23 December he was assured that although the mood in Washington was more 'rambunctious' than in Europe, and the President's remarks would be 'not only explosive but tough', they were 'just on the acceptable edge', announcing things that the allies were already aware of (note of telephone conversation by Mr F. N. Richards [APS], 23 December in FCO 28/4490; ENP 014/1).

[5] Both letters dated 23 December. President Reagan wrote to General Jaruzelski warning of serious consequences if the Polish Government continued to use violence against its populace and urging him to free those in arbitrary detention, to lift martial law, and to restore the internationally recognized rights of the Polish people to free speech and association. He also wrote to President Brezhnev urging him to permit the restoration of basic human rights in Poland provided for in the Helsinki Final Act and informed him that if repression continued, the USA would have no choice 'but to take further concrete political and economic measures affecting our relationship'. (Summaries of both letters can be found in PREM 19/871.)

[6] On 24 December President Reagan wrote to NATO leaders, and those in Spain, Australia, Japan and New Zealand, stressing the need 'to act in harmony to maximise the chances for peaceful evolution in Poland'. He hoped that they would agree 'on the importance of concerting our actions and the signals' to Warsaw and Moscow and act together if the suppression of civil liberties in Poland did not cease (PREM 19/871). Mrs Thatcher replied on 8 January (see *DBPO: Afghanistan*, No. 123).

No. 122

Letter from Mr Fall to Mr Whitmore (No. 10), 24 December 1981[1]

Confidential (PREM 19/871)

Dear Clive,

Poland

Since the Foreign and Commonwealth Secretary circulated a minute to his Cabinet colleagues last week[2] there have been further developments, some of which were touched on when he saw the Prime Minister yesterday.

The picture in Poland itself is clouded by the news black-out and the cutting of communications, so that it is impossible (for example) to be sure even of basic facts such as the number of deaths. But it seems that martial law has been successfully imposed in all but one or two places. Passive resistance however is

[1] The letter was copied to Mr Melhuish in Warsaw (FCO tel. No.778 of 24 December, FCO 28/4490; ENP 014/1).

[2] No. 117.

widespread, mostly taking the form of attending work places but not working. The military council has made no move either towards economic reform or towards resumption of the dialogue with the other elements, although there are some contacts with the Church. The economic situation must be deteriorating rapidly from the low level to which it had already sunk before martial law was imposed, but this is masked by special deliveries of food and consumer goods from the Soviet Union and Eastern Europe. We may see relaxations in some aspects of martial law, e.g. shorter curfews, but the prospects for the Polish people must be one of hardship and repression lasting certainly for months and possibly for years.

Western reactions are beginning to take shape. The tone in Washington naturally continues to be sharper than elsewhere, but there have been strong statements from most other NATO capitals (not including Ottawa) and from the Ten as a whole.

As regards actions, the problem is to devise measures constituting pressure on or inducement for the Polish leadership without imposing hardship on the Polish people; and measures which might impel the Soviet Union to help and not hinder such steps back towards normality as Jaruzelski may be able and willing to take. To these objectives the Americans would add the need to strike a firm pose in the context of US-Soviet and East/West relations as a whole. The latter, together with domestic considerations, are probably the main motives behind President Reagan's speech last night.[3]

There has been a great deal of consultation, bilaterally, among the Ten and in NATO. As agreed with the Prime Minister yesterday, Lord Carrington has invited his colleagues in the Ten to a special informal meeting in London on 30 December: its task would be to try to identify steps which we could usefully take, either as individual governments or as the Ten, or which we could promote in other groups such as NATO and the major creditors' club; and Lord Carrington has it very much in mind that such a meeting would provide an effective response to the kind of criticism levelled at the Ten for its inactivity during the Afghanistan crisis two years ago. We are in close touch with the Americans and will take account of their views, although it seems likely that the United States government intends to advance down the path of 'punishment' of both the military regime in Poland and the Soviet Union, using economic as well as political levers, whether or not its allies are in the mood to follow suit.

There are two particular problems which the Foreign and Commonwealth Secretary wishes to draw to the attention of his colleagues:

(*a*) *Refugees*

The Home Office have announced that any Pole already in Britain who does not wish to return to Poland may apply for his stay in Britain to be extended; that this will normally be granted, initially for two months. Lord Carrington hopes that there will be few if any refusals. A bigger question is how to respond to Chancellor Kreisky's[4] appeal to Western countries to help absorb the 30,000 Poles now in Austria. Lord Carrington hopes that we will consider with sympathy what part we may be able to play.

(*b*) *Economic aid*

Leaving aside aid from private sources and humanitarian aid (e.g. baby food and medical supplies) there are two main aspects here: first, the supply of food; and second all other forms of economic assistance (re-scheduling, fresh credits etc). On

[3] See No. 121, note 4.

[4] Bruno Kreisky, Chancellor of Austria.

food, Lord Carrington considers that supplies already agreed by the Community should go ahead, subject to reasonable satisfaction that the food is being distributed fairly in Poland. (We are already seeking assurances to this effect about the 8,000 tonnes of free beef from France and Ireland, but not so far about the uncompleted part of subsidised food supplies from various Community countries including Britain which were agreed before 13 December.) Meanwhile, the Community has agreed not to take decisions about supplies additional to those agreed before 13 December. As regards the other forms of economic assistance, the question is whether we should make some or all of them depend on our getting evidence that the regime in Warsaw is living up to its own assurances about an early return to the path of reform and renewal.

Lord Carrington's expectation is that it will be necessary to consult his colleagues again on various aspects of the Polish problem very early in the New Year. The French are at present making difficulties about having the proposed meeting of the Ten at Foreign Minister level (as are the Greeks, although we would be prepared to go ahead without them), and it may be that a first meeting will have to take place at Political/Economic Director level.[5] Either way, FCO officials have been in touch with their colleagues over the subjects likely to arise at the meeting and briefs will be cleared as necessary. If the meeting takes place, as we would wish, at Ministerial level, it is the rule at informal meetings of this kind that conclusions which may be reached will need to be processed formally in the appropriate political cooperation and Community institutions. Further consultations in the Alliance will no doubt also be necessary.

I am sending copies of this letter to the Private Secretaries of all members of OD and to Robert Armstrong.

Yours ever,
BRIAN

[5] The meeting eventually took place on 30 December but at Political Director rather than Foreign Minister level, as M. Cheysson had refused to attend, much to the annoyance of Lord Carrington and the Prime Minister.

No. 123

Record of a telephone conversation between Lord Carrington and Mrs Thatcher, 27 December 1981, 12 p.m.

(PREM 19/871)

LC: I ring you up really to let you know the latest on Poland.
PM: Yes, the news is very, very conflicting today, according to the press—some saying they're talking to the Church and others saying that they really are having a massive repression.
LC: I personally am inclined to think that, half-way between that is probably true. Cheysson has refused to meet on Wednesday.
PM: Well I saw that, but I thought you'd got it all sorted out.
LC: So did I. He agreed with me on the telephone, he then came back and said—I don't know whether Mitterrand has told him not to and so reserve their right to do their own thing—but the reason he gave was that he didn't want there to be a meeting out of which comes less or only the same as we'd already said and that this would do more harm than good. I think reading between the lines he doesn't

want to have a row with the Germans. There's no doubt about it, the Germans are being extremely unwilling to consider taking any measures even against the Poles, let alone the Russians, and I think that it may be that he doesn't want a row with the Germans. So what is now happening is that there is going to be a Political Directors meeting on Wednesday—I think I'll be up on Tuesday and Wednesday and see that all goes well there or at any rate be around—and then I think we shall have to see after the Political Directors' meeting whether we ought to have a Foreign Ministers meeting next week. This will depend a little bit on the Frenchman and where he stands. I think it's rather a pity really, but . . .

PM: Well I think it's a great pity, but I also think it's a pity you can't go ahead without the Frenchman.

LC: Yes, but it's a bit difficult to do that in terms of . . .

PM: Yes, but so long as it's known, so long as it's leaked—I'm now going to do counter leaking Peter, I've had enough of being leaked against me I'll have to do counter—so long as it is leaked that we've tried to call a meeting and everyone agreed except the French.

LC: Well, to be fair, the Italians were not overly keen either.

PM: Well they don't . . . we can do without them.

LC: But they were prepared to do it.

PM: But it's awful when you go to all the trouble . . .

LC: Yes, mounting it and so on . . .

PM: But it must be known that we tried to set one up.

LC: Well, everybody does know—certainly the Americans know because I talked personally to Al Haig about it on the telephone. The only other thing that's happening is Gibraltar—I don't know if you know anything about that?

PM: No.

[. . . *the next part of the conversation relates to Gibraltar*]

LC: Otherwise, there is literally nothing happening very much except the poor wretched Poles.

PM: I think the Polish thing is going to get worse Peter. As winter gets worse I think it's just going to get worse and worse.

LC: Unless they're so sort of beaten that they'll just sort of accept it.

PM: If life is terrible, you might just as well resist. And if life is terrible and you don't resist you might just as well resist. Passive resistance, because there's nothing any Government can do against it.

LC: It was quite well timed, wasn't it, what they did because it's too soon to know—I mean over Christmas and so on—it's too soon to know whether they are going to resist passively or not.

PM: Well, it seemed to mean that what they were doing was the way to do it. Yes, they turn up to the factories but they don't do any work.

LC: Well, there are so many conflicting stories, that may be so, one doesn't know.

PM: No.

LC: This is going to be our problem is to get the truth out of the place.

PM: Yes, you get some from the people who are coming over the border. But the most awful one was that they're kept in open detention camps.

LC: And having water thrown over them, and that sort of thing.

PM: Every hour, but Peter it can't be cold water because it would freeze.

LC: Well, you know, I think you've got to take some of these stories with a certain amount of scepticism.

PM: Well so do I, but I'm always—one took the stories out of Nazi Germany . . .

LC: Yes, and they were true.
PM: And they were true with scepticism. And that's why I'm—it's just the tyrants are the same these days, well the Communists and the Fascists were the same, and therefore there is no depths to which they cannot sink.
LC: Yes, but I don't know if this chap is as bad as that. I *really* don't know. Certainly Gierek wasn't you know.
PM: No . . . but didn't you say the news was it was virtually all the secret police that were doing this and not the ordinary army?
LC: Well, these are some of the rumours coming out, yes.
PM: And every Communist state has a secret police and in a way we have to avoid giving the impression that under Communism it was all right but under military rule it's not. And the fact was Solidarity was getting away from Communism.
LC: That's right, and the military. Anyway I think we've got to keep a very close eye on things and see which way we go.
PM: Yes, so do I.
LC: But as things are I'll give you a ring. You're going to be at Chequers all the week are you?
PM: I've got to go up on Wednesday night, because I've got to do something on the New Year for Thursday. There's no-one else doing anything. So I've got to keep it going and I've got to get a presentation together. It's not my job to do Government presentation but you know when I was doing it we used to arrange for three or four people to do something. Now this week has fallen through.
LC: Which is rather a bore. I can easily arrange to go on television but I don't know quite what one can say.
PM: Well I'll have to go on . . . either this week or next week.
LC: I'm perfectly prepared to do it of course, it's just . . .
PM: Well I shall be on on Thursday now Peter . . .
LC: On New Year's Day . . .
PM: On New Year's Eve . . .
LC: Well, if there's something to say I can easily get a slot, I'm not anxious to get up there and be asked 'what are you doing about it' when we've got the French . . .
PM: Right, well I shall say 'well we wanted to call a meeting now we're holding the Presidency but two of the big nations disagreed. They couldn't agree to come'
LC: There was a disagreement about that . . .
PM: And that's Europe, I'm afraid.
LC: Don't put the finger on France.
PM: No.
LC: Not in public. I think, you know, it's easier to let that be known around the backdoor to say that really.
PM: OK Peter.
LC: Sorry to bother you.
PM: No bother, bye.

No. 124

Sir N. Henderson (Washington) to Lord Carrington, 28 December 1981, 11.32 p.m.

Tel. No. 3941[1] Immediate, Confidential (FCO 49/916, RS 014/2)

MIPT[2] (Saving to some): EC lunch for Haig: Poland

1. After referring to the latest discussions on food for Poland in COREPER (UKREP Brussels Telno 5048)[2] and the determination of the Ten to ensure that this reached its proper recipients, I asked Haig to explain the aims of the Administration. To what extent had they completely written off Jaruzelski, or did they consider that some contact with the Polish administration should be maintained? What was the long-term objective?

2. Haig began by referring to his interview published yesterday in the *Washington Post* (text by Bag—not to all) in which he had addressed these questions. The US had not been surprised by the resort by the Poles to internal repression. If the Soviets themselves had done it by direct intervention the cost to them would obviously have been very high. The long catalogue of hard intelligence about Russian movements including the printing in Russia of the martial law leaflet, gave the lie to the appalling claims, even by some in the West, that Solidarity was to blame for the crack-down. Solidarity may have contributed to the timing of events, but the repression could not be attributed to its excesses. It was equally wrong, though closer to the truth, to see Moscow's hand behind everything Jaruzelski had done.

3. It was vital that no-one on either side of the Atlantic engaged in activities which served the Russian aims. Neither he nor the President believed, as he said in his interview, that the Russians were totally in control of events in Poland. Forces still existed there who were trying to pursue the original objectives of the reform movement and keep the Russians out.

4. On food aid, those who waved their finger at the US (as Genscher appeared to have done today) had not understood Washington's policy. Long before the present crisis Haig had urged Genscher, Cheysson and yourself [of] the need to establish conditionality both in the political sphere as a restraint to repression, and as an element in the Polish economic reforms. Western governments could not be expected to continue pouring money down the Polish rat-hole. Present US policy on food was not to deprive the starving Poles, but to refuse to refurbish the larders of the repressors. The assurances of the regime were not sufficient and the West should think imaginatively about expanding our ideas on assistance to include on-the-spot monitoring by donor countries, with help perhaps from the Polish Church. (He showed particular interest in this respect in what I had said about EC countries monitoring.)

5. In dealing with the Russians, the Administration had not responded in the old-fashioned way, posing challenges to Soviet vital interests or trying to roll back the Soviet empire. However, two recent events—Poland and Afghanistan—represented a direct contravention of the Helsinki Final Act. The West had the right and the obligation to raise this with the Russians and other international fora, if East/West relations and détente were to be pursued with success. A US or Western

[1] Repeated for Information Routine to UKDEL NATO, Bonn, Paris, Moscow, MODUK, UKREP Brussels, Warsaw, Rome, UKMIS New York. Information Saving to other NATO posts, Dublin.

[2] Not printed.

failure to act would diminish our credibility in Moscow and do lasting damage to the Alliance.

6. Haig believed that, with the possible exception of France, the European governments lagged behind the US in their attitudes to Moscow's involvement. He had the feeling that public opinion throughout the West was upset and frustrated at the lack of Western activity. We could not ignore that pressure. The US would not tackle the Russians in a spirit of confrontation or isolationism but we must recognise that the Polish problem would be easier to solve with the public and private assistance of Moscow.

7. While he recognised the great historical importance of events in Poland, Haig repeatedly emphasised that the greatest danger was the impact Soviet moves might have on Western unity. It was clear from intelligence reports that the Russians had focussed their attack on the FRG where they were using every available channel to claim their support for moderation. Neither publicly nor in private to the US were they making such claims. In other words, the Russians were continuing their peace offensive and their approach to arms control which were specifically designed to split Western Europe, especially Western Germany, from the US. If they succeeded, events in Poland would pale in contrast. Whatever happened there, the outcome would be the worst possible for the West.

8. He himself had been frequently in touch by telephone and numerous messages with his Western colleagues, and was disappointed that there would be no EC meeting at Ministerial level this week.[3] I interjected that nonetheless the meeting of Political Directors would be important. He repeated his earlier suggestion in NATO that a Ministerial meeting of the Alliance should be considered for early (repeat early) January. The Alliance had never suffered from an exchange of views at the Ministerial level on a subject of such historic importance. If we did nothing, we would deserve the criticism we were already getting. (Comment: I think that this proposal has more significance now than when it was made before the Polish crack-down.)

9. Haig continued that as a result of today's meeting at the White House, he expected an announcement, on which the Allies would be consulted, to be made shortly about further steps.[4] These would not be cataclysmic in character but if the Russians remained uncooperative further steps beyond these would be taken. Discussing available Western leverage, Haig distinguished two types: internal and external. The restraint the Russians had exercised over the past eighteen months, despite the rise of an independent trades union movement and the challenge to the political authority of the Party, demonstrated that the Eastern Europe of 1981 had changed from 1968 or 1956. The serious inhibitions against Soviet intervention had not disappeared with martial law. It was up to the West to discover the true nature of these and to apply our limited assets in order to reinforce them. It was unrealistic to expect, as the Russians and some in the West claimed, that the Polish revolution was over and the repression should soon pass. The results of the economic shambles in Poland had still to be felt and the potential for destabilisation remained great. Poland depended on the West for her economic vitality, which improved our internal leverage. It was therefore all the more important to ensure close cooperation on food supplies, and not to lift prematurely our pressure in this area.

10. However, the real leverage on the Russians was external. They had shown massive misjudgement over Afghanistan, earning international opprobrium

[3] See No. 123.
[4] See No. 125.

especially from the Third World. Moscow needed a deal on arms control and economic aid from the West. They faced demographic problems themselves and further trouble in Eastern Europe as a result of Poland. If however they saw a chance of splitting the Alliance especially the FRG from the US, they would continue their present course. We had unprecedented leverage, and should do all we could to enhance it.

11. Questioned about specific steps, Haig said the worst thing the Administration could do would be to threaten cancellation of the INF negotiations or to add them to a package of other moves. The US had passed the point of treating arms control as normal business. Western public opinion was hostile to the repression in Poland. We must not let it be turned against ourselves. The President felt very strongly on this point. Arms control was a different and separate part of the Administration policy. For the moment, while the US could not afford to give the impression that negotiations would continue irrespective and in ignorance of what the Soviets did elsewhere, it was best to keep future policy fuzzy, with an emphasis on the positive, and to avoid raising public concerns about possible cancellation.

12. On CSCE Haig said that it would be a tragedy if the next meeting were cancelled. Indeed he hoped within the next day to get Reagan's agreement that an emergency session be convened. Although some people in Washington thought that the continuation of CSCE was an affront while repression continued in Poland, to cancel it would remove the fundamental legitimacy of our own position in criticising the repression. Western public opinion could easily understand the point that Helsinki represented a solemn agreement to which all signatories were bound. To that extent, as he pointed out in his press interview of 27 December,[5] Helsinki had changed the political map of Europe established after Yalta.[6] To argue about rolling back the Soviet Empire would immediately involve us in debates about spheres of influence and even condominia. This the West and US must avoid (even though the Russians did not observe the practical spheres of influence elsewhere in the world). We should play on the Soviet concern about legitimacy.

13. On economic sanctions, about which I expressed European scepticism in the light of previous experience (Rhodesia[7] and Afghanistan[8]) and the US lifting of the grain embargo,[9] Haig agreed there could be no double standards or half-sanctions. He had personally opposed the lifting of the embargo (though he noted, acknowledging that he was being Jesuitical in doing so, that if this had not happened we would not have our present leverage). He shared the scepticism about the effectiveness of partial sanctions, but emphasised that an embargo imposed by all grain-producers would have a tremendous impact on the Russians, even if they

[5] In the *Washington Post* Mr Haig had stated that the events in Poland had historical importance not only for the Polish nation but the entire post-1945 international system.

[6] The Yalta Conference, from 4 to 11 February 1945, where US President Franklin D. Roosevelt, British Prime Minister Winston Churchill, and Soviet Premier Joseph Stalin made important decisions regarding the future of the post-war world.

[7] Following the Unilateral Declaration of Independence from the United Kingdom by Rhodesia, on 11 November 1965, the British Government announced a full range of economic sanctions against Rhodesia. However some countries continued to trade with Rhodesia, undermining their effectiveness.

[8] See *DBPO: Afghanistan*.

[9] A grain embargo, imposed by President Carter on the Soviet Union following the invasion of Afghanistan, had been lifted by President Reagan in April 1981.

would not necessarily be compelled to act against their vital interests. Any sanctions had to be imposed on a broad front and in unison. Otherwise they would not work, and those who imposed them would be singled out for Soviet reaction. Haig also noted that their growing international isolation was a further important restraint on the Soviet leadership.

14. In summary Haig made the following point:

(i) We must maintain Western cohesion.

(ii) The Russians had a responsibility for what was happening in Poland. If we ignored the unequivocable evidence it could produce unpleasant results.

(iii) We had considerable leverage to work for a compromise in Poland. Jaruzelski was not a total stooge of the Russians. We should aim to strengthen the hand of the Church, Solidarity and others responsible for disbursing humanitarian aid.

No. 125

Note of conversation between Mrs Thatcher and Lord Carrington, 29 December 1981

(PREM 19/871)

Poland

Lord Carrington telephoned the Prime Minister this afternoon at 1230. He said that he had just received a message from Secretary of State Haig.[1] The Americans would be announcing some fairly severe sanctions against the USSR later today. The sanctions would not include the cancellation of the disarmament talks in Geneva. But they would include measures such as the cancellation of Aeroflot landing rights, a halt to negotiations on the sale of grain, a halt to the export material for constructing natural gas pipelines etc.[2] The message from Haig asked the Ten to take comparable measures.

Lord Carrington said that a meeting of the Foreign Ministers of the Ten was now urgent. He had sent a message to Cheysson asking him to change his mind, and agree to such a meeting on Thursday. Cheysson was in Athens today, and would be in Ethiopia tomorrow, and communicating with him was very difficult. A meeting of Foreign Ministers tomorrow would be impossible to arrange. But Haig's message could be considered by Political Directors on Wednesday, and by Foreign Ministers on Thursday. In case this proved impossible, Lord Carrington said that he had told Tindemans, who would be taking over the Presidency on Friday, that he considered a meeting should be held before next week.

Lord Carrington said that he had now made it public that the UK wanted a meeting to be held, and that it was the French who had been dragging their feet. He had been prompted to do this partly by the fact that the French had now blamed us for dragging our feet over the setting up of the meeting.

[1] Mr Haig said that there was no indication that the repression in Poland, or Moscow's complicity, had lessened, and the President had no alternative but to take concrete measures against the Soviet Union aimed at re-establishing the conditions for reconciliation and the resumption of Renewal in Poland. Haig went on to urge the UK to take parallel steps, 'to demonstrate our common resolve', and called for an early meeting of NATO foreign ministers.

[2] See *Public Papers: Reagan (1981)*, p. 1209.

On substance, Lord Carrington said that it would be very difficult to reach a consensus in the Ten. He felt that the Americans were focussing more on East-West relations than on the situation in Poland. President Reagan had received a rude response to his message to Brezhnev.[3] The measures they intended to announce today were a gesture against Russian interference in Polish affairs. In Lord Carrington's view, the Americans were playing the sanctions card far too soon.

Lord Carrington ended by saying that he would report to the Prime Minister again after the meeting of the Political Directors of the Ten.[4]

[3] On 23 and 25 December President Reagan and President Brezhnev exchanged letters each accusing the other of interfering in the internal affairs of Poland contrary to the principles of the Helsinki Final Act. (The letters are reproduced at http://www.thereaganfiles.com/.)

[4] At this meeting on 30 December it was agreed that foreign ministers of the Ten would meet in Brussels on 4 January. On Poland it was agreed that the short-term objectives were to get martial law lifted, detainees released and internal dialogue resumed. In the longer-term, the objectives were: not to accept the situation as irreversible, keep international aspects of the crisis under control, prevent foreign military intervention, ensure the process of reform and renewal was resumed, and to maintain unity amongst the Ten and in the Alliance. On the USSR, there was agreement that the US had given a lead in a direction which the European allies would find hard to follow. But they agreed to avoid action which would make Western unity worse, make maximum use of political measures (where the Ten were less constrained than in economic field), and each look for national ways to reflect disapproval of the Soviet role in Poland (FCO tel. No.159 of 30 December to Brussels; FCO 28/4491, ENP 014/1).

No. 126

Letter from Mr Fall to Mr Whitmore (No. 10), 31 December 1981
Confidential (FCO 28/4491, ENP 014/1)

Dear Clive,

Poland

Since I wrote to you on 24 December[1] the military regime has established firm control throughout Poland. Major centres of resistance appear to have been eliminated through a combination of pressure, shows of force and on occasion some brutality, although the authorities seem to have tried to avoid violence in the knowledge that this could make the matters worse for themselves. They are now seeking to convince the world that the situation is rapidly returning to normal, that the Polish people are now working more efficiently than before and that the harsh martial law restrictions will soon be relaxed. Though we still have only fragmentary information, it is clear that the reality is far from this rosy picture. Initial resistance may have been broken, including that at Gdansk and the mines in the South-West, but at least 5,000 people including many leading intellectuals are being detained without trial; the Polish people are back in the factories, but they are not working with a will; and the continuing restrictions on travel and communication are preventing any early return to normal civil or business activity. It is not clear how the authorities can begin to implement their promises to continue the renewal and pursue economic reforms in the face of a sullen and embittered populace. The only logical course must be a resumption of the dialogue

[1] No. 122.

approach the neutral and non-aligned countries, seeking their views about the possible early reconvening of the meeting.

Dispatch of emissary to Poland

6. The idea received widespread support from most Ministers, especially Genscher and Colombo, with the former suggesting also that the emissary—Tindemans—should also go to Moscow. But the suggestions was blocked by Cheysson who adamantly refused to permit the communiqué to make any mention of the idea which, he maintained, would amount to authorising one representative to speak at the highest level on the whole of East-West relations and would thus be a major step forward in political cooperation.[3] He was supported by Fotilas (Greece). It was therefore omitted from the communiqué. It is widely believed that Cheysson has been invited to visit Poland.[4]

US-Europe relations

7. Most Ministers spoke firmly on the need to avoid a crisis of western unity. I emphasised that we should focus on the crisis in the communist system which the events in Poland showed. Denmark and the Netherlands doubted whether the Ten should endorse US measures, but agreed that the Ten should not stand in the Americans' way. Dooge (Ireland) said that his country would examine the impact of US measures in order to ensure as far as possible that they would not be undermined or circumvented. Thorn (Commission) warned against antagonising the US in view of other EC-US problems such as steel. The only really discordant note was struck by Fotilas (Greece) who said that he could not conceal his bitterness at the unilateral nature of the US measures. The text in paragraph 7[5] of the communiqué emerged in satisfactory form—the last sentence refers to the need to avoid any step 'which could undermine' the US actions. (Presidency text of English version which says 'compromise' is wrong.)

Measures against Poland

9. [*sic*] Other measures against Poland which I had sought to have incorporated in the communiqué were edited out after objections from partners. As regards the possible imposition of restrictions on Polish embassies by the Ten, the principal objection came from Fotilas (Greece) who argued that to impose such restrictions might lead to those in Warsaw becoming permanent. He received some support from Olesen (Denmark) on the grounds that it was not Danish national practice to restrict any embassy, even that of the Soviet Union, in the way proposed. The inclusion in the communiqué of reference to the increase in broadcasting to Poland by those members of the Ten with international radio services was also opposed by

[3] On the same day as the meeting in Brussels, General Jaruzelski spent nearly two hours with the eight EC Heads of Mission represented in Warsaw. However he did not offer any new concessions but largely repeated past justifications for the imposition of martial law (Warsaw tel. No.12 of 4 January). Mr Melhuish had earlier, in Warsaw tel. No. 1098 of 31 December, advised trying to pursue a political dialogue between the Ten and the Polish military authorities, if they were willing to accept this channel. (Poland did not formally recognise any political activity on the part of the Ten.) The eight EC embassies (Luxembourg and Ireland were not represented) were currently meeting regularly twice a week.

[4] Sir R. Hibbert, in Paris tel. No. 12 of 6 January, commented that M. Cheysson's behaviour 'was probably no more than the usual French effort to ensure that if there are going to be colourful initiatives the option is left open for them to be French' (FCO 28/4946; ENP 021/2).

[5] This read: 'The Ten have taken note of the economic measures taken by the United States Government with regard to the USSR. The Ten will undertake in this context close and positive consultations with the United States Government and with the governments of other Western states in order to define what decisions will best serve their common objectives and to avoid any step which could undermine their respective actions.'

Olesen, although it was agreed that the Presidency could mention the subject at the Presidency press conference immediately after the meeting.

Comment

10. The outcome of the meeting was satisfactory, if not all that we might have hoped for. The meeting's most striking feature, however, was the contrast between French words, which were strongly critical of events in Poland, and French actions, which consisted in pressing for food aid to continue, opposing the early reconvening of the CSCE and scuttling the idea of sending an emissary. On this latter point in particular, there was a strong clash between Cheysson and Genscher. If the Americans are critical of the results of the Ten's meeting, you may wish to make sure that they know where the blame lies.[6]

[6] On 7 January Polish Deputy Foreign Minister, M. Wiejacz, handed Mr Melhuish a letter from General Jaruzelski to Mrs Thatcher. The letter sought to justify the Polish Government's actions, in particular the need to preserve Poland's national independence and freedom which he considered were under threat unless some action was taken. He also asked for the British Government to show understanding for the situation and his Government's efforts which were aimed at 'a return to political and economic stabilisation and the creation of conditions for the future democratic stabilisation of Poland' (Warsaw tel. Nos. 56 and 57 of 7 January, FCO 28/4924, ENP 020/1).

No. 128

Sir A. Parsons (UKMIS New York) to Lord Carrington, 6 January 1982, 6.05 p.m.

Tel. No. 16 Priority, Confidential (FCO 28/4968, ENP 022/4)

Poland in the UN

1. I see that the communiqué of the foreign ministers of the Ten about Poland (Brussels Tel. No. 2)[1] mentions action in the United Nations and its specialised agencies to denounce violations of human rights and acts of violence. A similar phrase appears in the joint communiqué published in today's (6 January) *New York Times* following Schmidt's meeting with Reagan.

2. If the Americans or the Ten or both decide to involve the UN in the question of Poland before there has been overt military intervention by the Russians or others, it is most important that we should not simply end up by shooting ourselves in the foot. You already know my views on the American idea of bringing the question of human rights in Poland to the Security Council (my tels Nos. 1614 and 1618).[2]

3. As regards making use of the General Assembly, the Human Rights Commission and/or relevant specialised agencies, the key point is that the majority of the Third World must be brought on board: otherwise the exercise would be a fiasco. In this sense, we have two main problems to face, first, the accusation of double standards and second the risk of inviting damaging counter-attacks.

4. On the first point—double standards—there would be a tendency amongst the Third World majority, which would be actively fostered by the Soviet Union and their friends, to argue that the West was getting into a great state about Poland

[1] Not printed. The communiqué (see No. 127, note 2) stated that 'The ten will work in the United Nations and its specialised agencies for a denunciation of violations of human rights and acts of violence' (FCO 28/4954, ENP 022/1).

[2] No. 120.

whereas it appeared unconcerned about habitual violators of human rights who happened to be in the Western camp *viz* South Korea and the Philippines, not to speak of Jerry Rawlings[3] *et al* and, as regards the Americans, the Central and South American dictatorships. The argument would continue that the West was simply using Poland as an arena in the East/West ideological battle and was trying to recruit the Non-Aligned Movement into its camp. Skilful deployment of this argument by the Russians would not only deny us the necessary majority over Poland, it could also erode the Non-Aligned support we have so laboriously built up over Cambodia and Afghanistan, even though these are not analogous cases.

5. The second point—the danger of counter-attacks—is most relevant to the United States and ourselves. The Russians have small skeletons in the cupboards of all Western countries to be rattled if need be e.g. Eskimos in Canada and the Moluccans[4] in the Netherlands. The only substantial skeletons in their possession are the racial situation in the United States and Northern Ireland. In retaliation for Western action over Poland, they would not hesitate to use these to the full.

6. As regards Northern Ireland, we know that some of the nasties tried to promote a resolution in the Third Committee of the General Assembly a month or so ago. They were driven off by the admirable Irish chairman of the Committee. If we were seen to be at the front of the pack over Poland in the UN context, this would increase the already present danger that the Soviet Union would retaliate by promoting the introduction of a resolution on Northern Ireland at the Human Rights Commission and/or elsewhere. It would be unfortunate to say the least if, having just rid ourselves of virtually all our historical national problems in the UN e.g. Rhodesia and colonialism, we inadvertently helped to forge a new weapon for our enemies to use against us year after year.

7. With the above considerations in mind, my present advice is that we would do better to stick to the relevant European organs such as the CSCE where the need to mobilise the Third World with its attendant risks does not apply. If it is decided that we must involve the UN at some stage on the question of human rights in Poland, we must think very carefully about the consequences before finally deciding to act. In this context, the ILO looks like one of the most promising areas.[5] The risks to which I have drawn attention above would be less if action was seen to be primarily an effort by Western trade unionists to protect the rights of their brothers and sisters in Poland. Beyond this, we must co-ordinate very carefully with the Western like-minded group (which includes the United States) in advance of the Human Rights Commission.[6] The group will meet informally in New York on 11 and 12 January to prepare for the Commission on Human Rights, and it would be very useful to have your comments by 111300Z.[7]

[3] He twice became President of Ghana following coups (June-September 1979 and 1981-2001). His coup in 1979 was followed by a series of executions of the elites and military associates of the former president. Following his coup on 31 December 1981, he suspended the constitution of Ghana, dissolved parliament and banned political parties.

[4] When Indonesia gained independence in 1949 the Dutch did not keep their undertaking to make the Moluccans (indigenous inhabitants of the Maluku Islands) independent, and they became part of Indonesia.

[5] See No. 153, paragraph 16.

[6] On 8 January the Ten's Permanent Representatives discussed Poland and agreed that there was no specific occasion for action until the spring Economic and Social Council and that in the meantime the appropriate fora for potential action were the ILO and the Commission on Human Rights.

[7] 1 p.m. GMT on 11 January. The annual meeting of the Human Rights Commission in Geneva discussed Poland on 2 February. The Canadians (on behalf of the Western members except Greece) called for the question of human rights in Poland to be given priority. The Canadians and the Danes

(speaking in support of the Ten) were interrupted by points of order from the Soviet Bloc countries, and the Bulgarian chairman suspended the session. Mr Marshall, the UK Representative to the UN (Geneva) concluded that although the proceedings brought little credit to the Commission, the result was 'pretty good' as the West had stood together and Poland had been put firmly on the agenda (UKMIS Geneva tel. No. 34 of 2 February).

No. 129

Record of call by the Soviet Ambassador on Lord Trefgarne, 6 January 1982, 11.30 a.m.
(FCO 28/4788, EN 306/1)

Present:

Lord Trefgarne	HE Mr V. I. Popov
Mr Macgregor	Mr Ouspenskiy
Mr Johnson	

BBC jamming[1]

1. *Lord Trefgarne* reminded the Ambassador that on 31 December he had told him of HMG's displeasure at hearing reports that the BBC's Polish language radio broadcasts were being jammed. The Ambassador had then declined to comment on the grounds that Poland was a sovereign and independent state on whose internal affairs it would be wrong for the Ambassador to pronounce. However, it has now been learned that the jamming of these Polish language broadcasts came from sources inside the Soviet Union. The jamming had become more extensive in the past two days. Lord Trefgarne therefore wished to repeat in stronger terms what he had said to the Ambassador last week. The British Government totally deplored this unjustified interference in radio broadcasts. Such action ran counter to the letter and spirit of the Helsinki Final Act whose signatory states had noted the expansion in the dissemination of information broadcast by radio and had expressed the hope for the continuation of this process so as to meet the interest of mutual understanding among peoples and the aims set forth by the CSCE. Lord Trefgarne requested the Ambassador to inform his authorities that the British Government strongly condemned Soviet actions in this regard and called for the lifting of the jamming forthwith.

2. *Mr Popov* rejected this condemnation as being without foundation. He regretted that Lord Trefgarne's sources of information were unreliable. The Soviet Union did not interfere in the internal affairs of other states, including Poland. Any talk of Soviet complicity in the so-called jamming was unfounded. This was an attempt to shift responsibility for violations of the Helsinki Final Act away from Western countries and in the first place the United States. As TASS had made clear President Reagan's attempt to throw responsibility for developments in Poland on the Soviet Union was a flagrant distortion of the Soviet position. There was no ground for raising questions about Soviet fulfilment of the provisions of the Final Act, including those concerning radio broadcasts. Unfortunately the same thing could not always be said of BBC broadcasts to the Soviet Union which did nothing

[1] A week after martial law was imposed BBC Polish Service transmissions were increased from just over 21 hours a week to 26.5 hours a week. On 30 December the Polish Service began to be jammed.

to illustrate British life or promote mutual understanding. BBC broadcasts constituted interference in others' internal affairs and were thus in contravention of the Final Act. As for BBC broadcasts in Polish, the Ambassador noted that the Polish press had denounced these as subversive, designed to turn Poles against one another and encourage them to infringe Polish regulations. But this was an affair between the British and Polish governments and the Soviet Union did not interfere in it.

3. *Lord Trefgarne* asked whether the Ambassador was saying that the Soviet Union was not jamming BBC broadcasts in Polish. *Mr Popov* repeated that the Soviet Union had not interfered in anyone else's internal affairs and were not violating the Helsinki agreements. *Lord Trefgarne* said that this was an equivocal reply. The fact was that the Soviet authorities were jamming BBC Polish broadcasts: the sources of such jamming had been located at Smolensk and Kaliningrad. Location was a simple procedure and there could be no doubt about it. HMG took the greatest exception to this Soviet action. As for Mr Popov's allegations about the BBC, as the Ambassador knew the BBC was independent of Government control. But it was quite wrong to suggest that BBC broadcasts had incited dissention in Poland. The BBC aimed merely to give the Polish people a more balanced view of events in their own country and in the world than was available to them from domestic sources. Lord Trefgarne reminded the Ambassador that HMG had never interfered in any way with Soviet broadcasts to the United Kingdom even though we took exception to some transmissions from Radio Moscow. He repeated the gravity with which HMG viewed this matter and their expectation the jamming would be stopped forthwith.

4. *Mr Popov* said that they could discuss this forever. He would merely comment that it was only natural that Soviet broadcasts were not jammed since they were entirely 'loyal' and objective. He repeated that Lord Trefgarne's sources of information about the mythical jamming were unreliable and regretted that Lord Trefgarne had made use of them. *Lord Trefgarne* asked again if the Ambassador was saying that the Soviet Union was not responsible for the jamming of the BBC Polish transmissions. *Mr Popov* replied that he was not aware of the fact of any jamming and that the Soviet Union could not bear any responsibility for something it was not doing.

5. The meeting ended at 12 noon.

No. 130

Letter from Mr Fall to Mr Coles (No. 10), 6 January 1982
Confidential (PREM 19/872)

Dear John,

Poland

I understand that the Prime Minister is to hold a meeting at 1700 hrs tomorrow.[1] You will wish to know where matters stand on Poland, and in particular what response we and our partners in the Ten might be able to make to the US request for support for the measures against Poland and the Soviet Union announced by

[1] See No. 131. This was an ad-hoc ministerial meeting held at Lord Carrington's suggestion to decide what lines to take on economic measures for Poland and, in the Polish context, the USSR at various forthcoming international meetings.

President Reagan on 23 and 29 December.[2] There is quite a lot of ground to be covered and I apologise for the length of what follows.

The regime in Poland following the imposition of martial law on 13 December is now entering its fourth week. The repressive nature of the regime has become clear although it would be premature to reach any final judgements about General Jaruzelski's long-term intentions or his room for manoeuvre. Meanwhile our public stance has, as you know, been adjusted to reflect sharp condemnation of what has happened in Poland as well as the Soviet Union's role.

At the meeting of the Ten Foreign Ministers on 4 January there was no fundamental disagreement over the Soviet Union's complicity in and responsibility for the imposition of martial law in Poland. This is an encouraging step forward, as is the fact that most Ministers present spoke firmly of the need to preserve Western unity and particularly not to undermine the US measures. We are at one with the United States on our immediate objectives to press for the lifting of martial law, the release of the detainees and the resumption of a dialogue between the Polish authorities, the Church and Solidarity.

A very intense period of consultation both within the Alliance and the Community lies ahead. The NATO Ministerial meeting on 11 January could prove difficult, given the existing differences of interest and opinion among the Ten. Nevertheless attention must remain focussed on the real crisis in Poland and not on diversions among the Alliance partners. We need therefore to join with them in measures which, while not identical with those the US have announced, do show our clear support.

It will not be possible to take final decisions on all these questions on 11 January. A number of them fall to be taken in the Community, through preparation in COREPER leading to decisions at the Foreign Affairs Council on 25-26 January. There may be some discussion at the EC Foreign Ministers' meeting on 14 January, but that is of course intended to deal with the mandate.

This is the background against which, bilaterally and in the Ten, we have made our views clear about developments in Poland. The scope for political action against the Soviet Union is not great. Following Afghanistan we have already reduced our contacts to the essential minimum.[3] One obvious opening is to use the Madrid Review Conference. At the meeting of Foreign Ministers of the Ten on 4 January we agreed to press for the early reconvening of the Review Conference at Ministerial level to discuss the grave violations of the Helsinki Final Act and, if this takes place, it will give a further early opportunity to put the Soviet Union and Poland back in the dock.

The following are specific points which now arise for decision in connection with Poland and the Soviet Union (against whom the Americans are pressing us to take economic measures).

Poland. I attach a note by officials[4] for making recommendations on a number of economic aspects of our relations with Poland. Lord Carrington hopes that these can be agreed. He would like to draw attention to two points in particular.

[2] See No. 121, note 4 and No. 125.

[3] For the UK response to the Soviet invasion of Afghanistan see *DBPO: Afghanistan*. HM Ambassador in Moscow, Sir C. Keeble, thought there was an important distinction between Afghanistan and the Polish crisis. In a note of 7 January, he stated that room to influence the course of events, though slight, did exist in relation to Poland in a way which it did not in Afghanistan, as Soviet troops had not intervened directly and General Jaruzelski would have to try to move back to normality if he wanted the country to function (FCO 28/4954, ENP 022/1).

[4] Not printed.

The Ursus project.[5] We need to think further about the balance of advantage, political, economic and industrial in the continuation or otherwise of this project. I understand that officials of the Department of Trade are examining these issues in consultation with Massey-Ferguson.[6] We should await their report before taking decisions. Meanwhile, a summary of the present position is contained in an annex to the officials' paper.[7]

EC Food Supplies. Lord Carrington thinks that it would be wrong for the Community to offer further subsidised food to Poland. Although there will be opposition to this view within the Community from those who have a national interest in continuing to export Community surpluses to Poland, he asks his colleagues to agree that any consideration of further supplies of subsidised food to Poland must be made dependent on significant movement towards lifting martial law and resuming the reform process. As there will be strong public and Parliamentary pressure on governments to respond urgently to the serious shortages of food in Poland, he would like to ask the EC to agree that further community funds be made available for humanitarian supplies to be distributed by voluntary and church agencies in Poland. This would be a humanitarian gesture most likely to serve the interests of the Polish people.

Two other questions should be mentioned. Poland has applied for readmission to the *IMF*. The application is now under consideration by the Fund's authorities but will move very slowly. We need not take specific blocking action for the time being. But we should look again at this later in the year when substantive decisions are more imminent.

The Americans have announced that they will be proposing a tightening of the restrictions on high technology exports to Poland under *Cocom* rules. Given the very small percentage of our trade that would be affected by such a move we would see no reason to oppose this if our other Allies were also willing to go along with the Americans.

Then there is the question of *Polish refugees*. The question is sensitive and has already aroused a considerable amount of Parliamentary interest. The Home Secretary has agreed not to return any Pole to Poland against his will. Lord Carrington welcomes this, and hopes that we can also play a helpful part in response to the request from Chancellor Kreisky (now supported by the UN High Commissioner for Refugees) for assistance in the re-settlement of the large number of Polish refugees in Austria. He will be pursuing this question separately with the Home Secretary.

There is also the question of what we should say to the *Poles, Parliament and press* about these decisions. As far as the Poles are concerned, until we are in a position to make a collective announcement with our other allies, we should continue to take the line that while we are willing when circumstances permit to return our relations, including economic relations, to their former level, present circumstances make this impossible. We will need to see how far we have got in taking decisions before deciding whether to make a formal announcement of these measures in Parliament when it reconvenes on 14 January. The press line should continue to be that reflected in the communiqué following the 4 January meeting,

[5] See Nos. 99, 109 and 117.

[6] The multinational company Massey-Ferguson was involved in modernisation and investment at the Ursus tractor plant.

[7] Not printed.

which was that measures including those concerning credit and economic assistance to Poland would be considered as the situation in Poland developed.[8]

Soviet Union. I attach the text of President Reagan's statement of 29 December setting out US measures against the Soviet Union.[9] It is not entirely clear what the impact of these measures will be on Europe's trade with the Soviet Union, especially as regards the gas pipeline and high technology exports. I understand that officials are looking further into these aspects.

The Americans have pressed the allies to take complementary action. While they are not necessarily looking for measures identical to their own, they have made it clear that they want a convincing display of unity and support through concerted action. Lord Carrington thinks it important that we should make a positive response and that our approach should be guided by the following two considerations: first, any action which we take should be closely coordinated with our Community partners and with other main Western industrialised countries; and, second, existing contracts should not be affected.

Our broad objectives should be to secure agreement on means to ensure that the United States' measures are not undermined. How we give effect to the commitment not to undermine the US measures gives rise to a number of important and complex questions which will need to be carefully studied by officials and worked out with our EC partners to ensure that we are in line. We should also seek agreement to measures which would generally support those taken by the US but would not be identical.

Restriction on Imports of Soviet Manufactures. At the meeting on 4 January the Commission raised the possibility of increasing restrictions on imports of Soviet manufactured goods into the Community. A reference was made to this in the communiqué. We should encourage the Commission to produce proposals. These are likely to be either increases in quantitative restrictions or in tariffs. Lord Carrington hopes that on examination we shall be able to agree to some form of restrictions on these lines. This is a field where he believes that, provided we act collectively, we could achieve a significant political gesture at very limited economic cost.

COCOM. The Americans have asked for our support in placing further limitations on exports of high technology goods to the Soviet Union. This is something we shall need to look at carefully at the high-level meeting of officials planned for 16/18 January where the Americans will no doubt make their views clearer.

Maritime Agreement. The Americans have suspended negotiations on a new maritime agreement with the Soviet Union. Our own Maritime Agreement has not worked in our favour. Lord Carrington hopes that it can be agreed that he should be able to say that we are prepared to give notice of termination of the Agreement. We shall of course have to consider the position of those of our partners who have similar agreements and who could usefully be encouraged to take similar action.

Factory Fishing. Lord Carrington has circulated to colleagues a minute he sent to the Minister of Agriculture on the possibility of using the proposed new licensing system for the transfer of fish caught by UK fishermen, to discriminate against Soviet factory ships. While the introduction of licensing is a measure we may be taking for conservation reasons, he thinks it would be wrong to miss the

[8] See No. 127, note. 2.

[9] Not printed. See No. 125, and for further detail see *DBPO: Afghanistan*.

opportunity of presenting this as part of a package of measures we might be prepared to take against the Soviet Union.

Bilateral Exchange Agreements. Lord Carrington thinks we ought to be prepared to follow the US lead and, in conjunction with our partners, state that we will not renew any scientific, technical or similar exchange agreements with the Soviet Union that fall due for renewal and will confine the implementation of existing agreements in these fields to routine exchanges. If a package along these lines is to be agreed, we will need to think carefully about ministerial and other contacts with the Soviet Union. These have already been reduced to a routine level and confined to essential business, mainly in the trade field. He believes that such contacts should continue. At present these include a CBI Economic Round Table visit to the Soviet Union in February, the Anglo/Soviet Joint Commission meeting in May and indeed Mr Rees' speech at the British-Soviet Chamber of Commerce lunch on 21 January.

I am copying this letter to John Kerr (HM Treasury), Kate Timms (MAFF), John Rhodes (Department of Trade), Ian Ellison (Department of Industry) and David Wright (Cabinet Office).

Yours ever,
B. J. P. FALL

No. 131

Letter from Mr Coles (No. 10) to Mr Fall, 8 January 1982
Confidential (PREM 19/872)

Dear Brian,

Poland

The Prime Minister held a meeting at 5 p.m. on 7 January to consider the proposals in your letter to me of 6 January.[1] The meeting also had before it the Foreign and Commonwealth Secretary's minute of 5 January (FCS/82/3) to the Minister of Agriculture;[2] and some of those present had seen the latter's reply, in Robert Lowson's letter to you of 7 January.[3] The meeting was attended by the Foreign and Commonwealth Secretary, the Chancellor of the Exchequer, the Secretary of State for Industry, the Secretary of State for Trade and Mr Wade-Gery.[4]

The Foreign and Commonwealth Secretary said that the communiqué issued by the Foreign Ministers of the Ten Member countries of the European Community on 4 January had been helpful in condemning both repression by the Polish authorities and the hostile role of the Soviet Union; and in undertaking not to undermine American economic measures against the Russians, although it had naturally not been possible to spell out what this would involve. The communiqué had been well received by the United States Government, and the subsequent meeting between President Reagan and Chancellor Schmidt had also gone reasonably well. American public opinion was nevertheless deeply concerned about what was seen as weakness among the European allies. The United States Government were therefore very anxious to see the Europeans take some concrete steps against the

[1] No. 130.
[2] Not printed.
[3] Not printed. Mr Lowson was Principal Private Secretary to the Minister of Agriculture, Fisheries and Food.
[4] Deputy Secretary to the Cabinet.

Soviet Union as well as Poland; but they recognised that these need not exactly match the steps they themselves had already taken. The Americans had chosen measures which signalled their displeasure while not doing great harm to their material interests; and they tacitly accepted that it would be reasonable for the EC to do the same. It would now be necessary to discuss the matter at the meeting of NATO Foreign Ministers on 11 January[5] and subsequently among the Ten. European action against the Soviet Union, to which some of the Ten were wholly opposed, would be harder to agree on than on action against Poland. But there should be a reasonable chance of progress if he could put forward a package of possible measures, on the lines of those listed in your letter under reference, which would convey a clear signal both to the Americans and to the Russians and Poles without seriously damaging European interests. If agreement on such a package proved impossible, it would be necessary to consider how far Britain might take action on her own; but for the present that difficult decision did not arise.

The Secretary of State for Trade welcomed the Foreign and Commonwealth Secretary's proposals as a well-judged response to a difficult situation. A signal was clearly needed. But he was glad that comprehensive economic sanctions were not being suggested, given their uncertain efficacy and the considerable damage to British interests they would involve.

In discussion there was general agreement with the course proposed by the Foreign and Commonwealth Secretary. The following points in particular were noted.

(*a*) Of the proposed measures against Poland, the suspension of subsidised sales of EC food might prove the hardest to agree on, in the face of opposition from the French and possibly the Germans. Britain had a right of veto; but if the prospect were that this would have to be used in uncomfortable isolation it might be preferable simply to make clear that there would be no British participation in such sales.

(*b*) Among the proposed measures against the Soviet Union, termination of the Maritime Agreement would do little harm to British interests and might have incidental advantages if the number of Soviet sailors visiting British ports were reduced. It would irritate more than harm the Soviet Union, and would not take effect until 12 months' notice had expired; but it would be welcomed by the Americans as an appropriate gesture.

(*c*) As regards factory fishing, the Minister of Agriculture's need to consult the fishing industry about the proposed new licensing system was understood. But the idea of using that system to discriminate against the Russians would do no harm to British interests and would need to be canvassed with Britain's partners in the coming week. Any prior consultation needed should therefore be undertaken on 8 January.

(*d*) Possible COCOM measures against Poland and against the Soviet Union were further examined in a minute which the Foreign and Commonwealth Secretary was on the point of circulating to the Prime Minister and others concerned. In this context it was not clear whether the measures already taken by the Americans against the Soviet Union applied to existing contracts as well as new ones. It was to be hoped that they did not, as the EC had strongly urged. Otherwise serious difficulties could arise for British, German and Italian firms over contracts for equipment for the West Siberian pipeline[6] which involved

[5] See No. 132, note 2.
[6] The pipeline issue is covered in greater depth in *DBPO: Afghanistan.*

components made in the United States or under United States licence. It would be unwise of the Americans to press this point, since the European firms could if necessary find ways round any American ban; but the process of doing so would be highly inconvenient.

(*e*) Some of the Government's supporters in Parliament were critical of the United States Government's measures against the Soviet Union, which were seen as precipitate and probably ineffective. There would therefore be advantage in any British measures being so far as possible seen to be part of a distinct European response to the present crisis. In practice, however, there would be little scope for disguising the fact that European and American policies were being coordinated, e.g. in the NATO forum; nor would it be desirable to underplay the extent of such coordination, given the importance of unity of purpose within the Western Alliance.

Summing up the discussion the Prime Minister said that it was right to deny any help to Poland which would assist the regime in its present repressive policies; and to work for a series of European gestures against the Soviet Union which would echo but not necessarily copy the gestures being made by the United States. The Foreign and Commonwealth Secretary should therefore proceed as he had suggested. The Americans had chosen measures which were not likely to do serious harm to their interests, and it was reasonable that the members of the EC should do the same. It was important that American restrictions on technology exports should not be allowed to damage the current contracts of British firms such as John Brown;[7] and the Foreign and Commonwealth Secretary, in consultation with the Secretary of State for Trade, should report further if this problem could not be satisfactorily clarified. The Minister of Agriculture's proposed consultations with the fishing industry over licensing in relation to factory fishing should be begun at once, i.e. on 8 January (you will have seen the separate letter on this which I sent to Robert Lowson last night).

I am sending copies of this letter to the Private Secretaries to the Chancellor of the Exchequer, the Secretaries of State for Industry and Trade and the Minister of Agriculture; and to David Wright (Cabinet Office).

Yours ever,
JOHN COLES

[7] John Brown Engineering was involved in a substantial contract for gas pipelines.

No. 132

Submission from Mr Broomfield to Mr J. Bullard, 14 January 1982

Confidential (FCO 28/4772, EN 122/1)

Economic sanctions against Poland and the Soviet Union[1]

1. I have discussed the effect of the measures referred to in the NATO communiqué[2] on Poland and the Soviet Union with Mr Williamson.[3] What follows draws heavily on his advice. The judgements are, however, my own.

[1] Mr Bullard had asked for an assessment of the political and economic consequences of the various kinds of sanctions being considered against Poland and the USSR, ahead of a meeting of his opposite numbers in the Ten.

Soviet Union

2. It is not possible to make an estimate of the consequences of the sanctions currently under discussion. Their exact scope is not yet clear. At one end, if the energy regulations and high technology licence procedures are interpreted restrictively they could make a considerable difference to the Soviet Union's economy. At the other the difference is likely to be marginal.

Poland

3. It is likely that at the Western Creditors' meeting today in Paris all of Poland's sixteen major creditors will agree to suspend new export credit and also negotiations on rescheduling Poland's 1982 official debt obligations.

4. In strict economic terms the effects of these two actions will be minimal. That is the Polish economy will not be forced to operate at a significantly lower level than it is at the moment.

5. By December 1981 the Polish economy looked as if it would be in surplus on current trade in hard currency in 1982. Poland's main requirement for new credit was to finance debt service payments. They required some $4 billion to meet residual debt service obligations even if debt rescheduling had been agreed with official Western creditors and banks. The Polish trade surplus was expected to be about $1 billion. This would have been inadequate to meet their debt service obligations.

6. The point reached before 13 December was that the West was likely to make available $2-2.5 billion towards paying debt service obligations. It was thought unlikely that the Soviet Union would offer $1.5-2 billion to bridge the gap between the Western offer and default.

Effects of Present Western Position

7. Although the effect of suspending credits makes little difference to the economy as it now is, the present position is already highly unsatisfactory. Output is down by 15% on 1980. Many factories are suffering severe dislocations. At the consumer end the shops are empty and the Polish authorities' hopes of mopping up

[2] The communiqué of 11 January acknowledged that economic relations with Poland and the Soviet Union were bound to be affected by the current situation in Poland. Regarding economic relations with Poland it noted that: future non-food commercial credits would be placed in abeyance; negotiations about Poland's official debt payments for 1982 should be suspended; humanitarian aid to the Polish people would continue to be distributed and monitored by non-governmental organisations, and those Allies who sold food to Poland would seek the clearest possible Polish commitments with regard to the use of the food. Each of the Allies also agreed to examine measures regarding imports from the Soviet Union, maritime and air services agreements, the size of Soviet commercial representation, and the conditions surrounding export credits. They also resolved not to undermine the effect of each other's measures, and to reflect on longer-term East-West economic relations, particularly energy, agricultural commodities and other goods, and the export of technology, in light of the changed situation (A copy of the communiqué can be found on the NATO website: www.nato.int.).

[3] Economic adviser at the FCO. Mr Broomfield also asked Mr Manning to consider what leverage economic sanctions offered in Poland. In a minute of 14 January Mr Manning thought sanctions represented 'the one really effective weapon in the Western armoury'. The threat or imposition of sanctions should be used vigorously by the West to force Jaruzelski to accept a measure of reform in Poland. If this failed the maintenance of sanctions would force the Soviet system to bear the whole economic burden of the Polish crisis, which may well have serious long-term economic and political consequences. Mr Meluish, in Warsaw tel. No. 113 of 14 January, agreed but he warned that they would cause hardship to the Polish people. Industry would suffer from a lack of raw materials, spare parts and components, whilst levels of food and livestock would drop even further. The authorities would attempt to pin the blame on Western governments and Poland's economic, and therefore political, dependence on the USSR would increase (FCO 28/4989, ENP 093/1).

liquidity through price rises and by making many more goods available, will be disappointed.

8. If the Western creditors maintained for some time their position, they would be condemning the Polish economy to a long period of relative stagnation. For some ten years economic planning has been based on large Western inputs of capital and technology and a requirement for exports to the West to pay for these. An exceedingly painful process of reorientation would be necessary. It is doubtful whether the Soviet Union would make available sufficient resources to smooth out the problems that would arise during the interim phase.

9. If, therefore, General Jaruzelski's hope is to buy political calm through increasing material prosperity, the Western move will considerably reduce his chances of success.

Polish Imports

10. If the West wished to take action that would significantly reduce the already reduced level of economic activity the most effective way would be through quantitative restrictions on Polish imports. If the Community were to take this action against shoes, television sets, etc. Poland's ability to earn hard currency to keep its industry turning over even at the present level would be seriously affected.

Rescheduling

11. By agreeing to postpone rescheduling the West is currently granting 100% rescheduling benefits to Poland. It is significant that a report from Warsaw recently stated that the Poles hoped for a year's grace period for debt service payments. They combined this with a request for Western credits.

12. To exert pressure the West should start rescheduling talks and demand more stringent terms than the 90% on interest and principal that was being contemplated before 13 December. But this will effectively force the Poles to declare a moratorium or the West to declare them in default. Without new credits there is little hope of Poland meeting their residual debt service obligations either to their official creditors or to the commercial banks, unless the West agreed formally to 100% rescheduling.

13. At the Cabinet Office meeting this afternoon[4] I will be pressing ECGD and the Bank of England to put a figure on what it might cost the UK in PSBR terms if we were to force a moratorium/default at the Rescheduling Talks. (ECGD confirm that they expect to be repaid £155 million in 1982 by the Poles.)

Conclusion

14. (*a*) The effects of what the West had already done in suspending credit should be severe.

(*b*) Jaruzelski will be forced to turn to the Soviet Union for increased assistance, but would probably have to pay an increased political price in terms of his attitude to Solidarity, which in turn will have an effect on Western attitudes to Poland (and the Soviet Union).

(*c*) The logical way out would be to offer a major rescue operation in return for political improvement (the major rescue operation being necessary economically/financially anyway).

(*d*) If a major operation is not on then we are left with the leverage of suspended credits but the problem of default/moratorium towards the middle of 1982 (the gap of $1.5-2 billion) even if the situation improves and credits are unblocked.

[4] The 2nd meeting of the cross-Whitehall official Group on Economic Policy towards Eastern Europe—MISC 64—which discussed possible economic measures against Poland and the Soviet Union.

No. 133

Lord Carrington to Sir N. Henderson (Washington), 15 January 1982, 6.31 p.m.

Tel. No. 50[1] Immediate, Confidential (FCO 28/ 4905, ENP 014/1)

Poland

This telegram updates FCO telno 1974[2] to Washington and can be drawn on freely except where indicated.

Internal situation

The situation inside Poland has stabilised. The authorities have succeeded in establishing tight control throughout the country. Active resistance has ceased, although passive resistance may continue and is most likely to be seen in shipyards, coal mines and large industrial enterprises. The authorities have announced some minor relaxation of the martial law provisions (some travel is permitted, some telephones reconnected, foreign journalists are again allowed to file) but these are largely cosmetic adjustments.

Although many of those detained when martial law was first imposed have now been released, the authorities admit that there are still over 5,000 people in detention (the real figure may well be higher). Trials have begun of Solidarity activists arrested for contravening martial law (e.g. organising strikes or sit ins or distributing leaflets). It is impossible to say how many people were killed in clashes with the security forces when martial law was imposed, but the numbers may well be higher that the officially admitted figure of nine dead.

Solidarity

Some Solidarity leaders eluded the authorities and remain at large. The most prominent of these is Bujak, the radical leader of Solidarity's Warsaw region. Solidarity has produced a number of underground bulletins which have included messages from Bujak that Solidarity continues to function. Walesa remains under restraint and is apparently refusing to cooperate with the authorities, although there are persistent rumours that they are continuing to try to engage him in some form of dialogue. Foreign journalists visiting Poznan under official auspices on 14 January noted badges and other evidence that Solidarity still commands much support among ordinary workers.

The economy

The authorities are claiming that work in the mines, shipyards and enterprises is fast returning to normal. This claim should be treated with considerable caution: here too the evidence from Poznan was to the contrary. It will not be easy to make people work effectively at gunpoint: and Polish industry is crippled by shortage of raw materials and spare parts and by the restrictions on telecommunications. The reintroduction of Saturday working may however help to increase production e.g. of coal.

[1] Repeated for Information Priority to Moscow, Paris, Bonn, Belgrade, Bucharest, Budapest, Prague, Sofia, East Berlin, Rome, The Hague, Luxembourg, Brussels, Copenhagen, Athens, Dublin, Ankara, Lisbon, Oslo, Ottawa, Reykjavik, UKDEL NATO, Stockholm, Helsinki, Vienna, Berne, Madrid, Canberra, Wellington, Peking, Tokyo, New Delhi, Islamabad, Tel Aviv, Cairo, Pretoria, Buenos Aires, Mexico City, Strasbourg, UKDEL Madrid, UKMIS New York, UKMIS Geneva and Kathmandu.

[2] No. 119.

Preliminary Polish estimates for 1981 confirm the downward spiral of the economy last year. National income fell by 15 percent and industrial output in the state sector by 13 percent. Exports were down by 14 percent, largely because of shortfalls in hard coal production. (Preliminary Polish estimates put output in 1981 at 163 mt, 30 mt lower than in 1980). In an attempt to curb demand the authorities have proposed substantial retail price increases (in some cases more than 3 fold) for basic food stuffs, fuel and power. These increases, which are technically open for debate this month (but which is unlikely to mean much in the present situation) will probably add to existing hardship and to popular resentment.

The Party

Eclipsed by the military takeover, the Party is now being purged and rebuilt. The outcome of this process is likely to be a Party which is smaller and more orthodox. But there are rumours that if the authorities decide that this process is not working satisfactorily, they will disband the present Party altogether and build an entirely new one. It is not clear how and when Jaruzelski intends to return power to the present party or any successor. But he is likely to come under increasing pressure from Moscow to do so since the present military government is highly unorthodox in ideological terms.

The Church

The initial reaction of the Polish Primate, Archbishop Glemp, to the clampdown was to counsel moderation in an attempt to avoid bloodshed. But this line attracted considerable criticism within the Church as weak and unconvincing, and he has since come out much more strongly in condemning martial law and the repression that has followed.

The regime has been anxious to find someone to talk to, in order to suggest that it is conducting some sort of dialogue with society, and it has therefore been trying to enmesh the Church in negotiations. Jaruzelski will calculate that such negotiations would also confer a measure of respectability on him that only the Church can offer. For its part the Church has been active in trying to promote discussions between the authorities and Solidarity, but the preconditions laid down by both sides have so far proved too much. There is nevertheless a good deal of talking going on behind the scenes and the Episcopate is likely to continue to press the regime to resume the dialogue with Solidarity as the only way out of the crisis. The predominant fear of the Church is that the situation will deteriorate to the point where the Russians feel bound to intervene, with sharply adverse consequences for the Church's present influential position.

The UK reaction

Ministers have confirmed what is happening in Poland and have made it clear that they look to Jaruzelski to live up to his initial promises that martial law would be short lived and that there would be a return to the path of reform. You should draw on the Lord Privy Seal's speech in the House on 22 December,[3] the Prime Minister's interview with the BBC on New Year's Eve (RETRACT 21431), my interview with Kate Adie on 4 January (Verbatim 002/82), and the interview I gave on Panorama on 6 January (Verbatim 006/82).[4]

We have so far taken the following steps in response to developments in Poland:

(*a*) Strong and repeated condemnation of the Polish clampdown;

(*b*) Increased BBC broadcasting to Poland (by forty five minutes a day in the Polish Language Service);

[3] *Parl. Debs., 5th Ser., H. of C.*, vol. 15, col. 933.

[4] Not printed.

(*c*) The supply of 8,000 tonnes of free EC beef to Poland was held up until the Polish authorities gave assurances that those supplies will reach the civilian population;

(*d*) Decisions with the Community on further sales of food at special subsidised prices have been held up, and we are exploring within the Community the possibility of channelling food supplies through voluntary agencies;[5]

(*e*) The Community have allocated 2 million ECUS for humanitarian aid through voluntary and Church agencies.

In addition, but strictly for your own information, we are considering other measures of which the following are illustrative examples:

(*f*) Suspension of official credit (except in cases where a legally binding commitment already exists);

(*g*) Postponement of negotiations about rescheduling Poland's 1982 official debt;

(*h*) Tighter COCOM controls on high technology exports to Poland;

(*i*) Travel restrictions on Polish diplomatic missions and other organisations.

12. Again strictly for your own information we are also considering taking measures[6] of the following kinds against the Soviet Union:

(*a*) Restricting imports, together with our EC partners, of Soviet manufactures;

(*b*) Terminating the UK/USSR Maritime Agreement;

(*c*) Reducing scientific and technical cooperation or not renewing exchange agreements;

(*d*) Reviewing the conditions surrounding export credits (see para 16 below).

The US reaction

13. President Reagan made major policy speeches on 23 and 29 December.[7] In the first he announced measures against the Polish military regime, and in the second measures against the Soviet Union in protest at the latter's undoubted complicity in the suppression of the Polish Renewal. (For your own information, the Americans have revealed to their allies that they possess material showing that the Russians were closely involved in the planning of Polish clampdown. Marshal Kulikov[8] spent long periods in Poland during 1981 and was present in Warsaw when martial law was declared. He appears to have been an important channel of Soviet pressure on the Polish authorities.)

14. The Americans have emphasised that the measures announced by the President are aimed at achieving the common Western objective of re-establishing conditions for reconciliation and a resumption of the process of Renewal. This would involve the lifting of martial law, the release of those detained, and the resumption of a genuine dialogue between the authorities, Solidarity and the Church.[9] (For your own information, we were only given a few hours' notice of the

[5] Lord Carrington had explained to the Cabinet on 14 January that there might be difficulties in the Community over subsidised food aid, which he thought should be discontinued. However, the French and the Germans wanted to maintain them for a 'mixture of commercial and humanitarian reasons' (CC(82)1, 14 January 1982, CAB 128/73).

[6] Lord Carrington suggested 'measures' rather than 'sanctions' (CC(82)1, 14 January 1982, CAB 128/73).

[7] See No. 121, note 4 and No. 125.

[8] Commander-in-Chief of the Warsaw Pact, 1977-89.

[9] In a telegram on the same day, Mr Melhuish assessed that the hardening of Western displeasure and the probability of economic sanctions worried the Polish authorities, who were concentrating their attention on the three issues identified by the West: abolition of martial law; release of detainees and resumption of dialogue. Although Western pressure had undoubtedly been

measures the Americans proposed to take against the Soviet Union. This lack of prior consultation caused difficulties for us and for our EC partners and contributed to the impression of disarray in the Alliance.)

The EC Reaction

15. Efforts to convene a special meeting of EC Foreign Ministers in London during the last week of December foundered on difficulties raised mainly by the French. It was therefore not until 4 January that such a meeting took place in Brussels under the Belgian Presidency. Ministers agreed on the need to preserve Western unity and not to undermine the US measures that had been announced. They also agreed on the Soviet Union's complicity in and co-responsibility for the imposition of martial law in Poland. (For the communiqué issued after the meeting, see Verbatim 001/82).[10]

16. As well as discussing the question of further humanitarian aid including food (which we are encouraging), and further specially subsidised food sales (which we are opposing on the grounds that channelling food through voluntary agencies is preferable to ensure that it gets to the right people), the Community is also considering possible restrictions on Soviet exports and is working out a coordinated policy on not undermining the US measures. We hope that decisions on these various issues will be taken at the 25/26 January Foreign Affairs Council.[11] We shall also be exploring within the Community the possibility of reclassifying the Soviet Union's credit rating. There is a good technical case for classifying the Soviet Union as 'relatively rich', which would mean the minima for official credits would be higher. The effect would be to reduce credit subsidies to the Soviet Union. As the Russians attach importance to cheap credits, the signal would be a clear one.

17. (NOT FOR USE). We do not underestimate the difficulties involved in agreeing a concerted Allied response. Nor do we believe that the sanctions at present being considered against Poland and the Soviet Union will have a significant effect on the Polish or Soviet economies to the point where either economy will be forced to operate at a significantly lower level than at present. Both sets of measures are directed as much towards maintaining alliance cohesion as influencing Poland or the Soviet Union. But we believe that they constitute a clear and valuable warning to both the Poles and the Soviets that failure to return to Renewal and reform in Poland would carry severe political and economic penalties. In particular the withdrawal of Western financial support from the Poles will give them a psychological jolt and force them to declare a moratorium on debt servicing even though their economy could continue to function at its present low level of activity by trading on a cash basis.

The NATO reaction

18. The EC meeting on 4 January did much to bring European and US reactions into line. It was possible to build on this at the NATO Foreign Ministers' Meeting on 11 January, when there was a substantial closing of ranks. The Foreign

instrumental in some minor relaxations, he reiterated that despite Archbishop Glemp's and General Jaruzelski's meeting, there had been few signs of serious discussions with Solidarity, largely it seemed because Wałęsa refused to talk to the authorities without his Presidium and closest advisers (Warsaw tel. No. 122, FCO 28/4905, ENP 014/1).

[10] See No. 127.

[11] The EC agreed on 26 January to suspend its programme of subsidised food sales to Poland and redirect Community funds to humanitarian assistance through voluntary agencies (CC(82)3, 28 January 1982, CAB 128/73).

Ministers issued a strongly worded declaration (Verbatim 004/82).[12] This condemns the imposition of martial law, holds the Soviet Union co-responsible for developments in Poland, and warns the Poles and the Russians that 'business as usual' is impossible in the present situation. While re-affirming NATO's commitment to the pursuit of arms control, it warns the Soviet Union that it will be held responsible if this process is damaged because of the Soviet Union's failure to live up to its existing obligations, in particular those enshrined in the Helsinki Final Act. In recognition of the Russians' serious violation of those obligations, attendance by NATO member states at the reconvening of the Madrid review meeting on 9 February will be at Foreign Minister level.

19. The Declaration also announces that there will be an early follow-up meeting of the NATO Council to consider economic measures in particular (see paragraphs 13 to 16 of the Declaration). For your own information we hope that it will prove possible to draw up a respectable list of national measures against Poland and Soviet Union. UK measures will be announced in concert with those of our Allies. The most likely timing for this is during the fortnight beginning 25 January.[13]

20. In speaking to your contacts, you should stress that the NATO Declaration illustrates the unity and determination of the Alliance. Martial law in Poland is a breach of the commitments entered into by Poland and the Soviet Union in the Final Act of the CSCE at Helsinki in 1975. (This is the answer to charges of NATO interference and double standards compared with e.g. El Salvador).[14] The measures outlined in the NATO Declaration are an important symbol of the West's determination not to accept the present repression in Poland and to take further steps if the Soviet Union resorts to overt intervention.

21. More important still, what has happened in Poland is a major defeat for the communist system. Thirty six years of communist government have lead to martial law, internment camps, special courts, food shortages, economic bankruptcy, and a political dead-end. The socialist system has been shown to be a political and economic failure on a huge scale. As I have said in interviews and speeches, it is important that you should concentrate on this aspect of the crisis so that this disaster for the East should not be obscured by stories about differences among western allies.

Representation at Polish functions

22. You will see in paragraph 11 of the NATO communiqué that the quality of our relations with the Poles should reflect the abnormal nature of the present situation and our refusal to accept this as permanent. This has been interpreted in Warsaw by most of the Western allies to mean that attendance at official functions should be at middle ranking level rather than by Heads of Post. We are currently consulting with our EC partners on the level of representation at official Polish functions worldwide. Guidance will be sent to you shortly on this and on relations with the Soviet Union.

23. For non EC/NATO Posts: You should draw on this telegram when appropriate opportunities arise to explain the Western position to the governments to which you are accredited. Please report reactions.

[12] See No. 132, note 2.

[13] See No. 137.

[14] In the civil war (1979–92) between the military-led Government of El Salvador and the Farabundo Martí National Liberation Front there were many violations of human rights. The USA provided military aid to the Government.

No. 134

Letter from Sir J. Taylor (Bonn) to Mr J. Bullard, 15 January 1982
Confidential (FCO 28/4719, EN 021/10)

Dear Julian,

Poland: The Federal German Response

1. In the four weeks since the military takeover in Poland, the Federal German stance in East-West relations has come in for strong criticism, public as well as private, in some other major countries of the Alliance and particularly the United States. Both the Germans and the Americans have made strenuous efforts to reconcile their differences, and the Germans at least believe they have succeeded. I am not so sure. The underlying differences of philosophy and interest remain, rooted in each country's political and economic interests and in history, geography and culture, and are likely to continue to cause trouble as the Alliance considers what practical measures to take to demonstrate its concern, and (later) whether specific steps taken by the Poles amount to a genuine return to reform.

2. It may therefore be helpful if, at risk of going over some well-trodden ground, I try to explain the German philosophy, and why they have reacted in the way they have. I should refer first to two fundamental points which are, perhaps, so well known that they do not need restating in full. First, the deep-rooted German fear of further war in Europe, arising from their memories of the destruction of their country in 1944-45 and the knowledge that Germany would be the main battle ground again next time.[1] The fear is a real and a widespread one—*viz*, the reasons given by many Germans applying to emigrate to Australasia—and it is one reason why *Sicherheitspolitik*—security policy—is so much more central a word in German political vocabulary than it is in English. Secondly, the fact that, ever since the creation of the Federal Republic, the core of German security policy has been and continues to be membership of NATO, which all the main political parties and a clear majority of the public continue to accept as indispensable. In from time to time questioning the strength of the FRG's continuing commitment to NATO, the Americans tend to take for granted the understanding which the great majority of Germans show about the presence on their soil of tens of thousands of foreign NATO troops.

3. Since the late Sixties, however, there has developed an important second plank in FRG security policy—the dialogue with the East. Twelve years of détente have, in German eyes, produced considerable benefits not only for the whole of Europe (the Helsinki Final Act, the network of arms control negotiations) but also specifically for the Germans themselves, in Berlin, in the reopening of contact with the other half of their divided country and in the atmosphere of confidence created by increasing dialogue and contacts with the Soviet Union and Eastern Europe. It is now a cardinal thesis of German foreign policy—clung to tenaciously by the electorate, and therefore endorsed with varying degrees of enthusiasm by the Opposition as well as by the Government—that the dialogue with the East must be kept going at almost all costs, since Europe would be a less secure place without it. Helmut Schmidt's success in continuing and developing the dialogue—in making himself Brezhnev's chief interlocutor in Europe while adhering scrupulously to agreed Western positions—is a major reason why his personal popularity continues

[1] Mr Bullard annotated: 'He does not mention another powerful factor: German unwillingness to appear to be hitting Poland when she is down, given what Germany did to Poland in 1939-45.'

despite the misfortunes of his party. If circumstances drove him to abandon it, it would be another nail in his and the Coalition's coffin.[2]

4. Underlying Schmidt's own approach to the dialogue is a concept which for some 15 years at least has been an important part of his thinking—the concept which, in his 1969 book 'The Balance of Power', he called the strategy of equilibrium. He believes that the East-West balance of power in Europe has developed into a major force for stability and for the preservation of peace, and that he who attempts to upset the balance too violently endangers peace. Hence his initial hesitation (now overridden by other considerations) about Spanish entry into NATO, and his unhappiness with the Reagan Administration's talk about regaining something like strategic superiority. Only in a situation of equilibrium does deterrence work, giving both sides an interest in maintaining the dialogue. While, therefore, political change in Eastern Europe is to be welcomed, it will risk being counterproductive if it goes too far too fast and upsets the confidence brought about by balance. Witness Hungary, where an attempt at too sudden a change in 1956 brought a frightened Soviet counter strike, but where encouraging progress towards liberalisation has slowly and unobtrusively been made since then. This is the philosophy behind Schmidt's remark to the *New York Times* last week, about not seeking to disturb the European order created at Yalta.

5. Ever since August 1980 the Germans have been less unambiguously enthusiastic about Solidarity's actions than some other Western countries, because they feared such action would lead to Soviet intervention in Poland. This was not only because they feared the economic consequences of Soviet intervention but because they felt it would destroy hard-won confidence between East and West in Europe and force even the Germans themselves to put their contacts with the East into cold storage. In their judgement these effects would be good for no-one, though inevitable if the Russians so blatantly ignored Western warnings against interference in Polish external affairs. When military take-over in Poland came on 13 December, therefore, they were reluctant to see it as Soviet intervention by proxy, hoping instinctively that it would turn out to be a Polish solution to a Polish problem, and preferring to give it a chance to work. I took the Governor of the Bank of England to the Federal Chancellery on 15 December. Lahnstein[3] (uniquely close to the Federal Chancellor) then said that, as a cynic, he might be encouraged by the take-over. Stability might give the Poles a chance. Similarly, hopes that the Poles would save themselves probably explain Schmidt's immediate reaction at Werbellinsee[4] to the news of the take-over—in retrospect a serious tactical mistake. With the instinctive caution which the Germans showed after the Soviet invasion of Afghanistan they declined to make a firm judgement until sufficient information was available. They increasingly disliked what they saw, and five days after the take-over came the Chancellor's strong statement in the Bundestag and the Bundestag resolution.[5] Rakowski's visit[6] (which it would have been quite

[2] Coalition between the Social Democrats and the Free Democratic Party.

[3] Chief of Herr Schmidt's Chancellery.

[4] Werbellinsee in the GDR, where Chancellor Schmidt was on a visit.

[5] Chancellor Schmidt pledged wholehearted support for the Polish workers and expressed deep concern at the imposition of martial law. The Bundestag resolution, supported by all but one abstention, called on Polish authorities to free everybody arrested since martial law (*The Times*, 19 December 1981).

[6] The Polish Deputy Prime Minister had visited Bonn on 30 and 31 December, where he had a four-hour talk with Herr Genscher who had made clear that that the FRG's moderate language should

contrary to their philosophy of dialogue not to have agreed to) gave them new hope; but within a further week their hopes had been dashed by the lack of any signs of normalisation which Rakowski had promised. It is still not clear whether, when Schmidt took up the theme of Soviet involvement in Washington on 5 January, he did so from conviction or out of tactical considerations *vis-à-vis* the Americans. German officials still see the actual decision to impose martial law as a Polish one, though they fully agree that it would not have had to be taken if Poland had not been part of the Soviet Empire. Genscher himself spoke to Rakowski of the Soviet fist behind the Polish decision. But the Germans regard the question of instigation as essentially academic, given the distance things have moved since. What they have been doing, in the four weeks since 13 December, is to grope towards a *Gesamtkonzept*—a considered overall view of the Polish situation based on reliable information—and as always they have not been prepared to act until they had got one.

6. President Reagan's sanctions announcements of 23 and 29 December were badly received in Bonn, not only because of the lack of high-level consultation and the apparent haste with which the decisions were taken but also because of the Germans' instinctive abhorrence of sanctions as a weapon. They do not like anything which interferes with the free play of market forces which they believe is central to economic good sense. They believe that sanctions are usually ineffective against the intended target and often do more damage to those who apply them—and they are aware that they have much more to lose from such sanctions than the Americans. They are prepared to take some action against the Poles—and even against the Russians—to demonstrate Western disapproval of what has happened. But they do not want the political dialogue interrupted, and they do not want to suspend existing trade. As far as the dialogue is concerned, they are delighted to have (apparently) persuaded the Americans of their point. On economic sanctions, they are concerned to use carrots rather than sticks—not to punish by stopping what is already going on, but to make it clear that further Western aid to Poland is dependent on the Polish authorities showing that they mean what they say about a return to the path of reform.

7. Genscher's odd remark in Stuttgart on 6 January, in which he appeared without Alliance or Community consultation to commit not only the FRG but her allies to giving large-scale further aid to Poland once she was on the road to reform, is a good example of the German preference for carrots over sticks. It raises the questions whether it will get Alliance support, and if so whether the Finance Ministry would go along with the implicit assumption that the Federal budget would stretch to extensive further aid.

8. I am not trying to defend the German performance since 13 December. They could have presented their case much better—it comes over on occasion with an irritating air of self-righteousness, and the accident-prone Government press spokesman has said things better not said.[7] The Germans seem not to understand that for Chancellor Schmidt to write to Brezhnev without consulting his Allies is as open to objection as for President Reagan to announce sanctions without consulting his—though they are not looking to their allies to write too. But at least

not be misunderstood, as his country was extremely concerned with the fate of the Polish people and wanted a return to the reform policy.

[7] Herr Kurt Becker had said that the decision to invoke sanctions against the Soviet Union was purely American and that Germany had been given only a few hours' notice (*The Times,* 31 December 1981).

the German viewpoint on Poland is consistent and logical in their own terms, and is based on deeply-held convictions and on arguments thoroughly thought through. They will not easily be shifted from it.

Yours ever,
JOCK TAYLOR

No. 135

Letter from Lord Trefgarne to Dr David Owen MP, 19 January 1982
(FCO 28/4797, ENA 020/1)

[No salutation]
Thank you for your letter of 7 January to Douglas Hurd about diplomatic relations with Albania and the question of the gold claimed by Albania.[1]

We believe that it would be desirable to re-establish diplomatic relations with Albania. We therefore told the Albanians in 1980 that we were ready to do so without preconditions and without waiting for a resolution of the financial problems which had previously stood in the way. We made this offer despite the fact that the Albanians have not so far been prepared to comply with the judgement of the International Court of Justice in the Corfu Channel case. The offer was thus a significant gesture of goodwill towards Albania and a clear indication of our genuine wish to settle our differences.

Unfortunately, the Albanians have not accepted this offer. Instead, they have reiterated their demand for the delivery to them 'with interest' of the gold allocated to them in partial compensation for the much larger sum looted by the Germans during the war. The gold allocated to Albania is presently held in the Bank of England on behalf of the Tripartite Commission for the Restitution of Monetary Gold. There are, however, a number of claims against Albania or on the gold itself and since we, the Americans and the French are equal members of this Commission, the British Government cannot act unilaterally to deliver the gold to Albania before there has been a mutually satisfactory resolution of the financial problems. We are continuing to discuss with the French and American governments ways of achieving such a resolution. In the meantime our offer to resume diplomatic relations without strings attached remains open.

One of the financial problems, though not the only or even the major one, is the Albanians' failure to meet the International Court's judgement in the Corfu Channel case. But the damages awarded to the UK were not exacted from Albania by unilateral action. The Albanians freely agreed to take the case to the International Court and should in our view have accepted the Court's judicial award against them in 1949. We therefore still maintain that they should do so, even now. But for our part we do not see this as an obstacle to the resumption of relations. Indeed, in our view, such a resumption could only help to promote a settlement by making it easier for us to communicate directly with the Albanian Government.[2]

TREFGARNE

[1] See No. 97.
[2] The Albanians saw things rather differently. On 18 February 1982 Mr Bolland (Belgrade) reported a meeting with the Albanian Ambassador, who reminded him that Albania had offered, in February 1981, to solve two questions at once by agreeing to establish diplomatic relations if Britain agreed to hand over the gold with interest. He did not agree that Britain, as only one of three TGC members, was not competent to settle the gold question, and did not accept the legality of the

International Court's award. Both Ambassadors thought the ball was in the other's court. Mr Bolland said he 'would report what he had said to London but meanwhile awaited a reply from him. He said he would report what I had said and now awaited a response from me.' The Albanian Ambassador did admit Albania would like more contact with Britain: 'She would send her folk dancers to any country who would receive them.'

No. 136

Lord Carrington to Mr James (Warsaw), 20 January 1982, 9.10 p.m.
Tel. No. 85[1] Priority, Confidential (FCO 28/4958, ENP 022/2)

Warsaw: views of the Pope

1. At the Political Directors' lunch in Brussels on 19 January Dupont (France) gave an account of Cheysson's conversation with the Pope about Poland.[2]

2. The Pope had been very pessimistic, using the word 'humiliation' and describing recent events as having carried the situation in Poland back to long before 1980. He doubted the possibility of re-establishing a genuine dialogue within Poland. The Polish Church had no choice but to take their present attitude, but the idea of saving part of what had been achieved in 1980/81 was an illusion. The Pope even feared that religious freedoms might eventually be called into question in Poland. Jaruzelski was totally devalued in the eyes of the population, and the military could not effectively replace the Party. The Pope asked Cheysson to distinguish between the system, which was to be condemned, and the Polish nation, which should be helped by the West, provided it could be made sure that help was reaching the right people.

[1] Repeated for Information Priority to Holy See, Washington, Paris, Bonn, UKDEL NATO and Routine to Moscow.

[2] The French Foreign Minister had a one-hour private audience with Pope John Paul II on 9 January.

No. 137

Minute from Lord Carrington to Mrs Thatcher, 20 January 1982
PM/82/5 Confidential (FCO 28/4770, EN 122/1)

Poland

You will wish to know where we stand before the follow up meeting of the North Atlantic Council on 23 January to discuss measures to be taken against the Soviet Union and Poland. I enclose a steering brief for the meeting which has been agreed interdepartmentally among officials.

The Americans are continuing to exert pressure for their allies to declare and announce decisions on 23 January. I think there is a danger that the meeting might go seriously wrong and end in acrimony if they feel that they are not getting the support they were led to expect at the meeting on 11 January. This would be a major setback to Alliance unity and send the wrong signals both to the Russians and to Western public opinion.

In all exercises of this nature the burden-sharing aspect is uppermost in everybody's mind. From that, in my view, flow the following consequences. The first is that the US should be prepared to exempt existing contracts from the application of the draft legislation they have published. The second is that our allies should be prepared to take broadly comparable measures.

While I think it is unlikely that both these conditions will be met on 23 January, I believe nevertheless we should be prepared for that contingency. In that case I would hope that it can be agreed that the UK representative should state that we are prepared to take the measures concerning Poland set out in paragraph 11(*a*), (*c*) (*d*) and (*e*) and (*g*). As far as the Soviet Union is concerned he would have authority to say that we were prepared to take the measures set out in paragraph 12 (*a*) (*b*) (*d*) (*h*) and (*i*). As to Community matters, he would indicate our willingness to pursue actively in the Community the possibility of other measures such as those in paragraph 11 (*e*) and 12 (*c*) and (*g*).

Even if the two conditions in para 3 above are not specifically met, I hope it can be agreed that our representatives should have authority, without committing us finally, to describe on 23 January the areas in which we might be prepared to take decisions.

At the same meeting on 23 January we would urge that decisions should be finally taken at a single further NATO meeting to be held as soon as possible after the Foreign Affairs Council on 25-26 January.

In the meantime we are taking action to reduce American expectations of Saturday's meeting, which at the moment seem to be excessive, and to put into their minds the 'reverse linkage' idea described in your Private Secretary's letter of 19 January[1].

I am copying this minute to the Chancellor of the Exchequer and to the Secretaries of State for Industry, Trade, Agriculture, Environment, Energy and Health, and to Sir Robert Armstrong.[2]

CARRINGTON

ENCLOSURE IN NO. 137

Meeting of the North Atlantic Council on 23 January: Poland
Steering brief

Introduction

1. The North Atlantic Council will meet on 23 January together with senior officials from capitals to consider how to implement the Ministerial Declaration of 11 January (text at Annex A).[3] This steering brief contains general guidance for our representatives; they should also draw on the papers prepared by MISC 64, especially the record of the meeting held on 14 January.

[1] In this letter from Mr Coles to Mr Richards of 19 January it was suggested, in light of US tactics over the gas pipeline, that Lord Carrington might wish to consider the possibility of reverse linkage 'whereby we might suggest to the Americans that it would be easier for us to put together what they would regard as an adequate package of measures if they were prepared to be helpful over existing contracts'.

[2] The Prime Minister agreed with the conditions set out in the third paragraph and also with the fact that they were unlikely to be satisfied at the NATO meeting. Even if they were, she thought it essential that Ministers should be consulted before any firm commitment was made (a point the Department for Trade had emphasised). But she was content with the proposal in the fifth paragraph and the tactics suggested in the sixth (Mr Coles (No. 10) to Mr Francis, 22 January; FCO 28/4959, ENP 022/2).

[3] Not printed.

Objectives

2. Our broad objectives are the following:

(*a*) To assemble a credible package of measures to be implemented by NATO members as a demonstration of our strong disapproval of events in Poland and to bring about real political change. We wish to show that Soviet involvement is unacceptable and that further (especially military) intervention would have the gravest consequences. We also wish to stress our desire to maintain Alliance cohesion. Measures taken by each member state should be broadly comparable but need not be identical. Their economic cost to the West should not be excessive and should be fairly shared.

(*b*) To ensure that the measures already taken by the United States are not applied in such a manner as to frustrate existing contracts undertaken by European firm, if necessary by linking progress on national measures to a solution of this problem.

(*c*) To make suitable arrangements for ensuring that non-Alliance members, particularly the Japanese, keep in step and that there are effective arrangements to monitor our partners' performance.

(*d*) To minimise the risks of retaliation by the Soviet Union.

Tactics

3. In the interest of the Alliance, we wish to encourage our partners to assemble a convincing package rather than to settle for the lowest common factor. The Delegation should therefore give an early indication of our willingness to take some or all of the measures outlined below as part of a NATO response to which all partners would make a comparable contribution. They should include a suitable reference to the problem of existing contacts. They should encourage others to make a similarly positive statement.

4. Final decisions should be reserved for Ministers who will wish to assess the contributions by other governments before making commitments. So far as possible, we should ensure that measures chosen are reversible if there is an improvement in the Polish situation. Sufficient measures should be kept in reserve to deter the Soviet Union from military intervention in Poland and to constitute an effective Alliance response should she nonetheless intervene by force.

5. The outcome is likely to depend on reaching a balance between American willingness to interpret their own measures with sufficient flexibility to permit existing European contracts (especially for the Siberian gas pipeline) to continue, and European willingness to participate in a plausible package of measures. The Delegation should therefore, after demonstrating our own willingness to act, concentrate on probing the position of other governments, especially the United States and the FRG.

Attitudes of the other governments

6. The German position will be crucial. So far, they have indicated that they can do no more than enter into positive consultations on how to avoid undermining the American measures.

7. The French have been more robust in tone. They attach particular importance to acting within international law as well as maintaining existing contractual commitments. They are, however, willing to redress the balance in areas (such as their air services and maritime agreements) where the Russians gained undue

advantage during the détente period. In the longer term, they say they favour a fundamental review of relations with the Soviet Union.[4]

8. The Japanese are lying low. They have been asked by the Americans not to circumvent their measures but their basis for action is different since they are not committed to the Helsinki Final Act. Their broad intention is to keep in step with the Europeans, by administrative rather than legislative action. They have stated publicly that they will 'pay due attention not to undermine the measures taken by other Western countries'.

European Community

9. A number of issues are also being discussed in the European Community:

(*a*) subsidised food supplies and EC humanitarian aid for Poland; there is growing support for our preference for the latter. (Brief No. 3)[5]

(*b*) restrictions on imports from Soviet Union; Foreign Affairs Council will consider on 25/26 January on the basis of a neutrally drafted 'annotated catalogue' provided by the Commission. (Brief No. 7)[5]

(*c*) non-circumvention of US measures; Foreign Affairs Council are expected to instruct officials to carry out further work; a relatively slow tempo in the Community is satisfactory while the main discussion is pursued in NATO. (Brief No. 11)[6]

(*d*) export credit. The question whether the Community should adopt a position in favour of up-grading the Soviet Union to the category of relatively rich countries may come before the Council. (Brief No. 9)[6]

Decisions on (*a*), (*b*) and (*d*) will have to be taken in the Community before we can enter into detailed discussion of them in NATO.

West Siberian Gas Pipeline

10. This project is a particular, but important, case of the general difficulty surrounding existing contracts. The Department of Trade have produced a paper on the industrial and other implications (Brief No. 11)[6]. This will be the basis for consultation with those countries most directly concerned in the project (France, Germany and Italy). These consultations will be distinct from the general Community discussions referred to in paragraph 8 above.

Measures concerning Poland

11. This paragraph takes the measures in the order they are mentioned in the communiqué; they will be discussed in this order.

(*a*) *Restrictions on Diplomats*

We are prepared to impose travel restrictions on Polish diplomats and official representatives in the UK.

(*b*) *Scientific Exchange Agreements*

No action contemplated.

(*c*) *Future Commercial Credits*

The UK has placed undrawn officially guaranteed credits in suspense, except where legal or administrative difficulties prevent us from doing so. No new credits will be offered in present circumstances.

(*d*) *Rescheduling*

[4] Mr Gladstone, in a letter to Sir R. Hibbert of 20 January, acknowledging the Ambassador's reporting on French reaction to the Polish crisis, conceded that the French attitude 'with its yawning gap between rhetoric and action, has provoked some irritation on this side of the Channel' (FCO 28/4946, ENP 021/2).

[5] Not printed.

[6] Not printed.

The Group of Western creditor governments has agreed that negotiations on rescheduling Poland's official debts in 1982 should be postponed for the time being.

(*e*) *Humanitarian Aid*

We shall act as the communiqué suggests. Humanitarian aid is also being considered in the EC.

(*f*) *Food Sales*

We have stopped our government credit for food sales to Poland. We are discouraging the Community from further specially subsidised food sales and hope that finance can be diverted to providing some food in the context of humanitarian aid.

(*g*) *Tightening COCOM Restrictions*

This is not included in the communiqué nor would we wish it to be in the public arena. However, we are prepared to support in COCOM the extension to Poland of the 'no general exemptions policy' applied to the Soviet Union after Afghanistan.

Measures against the Soviet Union

12. The following summarises our reaction to the measures proposed against the Soviet Union.

(*a*) *Restrictions on Diplomats*

We would reduce the free travel area from 35 to 25 miles.

(*b*) *Scientific Exchange Agreements*

We are prepared to reduce activity under the four Anglo-Soviet agreements. None of these come up for early renewal but nevertheless prepared to consider possibility of termination. Levels of activity are already low.

(*c*) *Imports from the Soviet Union*

To be considered by EC.

(*d*) *Maritime Agreements*

Willing to give notice of termination as part of a suitable package.

(*e*) *Air Services Agreement*

Not, in our view, a suitable field for action.

(*f*) *Reduction of Commercial Representation*

We have no plans to reduce Soviet commercial representation which is already controlled by ceilings (such a measure would be more appropriate to a general trade embargo).

(*g*) *Export Credits*

We are prepared to give positive consideration in the Community, and later in the OECD consensus forum, to the possibility that Soviet Union might be reclassified as a relatively rich country.

(*h*) *High Technology*

Willing to examine carefully any US proposals in COCOM.

(*i*) *Factory Fishing*

We intend to introduce, probably from 1 February, a licensing system. This will enable us to discriminate against Soviet factory ships.

(*j*) *Longer Term Issues*

The Delegation should argue that these matters should be addressed later.

COCOM

13. We accept that, in the current circumstances, there is scope for some action in COCOM. But we believe that COCOM machinery should be essentially addressed to longer term strategic and technical considerations. It should also be

kept as confidential as possible. A High Level Meeting of officials will take place in Paris on 19/20 January. Its result should be available to the meeting.

Timetable for further discussions

14. We hope that EC Foreign Affairs Council on 25/26 January will make progress on the matters contained in paragraph 8 above. Thereafter, we envisage a further meeting or meetings of the North Atlantic Council. We should seek a final meeting in the series as soon as possible. At this meeting, governments should inform each other of the decisions that they had taken or intended to take. It is likely that several allies will insist that announcements should be made subsequently on a national basis; the timing of these announcements should be co-ordinated.

The Press

15. We share the American view that we should try to keep this first meeting out of the limelight. But we wish to ensure that the press gain the impression that effective and substantial work is being urgently undertaken and that Alliance unity is being maintained.

No. 138

Mr Melhuish (Warsaw) to Lord Carrington, 22 January 1982[1]
Confidential (FCO 28/4954, ENP 022/1)

Martial Law in Poland I: the Gathering Storm

Summary . . .[2]

My Lord,

Now that the tempo of life in Warsaw has begun to settle down to near-normality again, I would like to examine in greater detail the events leading up to the declaration of martial law and a number of other related subjects. The aim of this particular despatch is to assess the reasons why, on the night of 12/13 December, martial law was declared in Poland. In a separate despatch I will consider the part that Solidarity played in the events that led up to martial law. And in subsequent despatches I will deal with the imposition of martial law itself, the functioning of the Embassy during it and the future of Poland.

Introduction

2. It is worth stating at the outset two opposite and extreme theories of the last few years in Poland. Neither, I believe, is correct. But both contain elements of the truth and shed useful light on some aspects of the Polish crisis. The first is the Conspiracy Theory. This is that, since the Pope's election in October 1978, and, more particularly, since his visit to Poland in the following year, certain far-seeing elements in the régime regarded a period of liberal ferment as inevitable. They decided to make a virtue of necessity by letting this ferment bubble freely for a few years. This would lull the opposition into a false sense of security and make it easier to identify the enemies of Communism when the inevitable clampdown came. By this theory, martial law—or something very similar—was inevitable from 1978, or at least from August 1980. This theory would explain the way

[1] This was the first of a quartet of despatches on the causes, impact and likely future developments of martial law (see Nos. 140, 144 and 147).

[2] Not printed.

successive Polish leaders repeatedly conceded the unthinkable to Solidarity and thought the impossible, secure in the knowledge that eventually all these concessions would be clawed back. Its validity rests on the continuity of the security apparatus throughout this period. And it explains why the Soviet Union was prepared to stomach such setbacks to the cause of socialism. It is also true, and important, that whereas the seeds of dissent were taking root in Polish soil from the late 'seventies onwards, there was nothing, apart from the odd manifestation, on which to clamp down until August 1980.

3. As the Ambassador said in his Annual Review[3] however, the Conspiracy Theory is too neat: too neat for Poland at least. It assumes that the leadership were willing to play for very high stakes; it assumes a degree of forward planning and subtlety of thought which has ever been absent in this country; it ignores the disastrous effects which such a policy was bound to have on the economy; and finally it goes against the instinctive but, I think, accurate assessment of most observers that, if the Polish authorities (and the Soviet Union) had known in August 1980 what they know now, they would have clamped down there and then.

4. The lack of direction shown by the Polish leadership in the Polish crisis has given rise to the Confusion Theory. This is not as easily defined as the Conspiracy Theory; but that is part of its attraction. (As a citizen of Belfast said: 'Anyone who isn't confused here doesn't understand the situation.') This theory assumes a lack of planning by the authorities, and the Soviet Union—a series of blunders of which martial law was the last. It assumes a similar lack of forethought by Solidarity, who lost sight of the limits within which they should have operated, and thus overstepped them. And it suggests a trail of mistrust between the two sides leading to ultimate calamity with all the inevitability of a Greek tragedy.

5. This theory has much to commend it. No historian should try to be too neat. No historian of Poland especially is likely to fall into that trap. More particularly, the Polish crisis broke new ground in Eastern Europe, defying the rules that had held good for thirty-five years. But while I accept that the Polish leadership probably behaved throughout as the moment dictated, I doubt if this is true of the Soviet leadership. And while I agree that the Conspiracy Theory suffers from trying to impose a pattern where there is none, the Confusion Theory suffers from denying any pattern at all.[4] The truth lies somewhere in the middle. I believe that there is a reasonable explanation of much of what happened in the run-up to martial law. Where we cannot explain logically, we must just accept the confusion. Against this background, I propose to consider the part the most important elements in Polish society played in the events leading to martial law.

The Church

6. The Polish Church is worth considering first. It was a power in Poland before Solidarity, the Government or the Party.[5] And it is a power still, when Solidarity is proscribed, the Party is in tatters and the government has surrendered its power to the Army. It has a powerful stake in the political direction of this country. The

[3] Not printed.

[4] Mr J. Bullard, in thanking Mr James on 6 April 1982 for the four despatches, agreed with the Embassy that both the 'conspiracy' and 'confusion' theories should be discounted (FCO 28/4907, ENP 014/1).

[5] Mr Jenkins did not think that the Church was a power, but he agreed that it had a considerable authority and influence. He thought that Cardinal Glemp—although condemning martial law—believed that General Jaruzeleski was better than the other alternatives and that for that reason the Church was probably irritated by Mr Wałęsa's intransigence (Mr Jenkins to Miss Brown, 16 March 1982; FCO 28/4907, ENP 014/1).

Church's interests were strongly opposed, therefore, to any declaration of martial law. Glemp, and Wyszynski before him, strove to avoid such a catastrophe. Unfortunately, however, I do not think that the Church played its difficult hand in the best possible way.

7. Wyszynski did not really understand the *odnowa*. He grew up in pre-war Poland and began his primacy with three years' internment during the Stalinist era. He fought the battles of the fifties, sixties and seventies with courage and skill. But the eighties found him an old and, as it subsequently turned out, dying man. He maintained close contact with few advisers and became out of touch with what was going on in Poland. The events of August 1980 surprised him. His reaction—a sermon in Częstochowa calling for calm—was mistimed and ignored. Consequently he made few public pronouncements during the autumn of 1980. Only in spring 1981 did the Church unequivocally declare some of the demands of the workers to be just when the Chief Council of the episcopate demanded the registration of Rural Solidarity. Meanwhile, Wyszynski had formed a close relationship with Wałęsa. At the time of tension after the Bydgoszcz incident, he begged Wałęsa on his knees to avoid a general strike. In fact, the strike was averted by a Government climb-down.

8. After Wyszynski's death, his successor, Glemp, pursued a different policy. He showed himself straightaway to be sympathetic to Solidarity, most of whose demands he considered to be just. This gave him a much better chance of acting as an effective moderating influence. But it was too late by then to restrain the extreme elements in Solidarity. Glemp almost certainly acted as a catalyst for the tripartite meeting between himself, Wałęsa and Jaruzelski.[6] He took an active part in politics, and understood the situation well. Had he been Primate from the start of the *odnowa,* he might have been able to influence the course of events more decisively. But it is unlikely that the Church by itself, could have averted martial law.[7]

Solidarity

9. Solidarity must bear some share of the blame for bringing Poland to martial law.[8] From the beginning, the movement demanded what was, in Communist terms, unthinkable and won it. The Gdańsk agreements in August 1980, the Union's registration in November, Rural Solidarity and Bydgoszcz: each represented a further concession by the embattled authorities. It was little wonder then that some elements—and increasingly large proportion of the active membership—came to believe that there were *no* limits within which they had to operate, no boundaries that could not be crossed. Solidarity began to move into the overtly political sphere by demanding *inter alia* free elections to the local councils and a Social Council for the National Economy, which was to have a veto on Government policy.

[6] See No. 98.

[7] Mr J. Bullard in his comments to Mr James on 6 April thought that despite the Cardinal's initial misjudgement of the popular mood in August 1980, his courage and prestige had been instrumental in defusing the Bydgoszcz crisis in March 1981. But Cardinal Glemp exposed the Church by identifying it with Solidarity, which encouraged the Union's more radical members to go further.

[8] Mr Manning did not find the term 'blame' helpful, as he thought that a 'huge and disparate organisation like Solidarity cannot be fine-tuned in its responses' and 'it might be more profitable to ask how it was that the Solidarity leadership managed to contain and focus popular pressure for so long, without people taking to the streets' (Mr Manning to Miss Brown, 15 March 1982; FCO 28/4907, ENP 014/1).

10. It is a separate question whether the turn that Solidarity had taken by mid-December 1981 justified the imposition of martial law. But it is worth considering here whether Solidarity could not, at least for tactical reasons, have played its hand more gently. It might still have reached its goal in the end. On the one hand, there is no doubt that a revolutionary movement must always be on the advance. The momentum must be sustained at all costs. Faced with a régime on the retreat, Solidarity had a double incentive. But, despite the Gdańsk Congress which theoretically gave Solidarity a programme, there rarely seemed to be a coherent set of aims that linked the union's activities in the workplace to its social and political acts. There was neither agreement amongst the leadership about the ultimate goal—social democracy, Communism with a human face or simply free trade unions within a totalitarian State—nor on the best method of achieving them. So the union came higgledy-piggledy to the point of being a radical and threatening political force. Could Wałęsa and the other moderates have restrained this tendency? They certainly tried. But Wałęsa was up against the natural momentum of the union. Whilst his prestige never diminished, his authority did. He found the powerful (and radical) regional barons such as Bujak, Slowik and Waliszewski increasingly difficult to deal with. And he himself became disenchanted with the Government. He was determined, for example, not to be drawn into the proposed Front of National Understanding.[9] Yet the radical Radom declaration,[10] which arguably sparked off martial law, was a defeat for him. His moderate counter-proposal gained only three votes!

The Party

11. Solidarity's development into a political force was partly because of the political vacuum that was left by the Communist Party. During the Gierek era total Party numbers had expanded considerably with an accompanying decline in the quality and conviction of the membership. As such the Party was in no position in the summer and autumn of 1980 to counter the threat of Solidarity. Instead, it turned on itself and dismissed its leadership one by one. Only after Gierek's fall did it address itself to the political response it should make to the emergence of free trades unions. The crucial VI Plenum of October 1980[11] decided upon the path of dialogue, the policy that the Party claimed to maintain from then until martial law. But the Party spent most of the intervening time between October 1980 and the IX Congress[12] in July 1981 on continued in-house bickering. Kania's initial policy, which was probably right, was to hold a quick Congress late in 1980 which would purge the old leadership and give the Party the political impetus it needed to play an effective role in the new situation. But the Congress slipped back and back and, even when it finally took place more than six months later, it concentrated far more on personalities and the minutiae of new-found democracy than on developing a coherent political programme. What is more, the party still had not finished with its own internal problems. Kania, who looked so strong in July, fell three months later. During this period Solidarity sympathisers began to infiltrate

[9] General Jaruzelski had appealed for national unity and invited Solidarity and the Church to cooperate with the PZPR on economic recovery within such a Front. Mr J. Bullard put it to Mr James that Solidarity's 'scornful rejection' demonstrated to the Government that the Union would never agree to cooperate on the terms of the Government as it believed it had no intention of accepting the Union as a political partner. This undermined the moderates in Solidarity and led to the radical declarations of Radom and Gdańsk and the hardening of respective positions.

[10] See No. 111, note 4.

[11] See No. 36.

[12] See No. 71.

the active Party cells and fresh elections were held up to the level of local First Secretaries. The Party became not so much the natural opposition to Solidarity as a vehicle for it.

12. It seems to me that the Party made two fundamental errors. Firstly, it failed to take a firm decision at the earliest possible moment after August 1980 about its attitude to Solidarity and the *odnowa*. Had it been sufficiently resolute and sufficiently faithful to its Marxist-Leninist principles, it could have become a strong hard-line force opposed to the *odnowa*, a role it will almost certainly pick up with enthusiasm in the next few weeks. Or it could have jumped firmly and whole-heartedly on the back of the *odnowa* and tried to steal Solidarity's thunder. In fact it fell between two stools. The second error was very similar to that of the Church. The Party did too little too late. Its Congress was hopelessly delayed and its membership spent too much time fighting amongst themselves.[13]

The Government

13. In this part of the world it is always difficult and sometimes misleading to draw too precise a dividing line between the Party and the Government. As a general rule, it is the party which makes policy and the Government, all good Party men themselves (or, in the case of Poland, for the most part good Party men) who carry it out. But there is an interaction. The Government, being, with a bit of luck, more practical men than the Party ideologists, can not only amend and change policy when it becomes too theoretical but can offer up recommendations which, with the consent of the Party, become policy. So it has been with Poland in the last 16 months.

14. From the first the Government clearly had no real idea of how to deal with the effervescent mass movement which quickly swept the country. Unaccustomed to democratic processes and woefully ignorant of political psychology or even industrial relations, the Government tried to oppose Solidarity's growing appetite for change by an outdated mixture of bluster and threat. Their bluff was called time after time as Solidarity, confident in the strength of its 10 million members, marched from minor triumphs to major successes. Bydgoszcz in March 1981 was an important watershed. The Government found themselves faced with the threat of a general strike and could avert it only by major concessions. Rakowski, who had been brought in to replace the discredited Jagielski, started off well after a promising round of discussions with Solidarity, but then found that he could not cope with the union's dispersed power centres and ambitious demands. Through a summer of sterile exchanges the increasing despair of the Government was not lifted by Solidarity's national congress. And the last flicker of hope brought about by the talks in October between Jaruzelski, Glemp and Wałęsa faded into subsequent bickering. The impact of this clash of wills was bad for both sides; for the Government because it eroded their self-confidence and cast doubt on their

[13] Mr Manning wondered whether Mr Melhuish's comment that the Party had become a vehicle for Solidarity was not exaggerated (Mr Manning to Miss Brown, 15 March 1982; FCO 28/4907, ENP 014/1). Mr Jenkins for his part blamed mainly the PZPR for the unrest in Poland, which led to the founding of Solidarity. The Party having failed to undertake necessary economic reforms since 1956 had alienated the workers, the intellectuals and the peasantry. Its false confidence in its ability to divide and rule led to the 1980 events, when those who it had alienated came together. It was therefore paramount for General Jaruzelski to rebuild the Party (Mr Jenkins to Miss Brown, 16 March 1982; FCO 28/4907, ENP 014/1). Mr Bullard incorporated these comments in his letter to Mr James of 6 April. He commented that the weakness of the party was clearly revealed in August 1980 and 'the stage set for what was in effect was a broad-based popular revolt against a system which plainly did not work'.

ability to govern; and for Solidarity because it pandered to their excessive ambitions and encouraged their built-in tendency to become in effect a political party.

The Timing

15. This examination of the four most important elements in the period of the Polish *odnowa* reveals a complex web of inter-related factors. The weakness of the Party, the indecision of the Government, the recklessness of Solidarity and some errors on the part of the Church all contributed towards the decision to impose martial law. But, in one form or another, the distinctive weaknesses of the constituent elements had been apparent to most observers from August 1980 on. The chances of an abrupt and physical end to the *odnowa* were always rated high. The question then of why the decision was taken to act over the weekend of 12/13 December needs to be posed.

16. The Conspiracy theorists would argue that the decision to crush dissent and to impose martial law had been taken in August 1980 or even earlier. The Confusion theorists would suggest that it was taken, or blundered into, just before it was put into practice. I suggest that neither is correct. In July and August 1980 when Solidarity was born, Gierek was still mindful of the Gdańsk killings in December 1970[14] which had preceded his coming to power and which had persuaded him not to use troops against the strikers. Kania also set his face against physical confrontation. In the first six months of his reign as First Secretary, he was almost certainly sincere in seeking out a dialogue with Solidarity. What I think changed the attitude both of the Government and of Solidarity was the Bydgoszcz incident. This sharp reminder of the physical aspects of confrontation and the subsequent escalation of the conflict almost certainly induced the Government to start secret planning for martial law. It may indeed have been only a contingency measure, but such plans tend to acquire a momentum of their own.

17. There are good indications that once Jaruzelski came to power the plan moved from the contingency to the operational phase. The military task-forces that were sent into the countryside in the autumn probably had a two-fold role: to test the infrastructure and to gather intelligence. The decision to prolong military service for a further two months in October also probably had two purposes. The first was to retain a cadre of fully trained soldiers. The second was more subtle. There is good evidence that throughout the *odnowa* the Army maintained a high level of political indoctrination. The recruits who should have been released in October 1981 had been in the Army since well before the formation of Solidarity. Their isolation from the rest of the country is confirmed by the stories that many of them, going home on leave, were astonished to find that their families had joined a subversive organisation about which they had been told so many unpleasant things. Had they finished their time in October their places would have been taken by young men exposed for over a year to Solidarity's beguilement. By extending military service by two months, Jaruzelski ensured the continuation of a well-trained and politically sound Army. He could probably have extended once again but there would have been a serious effect on morale. By this token, therefore, mid-December 1981 was the last date on which martial law could safely be declared.

18. The neatness of this theory is somewhat invalidated by the events which preceded the imposition of martial law. Solidarity's radical demands at Radom and

[14] See No. 11, note 4.

their subsequent endorsement by Solidarity's National Commission in Gdańsk would probably have convinced any Communist Government that it would be difficult to go on pursuing the path of conciliation. The double bonus of having all Solidarity leadership concentrated in Gdańsk and the Gdańsk endorsement arriving on a Saturday, the best possible time to take pre-emptive action against Solidarity, must also cast doubt on the belief that Jaruzelski had decided to act by mid-December. We shall probably never know the real answer. Solidarity may have accidentally played into Jaruzelski's hands; or, perhaps more likely, he might have retained flexibility to impose martial law at any weekend leading up to Christmas and had then struck quickly on 12/13 December to take advantage of good luck and Solidarity's gift to him.

The Soviet Union

19. Whilst it is obviously for Sir C. Keeble to comment on the policy of the Soviet Union, it is clear that no Polish Government would take the important step of declaring martial law without consulting its principal ally. The growing impatience with events in Poland on the part of the Soviet Union was demonstrated by repeated Polish/Soviet summits and in particular by the letter sent by the Central Committee of the Soviet party to its Polish counterpart in June 1981.[15] It is well attested that Kulikov visited Warsaw on the Friday before martial law was actually imposed. I venture to suggest that the Soviet Union came to the conclusion that martial law was the only way (short of intervention) to arrest the disturbing trends in Poland. It does not really matter from our point of view whether the actual idea came from Warsaw or Moscow.[16] Clearly Jaruzelski would not have gone ahead without Soviet assurance that if things went wrong they would help.

Conclusion

20. With hindsight, therefore, martial law might have been predictable. Indeed, many of us in the Embassy in the weeks immediately preceding 12/13 December were more worried about Poland than we had been since the crisis began without actually being able to point precisely to reasons why. Believers in the inevitability of physical confrontation had found it difficult to sustain the clarity of their forecasts and the passion of their convictions through the 16 months of bewildering movement that characterised the *odnowa*. Several apparent points of no return had been reached and passed. Lines beyond which none of us thought the Soviet Union or the Party/Government here would permit Solidarity to trespass had been safely crossed. We even began to wonder whether, against all logic and with more luck than their history would suggest, the Poles might get away with it. But such romantic illusions rarely survive the next morning's appraisal of events on the ground and in our hearts, or perhaps more accurately in our heads, we still believed it would all end in tears.[17] And that, finally, is how it has ended—though none of us managed to get our dates right.

[15] See No. 62, paragraph 15.

[16] Mr J. Bullard disagreed and on 5 February 1982 wrote to Mr Broomfield that the Soviet angle was a much more important question than the conspiracy or confusion theories, which presupposed a Polish initiative (FCO 28/4906, ENP 014/1). Bullard regarded Jaruzelski as a Polish General in Soviet uniform, who would ensure a Poland anchored in the Soviet sphere, but with Polish traditions and culture (Bullard to James, 6 April 1982; FCO 28/4907, ENP 014/1).

[17] Mr Manning thought that the conclusion omitted to mention the strong feeling that prevailed at the end of 1981 that 'any attempt to impose martial law would be unsuccessful because things had deteriorated so far in Poland' and this was believed by Solidarity which had become over-confident. And to some extent 'we also believed it' (Mr Manning to Miss Brown, 15 March 1982; FCO 28/4907, ENP 014/1).

21. For the time being therefore—and perhaps for longer than that—the *odnowa* is over. The aspirations of the Polish people for a different sort of life from the drabness they had experienced since 1948 have been frustrated. Martial law, now finishing its sixth week, has an ominous air of permanence and there are no signs of any re-emergence of genuine political dialogue. For those of us who lived here through the heady days of the *odnowa*, it is difficult, however, to believe that it has not left a lasting impression on Poland and further afield. Or even sometimes, that some of its hard-won gains will not re-emerge.[18]

22. I am sending copies of this dispatch to Her Majesty's Ambassadors at Moscow, East Berlin, Budapest, Bucharest, Sofia, Prague, Belgrade, Washington, Paris, Bonn, Helsinki and Stockholm, to the UK Permanent Representatives on the North Atlantic Council and to the European Community, and to the Secretaries of State for Defence and Trade.

I am, etc,
M. R. MELHUISH

[18] Mr Bullard praised the despatches for their long view which would be of 'keen interest to historians'.

No. 139

Minute from Mr Jay to Mr Mallaby (Planning Staff), 25 January 1982
Confidential (FCO 28/4905, ENP 014/1)

The Course of Events in Poland

1. We are beginning to turn our attention towards possible future developments in Poland. For example, at our instigation, one item on the agenda for the meeting with some of our allies to be held on January 29[1] or February 5 is the Western reaction to the apparent satisfaction by Jaruzelski of our three conditions.[2]

2. As a contribution towards this forward look, I attach a draft note[3] which (i) looks at four possible scenarios in Poland over the next few months (ii) sets out the likely Alliance response to them, (iii) assesses (inevitably somewhat arbitrarily) their probability, and their desirability from a Western and a Soviet view point, and (iv) draws some tentative conclusions.

Developments in Poland: Four Possible Scenarios

1. *Return to Renewal*

(*a*) *Inside Poland*: 3 conditions satisfied; dialogue with Solidarity results in return to path of genuine reform.

(*b*) *Allied response*: Sanctions against Poland and Soviet Union reversed over time; financial assistance given to Poland in 1982 and beyond. INF and CSCE continue; START starts; Reagan/Brezhnev summit end 1982.

(*c*) *Medium term outcome*: Renewal continues, but set back; victory for Western Alliance, with hawks and doves both claiming credit; dilemma remains for Soviet Union.

[1] See No. 142, paragraph 2.
[2] That is the release of detainees, the restoration of civil rights and the opening of a dialogue with Solidarity (see No. 127). The word 'apparent' is important as Mr Melhuish, ten days earlier, had noted that these conditions were being looked at by the Polish authorities, but in spite of some relaxations, there had been no sign of serious governmental discussion with Solidarity.
[3] Not printed.

(*d*) *Probability* on a scale of 1 to 5: 1.
(*e*) *Desirability* on a scale of 1 to 5: To the West: 5. To the Soviet Union: 1.

2. *Maintenance of status quo*

(*a*) *Inside Poland*: Solidarity is effectively crushed. Controls remain, but some liberalisation.
(*b*) *Allied response*: Initial package announced around end-January. American pressure for further measures resisted by most of Europe; US goes it alone with Europe split. INF and CSCE continue (just); START probably postponed; no Reagan/Brezhnev summit.
(*c*) *Medium term outcome*: Renewal quashed; East/West relations set back; disarray in Western Alliance; European anti-militarism/anti-Americanism grows.
(*d*) *Probability* on a scale of 1 to 5: 3.
(*e*) *Desirability* on a scale of 1 to 5: To West: 4 if the Alliance holds; otherwise 2. To Soviet Union: 2 if the Alliance holds and INF talks broken off, otherwise 4.

3. *Further Polish repression: no direct Soviet military intervention*

(*a*) *Inside Poland*: Solidarity regroups underground; violence erupts in early spring as frustration grows, and prices rises, shortages hurt more. More detained; more deaths; but violence contained by Polish forces with Soviet advice and perhaps support, e.g. logistics, but not direct military intervention.
(*b*) *Allied response*: Initial package against Soviet Union and Poland followed by further measures; Europe follows US lead as softly-softly approach seen to fail; US breaks off INF talks; postpones START indefinitely. No Reagan/Brezhnev summit.
(*c*) *Medium term outcome*: Renewal crushed; Poland remains firmly in eastern bloc; major setback to East/West relations; arms control talks indefinitely postponed; Western Alliance holds.
(*d*) *Probability* on a scale of 1 to 5: 3.
(*e*) *Desirability* on a scale of 1 to 5: To West: 2. To Soviet Union: 3.

4. *Soviet military intervention*

(*a*) *Inside Poland*: as for 3A, but uncontainable by Polish authorities; direct Soviet military intervention (distinction between limited intervention, e.g. with troops already in Poland, and intervention with troops now outside Poland, probably academic); puppet government installed (Jaruzelski or successor).
(*b*) *Allied response*: Imposition of sanctions as envisaged in NATO contingency plan, including full export embargo; US may wish to go further, e.g. by interfering with existing contracts. CSCE, INF broken off; START postponed indefinitely.
(*c*) *Medium term outcome*: end of détente; major setback to East/West relations; end of *Ostpolitik* presents problems for FRG; economic and military commitments to Poland present problems for Soviet Union.
(*d*) *Probability*: on a scale of 1 to 5: 2
(*e*) *Desirability*: on a scale of 1 to 5: To Western Alliance: 1. To Soviet Union: 3

Tentative Conclusions:

1. Return to renewal is highly unlikely. Soviet military intervention in Poland is in neither the West's nor the Soviet Union's interest, though the Soviet Union will intervene if necessary. Interests of both West and Soviet Union should realistically be centred on outcomes 2 and 3 (although the West must continue to state return to Renewal as its objective).

2. Soviet Union's objectives are likely to be:
(i) the crushing of genuine reform without their own direct involvement;
(ii) the preservation of economic ties with the West;
(iii) the continuation of INF talks, and the start of START;

(iv) dissension in the Western Alliance.

3. The West's objectives are harder to state, partly because members of the Alliance would differ over them. They would include:
(i) a return to genuine but gradual reform in Poland which will carry with it the hope of gradual reform in other Eastern European countries;
(ii) the cohesion of the Alliance;
(iii) sufficiently strong action towards Poland and the Soviet Union to deter the Soviet Union from expansionism, either direct or through surrogates, elsewhere in the world.

4. The difficulty is that some Europeans, notably the Germans, are likely to emphasise (i) which argues for the maintenance of contact with and perhaps economic assistance to Poland, which may in turn make measures against the Soviet Union harder to justify; while the US is likely to emphasis (iii), which argues for strong measures against the Soviet Union, though not necessarily Poland. This conflict will make the achievement of (ii) much harder. One possible way out of this, at least under scenario 2 (maintenance of status quo), would be Alliance agreement on tough measures against the Soviet Union (though sparing the trans-Siberian pipeline), but a more relaxed attitude towards Poland, including possibly economic aid, thereby protecting outstanding Western loans.

5. This would be a more difficult solution under scenario 3, since increased Polish repression would make a relaxed attitude towards Poland hard to justify; but it would also be less necessary, since agreement on measures against Poland and the Soviet Union, and thus the maintenance of Alliance cohesion, will be more likely if Polish repression is seen to increase.[4]

[4] In Cabinet on 28 January the Lord Privy Seal noted that the situation appeared to have stabilised, with merely passive resistance, although there might be 'more serious trouble with Solidarity' in the spring. He did not expect more than cosmetic changes in martial law. He also reported the potential divisions and damaging public split among Allies, as the Americans pressed for a stronger response than many Europeans (CC(82)3, 28 January 1982, CAB 128/73).

No. 140

Mr Melhuish (Warsaw) to Lord Carrington, 29 January 1982
Confidential (FCO 28/4905, ENP 014/1A)

Martial Law in Poland II: The Rise and Fall of Solidarity

Summary . . .[1]

My Lord,

In my first despatch on martial law in Poland,[2] I said that some of the blame for it must be ascribed to Solidarity. In this despatch I have the honour to examine more closely the brief history of the union up to the events of the weekend of 12/13 December 1981.

[1] Not printed.
[2] No. 138.

Introduction

2. Solidarity formally came into existence on 10 November, 1980, when the Supreme Court upheld its founding committee's appeal against an earlier ruling that forbade it to register as an independent trade union. But its history goes back to the Gdańsk agreements; and beyond. There had been miniscule 'free trades unions' in Gdańsk for many years and labour troubles for much longer. In 1970 the Baltic ports erupted when Gomułka's Government attempted to introduce price rises. Wałęsa was present when the workers were fired on outside the Lenin shipyard in Gdańsk. During the following decade he was dismissed from three successive jobs for illegal union activity. Most recently, in December 1979, he was sacked for organising a mass demonstration at the shipyard gates on the ninth anniversary of the death of his colleagues. Wałęsa was not the only one of Solidarity's founders to grow up against this background. Solidarity's roots in Gdańsk were deep. But until 1976 the underlying labour unrest lacked support and co-ordination throughout Poland. After the foundation of KOR (the Committee for the Defence of the Workers) this changed somewhat. In July 1980, after Gierek introduced price rises, KOR was able to co-ordinate the industrial unrest that resulted. But it was only in mid-August that the 'Baltic Free Trades Unions', led by Wałęsa, staged a strike in Gdańsk, concentrated on the shipyards, which led to the dramatic negotiations with the government represented by Deputy Prime Minister Jagielski. From these emerged the Gdańsk agreements later to be joined by the similar Szczecin and Jastrzębie agreements and the birth of free trades unions. After two months of argument, Solidarity was legally born.

3. Many of the distinguishing features of the national movement that Solidarity quickly became were thus apparent when the union was registered. Solidarity had its roots and its spiritual home in Gdańsk and was supported by a ready-made tradition of workers' dissent stretching back over a decade. It had a charismatic and popular leader in Wałęsa, whose unaffected piety epitomised the union's close association with the Catholic Church in Poland. It owed a deep debt to the advice and help of the radical intellectuals of KOR. For the first time in the history of the Polish protest movement, the brawn of industrial muscle was allied to the guile of experienced anti-government dissenters. Finally, by the time of its registration, it had already twice taken on the authorities and won hands down.

The first phase (registration to Bydgoszcz)

4. The future historian of Solidarity will probably distinguish three phases in its existence before martial law. The first, from November 1980 to March 1981, saw the union pursuing mainly industrial objectives, behaving almost as if it were a Western trade union. This was a time of reinforcement and consolidation when the union was probing the Government's position in an attempt to ensure the implementation of the important gains it had secured in the Gdańsk/Szczecin/Jastrzębie agreements. Inevitably, this led to a series of differences with the government of which the most visible was the dispute over free Saturdays. With the help of a few well-placed strikes and other threats to strike, Solidarity secured an ignominious climb-down by the government on this issue. The Bydgoszcz incident in March, when some local Solidarity officials were roughed up by the Milicja, had a number of important effects on the union. It sparked off the first major political row between the moderates led by Wałęsa and the more radical elements. Wałęsa was persuaded, partly by pressure from the radicals and partly by his own sense of shock at the incident, to take a firm line. The union took Poland to the precipice and forced the Government to back down

and make further major concessions. I am not concerned here about the effects of Bydgoszcz on the authorities. It may well be that it was after this that they began to make plans to implement martial law. But there can also be little doubt that it gave the union renewed self-confidence—some might say over-confidence—and set it on a more radical path.

The second phase (Bydgoszcz to Gdańsk)

5. The period April to September 1981 saw Solidarity embarking on a gradual process of increased politicisation. It was marked by a considerable number of increasingly bitter disputes with the government. The most important centred on the control of the economy and led to the hunger marches of August. During much of this period, however, the union was engrossed with organising its own elections in preparation for its first national congress in Gdańsk. And it was finally during this period that the radicals were securing the support at grass roots level which eventually enabled them to dominate the Gdańsk congress. Solidarity had not yet turned into an overtly political organisation, but it must have been clear to many of the leaders that the union's interests could only be protected by overt political means. Their reasoning must have run something like this. 'Strikes and hunger marches are not going to make any difference to food supplies. The only thing for us to do is to take control of the economy ourselves.' Another important development was that Solidarity and the government were rapidly parting company. Negotiations between Rakowski and Wałęsa in August broke down with bitterness on both sides. It was accordingly a frustrated but still very self-confident union that gathered for its first congress in Gdańsk in early September. Wałęsa's position was felt to be weaker than it had been but there was no other serious challenger for the presidency.

The third phase (Gdańsk to Radom)

6. The Gdańsk congress effectively completed the transformation of the union into a political movement. By its own admission it described itself thereafter as a 'social movement' and was accepted as such by the government. The programme agreed upon at Gdańsk included demands for a social council dominated by Solidarity which would oversee the national economy and which would effectively hold a veto over the Government. The congress also demanded free elections to the local councils which were due to be held early this year. Its appeal to free trade unions elsewhere in Eastern Europe was provocative by any standard. There were signs in the autumn that Solidarity's more responsible leaders, including Wałęsa himself, realised that the union had gone too far in Gdańsk. The replacement of Kania by Jaruzelski at the IVth Plenum in October opened the way for another attempt at reconciliation. Encouraged by the Church, Solidarity accepted an invitation to tripartite discussions and the one and only meeting between Wałęsa, Glemp and Jaruzelski was arranged. Nothing of substance emerged, however, and the possibility of further tripartite meetings became swiftly bogged down in an argument over the composition of a possible Front of National Unity. From then on relations with the Government deteriorated rapidly. The Government elected to use force to end a sit-in at the Warsaw Fire School and Solidarity replied with a strident declaration at Radom, later endorsed by the National Council in Gdańsk. This was followed by martial law.

Solidarity's organisation

7. At this stage it is worth saying a word about the pre-martial law organisation of the union. Solidarity never had time to become a closely-knit movement with a coherent philosophy or structure. It had very little by way of hierarchy and no

clearly defined chain of command. From the outset it simply sucked in the overwhelming majority of the Polish workforce, professionals and most other employees and its rambling decentralised organisation reflected the separate character of Polish industry and society. Solidarity was led throughout by Wałęsa from Gdańsk but its various regional, town and enterprise branches often acted independently. The National Praesidium, starting at first with seven or eight close colleagues of Wałęsa and growing to about 20 after the Gdańsk congress, acted as a sort of top-level body but its deliberations rarely came to any sort of neat conclusion which could be passed on to the movement as a whole. After the congress, Solidarity's National Council, drawn from all over the country and numbering some 120 delegates, met once a month and was the closest thing to a central policy-making body. The only real national forum was the union congress held only once in Gdańsk in September which did not succeed in registering a mandate on most issues it debated. Power tended therefore to be concentrated in the hands of individual Solidarity leaders, normally of strong personality and often of extremist views, ensconced in their own areas. Some of these regional barons, like their mediaeval forebears, became self-willed and difficult as the movement developed.

8. Solidarity was an amorphous, sprawling, ill-organised and often bickering movement. But, when it chose to get its act together, it moved with impressive speed and decision. It demonstrated its ability to organise a disciplined one, two or four hour strike at local, regional or even national, basis. It made effective use of the telex and telephone to keep regions closely in touch so that, for example, a quickly-staged strike by Rural Solidarity in Rzeszów in the south-east would be supported almost simultaneously by a shipyard workers' sit-in strike at Szczecin, the other end of the country. It relied on the enthusiasm of its officials and helpers and the support of the traditionally anti-government workforce of Poland. It swiftly became, and remained, a national movement of protest. Its strength lay in its size; but its size was in a sense its undoing.

Its undoing

9. As I noted in my earlier despatch, Solidarity's gravest weakness and its ultimate undoing was its self-confidence, bordering on arrogance, and its effective transformation into a political party with a growing radical flavour. These trends interacted in a complex way with each other. The union became more political as it became more self-assured. As it became self-assured and more successful, it increasingly turned to political objectives. As it began to show signs of splitting, it patched over these divisions by making ever greater political demands and thus putting itself under pressure from the authorities. It thus became a close race whether the union would destroy itself and split up into a number of squabbling factions or be destroyed by some outside force.[3]

10. My earlier despatch pointed out that the imposition of martial law in Poland could not be attributed to any one cause. Solidarity's failures, listed in paragraph 9 above, certainly constituted one of these causes. But of equal importance was the

[3] Mr Manning in a letter to Miss Brown of 15 March pointed out that the despatch should also have examined ideological rifts in Solidarity, which 'included those whose views might broadly be described as Christian Democrat or Social Democrat on the one hand and Trotskyite sympathisers (such as Michnik and Kuron of KOR) on the other . . .'. Also, although he agreed that the Solidarity Congress was a turning point, he thought that Mr Melhuish should have mentioned its impact on Soviet perceptions, who after the Congress 'began accusing Solidarity of being a political organisation that was bent on taking power' (FCO 28/4907, ENP 014/1).

weakness of the Government. By constantly retreating in the face of Solidarity pressure, the Government encouraged the union to become over-confident and to drive constantly forward in a conscious attempt to sustain the momentum. By its unintelligent opposition, particularly in the summer of 1981, it encouraged Solidarity to believe that its trade union goals could only be achieved by radical political means. Had the Government stood firmer at an early stage or co-operated more constructively in selected areas at a later stage, it might have strengthened the position of Wałęsa and the moderates so that some reasonable compromise could have been achieved.

11. Ultimately, however, the aims of Solidarity were irreconcilable with the political requirements of the Polish Government and the ideological concepts of the Polish party. And behind the Polish Government and the party there lurked the constant critical presence of the Soviet leadership. With hindsight we could probably identify moments in the history of the last 16 months when the two sides, with a lot of luck, infinite patience and political wisdom, might have come together. But a more honest verdict would have to be that the seeds of conflict were always there. Most experienced observers would have to admit their surprise that it took until 13 December, 1981 to reach the point of no return.

Its achievements

12. No account of the 16 months of Solidarity before martial law would be complete without some assessment of its impact on Poland and further afield. In many respects it is probably too soon to make a definitive judgement but there can be little doubt that Solidarity's achievements were by any yardstick impressive. Pursuing its own opportunistic aims, Solidarity, which in the context of the *odnowa* really meant the Polish people, reacted strongly against the mismanagement and corruption which has characterised Polish politics for the past 10 years. It underlined the point that those who govern must in some clearly-defined way be accountable for their actions to the mass of the people. It also rebelled against the monopoly of authority wielded by the regime. Instead of a totalitarian system, it would have liked to have established a pluralist political framework based on secret voting from an unlimited list of candidates. At the same time it reasserted the traditional virtues of religion and nationalism. There is of course a danger in drawing up a catalogue of this sort. It is all too easy to impart a conscious and coherent pattern of what was essentially a protest movement working in a bloody-minded and often narrow-minded way. But whether Solidarity achieved those aims more by luck than by good judgement, there can be no doubt that their impact was real.

13. In a wider context Solidarity has taken Poland further away from the path of orthodox Communism than any other Eastern European country since the war. In the process, the ideological pretensions of Marxism/Leninism have taken a nasty knock. Every apologist for the Communist regime here in the past 16 months, from Kania through the IXth Party Congress, has argued that the *odnowa,* with Solidarity behind it, was not attacking socialism as such, but the abuses of socialism which had disfigured the history of Poland in the last 10 years. This glib half-truth misses the point that, in opposing the barren, inefficient, deadening and corrupt way this country has been governed, Solidarity was at the same time publicly pointing up the intrinsic ugliness and unworkability of the Marxist/Leninist philosophy of government.

14. A country subject to a Communist Government for over 30 years has thus demonstrated that it would far rather have freedom. Jaruzelski's resort to force on

13 December to crush Solidarity underlines both the political sterility of his thinking and the immense difficulties that lie ahead of him. The latest Solidarity slogan in Warsaw is 'the winter may be theirs; the summer will be ours'.[4]

15. I am sending copies of this dispatch to Her Majesty's Ambassadors at Moscow, East Berlin, Budapest, Bucharest, Sofia, Prague, Belgrade, Washington, Paris, Bonn, Helsinki and Stockholm, to the UK Permanent Representatives on the North Atlantic Council and to the European Community, and to the Secretaries of State for Defence and Trade.

I am, etc,
M. R. MELHUISH

[4] For his despatch, Mr Melhuish had built on Mr James's Annual Review, which the Ambassador had composed while in hospital over Christmas. James had concluded that: 'Soviet pressure and the country's drift into anarchy probably caused martial law' and predicted that: 'Poland faces a dark, hard winter. The clamps will not be lifted soon' (James to Carrington, 30 December 1981; FCO 28/4921, ENP 014/5).

No. 141

Background Brief by the East European and Soviet Department for the 38th Session of the UN Human Rights Commission on the Question of Human Rights in Czechoslovakia (1 February to 12 March 1982), 1 February 1982

Confidential (FCO 28/4837, ENC 241/1)

Introduction

1. Czechoslovakia's human rights record is poor. There are no signs that there is likely to be any improvement in the near future.

UK Aims

2. (i) To avoid mounting any major public attack on Czechoslovakia's record since we believe that more can be achieved at this stage by taking up human rights issues confidentially with the Czechoslovak authorities;

(ii) If however there is a strong general move among our Western partners to raise human rights abuses in Czechoslovakia we should join in.

Tactics

3. (i) To consult closely with our partners in the Ten and other Western countries.

(ii) In such coordination, to suggest that strong condemnation in the UN could provoke the Czechoslovaks into retaliating by imposing harsher sentences on those involved in a major trial which is still outstanding (para 6). There are indications that repeated confidential approaches could have more effect.

(iii) However, if there is a powerful move to specifically raise Czechoslovakia, we should associate ourselves with general criticism.

Points to make (if there is a general Western consensus)

4. Deplore harassment and trials of people who merely seek the freedom to express their beliefs. Not compatible with UN Covenant on Civil and Political Rights or the Declaration on the Elimination on Civil and Political Rights, or the Declaration on the Elimination of All forms of Intolerance based on Religion or Belief.

Background (may be drawn on if appropriate)

Charter 77 and VONS

5. The Czechoslovak authorities consistently harass members of the dissident groups, in particular supporters of Charter 77 and members of VONS (the Committee for the Defence of the Unjustly Prosecuted). The aim of this harassment appears to be to force some dissidents to leave the country and the others to give up their activities.

6. The UK and other Western countries protested strongly in 1979 when a number of VONS members were arrested, five subsequently receiving jail sentences ranging from 3 years to 5 years. In May this year around 30 dissidents were detained in Prague, Brno and Bratislava. Most of them were released but eight are still in detention facing trial on charges of subversion. Approximately 8 others, including Jiri Hajek, who was Minister of Foreign Affairs in Dubcek's government, were also charged but were released pending trial. There are indications that the government is split over whether or not to hold a show trial.

Rudolf Battek

7. A recent trial which attracted considerable publicity was that of Rudolf Battek, a former Minister of the Czechoslovak Parliament who until his arrest had been spokesman for Charter 77. He spent nearly a year in detention before being brought to trial on charges of subversion and assault on a policeman. In July of this year he was sentenced to 7 years 6 months imprisonment. On appeal the sentence was reduced to 5 years 6 months. Prior to his sentencing the European Parliament passed a resolution on arrests in Czechoslovakia which called for his immediate liberation.

Religious Activities

8. The Czechoslovaks, perhaps because of events in Poland, have also started to crack down on religious activists. There have been several recent reports of foreigners being detained for 14 days before being expelled from the country after being discovered in possession of religious literature at border posts. In September trials were held in Olomouc, Bratislava and Louny of 8 Catholics. The trials in Bratislava and Louny were of men charged with illegal religious activity. (Both men are priests. But in Czechoslovakia it is necessary to obtain a government licence before religious duties may be carried out. Neither of these had a licence.) In Olomouc, five men were charged with illegal trading (in religious books) and another of theft of socialist property (the paper on which the books were printed). Sentences in these trials ranged from a suspended sentence (for one of the unlicensed priests) to 3 years imprisonment (for one of the religious books case).

General Harassment

9. Apart from the danger of arrest dissidents also endure other forms of harassment. One of the most unpleasant recently was a serious assault on a young woman, probably by the secret police, in her own home.[1] Often the families of dissidents are also made to suffer restriction of job or education opportunities.

Reactions by the UK and the Ten

10. The last reference to human rights in Czechoslovakia in the CSCE talks was made on 27 October at the Madrid Review Conference. Mr Wilberforce, speaking on behalf of the Ten, said 'In Czechoslovakia too the record seems to be growing worse rather than better. Following the wave of arrests in May, 8 people remain under arrest awaiting trial; Rudolf Battek, a Charter 77 signatory arrested a year earlier, has been sentenced to five and a half years imprisonment; and there have been reports of trials of a number of religious personalities in recent weeks.'

[1] On these arrests and trials, see Nos. 14 (note 2), 86 and 88.

11. After the three recent trials of religious activists the UK, on behalf of the Ten, made a démarche in both London and Prague (Ref A).[2] It was pointed out that the Czechoslovak actions were difficult to reconcile with the Helsinki Final Act, by which all signatory states undertook to respect religious as well as civil liberties, or with the terms of the UN Covenant on Civil and Political Rights. It was made clear that the démarche also applied to any prospective trials of Charter 77 signatories. By agreement within the Ten this démarche was confidential.

12. The Ten have prepared on a contingency basis a public statement for use should the prospective trials be held. (Text at Ref B) It would be released only after sentencing to avoid the possibility of the Czechoslovaks retaliating by imposing harsher sentences.

International Obligations

13. Czechoslovakia is a signatory to the Helsinki Final Act and is a party to the UN Covenant on Civil and Political Rights. It also joined the consensus in adopting the Declaration on the Elimination of All Forms of Religious Intolerance at the General Assembly (not legally binding but it clearly carries moral weight).

[2] See No. 88.

No. 142

Letter from Mr Coles (No. 10) to Mr Fuller (Lord Privy Seal's Office), 3 February 1982

Confidential (FCO 28/4925, ENP 020/1)

Dear Simon,

Poland

The Prime Minister held a meeting on 2 February at 1600 hours to consider possible British measures against Poland and against the Soviet Union in the light of the situation in Poland and current discussion between members of the Western Alliance. The Minister of Agriculture, the Lord Privy Seal, the Secretary of State for Industry, the Chief Secretary and the Minister for Trade[1] were present, together with Sir Robert Armstrong and other officials. They had before them your letter to me of 1 February[2] indicating the line which British representatives were to take at the five-power meeting in London earlier on 2 February.

2. The meeting was informed of the outcome of the five-power meeting, which had been arranged following the Prime Minister's meeting with Mr Haig on 29 January and subsequent message to President Reagan.[3] It had been accepted that the North Atlantic Council meeting on 3 February should be steered towards reaching and announcing agreement in areas where little difficulty was expected, while more difficult issues were held over for further consideration. The United States representatives had adopted a more moderate approach than had seemed likely before the Prime Minister's contacts with Mr Haig and President Reagan. But they had made it clear that moderation in Washington would be easier to sustain if there was a reasonably wide measure of agreement on 3 February. In the light of this it had been indicated that Britain might be willing to announce the

[1] Peter Walker (Agriculture), Humphrey Atkins (Lord Privy Seal), Patrick Jenkin (Industry), Leon Brittan (Chief Secretary), John Biffen (Trade).

[2] Not printed.

[3] See *DBPO: Afghanistan*, No. 127.

political and economic measures against Poland listed in the first part of the note enclosed with your letter and the political measures against the Soviet Union listed in the second part of that note. As regards the five economic measures against the Soviet Union in the same list, the position was as follows:

(i) On export credit, action by the European Community would be required. There was a good chance that this would prove possible, but opinion within the French Government was still divided and no announcement would be possible on 3 February.

(ii) On import of Soviet manufactures, EC action would be similarly required. Britain had suggested raising tariffs in certain cases but this had not been agreed. Further consideration would now be given to the alternative possibility of tightening some of the quotas restrictions which still existed. But it was not clear whether this would be generally acceptable.

(iii) and (iv) On Soviet factory ships and the Anglo-Soviet Maritime Agreement, Britain had indicated a readiness to take action if her partners' intentions were broadly comparable. The Germans and Italians had certain steps in mind, but the French position was less clear.

(v) On non-undermining, it seemed possible that agreement might be attainable on the basis that the Americans would not frustrate existing European contracts in return for the Europeans undertaking not to take up future contracts with the Soviet Union which there were reasonable grounds to suppose would in normal circumstances have been awarded to United States companies. The British representatives had made clear that as things stood they had no authority to accept such an arrangement. But it had been agreed that the five Governments would now consider the possibility and resume discussion later in the month; that meanwhile the issue would not be substantively discussed in the NAC and no announcement would be made on 3 February; and that it would be important to ensure that neither the Japanese nor other major non-NATO industrial states picked up any contracts which the Europeans undertook to forgo.

3. Ministers agreed that on 3 February the British representatives at the NAC meeting might authorise the announcement of the proposed political and economic measures against Poland and of the proposed political measures against the Soviet Union. As regards item A(iv) in your list of measures against Poland, they agreed that it would be wrong to specify a contribution of £5,000, which might seem too small, and that the Government should instead indicate a general willingness to cover all reasonable costs of co-ordinating the humanitarian efforts of the voluntary and church agencies. As regards item B(iii) in the same list, they agreed that, if possible, it should be made clear how much money was to be allocated by the EC to the provision of humanitarian aid. Turning to economic measures against the Soviet Union, Ministers took note of the position on points (i) and (ii) above. On point (iii), they agreed that on 3 February public attention could be drawn to the fact that the government had introduced licensing control over the fish factory ships. But no actual restrictions should be imposed for the time being, since these might involve British fishermen in financial loss. The possibility of such restrictions could be reviewed in the summer. On point (iv), Ministers agreed that the NATO spokesman on 3 February could be authorised to say publicly that certain Maritime Agreements with the Soviet Union were to be terminated, but without identifying Britain as one of the countries involved in this. On point (v), they agreed that a deal on the basis canvassed would be acceptable to Britain if it was to others. In taking the necessary powers to prevent British firms undertaking

contracts in the circumstances specified, the Government would have to retain considerable discretion over the definition of these circumstances. This might give rise to argument over the borderline cases, but there should be no danger of challenge in the courts. It would be very important to ensure that the Japanese were not able to pick up contracts forgone by British firms.

4. Ministers agreed that Parliament should be informed of the public position taken by Britain at the NAC on 3 February, but that this should if possible be done by Written Answer in order to avoid damaging cross-examination.[4]

5. Ministers noted with satisfaction that the United States Government were now reported to have abandoned the idea of precipitating a default by Poland on her debts; that the importance of existing European contracts was now better appreciated in Washington; that there were signs of a growing awareness on the part of the Americans that measures taken by their allies should not impose a burden out of scale with what their own measures involved; and that in general they appeared to be reasonably pleased with their European partners' approach at the five-power meeting.

I am sending copies of this letter to the Private Secretaries of other Ministers present and to Sir Robert Armstrong.

Yours sincerely,
JOHN COLES

[4] The measures were announced by Mr Atkins in a Written Answer to Sir Anthony Kershaw (see *Parl. Debs., 6th ser., H. of C.*, 5 February 1982, vol. 17, cols. 221-2).

No. 143

Teleletter from Mr Montgomery to Mr Fell (Warsaw), 16 February 1982
Confidential (FCO 28/5034, ENP 384/1)

Your Telno 245: Detainees[1]

1. We see some advantage in bringing home to the Polish authorities the fact that politicians and other prominent figures in the UK are taking active interest in the fate of named individuals who have been detained under martial law. We believe that the pattern of developments so far has shown that the regime are not entirely insensitive to Western public opinion. While there can clearly be little hope of their releasing the major Solidarity organisers, we think that they might be inclined to adopt a more lenient attitude towards some academics and intellectuals who have been arrested purely on account of their known views rather than for any 'anti-state activities'.

2. Clearly we would not wish to push a case where you felt that to do so would be counter-productive. But we know that Bartoszewski's case has already been raised by the Germans. Our thought was that you might prefer to present a list of known detainees, partly because it might appear invidious to single out any one individual to make representations on his/her behalf, and also in the hope that if several cases were raised there would be less chance of provoking any kind of retaliation.

3. In any case, it was not our intention that you should seek an appointment specifically for this purpose, but rather that you might take the opportunity when

[1] Not printed.

calling at the Ministry on some other business to raise the subject and if appropriate name a few names, including the fact that their situation was the subject of considerable interest on the part of leading personalities in the UK.

4. We shall be sending you, in the next bag, a list of some of the names which have been raised with us in correspondence to Ministers. However we are content to leave it to your discretion as to which, if any, should be mentioned to the Poles. Clearly in such a sensitive area as this the last word must rest with those on the spot. When you do raise this with the Polish authorities, however, it would be helpful to know that you have done so, which names have been mentioned and the Polish reaction if any so that we can refer to these representations in correspondence.

A. E. MONTGOMERY

No. 144

Mr Melhuish (Warsaw) to Lord Carrington, 16 February 1982
Confidential (FCO 28/4906, ENP 014/1)

Martial Law in Poland III: Darkness and Silence

Summary . . . [1]

My Lord,

'A cruel night of darkness and silence has descended over my country'
(Romuald Spasowski, former Polish Ambassador in the United States)[2]

1. In two earlier despatches I examined the background to General Jaruzelski's decision to impose martial law in Poland, and the role played in the process by Solidarity. In this despatch I have the honour to describe the first phase of martial law. With the advantage of hindsight it is possible to see more clearly the pattern of events in the early weeks of martial law, which was impossible at the time due to lack of news from outside Warsaw. I attach a chronology of events from 13 December 1981 to the end of January 1982. This is a convenient point at which to break off the narrative since the events in Gdańsk of 30 January[3] marked the beginning of a new stage in the progress of martial law.

Introduction

2. Looking back, it is possible to discern three phases in the first fortnight of martial law. First there was the clinically efficient imposition of martial law which stunned the population for a day or two. Secondly there was a wave of sit-in strikes which was crushed ruthlessly by the riot police and the army. Thirdly, following the period of initial resistance, there was a period of calm. Thereafter analysis of what was happening gets more difficult. It looked for a while as if dialogue was beginning between the authorities and the Church and also as if the authorities were considering lifting martial law in January and perhaps replacing it by something not quite so harsh. In the event, neither of these eventualities happened. But it may be instructive to assess whether the authorities did seriously consider lifting martial law because it may give a clue to their thinking in the next few

[1] Not printed.
[2] He had defected on 19 December 1981.
[3] Riots in the town on that date resulted in 205 detentions and the extension of the curfew from 8 p.m. to 5 a.m.

months. This is still for the future however. This account really begins on the night of 12/13 December 1981.

The crackdown

3. The actual imposition of martial law was carried out according to what must have been a pre-arranged timetable. In the early hours of Sunday 13 December troops were deployed on the streets of Warsaw and other major towns to set up road blocks and to keep a close check on the movement of people and particularly vehicles. At the same time, practically the whole Solidarity leadership was arrested (most of them conveniently concentrated in Gdańsk for a meeting of the National Commission). As the clamp-down proceeded over the next few days, troops were moved to other big towns as necessary and further arrests were made of the smaller fry in Solidarity, prominent intellectuals and sympathisers. Military commissars moved in to local government and factories. Jaruzelski broadcast on the radio and the newly set up Military Council of National Salvation issued decrees which suspended many civil liberties as well as the trade unions and the Sejm and which introduced countless other restrictions into the life of the Polish citizen. At the very beginning all telephones and telexes were turned off, then Polish air space was closed and all the other obstructive decisions were taken. The whole process of establishing martial law took only a few hours.

4. It was hardly surprising therefore that the initial reaction of the man in the street and the trade unionist on the shop floor was stunned surprise. In a way they—and we with them—should not really have been so surprised, since action against Solidarity had been predicted for some time but there was an insidious and pervading conviction that, in some unspecified way, Solidarity had become immune from persecution. In most cases this sense of shock lasted throughout Sunday 13 December and on into the following day. Some people stayed away from work on the Monday, others did not. A half-hearted call for a general strike did not seem to be heeded. In most places where there were later sit-in strikes they did not begin for a day or two. The fact that martial law took everybody by surprise was one reason for this but another was the arrest of virtually the entire Solidarity leadership. Equally important was the ban on communications and travel which effectively prevented any coordination between potential strike leaders in different parts of the country. This false calm lasted only a day or two in some areas and up to a week in others. It is important to remember when talking about a 'wave' of sit-in strikes or different phases in martial law that there was no coordination and that the same process moved at different speed in different parts of the country.

The response

5. In those early days of martial law the remaining Solidarity activists moved into action in two ways. Firstly, virtually all factories started 'Italian strikes'. The workers turned up but did the minimum amount of work possible. Productivity dropped to around 30-40% and in most factories that is the figure at which it still remains. Secondly, workers in a small minority of more militant factories staged sit-in strikes. This was the weapon that had proved so effective in August 1980 and at the many confrontations with the government since. It was a piece of received wisdom that it was impossible to break a strike with a tank. In some places this proved to be literally true. The tactics adopted by the authorities were for the army to breach the factory walls (in Wroclaw it is rumoured that tanks were actually used for this purpose) and for the riot police to follow through and clear out the strikers. There were a series of bitter and often bloody clashes between strikers and the authorities. At the Wujek mine in Silesia seven miners died. We have heard

rumours of deaths in many other incidents, although the government has not admitted them. In most cases the authorities wasted a day or so before moving in once they judged that this would be the only way to clear the factory concerned. In some cases, once the sitting-in workers had been cleared from the factory, the next shift 'sat-in' again. The Lenin shipyard, for example, was reoccupied at least twice. The army and the police obviously did not have the manpower to mount a 24-hour guard on the factories they had cleared and in any case production in the shipyards, the steelworks and the other factories was vital for the country's economic survival. But it is also possible that the authorities saw the forcible eviction of strikers as a means of teaching them a lesson. If the lesson needed to be repeated the authorities were quite prepared to do so.

6. Not all strikes were broken by violence. Some miners in Silesia were starved or simply laid siege to until they gave up. But where practical the military authorities, usually through the agency of ZOMO riot police, acted quickly and decisively. After breaking up the sit-in, the security forces then swiftly carted off all Solidarity activists, often working from a list of names presumably obtained from the 13 December swoop on all Solidarity headquarter offices. Realisation dawned on members of Solidarity that they were facing a regime which was acting in quite a different fashion to successive Polish governments since August 1980. They soon realised that this regime was ruthless enough to use violence, even to the point of causing deaths, and to go on doing so more or less *ad infinitum*. They thus drew the conclusion that an occupation strike was no longer the most effective weapon to use against the military government. (Some Solidarity activists admitted as much to Western journalists in Poznań last month.) So the second phase of martial law was eventually brought to a close by the regime's tough methods and by Solidarity's realisation that different tactics would have to be employed. The Solidarity organisation went underground and waited, it knew not for what. It is still waiting, although rumours suggest that an active wave of opposition will start in the spring.

7. Meanwhile, military courts began dealing out harsh sentences to those who organised strikes after the start of martial law. Two or three years' imprisonment seems to be the standard sentence although more recently some strike leaders in the north have been given up to ten years. This judicial harshness complemented the willingness to use force to break strikes. The policy of effective opposition to strikes and harsh punishment thereafter was calculated to deter all but the bravest (or the most foolhardy).

Relaxation

8. Once the first wave of opposition had been put down in any particular locality (and it has to be remembered that throughout most of the country there was no opposition) the process of relaxation of the restrictions of martial law began. This process has been going on steadily since just before Christmas. So far, none of the substantive political restrictions of martial law has been affected. But gradually life for the average citizen has begun to return more or less to normal, with the melting-away of most of the road-blocks and other visible evidence of the military presence, the gradual reintroduction of telephones, and the steady lifting of travel restrictions etc. This process has not proceeded entirely smoothly. There have been periods when few relaxations have been made and other periods when there have been spates of them. In the middle of January it looked as if martial law might be lifted and replaced by a state of emergency or simply by an institutionalisation of its political restrictions. We and most other Missions in Warsaw were told as much

by senior MFA officials. The Polish government would no doubt have presented this as a significant step forward whereas in fact it would have been a backward step. Any institutionalisation of the political restrictions of martial law would have driven this country more permanently towards the political status of say Czechoslovakia. But in fact rumours of such a step died away and Jaruzelski's speech to Sejm, which went through several different drafts, and whose date of delivery was put back from 20 to 25 January, made no concessions at all. He contended himself with a vague promise about further relaxations at the end of February, whilst stressing that this would not mean an end to martial law or the release of internees. In so far as further minor concessions have now been made, that process of relaxation could be said to be continuing.

Jaruzelski's aims

9. The questions I touched on in para 2 above are important. Did Jaruzelski ever intend to lift martial law at this early stage, and if so, why did he change his mind? An answer to these questions must rest on an analysis of Jaruzelski's aims so far as we can perceive them. The important characteristics of the three phases of martial law which I have outlined above are that Jaruzelski clearly intended to deliver a 'short sharp shock' to the Polish people and to Solidarity in particular; that he saw force as a means of breaking the cycle of industrial unrest; and that he was quite determined to use violent methods as often as necessary until the strikers learnt their lessons. In short, he wanted above everything else calm, and law and order; and he was prepared to use force to get it.[4]

10. Against this background I believe that Jaruzelski may seriously have considered lifting martial law by mid-January. If he saw martial law as a short sharp shock, then it should not last longer than about a month. By mid-January there were no further strikes against which to use violence and all strikers seemed to have learnt their lesson. He had the law and order which he obviously wanted. It would seem that martial law had achieved what it set out to do. But the fact that the Sejm session was postponed from 20 to 25 January is a sure indicator that there was fierce debate among the Polish leadership.[5] Jaruzelski's unnamed opponents, who probably included politically aware hard-liners such as Olszowksi, cannot have questioned the fact that martial law had restored law and order to Poland. But they must have been fearful of the consequences if martial law were lifted. And his own military colleagues, perhaps aware through their intelligence coverage of the country that there was more underground opposition than the peaceful surface indicated, might also have advised against a premature lifting of martial law. Martial law had achieved what it set out to do but he could not then risk lifting it.

11. Almost a month on this analysis continues to hold good. The country is calm, surprisingly calm considering that swingeing price rises were introduced on

[4] Mr Manning had a slightly different reading of General Jaruzelski's intentions. Although he agreed that Jaruzelski wanted to use strong methods he thought he wanted to avoid severe violence and bloodshed at all costs for fear of provoking a popular reaction of the 1970 model. Mr Manning thought that 'the fact that there was comparatively little actual violence was one reason why Jaruzelski managed to impose martial law so successfully' (Mr Manning to Miss Brown, 15 March 1982; FCO 28/4907, ENP 014/1).

[5] Mr Manning did not believe that there had been a genuine debate in the Polish hierarchy, but that 'more probably the debate had turned on whether to replace martial law by administrative measures that would have the same practical consequences' (Mr Manning to Miss Brown, 15 March 1982; FCO 28/4907, ENP 014/1). Mr Bullard put that point to Mr James, himself believing that 'General Jaruzelski would only lift martial law on his own terms and at his own pace' with no unnecessary risks (Mr Bullard to Mr James, 6 April 1982; FCO 28/4907, ENP 014/1).

1 February. But there is little doubt about the tension beneath the surface. If martial law were lifted, opposition would be both vocal and active. Gdańsk on 30 January and Poznań on 13 February support this interpretation.[6]

12. The renewal of opposition is not in itself enough to explain Jaruzelski's decision not to lift martial law in mid-January. He could still have done so if there had been an alternative apparatus to take over the job that the military were doing so successfully. This is the most serious obstacle to any plans to lift martial law. The demoralised police and security forces, who might have been a candidate to take over from the military, had proved singularly incapable in the late 70s and early 80s of keeping down the opposition. Not only that, they had allowed common crime to increase immeasurably. With the military to help them, the police, and in particular the nasty riot police, have been much more self-confident and effective since martial law. But there is no doubt that they rely on that military help. Without the military structure of security, Poland would quickly lapse back into what it was before 13 December. Politically, the Party is not yet in any shape to take back power from the Military Council. Nor does the government, which has taken advantage of the political breathing space to push through price rises and other economic reforms, show any sign of wanting to resume the responsibilities it handled so badly.

Conclusion

13. There was a natural sequence in the first three phases of martial law, as the internal crack-down produced its response which led in turn to a period of outward calm. But this third phase leads nowhere. And, in the absence of a constructive solution to the crucial problem of what political structure comes next in Poland, I believe that martial law is likely to remain in force here for a long time. In this description of the first seven weeks of martial law I have gestured at some of the formidable political tasks that lie ahead of Jaruzelski and the Military Council before they can think of returning power to the civilian authorities. In a further despatch, the last in the series about martial law, I will examine in more detail Jaruzelski's long-term aims and the inevitably bleak prospects for the future.

14. I am sending copies of this dispatch to Her Majesty's Ambassadors at Moscow, East Berlin, Budapest, Bucharest, Sofia, Prague, Belgrade, Washington, Paris, Bonn, Helsinki and Stockholm, to the UK Permanent Representatives on the North Atlantic Council and to the European Community, and to the Secretaries of State for Defence and Trade.

I am, etc,

M. R. MELHUISH

[6] The Polish News Agency, PAP, reported that the police had arrested 194 people, many of them students, during demonstrations in Poznań. As a result private cars were banned and theatres and cinemas closed.

No. 145

Letter from Mr Broomfield to Mr Cartledge (Budapest), 22 February 1982[1]
Confidential (FCO 28/4877, ENH 014/1)

My dear Bryan,

Hungary: Economics and Politics

1. Thank you for your interesting letter of 1 February.[2]

2. We are of course aware of the distinction Timar[3] was trying to draw, that Hungary is in a different category from countries like Poland, Romania and Yugoslavia. ECGD rate Hungary in Category 'B' (Romania, by way of comparison, is rated 'D'): and a recent paper by Whitehall officials which Ministers approved concluded that in the case of Hungary no immediate economic problems were foreseen. (A copy of this paper has already been sent to Budapest under separate cover).

3. The ripples from the storms in Poland and elsewhere are, however, spreading widely. You mentioned that Ede Bako[4] admitted that Hungary would suffer from the cumulatively harmful effect of the disruption of intra-CMEA trading patterns which resulted from the Polish crisis. This knock-on effect is of course precisely what worries possible Western creditors, and it does not affect Hungary alone: for example, Giles Bullard has also expressed concern that other countries' problems may spill over and affect Bulgaria, and that the Bulgarians may find credits much harder to find in future. It is therefore neither surprising nor unreasonable that the Hungarians should be worried that they may face similar problems.

4. The Governor of the Bank of England has gone on record with a speech emphasising that borrowing countries should be treated on their merits. There is, of course, no way of forcing the banks to accept this advice. But the banks are understandably running scared given their recent experiences in Poland and Romania. Their previous overconfidence in the efficacy of the 'umbrella theory'[5] has been profoundly disturbed and they are going to be very cautious until the situation in Eastern Europe becomes clearer. Western Governments have had much the same experience and export credit organisations like ECGD are naturally reluctant to increase their liability, particularly those who feel dangerously over-exposed already.

[1] The letter was copied to Ambassadors in Moscow, Warsaw, East Berlin, Prague, Bucharest, Belgrade and Sofia.

[2] In this letter Mr Cartledge reported on Hungarian concerns that Western policies of differentiation towards Eastern Europe might be changing due to the cooling in East-West relations following the imposition of martial law in Poland. In a further letter, on 19 February, Mr Cartledge sent evidence of a clear re-affirmation of Hungary's position across a range of issues—economic management, foreign policy and industrial relations. He ended: 'The Hungarian leadership will also hope that the re-statement may encourage the West to continue to differentiate between Hungary and some of her less fortunate and less independently-minded partners.'

[3] Mr Cartledge had reported in his letter of 1 February that Mátyás Tímár, Governor of the Hungarian National Bank, 1975-88, had expressed 'chagrin and anxiety' over the fact that Hungary's ability to borrow in the West was being impaired by the economic crisis in Poland. He stated that Hungary was not Poland and should be judged on its own merits.

[4] Senior official at the Hungarian National Bank.

[5] See No. 55.

5. The pendulum almost certainly swung too far in the direction of the Eastern Europeans in the 1970s when *Ostpolitik*, Kissingerism[6] and petro-dollar surpluses came together in a way which is unlikely to be repeated. The pendulum is now swinging the other way pushed by a world-recession, strong doubts about the Soviet Union as the lender of the last resort for Eastern Europe and a new mood in the US which is summed up by the desire to 'let the costs of a bankrupt system, lie where they truly fall'. To some extent therefore, the Hungarians are going to have to live with the fact that despite their good record and good intentions they will find it more difficult to get credit from the West in future.

6. All this as you know from recent telegrams and a Planning Staff paper on policy on Poland which has just issued, is now the subject of lively debate, (a sufficiently neutral term), between the Americans and the West Europeans. The specific focus of this debate is the gas-pipeline but the principles go much wider. A fair amount of work is in hand in the Assessments Staff on the political and economic effects of East/West trade (not for the first time as you will recall). We hope to air the subject in the run-up to the NATO Summit in June and we are of course committed under paragraph 16 of the NATO Declaration of 11 January to look at the long term effects in discussions with our NATO partners.

7. To return, against this background, to what Marjai said to Corti.[7] On the one hand Marjai hopes the present tension will be as short as possible. But I fear this is unlikely. Martial law and repression in Poland are unlikely to be ended soon. Marjai then spoke, from our point of view, more hopefully in indicating that even if forced to conform more to CMEA practices it would be only temporary 'since in the end the economic realities would be bound to prevail'. To which you add your comment that the Russians do not always take a rational view of where their best interests lie. Or put another way, they sometimes in our view take a disproportionately pessimistic view of the threat to their political/security interests from any deviations from their self-proclaimed norm.

8. To conclude therefore I can only refer to our policy of discrimination towards the countries of Eastern Europe. To the extent that we can, we will, but there are powerful economic and political currents pulling in the opposite direction. I hope even if they temporarily prevail and Hungary is forced to adapt more to CMEA practices, which would of course have a disincentive effect on Western creditors, that in the end economic sense will prevail. 1982 will prove an interesting and testing year from that point of view. Perhaps the best thing that Hungary can do is to press ahead with its application to join the IMF. We see no reason why this should be prevented by developments in Poland. If as we hope the application is successful, the Hungarians will have strengthened their links with the West,

[6] The application of Continental *realpolitik* to American strategy-making during the Cold War by Dr Henry Kissinger.

[7] Jozsef Marjai, Deputy Prime Minister of Hungary, and Bruno Corti, an Under-Secretary of the Italian Foreign Ministry. In his letter of 1 February Mr Cartledge reported that M. Marjai feared that Hungary may be forced by the Soviet Union, for CMEA purposes, to change her economic policies and put the reform process 'in cold storage for the time being' and 'give priority to CMEA rather than Western markets'. He also expressed the view that the economic dimension of the Polish crisis, and Western sanctions, could lead to the re-emergence of neo-Stalinism in Eastern Europe. Whilst thinking this view unduly pessimistic Mr Cartledge added that for Hungarians 'a reversion to the politics, and hence to the personalities, of the period before 1968 . . . would constitute a severe setback to their efforts to carve out for themselves a more individual and a more comfortable situation within the overall alliance relationship from which they cannot, of course, escape.'

enhanced their credibility and perhaps prepared themselves a small insurance policy for the future.

Yours, NIGEL

No. 146

Minute from Mr Mallaby (Planning Staff) to Mr Broomfield, 25 February 1982

Confidential (FCO 28/4989, ENP 093/1)

Withholding of credit to Poland

1. The paper attached to my minute of 19 February to PS/PUS[1] stated that the purpose of our measures against Poland, of which the withholding of credit is by far the most important, was to increase the pressure on Jaruzelski to relax the repression when he thinks it safe to do so. When this paper was discussed by DUSs on 23 February, the PUS pointed out that various questions are begged by this statement. The meeting concluded that we should prepare a list of questions about Poland for discussion at a meeting with the Secretary of State after his return from Africa. I shall cover the point about the purposes of our measures in drafting those questions, and will consult you about the draft. In essence, my view is that Jaruzelski's overriding aim is to keep the lid on the political situation in Poland and that this consideration will outweigh the desire for Western credits; but that, when the Polish leadership begin to see the possibility of genuine relaxations in the repression, the desire for credits will provide a motive for moving [more] quickly in this direction than otherwise might have been the case.

2. Warsaw telegrams numbers 301 and 302[1] about Wehner's[2] visit to Warsaw confirm our existing impressions that the withholding of new credit is biting hard on the Polish economy.[3] I have my doubts about the view that Poland can adjust relatively easily to the absence of credit by simply beginning to trade on a cash basis. In any case, such an adjustment does not seem to be happening yet.

3. If Poland continues to need Western credit and if the three Western political demands are not met, we shall need to consider whether the effects on the Polish people, as distinct from the regime, of the withholding of credit should cause us to reconsider our decision.

4. If we continue to withhold credit, the Polish leadership will continue to claim that the West is partly responsible for the situation in Poland and the impossibility of lifting martial law. If food supplies reach dangerously low levels, and ordinary people begin to suffer from hunger, there may well be pressures within Western countries for a resumption of credit, at least for supplies to Polish agriculture. If food shortages lead to widespread unrest, and perhaps violence, some people in the East and the West might accuse Western governments of being co-responsible for such incidents. If the incidents led to Soviet invasion, the same charge would be made with more force.

5. Against these points, the real position would be that the Polish people were being made to suffer for the sake of the reimposition of authoritarian Marxist-Leninist rule in Poland. The people who really ought to be preventing the suffering

[1] Not printed.

[2] Herbert Wehner, parliamentary leader of West Germany's ruling Social Democratic Party.

[3] In a despatch entitled 'Poland: The Economy under Martial Law', dated 4 March, Mr Melhuish reported that the economic measures taken by the West had aggravated an already parlous situation.

of the Polish people would be the Russians. In the face of domestic criticism, we could point this out and draw attention to the things for which the Russians *do* find money, notably military expenditure.

6. If we were to decide for humanitarian reasons to resume credit to Poland, this would be inconsistent with our stated policy. It would involve the cessation or severe weakening of our attempts to put pressure on the Polish regime to relax the repression. This would look ineffectual, to say the least. Indeed, it could be argued that, by reducing the need for Soviet credits to Poland, we were collaborating in the maintenance of Soviet control in that country at a time when the Soviet system had shown itself unable to cope economically.

7. It is possible that Schmidt will be influenced by Wehner towards concessions concerning credit to Poland. The American position is likely to be much closer to the views in my previous paragraph.

8. These considerations, I suggest, confirm the importance of humanitarian and especially food aid from the West to Poland. The more we can give, the easier we can demolish the accusation of hard-heartedness towards the Polish people. I wonder whether ECD(E)[4] consider that even more could be done by the Community? These considerations also suggest that we should not flinch for now in our policy of withholding credit, but should keep the questions under review.[5]

C. L. G. MALLABY

[4] European Community Department (External), FCO.

[5] On 26 February the Chancellor of the Exchequer sent Lord Carrington a paper which favoured a resumption of official debt rescheduling renegotiations with the Poles in 1982 if, as expected, the Poles concluded an agreement with the commercial banks for rescheduling commercial debts for 1981—provided that political conditions would allow. He argued the continued refusal of Western Creditor governments to resume rescheduling talks was doing more damage to the West than to the Poles. There was a substantial UK financial interest in achieving an orderly rescheduling programme rather than simply allowing the Poles to default completely (worth some £300m to the PSBR over 1982-85). Whilst Polish debts were rolled over they were obtaining 100% *de facto* relief—a position more favourable than before martial law. However he recognised that resuming negotiations might look like a return to 'business as usual'. In a reply of 3 March from the Lord Privy Seal, the FCO agreed broadly with the paper but thought that the prospect of the Poles making significant net repayments was still small and the risk of default remained even if rescheduling were to take place. Nevertheless they agreed to an informal discussion in the margins of the March meeting of the Paris (creditors) Club ahead of a full meeting of the group of creditors to assess the position. Mr J. Bullard meanwhile noted that the question of rescheduling was going to be 'a problem of major difficulty'.

No. 147

Mr Melhuish (Warsaw) to Lord Carrington, 3 March 1982

Confidential (FCO 28/4906, ENP 014/1)

Martial Law in Poland IV: After the War

Summary . . .[1]

My Lord,

1. The preceding 3 despatches in this series on martial law in Poland covered the causes of the military takeover on 12/13 December, the part played by Solidarity

[1] Not printed.

and subsequent developments in the first 7 weeks of martial law. In this concluding despatch, I have the honour to examine where the present Polish leadership now wants to take this country and how far they look like being able to do so. It is notoriously rash to make a forecast of what is likely to happen in any country, let alone one so precariously balanced as Poland in 1982. But I hope it may be helpful to examine some of the things that might come to pass in Poland, in order to test some of the current assumptions of British and Western policy.

2. This despatch assumes that General Jaruzelski will remain in supreme power as Chairman of the Military Council, Prime Minister, First Secretary of the Party and Minister of Defence, at least until the end of this year. This is in fact the assumption on which all of us here have been working since the imposition of martial law.[2] Its validity has been strongly reinforced over the past weeks. There is now an air of permanence about Jaruzelski which has been particularly marked in his recent appearances in the Central Committee, the Sejm and in Moscow. He has never lacked authority and self-control in his public (and private) image. To this he has now added increasing self-confidence and a marked aura of power. On the day after his return from what seems to have been a successful visit to Moscow,[3] it is difficult to envisage any voluntary abdication from his supreme position here nor, for the foreseeable future, any chance of his being ousted by someone else. There seems, therefore, little point at present in speculating too much on 'After Jaruzelski—who?' lines, except to point out that, whether from Western or Polish (or indeed Soviet) points of view, little comfort could be derived if Jaruzelski fell from power.

3. All the evidence we have received suggests that, leaving on one side his undoubted Polish patriotism, Jaruzelski is a military man first and a Communist second. The support of the army seems crucial to his present hold on all the levels of power. His appointment of military figures to senior civilian posts adds to the military aspect of his regime which is already obvious enough under martial law. There must be few Generals left who are not now members of the WRON, Ministers, Provincial Governors or holders of other important official positions (e.g. Mayor of Warsaw)[4]. His speeches bear the stamp of his military training, backed up by strong elements of austerity and puritanical zeal. He hammers away at the virtues of hard work, law and order, discipline, conformity, responsibility and political stability. Under Jaruzelski's leadership, therefore, the army seems unlikely to retire very far from the forefront of Polish life. With this help, he can be assured that the country will conform to the image in which he would like to see it refashioned. The army is an effective instrument to control what has always been an ungovernable and non-conformist society. This is not to say that he believes that martial law is forever. In his speeches he insist on the desirability of lifting at least

[2] This was echoed by Mr Jenkins whose analysis was that General Jaruzelski had the 'wherewithal to govern the country for the foreseeable future' as he had the muscle of the army and the security forces and also, and possibly more importantly, an administrative framework, the National Defence Committee, which had extensive links throughout the country down to village level (Mr Jenkins to Miss Brown, 16 March 1982; FCO 28/4907, ENP 014/1). Mr Bullard included this point in the reply to Mr James of 6 April, adding however that in the longer term General Jaruzelski's position was quite vulnerable as there was a danger from both extremes—Solidarity's and Security Forces' hard-liners (FCO 28/4907, ENP 014/1).

[3] General Jaruzelski visited Moscow on 1-2 March where he announced his 'normalization' plan (see No. 153, paragraph 7).

[4] Mieczysław Dębicki (1982-86), Chief of the Polish Defence Secretariat, had replaced the civilian Jerzy Majewski as Mayor of Warsaw.

some of the martial law restrictions, but he does not appear to envisage the early ending of martial law itself, given the conditions that he says would have to be fulfilled before he does. And, even if more restrictions are gradually lifted over a period of time, as the situation is deemed by the authorities to be returning to 'normal', a loyal army would constantly provide the means of re-establishing the apparatus of military rule within a very few hours.

4. Jaruzelski's credentials as an ideological leader have appeared to be rather hazy. As leader of the Party since October 1981, he has stood aloof from its in-fighting, and he still appears reluctant to describe himself as First Secretary of the Party, rather than as Prime Minister or Chairman of the Military Council. One could be forgiven for thinking that he believed that the military virtues which he sees as necessary for Poland as a whole could also with benefit be applied to the Party, as though a brisk period of re-training would soon set it to rights. Yet there seems every reason to suppose that insofar as his views on the Party have been developed, they have done so on highly orthodox lines. In his most recent pronouncements, particularly his opening speech at the VII Plenum,[5] he has clearly tried to emphasise his orthodoxy from the ideological point of view. This emphasis will no doubt have partly been designed to reassure his Soviet neighbours on this score, but it also, I believe, reflects his own preference for discipline and conformity.

5. It follows from this that Jaruzelski's policies are likely to be unimaginative, inflexible and even unambitious for Poland. What he would like is a stable and disciplined country, working hard and tightening its belt in order to revive the economy, eschewing dangerous dreams of pluralism and democracy and remaining a faithful ally to the Soviet Union and a member of the Warsaw Pact. He would like to reconstruct the trade unions in Poland as strictly social and economic organisations, as described in the recently published discussion paper. The void left by Solidarity's demise would be filled in this scheme of things by a coming together of the various strains of Polish society, the Party, lay Catholics, unionists, into a widespread coalition movement working in local groups but eventually represented in the Sejm on a national scale. The Party would be revived and reconstructed and reminded that it should be working to play a leading role in the State. But in his mind, it would still be one regiment among others. And under his command.

6. This picture of everyone in Poland working hard with their heads down and asking no questions (unless the correct answers are known in advance) is a grim and depressing one. Nor does it seem likely to deal very successfully with the four main constraints on Polish policy, which I outlined telegraphically to the Department six days after martial law. These were local opposition (in its wider sense), economic problems, the attitude of the Soviet Union and the activities of the West.

7. Jaruzelski has demonstrated in the last 10 weeks that he intends to permit no active opposition to his regime. With the support of the Army, he is likely to continue to be able to keep Poland quiet. Of course the opposition, by which I mean Solidarity supporters and, to a certain extent, the Church, can be grudging

[5] In opening the Plenum (24-25 February 1982), the first since the imposition of martial law, Jaruzelski reiterated his willingness to relax measures but warned that he would continue to confront the enemies of socialism. He suggested that the Party should facilitate greater involvement of the Polish people in public life and continue the dialogue with the Church. He also stated that the leadership was determined to pursue the programme of economic changes.

about the degree of cooperation they give the military regime but they cannot overthrow it or perhaps even seriously disrupt it. This may not stop them from beginning to stir up trouble when the weather gets better and the more obstructive measures of martial law are lifted. But I do not think they will get very far; and they will suffer a bloody nose, or worse, in the process.

8. While Jaruzelski can probably keep the opposition more or less at bay, with his road blocks, his curfew and his military courts, these can do little [to] solve Poland's enormous economic difficulties. This is the real weakness of his position. In Jaruzelski's scheme of things the 6-day week, no absenteeism and no strikes were intended to ensure higher productivity and a reviving economy. But, because of the legacy of past mistakes, the accelerating economic decline since the summer of 1980 and recent external financial constraints, the economy is far too disorganised to be revived in such a simple way, even if one assumed that there was no internal passive resistance in factories. Hard work is beside the point when there is nothing to work with. Industrial production, apart from a few favoured areas—mining is the most obvious—continues to decline. Even the official government forecasts suggest further deterioration in many sectors before things can improve.

9. The attitude of the Soviet Union is less easy to assess, at least as seen from Warsaw. The Soviet leadership would seem to have three main concerns in Poland, the geo-political security of their Warsaw Pact communication links with East Germany, the ideological sanctity of orthodox Marxist/Leninist concepts with particular emphasis on the leading role of the Party, and the practical importance of having a Polish political leadership that is visibly in control of Poland. So long as these concerns are more or less met, the Soviets will be satisfied. For, above all, as the events of the last 18 months have shown, the Soviet Union does not want to intervene directly in Poland. Judged by these criteria, Jaruzelski should be able to continue to count on Soviet support at least for the time being. The country is quiet. It will be a model ally, increasingly dependent for its economic health on Soviet and CMEA help and, although Jaruzelski may not be a brilliant student of ideological orthodoxy, by Polish standards he tries hard and there is no obvious heresy. I would guess that for the next few months anyhow, the Soviet leadership would prefer Jaruzelski to any alternative Polish leader, even a more orthodox one. The potential gain from a greater ideological purity or a more subservient leadership in Warsaw would not compensate for the increasing chances of strife in Poland which in turn could bring Soviet intervention closer.

10. The constraints imposed by the West must be considered of less importance in the list of problems facing Jaruzelski or his successor. These constraints are partly political, concentrating on condemnation of Poland's policy in a number of international *fora*, and partly economic. Both matter, the political because the Poles do care about Western reactions, and the economic because Poland needs new credits to supply crucial inputs to the economy. Their impact, however, is marginal to Jaruzelski's main preoccupation with order and discipline. He hopes to be able to avoid economic collapse by Soviet help and by Polish acceptance of a much reduced standard of living. He will also convince himself that there is no way he can safely (from his point of view) satisfy Western demands, even if he wanted to.

11. This analysis leaves little room for any chances of the West securing satisfaction on their three basic conditions. The problem is that the lifting of martial law and the release of detainees would undoubtedly add to the regime's internal security preoccupations, while resumption of a genuine dialogue would

conjure up for Jaruzelski visions of the anarchic state of pre-13 December Poland. As the consequences of economic decline in Poland become more obvious, the scope for embarking on more liberal policies would seem to grow even less.

12. The most severe constraint on Jaruzelski over the remainder of this year is likely to be Poland's appalling economic situation. But I very much doubt whether the effect of this economic debacle, even if it is exacerbated by some or all of the other constraints, will be enough to topple Jaruzelski from power. In theory, he could at any time be replaced either by a more hard-line leadership (Kociołek, Milewski[6] or some other currently unknown) that would openly abandon any pretence of looking forward to relaxing the rigours of central control. Or he might be replaced by a more pragmatic leadership (Olszowski or maybe Barcikowski)[7] that would concentrate on trying to revive the economy and might be willing to contemplate paying the price, as they would see it, for resumption of Western help. Either of these alternatives would, as far as one can see, be most unlikely to produce a happier ending to the Polish problems than the depressing course that Jaruzelski has set. It is difficult to believe that a hard-line regime could cope more satisfactorily with the constraints facing Poland than Jaruzelski, and even the Russians might be unenthusiastic about it if it meant leading to more practical trouble in their troublesome neighbour.[8] A more pragmatic leadership willing to gamble on being able to exploit the possibilities for negotiation with the Church[9] or with Solidarity and willing to contemplate a further wooing of the West seems unlikely to get very far without provoking another bout of repression from the Polish Army or from the Soviet Union.

13. Against this background of Poland's deep-seated difficulties described above, there seems to be no chance that Jaruzelski or any successor can overcome Poland's political and economic problems, while meeting the requirements of both the Soviet Union and the West. The maze in which Poland's leaders find themselves has no easy way out and a lot of nasty blind alleys. This is a bleak prospect for the Poles. It is also, but much less directly, a worrying one for the West. The only countries that can derive some satisfaction from what is going on here, at least in the short-term, are the Soviet Union and most of its CMEA allies. And even they must be concerned about the longer-term prospects. The Polish crisis may yet surprise us all by how long it is going to last.

[6] Stanisław Kociołek, First Secretary of the Communist Party in Gdańsk, who had served as Deputy Prime Minister during the massacres in the shipyard in 1970, was Ambassador in Moscow during martial law. General Miroslaw Milewski was an officer in the State Security Police, Minister of Interior until July 1981, and National Party Secretary responsible for the police and the security services in the Politburo.

[7] Stefan Olszowski was the Party's Central Committee Secretary for ideology and media. Kazimierz Barcikowski served on the Central Committee and on the Political Bureau of the Party and had headed the Government negotiations with striking workers in Szczecin in 1980.

[8] Although Mr Manning agreed that the Russians might be discomfited by Jaruzelski's fall, he thought that they might get restive if there were no signs of the re-emergence of the Party, commenting: 'The present unorthodoxy of Bonapartist rule is uncomfortable and embarrassing' (Mr Manning to Miss Brown, 15 March 1982; FCO 28/4907, ENP 014/1).

[9] The Polish Bishops had given their assessments of the situation to the Council of European Bishops' conferences on 5 and 6 February 1982. They hoped for cooperation between the Government and Solidarity but believed that the authorities would not allow an old-style Solidarity to re-emerge. They were concerned about: the danger to children, the sick and the old from a lack of supplies; the catastrophic fall in production; the struggle between Party hardliners wanting a 'Czech' solution and those around General Jaruzelski wanting to prolong the state of emergency to achieve a 'Hungarian' solution (Cardinal Hume to Lord Carrington, 20 February 1982; FCO 28/5007, ENP 226/1).

14. I am sending copies of this despatch to Her Majesty's Ambassadors at Moscow, East Berlin, Budapest, Bucharest, Sofia, Prague, Belgrade, Washington, Paris, Bonn, Helsinki and Stockholm, to the UK Permanent Representatives of the North Atlantic Council and to the European Community, and to the Secretaries of State for Defence and Trade.[10]

I am, etc,
M. R. MELHUISH

[10] Mr Manning thought that there was an ironic conclusion to be drawn from Mr Melhuish's despatches: 'The Solidarity revolution had to be stopped because of the immediate political and ideological threat it posed to the Soviet system, but having halted the renewal movement, the Russians are now faced with a bankrupt and resentful Poland that is likely to be a long-term economic burden, and liable to renewed political upheaval . . . The lesson may be that Poland is indigestible' (Mr Manning to Miss Brown, 15 March 1982; FCO 28/4907, ENP 014/1). On 6 April, Mr Bullard, in thanking Mr James for the Embassy's four despatches on martial law closed by commenting: 'It is difficult not to reflect upon the sad history of Poland and to wonder whether even a communist government is incapable of providing consistent and effective government to a people so perversely individualist as the Poles' (FCO 28/4907, ENP 014/1).

No. 148

Mr Rich (Prague) to Lord Carrington, 8 March 1982
Confidential (FCO 28/4834, ENC 104/1)

My Lord,

Czechoslovak Gold and UK claims: the end of the affair

1. On 19 December, in the presence of Lord Trefgarne, I initialled in Prague an Agreement between the United Kingdom and Czechoslovak Governments on the settlement of certain outstanding claims and financial issues. On 29 January 1982, on your instructions, my Lord, I signed the Agreement. Four days later an Exchange of Notifications took place bringing the Agreement into force. In Zurich on 20 February the terms of the Agreement were implemented; by means of a complicated simultaneous transaction the Czechoslovaks took custody of 18.4 tons of gold, and we received £24,266,619 payment in settlement of UK claims.

2. The history of the gold and claims problem starts with the Munich Agreement of 1938. The background is covered in a memorandum of 22 January 1979[1] prepared in East European and Soviet Department and I will not repeat here the mass of detail contained in that memorandum. A brief summary will however set the scene for an account of the latest round of negotiations, concluded successfully in Zurich.

The Gold

3. During the last War Nazi Germany removed gold from a number of occupied countries, including Czechoslovakia. A large part of this was recovered in 1945 after being discovered in caves near Frankfurt by advancing American troops. At the end of the War a Tripartite Commission, composed of representatives of the United States, France and the United Kingdom, was formed to return the allocation of gold to each country in proportion to what they had lost.[2] As an interim measure

[1] Not printed.

[2] See Nos. 97 and 135. In respect of UK claims also see FCO History Note 13, *British policy towards enemy property during and after the Second World War* (FCO, 1998) available at www.issuu.com/fcohistorians.

6 tons of gold was returned to Czechoslovakia in 1948 and in the late 1950s a further 18.4 tons was allocated to Czechoslovakia. The recaptured gold had been transferred in 1948 to the Bank of England in London and the Federal Reserve Bank in New York. The Bank of England held approximately 10.4 tons of the Czechoslovak allocation, and the Federal Reserve Bank the other 8 tons. This could not be handed over, however, because the United States refused to agree to this until certain US claims against Czechoslovakia had been settled. The US Government or Congress continued to block possible settlements throughout the 1950s, 60s and 70s.

UK Claims

4. The United Kingdom claims against Czechoslovakia were based on Inter-Governmental debts and some private claims. In 1949 an Agreement was reached with the Czechoslovaks for the payment of the Government debt, but later they refused to make any repayments under the terms of the 1949 Agreement and instead linked the settlement of the UK claims to the return of the gold. The United Kingdom rejected this linkage until 1963, when it looked as though the settlement of both French and US claims was imminent. The result of this reassessment of the UK position and further negotiations with the Czechoslovaks was the signing in November 1964 of an Agreed Minute. In brief this provided that, on the transfer of the gold to Czechoslovakia, the UK would be given £1 million as a first payment towards the settlement of its claims. The sum to be paid in final settlement was to be agreed in subsequent negotiations. France did settle its claim in 1964 but the US had second thoughts and did not; so the 1964 Agreed Minute did not become operative.

5. In 1974, the US Government initialled a new draft agreement, but this was rejected by Congress, which demanded that US claims be met in full. An amendment to this effect was included in the Trade Reform Act passed by Congress that year. At the same time several Senators argued that the US should sell the gold held by the Federal Reserve Bank and use the proceeds to satisfy the American claimants. The US Government pointed out that it had no legal authority to do this, since the gold was held on behalf of the Tripartite Commission.

1980

6. It was the renewal of the Senators' 1974 proposal which brought the gold question to a head in 1980. A draft Bill was introduced into Congress in May 1980, requiring the US to sell the gold held in New York, invest the proceeds, compensate US creditors with the interest, and return the capital to Czechoslovakia only when all the claims were met in full. In view of this development it was decided in July 1980 that we should inform the Czechoslovaks verbally that Her Majesty's Government were unwilling to negotiate UK claims on the basis of the 1964 Agreed Minute. In November we repeated this in a Note to the Ministry of Foreign Affairs and the subject was raised at the end of that month by Foreign Minister Chňoupek with the visiting Minister of State, Mr Peter Blaker. In December, the Czechoslovaks responded to our Note saying that they still considered the 1964 Agreed Minute the proper instrument by which to proceed.

1981

7. The pace of developments quickened in 1981 as Congress threatened to pass its Bill. With this threat as a spur the Czechoslovaks agreed to reopen negotiations with the Americans. The first round of these took place in Prague in March and three months and three rounds of negotiations later the two sides agreed a settlement of US claims worth 81.5 million dollars. The US Administration had

still to win Congress' approval for this Agreement, but urged us to proceed swiftly to negotiations with the Czechoslovaks. This we had already tried to do, but the Czechoslovaks had rejected our advances. However, in August the first round of renewed British negotiations opened in Prague, at which time the Czechoslovaks had still not abandoned their position on the Agreed Minute. The British team put forward a claim for £47 million, which was based on £19.5 million for the Government debt, £6.025 million for private claims, plus varying levels of interest over different periods for both these items.

8. Our delegation, ably led by the Assistant Head of East European and Soviet Department, Mr Alan Montgomery, were involved in four rounds of negotiations before the Czechoslovaks came up in November with an offer that fulfilled our requirement for 100% payment of the UK claims plus an element of interest. After taking into account an offer for blocked Czechoslovak assets in the UK, the Czechoslovaks agreed to pay £24,266,619. This was an excellent result, a considerably higher percentage settlement than any previously obtained by the UK in the post-War period. The Czechoslovaks were not unaware that they were being forced to pay a high price and this heightened the sometimes harsh and emotional nature of the arguments. Being in effect forced to repay the 'Munich Loan'[3] could not have been an easy decision for them, even though the figures could be so fudged for the general public that the Munich payment need not be openly acknowledged. The Czechoslovak decision to yield on this question was dictated principally by the threat of unilateral legislation by the US Congress, though factors such as a wish to obtain most favoured nation status from the US, a perhaps surprising concern for their bilateral relations with Western countries, and the economic advantages of a large boost to the State Bank's reserves during a difficult period for the economy came in to it.

1982

9. In the event reaching agreement on a settlement proved in some ways an easier task than arranging the detailed practical procedure for the simultaneous transfer of the payments and the gold. Mr Whomersley, of your Legal Advisers, colleagues in the Bank of England and the Acting British Tripartite Commissioner in the Brussels Embassy were active in the negotiation of the agreed procedure which involved four governments, the Tripartite Commission and the Swiss Bank Corporation. At the end of this tortuous tale the transfer took place in a room in Zurich belonging to the Swiss bank. The Czechoslovaks had pressed for this venue from an early stage, a decision which they, we, and the Americans regretted for some weeks before the transaction took place, because of the additional complications it caused. For the gnomes of Zurich it was a profitable exercise; Socialist Czechoslovakia paid their bill.

Conclusions

10. It is my view that we correctly judged how far the Czechoslovaks could be pushed on this question by exploiting the various pressures they faced. Standing firm on a demand for an even higher settlement might have led to a collapse of negotiations as Czechoslovakia's leaders might well have regarded the price as impossibly high from a presentational point of view. Our and the US Administration's positions might have collapsed amidst considerable recrimination

[3] A loan made to Czechoslovakia by the British Government following the Munich Agreement of 1938. For the background see *Documents on British Foreign Policy*, Series 3, Volume 3 (London, HMSO: 1950).

and the near certainty of unilateral action by Congress. Alternatively, we might have come under heavy and high-level pressure from the Americans to lower our sights.

11. Instead the solution of this long outstanding problem has disposed of a major irritant in our (and US) relations with Czechoslovakia. Whilst there will be no sudden improvement in our relations as a result of the Agreement, a barrier to the promotion of British interests in Czechoslovakia has been removed. And Britain has gained £24 million from the exercise, terms much more favourable than any of our predecessors from the 1950s and 1970s would have foreseen.

12. I am sending copies of this despatch to Her Majesty's Representatives in Washington, Paris, Brussels, Berne and Vienna, to HM Treasury and to the Bank of England.

I am, etc,
JOHN RICH

No. 149

Mr James (Warsaw) to Lord Carrington, 15 March 1982, 4 p.m.
Tel. No. 359[1] Immediate, Confidential (FCO 28/4930, ENP 020/3)

Your Telno 223[2] (not to all): *Call on Czyrek*

1. I called today on Czyrek.[3] After initial courtesies I spoke to him as instructed in your telegram under reference. I made hardly any alterations to the wording or the order. I ended by saying that I thought it important, as British Ambassador, to keep the channels of communication open, even in these difficult times and even when I had to say unpalatable things. I would be particularly interested to know how he saw the future developing and when the apparatus of martial law would be lifted. Czyrek listened to me attentively and without interruption. He replied in a mild and courteous manner. Our talk lasted nearly an hour and a half.

2. He said that he was glad that you were still a friend of Poland and wanted to maintain a dialogue. He too attached importance to this. He claimed that in autumn 1981[4] you had asked him why Solidarity did not consolidate its gains rather than risk destabilising the situation in Poland. Czyrek had replied that he did not know the answer and was fearful of a Polish tragedy. This fear had proved to be well grounded. He had told you in November[5] that Solidarity was strangling the economy by holding down coal production, blocking exports and frustrating

[1] Repeated for Information Routine to Moscow, Washington, UKDEL NATO, UKMIS Geneva and Saving to East Berlin, Prague, Budapest, Paris, Bonn, MODUK, Sofia, Bucharest, Belgrade, Helsinki, Stockholm, UKMIS New York and UKREP Brussels.

[2] In this telegram of 8 March Lord Carrington instructed Mr James to convey to the Foreign Minister that: 'I count myself as a friend of Poland, but shall find it difficult to remain one so long as the martial law regime continues on its present course.' He also suggested reminding Mr Czyrek of his statement when he visited London in November that the Government believed in dialogue to solve problems. He ought also to make clear that the British Government was unhappy that three months after the imposition of martial law—and in spite of Mr Czyrek's and General Jaruzelski's past assurances that it would not be permanent—there were still no firm indications of when it would end. Finally, he should also state that Britain and the West were concerned about the consequences for East-West relations, and reject any suggestion of Western interference in Polish affairs.

[3] Mr James had just returned to his duties after a heart attack.

[4] This must refer to their meeting in September (No. 83).

[5] See No. 104.

economic reforms by demanding political concessions in return; and that unless economic breakdown were averted, the situation would develop adversely for Poland and for detente. So it should not have been a complete surprise to the British Government that Martial Law had later been declared. It was clear after the demands made by Solidarity at Radom and Gdańsk where Solidarity was leading Poland, to anarchy, economic breakdown and destabilisation. The Polish Government would have preferred a political solution and did not like imposing martial law. But its readiness to hold a dialogue had been taken as a manifestation of weakness, an error now admitted even by a dissident like Michnik. Despite the emergency measures there had been no change in the Government's basic policy of dialogue and conciliation.

3. Czyrek said that from the start the Polish Government had said that martial law would continue as long as was necessary. The political situation was now improving and confrontations were becoming less frequent, even though some internees and members of Solidarity were not prepared to declare their loyalty to Poland. But the main reason for keeping Martial Law was to allow economic stabilisation. Martial law provided the conditions under which economic reform could be introduced. The only answer to Poland's economic problems was to lower the standard of living by introducing price rises. This had now been successfully achieved. The Polish Government did not want to use martial law as a means of ruling but as an umbrella under which necessary reforms could be made. The situation in Poland was being exploited in East-West confrontation.

4. Czyrek said that it was unreasonable for other countries to tell the Polish Government with whom it must conduct dialogue. Dialogue was going on with the Church in the context of the Mixed Commission, the meeting between Glemp and Jaruzelski and in other ways. This dialogue would continue because the Church had a special place in Poland. But no dialogue could be held with the former leadership of Solidarity who had declared at Radom that dialogue with the Government was only to be undertaken for tactical reasons. Solidarity must be a trade union and not a political party. But the Government would continue dialogue with all sectors of Polish society.

5. The Polish Government had done nothing which worsened East-West relations. It was respecting both international and Polish law and had, for example, notified the introduction of martial law to the UN. Martial Law had been introduced with full respect for humanitarian principles. In this respect, it compared well with states of emergency elsewhere in the world.

6. British Government had assumed an attitude of moral disgust towards internees who wished to leave Poland and said that it would not accept those who were not leaving of their own free will. The Polish Government did not intend to force anybody to leave the country but would not stand in the way of those who wished to do so. The question of whether any individual leaves Poland would depend on the receiving country. Poland had said that people who wished to leave would be allowed to do so in order to pre-empt allegations that the country was being surrounded by an iron curtain. If the Government had wished to expel people forcibly then it would not have been necessary to make any statement since such people could have been thrown out in any direction. (At this point I expressed surprise and said that this would not be possible in my own country for good reasons.)

7. Czyrek then cited a leaflet published by Radio Free Europe as an example of interference in Poland's affairs. But when I pressed him on possible British interference, he did not pursue the matter.

8. Czyrek said that internees were being released all the time and that more than 50% had now been released. Less than three and a half thousand people remained interned. How quickly the process continued depended on the stance adopted by individual internees and the situation in the country.

9. He then said again that he valued highly your declaration of friendship but asked how it could be translated into practice. He asked whether economic sanctions helped Poland, eased the social situation and assisted the progress of reform or whether they had the opposite effect. Had they in fact stimulated social tension, harmed the economy and deprived Poland of her economic sovereignty? He referred to the problems of agriculture and the suspension of credit for Massey Ferguson project. I said that I took note of this last point.

10. Czyrek concluded by saying that he now believed that you were right when you told him in New York in autumn 1980 that he lacked experience of relations between trade unions and the State. You had implied then that he was over-optimistic and he believed you were wise. Poland was now aiming for political and economic stability but this would cost something and would need time. The Polish Government would do all it could to lessen the damage to East-West relations.

11. I said that British policy towards Poland was part of a joint Western policy. The evolution of Western attitudes in a direction more favourable to Poland depended on events in Poland. Did he have anything further to say about the future? Czyrek said that events in Poland in part depended upon the actions of the West. I said that I did not wish to indulge further in polemics on this matter. There was an element of the chicken and the egg. But he knew clearly from what I had said what the attitude of the British Government was to martial law in its present form.

12. Finally I asked him directly whether he thought Poland would become a tidy, well-disciplined authoritarian state or a less clear-cut nation which maintained aspirations towards freedom and democracy. It would be important for the West to try to assess this. Czyrek said that every nation was a product of its own history and there was no trace in Polish history of durable dictatorship. He was not afraid for the future of democracy in Poland. Poland's downfall in the past had been caused not by dictatorship but by anarchy. The Polish Government was now trying to reverse the trend towards anarchy in Poland.

13. I found Czyrek looking well and in reasonably buoyant form. He was well briefed and obviously enjoyed referring to his earlier meetings with you, even if he gave some favourable twists to his recollections. He seemed anxious to continue dialogue with us, although on this occasion he said little that was really new. I was struck by the way he tried to justify martial law on economic grounds.

14. My overall impression is that he has no clear idea when or how martial law will end. It is very probable that he has little hand in the decision.

No. 150

Mr G. Bullard (Sofia) to Lord Carrington, 16 March 1982
Confidential (FCO 28/4849, ENG 014/1)

My Lord,

What price the Bulgarians?

1. Bulgaria is not a well-known country to the British, even to members of the Diplomatic Service. Before my appointment to Sofia I had met no Bulgarians socially and very few professionally—Bulgaria had a resident mission in only two of the six posts in which I previously served. Restrictions on travel to Communist countries kept me out of Bulgaria on two occasions when I was in the neighbourhood and might have visited it. Even in Boston,[1] where they know most things, information about Bulgaria was hard to come by. The Bulgarian section of the local library on Beacon Hill contained only two books. One was called 'Gay Bulgaria'. The other, published in 1869, had last been taken out in 1904.

2. Now, nearly two years later, Bulgaria and the Bulgarians are less of a mystery than they were. The aim of this despatch is to summarise what has been learnt and to draw some tentative conclusions from it. There will be areas of darkness, partly because of the fence by which the Western diplomatic community is surrounded in its non-official dealings with the Bulgarians, but there are cracks in the fence which a resident foreigner can occasionally put to good use, and the country is small enough to be comprehensible. Now that first impressions are back in favour this personal and necessarily somewhat superficial account may have some value.

3. After the beauty and variety of the landscape the first thing one notices travelling round Bulgaria is how few people there are, only 9 million in a country the size of England. The second is the predominance of one particular physical type—dark-haired, strong-features, chunkily built, with no back to its head. This racial homogeneity in part reflects losses of territory in successive wars which reduced Simeon's Bulgarian kingdom of the 10th century and the Greater Bulgaria envisaged in the Treaty of San Stefano[2] to a more manageable size, severe blows to a national pride at the time but now probably a source of strength. The only sizeable minority in Bulgaria today is that of the Turks, and they since the expulsions of the 1950s have given little trouble.

4. The Bulgarian type is a Slav one; all links with the early inhabitants of the area, the graceful, aristocratic Thracians, have long disappeared, together with any obvious legacy from Rome, ancient Greece or Byzantium. The Proto-Bulgarians, nomadic horsemen from Central Asia who crossed the Danube in the 7th century and set up a Bulgarian state with its capital at Pliska, have also vanished, leaving only a name behind them. Whether one likes the Slav type or not seems to be very much a matter of taste. St Clair and Brophy,[3] two British Army officers who spent some years in Bulgaria in the 1860s when it was still a Turkish province, found the Bulgarians 'brutish, obstinate, idle superstitious [and] dirty', and Brailsford in 1906[4] called them 'a race with few external attractions . . . dull, reserved,

[1] His previous posting was as Consul-General in Boston.

[2] The Treaty of 1878 envisaged an independent Bulgarian principality which included most of Macedonia and extended to the Danube and from the Aegean to the Black Sea.

[3] *A 'Residence in Bulgaria' or Notes on the Resources and Administration of Turkey* by S.G.B. St. Clair, and Charles A. Brophy (London: John Murray, 1869).

[4] *Macedonia: its races and their future* by H. N. Brailsford (Methuen & Co., London, 1906).

unprepossessing'. A more recent and sympathetic British observer however finds them 'sturdy and compact in build . . . handsome in a Mediterranean way . . . less volatile than their neighbours the Serbs, the Romanians and Greeks . . . industrious, tolerant and hospitable'. Most Westerners certainly find the present-day Bulgarian, with his open, straightforward manner, his ready hospitality and his uninhibited patriotism, easy and pleasant to deal with at first sight.

5. A second glance reveals other characteristics. One of these is the average Bulgarian's close attachment to the land and to the countryside. This is partly because the industrialisation of Bulgaria began so recently, most of it in the last 35 years. Nearly 25% of the workforce is still on the farm. But it goes deeper than that. The link between town and village is still very strong; every Bulgarian in Sofia seems to have friends or relations in the country with whom he can spend a summer weekend, coming back with the boot of his Lada or Moskvich full of fruit and vegetables and flowers. Those Bulgarians who can afford them build or buy second houses well away from the capital where they can walk or fish or grow raspberries. The habit persists even among senior officials, some of whom go to almost British lengths to get away. Guinev, one of the Deputy Ministers for Foreign Trade, has a house near Bourgas which takes him three hours to get to from Sofia—one in the plane and two by car. Zhelyazkov, the Head of the Legal Department of the MFA, spends part of each summer walking in the Rila or Balkan Mountains, cooking for himself and sleeping in a tent or in the Bulgarian equivalent of youth hostels. 'You have to remember', I was told by a Bulgarian defector in the United States, 'that every Bulgarian is either a peasant or the son of a peasant'. This is no longer literally true, but it must be more true of Bulgaria than of any other European country, except perhaps Albania.

5. The Bulgarians' peasant streak is important in two respects. First it helps to explain why their agriculture, particularly private agriculture, is more efficient than their industry. The original Slav settlers were farmers, and the modern Bulgarian still has a gift for making things grow. Tsar Ferdinand,[5] who thought little of their other skills (his remarks about their cooking are unprintable) conceded that they made the world's best gardeners and used them exclusively in building up his estates at Euxinograd and Vranya. Secondly the fact that most Bulgarians are able to escape to the country when they want to and find such pleasure in doing so is one of the reasons, in my view, why there is not more dissatisfaction with the regime and its failings. It will be interesting to see whether the safety valve continues to be effective as the ratio of town to country dwellers increases.

6. Another aspect of the Bulgarian character worth mentioning is a sense of cultural inferiority to the rest of Europe. This does not reveal itself immediately; indeed one's first impression of Bulgaria is of how much time and money is spent on publicising Bulgaria's cultural achievements. Every provincial town of any size has its theatre and library, there are regular seasons of concerts and plays, and cultural events get excellent coverage in the press and on radio and on television. Looked at more closely however the evidence is less flattering to the home team. Events attract the biggest crowds in proportion to their foreign element: an opera with a Soviet guest soprano, the La Scala Orchestra of Milan, the Stuttgart Ballet. Most Bulgarian cultural manifestations are less well attended, at home and abroad. The Thracian Art Exhibition, itself a great success, underlined the poor quality of most modern Bulgarian work.

[5] Ferdinand I, ruler of Bulgaria from 1887 to 1918.

7. Some Bulgarians attribute this falling-off in artistic achievement to the Turkish occupation, and it is true that the Turks did little in their 500 years as rulers of the country to encourage the arts. But Bulgarian indolence must have played a part in for instance delaying until 1824 the publication of the first book to appear in colloquial Bulgarian, as opposed to Church Slavonic. Even the staunchly pro-Bulgarian historian Mercia McDermott concedes that the so-called National Revival (*Bulgarskoto Vuzrazhdane*) never amounted to much in artistic terms. The first Bulgarian school did not open until 1835, and the first Bulgarian newspaper in 1846. The great names of 19th century Bulgarian history are those of revolutionaries who wrote, not of writers who were revolutionaries. Almost the only artistic skills the Bulgarians possessed at independence were those of metal-working and the making of jewellery, wood-carving, and ikon-painting, along with a tradition of ballad-singing, story-telling and rustic dancing. No wonder President Zhivkov in his speech last October on the occasion of Bulgaria's 1300th Anniversary, spoke of the Bulgarian people's 'thirst for knowledge'. They have a lot of ground to make up, and they know it.

9. This sense of cultural inferiority would count for less if the Bulgarian Government did not itself take culture so seriously. In the words of a Deputy Minister, Emil Alexandrov, 'Scientifically substantiated solutions are sought for the future cultural advance . . . and for the aesthetic education of the nation. These objectives call for the appropriate approval and activity in the international arena.' But international approval is exactly what the Bulgarians are not going to get so long as their artists are subject to political control. This is an artistic judgement, not a political one. I find it significant that the Bulgarian artists best known in the West are singers and musicians rather than composers, writers or painters; executors that is to say of other people's work rather than their own. If, as Alexandrov maintains, cultural cooperation with the West is 'the area in which our two ideologies are opposed' the Bulgarians are fighting with one hand tied behind their backs. It would be worth our while investing in more money and effort in a battle we cannot fail to win.

10. The 'thirst for knowledge' shows itself too in the policy followed by the Bulgarian government of exploiting the technical discoveries of other countries, and at a lower level in what a recent British visitor has called 'an obsessive interest in material possessions'. I confess I regard the latter as a good sign. The more bourgeois the Bulgarians become the better, I should have thought, and I look on their fur coats and hang-gliders with an indulgent eye. But I wonder sometimes whether our generous attitude towards information-sharing does not work to our disadvantage. It is one thing for a group of British surgeons to exchange experiences with their Bulgarian opposite numbers, but if the subject under discussion is the most effective way of using computers or if, as recently happened, the Bulgarians tell a British firm of consulting engineers with which they have been negotiating for four years that they have decided after all to do the bulk of the work themselves, it is pretty clear who is doing whom the favour. This is a point to be borne in mind when considering requests from the Bulgarians for commercial and professional collaboration.

11. Another Bulgarian characteristic is a liking and admiration for things Russian. I use the word 'Russian' deliberately, since the link pre-dates by many years the post-1944 relationship with the Soviet Union and has not suffered in the same way from over-exposure. Many of the subversive jokes doing the rounds in Sofia make fun of the unequal nature of the present relationship, like the one about

President Zhivkov coming back from Moscow with a new raincoat which only reaches his hips 'because I was kneeling down when they took my measurements'—whereas the monuments to the Russian soldiers who died in liberating the country from the Turks a century ago are still places of pilgrimage, and no-one has yet thought to move the equestrian statue of Tsar Alexander II from its plinth opposite the National Assembly. It is of course in Moscow's interest and that of the BCP[6] to blur this distinction, to behave as though the Soviet Union were the natural inheritor of this century-old goodwill. There is a connexion of sorts, but the relationship between Bulgaria and the Soviet Union is more complex than either country cares to admit. A sure way of getting a rise out of a Bulgarian official is to ask him in what way Bulgaria's foreign policy differs from that of the Soviet Union. And the same student who tells you the joke about Zhivkov's raincoat will react angrily to a suggestion that the Soviet Union is at fault over Afghanistan or Poland. Each man combines a mild resentment at Bulgaria's secondary role in the alliance with the knowledge that Bulgaria owes much to Soviet protection.

12. In individuals this ambient attitude does not create serious problems for the regime. It is different though when Bulgarian national interests come into conflict with those of the Soviet Union, as is believed to have happened over the 1300th Anniversary when Moscow is suspected of having tried to have the occasion toned down on the grounds that it would encourage a sense of nationalism. Even after 37 years of Soviet domination Bulgaria is still some way short of becoming the Soviet Union's 16th Republic. On the other hand it shows no signs either of becoming the same kind of threat to Soviet control of Eastern Europe that Hungary, Czechoslovakia and Poland have posed at different times. There are a number of reasons for this, one being that Bulgaria has done pretty well out of its relationship with the Soviet Union, receiving raw materials, including oil, at reduced prices and having a guaranteed market for much of what it has produced. Most Bulgarians, starting as they did from a very low base, can look back on 35 years of gradually increasing prosperity, an increase which has been particularly marked in the past five years. They are too, at any rate compared with the Poles, an unimaginative lot, 'an industrious, plodding race', wrote one 19th century traveller, and their submissiveness has been rewarded by a slackening of control, to the point where their country gives few visitors the impression of being a police state. It took the Bulgarians 500 years to get round to doing anything about the Turks, who they say so ferociously opposed them. It would not be out of character if they allowed 50 years or more to the socialist experiment, especially if it continues in small ways to show itself adaptable to their needs. I can see Bulgaria copying a change that has proved successful in another CMEA country, like the New Economic Mechanism in Hungary. I cannot see them initiating reform.

13. But the Bulgarians are changing, though certain national characteristics remain. The very achievements of which their Government so tirelessly boasts would ensure this, even if there were no outside influences. Better food makes them taller and more energetic, better education makes them more inquisitive, better health care improves their appearance and lets them live longer. There is still much to be done; Bulgaria's per capita income of £1,700 (the 1980 figure) is one of the lowest in Europe, and for most Bulgarians, particularly in the rural districts, life is very hard by Western standards. Townspeople are on the whole better off

[6] Bulgarian Communist Party.

financially, but urban housing is tight even for the professional classes. The Christov family in my Bulgarian primer (father a magistrate, mother a dentist) are inordinately proud of their two-bedroom flat they share with their one grown-up and two younger children. The Sofia shops look reasonably well-stocked but there are periodic shortages of semi-essentials like torch batteries and car parts; it is unwise to leave a car parked with windscreen wipers in place. Yet the overall progress made since I last served in this part of the world over 25 years ago[7] is remarkable: the state of the roads, the number of things that can be bought, the look of the people and the way they dress, their contacts with the West, the amount of criticism that is permitted in the press and on television. Members of the Everest expedition of 1953 noticed on their way down to base camp that the route which they had laboriously hacked out of the icefall several weeks earlier had been swallowed up by the glacier. So it is with Bulgaria: the ice is moving, though it appears stationary.

14. I was reading the other day a book by Hedrick Smith[8] called 'The Russians'. Many of the things he describes as Russian characteristics are to be found in Bulgaria also: the respect for strong leadership, the intense curiosity about the outside world, the importance of personal contacts, the ingenuity devoted to manipulating the system for personal gain , the growing interests in the country's past, the love of simple pleasures like fresh air and talking with friends, the pre-occupation with health (Bulgaria is a nation of pill-takers) and the slightly old-fashioned attitude to morals. The resemblance struck me again when I read Sir Curtis Keeble's despatch of 4 March about relations between Britain and the Soviet Union.[9] At this much lower and less important level our political relations with Bulgaria reflect a similar decline. The change is less marked than in Moscow, partly because the peak was never so high, partly because the full force of Western displeasure over Soviet behaviour in Afghanistan and Poland has not been so strongly felt here. Trade continues (our exports to Bulgaria were up 30% last year) and there is a steady flow of cultural and professional exchanges. But political dialogue, even when formalised in our annual meetings at junior Minister/senior official level, produces little of value to either side, and in Sofia as in Moscow there are no opportunities for me or my staff to get on good terms with senior Bulgarians. It is permissible to ask what the British taxpayer gets in return for the £600,000 a year it costs to run this Embassy.

15. The answer I think is that we need to be on the spot as Bulgaria changes in order to be able to help steer the changes the way we want them to go. What steering we can do amounts to very little by itself, but the combined EC/NATO presence here is by no means negligible or without influence. The next five years are likely to be difficult ones for Bulgaria, with various pressures working to stunt economic growth and a question mark hanging over the leadership. President Zhivkov looks to be in much better shape than Mr Brezhnev, but he is only five years his junior and the odds must be against his lasting out the decade. While he lives there are channels to be kept open to what might be called the pragmatists in the Bulgarian Government, people like Doinov, the Politburo member responsible for the economy, and his protégé Lukanov, as opposed to the ideologues like Filipov and Lilov. When he goes, after more than a quarter of a century in power, it

[7] He served as 3rd Secretary in Bucharest, 1957-58.

[8] US journalist and author. The book was based on his experiences as the *New York Times* Moscow Bureau Chief from 1971-74.

[9] See *DBPO: Afghanistan*, No. 138.

will be more important for Bulgaria and for the West that the pragmatists should continue to be allowed their freedom to experiment chiefly with the economy but also with culture and education, where some departures have already been noted from the strict Party line. Politically I fear Bulgaria is doomed to be the instrument of Soviet policy for the foreseeable future, but that too argues for the maintenance of diplomatic relations: if for example Bulgaria continues to be used as a means of extending the bloc's influence in the Third World, or in reverse if Western pressure can be exerted on the Soviet Union through Sofia, for instance over Afghanistan where Bulgarian enthusiasm for the Soviet line has at times seemed less than total. There are opportunities for us here if we are clear-headed enough to spot them and tenacious in their exploitation.

16. I am sending copies of this despatch to Her Majesty's Ambassadors at Belgrade, Bucharest, Budapest, East Berlin, Moscow, Prague, Warsaw and Washington, and to the United Kingdom Permanent Representative on the North Atlantic Council.[10]

I am, etc,
GILES BULLARD

[10] In a reply dated 5 April Mr Montgomery agreed that there was little prospect 'of radical transformation of Bulgaria from its self-appointed role as Moscow's most obedient and willing acolyte'. He also agreed that there were grounds for hope that 'if we can encourage the development of Western values and plant here and there the seeds of greater freedom and a sensitivity to fundamentally democratic concepts, we may hope to introduce a leavening into the machinery of the Eastern Bloc which may in due course permeate to the Russians themselves.'

No. 151

Letter from Mr Munro (Bucharest) to Mr Gray, 30 March 1982
Restricted (FCO 28/5055, ENR 021/2)

Dear Charles,

Romanian foreign policy

1. There is evidence that President Ceausescu is currently engaged on a major effort to maintain the momentum of his foreign policy, in order to enhance Romania's role as an internationally significant intermediary between military blocs and warring nations (see my letter of 22 March about the Titulescu celebrations).[1] Romanian diplomacy is particularly active in the following fields:

(i) arms control and disarmament;
(ii) the Balkans;
(iii) the Middle East;
(iv) East/West relations;
(v) China.

The current basic operating text, according to Ministry of Foreign Affairs officials in conversation with two visiting Australian diplomats (accredited here, resident in Belgrade) is the interview Ceausescu gave to the Brabant Press, a group of Dutch newspapers. The interview took place on 3 March but was not published here until 22 March. As of the middle of last week the Netherlands Embassy did not know how much material had actually appeared in the Dutch press. MFA officials told

[1] Not printed.

the Australians that this text contained everything that a foreign observer, or indeed a Romanian needed to know about current Romanian thinking.

2. *The Domestic Political Background*

The domestic political requirement for an active foreign policy has never been stronger. Compared even with November 1981 when Ceausescu's Romanian peace movement was at its most active, the food queues have grown longer, the debts have piled up further, and Romania's 'friends' in the East and West are more suspicious (and strapped for cash themselves) than ever. Thus the need to keep a diversionary circus on the road is considerable. Ceausescu is off to China and North Korea (at this post at least we shall be interested to see if Kim II Sung gets any publicity) in April and to Greece in May. The Turkish Leader, General Evren, is expected to visit Romania in early April and the Governor General of Canada in the first half of May. The Secretary General of the Arab League arrived in Bucharest (on a hitherto unpublicised visit) on 29 March. It also seems likely that the Romanians are seeking to make a foreign policy virtue out of an economic necessity by pretending that their economic missions to various Western countries are connected not only with the development of trade and debt rescheduling, but also with conveying Ceausescu's latest political thinking at the highest level.

3. *Arms Control and Disarmament*

Ceausescu sees himself as a man of peace and professes to believe (the reverse of our own view) that the security of all European peoples can be best served by a nuclear free Europe. He and his Lieutenants use every opportunity to call for a reduction in nuclear inventories and the peaceful settlement of disputes. The extent of Ceausescu's willingness to risk offending the Soviet Union for the sake of peace by actually welcoming Western negotiating proposals (notably the zero option) and by calling for the destruction (as opposed to mere withdrawal, which even he must know is worthless) of Soviet missiles has varied in recent months. Before the visit of FRG President Carstens in October 1981, Ceausescu seemed ready to risk some Soviet displeasure in the hope of being rewarded with a large DM loan. By the time of the Warsaw Pact Foreign Ministers Meeting in Bucharest in early December, when peace demonstration activity in Romania had reached its apotheosis, much less was heard of calls for the destruction of Soviet rocketry. In the Brabant Press interview Ceausescu has reverted to his bolder, pre-Carstens' visit, formulation. He said that both US and Soviet missiles affected Europe directly and threatened the existence of life on the continent. Therefore he considered that everything should be done to stop the deployment of new medium range US missiles and to achieve the withdrawal and destruction of existing medium range Soviet missiles. In this respect, action should be taken with a view to diminishing, and eventually completely eliminating nuclear armaments in Europe altogether. This would correspond with the interests of all European peoples. Brezhnev's revamped moratorium offer (as I understand it, announcing completion of the current SS-20 deployment programme) came after Ceausescu's interview with the Brabant Press. But he lost no time in welcoming it. In the course of a 2½ hour marathon speech on the 60th anniversary of the communist youth movement on 19 March Ceausescu said: 'We welcome President Brezhnev's commitment not to deploy any more new medium range missiles in Europe during the current negotiations on stopping new deployments and reducing existing inventories. And we welcome the Soviet Union's declared readiness to implement unilaterally a reduction in its existing inventories. We consider that this declaration and this step are particularly important moves on the road to freeing Europe completely from medium and short range nuclear missiles.' He went on to call for an appropriate response from the US and other NATO countries and added that if the Soviet offer was propaganda, matching propaganda measures from the West would be most welcome. Ceausescu has thus sought to maintain a balanced position between East and West.

4. *The Balkans*

Proposals for a nuclear weapon free zone (NWFZ) in the Balkans and a possible meeting of all Balkan leaders to discuss this and other matters of mutual interest, have been the subject of recent correspondence from this and other posts. In speaking to the Brabant Press, Ceausescu said that he was in favour of a meeting at top level by the Heads of State and Governments of the Balkan countries, to develop cooperation in economic, technical and scientific fields and to encourage progress towards disarmament and the establishment of a Balkan NWFZ. He emphasised that he believed that at the present juncture it was both possible and necessary to arrange such a meeting. Ceausescu recognised that although the Balkans were no longer a 'powder keg' there were still many problems, including that of Cyprus. Ceausescu no doubt sees his forthcoming meetings with General Evren and Mr Papandreou as opportunities to deploy his good offices in the resolution of the Cyprus dispute and the many other neuralgic points of conflict between Turkey and Greece.

5. *The Middle East*

The Romanians like to claim that they were among the prime movers of the process that led to Camp David and the reconciliation between Egypt and Israel. It is true that Romania alone in the Warsaw Pact maintains full, and quite good relations with Israel. Shortly after the visit to Romania by the US Secretary of State Mr Alexander Haig on 12-13 February (our telno 31 of 18 February),[2] the Egyptian Embassy approached us and the US Embassy in some concern. They had noticed that just after Haig left Bucharest Ceausescu had despatched envoys to both the Lebanon and to Syria. The envoys met Arafat in Beirut and Assad in Damascus. The Egyptians suspected that the Romanians had been commissioned by the Americans to carry special messages to Arafat and Assad, calling on the PLO and Syria to be on their best behaviour until 26 April, the date for the final Egyptian withdrawal from Sinai. As seen from here the Egyptians were merely, and quite unnecessarily, nervous about possible crossed wires. The US Embassy have reassured them that these Romanian contacts in the Middle East have taken place on their own initiative. But be that as it may, the Romanians are constantly campaigning as intermediaries in the Middle East. The Secretary General of the Arab League may be followed before the year is out by Messrs Begin and Mubarak who have both accepted in principle invitations to visit Romania in 1982.

6. *East/West Relations*

Ceausescu continues to play down the fact of Romania's membership of the Warsaw Pact. His formula in the interview with the Brabant Press was: 'As far as military alliances are concerned, they are the result of a specific political situation existing at a given moment. We hope that we will reach a situation where these military alliances will be abandoned and a climate of trust will have been created which renders them unnecessary. Certainly it is necessary to take action in this direction.' The reality, of course, is rather different. On 3 March Ceausescu still felt it appropriate to call for all efforts to achieve a positive result to the Madrid

[2] Not printed.

Review Meeting and the convening of a conference on military détente and disarmament (CMDD). And inevitably he repeated his call for the European states to be involved in one form or another in the US/Soviet IMF negotiations at Geneva.

7. *China*

Since Ceausescu spoke to the Brabant Press, Brezhnev has held out an olive branch to the Chinese. Quite exceptionally, the Romanian television news last week carried pictures of Brezhnev making the offer. The accompanying Romanian commentary reported Brezhnev's proposals fairly but made no mention of the initial Chinese reply that the Soviet Union would be judged by its actions. One may assume that Ceausescu will have offered his services to both the Russians and the Chinese but, according to the Chinese here at least, his offer is unlikely to be picked up by either side.

8. *The Role of the RCP*

Unusually in a communist country the MFA here does seem to count for something—perhaps more than the international relations secretariat of the Central Committee. Stefan Andrei[3] certainly appears to be a more important man (to the extent that anyone other than Ceausescu can be important) in Romania than Virgil Cazacu the CC Secretary responsible for foreign relations. As far as we can judge the RCP is devoting its energies to the advocacy of the right of each communist party to follow its own policy in the light of domestic conditions. Thus the RCP disagree with the PCI[4] policy in its dispute with the CPSU but would defend vigorously PCI's right to an autonomous policy. The Romanians are willing to make demonstrative gestures of support for a party with which they disagree. The visit of Giancarlo Pajetta[5] (reported in the Ambassador's letter of 15 February to Nigel Broomfield and my letter of 8 February to you),[6] has now been followed up by a meeting in Italy on 29 March between Pajetta and Virgil Cazacu. According to Romanian press reports Cazacu has done the rounds in Italy seeing leaders of all parties which the Romanians regard as 'progressive'. Above all the Romanians are opportunist in their choice of channel. After the election of Mitterrand for example they issued an invitation on the party set to the First Secretary of the French Socialist Party Lionel Jospin but he had no hesitation in turning it into a governmental visit when Jospin was in Bucharest (this comedy was reported in my letter of 22 October 1981).[6]

Conclusion:

9. I would suggest that the picture which emerges from this report is one of a small nation ruled by a dictator in deep trouble at home, trying the gimmick he knows best and which costs least—a further effort to establish himself (and Romania) as an indispensable factor for peace and stability in a troubled world. Ceausescu's frantic efforts to have First Deputy Prime Minister Oprea received by Mrs Thatcher suggest that he still attaches much more importance to apparently prestigious meetings than to hard decisions on economic reform. The reaction of countries chosen as Ceausescu's partners in his diplomatic enterprise ranges from indifference (the Chinese and perhaps the Russians) to irritation at his false priorities (UK, France, FRG, US) and some nervousness (the Egyptians). If I were

[3] Romanian Minister of Foreign Affairs.

[4] Communist Party of Italy.

[5] Italian communist politician, well-known for dissenting from the official line of the Italian Communist leadership.

[6] Not printed.

Ceausescu what would worry me most would be the fact that no country which counts for something in the world feels strongly enough to be genuinely interested positively or negatively in Romanian foreign policy initiatives: we are all much too busy monitoring Romania's faltering economic performance and wondering if, when, and how Romania will repay its mounting debts.

Yours ever,
COLIN

No. 152

Mr James (Warsaw) to Lord Carrington, 5 April 1982, 10 a.m.
Tel. No. 415[1] Priority, Restricted (FCO 28/4935, ENP 020/6)

Polish Coverage of the Falkland Islands[2]

1. The Polish press and television coverage of the events in and around the Falkland Islands has been low key and fairly factual. The military situation has been given curt but straightforward coverage, and the pronouncements of British and Argentinean ministers and officials have also been reported without comment. The Security Council vote,[3] and the fact that Poland was among those abstaining, have also been reported, but without any explanation beyond a brief paragraph in today's press reporting Wyzner's[4] remarks in New York.

2. We will report further only if there is any significant change in the tone of Polish comment.[5]

[1] Repeated for Information Routine to UKMIS New York.

[2] For the Argentine attack on the Falkland Islands on 2 April, leading to the despatch of a British naval task force on 5 April, see Sir L. Freedman, *The Official History of the Falklands Campaign*, vol. ii, *War and Diplomacy* (Routledge, 2005). Lord Carrington resigned as Foreign Secretary on 5 April, taking full responsibility for the FCO not having foreseen the invasion. He was succeeded by Mr Francis Pym.

[3] On 3 April 1982 the UN Security Council passed Resolution 502, expressing concern at the invasion of the Falkland Islands and demanding an immediate cessation of hostilities and complete withdrawal of Argentine forces: see *The Official History of the Falklands Campaign*, vol. ii, Chapter 3. The conflict ended after 74 days with Argentina's surrender and British recovery of the Islands.

[4] Eugeniusz Wyzner, Polish Ambassador to the UN, 1981-82.

[5] On 21 April Mr James reported that the press in Poland continued to be even-handed 'with only occasional echoes of the Soviet line that Britain was largely to blame for not having solved this colonial problem long ago' (Warsaw tel. No. 448, FCO 28/4935, ENP 020/6). However, two months later London received reliable evidence from the international arms market that Argentina was negotiating for a consignment of Polish made SAM-7 anti-aircraft missiles. Mr James was asked to make urgent representation to the Poles that if this were true it was bound to become public and have serious long-term implications for their bilateral relations (FCO tel. No. 365 to Warsaw, 7 June 1982). James discussed the issue with Vice-Minister Wiejacz, who did not give him assurances that this was not the case, but said that he doubted the reliability of the report and would look into the matter urgently (Warsaw tel. No. 598, 8 June 1982). In a further meeting Wiejacz again reiterated that he had no knowledge of any such transaction and James thought that this was as much of an assurance as they would ever get (Warsaw tel. No. 623, 22 June 1982).

No. 153

Mr Pym to Certain Missions and Dependent Territories, 13 April 1982, 10.30 a.m.

Guidance Tel. No. 56 Saving, Confidential (FCO 28/4907, ENP 014/1)

Poland

This telegram updates FCO telno 50[1] to Washington (not to all) and can be drawn on freely except where indicated.

Internal Situation

1. The situation inside Poland has stabilised and is calm. Military control is firmly established throughout the country. General Jaruzelski formally runs Poland through an extra-Constitutional Military Council of National Salvation (WRON); real power however lies in an informal 8-man directorate (four Generals and four civilians). Measures introduced to impose martial law on 13 December were approved by the Polish Parliament at the end of January.

2. Some martial law restrictions have now been relaxed: telex and telecommunications links within Poland have been restored and travel within the country is generally unrestricted except for foreign journalists. The basic political restrictions however remain. Solidarity is still suspended and an estimated 3,500 of its members and sympathisers remain in detention. All political meetings are banned; censorship of press and private mail continues and a curfew remains in force throughout Poland. 275 people have been convicted of offences under martial law; and a similar [*sic* number?] await trial. Sentences of up to ten years have been imposed in some cases. The Military Government has said that martial law restrictions will remain in force as long as the security situation requires this.

Popular Opposition

3. Poland has not been stabilised without cost. At least 10 people are known to have been killed in clashes with the security forces in the Baltic ports and Silesian coal fields in December. Many hundreds more are believed to have been seriously injured. Popular opposition has shown itself in passive resistance at the work place, silent marches in city centres, lighted candles in windows on the 13th of each month and violent demonstrations, in Gdansk and Poznan earlier in the year. The more co-ordinated opposition in the spring which was rumoured earlier has not so far materialised. It is unlikely that this would be on a scale that the Military authorities could not contain, even though more widespread resistance could grow as the full consequences of martial law for the Polish people become clear.

Solidarity

4. The Military Government's attempts to gag Solidarity seem to have been largely successful. Those Solidarity leaders who are free have been attempting some underground activity but this seems neither particularly widespread nor effective. Walesa remains under house arrest and is unlikely to be released soon. He continues to refuse a dialogue without the presence of his advisers and other members of the Solidarity Praesidium, most of whom are interned. New Government proposals for future trade union activity in Poland speak of a free trade Union but make it clear that a reconstituted Solidarity would enjoy little if any of its former powers.

The Party

[1] No. 133.

5. The Party continues to be eclipsed by the military. Party membership has fallen by some 500,000 since July 1980 and resignations, suspensions and expulsions continue. The Party Plenum on 29 February, the only full meeting of the Central Committee to have been held since martial law, gave full support to Jaruzelski's policies and agreed on the need for greater unity and discipline within the Party. Despite this however, there is no sign that the Party is any nearer to resolving its organisational and personnel problems. The rebuilding of the Party and the regaining of at least some public acceptance of its authority is a vital pre-requisite for a return to civilian Government.

The Church

6. The Church in recent weeks has taken an increasingly militant stand in condemning martial law and the infringement of human rights. It continues however to urge its followers against violence and confrontation and the authorities no doubt assess that the Church will remain a moderating force whose support may be enlisted. There is evidence to suggest that Archbishop Glemp finds Walesa's intransigence excessive and that he is continuing to work for a dialogue, however circumscribed, as the best hope for overcoming the present impasse.[2] It seems unlikely in the present circumstances that the Pope will be able to visit Poland in August as planned.

The Soviet Union

7. Jaruzelski's successful visit to Moscow at the beginning of March underlined the ties between Poland and the Soviet Union and confirmed the latter's support for the Polish Government's policies. The visit also apparently secured further promises of Soviet economic assistance: in particular, to supply raw materials and semi-manufactures to complete a number of industrial projects hitherto dependent on Western supplies.[3] Poland's trade deficit with the Soviet Union in 1982 will, according to the Trade Protocol, be 1.2 billion roubles (in addition to the 1.5bn (in 1981)) and the Soviet Union has made available a new credit line of 2.76bn roubles on very easy terms to cover the deficit. Soviet support for Jaruzelski will however be dependent upon his success in tackling Poland's economic problems; in maintaining tight social discipline, including the suppression of Solidarity, and in re-establishing the leading role of the Polish Party.

The Economy

8. The Polish economy continues to deteriorate at a serious rate. Industrial production in January and February was down by 13.6% and 11.6% on the same months in 1981 which were themselves sharply down on 1980. Shortages of raw

[2] See No. 138, paragraph 6 and No. 155, paragraph 2. On 13 April, Mr James met Archbishop Glemp, who firmly believed that genuine dialogue had not resumed and said that he had written to the Episcopate explaining that 'the alternative to dialogue would be the creation of a "second state" in which resistance would go underground'. He was concerned about Mr Wałęsa's long period of isolation, but thought he was resilient (Warsaw tel. No. 428 of 14 April 1982; FCO 28/5007, ENP 226/1).

[3] On 2 March Sir C. Keeble reported that General Jaruzelski appeared to have said what the Soviet leaders expected. He acknowledged that Poland needed to be a reliable partner of the Soviet Union, which in turn needed to provide economic help, but he also asserted 'Polish traditions and culture'. Mr Brezhnev said that the 'measures' taken by 'our Polish friends' met with full Soviet understanding, that the USSR had done all it could to help Poland and he pledged future help. Both leaders emphasized that martial law had been a Polish decision (Moscow tel. Nos. 111 and 112, FCO 28/4977, ENP 026/6). On 8 March Mr James informed London that the Council of Ministers had taken stock of the Moscow visit and spoken of 'new higher forms of cooperation with the USSR'. It was claimed that hundreds of factories that would otherwise have to close would remain in business (Warsaw tel. No. 336, FCO 28/ 4906, ENP 014/1).

materials and spare parts are leading to continuing under-utilisation of manufacturing capacity. All key areas of industrial production have been affected and the continuing shortfalls in the production of raw and semi-finished materials mean that problems will continue to grow further down the production chain. The one exception is coal production, which is claimed to be 14% up on 1981. There is however no way of verifying the accuracy of the Polish figures; although there may have been some improvement, the figures are probably inflated. Food supplies are likely to be very limited (although sharp prices rises have in some places reduced the length of queues) and existing shortages are compounded by the reluctance of private farmers to sell their foodstuffs to the State. Foreign Trade continues to decline: imports in February were 50% down from the West and 17% down from the CMEA compared with the same period last year.[4]

Economic Reform

9. Notwithstanding this deterioration the authorities are proceeding with a modified version of the economic reforms drafted before 13 December. Price rises of up to 400% on foodstuffs were implemented on 1 February and a degree of economic decentralisation in planning has been introduced. A number of material incentives have been granted to Poland's peasant farmers and various political incentives to secure inheritance and land consolidation are under consideration. But the introduction of workers' self-management on the scale envisaged before 13 December has been suspended. The fuller implementation of economic reform in the longer term will depend on various political factors, in particular the final complexion of the Party. A sudden setback, such as a bad harvest, could have serious political consequences.

Poland's Debt

10. Poland's hard currency requirement in 1982 is estimated at some $10.3 billion. Even if Poland's Western creditors agreed to reschedule her 1982 debts on the same basis as 1981 this would account for only $5.6 billion. Even after the $1 billion trade surplus the Poles hope to achieve in 1982, $3.7 billion would be required to service Poland's debt obligations. Western banks ruled out the provision of further credits in 1981 and while martial law continues Western Governments will be unwilling to make any additional money available. Nor is it conceivable that the Soviet Union or other CMEA countries will be able to provide assistance on the scale required, given their own serious economic difficulties. It therefore seems certain that Poland's arrears will continue to mount, increasing the risk of a default or moratorium in the near future.

11. A meeting of Western creditor governments in Paris on 18 March confirmed their 14 January decision not to resume negotiations on an agreement for the rescheduling of 1982 official debt for the time being. However, the Poles concluded a 1981 rescheduling agreement with the banks on 6 April, and if, as seems likely, Western Governments remain unwilling to resume negotiations on 1982 debt rescheduling, it is possible that the Poles will attempt to negotiate with the Banks alone on a 1982 Agreement. The Poles' ability to make the payment that would be due under such an agreement must however be open to doubt: nor is the attitude of the banks towards such a proposition known. At present Poland is

[4] In order to bolster economic cooperation, Jaruzelski had also visited East Berlin on 29 March and Czechoslovakia on 5 April. Mr James thought that the sight of the General 'hobnobbing within a week with two of the most orthodox communist leaders in Eastern Europe will not have been lost on the Poles' (Warsaw tel. No. 419 of 6 April 1982; FCO 28/ 4976, ENP 026/5).

trading on a cash basis and so far as we know is not repaying arrears outstanding in 1982.

The Future

12. The prospects for an early end to martial law and a return to genuine renewal are bleak. Jaruzelski's main aim is to maintain law and order and to prevent a return to the situation prevailing in Poland before 13 December. He is unlikely at the present time to take any unnecessary risks either to woo Solidarity or to court Western opinion. Without a genuine internal dialogue however it is difficult to see how Poland can achieve lasting political and economic stability. Without some economic cooperation with the West it is most unlikely that Jaruzelski will be able to secure the economic recovery he seeks to buttress his policies and achieve the economic reforms which might lead in the long term to popular acquiescence in continuance of the communist system in Poland.

Western Reactions

13. In their declarations of 4 and 11 January, Foreign Ministers of the Ten and the North Atlantic Alliance condemned developments in Poland and called upon the Polish authorities to lift martial law, release those in detention and restore a genuine dialogue with the Church and Solidarity. This appeal was recently endorsed by Heads of Government and State of the Ten in their Statement of 30 March (UKREP Brussels telno 1298 (not to all) refers).[5]

Western Measures

14. In addition, the UK and a number of our Western partners have taken measures in respect of Poland and the Soviet Union to demonstrate our concern at the situation in Poland and our refusal to accept as permanent the repression in that country. Details of measures announced by the UK on 5 February have been circulated in the Retract series. Similar measures have now been announced by the FRG, Belgian, Canadian, Japanese, Australian and New Zealand Governments. (For your own information, other Governments, such as the Italian and French, have taken some measures but have not publicly announced these.)

Community Action

15. In response to the situation in Poland the European Community has decided to reduce Community imports of certain manufactured and luxury products from the Soviet Union (guidance telnos 34 and 38).[5] The Community has also proposed the upgrading of the Soviet credit rating in the OECD Consensus to 'the relatively rich country' status. This was welcomed by the US and some others but has met with objections from OECD neutrals. (For your own information, we expect neutrals to accept the Soviet upgrading in the context of the general revision of Consensus rates in May.)

Action in UN/CSCE

16. Apart from these measures, the UK and other Western Governments have taken appropriate opportunities in the United Nations and its specialised agencies to draw attention to the violation of human and civil rights in Poland and the Soviet responsibility for this. At the recent session of the UN Commission for Human Rights, Western Governments supported the adoption of a resolution calling upon the Polish Government to restore human rights in Poland and requesting the UN Secretary-General to investigate the human rights situation there. Within the ILO we have supported the efforts of the Director-General to send a fact-finding mission to Poland. At the resumed session of the CSCE Review Meeting in Madrid

[5] Not printed.

in February, Western and a large number of neutral Governments emphasised that repression in Poland was incompatible not only with the letter of the Final Act but also with its political purpose of creating a healthier framework for the development of East/West relations.[6]

Humanitarian Aid

17. In parallel with these measures, we and other Western Governments have increased our humanitarian assistance to Poland. A European Commission proposal of 8 million ECU (£4.5 million) humanitarian aid to Poland was approved by EC Foreign Ministers on 23 February. Funds are currently being allocated to a number of Western Charities including the British Agencies: the Sue Ryder Foundation[7] and the Ockenden Venture.[8] (For your information, the Commission is likely to put forward further proposals for humanitarian aid to Poland in due course.) In addition HMG have given a grant-in-aid of £5,000 to the Ockenden Venture to help coordinate the efforts of British agencies providing food and medical supplies to Poland.

Polish Refugees

18. The announcement by the Polish authorities that those Poles now in detention could apply to emigrate from Poland has been condemned by a number of Western Governments (most recently in the European Council statement of 30 March).[9] We and our partners have made it clear that only applications from Poles genuinely wishing to leave Poland will be considered. Poles, present in the UK at the time of martial law, who do not wish to return to Poland in the present circumstances, have had their leave of stay extended. No Pole is being returned to Poland against his will.

Austrian Appeal

19. If asked about the Austrian appeal to Western Governments for assistance in resettling the large numbers of Poles in Austria, you should indicate that this is under active consideration and that we hope to respond as sympathetically as possible. If pressed, you should say that in our response we will need to take into account the other priorities we face, in particular our international obligations in respect of those Poles already in the UK who may seek asylum here.

Western Policy

20. In any discussion of the Western reaction to Poland you should indicate that we and our partners have taken significant action to demonstrate our abhorrence of the present repression in Poland. Some of these measures, notably the imposition of travel restrictions on Polish diplomats, appear to have had a rapid effect and we

[6] The imposition of martial law had become the focus of the CSCE meeting between February and March. The US Secretary of State and Foreign Ministers of all NATO countries, as well as some NNA countries, denounced it, as well as Soviet complicity in it. The effect was such that it was agreed to suspend further discussions until November 1982.

[7] Sue Ryder, who had served in the Polish section of Special Operations Executive, began to help refugees in Europe after the Second World War. She first volunteered for relief work in concentration camps and prisons in Poland. In 1953, she established the Sue Ryder Foundation with homes and charity shops worldwide.

[8] The Ockenden Venture, founded in 1951 by three schoolteachers, took its name from the family home of one of the founders, Joyce Pearce. Its objective was to receive young East Europeans from displaced persons' camps set up after the Second World War and to provide for their maintenance, clothing, education, recreation, health and general welfare.

[9] The Ten opposed any attempt to put pressure on those concerned. They declared that they would interpret such a policy as a further deterioration of the situation in Poland and a grave breach of fundamental human rights (*Bulletin of the European Communities*, European Union website, http://europa.eu/).

believe that the withholding of Western economic assistance to Poland has brought home strongly to the Polish authorities the heavy cost of persisting with their present policies. Our measures are reversible and will be reviewed in the light of developments in Poland. The hope must be that the Polish Government may yet be persuaded to modify their policies in order to obtain dialogue in Poland, and the prospect of Western help. Although prospects for this cannot be rated very high, the Polish Government can be in no doubt that their continued repressive actions constitute unacceptable behaviour and that we cannot do 'business as usual' with them while the present situation continues.

21. You should emphasise that our measures do not constitute 'sanctions'. Our aim, and that of our allies, has been to send a signal to the Polish and Soviet authorities as an expression of our concern at the present situation in Poland and as an indication of our willingness to go further in the event of any more overt Soviet intervention in Poland. We believe the Russians have been surprised that the West has been almost unanimous in its view of Soviet complicity in the Polish repression, and disappointed by the adverse consequences this has had for Soviet relations with Western countries.

No. 154

Submission from Mr Broomfield to Mr Fergusson, 19 April 1982
Confidential (FCO 28/5035, ENP 384/1)

Forced Emigration of Solidarity Members

Problem

1. HM Embassy, Warsaw, have asked for instructions on how to respond to an application for settlement in the UK by Piotr Mroczyk, a prominent Solidarity activist currently in detention.[1]

Recommendation

2. That we should send the Embassy instructions in the terms of the attached draft telegram.[2] MVD, UND, Consular Department and the Home Office agree.

Background and Argument

3. The background to this is set out in Warsaw telno 436 of 14 April.[2]

4. Mr Mroczyk's application to resettle in the UK is the latest in a series of requests that the Embassy have received since the Polish Government announced on 3 March that Poles in detention wishing to leave Poland would be given permission to emigrate.

5. The decision by the Polish Government has been criticised by the UK, US, French and Swedish Governments, who have indicated that their Governments will only consider applications from Polish citizens who genuinely wish to leave Poland. This line was reaffirmed by the European Council on 31 March[3] and a possible further statement on similar lines is now under discussion in NATO.[4]

[1] In 1980 he founded and became chairman of Solidarity for Polish Radio and Television. When martial law was imposed, he was imprisoned for a year on charges of attempting to overthrow the Government.

[2] Not printed.

[3] The Council meeting actually took place on 29-30 March.

[4] British representatives to NATO argued that interviewing detainees gave the wrong signal to the Polish authorities. It surrendered a modest opportunity to put pressure on them to accelerate the

6. Since the Polish Government's announcement, the Embassy in Warsaw have received a total of 57 enquiries about settlement in the UK and have interviewed 28 applicants. Two applications have been received from Solidarity members in detention. Comparable or possibly larger numbers of applications have been received by other Western Embassies but in view of known duplication of applications, the overall total of applications is believed to be no more than 200 at the present time.

7. There has been general agreement so far among Western Governments, that we should resist the Polish Government's attempts to put pressure on Solidarity members to leave Poland. As far as we know, no application for settlement abroad by a Pole in detention has been granted by any Western country. A suggestion by the US Government that an international clearing house should be established in Warsaw to process visa applications has been rejected by most Western Governments on the grounds that the proposal is premature and would indicate, notwithstanding our public condemnation, that we were prepared to go along with the Polish Government's actions.

8. Western policy at present therefore is to continue to take every opportunity to express our dislike of the Polish Government's policy and to maintain our refusal to accept applications for resettlement from Poles acting under pressure of this kind. At the same time, we and our partners are considering the applications for asylum that have been received, in accordance with our national immigration procedures (the Home Office's views on this were set out in Mr Whitelaw's letter of 3 April to the Secretary of State).[5] Final decisions on these applications will not however be taken until we have assessed the effect of Western statements and have a clearer idea of the total numbers of Poles wishing to leave Poland. As indicated in Mr Montgomery's submission of 14 April, this question will need to be considered in the light of our overall policy on Polish refugees, including those now in the UK and Austria.

9. The Embassy's response to the application put forward by Mr Mroczyk should fall within the guidelines described above. In view of our repeated refusal to consider applications from Poles acting under duress it would be inappropriate to agree that Mr Mroczyk should be brought under armed guard to the Embassy for interview or alternatively arrangements should be made to see him at his place of detention. However this were handled, our agreement to take the application further in this way would signal our willingness to go along with the Polish

process of release and would be difficult to justify to public opinion (UKDEL NATO tel. No. 181 of 22 April).

[5] Not printed. Mr Whitelaw, in this letter to the Foreign Secretary, explained that Home Office officials recommended giving first priority to an estimated 2,000 Poles already in the UK on a temporary basis. It was likely that around 1,000 could be recognised as refugees, and it had been agreed they could not be returned to Poland according to the 1951 Convention on refugees as they feared persecution. The Polish Government had also indicated its intention to enforce exile on some, or all, of the estimated 4,000 Poles, who had been detained without trial. There had furthermore been an Austrian appeal to share the burden of some 40,000 Poles accommodated in reception camps in Austria. The Home Secretary suggested criteria for any potential admission of Poles from those camps: be recognised refugees; have 'substantial' ties with the UK; receive private—not State—funding, including for accommodation; be security checked. On the same day Mrs Thatcher annotated: 'We may have to take a lot of Falkland Islanders' (PREM 19/874). Mr Pym replied on 19 April that, although he agreed on most points, he had hoped for a more flexible approach regarding the Austrian request, especially as several partners faced a much larger demand, for example 300,000 Poles temporarily residing in the FRG (FCO 28/ 5013, ENP 243/1).

Government's aims and might also prompt similar bids from other Solidarity members in detention camps.

10. There is the further question of the advisability of allowing an interview of the kind to take place on Embassy premises. I agree with the Embassy that to admit Mroczyk in this way risks a possible request for asylum which would be extremely difficult to refuse and which could establish an unfortunate precedent.

11. In the circumstances therefore I consider we should instruct the Embassy to decline to interview Mroczyk but, as with the two earlier applications, received from Poles in detention, to complete the necessary documentation with the assistance of Mroczyk's wife and family.

12. I note the Embassy's anxieties concerning possible media interest in this case. The latter however have shown strong sympathy and support for the Western refusal to help the Polish Government rid itself of those who do not conform with its policies. If asked about our response to Mr Mroczyk's application, I believe it would be perfectly defensible to say that at the request of his family we have taken details of his application, but, as previously stated, we will only consider applications for resettlement from Poles who are free agents and who are not acting under duress. Should these conditions be satisfied, and Mr Mroczyk still wish to leave Poland upon release from detention, we would be prepared to look at Mr Mroczyk's application in accordance with normal procedures.[6]

[6] Mr A.C. Goodison (AUS) annotated that it was 'disagreeable' to have to inform a man that we will not help him to get out of internment, which is how M. Mroczyk and the media might wish to present the recommended action. Yet there was no other reply compatible with the UK's repeated condemnation of the Polish Government's wish to expel Poles. Mr Bullard agreed with the line adopted, annotating that 'having handled policy on this matter from the start, I am sure this is right. Otherwise our statements agreed in the Ten will be meaningless.' On 20 April Mr James was instructed not to interview M. Mroczyk on 23 April as originally planned, unless he was completely satisfied that he had been released (FCO tel. No. 122 to Warsaw). M. Mroczyk remained in detention until December 1982 when he was expelled from Poland, living subsequently in the UK and the US.

No. 155

Mr James (Warsaw) to Mr Pym, 23 April 1982, 9.15 a.m.

Tel. No. 456[1] Priority, Confidential (FCO 28/4907, ENP 014/1)

Poland: the Present Mood

1. The political and social situation in Poland is still quiet on the surface and I have no reason to alter the general assessment in my telno 395 of 26 March.[2] But there are signs of discontent, resentment and hatred bubbling away below the surface. Evidence for this has come mainly from the Church, University and intellectual circles. But there have been signs of restiveness on the factory floor as well.[3]

[1] Repeated for Information Routine to Washington, Paris, Bonn, UKDEL NATO and Moscow and Information Saving to East Berlin, Prague, Budapest, Sofia, MODUK, Bucharest, Belgrade, Helsinki, Stockholm, UKMIS New York, UKMIS Geneva and UKREP Brussels.

[2] Not printed: cf No. 147.

[3] On 14 April Mr Furness, Head of Chancery in Warsaw, described to Mr Montgomery the atmosphere in a Benedictine monastery close to Krakow where he had spent Easter. He reported a mood of deep pessimism but 'despite the shortages there seemed no inclination to criticise the West for its measures against the present regime; these were rather welcomed for the difficulties they

2. The Church took a bold step in publicising its paper on 'Social Agreement'.[4] It is a hard-hitting document with a formidable list of criticisms of the Government and martial law. Archbishop Glemp told me last week that he had detected no direct response to it from the Government, but he said that he thought it was less likely that Jaruzelski would wish to meet him when he had read it. This is not surprising since the Government will find it hard to swallow something so direct and well-expressed. I think that the Church, who say that the document is meant to be a basis for dialogue, consider that there is now a political vacuum in Poland and wish to see it filled. The document is also designed to alert the Government to the dangers of inaction and to spur it into taking initiatives, and to calm down some of the fiercer spirits, particularly among the young, who would like to take more determined action, in some cases violent action. There are persistent rumours that there will soon be a big release of detainees. This could sweeten the climate for a while.

3. There is obviously a terrific argument going on in the Party. Broadly speaking the need for some form of economic change has been accepted by both the conservatives and the moderates in the Party leadership. It is the degree of freedom to be allowed to non-Party organisations like trade unions which is under discussion. The fact that a letter calling for the reconstitution of Solidarity by an ex-member of Solidarity was allowed to appear in *Zycie Warsawy*[5] was probably a product of manoeuvring between the factions. Beneath the leadership there is an inert mass of *Apparatchiki* at the *Voivodship* level awaiting instruction from the centre. And the army has become increasingly politicised, partly through the appointment of senior military men to key posts both in the *Voivodships* and in the central state authorities.

4. We believe that men such as Radowski and Barcikowski are in the more moderate camp. Olszowski is a wild card, who seems to see his future for the moment on the hard line side. Jaruzelski's political views, such as they are, seem pretty much in the centre.

5. In their different ways both the Church and the Government are preoccupied with the problems of disaffected youth. Most of all, the Party has lost the support of the young generation. We hear various reports from the universities about the mood of the students. I was told by one normally good informant that the authorities were considering temporarily dissolving certain sections of the University of Warsaw (e.g. history and political science). The dismissal of the Rector of Warsaw University[6] has stirred up a great deal of resentment. The new

caused the regime.' He commented that perhaps the unspoken thoughts of the congregation were 'crudely summed up by the slogan (in English) on the bomber jacket of a young man . . . : Fuck "the Commies"'. On 27 April Mr Montgomery thanked Mr Furness for a valuable insight into 'aspects of life in Eastern Europe of which we are not usually aware'.

[4] The paper had been drawn up on 27 February 1982 after discussion in the Primate's Social Council to find ways of reconciliation to end the crisis in Poland. It condemned the offensive tone of official propaganda but also advised Solidarity to critically examine its own behaviour. It called for: dialogue between the authorities and the Church; the reactivation of Solidarity on an apolitical basis; the release of internees; an amnesty for those convicted for non-criminal acts; the restoration of free creative associations; permission for the Catholic press to resume its activities; and separate elections for local councils (Warsaw tel. No 437, 6 April 1982; FCO 28/5007, ENP 226/1).

[5] Founded in 1944 by the Polish Workers' Party, it was a semi-official organ of the Polish Government.

[6] Henryk Samsonowicz, a supporter of Solidarity and a renowned medieval historian, had become Head of the 16,000-student university in September 1980 following limited campus liberalization. A member of the Communist Party member, he was expelled in February 1982 having refused to subject the faculty to a purge, or 'ideological verification' after martial law.

Rector, a Government place man, had interviewed numerous colleagues for the jobs of Pro-Rectors but most of them had spurned his offers.

6. The Church's document speaks of 'the great and deepening chasm between society and the authorities'. Whilst I think this description is justified, I do not think that Jaruzelski's personal position is threatened. He can contain any sporadic eruptions or demonstrations. He has the Army firmly behind him and I see no disposition to hand over more power to a Party in disarray. But the dilemma that he and the Soviet Union face is that they both want law and order (for which they need the Army and martial law) but they also want the reconstitution of a strong Party which can reassume its leading role. This is incompatible with rule by a military oligarchy. Jaruzelski's only course, therefore, is to remain relatively immobile, and this probably accords with his own stiff and somewhat narrow views. Better go slowly than take risks. This immobility has its dangers—not immediate perhaps, but real none-the-less in a country as volatile as Poland.

No. 156

Mr James (Warsaw) to Mr Pym, 7 May 1982, 1.35 p.m.
Tel. No. 513[1] Priority, Confidential (FCO 28/4908, ENP 014/1)

Poland: The Situation after May 3[2]

1. The present situation must cause General Jaruzelski concern. It is clear that he hoped his programme of 'normalisation', including the release of detainees and the lightening of certain other aspects of martial law would be accepted and even welcomed as a token of his good intentions. The demonstrations throughout Poland were clearly a blow to his hopes. It is difficult to judge how well the Government handled the whole thing. They showed marked restraint on 1 May in allowing a peaceful demonstration to take place. Perhaps they now regret that they did so. In Warsaw, they could probably have prevented so much street violence on 3 May if they had wanted to. They allowed crowds to assemble in well-known areas and then moved to disperse them with tear gas. So far as we know, this pattern was followed in other centres; it is arguable that the Government wanted to teach the demonstrators a sharp lesson. It is possible that there were deliberate provocations. We have heard further manifestations are planned for the 9th, 12th, 13th and 25/26 May (first anniversary of Wyszynski's death).[3]

2. The Church is not pleased with the way things have developed. I have been told that at a meeting with the authorities at a high level they were severely criticised for allowing churches to become places where demonstrators congregated. They have consistently condemned violence and resort to the street. The communiqué of the last Episcopal conference said that the recent disturbances

[1] Repeated Routine to Bonn, Paris, UKDEL NATO, Washington, UK Brussels and Moscow; for Information Saving to East European posts, including W. Berlin, Sofia, Prague, East Berlin, Budapest, Bucharest, Belgrade, Stockholm and Helsinki.

[2] On 3 May there were demonstrations throughout the country with serious clashes in important cities leading to further detentions. On 5 May Mr James commented that the demonstrations 'indicate a surprising degree of co-ordination' despite the difficulties of communication under martial law and reported that a reliable source had told him that Solidarity underground committees had been very active in Warsaw, Gdańsk, Wrocław and Krakow (Warsaw tel. No. 497).

[3] See No. 76.

would delay normalisation, but at the same time it exhorted the authorities to continue relaxation of martial law and to release detainees and to permit the return of trade union activities. There are other people outside the Government and Party who also think that the recent tactics of Solidarity were mistaken and that if persisted in they would lead to repression and to harsher Government policies. There are some signs that Solidarity itself was divided.

3. So far—and these are of course very early days—the indications are that the Government still wish to hold a moderate line. They restored telephonic communication quickly, they have given light sentences to most of the demonstrators and have tried to present the troubles as the protest of youth rather than of the whole population. It is indeed very difficult to know how many workers were involved in the demonstration, although some were in Warsaw and more were probably in Gdansk and Szczecin.

4. Jaruzelski will also have trouble with the Soviet Union and the East Europeans who will surely be saying that this sort of thing cannot go on (and would certainly not be allowed to go on where they came from). There will be hard-line pressures inside the Party for tougher measures and I am sure that there is an acute debate going on at the moment on what policies to pursue. So far the Government seems to have resisted the hard-liners and declarations and actions have not, within the realities of the present situation in Poland, been immoderate. But it is difficult for Jaruzelski, and the moderate elements, such as they are. No sooner does he lift his head above the parapet of martial law than he gets a great sock on the nose from the Polish people.

No. 157

Letter from Mr James (Warsaw) to Mr J. Bullard, 14 May 1982
Confidential (FCO 28/4925, ENP 020/1)

Dear Julian,

1. I have been thinking about your letter of April 6[1] on martial law and about the future of our policy towards Poland. I will deal separately with the specific points raised in your letter. In this letter, I should like to raise some questions about our future policy towards Poland. I find it difficult to draw any but the most tentative of conclusions but I would be very interested to have your views.

2. First a general assumption. Policy towards Poland is a part, but only a part, of our general policy towards the Soviet Union. The two cannot be separated and the dog is Russian and the tail is Poland. I accept that we must not let the tail wag the dog.

3. None of the three Western conditions laid down in January, for the restoration of normal relations with Poland, has yet been met. Some of the detainees are still in detention, martial law has not yet been dismantled, though it is has been lightened, and there is no resumption of a meaningful dialogue between the authorities, Solidarity and the Church. Do we really still expect Poland within any realistic timetable to be able to satisfy our criteria fully? Do we think it realistic to keep

[1] Not printed. This was Mr Bullard's reply to Mr Melhuish's quartet of despatches (Nos. 138, 140, 144 and 147).

Poland at arm's length so long as some aspects of martial law continue to exist? Or do we think we shall have to take a new look at the whole question before then?

4. The problem is complicated by the uncertainty of events in Poland. Political structures are fragile, the economy is weak and popular discontent can still bubble up and cause the regime great trouble.

5. What sort of regime can we in fact expect here, given the overpowering strength of the Soviet Union and the determination of the Polish military not to let matters get out of hand again? Probably a military backed regime of some sort for some years. Are our present policies designed to help the liberal elements in the Polish government bring about a gradual change or are they likely to promote further convulsion? Which do we really want? Is there still the possibility that Polish links with the West and comparatively liberal internal policies could be revived by relaxing Western pressures on her? Or while some Poles might be influenced by a resumption of normal relations with the Polish regime and particularly by a resumption of fresh credits, would others see these as bolstering the martial law regime and smacking of collaborationist tactics? Our present policy was articulated partly to express Western disapproval, partly to put as much pressure as we could on Jaruzelski to retain some parts of *odnowa* and partly to show the Polish people that we in the West cared.

6. I know there is an argument in favour of maintaining Poland as a centre of trouble in Eastern Europe and as a continuing embarrassment to the Soviet Union. Should the West therefore deliberately set out to play the role that the Soviet leaders, strongly echoed by the present Polish leaders, accuse it of playing? As regards the questions of credit, for example, it seems very difficult to disentangle the question of applying pressure on the Polish Government from resultant deprivation of the Polish people. Deprivation of the people will mean the continuation of social unrest. Do we wash our hands of the problem, or do our own economic problems make it unlikely that we could extend further credits to Poland whatever the political climate here (except perhaps as a way of getting back our own past loans)?

7. Until now I have taken the view that Western policy was justified and about right. I have believed that the present regime must be made aware whether they like it or not that they are on a sort of probation, both in the eyes of Western governments and in the eyes of Western public opinion. I see no reason to do normal business with Poland while a lot of Solidarity people remain in detention. But it seems unrealistic to expect that this present Government or any foreseeable Polish Government acceptable to the Soviet Union will allow Solidarity to re-establish itself. Even so, realities here are complex, and the authorities may have to take account of what happened in 1980-81 in conducting their future industrial relations, even if they set out to be restrictive. Solidarity itself, however, may wreck the Government's moves towards a new, more controlled, but still not wholly facade-like trade unionism.

8. Whatever happens here, I see some degree of stand pat-ism in our future handling of our relations with Poland. The Germans clearly believe that economic restrictions do not really correspond to what is necessary for Poland and I am sure we shall see growing pressure on their side to re-open the economic and the political dialogue. Already Schmidt is reported to have made statements which run counter to the Western position. The visit of Kowalczyk[2] at Genscher's invitation

[2] Edward Kowalczyk, Vice-Premier of Poland.

is another sign that the FDP for their part also want to start moving in the direction of normalisation. The Germans always take the view that tension between East and West is to be avoided and they will only be held back from pursuing normalisation by continuing outbursts of popular opposition in Poland and by the resort of the Polish Government to repressive measures. Their argument, and it has some force, is that to stand pat on our three conditions for too long will make it easier for the illiberal elements in Poland to demonstrate that there is no Western carrot at the end of the road and that there is no reason why the manacles should not be clamped on to the hands of the Polish people more firmly than they have been. On the other hand, it can be argued that Jaruzelski is so boxed in that he cannot go too far in a liberal direction even if he wishes to because of opposition from hard-liners, from the Army and from the Soviet Union; and that even if he persists in trying to embark on a restricted path of reform he will get no response from society or from the workers.

9. I ask a lot of questions to which I have no clear answers. It is quite possible that the situation will deteriorate and that by next winter the Polish economy will be in a worse plight, the population even more sullen and the Government have little option but to resort to harsher measures. The chances of political initiatives which will give Jaruzelski more room to manoeuvre or improve his standing with the population seem dim. The pressure from the Soviet Union will remain heavy on the Polish Government to maintain a tough line and we may yet see popular demonstrations put to the sword.

10. The only conclusion I want to draw from all this is that we cannot assume that the NATO convoy on Poland will move at the same pace. The Federal Republic shows every sign of wanting to see political initiatives and I believe that the German ship is already trying to detach itself, drawn by the magnet of *Ostpolitik*.[3] Nor will I be surprised if some others like the Danes, Norwegians and Canadians, will not soon become restive and be tempted to follow the Germans. The French have strong trade union and public opinion to cope with and for the time being this seems to keep them firmly with the Americans and ourselves. But I wonder at times even about the United States, despite the fact that US-Polish relations are at present going through a pretty rough patch. Poland is only part of the larger game of relations with the Soviet Union. If these were to take a move forward, Poland might fall into a place which is an adjunct to that policy. In short, I am not suggesting any changes in our policies towards Poland at present or in the three criteria (though these will need refinement as time goes on). But I believe there is a possibility that changes may occur in our allies' attitude and you will no doubt have this in mind in the briefing for the NATO meeting in June.[4]

Yours ever,
C. M. JAMES

[3] On 15 June Sir J. Taylor commented to Bullard that James was going rather too far. He argued that, as he had shown in his letter of 15 January 1982 (No. 134), the FRG Government was inclined towards dialogue, but that they had moderated their initial reaction to events in Poland, which had displeased their allies, especially the Americans. He thought that the FRG had then remained in the centre of the 'NATO convoy' (FCO 28/4926, ENP 020/1).

[4] Mr Bullard replied on 14 May that it was not any easier to find answers in London than in Warsaw. He agreed that HMG had to continue its disapproval of the Polish regime's measures, whilst also maintaining pressure on Jaruzelski to preserve some of the *Odnowa*, and using humanitarian aid to show that the West did care. He concluded that a *modus operandi* with Poland would have to be found and that 'we will continue to be guided by our long-term aim of seeing evolutionary change in the countries of Eastern Europe' (FCO 28/4926, ENP 020/1).

No. 158

Minute from Mr Rifkind to Mr Pym, 18 May 1982

Confidential (FCO 28/4926, ENP 020/1)

Poland

1. You may wish to see a brief summary of the conclusions reached at a meeting I held with officials on 12 May. Discussion was based on two notes submitted on 7 May.[1]

General

2. At the meeting we reviewed the policy options outlined in the second note and considered a number of practical bilateral and multi-lateral issues on which we and our partners need to take decisions. We assessed these in the light of our domestic political requirements, the likely attitude of our partners and allies and the possible effect on the situation in Poland. We agreed that, on the latter, Western governments would have to accept that they were relatively impotent to shape events in Poland, although this view would be resisted by some, notably the US.

Economic Assistance to Poland

3. We looked at the possibility that the West should take the initiative and offer General Jaruzelski substantial political and economic assistance in return for the fulfilment of the three criteria and noted that President Reagan had appeared to refer to this idea in his letter of 7 May to the Prime Minister.[2] We considered it extremely unlikely, however, that the West could provide an economic package large enough to fulfil the Poles' requirements ($10 billion in 1982 alone) or to persuade Jaruzelski to act as the West wished, given the contrary influences upon him.

4. We recognised there could nonetheless be political advantage in holding out such an offer to the Poles but believed this could become an unwelcome hostage to fortune as other East European countries with economic problems might seek similar assurances of major economic support. There was no evidence to suggest the US had taken the idea very far. American intentions on this should be probed.

Rescheduling

5. The conclusions of our discussion pointed to the continuation of our existing policy. We agreed however that the present decision to suspend 1982 debt rescheduling negotiations with Poland was illogical and gave the latter *de facto* 100% relief. The Poles were known to be repaying some creditor governments individually and were pressing hard for a 1982 agreement with the banks. A

[1] Not printed. The two notes reviewing the situation in Poland had been prepared by EESD. The first was intended to provide a snapshot of the present situation, the second made recommendations about future policy. Mr Broomfield noted to Mr Bullard, to whom he sent the notes on 7 May, that in conducting this exercise he was 'struck by the "Polishness" of the martial law regime. It is at times brutal and at others surprisingly liberal. Within days of tear gas and baton attacks in Warsaw the Sejm was reported as passing a remarkably liberal bill on higher education.' Mr Goodison commented that more attention should be given to the Soviet Union and that 'we can't be nicer to the Poles in isolation, or can we?' Mr Montgomery responded: 'I don't see why we shouldn't separate the Poles from the Soviet Union. The Americans will certainly wish to continue being beastly to the Russians, even if martial law was lifted tomorrow' (FCO 28/ 4908, ENP 014/1).

[2] Not printed. President Reagan wrote to Mrs Thatcher, ahead of the G7 and NATO summits: 'We should reaffirm our measures against the Soviet Union and Polish regime if circumstances so dictate, while showing our willingness to join in a programme of economic reconstruction for Poland if Western conditions are met.' (A copy of this letter can be found on the Margaret Thatcher Foundation website: http://www.margaretthatcher.org.)

decision to resume negotiations could be defended on the grounds that we were calling the Poles to account and attempting to recover our money in an orderly and controlled manner.

6. In these circumstances we agreed that it would be sensible to explore the question with our partners, particularly the US, and to seek a reappraisal of the situation. It would be necessary within the UK to be in a position to defend the outcome of any rescheduling talks on the grounds that we were confident that we had extracted from the Poles the highest amount they were capable of repaying to their Western creditors. A decision to re-negotiate would also take account of the development of the situation in Poland. We would raise this informally with our US, French and German partners.

New Credits/IMF Membership

7. We noted that a resumption of rescheduling talks might provoke fresh requests from the Poles for credits. These would have to be resisted.

8. We saw no good reason on either political or economic grounds to block Poland's membership of the IMF. There was no benefit to the West in isolating Poland from the world economic community.

Political Relations

9. We recognised that in time we would need to move towards a normalisation of our political relations with Poland. Any overt movement in this direction at the present time, however, would not be understood either domestically or by our partners and would give the wrong signal to the Poles. For relations to normalise, it would be necessary either for Jaruzelski to have stabilised his position to such an extent and over such a period of time that his regime could only be regarded as [a] *fait accompli*, or for there to be significant movement on the West's three criteria. In the light of the recent demonstrations,[3] which indicated that the population had by no means come to terms with Jaruzelski's policies, our best course was to maintain our existing stance while keeping this under careful review.

Conclusion

10. It was agreed that problems such as the question of the level of Anglo-Polish bilateral contacts, the attitude to be adopted towards Poland in the UN and its specialised agencies and the position to be taken at the resumed CSCE Conference in November should continue to be determined on a case by case basis, in the light of circumstances in Poland and in close consultation with our partners and allies. Meanwhile HM Ambassador should pursue his official contacts with the Polish leadership in Warsaw and reinforce our present policy objectives. We would do the same with the Polish Ambassador here.[4]

MALCOLM RIFKIND

[3] See No. 156, note 2.

[4] Mr Macgregor, Private Secretary to Mr Rifkind, noted: 'We should now work on the assumption that these are now the agreed guidelines on policy towards Poland.'

No. 159

Letter from Mr Nichols (Budapest) to Mr Wilson, 18 May 1982
Restricted (FCO 28/4902, ENH 400/3)

Dear Fraser,

Embassy film week

1. I am writing to let you know about a problem we have had with the Ministry of Foreign Affairs over our Embassy Film Week.

2. The Film Week is now an annual event. We show three or four of the latest British films to an invited audience in the Embassy hall: invitations are sent to about 700 people, mostly Hungarians.

3. This year, the film on the opening night of the week—Monday 10 May—was the James Bond film 'For Your Eyes Only'. I was summoned to the MFA at 12 p.m. that day and the Deputy Head of the Press Department asked me to arrange for the showing of the Bond film to be cancelled because 'the film shows the Cubans and the Soviet Union in an unfavourable light . . . Hungary had to be careful not to give offence to fraternal countries.'[1]

4. After consultation in the Embassy we decided to comply out of deference to our audience and showed 'The Day of the Jackal'. But next day the Head of Chancery made a formal protest to the Head of the Press Department at the Ministry. Birch said that the action by the Ministry was unacceptable to us because:

(*a*) the stated objections to the film had no foundation. James Bond was a frivolous light entertainment which no one could take seriously. The film had not been seen by the Hungarian authorities who should give the Embassy some credit for deciding what might be offensive to Hungarians;

(*b*) it was arrogant and discourteous both to the Embassy and to our guests to demand a cancellation at six hours notice;

(*c*) the Embassy did not accept that the Hungarian authorities should seek to interfere with whatever entertainment the Embassy wished to offer its guests.

5. He went on to say that we had nevertheless, through concern to avoid embarrassment to our guests, decided to substitute another film. The Ministry's action was harmful to our bilateral relations. We were asked to treat Hungary on her merits and to recognise the factors which differentiated her from other East European countries. This action made it more difficult. It could suggest to some people that Hungary was attempting to put the clock back.

6. Mr Ivan was upset by the reference to our bilateral relations and denied that there was any attempt to put the clock back. There was, however, an MFA ruling of long standing that Embassies should not indulge in any activity which might be offensive to third countries. The Bond film was in this category. Birch concluded that we had both made our views clear and would now draw a line under the incident.

7. We hope there will be no further repercussions but thought it best to let you know that we have had this row. In explaining the change of film to the audience we explained that their authorities believed there might be passages in 'For Your Eyes Only' which could be embarrassing to a Hungarian audience. We said that we

[1] In the film Bond attempts to prevent a missile command system from falling into Soviet hands, and is assisted by a woman who is seeking revenge for the murder of her parents by a Cuban hit-man.

did not share this view but in order to avoid the risk we were changing the programme. Needless to say, the audience regarded the ban as petty and ridiculous.

Yours ever,
JOHN NICHOLS

No. 160

Mr James (Warsaw) to Mr Pym, 1 June 1982, 3.15 p.m.
Tel. No. 586[1] Priority, Confidential (FCO 28/5001, ENP 212/1)

Walesa

1. There are indications in Warsaw that Walesa's release from internment may be becoming an issue among the leadership. Walesa has recently been moved from his quarters in Warsaw to the remote south-east corner of Poland (not far from where Gierek used to shoot with Giscard). Reliable reports indicate that over the last month access to Walesa has become very difficult. His wife has been subjected to vigorous searches before she was allowed to visit him. Once she was refused permission to visit him at all. Since his move, his priest, Father Jankowski,[2] has been refused permission to visit him.

2. There is something odd about Ozdowski's interview on American television in which he was reported to have said that Walesa would soon return to normal life including Trade Union activities in Gdansk. Urban, the government press spokesman,[3] then denied yesterday that this was what Ozdowski had said and said that he had been quoted out of context. But Urban's office subsequently issued a counter-denial which has muddied the waters still further. The only thing that is clear is that the government cannot get its act together over what it wants to say about Walesa, perhaps because it has not yet got an agreed policy.

3. It is all too likely that there is an argument going on in the Government and in the party. There must be those who would argue that Walesa is an embarrassment to the government while he is interned, that his release would have a most beneficial effect on public opinion in the West, particularly in the United States at a time when the Western leaders are about to meet in Versailles and Bonn.[4] They would say that the risk of Walesa being looked upon as a martyr is higher while he is in internment. Others would argue that Walesa should not be released for some time, or at least unless he is prepared to give an undertaking to collaborate with the government or to refrain from political activity. It could be that his new confinement is intended to push him in this direction.

4. When he spoke to party activists yesterday, Vice Premier Rakowki said that Solidarity had not changed its position since 13 December. He thus implied that overtures to Walesa have not been successful. Those in the government who would not wish to release him would no doubt argue also that from the government's

[1] Repeated for Information Routine to Moscow, Washington, UKDEL NATO and UKMIS Geneva and Information Saving to East Berlin, Prague, Budapest, Paris, Bonn, MODUK, Sofia, Bucharest, Belgrade, Helsinki, Stockholm, UKMIS New York and UKREP Brussels.

[2] Father Henryk Jankowski, the provost of St Bridget's Church in Gdańsk, was a member of Solidarity.

[3] Jerzy Ozdowski was Deputy Prime Minister and Jerzy Urban the Government spokesman and Press Secretary to General Jaruzelski.

[4] The G7 met at Versailles from 4-6 June and the NAC met in Bonn on 19 June. For the NAC declaration see No. 162, note 3.

point of view the worst of all worlds would be to release Walesa and then subsequently to re-intern him because of his activities.

5. I think it must be quite a poser for Jaruzelski. Walesa is now nearing six months of internment. Beyond six months, his internment will seem long to both the Polish people and to the West. The Government may be worried also about the possibility of demonstrations on 13 June, six months after martial law has been imposed. If they want to pursue a conciliatory path, they must be looking for ways of cooling the situation. We have heard persistent rumours, which we are checking, that passport policy may be somewhat relaxed at about that time. It is just possible that this may be part of a larger package which might include the release of Walesa and other relaxations designed to draw the sting from possible protest actions.

6. On past record, Jaruzelski will play safe. But it must be difficult for him to judge what safe really means, even if his Soviet allies and the hard-liners in his own party urge him to keep a firm hand on the situation.[5]

[5] On 9 July, Mr Barnett, who had just arrived at the Embassy in Warsaw, explained that Solidarity leaders were adopting a more pragmatic and moderate stance given the realities of life under martial law. Support for Solidarity remained very firm at the factory floor level, but individual workers were less than eager to engage in short-lived strikes as the underground press reported accounts of harsh punishment. Some splinter groups were advocating terrorism. He concluded: 'To a degree, the *immobilisme* of the authorities is matched by that of Solidarity.'

No. 161

Mr James (Warsaw) to Mr Pym, 9 June 1982, 3.45 p.m.
Tel. No. 601[1] Priority, Confidential (FCO 28/5036, ENP 384/1)

Settlement Applications from Solidarnosc Members[2]

1. We are not certain that you receive copies of telegrams that we send in the VISFO[3] series to MVD concerning settlement applications from *Solidarnosc* members. Many of them even in condensed form convey accurate descriptions of the circumstances surrounding their arrest, subsequent release from internment, and the current conditions under which they are compelled to exist.

2. In the past week or so some applicants have been subject to a new kind of pressure from the Polish authorities which seems to indicate a hardening of policy towards ex-detainees. Wladyslaw Stanislaw Komorek[4] (our telno visa 65)[5] is a typical example. He has told us that he has been instructed to sell his apartment, liquidate his assets and that he would then be given a passport and should leave Poland before the end of July. He said that if he did not comply he had been told that he would be re-interned for a period of up to three years or dumped on the Austrian border to take his chances as a refugee. Komorek also said that he had heard that the BBC Polish service had announced that HMG were prepared to offer settlement to *Solidarnosc* members but he was unable to quote dates of broadcasts.

[1] Repeated for Information Routine to Vienna and UKDEL NATO.
[2] For policy on forced settlements see No. 154.
[3] Traffic specific to visa operations.
[4] A mechanical engineer and Solidarity member, interned on 16 December 1981 and released on 1 February 1982.
[5] Not printed.

3. It is not possible for us to verify whether what Komorek tells us is true. Nor can we judge what action the authorities might take if they are unable to squeeze out selected members of *Solidarnosc*. It would seem unlikely that they would wish to re-intern large numbers of people. This is not however a possibility that can be excluded if there are further demonstrations.

4. We offer *Solidarnosc* applicants little hope of a speedy positive response. However you should be aware that they in common with our present visa applicants have reached the state of pleading for our help. We are checking with other Western embassies whether they have heard similar stories of Government pressure and threats of re-internment. It is clear that their staff like ours are being subjected to increasingly harrowing emotional scenes. If we find out that the pressure from the Polish authorities is general, we should consider publicity in concert with our allies and friends.

No. 162

Note by Mr Goodison (AUS) of a visit to Prague, 4-9 June 1982, 10 June 1982

Confidential (FCO 28/4825, ENC 026/4)

1. Prague is a Western European city. It lies West of Vienna in much the same longitude as Berlin, but it is not merely its geographical position which makes it Western; its architecture, its history, its culture strike the visiting Englishman at once as part of his own European heritage.

2. And the people too. I was particularly struck by the way a number of officials avoided putting conviction into such official lines as they conveyed. One of them is reported to have said, on an earlier occasion, 'There are official explanations and there are real explanations, but you must never ask for the real ones.' Another made no bones, in answer to a question, about hinting to HM Ambassador that he would do well to stay away from a Lidice commemoration, if he was concerned that the President of the Republic would say disobliging things about NATO and Western Governments in his speech. I talked to a banker about the artificiality of the currency controls and to a professor of economics about the reform of the CMEA. Both were ready to criticize the current system constructively and without any apparent ideological constraints, even though my appointments with them had had to be made through the Ministry of Foreign Affairs. (According to the professor, the reason the Czechoslovaks have no international debts to compare with those of their Socialist allies is that they are too unadventurous to contract them.)

3. Admittedly, the Embassy has no access to the Party dogmatists, except by reading the dreary pages of *Rude Pravo*,[1] and the diplomatic visitor is protected from the most oppressive aspects of the regime. The empty shops contrast painfully with the country's export achievements, which, though naturally regarded as inadequate, are substantial. Rent-a-crowd occasions are not far to seek, and Mrs Rich impressed me with an account of how they stay silent and unmoved except when instructed to cheer. One gathers that the Western diplomats have to spend

[1] The official paper of the Communist Party of Czechoslovakia.

quite a lot of time exchanging rather small crumbs of information, and the Attachés even smaller crumbs.

4. Perhaps I got the standard line best, though briefly, from Deputy Foreign Minister Spačil, an urbane and witty pipe-smoker who is likely, he gave me to understand, to be appointed Ambassador to London next year. He stressed the differences between Eastern and Western Europe, and the complete lack of difference between the countries of the East; he said that they had their way of life and we had ours and we should let one another get on with it. I quoted the UN Charter, Human Rights covenants and the Helsinki Final Act to show that we had entered into mutual commitments to keep up certain standards. He did not bother to reply; nor did he reply when I spoke sharply about the Czechoslovak attitude on the Falklands. It seemed that he was not particularly interested in exchanging views on political subjects.

5. He showed animation only on the topic of visits. He appeared to accept that the Secretary of State might not be able to come in November, as Lord Carrington had intended. He said what would be even better was someone more important, and a delicate allusion to the recent private visit of Prince and Princess Michael led us to suppose that he was talking about The Queen! HM Ambassador assures me that it is useful to promote as many visits as possible, given the insatiable appetite of the Czechoslovaks and their potential to manipulate our political and commercial relations in response. However, a State Visit to this régime is not something to be recommended. I admire their cheek while deploring the lack of self-confidence which makes them demand such continual proofs of friendship from people they daily revile in public. They seem to need us much more than we need them.

6. But I think it is worthwhile all the same to go on cultivating the Czechoslovaks, within the limits of our resources. There is a useful market for our exports which HM Ambassador is working hard to exploit further. But, as I have tried to show, there is also a substantial volume of Western sympathy, of decent intelligent understanding of our way of doing things, which we ought, as far as we can, to encourage and maintain; I am not suggesting that we have the powers to induce the kind of change the Czechoslovaks produced themselves in 1968 or that it would be wise to do so if we could. I am afraid of proposals to unravel Eastern Europe now. But we should, as far as we can, nurture the good instincts of the Czechoslovaks so that they can flower in their own good time. No doubt we shall be giving further thought to these matters in the light of President Reagan's speech to Parliament[2] and the Bonn Summit declaration.[3]

7. HM Embassy will be sending us detailed records of my talks.

A. C. GOODISON

[2] The President visited the UK from 7-9 June 1982. In a speech to both Houses of Parliament on 8 June, he spoke of his hope that 'the march of freedom and democracy . . . will leave Marxism-Leninism on the ash-heap of history as it has left other tyrannies which stifle the freedom and muzzle the self-expression of the people' (see *Public Papers: Reagan* (1982), Book I, pp. 742-48).

[3] Following a Summit meeting of the North Atlantic Council held in Bonn on 10 June a Declaration was issued setting out a six-point programme for Peace in Freedom. The programme called for greater Soviet restraint and responsibility in order to allow the development of a more constructive East-West relationship. It also addressed the objectives sought by the Alliance in nuclear and conventional arms control negotiations, as well as in the field of human rights issues and the principles and provisions of the Helsinki Final Act (the declaration is available on the NATO website: www.nato.int).

No. 163

Letter from Mr Longworth (Sofia) to Mr Montgomery, 10 June 1982
Confidential (FCO 28/4849, ENG 014/1)

[Opening salutation omitted]

Bulgaria: The Generation Gap

1. In the light of last year's changes in the *Komsomol*[1] leadership (Richard Stagg's letter of 28 December 1981),[2] the 14th Congress of the Dimitrov Young Communist League was of more than usual interest. As it turned out, however, the considerations prompted by the event were less to do with structures and personalities than with the generation gap and its implications for the Party.

2. Much of the plenary discussion was devoted to old chestnuts—the importance of raising workers' qualifications, the birth rate etc—and the official line on the conference was 'the Party and the People have confidence in Youth'. But the guts of matter came in Zhivkov's keynote speech when he referred to manifestations of idleness among young people, a lack of stable and meaningful interests, negative phenomena influenced by the bourgeois world. He called for 'an irreconcilable struggle' against these manifestations. It was a principal task of the *Komsomol* to educate the country's youth in the Communist ideal. But more significantly he stressed the role of 'radio, television, cinema, theatre, literature and all the public factors' in carrying out this campaign.

3. The speech therefore provides a useful pretext for drawing together some of the developments on which we have reported ad hoc over the past few months: the Lilov speech at Yordanov's inauguration as Chairman of the Committee for Culture, the disappearance from our cinema screens of 'A Woman of 33',[3] the amalgamation of radio and TV administration. It confirms the theme of Richard Stagg's letter of 27 May to Fraser Wilson[2] that the hierarchy has decided to blow the whistle on cultural experimentation and the Westward drift of intellectual thought. But further, it suggests a deep unease over the future of the system once its present guardians have passed the baton. In particular Zhivkov himself seems seriously preoccupied with the problem of selling Communism to the new generation.

4. On a superficial level, this concern shows itself throughout society, with the older generation expressing concern over modes of dress, the encroachment of pop music and increasing disrespect for the law amongst young people. In the National Assembly debate on changes in the Penal Code, at least one deputy spoke about Youth in terms that would not have been out of place in more right wing fora—long-haired layabouts etc. And while young people in Bulgaria seem quite tame to Westerners compared with our domestic product, stories of vandalism etc. become more prevalent and I have witnessed mass disregard for the Militia at a rock concert which took the organisers obviously aback.

5. But Zhivkov indicated in the *Komsomol* speech that he recognised the nature of the problem as much as its manifestations. He refers to the country's three generations: those who fought Fascism, those who have built Socialism in the wake of the Revolution and those who have to bring the Socialist state into its new

[1] The youth wing of the Communist Party.
[2] Not printed.
[3] A film by director Hristo Hristov chronicling the trials and tribulations of a divorced mother in Bulgarian society.

technological phase. There have been several indications that he regards this third generation as ideologically vulnerable—in its best light: they are too far removed from the ideological struggle to appreciate the nature of the task. Or, as we might see it: they cannot cope with the startling gap between the pretence of Communist hyperbole and the reality of the mess around them. For the failings of the state have become apparent to an increasing number of Bulgarians through foreign trade, wider cultural contacts and the influx of Western tourists.

6. It seems from recent developments that the corrective is not to be freer discussion, but tougher control on expression, and it is significant in this context that the FRG Ambassador has described how, at a recent lunch in honour of Frau Schmidt, Zhivkov launched into a heated discussion of ideology with the Bulgarians present, mostly distinguished cultural figures. The argument was not translated and went over the heads of the German guests, but the FRG Ambassador was struck by Zhivkov's animation.

7. How this trend of thinking will work out in practice is not yet clear. But the need for a better educated workforce and greater flexibility in economic management is likely to open decision-making and influence to a wider circle than that of the Party elite who have managed hitherto to contain discontent with skilfully applied patronage. It seems to me that the leadership feel the message needs a harder sell than the traditional institutions can provide: *Komsomol* is certainly not up to a task of this magnitude; hence the decision to appoint Tikchev as radio and TV overlord. Just before this had been announced, Zhivkov told Cheysson that he was not satisfied with the existing structure and that he wanted radio and television 'co-ordinated under very firm direction'. Our subsequent contacts with TV people have indicated a significant drop in morale, and it is clear that whatever lies behind this move, it is not in the interests of higher quality broadcasting. A more recent and more blatant development was the signature last week of a plan for 'joint activity' between the Bulgarian Union of Journalists and the Committee for State and Peoples' Control; the plan is to consider the problems discussed by Zhivkov in his speech to *Komsomol* and, last October, to the Trade Unions.

7. [*sic*] I think we are at an interesting phase in Bulgaria. Not that the mood is particularly dangerous for the Government. But after Poland the leadership want to head off trouble before it starts. They are clearly doing a lot on the consumer goods/standard of living front. But it seems that they might not have thought out the spiritual side of the equation.[4]

Yours ever,
P. LONGWORTH

[4] Mr Stagg continued to report on official concerns over the alienation of the younger generation. In a letter of 17 June to Mr Wilson (EESD) he noted a series of press articles which attacked discotheques as, in his words, 'meeting places for feckless lay-abouts' who were 'unable or unwilling to do a decent day's work, who were happier to spend their afternoons drinking and gossiping, with Bony M blaring in the background, [than] to contributing to the building of real socialism in Bulgaria.' Later in the year Mr Stagg, in a letter to Mr Wilson of 2 September, noted that whilst the *Komsomol* was periodically purged for failing to sell the Bulgarian Communist Party to the young, they ignored the fact that it would require 'a combination of Goebbels and J. Walter Thompson to convince young Bulgarians that the Party is not an organisation largely made up of middle-aged mediocrities whose first (perhaps only) interest in life lies in doing well for themselves and their families'.

No. 164

Minute from Mr Rifkind to Mr Pym, 22 June 1982
(FCO 28/4892, ENH 026/5)

1. I visited Hungary from 16-18 June. I had talks with Foreign Minister Puja, State Secretary for Foreign Affairs Nagy, the Deputy Ministers for Foreign Affairs and Trade and the Presidential adviser to the Hungarian National Bank. I also visited a large heavy engineering factory on the outskirts of Budapest and a co-operative farm.

2. Everything I saw and heard confirmed the rightness of our 'differentiated approach' to Eastern European countries. Hungary apparently has little proclivity towards political reform at home and adopts a pro-Soviet stance on world issues. But in return for the latter she gets a qualified *carte blanche* to pursue economic experiments which verge on the free market economy. Incentives, rewards for personal initiatives, freedom to provide what the market needs are in evidence everywhere. There is a virtual absence of Russian and Polish-style queues and, in Budapest at least, the appearance of a reasonable standard of living. On the economy there is what amounts to a real national debate. Ministers' and officials' conversation proved refreshingly free of rehearsed statements of party-approved lines. This is a style of freedom which we should seek discreetly to sustain; it is more likely to prove infectious than the radicalism of Poland.

3. How can we sustain it? At the moment they need financial help; they are suffering badly from the domino effect of the Polish debt crisis. A rapid withdrawal of funds (by Arab banks among others) has led to a major liquidity problem. But the underlying state of the economy is good; they are in process of joining the World Bank, having just joined the International Monetary Fund, and have the prospect of substantial support in due course. I believe therefore that we should do everything we can to help the Hungarians through their short-term liquidity crisis; if the West cannot help them, they could be forced into a default in July. This means lending Ministerial weight to the Department's current representations to ECGD and talking to the Bank of England.

4. I believe we should accord Hungary a position of relative priority in our trade with East Europe. The present intention of ECGD to change Hungary from cover category B to C has already been challenged by the Department; it should be looked at carefully by our economists and, if they agree, challenged again. There are doubts in the Embassy as to whether a change is justified even in purely economic terms. And in psychological terms it will be seen as a vote of no confidence in Hungary's free enterprise system which I consider short sighted.

5. During my talks I was asked repeatedly about the meaning of the Versailles communiqué language on future credits for Eastern Europe.[1] I explained our understanding of a 'prudent and diversified' approach, emphasising that Hungary would be considered in a relatively favourable light according to these criteria. There was great resentment at the appearance while I was in Budapest of an article

[1] The Declaration at the conclusion of the G7 summit at Versailles stated that countries would handle cautiously financial relations with the USSR and other Eastern European countries in such a way as to ensure that they are conducted on a sound economic basis, including also the need for 'commercial prudence' in limiting export credits.

law met with resistance. But the lessons of the Hungarians' successful development of links with the West on the one hand and Czechoslovak and Polish failures to secure and consolidate and the liberalisation in their countries on the other, surely emphasize the need for gradualism and demonstrate the risks awaiting those who test Moscow's patience beyond its limits. In the next decade the conjunction of economic difficulties, increasing resurgent nationalism, and the succession problem in the Soviet Union may make the area prone to crisis. But it is not in the West's interest to encourage an upheaval which would jeopardise the forty year old peace of Europe. Our object, as in the past, must be to encourage an East-West climate which will permit both political and economic experimentation to push back the limits of Soviet tolerance.

4. In pursuing these aims we have consciously set out, in common with our major European allies, to identify and exploit the diversity of Eastern Europe—by adopting a policy of positive discrimination (Mr Fall's letter of 19 November 1980, covering Mr Walden's minute of 12 November 1980).[2] We have encouraged any East European country demonstrating some degree of independence to seek a more open and constructive relationship with the West. Thus we have rewarded Romania for its 'independent' foreign policy with high level visits and exchanges; encouraged economic experiments in Hungary; and offered economic help to Poland during the *odnowa*; but we have in the past had correspondingly less contact with the more orthodox regimes in Bulgaria, Czechoslovakia, and the GDR. (See paragraph 18 below.)

5. The Polish crisis has chilled the atmosphere within which we practise our policy of differentiation. The Eastern European Governments themselves still want political contacts. But all felt threatened by the Polish *odnowa*. All feel bound to back the Polish martial law regime, both for internal reasons and because they know that the Soviet Union expects it of them. They expect the West to recognise that they are not entirely free agents. But even now the parameters are not wholly rigid and they will all, to some extent, seek to widen these where they see advantage in doing so. In this respect they themselves will continue to be the best judges of what they can get away with.

6. Meanwhile, the economic crisis in Eastern Europe and the problem of Eastern European indebtedness has cast its shadow over the development of commercial relations, and made it more difficult for us to discriminate other than upon primarily prudential criteria.

Political Implications

7. We have always recognised that there are limits to the amount of substance we can put into our relationships. Ministerial exchanges have increased and flourished during the present administration. We should continue our general policy of building and developing contacts at all levels. Although such exchanges are frequently sterile they expose Eastern decision-makers to Western thinking and challenge the Communist regimes on their own ground—that of ideas. There is, of course, another side to the coin: the East Europeans prize visits as a mark of acceptability and recognition of their regimes and their policies. We should perhaps be more sparing in future of Secretary of State visits, which like those by the Prime Minister, should be offered as a mark of favour to the specially deserving—as in the recent case of Yugoslavia.

[2] No. 34. See also note 8 of the same document, which reported posts' reactions to the policy of 'discrimination'.

8. However, we cannot disregard the disappointment caused to the GDR and Czechoslovakia by the cancellation of Lord Carrington's visit: in the interests of common courtesy these visits should be reinstated before any further Secretary of State visits to Eastern Europe are planned. The GDR if offended would undoubtedly exercise its considerable influence within the bloc to make life difficult for us.[3]

9. No such problem attends visits by other Ministers where we should pursue the routine of regular exchanges approximately every other year by the minister responsible for Eastern European affairs. As for visits by Ministers from other Departments we should seek to promote these on an *ad hoc* basis as and when suitable opportunities can be created (an outline programme is set out in Annex 'B' to this submission).[4]

Economic Implications

10. The financial crisis in Eastern Europe will dominate our relations for the foreseeable future. Poland and Romania have had to reschedule. Yugoslavia, Hungary and even the GDR may yet follow suit. Western Banks and Governments have adopted a more prudent attitude towards Eastern Europe in order to protect their investments. Eastern European Governments have reviewed their economic relations with the West: most—with the notable exception of Hungary—have concluded that closer trading links within the CMEA are desirable. In these straitened circumstances we must try to ensure that Western governments and banks do not treat all Eastern European countries alike regardless of their economic situations and to the extent possible show sympathy to those whom for political reasons we wish to help.

11. There will still be commercial opportunities in Eastern Europe: a market of 130 million people should not be ignored. There may be few major projects but we should not rule large scale investment out of court. We must gauge with care whether we shall be repaid: we are not in the business of subsidising Eastern Europe. Equally, financial chaos in Eastern Europe which would sever those economic links which remain would not be in our interests. We must therefore work to promote financial confidence and be prepared to be particularly helpful to countries such as Yugoslavia and Hungary, whose economic management is creating problems but whose economic policies and political significance justify efforts to try to encourage still further the more liberal aspects of their unique brands of socialism. We may no longer be able to look to commerce as the mainspring of our relations—but we should do our best to ensure that investments already made are not wasted and that where a basis for the growth of fruitful commercial relationships has been laid this is preserved.

Culture

12. In present circumstances the cultural field still offers excellent opportunities to promote and foster fundamental Western concepts of freedom, and liberal ideas. Young people in particular watch events in our countries with careful attention. We have a tremendous advantage. These countries generally identify far more closely with the European tradition than does the Soviet Union. All are anxious to foster their own sense of historic independence and crave recognition of their own unique

[3] In March 1982 Lord Carrington had agreed to visit the GDR and Czechoslovakia that November. Following his resignation in April 1982, his successor, Mr Pym, decided that there should not be any visit to the GDR or Czechoslovakia in 1982 and it was suggested postponing them to the following year (FCO 28/4824, ENC 026/3).

[4] Not printed.

contribution to European culture. This was demonstrated most clearly recently by the Bulgarian efforts to promote their 1300th Anniversary and somewhat less effectively by the Romanians with their efforts to celebrate Titulescu.[5] This is an opportunity we are well placed to exploit. It would be a pity if because of economy measures we were unable to maintain the links established in the late 60s and 70s. The British Council, the GB/East European Centre (GB/EEC) and the British/Yugoslav Society and the BBC World Vernacular Service can and do play an important role in the promotion and sustain not merely contacts but ideas. In the absence of more substantive relations these cultural exchanges take on a specially important significance and we are currently re-examining whether the role of the GB/EEC can be expanded and developed.

Conclusion

13. *In sum* we should continue our policy of positive discrimination adapting our policies to each country in the light of its particular circumstances. In order that this policy should be more clearly recognisable and have a greater chance of success, we should try to keep in step with our European partners through consultation.

14. *Yugoslavia* by virtue of its independent stance retains pride of place as signified by the Secretary of State's recent visit. Yugoslavia needs economic help and is being treated as a special case. If the current difficulties lead to rescheduling we should promote the case for a generous settlement which will set the country back on the road to early recovery. But we must back the IMF if it concludes that a stronger programme is necessary.

15. *Hungary* too deserves special consideration: the Hungarians' economic experiments taking them closer to a market economy have positive implications not only for socialist economic management—but also for the credibility of orthodox socialist ideology. We can show sympathy for her current economic difficulties; support improvements in economic management in the context of an IMF programme; and maintain our political dialogue.

16. We are now more inclined to doubt the benefit to us of *Romania's* 'independent' foreign policy than in the early 1970s. Likewise the adverse features of Ceausescu's personality cult and the repressive character of the Romanian regime counterbalance to some extent the arguments for discriminating in Romania's favour e.g. in helping her out of her economic difficulties. We should continue to maintain the contacts which exist and encourage the preservation of a degree of independence in Romanian foreign policy. But Romania does not deserve the degree of special treatment accorded in the past.

17. In the past we have tended to discriminate against the *GDR*, Berlin considerations and the GDR's rigid orthodoxy being the determining factors. But it is clear that the GDR now shares the general desire to maintain the current calm in Berlin. We should not ignore a country of relative economic strength and increasing international stature, even though aspects of both its domestic and foreign policy are distasteful to us. It was for this reason that Lord Carrington decided to visit the GDR (and incidentally Czechoslovakia at the same time).

18. Neither *Bulgaria* nor *Czechoslovakia* as loyal allies of the Soviet Union have provided grounds for differentiating in their favour e.g. in the matter of visits. But recent developments in our relations with Czechoslovakia, e.g. the solution of the gold problem have created a very positive climate for the development of

[5] Nicolae Titulescu, Romanian statesman born in 1882.

cultural relationships and the promotion of trade. We should exploit this without implying acceptance of the oppressive nature of the regime. To a lesser degree the recent assertiveness by the Bulgarians of their national identity has created a similar opportunity in that country, although more recent indications suggest a step back from cultural progress there.

19. In the case of *Poland* the imposition of martial law forced us to discriminate in a negative sense to demonstrate disapproval. But as the situation in Poland gradually settles down, we shall wish to maximise the UK's share of Poland's trade on a cash basis and reinstate contacts. Poland's economic plight places strict constraints upon what we can do to maintain our economic relationship. But we shall wish to ensure that the political and cultural links which have distinguished Poland from her neighbours and kept alive her traditional ties with the West are restored and strengthened in such a way as to consolidate the uniquely antipathetic character of the Polish State within the Soviet Empire.[6]

[6] The paper was sent to Mr Goodison on 6 August, before going to Sir J. Bullard and finally to the Secretary of State, who asked for a meeting to be arranged to discuss the issue. This took place on 15 September and also considered a parallel paper on policy towards the Soviet Union (for the background to the latter paper see *DBPO: Afghanistan* pp. 360-361). For the outcome of the meeting see No. 174.

No. 171

Letter from Mr Furness (Warsaw) to Mr Broomfield, 20 August 1982
Confidential (FCO 28/4910, ENP 014/1)

Dear Nigel,

Hot August in Poland?

1. I have hesitated to send you very much by telegram on the fairly modest incidents and government announcements about them that have characterised this week. You may however like a few impressions, although after the events of Friday, 13 August and Monday, 16 August, not a great deal of much significance appears to have happened, so far as we know.[1] The meeting of NATO Heads of Mission here on 18 August found it very difficult to assess whether the further demonstrations Solidarity has called for, particularly on 31 August,[2] will make much impact on the authorities. On the whole, the feeling was that they would not, although we agreed to meet again on 2 September, to review what had happened by then.

2. The daily demonstrations around Wyszynski's floral cross in Victory Square have continued in an almost theatrical way with a nightly performance.[3] The ZOMO used water canon (but not very much, compared with May) and a little tear gas on 13 and 16 August. They were inhibited from doing this on 17 August when the Indonesian Ambassador gave his National Day Reception in the Victoria Hotel

[1] Mr James on 13 August had reported moves by the authorities against Solidarity, including the confiscation of printing equipment and reinternment of detainees who had been freed or granted parole (Warsaw tel. No. 763; FCO 28/5001, ENP 212/1). Mr Furness reported on 14 August that the Interior Ministry had published a communiqué that admitted disturbances in Gdańsk, Wrocław, Krakow and Warsaw the day before, leading to some arrests (Warsaw tel. No. 765).

[2] Solidarity, reorganised underground since April, had called for demonstrations to commemorate the second anniversary of the Gdańsk agreement and to protest against the Government having ignored their proposals for dialogue and release of internees.

[3] Over the summer, a cross appeared and reappeared each time the police took it away.

in Victory Square, although the ZOMO did hustle away the crowd (which was larger than the one dispersed with a spot of water cannon and a whiff of tear gas on 16 August) with staves after the reception was over. We may risk a few Polish jokes about the shortage of water in Warsaw, thanks to recent dry weather, affecting the water cannon. The Warsaw municipal authorities have announced their agreement this week that a permanent memorial to Cardinal Wyszynski can be erected, not in Victory Square, but just outside the Square in front of the Visitation Church (where a second cross of flowers had indeed been placed last Sunday, Assumption Day). It could be that the police will be less tolerant of the flower deposers in Victory Square itself as a result. There might be something of the theatre of the absurd there on 31 August itself when the Malaysian Ambassador gives a large reception at the Victoria Hotel for his National Day.

3. What we have heard from Gdansk indicates little activity after a considerable demonstration on Friday, 13 August. Opinions seem to be divided about whether something really big can be expected on 31 August. My guess is that it probably can. It seems a little odd (if rather Polish) that the plans for street demonstrations in Warsaw on 31 August are already well-known, even apart from the publicity given them by the BBC (which the MFA have now complained about) and other foreign broadcasting stations. It remains to be seen whether what happens will turn out to be what is now planned.

4. The authorities have been doing their best to play down the demonstrations that have taken place in the past few days, and are laying emphasis on the small numbers who have taken part and the little spontaneous support they have attracted. We are reporting separately on the various press reports on the lines of 'Small demonstration. Few take part.' At the same time, the tone of press comments on those few people who it is admitted do demonstrate is distinctly strident. It very much echoes the theme of the 'counter-revolutionary underground', supported from outside, in the phrase used in the statement issued after Jaruzelski's visit to Brezhnev in the Crimea.[4] One cannot help feeling that if the regime condemns the opposition in Poland in terms that appear to rule out the possibility of any reconciliation, then the authorities assert a standing excuse for maintaining martial law or a state of emergency indefinitely.

5. The Church's role is on the other hand the very opposite of strident at present and is probably too subtle to gain easy applause from opponents of the regime. It is striking that Archbishop Glemp's sermon to the pilgrims at Czestochowa on 15 August was given so much prominence in the official media. The main television news on Sunday evening gave him well over a quarter of an hour. Most of this sermon was devoted to Polish farmers. He touched on the mistakes on agricultural policy made in the early years of People's Poland and about the need for consultation and agreement among farmers, who should have the right to organise themselves without outside interference. He suggested that perhaps the longed for dialogue between the authorities and society in Poland could begin with farmers. He also referred to the Pope's postponed visit and expressed the hope that a date could be fixed in the near future and that the right atmosphere for a visit could be created. As I say, all this was given remarkable prominence in the official media, which also made the most of some rather deprecating remarks Glemp had made on

[4] On 16 August General Jaruzelski told the Soviet leader that 'the process of emergence from the crisis [was] being held back by the existence of a counterrevolutionary underground whose activities are inspired and supported from the outside, mainly from the United States' (*New York Times*, 17 August 1982).

the Saturday evening about the pilgrims to Czestochowa giving the 'V' for victory sign in the streets. Not a religious gesture, as the Primate put it. The enormous gathering at Czestochowa on 15 August took place without any disturbances and comparatively little police presence.

6. The Church/State Commission is due to meet on 25 August, i.e., the day before the actual anniversary of the Black Madonna, at Czestochowa, when the Pope had hoped to be present; but it seems a bit optimistic to expect that this meeting will enable the Primate to announce on 26 August (as some hope) a date agreed with the Government for a Papal visit next year. The effect on the regime of Soviet pressure against the papal visit is generally supposed here to be considerable.

7. Archbishop Glemp is, incidentally, due to visit Germany in the first week in September for a meeting of the German Catholic Association (the German Ambassador here fears that he may be a bit swept along on that occasion by the CDU. We shall see.)

Yours ever,
A. E. FURNESS

No. 172

Letter from Mr Furness (Warsaw) to Mr Broomfield, 3 September 1982

Confidential (FCO 28/4911, ENP 014/1)

Dear Nigel,

1. As most Western Embassies expected, I think, the events of 31 August have left us no more certain than before over where Poland is going.[1]

2. It will probably be some time before there is a clear picture of what happened, though very likely the full truth will never emerge. The demonstrations in many places seem to have been rather more spontaneous than organised, in the sense of bystanders, who may have come to see what happened, joining enthusiastically in demonstrations that passed (or possibly in some cases being almost obliged to do so after being tear gassed and water cannoned by the police). The authorities it turned out had brought more than enough police and army into Warsaw to disperse even the very large demonstrations that took place. Presumably many of the forces brought in were meant to deter. The Warsaw Party Headquarters (next door to this Embassy) was ringed by internal security troops with fixed bayonets (fixed on the spot under our noses) while there were several armoured personnel carriers just around the corner outside the Sejm besides hundreds more ZOMOS tucked away in a leafy side road. The URSUS tractor factory was sealed off by troops—we have still to hear from the Massey Ferguson people there how it was like inside.

3. In as far as one can readily judge the opinions of the Pole in the street in Warsaw, there seems to be a mood of some satisfaction that General Jaruzelski is not able to get away with what he wants without even a gesture of opposition. The size of the forces deployed and the quantity and insistent tone of the official propaganda beforehand seems to confirm that the authorities were indeed seriously worried over what might happen, although their statements in private were that

[1] Mr Furness reported on 1 September that possibly up to 50,000 people had demonstrated in several parts of Warsaw and that water cannons and heavy tear gas dispersed them (Warsaw tel. No. 819; FCO 28/4910, ENP 014/1).

some noise from hotheads was the most that could be expected (Olszowski was taking this line with the Danish Ambassador on the morning of 31 August when the latter called on him).

4. The idea of genuine national reconciliation à la Jaruzelski now clearly has even less plausibility than it did on 30 August. The authorities insist that they are determined to press on with their policies and they continue to dismiss the demonstrations as the work of evil-minded men, stimulated by foreign radio stations. Their propaganda that most of the demonstrators were youthful hooligans is however hardly consistent with their own statement that two thirds of the 4,000-odd demonstrators arrested on 31 August were under 30 (implying that one-third were not even as youthful as that). They take great credit from the fact that there were no strikes or go-slows on 31 August, even though Solidarity did not call for any, and some of the demonstrations notably at Nowa Huta,[2] took place as workers came out of factories at the end of a shift.

5. I was struck in Warsaw by how the authorities were determined to avoid bloodshed, despite a great deal of random brutality that one could easily see, such as firing gas canisters at individual passersby, including women and children, on the streets and at people taking their dogs for walks in the park. The ill-fated Malaysian Ambassador who gave his National Day Reception in the Victoria Hotel in Victory Square on 31 August, complained to me that his car had been tear gassed on his way there, despite its being the only car in the street at the time and his very non-European appearance. Many of the diplomatic corps gave up a hard struggle to get to the Victoria Hotel that evening, since it was one area in the centre of Warsaw where the police successfully kept out all demonstrators. The diplomat who suffered that evening most was arguably the Finnish Ambassador, who was called by his Norwegian neighbour to say that police were entering the garden in front of his Embassy apparently trying to arrest three Finnish secretaries whom they had followed during a walk around the town. When the Finnish Ambassador came to his gate to rescue his secretaries, both he and they were arrested and spent the next hour trying to get themselves released from the police station.

6. The chances seem at present to be that further demonstrations of the kind that happened this week, with some pre-arrangement but capable of gathering spontaneous support, may happen again. 13 December[3] strikes one as a very likely target date for country-wide demonstrations, although there are many other dates to commemorate before then. The authorities (and the Russians perhaps) must wonder how much further they could go to discourage such demonstrations in the future. Water cannons are nastier in December than in August, but there seem likely to be Poles brave enough to face them, and the authorities seem highly reluctant to order their forces to fire on crowds (to their credit I suppose one could admit, although there is obviously the calculation that bloodshed would rebound on them.) As far as I know, apart from Lubin, the one place where the authorities admit there was bloodshed, and Czestochowa, Poland was quiet on 1 and 2 September, which gives the political struggle here a distinctly symbolic if not ritual appearance. Warsaw is admittedly not the toughest town in Poland; but the fact that thousands of demonstrators could be swept through the centre of the town with great quantities of tear gas in the presence of thousands of armed troops, and really very little damage to people or property done (the authorities claim one passerby

[2] Easternmost district of Cracow and site of the biggest steelworks in Poland, with many workers belonging to Solidarity.

[3] First anniversary of the declaration of martial law.

and one bus driver were seriously injured after stones were thrown), shows how peculiar a country Poland is.

Yours ever,
A. E. FURNESS

No. 173

Letter from Mr Cartledge (Budapest) to Mr Montgomery, 6 September 1982
Confidential (FCO 28/4810, ENC 014/4)

My Dear Alan,

Impressions of Czechoslovakia

1. I paid a short 'familiarisation' visit to Czechoslovakia from 16-19 August, under our delegated authority scheme. The visit, like that which I plan to make to Poland next month, came rather late in my tour here, for a variety of practical reasons; but it was not wholly unfamiliar territory for me, as I had made two visits to Czechoslovakia during my time in EESD[1] and I believe that, in any case, there may be something to be said for visiting other parts of Eastern Europe after consolidating one's knowledge of one's own particular patch of it.

Although, because of commitments on both sides, the visit had to take place during the rather unpromising (from the business point of view) month of August, John Rich nevertheless arranged an extremely worthwhile and interesting programme for us (my wife came with me) and I am most grateful to him, to Rosemary Rich and to the other members of the Prague Embassy who were involved for all the help which they gave us. This letter records the inevitably superficial impressions which I derived from the visit, many of these may amount to no more than statements of the obvious: but the obvious sometimes tends, naturally, to be by-passed in more sophisticated day-to-day assessments of a country and its restatement from a lay viewpoint can perhaps be useful. One of the advantages of our system of familiarisation visits is that it provides occasions for this.

Visual Impressions

2. We entered Czechoslovakia by road at the Komarom/Komarno[2] border crossing and the scrupulously bilingual character of public signs and inscriptions (shop fronts etc.) in this part of Slovakia was a reminder of how relatively recently it had been part of Hungary; the waitress who served us in a Bratislava hotel spoke Hungarian with us with evident pleasure.[3] I found both the political slogans and the police presence less obtrusive than I had been led to expect: both are more evident than in Hungary but the slogans, at any rate, give the impression of having survived through inertia rather than continuing zeal. By comparison with Hungary, the roads of all classes are excellent. Hungary badly needs two motorways (north/south and west/east) of the standard of that between Bratislava and Prague; but although isolated stretches have been completed, the Hungarians have run out of money for this as for so many other infra-structural investments. A higher level

[1] Head of EESD, 1975-77.
[2] The original city was split between the Hungarian Komárom and the Slovak Komárno following the newly-created border of Czechoslovakia by the Treaty of Trianon in 1920.
[3] The city, despite a dominant Hungarian and German population, had been incorporated into the new State of Czechoslovakia in 1919.

of investment of a different kind was very evident in Prague itself: the numerous historic buildings and churches which, together with its physical situation, make it such an outstandingly beautiful city, have been restored and maintained with what must have been—and continue to be—a massive outlay of skill and money. Budapest, and Hungary as a whole, has in any case a very much smaller architectural heritage but has also been less successful in preserving it, or less able to afford to do so. New residential housing, on the other hand, struck us as being of even less imaginative design and of even poorer quality than in Hungary, which is saying a great deal; I was appalled by the 'socialist brutalism' of the new suburb south of Bratislava. The Czechoslovak countryside gives an impression of greater orderliness than the Hungarian mainly, I think, because there is less private agricultural and building activity but partly also because where such activity exists it is more strictly zoned, to the undoubted benefit of the landscape if to the detriment of the economy. Such villas and 'weekend houses' as we saw were (by contrast with the municipal housing) more substantial and more elegant than their Hungarian counterparts; but the predominance of lawns and flower-beds over vegetable patches indicated that they are designed more for relaxation than for economic profit—the Czechoslovaks do not, apparently, share the Hungarian obsession with utilising every square inch of cultivatable land.

3. Against this generally impressive and attractive (at least at the height of summer) backcloth, the anomalies of the Czechoslovak situation seem, to an outsider, to stand out in all the sharper relief. Despite an apparently high standard of husbandry in the countryside, the food shops both in Prague and in the villages seemed extraordinarily poorly stocked, particularly so far as fruit and vegetables were concerned; such fruit and vegetables as were on sale were of very indifferent quality and we were told that regular supplies could only be assured through carefully nurtured contacts. The pyramids of tinned fish in many shop windows, through the chinks of which one could discern empty shelves behind, were reminiscent of Moscow; and the bareness of the state or cooperative-owned stores was largely uncompensated by the street stalls or roadside retail outlets which are commonplace in Hungary. From superficial observation, there seemed to be a greater disparity than in Hungary between the supply situation in the two republican capitals and that in the villages through which we passed—the latter really looked very dismal indeed.

4. Even in Prague, for all its splendours, it was constantly obvious that the satisfaction of consumer needs is not the regime's first priority. Ready-made clothing, both adult and juvenile, seemed to be of a reasonable standard: but with that exception, the consumer seemed in general to be poorly served. Hairdressers and barbers, for example (admittedly ridiculously over-numerous in Hungary) seemed to be few and far between. Cafés and restaurants were notably fewer than in Hungary or in the west. Perhaps for these as well as for more important and enduring reasons the Czechoslovak shopper or passer-by seemed to me to be preoccupied, gloomy and unnaturally silent; after walking round the streets of Prague for a while, I realised that a contrast with Budapest even more striking than the supply situation in the shops was the absence of the constant background of animated chatter which Hungarians provide (in the process of pinning down this impression, I was interrupted by bursts of laughter from a group walking behind me which turned out, on closer inspection, to consist of British tourists). Hungarians talk loudly and continuously, pausing only to refuel with a bun or a cigarette, and are much given to physical contact; the Czechoslovaks are much

more reserved, to the point—at least in public—of dourness. In general—and this went for the countryside too—I missed the rather untidy, raffish hedonism of Hungary which helps to disguise and certainly compensates for this country's overall shabbiness.

5. Given all this, it was not perhaps surprising—although still striking—that the number of Western tourists in Czechoslovakia was so much smaller than in Hungary. Equally striking was the vast number of East German visitors—on the Bratislava/Prague motorway there were more DDR than Czechoslovak registered cars. Such experience as we had of the artificiality of the Czechoslovak exchange rate against hard currencies illustrated an even stronger disincentive for Western visitors: a light lunch in Bratislava which would have cost, at most, £1.50 a head in Budapest cost us the equivalent of nearly £5 a head.

Political Impressions

6. I have read with interest your exchange of letters with Richard Thomas in Prague about the contest between the proponents of orthodoxy and of pragmatism for the direction of Czechoslovak economic policy.[4] There seems to me to be no doubt, as a casual observer, that Czechoslovakia has the wherewithal to achieve a fair degree of material prosperity. Its failure to do so can, I think, be attributed only to the continuing reluctance of the Czechoslovak leadership to take any step which could be interpreted as a loss of confidence in socialism or as an admission of the fact that communism simply does not work. The Hungarians have become adept exponents of the syllogism that since socialism benefits all, anything from which all benefit must be socialist. The intellectual dishonesty involved has long ceased to trouble them and, even if it did, the recollection of 1956 is still a just sufficiently potent reminder that the retention of power is more important than ideological consistency or orthodoxy. John Rich, and his US and Canadian colleagues whom he kindly arranged for me to meet, were agreed that the Czechoslovak leadership is still too nervous of losing Moscow's confidence to deviate sufficiently strongly from orthodoxy to produce any significant economic improvement. Equally, they were in agreement that this fear was now probably exaggerated and that Moscow would be likely to tolerate a much greater degree of pragmatism than the Czechoslovaks are as yet willing to risk. Perhaps this is another facet of the difference between a revolution in which a Communist Party actually lost power (1956) and an intra-Party revolution (1968): the Hungarians have a stronger historical lever against Moscow.[5]

7. On the professional plane, I was struck by the difficulty of access to the Czechoslovak leadership as compared with the access which we enjoy here in Budapest. I was amazed to learn from the Canadian Ambassador (an old acquaintance from Moscow) who has now been in Prague for nearly a year that he has yet to meet the Czechoslovak Foreign Minister; John Rich told me that although the Foreign Ministry is particularly tiresome to deal with, other (economic) Ministries are easier. I was also told that in Prague there is no access

[4] Not printed.

[5] Mr Rich commented in a letter to Mr Montgomery on 5 October that although Mr Cartledge had recorded accurately his and Western colleagues' analysis, recent evidence especially from the Finance Minister, changed the picture somewhat. The pragmatists now believed that their most serious obstacle to economic change might not be Moscow or ideological theorists, but ingrained conservatism and habits of thoughts in the middle management, district party and local authority officials and 'even the workers themselves'. He suspected that if the leadership managed to dislodge the quiet-lifers and offered the right incentives, there would be an enthusiastic response, especially from the younger people.

for diplomats to the Party *apparat* whereas we here do, as you know, have regular access to at least the International Department of the Central Committee and occasionally access to other Departments as well. I was all the more grateful to John Rich for arranging for me to call, with him, on Deputy Foreign Minister Jablonsky, whom I had known during his time as Czechoslovak Ambassador in London. John Rich is better qualified than I to assess any points of significance in our discussion with Jablonsky and is preparing a note on it. From the point of view of my own local concerns, I was interested in Jablonsky's version of the recent difficulties in Czechoslovak/Hungarian relations which resulted from the growing number of Czechs and Slovaks (mostly the latter) who paid brief visits to Northern Hungary to do their shopping, thereby causing local shortages. I was also interested in Jablonsky's exposition of the Czechoslovak case for a CMEA summit and particularly by the fact that he said nothing to justify the flurry of speculation, following the communiqué on the Brezhnev/Husak meeting in the Crimea, that such a meeting may take place in the near future (the Hungarian line is that it could not take place before early 1983).[6]

8. Even a short glimpse of a fraternal neighbour helps one to look at one's own parish with a clearer eye and I valued this one. It is of some political significance here that most Hungarian visitors to Czechoslovakia are likely to have returned home with impressions not to dissimilar from my own.[7]

Yours ever,
BRYAN CARTLEDGE

[6] It did not take place until June 1984 and was the first CMEA summit since April 1969.

[7] Mr Montgomery commented on 16 September that Mr Cartledge's observations validated the thesis that 'even under communism the countries of Eastern Europe are distinguished as much by their diversity as by their uniformity.' Mr Rich on 5 October stated that he disagreed that 'the present regime had no disposition to improve the lot of the people'. He thought they would love to improve material benefits but were trapped in the rigidities of the system. The Finance Minister had described to him Mr Husák's instructions: 'Introduce flexibility, but avoid social dislocation'.

On 29 October Mr Montgomery replied to Mr Rich that 'an inability to overcome party sloth is in itself an indictment of the leadership's lack of will to promote more constructive policies' and 'moreover the repressive atmosphere under which the Czechoslovak population live, hardly seems to reflect the policies of a caring administration'.

No. 174

Summary of points agreed at the Secretary of State's meeting on relations with the Soviet Union and Eastern Europe, 15 September 1982[1]

Confidential (FCO 28/4745, EN 021/31)

A. *Eastern Europe*

1. Our policy should continue to be based on the principles of positive discrimination and the encouragement of evolution of more open societies.

Poland

2. Relations with *Poland* posed special problems. We had to accept that the Jaruzelski regime was here to stay. We should seek to move away from the stance that there could be no change in relations until all the three stated conditions (end of martial law, release of detainees, renewal of dialogue) had been fulfilled.

[1] See No. 170 for the background to this meeting.

Instead, we should think in terms of a graduated response to any gradual improvement that might occur.

3. The formal ending of martial law would be a significant symbolic and political event for public opinion in the West, even if at the same time new laws were introduced which maintained some of the restrictions currently in force. It would be desirable if any movement by the West on rescheduling could be linked to the ending of martial law, but in practice we might need to move much sooner, either as a result of moves by the commercial banks to conclude a rescheduling agreement for 1982 or in the event of signs that some of the official creditors were no longer prepared to maintain the unity of the official creditors group.

4. In the rest of Eastern Europe, the main thing was to maintain sufficiently active relations, particularly in the form of ministerial visits. Since the Secretary of State had already postponed the planned visits to East Berlin and Prague, these should be the first priorities when the Secretary of State's other commitments permitted him to visit Eastern Europe. The possibility should be looked at again at the end of the year. There would in any case be advantage in Mr Rifkind visiting the GDR in 1983.

5. The possibility of the Prime Minister visiting Hungary would be included in the letter about the Prime Minister's visits during 1983 which the Private Secretary would shortly be sending to No 10.

6. It would be useful for the Secretary of State to send personal letters to certain of his colleagues (Trade, Industry, Agriculture and Energy) suggesting that they might also consider the possibilities of visits by their Ministers to Eastern Europe or playing a part in receiving ministerial visitors from Eastern Europe.

7. Planning on the programme of visits to Eastern Europe should proceed on the basis of the annexes to the paper on policy towards Eastern Europe.

B. *Soviet Union*

8. There was a need to renew the dialogue with the Soviet Union, which because of the need to curtail relations after Afghanistan and Poland had almost ceased. No British Prime Minister had visited Moscow since Mr Wilson in 1975, and no Foreign Secretary since Dr Owen in 1977, apart from Lord Carrington's visit in 1981 to present the Ten's proposals on Afghanistan.[2]

9. A visit by the Prime Minister next year would be a rather dramatic way of changing our policy. An alternative would be to proceed more gradually by way of visits at junior and/or senior ministerial level. The Secretary of State would discuss the question with the Prime Minister after his meeting with Mr Gromyko in New York.

10. There was a need to bear in mind that a new leadership would probably be taking over soon in the Soviet Union. Visits next year might offer early opportunities to meet the new leaders, although obviously this was uncertain. Another factor was that if the INF talks did not reach agreement, INF deployment would be taking place next year. This would be easier to present to domestic public opinion if a dialogue with the Soviet Union were seen to be going ahead in parallel.

11. We should also look at the possibilities for reactivating cultural relations. The policy adopted since Afghanistan of avoiding major cultural manifestations had prevented us from doing anything to expose the Soviet public to Western cultural values, whereas the Russians were often able to arrange cultural manifestations in this country through private impresarios.

[2] See *DBPO: Afghanistan*, No. 107.

12. The Secretary of State agreed to circulate the papers on Eastern Europe and the Soviet Union (amended to remove references to a visit by the Prime Minister) to his colleagues in OD for their information.[3] In his covering minute the Secretary of State might refer to a paper on Policy in East/West Economic Relations which he hoped to circulate soon.[4]

[3] Both papers were circulated to OD on 27 September under cover of a minute from the Foreign Secretary to the Prime Minister (No. 160 in *DBPO: Afghanistan*).
[4] A summary of this paper is in *DBPO: Afghanistan*, No. 159.

No. 175

Briefing for a European Political Cooperation meeting of Foreign Ministers, 20 September 1982

Confidential (FCO 28/4956, ENP 022/1)

Poland

Points to Make

Internal Situation

1. Riots of 31 August[1] further evidence of widespread opposition to martial law which will continue to make itself felt.

Prospects

2. Demonstrations will not have broken political deadlock. Solidarity showed it could arouse and channel popular feeling; the regime that it could contain but not win over opposition. Uncertain how far Jaruzelski will now be able to maintain policy of cautious relaxation of martial law; pressure from hard-liners for a tougher approach to Solidarity will increase.

Western Policy

3. Must stand by our three criteria and urge Polish Government to fulfil undertaking to return to renewal and reform. See value however over the longer term in a more flexible approach in the interests both of encouraging the Polish authorities to moderation and of maintaining an influence over the situation in Poland. Should therefore keep latter under close scrutiny and review our response in light of developments in Poland. Important to maintain close co-ordination and ensure a united Western approach.

Political Contacts

4. Recognise that resumption of regular political contacts premature in present circumstances. See value however in exceptional contacts (e.g. at UNGA). Believe such contacts would not necessarily reflect an acceptance of situation in Poland by the West but would present opportunity to reinforce our views with Polish authorities. Important to maintain united approach both within Ten and with US.

Rescheduling (if raised)

5. No question of any change at present to policy not to provide new credits but have an economic interest in resumption of rescheduling negotiations. Accept however that resumption will have to wait until all Western Creditor Governments are agreed on this. Hope French proposal for meeting of technical experts may be pursued so that pros and cons may be considered in detail.

Relations with USSR (if raised)

[1] See No. 172, note 1.

6. Like partners, have always considered that Soviet Union bears heavy share of responsibility for events in Poland. Continuing close interest of Soviet leaders in Poland demonstrated by Jaruzelski's meeting with Brezhnev in Crimea in August and Olszowski's[2] visit to Moscow. Important to continue to make clear that Poland, like Afghanistan, a serious obstacle to development of East/West relations. UK announced measures to signal concern earlier in year which remain in force, and would not envisage any change in relations with Soviet Union as result of recent events.

Essential Facts

Situation in Poland

1. It has been officially confirmed that disturbances in Poland on 31 August took place in 35 of Poland's 49 provinces and involved at least 75,000 people (unofficial sources place this nearer 100,000). Some 4,000 people were arrested during the riots of which 3,000 have now been given sentences ranging from heavy fines to 18 months' imprisonment. Five people are reported to have been killed in the riots and some 300 seriously injured. The curfew has been reimposed in at least two cities. The authorities have announced their intention of pressing court proceedings against leading Polish dissidents (although not against Walesa); and trials against members of the Confederation for an Independent Poland,[3] an anti-communist opposition group in Poland, have now begun.

Western Policy

2. (*a*) *EC Response*

At its meeting on 1/2 September the Political Committee of the Ten concluded that although no change in policy towards Poland could be made in present circumstances, some modification on e.g. political contacts was not to be excluded at a later stage (Copenhagen telno 239).[4] The Political Committee therefore instructed the East European Working Group of the Ten (meeting on 16/17 September) to review the situation and as appropriate make policy recommendations in October.

(*b*) *NATO Response*

NAC Meeting on 15 September agreed that no change of policy was possible in present circumstances although NATO should be ready to review its response in the light of developments in Poland.

Political Contacts

3. The Political Committee of the Ten concluded that a resumption of political contacts did not necessarily imply an acceptance by the West of the situation in Poland, but an opportunity to reinforce our views with the Poles. This interpretation is not shared by all partners; some of whom (notably the Dutch) favour a more cautious approach. None of our EC partners however (except the Dutch) exclude the possibility of contacts with Polish Government in the margins of the UNGA.

Economic Assistance

4. The agreed position of Western Creditor Governments not to reschedule Poland's 1982 official debt repayments has come under increasing strain amongst the creditors. In discussions in NATO in July, the French proposed a technical

[2] Stephan Olszowski, who had succeeded Mr Czyrek as Minister of Foreign Affairs in July 1982 made a two-day visit for talks on 13-14 September. He met the Foreign Minister, Mr Gromyko, to discuss Soviet-Polish relations.

[3] See No. 11, paragraph 4.

[4] Not printed.

meeting of experts to discuss the Polish economy. At the NAC Meeting on 13 September there was some support for this proposal, although no date for a meeting has yet been fixed, but the French and US remain opposed to a resumption of talks with the Poles.

5. Meanwhile, negotiations between the Banks and the Poles on 1982 rescheduling are proceeding. Agreement seems near on a formula which would give the Poles 95% rescheduling of principal. They would also receive back in trade credits, 50% of interest payments they are to make this year.

Relations with USSR (if raised)

6. The Presidency has suggested that Ministers may wish to discuss the implications of events in Poland for relations with the Soviet Union. Relations with the Soviet Union were already restricted because of the invasion of Afghanistan, but following the declaration of martial law in Poland, HMG took additional measures against Poland and the Soviet Union. The text of the LPS' written answer of 5 February,[5] announcing these measures, is attached at Annex A.[6] Our national measures against the Soviet Union were not intended to be reversible. A number of other countries, including Belgium and the FRG, also announced national measures. In addition, the Community imposed certain restrictions on imports from the Soviet Union for one year; there will no doubt be discussions in the Community later this year as to whether these should be continued and in what form.

[5] See No. 142, note 4.
[6] Not printed.

No. 176

Minute from Mr Pym to Sir G. Howe (HM Treasury), 22 September 1982
FCS/82/137 Confidential (FCO 28/4897, ENH 101/1)

Possible BIS[1] Loan to Hungary

1. As you know, the Governors of the BIS member banks are due to meet in Basle on 27/28 September to discuss, among other things, a possible further $300 million facility for Hungary.

2. Malcolm Rifkind wrote to Leon Brittan on 7 July emphasising the importance we attach to helping Hungary to avoid being pushed into rescheduling.[2] My officials have also been in touch with yours. I remain strongly of the view that the Hungarian economic experiment deserves support. In spite of its present difficulties, the system does work, and provides a valuable model of the market-orientated approach to economic management to which other East European

[1] Bank for International Settlements.
[2] In July the Hungarians approached the BIS for a standby loan of $300 million (loans totalling $210 million had already been granted by the BIS earlier in the year). Mr Rifkind sought to persuade the Chancellor to encourage the Bank of England to participate in this limited loan to tide Hungary over 'a relatively short but crucial period'. If the Hungarians were forced to default, he warned, 'this will undermine the Hungarian experiment leaving the field clear for the dead hand of Soviet-style centralism'. In subsequent conversation with the Chief Secretary, Mr Rifkind found him 'sympathetic on all points except the possibility of a Treasury guarantee', which he did not consider possible in the present financial circumstances. In a submission of 21 September, Mr Broomfield felt that only a letter from the Secretary of State would be likely to carry weight with the Treasury at this stage. Sir J. Bullard agreed and believed the FCO might get support from those to whom the letter was copied.

countries may turn as a way of solving their own economic problems. The political consequences, as we have seen in Hungary, can be far-reaching.

3. The Hungarians appear to be genuinely determined to overcome their present difficulties; and you will by now have seen Budapest telnos 266 and 267[3], which record the considerable efforts the Hungarians are making. But in the short term they need help: if reform fails, Soviet-style orthodoxy can be the only winner, with all that this means in political as well as economic terms for Eastern Europe as a whole.

4. The BIS banks have deferred a decision on the $300 million standby loan once already this year. Without a clear lead from the BIS, further lending from commercial banks seems unlikely. If on the other hand the BIS could agree now to make the loan available, then we would hope that commercial banks would also be encouraged to make some further loans to Hungary, thus enabling it to pull through until IMF funds become available next year.

5. I am of course aware that, as Leon Brittan pointed out in his letter of 9 August[3] the Bank of England has already made an important contribution to the previous BIS loans for Hungary. But the chief purpose of these loans was to tide Hungary over until she could draw upon the IMF funds, which now seem likely to be delayed. It would be a doubtful economy if, having helped Hungary through the past six months, the West were now to withdraw its support and Hungary were to be forced into rescheduling as a result. It would also seriously reduce the creditors' prospects of being repaid not only by Hungary but by other Eastern European borrowers. A further financial crisis would almost certainly ensue, and the banks' increased reluctance to put any more funds in Eastern Europe could well precipitate defaults and/or requests for rescheduling by others.

6. Financially, economically and politically, therefore it is surely to the West's advantage to see Hungary overcome its present difficulties. I strongly hope that you will feel able to encourage the Bank of England to participate in this further loan.

7. I am copying this minute to the Prime Minister, the Secretary of State for Trade and the Governor of the Bank of England.

FRANCIS PYM

[3] Not printed.

No. 177

Letter from Mr Furness (Warsaw) to Mrs Macgregor, 22 September 1982
Confidential (FCO 28/5007, ENP 226/1)

Dear Judith,

Conversation with Bishop Jerzy Dąbrowski

1. I had a long conversation with Bishop Jerzy Dąbrowski on 20 September, when I called on him to discuss yet another showing of the video film of the Pope's visit to Britain[1] which you kindly arranged for us to receive.

2. He expressed a great deal of pessimism about likely future developments in Poland, although no pessimism at all about the position of the Polish Church. As

[1] The Pope visited the United Kingdom from 28 May to 2 June 1982. Over two million people attended events.

you know, Dąbrowski is the Primate's Special Assistant, and his views can, I think, be taken to echo pretty closely those of Archbishop Glemp. (For this reason, he is not a good source on account of the differences of view within the hierarchy and the Church in general.)

3. Dąbrowski said that the communiqué issued by the Bishops at the end of their conference last week,[2] on which we shall be reporting separately, will be followed by a separate paper that the Church would present to the State authorities, making a series of proposals on how to solve Poland's present difficulties. This further paper would not be published by the Church and he said, with a smile, that he was certain that the authorities would not publish it because of its content. He added that there seemed no chance that the regime would accept the Church's proposals. I asked him why in that case the Church thought it worthwhile to put forward these proposals—or indeed any other proposals. He said that the Bishops felt it important to put forward positive proposals, if only to get away from the whole negative nature of the current opposition in Poland to the regime. This led him on to a denunciation, in pretty fierce terms, of those small groups, as he called them, who had organised the street demonstrations on 31 August. These demonstrations—unlike demonstrations in Western countries—had called for nothing positive and those behind them had put forward no positive proposals for people to demonstrate about. I commented that this might be so, but that most Western observers were struck by how many people were ready to turn out on the streets on 31 August, and one could hardly say that such a sizeable cross-section of the population were all victims of political manipulators. Bishop Dąbrowski said that the people demonstrating were fired by their emotions, whether of hostility to the Soviet Union or hostility to the *régime*, but that such emotional demonstrations were wholly useless as a way of getting the authorities to change their minds. They provided a perfect vehicle for acts of provocation by the regime and stirred up further anger among the population against a system that it could not change, or at least change by this 'method'. (He excepted the KOR leaders from those who had no positive programme, although he said that it was hardly surprising that the *régime* had announced its intention of putting KOR leaders on trial.)

4. I went on to ask him his views about the release of detainees and an amnesty for those convicted of offences against martial law, which the Church continued to call for. If underground Solidarity was to be criticised for having no positive programme, how could it help for the Solidarity leaders in detention to be released? He said that in the Church's view on the release of the detainees would have a very valuable effect in lowering the political temperature by giving the impression that the regime could show at least some good will. He insisted that even the release of Wałęsa could have a calming effect and suggested—I am not sure with how much conviction—that it might be possible to imagine Wałęsa playing a useful role in organising trade union activity in Gdansk, without either becoming a focus for national opposition to the regime or a collaborator with the regime.

[2] In this communiqué of 17 September the bishops blamed the authorities for the violence of 31 August. It declared that Poland was 'being shaken by a number of crises. There are no definite indications that the social situation is improving, and we see no sign of any positive prospects. The future fills us with apprehension. The mounting wave of violence might well take a direction that would prove dangerous or even tragic for the existence of our nation and state.' It added that 'no appropriate steps' had been taken to re-establish a dialogue and urged for mutual concessions, reconciliation and forgiveness. The bishops regarded it as their duty to defend all those who had been injured (*The Tablet*, 25 September 1982).

5. Bishop Dąbrowski went on however to say that he was pretty certain that the suspended Solidarity organisation would soon be 'delegalised' by the authorities, and that there was now no possibility whatsoever of a dialogue between the authorities and Solidarity. Nor much chance of the leading Solidarity detainees being released. Indeed it was a mistake in his view to believe that the authorities had any intention of conducting anything that could be called a dialogue with society. How could, he asked rhetorically, periodic meetings between the State authorities and the Polish bishops be described as a dialogue with society? All the stuff we were now reading about the PRON (the movement for national rebirth) was simply a smoke screen to cover the fact that the Party was wholly inadequate to serve as a transmitter of the regime's requirements to society at large, and a new organisation had to be created for this purpose.[3]

6. On ecclesiastical matters, he said that the timing of the Pope's next visit to Poland was still completely open, and he spoke with some bitterness about the regime's lack of good faith on this issue. As far as the faithful were concerned, he did not think they were unduly disappointed by the Pope not having come this August as planned, and most people understood the reasons why he did not come. Speaking personally, he was not at all certain that the Pope would come to Poland next year, although it was likely that he would come 'within the next five years', as soon as the regime made up its mind. He said that it was all very well to talk of Soviet pressure against the Papal visit or against the Church generally in Poland, but in his view, this was a wholly speculative area and no-one knew for certain whether Soviet pressure was being applied or whether any was needed for the regime to act as it did. He said he was more amused than anything else by the interest aroused by criticism in the Government newspaper *Rzeczpospolita*[4] against Bishop Tokarczuk of Przemysl's fiery words at Czestochowa last month.[5] Bishop Tokarczuk could afford to have another fling against the authorities because he did not need any permits for new Churches to be built in his well-churched diocese. In the same vein he said that the installation of a Papal Nuncio in Warsaw, which the Minister for Religious Affairs had recently suggested the regime would welcome, would make little difference. He conceded that hierarchies often had ambivalent attitudes towards Papal Nuncios, but he said that the Polish Bishops would be happy to have one in Warsaw, even if this changed nothing in relations between the Church and State. The Papal Nuncio might find that his most laborious function was coping with enquiries of Western journalists about what he was doing.

7. Dąbrowski is of course used to speaking to Western diplomats and his remarks always have a degree of calculation about them. But even allowing for this, it is remarkable just how pessimistic the Primate's curia now is about the chances of the regime moving in a liberal direction. (And this is what is sometimes accused of being the 'collaborationist' wing of the Church!) This assessment is of

[3] The Patriotic Movement for National Rebirth (*Patriotyczny Ruch Odrodzenia Narodowego*), created in July 1982, replaced the Front of National Unity. It comprised pro-communist and pro-Government organisations aiming at showing unity and support for the Government and the Polish United Workers' Party.

[4] The daily newspaper, *Polish Republic*, became an organ of the provisional Government in 1944. It was discontinued in 1950 and in effect superseded by *Trybuna Ludu*, the Polish United Workers' Party's newspaper. It was relaunched in 1980 as a separate Government newspaper.

[5] On 8 September the newspaper criticised the Bishop who had denounced the 'blind and brutal force' used in the suppression of the protests against innocent people and said that 'the Church cannot remain indifferent . . . to the suffering and would have betrayed its mission [if it had done so] . . . thereby playing into the hands of those who are against God'.

course consistent with the Church's scepticism about the usefulness of Western measures against Poland. The degree of exasperation with underground Solidarity is also worth noting.

Yours ever,
A. E. FURNESS

No. 178

Letter from Mr Stagg (Sofia) to Mr Wilson, 23 September 1982
Restricted (FCO 28/4755, EN 062/2)

Dear Fraser,

Exercise Shield '82

1. Preparations for the forthcoming Warsaw Pact Exercise—due to begin on 25 September—are receiving widespread media coverage: film of various contingents arriving to extravagant welcomes, interviews with participants from other Pact countries (excluding so far Romania) and long analyses of the military threat to Eastern-Europe and Bulgaria in particular.

2. The over-riding theme of all the commentaries on Shield '82 is the stark difference between it and NATO manoeuvres. The former is merely the minimum preparation necessary to ensure the defensive security of the Warsaw Pact; the latter are ill-disguised exercises designed to prepare NATO troops for offensive operations in Europe and, indeed, throughout the world. To support this view, the Bulgarian press is full of photographs of soldiers kissing babies, hugging pretty girls, waving bunches of flowers and generally behaving in a friendly, relaxed and peace-loving manner. (The Bulgarians have even produced a Shield '82 car sticker.) In contrast, defence experts are producing a flood of articles describing, in words and diagrams, the threat from the West. A recent article in the military daily *Narodna Armia* showed a map of the Mediterranean basin in which almost every available square millimetre was covered with hostile tanks, troops, ships and aircraft (including a large cruiser parked in Algeria and a tank division stationed in Albania).

3. However the secrecy surrounding preparations for Shield '82, the paucity of factual information about who will participate and what they will do, and the decision to turn about two-thirds of the country into a restricted military zone (with its rules applying to Bulgarians as well as foreigners) must make intelligent Bulgarians wonder just how innocent and pacific the manoeuvres really are. And general public indifference to Shield '82 and, in particular, a current rumour—no doubt ill-founded—that that two villages near Bourgas have been totally evacuated so that they can be ceremoniously blown to pieces as the climax of the Exercise suggest that it is not quite the patriotic and popular event which the Ministry of Defence might like to claim.

Yours ever,
RICHARD

No. 179

Mr Bolland (Belgrade) to Mr Pym, 4 October 1982
Confidential (FCO 28/5193, ENU 014/5)

Valedictory: Britain's stake in Yugoslavia

Summary . . . [1]

Sir,

'Nothing that has been created must be so sacred for us that it cannot be surpassed and cede its place to what is still more progressive, more free, more humane.'
Last sentence in the Programme of the League of Communists of Yugoslavia.

I arrived here a few weeks before Tito died. My two-and-a-half years stay in Yugoslavia coincided therefore with the immediate post-Tito period which many forecasted would see the break-up of the country, opening the way for Soviet intervention. They were proved wrong. At the same time, Tito's successors have been faced with some very difficult internal problems which they have by no means resolved. Indeed, there are now signs that Yugoslavia is entering into a period of change. In my final despatch I would like to comment on this situation and to consider whether it is in Britain's interest to continue to support Yugoslavia as it advances along 'Tito's path'.

Political leadership

2. All Communist countries are faced, on the death of their leaders, with the problem of succession. Who will occupy the leader's seat? Will there be a struggle for power? Will there be change? It was not surprising that many expected, following the departure of a giant like Tito, particularly in a country as ethnically divided and recently united as Yugoslavia, that his former colleagues would contest the succession and one would emerge to ensure the country's unity and give it the required, decisive leadership.

3. It was in fact mainly to avoid such a struggle and to preserve Yugoslavia's unity that Tito devised a mechanism of collective and rotatory rule. This, he believed, would avoid any major ethnic group having to accept direction from another. So far the system has worked smoothly in that the leadership and country have remained united.

4. But collective and perpetually changing rule has its disadvantages. There is no single person to attract loyalty and give commands. This has strengthened particularist forces in the Republics and Provinces. More scope is afforded to the Yugoslav disease of endless consultation. Ordinary people I meet on the road hark back to Tito, saying when he was here they knew where they were and there were no shortages. Increasing economic difficulties generate such grumbles. Commentators, even Party leaders, talk of a crisis of confidence in the Party. There are differences among the leaders, although their general view remains, I am assured, that the need to keep Yugoslavia united and stable is best served by collective rule. And no public figure has yet questioned the strategic policies associated with Tito.

[1] Not printed.

5. It is, however, difficult to believe that this country, like almost all others, will not eventually accept a single leader. The only person now adopting the appropriate direct, commanding 'Yugoslav' tone is Ljubičić, the former Minister of Defence and now President of Serbia. Representatives of the Armed Forces in the Party call insistently for a stronger lead. Ribičić, the present Party President says the Party should be purged of incompetents and corrupt careerists. Even he has recently warned Party cadres that the Party must not delude itself that 'we are so dominant the question of political power is not posed'. All of which suggests that the political situation is becoming more fluid.

Nationalism: Kosovo

6. As Communists, Yugoslav leaders assert they have 'solved the national question'. Their doctrine insists that class consciousness is stronger than nationalism. But such a claim must ring hollow especially in Yugoslav ears. When wrestling in 1948 to free his country from the Soviet grasp, it was Tito himself who reminded Stalin that: 'No matter how much each of us loves the land of socialism, the USSR, he can in no case love his country less, which is developing socialism'. Croatian Party leaders said much the same in 1971 and Serbian Party leaders in 1972. Decentralisation was accepted and written into the Constitution and today there are few local leaders, and probably still fewer ordinary citizens, who do not think the best way to serve Yugoslavia as well as their local communities is to first serve themselves. In spite of the steep increase in those declaring themselves Yugoslavs in the last census, feelings of separate national identity predominate, nowhere more than in Croatia and Slovenia. These more advanced Republics consider that the country's economic problems could be more effectively solved by following their example. And the quiescent but strong national feelings of the Serbs have been violently stirred by the events in Kosovo.

7. Indeed, the main present nationalist threat to Yugoslav unity remains the resurgence of Albanian nationalism which followed Tito's death. In its policy platform of last December, the Party, whilst acknowledging the many other causes of disaffection in the Province, especially backwardness and the too rapid expansion of higher education, accepted that nationalism not class was the root cause of Albanian discontent. This is most acutely concentrated in the call for republican status which the Serbs in particular refuse to grant. The problem steadily worsens as the high Albanian birth rate coupled with the continued migration of Serbs and Montenegrins from the Province change Kosovo into an ethnically pure Albanian land.

8. The central authorities have shown they are determined to deal with Kosovo's underlying economical and social problems. They have also shown, at least for the present, that they can contain the security situation. But to do so they have been compelled to concentrate additional troops and police forces in the Province, to purge the local Party, educational and other institutions, and to arrest and pass stiff prison sentences on Albanian nationalists, mostly teachers and students, often for such minor political offences as distributing pamphlets and chalking up slogans. This hardly accords with the official policy of ethnic reconciliation and respect for human rights. The immediate alternative would, however, probably be worse: a stronger, better organised Albanian nationalist and probably irredentist movement which would not only disrupt the Federation but could also destabilise the whole region.

9. Eventually, Yugoslavia must devise ways to satisfy Kosovo's political demands, acceptable also to the Serbs. Meanwhile, it has to persuade the Albanians

in Kosovo that their material and other needs are best met within Yugoslavia. One line of advance would be to strengthen Kosovo's political links with the Federation at the expense of Serbia, e.g. by making it an autonomous Province of the former. But this is, unfortunately, not yet practical politics. So, for the time being, we can only welcome the central authorities' more rational plans for Kosovo's economic and social development and its care in not using excessive force to control the Province. The limited regard for human rights can be accepted as the lesser evil. But many other ethnic groups, including Serbs outside Serbia proper, criticise the Serbian handling of the Kosovo problem. It remains a major source of disunity.

Economic stability

10. The other major and growing challenge to Yugoslavia's stability is its serious economic situation. Mistakes were made in the seventies, in Tito's days, when Yugoslavia built too much and too extravagantly with too great reliance on foreign credits, some of which were perhaps too readily accorded. Now the creditors have to be paid at a time when foreign conditions, especially high interest rates and a world recession, make it more difficult for Yugoslavia to meet its obligations.

11. In this field, Tito's absence seems, initially at least, to have helped. All are agreed that he had little time for, or understanding of economics and this made it easier for others to squander. Soon after his death, the dinar was, however inadequately, devalued and a start made in putting Yugoslavia's economic house in order. This effort was put in the hands of a special Federal commission under the then President, Kraigher. So far, the commission has produced an all-embracing outline plan, important elements of which are an acknowledgement of the need to respect economic laws, to become more closely involved in the world market and to practise more self-reliance. The commission is now beginning to issue detailed guidelines on particular subjects: four of the projected sixteen have already emerged. The problem is to apply these plans to the economy and there is the rub. Present indications are that the leadership is still confronted by such obstacles as: the stubborn resistance of the Republics and Provinces to a unified Yugoslav market; the refusal of the workers, helped by the self-management institutions, to limit their wages to accord with the real value of what they produce; the failure sufficiently to increase exports to the convertible markets: the intractable problem of foreign financial obligations; and a deep seated ideological resistance to an emerging mixed economy.

12. But the leadership is clearly determined to push its policies through. Politically, it is trying to increase central control through the Party by strengthening discipline over its individual members and the local Republican, Provincial and lower Party organisations. It demands that laws and regulations, often disregarded, should be obeyed. Economically, the Party has put its weight behind some increasingly tough measures. It has now accepted as its most urgent task the servicing and repayment of its foreign debts; it has publicly rejected re-scheduling, saying it will not put off until a probably more difficult tomorrow the need to rationalise and to make necessary sacrifices today; it has ordered a reduction in investments and in personal incomes and whilst expressing its confidence in retaining the people's support, has made constitutional provision to deal with civil unrest. The leadership seems prepared to liberalise its economy still further by introducing more elements of private enterprise: the Prime Minister, Mrs Planinc, has spoken out in favour of 'rich peasants'. But, if it is to succeed, Yugoslavia must impose more effective economic constraints and accept even

greater exposure to market forces at home and abroad. Above all, it needs time and support from the West: the acceptance of more Yugoslav exports and the provision of credits to help meet the heavy repayments which are now falling due and to pay for essential imports. The problem for the West is to encourage Yugoslavia to follow sensible economic policies which take account of its political system but at the same time do not weaken its resolution to cure its economic ills. This will require not only willingness but nice judgment.

Democratic Communism?

13. Another potential cause of instability in Yugoslavia is the contradiction between Communism and democracy which its leaders continue to try, albeit reluctantly, to resolve. The problem arose as a major consequence of Yugoslavia's escape from Moscow's grasp which enabled and, indeed, partly compelled the leadership to develop a new and independent form of Communism. Djilas[2] went too far and was stopped. Kardelj,[3] Tito's theoretician, tried to bridge the gap bequeathing his tortuous writings as proof in itself he had failed. Tito's death suggested to many that, as in other fields, Yugoslavia could now advance to a more democratic system. And, as I have reported, the last Party Congress was preceded by a vigorous discussion of ways of democratising the system, including the Party itself, and was conducted in a refreshingly free atmosphere. Unfortunately, the outcome of the Congress revealed no major advance. But Yugoslavia has already in some respects moved closer towards a free society and I have seen no significant retreat.

14. Yugoslavs describe their path towards Communism as socialist self-management. This system is not, as its name suggests, limited to industrial democracy but also covers, under the curious title 'pluralism of self-managing interests', the people's participation in and control of all aspects of life, political and social as well as economic. The system in effect attempts to provide a unique theory and practice of socialism different from the 'real socialism' of the Soviet Union (which Yugoslavs never mention without a sneer) as well as Western social-democracy but combining the positive aspects of each. In theory, it inevitably emerges as a concatenation of contradictions and often, in practice, in plain dishonesty or patent excuse. All I need say here is that, neither in theory nor practice, can the Yugoslav people be considered to manage their lives themselves, in all their variety, if at the same time they must live in a society ruled in accordance with the (recently reaffirmed) principle of democratic centralism with the accent as in all Communist societies on the element of command. For the Party leaders to square the circle by acting as if they know better than individual Yugoslavs what they want in effect removes 'self' from the title of their system. Then, we are back to a form, albeit modified in practice, of Soviet Communism.

15. But accepting the limitations of socialist self-management, which is clearly no panacea, it is important to note that Yugoslav Communism has developed ahead of Soviet Communism and has the potential to advance even further. The Yugoslav system eschews dogmatism and, as the Party Programme proudly proclaims in its final sentence, positively welcomes change. It calls also for variety between countries, which is basic to freedom, and within countries for maximum participation by the people. In practice, it has created institutions and established a

[2] Milovan Djilas (1911-95), Yugoslav politician active in asserting the country's independence from the Soviet Union in 1948. He later became disillusioned with Communism and was at various times imprisoned for his critical writings.

[3] Edvard Kardelj (1910-79), Yugoslav revolutionary and politician, and close colleague of Tito.

way of life which strengthen freedom and encourage its expansion. Yugoslavia has, for example, already achieved extreme administrative devolution enabling the main ethnic groups largely to rule themselves; most peasants till their own land; the media is remarkably free; the frontiers are open; the Assembly system and even Party organs conduct their affairs increasingly in public; the Churches too enjoy considerable freedom; and so on. Not surprisingly, the Party keeps cracking the whip—against the popular press, over-demanding priests and the more root-and-branch dissidents—but it tends to do this discreetly as if somewhat ashamed and concerned at possible foreign reactions.

16. Yugoslavia certainly remains Communist and, even in its modified form, stops well short of Western systems. And friends within the Party here, when explaining the less attractive aspects of their country, are the first to admit that further progress is resisted by Party stalwarts, purblind and jealous of their power and privileges, who are strong in the *apparat* and Party organs, especially in the south-eastern backwoods. Half the new Central Committee, I should note, joined the Party before 1945 and are 56 years old or over: young critical intellectuals call the CC 'The Old People's Home'! But the trend towards more freedom, although in no way yet dominant, is clear. Hundreds of thousands of *gastarbeiter*[4] bring back, so the Orthodox Patriarch German confirmed to me, not only higher material standards but also Western democratic ideas. They are a strong force for desirable change. Progress towards more democracy continues to be made and it is in our interest that not only Yugoslavia should emerge from its traditional Communist shell but also that this possibility should exist as an example to others living under Communism. The fact that Yugoslavia moves forward without excessive haste is also to be welcomed. For the alternative could so easily be a setback similar to that suffered by other revisionists who went too far, too fast, in Hungary, Czechoslovakia and Poland.

Independence

17. Turning to Yugoslavia's international policies, pride of place must be given to its stubborn determination to maintain its independence. It has deep roots. But, going no further back than the Second World War, when Stalin took the opportunity to extend and consolidate Soviet Russian rule over Eastern Europe, the Yugoslav leadership refused, successfully, to submit. As a Communist *de souche*, a participant in the Russian Revolution and a believer in Stalin, Tito was very reluctant to accept a break with Moscow: but, as a Yugoslav, he would not bend the knee. Against all Khrushchev's wiles and bluster and Brezhnev's more discreet wooing, he persisted in this policy to his death. And his successors have not weakened. On the contrary, lacking Tito's emotional attachment, they may well prove to be more consistent. At their recent Party Congress, they even more firmly and insistently underlined Yugoslavia's independence. They asserted that Tito's major contribution to the international Communist and progressive movement was his re-statement of the theory of separate paths and they distributed blame equally to both blocs for endangering peace. All of which, we know, was anathema to the Soviet delegation. It is reassuring to us and bile to Moscow that Yugoslavia continues to publish books and articles condemning Stalinism and factual accounts of developments in e.g. Afghanistan and Poland which clearly show whence comes the major threat to independence and democratic change.

[4] 'Guest workers'.

18. By refusing to accept Moscow's diktat, Yugoslavia made and continues to make, an important contribution to weakening the Soviet Union as a world force. It called into question the Soviet concept and control of the so-called Socialist Community and the world Communist movement; it exposed Soviet expansionism and prevented Russia from taking over the central Balkans and so becoming a Mediterranean power; and, particularly by helping to establish the Non-Aligned Movement and, subsequently, by preventing Cuba lining up the Movement behind its 'natural ally', it obstructed Soviet efforts to extend its influence in the Third World. Yugoslavia does not falter in following these essentially anti-Soviet paths.

19. More generally, Yugoslavia has become a force for moderation and stability in world affairs. Of course, it remains anti-colonialist but there is now little Western colonialism to worry about in this context and, in the Falklands dispute, Yugoslavia proved fairly helpful. It continues to champion South against North in economic matters but it is trying to bridge rather than increase the gap between them. It is still obsessed by Bulgaria's alleged threat to 'Macedonia' and demonstrates an over-protective concern for its minorities in Austria and Italy, whilst denying it to Albania in Kosovo, but Yugoslavia puts good-neighbourliness first and so helps to maintain calm in this potentially dangerous region. Altogether, Yugoslavia can be irritatingly principled and impractical in pretending (though less convincingly without Tito) to be a leader of the world's 'progressive forces'. But even this we should welcome as a useful antidote to the spread of more poisonous doctrines and designs from further East.

To sum up

20. All that has happened in Yugoslavia since Tito died, taken with all he did inside and outside his country, confirms, I think, that we are responding to our interests in strengthening our links with Yugoslavia and doing what we can to help it remain stable, united and independent, even under a Communist government. This is particularly important at present when Yugoslavia is experiencing extremely serious economic problems and there are indications of political change. There are, I know, many other countries in similar or worse positions. But in the East-West confrontation, which remains the most serious threat to world peace and freedom, Yugoslavia is essentially on our side. Yugoslavia's leaders and people intend to keep it there and it seems to me clearly in Britain's interests that they should succeed.

Personal note

21. Unfortunately, my thirty-five years now end. They have been good years for me, made possible by the social changes following the War. In so many fields, including our Service, Britain then showed that, although our society is no exception in not being able to exist without privilege, it can adapt even its most exclusive institutions, including its Diplomatic Service, to meet the requirements of changing times. Britain has also showed that our Service can, certainly for its members serving overseas, without accepting any label, approach that demanding ideal: 'From each according to his ability, to each according to his needs'. It is this, together with the way we help each other both professionally and domestically, as I have found in all my posts in often difficult and even hostile environments, which makes working in our Service so worthwhile.

22. I am sending copies of this despatch to Her Majesty's Representatives at Moscow and Washington, to the UK Representative at NATO and also to Her Majesty's Consul-General at Zagreb.[5]

I am, etc,
EDWIN BOLLAND

[5] Mr Broomfield replied to the new Ambassador, Mr Scott, on 3 November. He thought the despatch bore out the predictions which were common ground between the Embassy and EESD in early 1980 (see No. 7). He did not think that the UK was doing enough to provide the Yugoslavs with the material help they badly needed: 'The Yugoslavs have chosen a bad time to go broke', and there were 'severe constraints' upon what the UK could do materially to help. 'The Polish and Romanian debacles and the Hungarian liquidity crisis have soured Western attitudes and created a much chillier climate than the Yugoslavs either expected or deserved to meet with in the West.' He hoped that in dealing with the economic crisis the UK would not call for measures which might precipitate a political crisis. 'Tito was fortunate to the extent that he was never really obliged to face up to the economic problems in which he took so little interest.' But for his successors time had run out. 'The problems exist; there are no easy answers: failure could well place the very survival of the Federation at risk.' But there were at least two factors in favour of workable solutions: the present leadership's own determination (and the Yugoslav's own toughness and instinct for survival) to work through things; and 'the slow burgeoning of democratic thought-processes and procedures' which suggested that perhaps 'its unique brand of socialism may be better adapted than Soviet Communism . . . to evolve flexible responses to intractable but unavoidable problems.'

No. 180

Note from Mr Rifkind to Mr Pym, 6 October 1982
Confidential (FCO 28/4859, ENG 026/2)

Secretary of State,

Visit to Bulgaria and Romania

1. I visited Bulgaria and Romania from 26 September to 3 October. In Bulgaria I had talks with First Deputy Foreign Minister Ivanov, with Deputy Minister Yordanov, with the Minister of Foreign Trade and the Chairman of the Agro-Industrial Union. I also spent a day at the Plovdiv Trade Fair where I briefly met the Prime Minister Mr Fillipov. In Romania I had talks with Mr Duma, the Minister Secretary of State (i.e. number two in the MFA) and with the Minister of Foreign Trade. I also visited the Rombac complex where BAC 111s[1] are being made under licence. In both countries the Foreign Ministers were away in New York at the General Assembly.

2. The visit confirmed my impression of the diversity of Eastern Europe. Not only are there differing interpretations of Marxism-Leninism, but national characteristics and in many cases a sense of nationalism often came through strongly.

3. Bulgaria has chosen the path of public conformity with the Soviet Union. There are historical reasons for this. The Russians liberated them from the Turks in 1876 and thus reinforced a feeling of common Slav identity with the Russians (the vocabulary of their languages for instance is almost identical). But increasingly if discreetly they seem to be emphasising their Bulgarian identity. The 1300th anniversary of the foundation of the Bulgarian state offered an obvious opportunity for this. When President Zhivkov told the Party Congress that Bulgarians had a

[1] See No. 2, note 43.

proud history, were nobody's slave and could stand on their own, the conference rose and cheered him to the echo with unscripted enthusiasm. The Panorama of Culture which I visited had only one exhibit among dozens which mentioned fraternal relations with Big Brother.

4. Helped by their outward conformity, the Bulgarians have successfully set about creating a better life. The first emphasis (a marked contrast with Poland or the Soviet Union) has been on agriculture, and the Bulgarians now claim to be 150% self-sufficient in food. In industry they have tried to skip a generation by concentrating on electronics. The new technocrats are gradually coming forward, and may ultimately provide a more flexible and pragmatic style of economic management than the first generation communists of solid peasant stock. At the moment Bulgaria with a population of only 8 million and relatively undeveloped, provides only a small market for British goods. But the representatives of British firms to whom I spoke at the Plovdiv Trade Fair confirmed that it was worth doing business if only on a small scale, and worth hanging on until the effects of greater prosperity increase Bulgaria's capacity to import from the West. In particular they were impressed by Bulgaria's success in avoiding the debt problems of their neighbours by modest economic investment.

5. I was driven by car from Bulgaria to Romania. The contrast was dramatic. Romania is a fertile country which is clearly failing to make the most of its potential. In the plains of the South we saw weed-ridden crops being gathered by hand. In the North's sub-alpine scenery things are better, but this is small scale sheep farming, some still in private hands. In Bucharest a faceless shabby concrete jungle is slowly enveloping what was justifiably called the Paris of Central Europe in the 19th century. At night the city is illuminated by 30 watt light-bulbs in order to reduce energy consumption, but it makes for a dingy impression, even by Eastern European standards. Politically, Romania is an unpleasant dictatorship where most law making appears to be done by capricious presidential decrees. They make extraordinary reading: one may not use a refrigerator in winter; all glassed-in verandas (of which we saw many) must be opened up and the glass removed so that food otherwise left in refrigerators can in winter be left in the open; with immediate effect, no-one may keep a dog in a flat. In the shops, coffee has not been available for 12 months, neither has flour, and meat is in such short supply that people even throw away their monthly ration cards. In an attempt to put the blame other than on the President, Ministers are being reshuffled with increasing regularity. As a result, the administration is coming slowly to a stand-still.

6. On the other hand Romania continues to plough its own furrow in foreign policy. Mr Duma was at pains to emphasise to me points where Romanian views are not synonymous with those of the Soviet Union: Afghanistan, the Reagan zero option, their non-acceptance of the philosophy of 'spheres of influence'. They clearly dislike the Russians deeply and during my visit to Moldavia the MFA officials accompanying me felt free enough to express this quite openly. And the Romanians continue to refuse to allow Warsaw Pact troops to be stationed in or pass through their country. It continues to be of some limited use to us to encourage this grey sheep in the Soviet flock but I believe that until there is a change in the style of their internal government, it would be impolitic to identify ourselves too closely with the Romanians. They are clearly aware of the impression that their financial mismanagement and political system have created on their Western interlocutors. With the gracelessness that characterises most

Romanian officials, Mr Duma treated me to an uninterrupted (and uninterruptable) discourse on the basic strengths of the Romanian economy and the unrivalled merits of their democracy. Perhaps there is no Romanian word for credibility gap.

7. The main bilateral point at issue is the aircraft plant which I visited and which has now completed the first BAC 111 under licence from BAe and Rolls Royce and with some supervisory help by British technicians. This and the petrochemical industry is Romania's major industrial achievement and they have invested a lot of national pride in it. The British technicians told me that their individual Romanian counterparts were very good. The problem is that they have no experience in managing a complex project of this sort and the habit of referring decisions upwards has the effect of delaying progress even further. I am sure that we will be confronted by some difficult political and financial decisions before long. The Romanians are already looking to BAe to sell the planes for them. They are also gradually realising that with its present engine the BAC 111 will be too noisy for most airports from 1986 onwards and probably too thirsty to attract hard currency buyers. They will argue that BAe and Rolls Royce should bear the major part of the development costs for a redesigned engine. While this is in the first place a matter for the companies, we will not be able to escape entirely. There is a large Government involvement through the provision of official credits. And President Ceausescu himself is politically committed and will look to HMG to help resolve any problems. If the project collapses Anglo-Romanian relations will be reduced to pretty well nothing while he remains in power.

8. An independent Romanian foreign policy is an embarrassment to the Soviet Union and a reproof to the more docile Communist regimes such as GDR and Czechoslovakia. It is in our interests that Romania should remain able to pursue such a policy and thus while we do not wish to identify too closely with the present regime we should not encourage developments that would force Romania to return to greater dependence on the Soviet Union.[2]

MALCOLM RIFKIND

[2] The PUS noted on 8 October: 'A rather optimistic description of Bulgaria which I was glad to read. I have not been there. The description of Romania tallies exactly with my own memories from Jan 1982. The BAC 111 problem could well be difficult. The fact is that it's a somewhat obsolete plane already.'

No. 181

Minute from Mr Broomfield to Sir J. Bullard, 7 October 1982

Confidential (FCO 28/5001, ENP 212/1)

Poland: Trade Union Legislation

1. It now seems certain that the Polish authorities will introduce a law on trade unions in the Sejm for discussion on 8 and 9 October. The result will be that suspended Solidarity will then be outlawed.[1]

2. You may wish to have a brief summary of where action now stands and our preliminary comments on the legislation.

Action

[1] The legislation was passed on 8 October (Warsaw tel. No. 935, 9 October; FCO 28/ 5001, ENP 212/1).

(*a*) Agreement has been reached in the Ten that a démarche will be made today in Warsaw to warn the Poles that measures of the kind they have in mind would constitute 'a most regrettable obstacle for more normal relations between their countries and Poland'.[2]
(*b*) The US, Canada and possibly other NATO countries may act similarly.
(*c*) The Presidency have undertaken to circulate a draft of the statement they might make on behalf of the Ten after the legislation has been passed. I have spoken to UKDEL NATO and asked them to stimulate discussion in NATO on 8 October to try to reach agreement on the common elements of individual NATO countries' responses to the passage of the legislation.[3] They will also seek to coordinate a line on the effect of the new legislation on the three NATO criteria.
(*d*) Our instructions are contained in FCO telno 263.[4] Our intention is to try to avoid statements which, by reaffirming rigidly the existing three criteria, make more difficult future development of relations between the West and Poland. Even though now is clearly not the time to change our existing policy.
Comments

3. I attach a note prepared by Research Department on what appear to be the points of difference between the new legislation and the Gdansk Agreement.[5] These can only be preliminary at this stage. We will be submitting more detailed comments as soon as we have received the full text of the new law and the Council of States' resolution from Warsaw.

4. It is clear that considerable care has been taken by the Polish authorities in retaining the words, if not the spirit, of the Gdansk Agreement. The fact is that the Gdansk Agreement was a lengthy document consisting of 21 points only three or four of which were directly relevant to trade union activities. The main substantive differences seem to me to be:

(*a*) The form of the unions is to be decided by the State and not the workers.
(*b*) The form chosen by the State is to have limited factory based unions and not a wide all-embracing structure such as Solidarity.
(*c*) It is to be a long process stretched until the end of 1984. Not until the end of 1983 will individual factory unions be able to combine into country-wide industrial unions.
(*d*) No unions are allowed for farmers, i.e., rural Solidarity (the Gdansk documents called for the creation of conditions to revive rural self-government).
(*e*) Labour courts or arbitration courts are to be set up to decide on strikes and whether the unions are acting legally. One report indicates that management are

[2] The Danish Ambassador delivered the text of the *démarche* to the deputy Foreign Minister Mr Olechowski (COREU CPE MUL 3749, 11 October 1982; FCO 28/ 4956, ENP 022/1).

[3] On 8 October Mr Graham reported that the US *chargé* said at the NAC meeting that it was inconceivable that the Soviet Union did not have a hand in the legislation banning Solidarity. The US hoped that NATO governments would reaffirm their January statement on the three conditions and indicate that NATO's position in the CSCE would not remain unaffected. They were also opposed to the rescheduling of the Polish debt (UKDEL NATO tel. No. 1386; FCO 28/ 4963, ENP 022/2).

[4] Not printed.

[5] Not printed. This undated note highlighted that the new draft legislation proposed the dissolution of *all* existing trade unions—including Solidarity—and the creation of single unions for each branch of industry. The main difference was that the Gdańsk agreement stipulated that pre-1981 unions and Solidarity would co-exist together.

to be heavily represented and would therefore be in a position to out-vote workers' representatives in these courts.

(*f*) Finally of course, no strikes are permitted under martial law. It remains to be seen how frequently the Sejm suspend the right to strike by particular resolutions (para 9 of Warsaw telno 919).[4]

5. I agree with Mr James that the draft law will probably provide a remarkably independent structure for trade unions if judged by existing standards in Eastern Europe. But the new law will be judged by standards set by Solidarity.

6. Much will now depend on the reaction to the new law by Solidarity and the Church. If both reject the limited opportunities offered in the legislation then it will indeed turn out to be as empty as its opponents suggest. The country's economic and political problems will be no nearer solution.

7. As far as the West is concerned the first occasion on which views on the new legislation are likely to be given is in the ILO. Mr James reports that a Polish delegation is on its way to Geneva to obtain ILO approval. Mr Thom,[6] reporting reactions from contacts in the TUC suggests, however, that with the possible exception of the French Communist CGT, there will be no support from the West in the ILO unless all detained Solidarity members are released and unless Lech Walesa and other leading Solidarity members are involved in some way with the new structure. We are checking to see whether HMG will have to voice an opinion in the ILO.

8. The legislation is also likely to have wider effects. Reports from Bonn indicate that the Germans are concerned that the US attitude to the CSCE will become even more resistant to the idea of negotiating the final document. I would expect the US position also to harden against rescheduling of Poland's official debts. This will be decided in the Experts Meeting in Paris on 25/26 October.

9. As far as the pipeline is concerned, the Americans (Secretary Baldridge—Washington telno 3721)[7] are continuing to emphasize that Poland alone is the President's concern. If that is still ostensibly true, the legislation will not make the resolution of the sanctions problem any easier.

10. As far as our own relations with Poland are concerned there is clearly no question of changing our present policy over such issues as political contacts, etc, for the time being. The legislation has, however, given an impetus to look at the longer term. The Dutch commented yesterday in the Political Committee that the three Western conditions risked becoming absurd. We should take this opportunity to try to focus attention on the need for some sort of longer term relationship with Poland which takes account of the new, if depressing, realities there. In public, rather than urging 'the Polish authorities to end the state of martial law, to release those arrested, and to restore immediately a dialogue with the Church and Solidarity' (11 Jan NATO declaration), we might move more towards the sentence which follows immediately on from that passage, which reads 'only with reconciliation and genuine negotiation can the basic rights of the Polish people and

[6] There appears to be a confusion of name between Mr Thom—the Commercial Secretary in Warsaw—and Mr Toms—the Overseas Labour Adviser at the FCO. Mr Toms had provided this analysis to Mrs Macgregor on 30 September.

[7] Not printed. There was disagreement within the US administration on how best to deal with the West Siberian pipeline issue. See *Foreign Relations of the United States*, 1981–1988, Volume III, Soviet Union, January 1981-January 1983, ed. James Graham Wilson (Washington: Government Printing Office 2016).

workers be protected and the economic and social progress of the country be secured'.[8]

N. H. R. A. BROOMFIELD

[8] On 7 October Mr Bullard summarized the new planned legislation as: 'no going back to August 1980, but no going back to December 1981 either'. On the 8th Mr Bone, the Foreign Secretary's APS, stated that the Foreign Secretary wanted to pursue the proposals in paragraph 10 of the submission as the Ten seem to be in an 'untenable posture now'. On the 9th an FCO statement strongly 'deplored' the recent action by the Polish regime against Solidarity as contrary to the spirit of the Helsinki Final Act and 'a further obstacle to the restoration of normal relations with Poland' (FCO to all COREU, 15 October 1982; FCO 28/4956, ENP 022/1). On 19 October Mr James reported to London a 'fairly disagreeable meeting' with the Polish Foreign Minister, whom he had informed of the content of the UK statement. The Foreign Minister 'rejected utterly' the 'objectionable' UK statement; said that martial law was intended to be abolished as soon as possible, that the situation would normalise and the economy would modernise (Warsaw tel. No. 979; FCO 28/4932, ENP 020/3).

No. 182

Mr Pym to Sir J. Graham (UKDEL NATO), 10 October 1982, 4.51 p.m.

Tel. No. 272[1] Immediate, Confidential (FCO 28/4963, ENP 022/2)

Poland: Trade Union Legislation

Your telno 390.[2]

1. MIFT[2] contains points for you to make at the special meeting of the North Atlantic Council (NAC) on 11 October.

2. At this meeting your first objective should be to maintain the alliance solidarity established between Foreign Ministers at La Sapinière[3] and to prevent the Polish trade union legislation becoming another apple of transatlantic discord. The mood in Washington and among American participants at this weekend's conference at Ditchley[4] suggests that there is a serious risk of this happening unless all concerned stick to the approach agreed upon at La Sapinière.

3. Secondly, you should seek to ensure that any national or joint action by NATO governments in response to the Polish events is taken on a rational basis and related to considered objectives. Here too we see a risk of emotion taking over in the American camp. Nevertheless, we could agree to concerted measures which while not particularly significant in themselves serve to maintain the unity of the alliance which is our primary objective.

4. Third, if the idea commands general acceptance we should like to use these developments as the occasion to launch a fresh look by the Alliance at our policy towards Poland, and towards the Soviet Union in the Polish context. Some of the hopes entertained immediately after the imposition of martial law that the situation

[1] Repeated for Immediate to Lisbon; Information Immediate to Damascus (for Private Secretary), Washington, Paris, Bonn, UKREP Brussels, UKMIS New York, Warsaw; Priority to other NATO posts, Dublin, Moscow; Routine to Budapest, Sofia, Prague, East Berlin and Bucharest.

[2] Not printed.

[3] A hotel in the Laurentian Mountains in Canada where NATO foreign ministers, including Mr Pym, met on 3 October. They agreed to aim to coordinate Western trade policy with the Soviet bloc and to initiate a number of studies on individual aspects of East-West economic relations such as strategic goods, high technology, credit policy and energy.

[4] The title of the conference from 8 to 10 October was: 'The Soviet Union: the internal situation and its implications for the West.'

inside Poland could be reversed seem certain to be disappointed. We believe that the time is right for the alliance to embark upon a thorough examination of its policy towards Poland. We are therefore suggesting that you propose a special meeting of the NAC which would be tasked to ensure that policy during the next year or two serves the Alliance as well as the decisions of 11 January 1982 have done during this year. We would envisage such a new policy being announced at the Ministerial meeting in December, when the imminent first anniversary of martial law will in any case necessitate some serious public statement by the Alliance.

5. If time permits, you should go over your instructions beforehand with the French and Germans. Bullard is hoping to reach Andreani[5] and Pfeffer[6] by telephone.

6. If you think it would be helpful, you should also compare notes in advance with the Americans. The point to impress on them is the one in the first sentence of Shultz's summing up at La Sapinière, namely that individual decisions in East/West relations need to be taken on the basis of a comprehensive policy, not piecemeal.

7. Lisbon: Williams[7] is aware of our general approach, but you should make some arrangement to ensure that he is informed of the contents of these telegrams after his arrival at Lisbon this evening and kept up to date with further developments during the meeting of Heads of NATO Delegations for the Madrid conference at Sintra on 11 October.[8]

8. These instructions have been approved by Mr Rifkind but are subject to any comments from the Secretary of State.

[5] Director of the Policy Planning Staff at the French Ministry of Foreign Affairs.

[6] Political Director at the Ministry of Foreign Affairs of the FRG.

[7] Leader of the UK Delegation to the CSCE Review Meeting in Madrid.

[8] The NATO Council meeting opened with the US representative announcing President Reagan's steps to suspend Poland's most-favoured-nation (MFN) status. He invited Allies to suggest further steps, repeated that they should reaffirm the declaration of 11 January, adopt a common position on the rescheduling of the Polish debt and acknowledge that NATO's position on the CSCE would be influenced by events in Poland. He recommended a unified approach to maximize pressure on the Soviet and Polish Governments. Sir J. Graham kept closely to his instructions. He stated that the UK recognised the need for solidarity in the Alliance's condemnation of the latest Polish developments, but that the declaration of 11 January no longer seemed entirely adequate or realistic. He agreed with the Danish delegate that Poland's MFN status was a matter for the EC. (The record of the Council meeting can be found on the NATO website: www.nato.int.)

No. 183

Mr James (Warsaw) to Lord Carrington, 13 October 1982, 10.10 a.m.
Tel. No. 951[1] Immediate, Confidential (FCO 28/4911, ENP 014/1)

Poland

1. Communications to Gdansk and other Polish coastal cities remained cut off yesterday. Reports reaching journalists in Warsaw indicated that the Lenin

[1] Repeated Priority to Moscow, Washington, UKDEL NATO, UKMIS Geneva; Saving to East Berlin, Prague, Sofia, Belgrade, Bucharest, Budapest, Helsinki, Stockholm, Paris, Bonn, UKMIS New York, UKREP Brussels and MODUK.

shipyard and a number of other factories in Gdansk had again gone on strike. Others were operating a go-slow.

2. Yesterday morning workers from morning and afternoon shifts arrived together at the Lenin shipyard at 6 a.m., fearing a lockout, but this did not take place. The strikers, who evidently comprised a significant part of the total workforce of 16,000, declared an intention to continue the strike daily from 6 a.m. to 2 p.m. until their demands were met (see my telno 944).[2] Thus only the afternoon maintenance shift continues normal work. At some stage during the day, the shipyard was placed under military control. It is not clear how this will affect planned continued strike action today.

3. There was an attempted march by some 3000 demonstrators through the streets to the local Communist party headquarters, and a gathering by the Solidarity monument near the shipyard. Both demonstrations were dispersed by security forces. According to one journalist, security forces then continued to patrol the streets of Gdansk in force in an apparent attempt to intimidate the population. It is said that they fired tear gas, smoke and percussion grenades at small groups of pedestrians or at random from their armoured vehicles.

4. There are few reports of unrest from elsewhere in the country, though telephone communications to Grudziaz, some 100 kilometres south of Gdansk were cut off during the day. Reports from Nowa Huta (near Krakow) indicate that some workers there are considering strike action today but others may wish to delay this until 10 November, on which day a general strike has been called for by underground Solidarity leaders (this is the second anniversary of the registration of Solidarity).

5. The authorities have again attempted to play down the significance of the strikes. At a lunchtime press conference yesterday given by Urban, the Government spokesman, it was stressed that normal work continued at most factories in the Gdansk area, and strike participation at the Lenin shipyard was limited to 10-13% of the workforce. On 11 October only 8 factories had gone on strike he said. An attempt was made to play up the hooligan nature of the riots. Urban said the authorities had made a considerable number of arrests (reports reaching journalists in Warsaw speak of at least 150). He admitted that rioters had attempted to build barricades and that unrest had continued late into the night. Polish TV also gave coverage to the rioting.

6. The riot control methods of the authorities in Gdansk are heavy-handed and indiscriminate. We have also had a number of reports of police harassment of some Western (but not British) news teams (and particularly of Polish nationals employed by them). This has taken the form of arrest, detention and temporary confiscation of documents.

7. FCO please pass to savings addressees.

[2] Not printed. In this telegram of 12 October, Mr James had reported to London the workers' reactions to the new trade union law, with up to 4,000 men setting up a strike committee in Gdańsk, which began a strike for the duration of their shift. They distributed leaflets calling for the reinstatement of Solidarity and the freeing of internees and promoting strike action in Gdynia and Szczecin (FCO 28/5001, ENP 212/1).

No. 184

Submission from Mr Broomfield to Sir J. Bullard, 14 October 1982
Confidential (FCO 28/4926, ENP 020/1)

Policy on Poland

1. UKDEL NATO telno 395[1] reports agreement to a reinforced NAC meeting on 20 October. Do you wish me to attend. The US 'expert' will be Deputy Assistant Secretary Blackwill.

2. I *submit* a policy paper on Poland[2] which might form the basis of our intervention at the NAC meeting. Comments from the other departments have been included.[3] There remain, however, two major problems, one economic and the other political.

3. The political problem relates to the three criteria. Solidarity is outlawed. I do not think that any organisation called Solidarity will be permitted again. To go on calling for the three criteria in the terms of the 11 January Declaration will impale us on an unfulfillable condition. But to drop any mention of Solidarity now will be seen as an act of political betrayal. We can in our speeches and statements draw a distinction between the structure and the spirit, etc. But at some stage on 20 October in NATO and thereafter at the Ministerial meetings running up to 13 December we will be asked the direct question, do we still subscribe to the three criteria? I do not think we can say no. And I am not very confident that we will be able to persuade the Americans to reformulate them.[4]

4. The economic problem is well known. The UK is not in a position to subscribe to an economic/financial inducement to the Polish authorities to make concessions in the social and political fields. President Reagan has restated the US offer. The FRG (cynically) may support them. We cannot. I would suggest that we see whether there is any support for the US position in the NAC before deciding whether to return to this in Whitehall. But without such an offer UK policy is virtually all stick and no carrot.

5. Mr Williamson (ESID) has drawn attention to another apparent inconsistency. Do we in fact wish the Polish economy to recover and pay back its debts? Or would we prefer the Polish economic crisis to continue and thereby prolong the divisive effect of Poland within the Warsaw Pact? I prefer the first choice, particularly if it can be accompanied by the sorts of economic reform introduced in Hungary.

6. We have to consider the question of Whitehall handling. Departments are aware of the NAC meeting and concerned that the US will put pressure on its allies to come up with further economic measures. Subject to your views we could either circulate a paper on the lines attached or inform the other Departments that we

[1] Not printed.

[2] See Enclosure.

[3] The British Embassy in Warsaw also commented on the draft.

[4] In UKDEL NATO tel. No. 405 of 20 October, Sir J. Graham reported that at the NAC meeting there was no support for further sanctions but widespread caution about changing Allied policies or public positions. The US insisted that the 'three criteria' should remain at the heart of Alliance policy. In the margins of the meeting the US representative had urged the UK against adding to current strains between the US and its allies by seeking to revise the policy set out in the 11 January Declaration, suggesting any reformulation of the three criteria or making any other changes might send the wrong signals at the present time (Mr Broomfield to Mr James, 28 October 1982; FCO 28/4963, ENP 022/2).

were not contemplating further economic measures. The NAC meeting would in our view be mainly concerned with the political aspects of our present policy. An opportunity to do this will arise at a meeting which the Cabinet Office have called for 1200 hours tomorrow, 15 October, to discuss EC Trade Policy towards Poland.

7. I also *submit* a draft brief[5] for the informal Foreign Ministers meeting on 16/17 October.[6]

N. H. R. A. BROOMFIELD

ENCLOSURE IN NO. 184

Policy towards Poland

Introduction

1. The present crisis in Poland is in some ways different in quality from previous crises in Eastern Europe. Poland has traditionally been the least receptive to the communist regime imposed since the end of the war. The present acute phase of the crisis has lasted since August 1980, although it has changed in character from an open attempt at a political and economic revolution to simmering rebellion at martial law. Any policies adopted by the West should take the long term nature of the problem into account.

Objectives

2. The West's objectives since the beginning of the Polish crisis have been:

(*a*) to avoid Soviet military intervention in Poland;

(*b*) to keep alive the prospect of a return by Poland to the path of renewal and reform;

(*c*) to preserve as much as possible of the gains made by Solidarity;

(*d*) to preserve Poland as a divisive and debilitating element in the Warsaw Pact and the CMEA;

(*e*) so far as possible to ensure that Western measures bite upon the Polish regime rather than upon the Polish people.

(*f*) to ensure that the international aspects of the Polish crisis do not get out of control;

(*g*) to do nothing which might prejudice the eventual repayment by the Poles of their international debts.

Western Measures

3. The measures adopted initially by Western Governments were intended:

(*a*) to express strong disapproval both to the Polish regime and to the Soviet Union;

(*b*) to make it clear to the Soviet Union that further actions such as military intervention in Poland would incur considerably greater costs;

(*c*) to make it clear to the Polish authorities that failure to live up to their own promises to return to the path of reform and renewal would have a damaging effect on their relations with the Western countries;

(*d*) to put pressure on the Polish regime to act with restraint;

[5] Not printed.

[6] Sir J. Bullard, commenting on 14 October, agreed with the line. He thought UKDEL NATO should say 'that we would envisage a strong public statement by Foreign Ministers in December, either as a paragraph in the communiqué or (perhaps better) as a separate statement: but that this should spring from agreement among the Allies about what are our objectives, what is feasible and what is the right policy. It is not *just* a question of public statements.'

(*e*) to put pressure on the regime to lift martial law, release those arrested and resume a dialogue with the Church and Solidarity.

Western Policy

4. Western Policy should be based on realism and consistency.

5. Realism consists in recognising what the West can expect to achieve by outside pressure, and in distinguishing between measures intended to demonstrate disapproval and those which could promote our concrete objectives.

6. Consistency lies in adopting policies which are sustainable over the long term and which match our aims. The policies should be 'reversible' when and if conditions improve.

7. The West cannot expect to be able to exert such pressure that the Polish, still less the Soviet authorities, will in the short term accept a transformation of a one party state acknowledging the leading role of the party, into a pluralist democracy on Western lines.

8. The West should therefore adopt a long term policy aimed at evolutionary, not revolutionary, change.

9. In the Polish context such a policy should seek to maximise the points of contact with the Polish people and maintain pressure on the authorities to enlarge the areas in which the majority of the population have a say in the way in which their country is run.

10. The factors working in the West's favour include:

(*a*) a realisation by the Polish authorities that the Party is, for the time being, discredited;

(*b*) the need to get some cooperation from the work force if the country is to escape from its economic crisis;

(*c*) the role and influence of the Polish Church and tradition of independence of the Polish people;

(*d*) the inability and unwillingness of the CMEA states to provide substantial assistance;

(*e*) the extreme reluctance of the Soviet Union to use direct military force.

11. It would be unwise to build a policy on assessments of Jaruzelski's character or intentions. His actions so far indicate an acknowledgement of the danger of adopting extreme hard line measures and a need to purge the party of corruption and incompetence. But he has equally been determined to use the force necessary to put down what he sees as a return to disorder as represented by Solidarity in its pre-13 December form. There is no prospect of his permitting Solidarity to revive in the future in the form in which it challenged the power of the State. It would be preferable to adopt a policy based on the known elements of the Polish situation (Soviet dominance, Church resistance, framework for trade unions with a legal right to strike etc.).

Points of Contact

12. The West has a number of points of contact with Poland. These are set out below with recommendations as to how they might be used to maintain contact with the people and put pressure on the authorities:

(*a*) Government to Government. Until martial law is lifted (even if thereafter some elements of emergency control are kept in place) official contacts should be limited. No bilateral ministerial visits should take place. Thereafter resumption of official contacts should take place on the basis of consultation and coordination in the Alliance. Contacts should be related to whether the internal situation in Poland shows signs of evolving towards greater recognition by the authorities of the wishes of their people. Ultimately Poland should be treated on the same basis of differentiation as other Eastern European countries where contacts are more regular and at a higher level with those, like Hungary, which adopt more liberal economic and political policies than those, like Czechoslovakia, which do not.

(*b*) International Organisations and Conferences.

(i) opportunities should be taken in the UN and its agencies e.g. ILO to criticise policies aimed at destroying expression of popular wishes. Pressure in the ILO also focuses attention on detained Solidarity leaders. The international trade union movement is playing a leading role which we should support.

(ii) the Polish record should be strongly criticised in the resumed CSCE Conference in Madrid.

(*c*) (i) Official public statements. We should continue to hold the Polish authorities to their promises to return to dialogue and renewal. If ultimately the Solidarity movement decides to enter the new trade union structure, the West should continue to insist that the structure is less important than the spirit and wishes which inspired Solidarity. The West should continue to condemn repression in Poland and call for the lifting of martial law and the release of those detained.

(ii) The West should not hesitate to refer to the collapse[7] of the system in Poland. This is acutely embarrassing to the Soviet Union and could weigh with them in their approach to the Polish and other similar problems in Eastern Europe.

(*d*) Information. Efforts should be made to maintain a high level of broadcast and other information to the Polish people.

(*e*) Cultural links. These should be maintained and if possible expanded provided we are clear that the parties on the Polish side are not being carefully selected to include only party hacks.

(*f*) Church links.

(i) links with the Polish Church should be maintained and strengthened both as a means of obtaining information and for passing messages;

(ii) the position of the Polish Church should be strengthened by insisting that it be used as the channel for humanitarian assistance to the Polish people;

(*g*) Humanitarian assistance. Humanitarian assistance to the Polish people should continue from both public and if possible private sources.

(*h*) Economic links.

(i) economic measures aimed at damaging the Polish economy should be carefully considered before being adopted. The revival of the Polish economy on a reformed and decentralised basis is in both the Polish and Western interests. We should avoid forcing them into greater dependence on the Soviet Union.

(ii) the West should press the Poles to repay both their official and commercial debts. (No new official credit should be made available until this is justified by the state of the Polish economy.)

(iii) the West should urge the Poles to adopt genuine economic reform.

(iv) the West should make it clear that it is prepared to return to a more normal economic relationship with Poland if the situation in the country returns to a position in which the wishes of the people are given greater weight by the authorities. It is only on this basis that the Polish economy is likely to recover.

[7] Sir J. Bullard queried whether this word should be 'failure'.

No. 185

Letter from Mr James (Warsaw) to Mr Broomfield, 14 October 1982
Confidential (FCO 28/5001, ENP 212/1)

Dear Nigel,

1. I have been reflecting on the timing of the trade union legislation and the abolition of Solidarity.[1] Why did the regime decide to do it now? What follows is highly speculative and uncertain. But I thought it was worth making an effort and I should be very interested to have your views.

2. We do not know what took place in the meeting between Jaruzelski and Brezhnev in August. But I would have thought that Brezhnev would have expressed concern at the continuation of counter-revolutionary activities in Poland and suggested to Jaruzelski that he should take a firm hand with Solidarity. It would seem to me very possible that Jaruzelski might have given him some general commitment to this effect. It is also possible that Jaruzelski planned to do this anyway, and the evidence for Soviet pressure is suggestive rather than conclusive.

3. We then come to the events of August 31.[2] The demonstrations were perhaps more widespread than we expected but I wonder what the Polish authorities expected? What is clear is that they were determined to take a thoroughly firm line with the demonstrators and to pursue intimidatory tactics. From a recent conversation which Nick Marden[3] and Judith Macgregor had with Wiatr, the Head of the Marxist-Leninist Institute, the regime were rather pleased with the way it had contained the violence. It may well have drawn the conclusion that now was a pretty good time to hit Solidarity and to introduce new legislation.

4. At the same time work on the new legislation was presumably proceeding, even though the subject of trade unions had almost disappeared from the media. It has generally been assumed that Rakowski and people around him provided a sort of Jaruzelski think tank on trade union legislation. Another factor in choosing early October to introduce the legislation was that it seems to be Jaruzelski's intention to lift a number of aspects of martial law before the end of the year, possibly before December 13. Several of my colleagues think that the Soviet Union wished to have the lifting of martial law as a sign of the return to the process of rehabilitating the Party and getting away from the military at every turn in the system. I myself have doubts about this and think that the Soviet Union is less concerned at this time with the return of the Party than with the maintenance of a certain degree of stability inside Poland. I think martial law could well be maintained for some time if this helps discipline in the factories.

5. If we accept, however, that Jaruzelski wanted to get rid of a number of aspects of martial law, we must also accept that the instrument for suspending Solidarity would be removed. Was there any way of doing this except by de-legalising? Personally I cannot believe that some means could not have been found constitutionally to have continued the suspension of Solidarity while dismantling martial law. But I report it for what it is worth that there does seem to be a view here that this would have been very difficult.

6. My own view is that the decision on Solidarity was taken by Jaruzelski and the Army people around him—though work may have been done on the legislation

[1] See Nos. 181 to 183.
[2] See Nos. 171 and 172.
[3] First Secretary in Warsaw since September 1982.

by Rakowski and company. I think Jaruzelski, with his military training and rather puritan attitude, felt that it was intolerable that opposition should be allowed to continue and that until some new structure was set up, the likelihood was that Solidarity would remain a vehicle for popular dissatisfaction with the regime. He must have hoped that by breaking the vehicle (Solidarity) and by putting a new one in its place, fake though this might be, he could start the process of manipulating the trade union movement once again. It might be that he is prepared genuinely to allow a certain degree of freedom and independence within the new trade union movement. But whether he thinks this or not is largely irrelevant in my view since the authorities both of the Army and the Party will see to it that the trade union movement becomes a creature. Did he also think that some of the members of Solidarity would join? There are grounds for thinking that the government believe that many Poles are fed up with Solidarity or tired of it or just plain weary with the whole situation and will go along with something different in the way of trade unions.

7. It is very difficult to know the extent of Soviet pressure. I have assumed that it is there, but in a general form rather than a specific one and that it is of course maintained constantly through various channels.

8. Does Jaruzelski really believe that there is such a thing as the 'majority' of 'good' Polish workers who will toe the line and get back to work and a small minority who are really the thorn in his side? It is impossible to say, but he is constantly repeating it (as is Czyrek and Rakowski). It must be very difficult for a Polish leader to accept the degree of disaffection in this country, when he is surrounded by people who are still prepared to support him in what he conceives to be the only responsible course, given the importance of Poland's relations with the Soviet Union.

9. It may also be that he hopes that a certain degree of tactical conciliation with the Church will help palliate an action against Solidarity.[4] But unless he has gravely miscalculated, he must hope to wear down Solidarity and opposition to the regime, although eruptions will continue to take place. His nightmare must be the thought of overt opposition spreading to large factories. If this were to happen, and the workers were determined to resist a mixture of intimidation and bribery, he could be facing again a real crisis. But it seems more probable at the moment that he will successfully grind away at his version of modified *odnowa*, containing still some elements of moderation.[5]

[4] On 18 October Mr James met Archbishop Glemp, who did not see the situation improving in the next two years and believed that Soviet pressure limited the Government's freedom of action: 'they could have found people in Solidarity to talk to if they had really tried.' He added that the trade union legislation gave the Government ample opportunity to manipulate the workforce and get their people into position of power. Nevertheless Solidarity was not dead. It would need to resist and find some new longer-term form. He felt unsure about potential Western sanctions, fearing they could drive Poland to the East and isolate the Polish people and did not find the Reagan Administration's ideas helpful. Aid was important, and the Church was doing most of the distribution, which worked well (Warsaw tel. No. 975, FCO 28/5008, ENP 226/1).

[5] In a meeting with Mr Rifkind the Polish Ambassador presented the new trade union legislation as the most liberal in Eastern Europe and he held Solidarity responsible for the failure of the Government's efforts to establish a dialogue. Mr Rifkind replied that the new legislation was a step backwards, confirming that the authorities had chosen confrontation over conciliation with Solidarity, which had overwhelming mass support. He contested the Ambassador's accusation that the West encouraged subversive elements, arguing that the demonstrations in Gdańsk had been a genuine anti-Government reaction. The Ambassador declined to say when the martial law might be lifted and Mr Wałęsa released (FCO tel. No. 577 to Warsaw of 12 October).

If Polish society accepts this, so much the better for them, as he can relax martial law and perhaps even abolish it. If it does not, he will still grind away.[6]

Yours ever,
KENNETH

[6] Mr Broomfield replied to Mr James on 25 November agreeing that the new law was essentially a Polish decision and that Jaruzelski would never have considered a re-emergence of Solidarity in its pre-December form, as he 'could never have stomached a quasi-political organisation'. Although he did not believe that Solidarity could be quickly forgotten he agreed with Mr James that Jaruzelski hoped that people would give a grudging approval to the new unions as their only realistic hope of preserving something of the *Odnowa* (FCO 28/5002, ENP 212/1).

No. 186

Note of a meeting between Mrs Thatcher and Herr Kohl in Bonn, 29 October 1982, 11 a.m.[1]

Secret (FCO 28/4989, ENP 093/1)

Present:		
Present:	Prime Minister	Chancellor Kohl
	Mr Coles	Mr. Genscher

Chancellor Kohl invited Mr. Genscher to give the Prime Minister an account of his recent contacts in respect of Poland. *Mr. Genscher* said that he had put through an intermediary the idea that he should have a meeting with Archbishop Glemp. The proposal had been accepted and he had had a secret meeting with the Archbishop in a building in the Vatican. He would be most grateful if the fact of the meeting, and what transpired, could be kept completely confidential.

It was clear from the meeting that Archbishop Glemp viewed the future with great concern. He was very depressed. His attitude towards Jaruzelski had been surprising. He had taken the line that we should try to keep Jaruzelski in power because whoever followed him would be worse. He was the lesser evil. This did not mean that the Archbishop agreed with Jaruzelski.

Archbishop Glemp was particularly concerned about the economic situation. He was very critical of the American attitude and could not understand why the United States imposed sanctions against Poland while sending wheat to the Soviet Union. It remained to be seen whether there would be a general strike in Poland. Glemp felt that street demonstrations could not be ruled out and that these could lead to bloodshed. The Polish church advised against street demonstrations because of their unpredictability.

Glemp advanced two possible explanations for the legislation against Solidarity. It might have been due to strong Soviet pressure. Alternatively, Jaruzelski might

[1] Mrs Thatcher had been attending the Anglo-German summit from 28 to 29 October. For a German account of discussions held during this visit see *Akten zur Auswärtigen Politik der Bundesrepublik Deutschland 1982* (Munich: Oldenbourg Verlag, 2013), Vol. 1, No. 288. During a visit to the Berlin Wall, she said that the 'lesson of Poland' under Soviet-backed martial law was that 'pitiless ideology only survives because it is maintained by force' and that at the end popular anger would overcome it and 'one day liberty will dawn on the other side of the wall'. (This speech at the 'Golden Book Ceremony' can be found on Margaret Thatcher Foundation website: http://www.margaretthatcher.org.)

have to step down fairly soon and might therefore wish to accomplish as much as possible before he did so.

The Archbishop identified four main groups in Poland—the totally desperate, those who co-operated with the regime, those who were prepared to fight and those who wished to create their own independent structures. The latter were the most interesting and the most deserving of help. They included the three million independent farmers and also large numbers of craftsmen. Glemp sought help from the West for these people.

He (Mr Genscher) had asked the Archbishop whether the Polish Government was at a loss to deal with its problems. Glemp had replied affirmatively. Until the summer, the Church had been ready to help with a dialogue. But the Government had rejected all its proposals, and by June it was clear that the views of Government and Church could not be reconciled.

He had asked Glemp for his view of Jaruzelski as a man. The reply had been that he was very difficult to assess. Jaruzelski wanted a strong state with peace and order and thought he could achieve this by forcing decisions on Poland. He would resist any return to earlier conditions. But on the other hand, he would do anything he could to avoid Soviet intervention. No one knew whether his main aim was to avoid this contingency or to please the Soviet Union. Perhaps both.

The Archbishop was worried that Poland might again become a cause of war. In this context, he was alarmed that the United States even considered the possibility of limited nuclear war. He had reiterated that it was worth regarding Jaruzelski as a man who should be supported because whoever followed him would be worse.

Glemp had made a plea for help and investment for small businesses so that areas of 'social freedom' could be created. He had described draft legislation that would make that possible and was discussing with the Polish Government a larger aid programme for the private sector. But his mind was now turning to more modest help which would take the form of investments in small companies by Western groups or individuals. He (Genscher) had told the Archbishop that he would discuss these ideas with appropriate German organisations to see how they could help. All this would be raised with President Reagan when the Chancellor went to Washington in November.[2]

The Prime Minister said that this was a most helpful account. It would be easier to take action if differences over the Siberian Pipeline could be cleared up.[3]

Mr. Genscher said that he was not sure that the Archbishop fully appreciated what economic conditions were necessary for private investment. Investors needed profits. Glemp appeared to be a very sincere, honest man who was heavily burdened by his responsibilities. He felt the shadow of his great predecessor.

[2] In their joint statement of 15 November, 'The President and the Chancellor . . . called upon the Polish leadership to lift martial law in Poland, to release all detainees, to reverse the ban on the trade union Solidarity and, through serious dialogue with the Church and appointed workers' representatives, to seek national consensus which is the only way to lead Poland out of its present crisis, free from any external interference. They hoped that the release of Lech Walesa will promote these objectives' (*Public Papers: Reagan (1982)*, p. 1473).

[3] The Prime Minister told Chancellor Kohl at a previous meeting in 10 Downing Street on 19 October that she had 'the clear impression that the Americans now recognised that the action which they had taken over the pipeline was a mistake and were looking for a way out'. She nevertheless defended the President as an 'honest politician with certain strong views' (PREM 19/765). The sanctions regarding the Siberian gas pipeline were lifted by President Reagan on 13 November (see *Public Papers: Reagan (1982)*, Book II, pp. 1464-65).

Chancellor Kohl said that Glemp only became Primate because it was the personal wish of Cardinal Wyszynski. Other sources in the Church thought Glemp was too pessimistic about the spirit of the resistance. It was clear that the Pope would like him to be more dynamic, and it was evident that Glemp did not understand economics. Nevertheless, we should find practical ways of helping Poland. The Government would not welcome it, but would probably tolerate it. The idea of giving practical help to farmers and small businessmen was good. They needed simple things like seed grain. Germany was working together with farming organisations in Germany and other European countries, on an initiative, to meet their needs. A small effort could have a big effect. If the private sector could be made interested in these ideas, it might not be necessary for Governments to be involved at all. The matter could be left to the Churches and to farming organisations.

The Prime Minister agreed that it should be possible to do something on the practical side. There would be a need anyway for an early discussion of Poland. There was still the question of debt re-scheduling and there was certainly a need to discuss food supplies.

The discussion ended at 11.30.

No. 187

Mr James (Warsaw) to Mr Pym, 12 November 1982, 10 a.m.
Tel. No. 1042[1] Priority, Confidential (FCO 28/4912, ENP 014/1)

The Political Situation in Poland

1. Before returning to the UK I thought you might like to have my view on the situation here.

2. November 10 was a flop from the point of view of Solidarity. The government are feeling bucked by the feeble reaction to the call for strikes in the factories and the demonstrations were easily dispersed. They are also very pleased at the agreement reached with the Church. The visit of the Pope has stymied a lot of opposition and has provided an expectation for a people bereft of it. I detect the hand of the Pope very much in the declarations of Archbishop Glemp on his return from Rome and in his meeting with General Jaruzelski (which was arranged at Glemp's request). I think that the release of Walesa may form part of the same process.[2] My expectation is that the government will declare the end of martial law by December 20 and the release of most of the detainees before Christmas.[3] This timetable could be upset by major disturbances but these seem unlikely.

3. This will mean that the three criteria of the West may be fulfilled next month, with the exception of the dialogue with Solidarity as such. Walesa's future is uncertain. There are those who think he may return to private life. But I would not

[1] Repeated Priority (for information) to Washington, Moscow, UKDEL NATO, Paris, Bonn; Saving (for information) to East Berlin, Prague, Budapest, MODUK, Sofia, Bucharest, Belgrade, Helsinki, Stockholm, UKMIS New York, UKREP Brussels.

[2] He was released on 14 November. HMG welcomed this 'positive development', but also noted that 700 people still remained interned (London COREU 4162 to all COREU; FCO 28/4956, ENP 022/1). Mr Pym, reporting the release of Wałęsa to the Cabinet on 18 November, thought that martial law would be lifted shortly. He announced that the Polish authorities had agreed that the Pope should visit Poland in 1983 (CC(82)49, CAB 128/74).

[3] See No. 194.

exclude him being drawn into some kind of discussion with the Government on trade union questions.

4. If things turn out this way, NATO will need to respond. I hope, therefore, that further thought will be given to renewing the ideas which the United Kingdom in particular have been examining and putting forward for a realistic evaluation of our long-term policy towards Poland, particularly in the context of the death of Brezhnev[4] and the new possibilities this may afford the United States administration to modify its stance on East-West relations generally and towards Poland in particular. It would not surprise me if the United States in due course were to make a *volte face* on Poland which will leave the rest of the Alliance clutching her coat tails.

[4] On 11 November at 11 a.m. local time, Soviet television announced that President Brezhnev had died suddenly at 8.30 a.m. on 10 November. For more on his death see *DBPO: Afghanistan*.

No. 188

Sir J. Fretwell (Paris) to Mr Pym, 25 November 1982, 7 p.m.
Tel. No. 1133[1] Immediate, Confidential (FCO 28/4699, EN 020/19)

Meeting between the PUS and the Secretary-General at the Quai: Poland

1. During his discussion with the Secretary-General at the Quai d'Orsay[2] this morning, the PUS asked how the French viewed recent developments in Poland.

2. Durfourcq (Director for Europe) said that developments should be examined against the three conditions imposed by the West at the beginning of the year:

(*a*) Release of detainees. Release of Walesa had been an important political act with regard to both domestic and international opinion. The Polish Government had taken the risk of releasing him because it felt it could limit his future action. It had succeeded in this. For the rest some 1,000 people remained in detention and another 3-4,000 had been arrested or imprisoned. So this condition had not been fulfilled;

(*b*) Dialogue with the Church and Solidarity. The Polish authorities had undertaken a limited dialogue with the Church. The Church had opted for stabilisation, and entertained some hopes that Catholics might be associated in the exercise of power. There was of course no dialogue with Solidarity, but the Government did have certain contacts with ex-members of the movement;

(*c*) A lifting of martial law. This seemed likely to take place around 13 December, but martial law would probably be replaced by measures with equivalent effect. A release of detainees and a pardon for some of those in prison was also possible. Fundamentally Jaruzelski's policy of normalisation by stealth was very firm. At the moment there was no reason for the West to modify its position at all.

3. Gutmann added that Jaruzelski was clearly not going to re-establish the system which had obtained before 13 December 1981. The Polish people would resist, but not in a spectacular way. The West could not ignore apparent normalisation, but should not be accomplice to Jaruzelski's hypocrisy. The fact that many detainees remained led him to the conclusion that the three conditions

[1] Repeated Priority (for information) to Washington, Bonn, UKDEL NATO, Warsaw.
[2] M. Francis Gutmann.

should be maintained. If there were further Polish gestures to the West it might however be necessary to try to 'globalise'[3] the conditions.

4. The PUS agreed that the problem was complex. After mid-December it was quite possible that certain of the three conditions would be met, or that all the conditions would be met in part. The West had to decide how to react and be ready to do so quickly.

5. Paye[4] (Economic Director) raised the problem of the rescheduling of guaranteed debt. If the West did not reschedule, this amounted to a moratorium. It was difficult to consider granting supplementary credits, for example for new purchases of cereals, if the three conditions were not fulfilled. Both the granting of new credits and rescheduling gave the West important means of pressure upon Poland.

6. Evans[5] said that the economic case for re-scheduling was strong, even if political considerations weighed against. At present the Poles were not paying interest on their debts, but the West had no recourse. Western governments should consider how to change the situation so that they did have recourse. The long-term problem was whether the Polish economy could be revived to the point where long-term debt could be repaid: this was open to question.

7. Gutmann stressed the absurdity of a position where rescheduling would be in the interest of the West and not the Poles. He recalled that the West had taken sanctions against Poland in righteous indignation a year ago. Now the West wanted to know how to lift sanctions without losing face. He agreed that Political Directors of the Community countries should begin to consider what statement should be made by the Community in the event that further liberalisation measures were announced by the Polish government in mid-December.[6] He concluded that Western countries should not get stuck on interpreting the detail of the three conditions but should maintain them globally. The West should maintain moral and political pressure on Poland, though without any hope of a very substantial return. The PUS agreed with this summing up.[7]

[3] This should be understood as referring to the French word 'globalité', meaning from all angles and as a whole, rather than the English meaning of 'worldwide'.

[4] Jean-Claude Paye, Director of Economic and Financial Affairs, French MFA.

[5] Richard Evans, Superintending Under-Secretary for Economic Relations.

[6] See No. 190.

[7] The Germans' views were also of interest to London. On 29 November Mr Taylor informed London that they had not yet received a Polish *démarche* about the lifting of martial law. Herr Gerold von Braunmühl, Herr Genscher's adviser on East-West relations, was pessimistic, as the Church expected oppression and intimidation to continue. He thought that the West should not give up its three demands, but go on repeating them. Although Chancellor Kohl had called for the lifting of the ban on Solidarity when in Washington, Braunmühl thought it was not realistic and the Chancellor had not repeated it in his statement to Parliament on 25 November. He said that the FRG would go along with any EC consensus on whether to lift sanctions against the USSR imposed because of Poland (Bonn tel. No. 1014, FCO 28/4698, EN 020/15).

No. 189

Letter from Mr Hurd to Sir B. Braine MP,[1] 1 December 1982
(FCO 28/4813, ENC 015/1)

Dear Bernard,

Thank you for your letter of 19 November about your meeting with Mr Josef Houzvicka from the Czechoslovak Embassy.[2]

I am grateful to you for letting me know about this meeting. It is possible that the Czech Embassy have come to the conclusion that friendly overtures may in the long run be a more effective way of defusing their critics than refusing to deal with them or replying aggressively. This would reflect the style of the present Ambassador and could well have been a follow-up to the lunch which he gave you last year. However, I agree that there could be a more sinister motive and think it would be as well to remain on your guard. I would of course be interested in hearing of any further approaches.

There has been a very recent indication that the Czechs may be easing up slightly on their treatment of certain dissidents. Karel Kyncl,[3] to whose case Houzvicka referred, has been trying to obtain permission to leave Czechoslovakia for some time.[4] This request has hit numerous obstacles but in the past couple of weeks he and two associates who wish to go to France and the FRG have been able to complete application forms for passports and exit visas. However we have had no indication that Rudolf Battek is likely to be released from his term of imprisonment.[5]

The Czech attitude towards dissidents seems inconsistent at times but in recent cases those who have requested to leave the country have been told to apply for a Presidential pardon. This Kyncl has done. Since it appears that Havel has not, I am doubtful that any easing in the treatment of dissidents is likely to extend as far as granting him permission to leave the country in the near future. But I am sure that your representations serve a useful purpose in reminding the Czech authorities that Havel's case has not been forgotten.

Yours ever,
DOUGLAS

[1] Conservative MP for Essex and President of the UK Committee for the Defence of the Unjustly Prosecuted (VONS), 1980–88.

[2] Sir Bernard reported that he had been invited to the Czech Embassy following his campaign for the release of Václav Havel where he was told that Havel had been offered the chance to go to the USA but had refused, 'preferring to be a martyr'. In the course of the conversation, Sir Bernard gathered that some prisoners of conscience were likely to be released soon, including, Messrs Kyncl and Battěk. He thought that he might have been invited to the Embassy to pave the way for him to be invited to the Eastern bloc to compromise him, as he had been an 'unrelenting opponent of the repressive Soviet system' and had been outspoken about human rights both in Czechoslovakia and Poland.

[3] See No. 110, paragraph 6 and note 7, and No. 166, note 4.

[4] Mr Makepeace, Press Secretary in Warsaw, believed that Kafkaesque delaying techniques had been deployed towards Kyncl, who had told him that together with other dissidents, who wanted to go to France and Germany, they were considering sending an open letter to the Governments of the UK, the FRG and France to publicise the treatment they had been subjected to in the press (Prague tel. No. 218 of 1 October 1982).

[5] The Czech sociologist, a founding member of VONS and spokesman for Charter 77 from 1980, had been convicted in 1980 to five and a half years' imprisonment for subversion in collaboration with foreigners.

No. 190

Letter from Mr Bone to Mr Coles (No. 10), 2 December 1982
(FCO 28/4957, ENP 022/1)

Dear John,

European Council: Poland

As you know, we received yesterday the Presidency's suggestions on the agenda for the European Council on 3/4 December. Poland is on the list of political cooperation subjects.[1]

Both the European Council and the NATO Ministerial meeting on 9/10 December fall before the anniversary of martial law on 13 December, when, according to the Polish Ambassador, martial law itself will be lifted and the detainees released, except for those to be charged with specific offences; both actions to be subject to there being 'calm' in Poland. Given the Solidarity Underground's decision to call off the protest actions planned for 13 December, and also the moderate line now being taken by the Church and by Walesa, it looks as if this condition may well be fulfilled.

Against this background, and in the light of the probable need to refer to Poland in statements and communiqués after the European Council, the NATO Ministerial Meeting and the Foreign Affairs Council on 13/14 December, we have been considering the line that the Prime Minister might take in Copenhagen and on which Mr Pym could thereafter build in Brussels. Discussion so far in NATO appears to be tending towards a consensus for a cautiously positive response if the Polish moves are actually announced on 13 December, followed thereafter by a pause during which the practical effects of the new measures would be assessed, together with the reactions of the Polish people. The Foreign and Commonwealth Secretary believes that this is the right approach. In formal terms, at least, the expected Polish moves would go a considerable way towards satisfying the three criteria set out in the 11 January Declaration. But everything depends on how far the situation in Poland actually improves as a result.

I enclose a note of the elements which Mr Pym suggests might be worked into public statements following the European Council and other meetings later in the month.

Mr Pym would be grateful to know whether the Prime Minister agrees. If so, her briefing will reflect this for the European Council and he will take a similar line—subject to any new developments—in his own later discussions in NATO and with the Ten.

Mr Pym's view is that our overriding aim in all this must be to maintain Alliance unity. He recognises that to judge the genuineness of any Polish moves on 13 December will not be easy. However, if the moves forecast for 13 December are implemented, and if they lead to tangible improvements in the situation in Poland,

[1] On 26 November the Ten's European Working Group recommended: maintaining the three demands; expressing their wish for further steps towards an acceptable situation; showing flexibility if such steps were to occur; stressing compassion towards the Polish people; and reiterating their desire to return to normal relations. For the latter, the criteria would be whether martial law regulations were replaced by 'temporary emergency powers'; internees were released; an amnesty for political prisoners was declared; enterprises were demilitarized; press censorship, checks on telephones, and restrictions on street gatherings and foreign travel were stopped (COREU CPE/MUL ETR 4362 to all COREU of 30 November 1982).

he believes the West should respond by sending a positive but controlled signal both to keep Jaruzelski on his present course and to avoid Poland turning still further towards the Soviet Union.

Yours ever,
ROGER BONE

ENCLOSURE IN NO. 190

Poland: Public Statements

The following are the elements which might be reflected in any public statements on Poland by the European Council or by NATO Ministers.

EC partners/NATO Ministers

(*a*) Wish to stress their desire to maintain and develop links with the Polish people;
(*b*) Recall the communiqué of 4 January 1982 or the NATO Declaration of 11 January; (Any reference to the three criteria to be inserted in a retrospective context);
(*c*) Note that the release of Lech Walesa and the Polish Government's expressed intention to lift martial law on 13 December are positive developments, but note also that Solidarity has been dissolved contrary to the Polish Government's expressed intention to pursue a policy of reconciliation;
(*d*) Will continue to follow the situation closely, particularly on how the Polish Government intends to implement its promise of lifting martial law;
(*e*) Draw to the attention of the Polish authorities the fact that in this regard their actions will be assessed by their effects;
(*f*) Reiterate the expectations of the International Community that the Polish authorities will fulfil their promise to return to path of renewal and reform;
(*g*) Hope that the situation will develop in such a way as to make it possible for the Ten/NATO to resume and develop the kind of relationship which they would wish to have with Poland and the Polish people.[2]

[2] Both the statement at the conclusion of the European Council meeting in Copenhagen on 4 December and the North Atlantic Council final communiqué of 10 December adopted these principles.

No. 191

Mr Pym to Mr James (Warsaw), 6 December 1982, 5.51 p.m.
Tel. No. 660[1] Priority, Confidential (FCO 28/5002, ENP 212/1)

Poland

1. Representatives of Solidarity working group in UK (linked to main Solidarity offices in Brussels and other capitals) told EESD in confidence on 2 December that Solidarity Temporary Coordinating Committee (TCC) would disband after 13 December. Full authority for union would then revert to Walesa and other Solidarity leaders that might be released.

2. The TCC's action would however be dependent upon action by the Government to:

(*a*) Amnesty political prisoners including those now under arrest;
(*b*) Reinstate Solidarity members sacked from their jobs;

[1] Repeated for Information to Bonn, Paris, Washington, UKDEL NATO and UKDEL Madrid.

(*c*) Move towards an understanding with Walesa.

3. Solidarity representatives believed that a deal with Walesa would be possible if Government wished this but emphasised necessity of Government making sufficient concessions to allow opposition to save face. Form of possible accommodation with Walesa was still unclear although Church authorities were actively seeking to involve him in plans for a new Catholic Democratic Party. Walesa would be wary however of giving impression that he was selling out and was reportedly unenthusiastic about the Church plans.

4. Solidarity representatives appeared overall despondent about prospects for further successful resistance to authorities in short term and said that Solidarity, as it had existed in Poland before 13 December 1981, was dead. Many Solidarity members now wanted moderation and compromise and Walesa reflected that mood. If a deal with latter was done, however, then more radical Solidarity groupings, particularly in large factories would break away and continue to fight underground.[2]

5. Further details by bag.

[2] On 3 December Mr Goodison reported to Mr Broomfield that he had met Mr Len Murray, the General Secretary of the TUC, at the German Embassy. Murray had said that the trade unions had very little interest in events in Poland. They were not demanding that HMG should insist on the reinstatement of Solidarity. He preferred to wait and see what happened after the lifting of martial law and was ready to accept that the Church had made a deal with Jaruzelski for the benefit of the Polish people.

No. 192

Minute from Mr Murrell (Research Department) to Mr Montgomery, 17 December 1982

Confidential (FCO 28/4745, EN 021/31)

Soviet policy towards Eastern Europe under Andropov

1. There is no clear evidence as yet as to whether Soviet policy towards Eastern Europe is likely to undergo any significant change with the accession of Andropov.[1] The Warsaw Pact Political Consultative Committee meeting now apparently scheduled for 4/5 January (it was first planned to take place on 8/9 December) will provide the first solid indications about any changes in atmosphere or substance in these relations, but in the meantime it may be worth reviewing some of the straws in the wind.

2. It is reasonable to assume that Andropov will take a special interest in Eastern Europe and that this could be one of the first areas where his personal influence will make itself felt. He was, of course, directly concerned with Eastern Europe between 1954 and 1967 successively as Ambassador in Hungary, Head of the Bloc Relations Department and Secretary of the Central Committee: and since 1967 as head of the KGB he must have had close links with his opposite numbers in each of the East European countries, and has been responsible for reporting to the Politburo on the security situation there. We have no evidence of any close personal relations between Andropov and any of the East European leaders except Kadar who, as well as his close involvement with Andropov around 1956, is the only one of them to have received him individually in the last 4 years (December

[1] Yuri Andropov was elected General Secretary of the Soviet Communist Party on 12 November following the death of President Brezhnev on 10 November.

1981). In recent years the East European Party leaders have probably had closer personal contact with Chernenko,[2] who was present at a number of Brezhnev's meetings with them in the Crimea. Some of the East European leaders appear to have put a certain amount of money on Chernenko to succeed—the Bulgarians (in May 1979 and September 1981), the East Germans (November 1981) and the Czechoslovaks (June 1982) conferred high State awards on him (which it was unusual for Politburo members other than Brezhnev to receive). Reports from our Embassies in Prague, East Berlin and Bucharest suggest that official circles had been surprised, and in the case of the Czechoslovaks and East Germans even somewhat disconcerted by Andropov's election (although both Strougal and Zhivkov had predicted it to Mr Nixon (Mr Cartledge's letter of 14 July to Mr Broomfield).[3] Chernenko might well have been regarded by some East European officials as a more reassuring choice and one may speculate there could be misgivings in some East European leadership circles about the fact that Andropov will presumably have established direct links with their own security services. There is however no real evidence of any significant unhappiness in East Europe about the Soviet succession although the Hungarians seem to be the only ones who particularly welcome the outcome.

3. It struck us a little odd that Andropov has not yet had any formal meetings with the East European party leaders. He greeted them at the funeral[4] but none of them have had the honour of a bilateral meeting which was accorded to *inter alia* the Yugoslav and Cuban leaders. This rather contrasts with the early meetings which Brezhnev (and Kosygin)[5] arranged following the ousting of Khrushchev in October 1964 (they had a meeting on the Soviet Polish Frontier with Gomulka within about 10 days of the change and also had separate meetings with the other East European leaders who came to Moscow for the November 7 Anniversary celebrations). On that occasion however, the Moscow changeover had been very sudden and somewhat irregular and the Soviet leaders may have felt the need to do some reassuring and explaining to their slightly rattled East European allies.

4. Andropov's own attitudes towards Eastern Europe are as yet more a matter for speculation than analysis. Much has been made in the press of the implications of his alleged interest in the Hungarian economic reforms. There is no evidence that he has encouraged, let alone sponsored, the Hungarian reform but since he has continued to take a close interest in Hungary and appears to be on good terms with Kadar it is reasonable to infer that he has taken a tolerant view at least. In his last major speech before he became party leader at the Lenin anniversary meetings in April, Andropov used a formulation which preserved the conventional balance between separate roads to, and the universal laws of socialism; 'we consider that for each country what is best is the form accepted by its people which corresponds to its interests and traditions. However, the basic principles of the socialist social system, its class nature, its essence, are the same for all countries and peoples.' In the rest of his remarks Andropov tended to put the accent on variety and individuality in socialist countries (without saying anything particularly new or original) e.g. 'socialism is in its essence alien to models and stereotypes . . . each ruling party proceeds from a concrete situation, specific national circumstances and

[2] Konstantin Chernenko, Member of the Soviet Politburo.

[3] Not printed.

[4] An account of Brezhnev's funeral, written by HM Ambassador in Moscow, can be found in *DBPO: Afghanistan*, No. 175.

[5] Aleksei Kosygin, Soviet Premier, 1964-80.

traditions. Whichever socialist state you consider—everywhere you see the manifestation of original national historical cultural and other particular features'. In the same passage Andropov attacked the 'bourgeois concept' of pluralism but in relatively moderate and sophisticated terms.

5. In his speeches since becoming Party Leader Andropov has spoken only in general terms about Eastern Europe without addressing specific issues or relations with individual countries. At the Central Committee Plenum on 22 November he said that the strength of the socialist community would continue to be 'the primary concern' of the CPSU and that 'comradely cooperation and socialist mutual help of fraternal countries should become deeper and more effective'. In discussing economic measures he spoke of the need to 'take account of the experience of fraternal countries'—echoing the sentiment expressed by Brezhnev at the 26th party congress.[6] Of more interest was the following passage: 'The CPSU and the Soviet State sincerely wish to develop and improve relations with all socialist countries. Mutual goodwill, respect for each others, legitimate interests, common solutions for the interests of socialism should indicate correct solutions even where for various reasons there is not yet the necessary trust and mutual understanding'. In the light of its position in the text and the reference to the 'Soviet State' it seems clear that this passage refers only to socialist countries which are not members of the socialist community proper i.e. China, which Andropov went on to single out specifically, Yugoslavia and Albania. That the message was partly intended for Albania was made clear when the *Izvestiya*[7] correspondent quoted from the above passage in an article of 29 November devoted to the Albanian national day. (See Mr Beel's minute to Mr Gray of 7 December.)[8]

6. The meeting on the occasion of Brezhnev's funeral between Andropov and the Yugoslav delegation underlined the importance which the Russians continue to attach to wooing Yugoslavia. In view of the level of Yugoslav representation (the current heads of both Party and State presidia, reciprocating Brezhnev's attendance at Tito's funeral) it was not however unexpected. The Yugoslavs who are extremely sensitive to any change in temperature in Moscow especially as regards relations with Eastern Europe seem to have taken Andropov's election equably and even optimistically, e.g. the Yugoslav Counsellor in Moscow referred to Andropov's particular interest in developing relations with Eastern Europe and described him as a realistic, clever, versatile and capable politician (Mr Butt's teleletter of 8 December).[10]

Poland

7. At his meeting with President Carstens at Brezhnev's funeral, Andropov seemed implicitly to rule out direct Soviet intervention in Poland when he said that the Soviet Union would have invaded Poland 2 years ago if it had intended to take that course. Andropov has not referred to Poland in any of his public speeches since becoming Party Leader and there has been no authoritative comment in the Soviet press on Poland since Brezhnev's death. This reticence is probably not significant although the disappearance of the kind of carping comment which was occasionally appearing in the weeks before Brezhnev's death is interesting. The succession in Moscow coincided with a number of fairly important and sensitive developments—the announcement of the Pope's visit to Poland, the release of Walesa, the lifting/suspension of martial law, towards which one would in any case

[6] For an account of his speech by Sir C. Keeble see *DBPO: Afghanistan*, No. 86.

[7] The official national publication of the Soviet Government until 1991.

[8] Not printed.

have expected a fairly cautious and non-committal attitude on the part of the Russians. However, *Pravda* of 17 November carried a reasonably full account of the Jaruzelski interview with the *Guardian* which quoted his remarks to the effect that the Polish reforms had found an understanding response from her allies; that Polish questions were decided by the Poles independently; and that while ideological principles of socialism were immutable their realisation required a 'creative approach'.

8. There is no evidence that Andropov has intervened in order to influence recent Polish policies. It seems possible that the Poles announced the release of Walesa on the same day as Brezhnev's death in order to pre-empt any possibility that an earlier Soviet agreement to this move would be revoked. (It must have been planned well in advance.) The apparent change of mind in Warsaw on the lifting or suspension of martial law occurred when Andropov was firmly installed. The Russians might have intervened in this matter but on past evidence the Russians appear to have a fair degree of confidence in Jaruzelski's judgement of the security situation in Poland. Moscow's attitude towards martial law is in any case probably ambivalent. The Russians are reluctant to take any risks with the security situation but on the other hand would probably be glad to see the army move into the background and allow the PZPR more scope.

CMEA

9. There has been no recent mention of the CMEA Summit which according to some reports is due to take place in spring and no authoritative pronouncements on economic policy towards Eastern Europe. However, a *Pravda* editorial of 19 November addressed the question of CMEA cohesion and East-West economic relations in unusually robust terms. *Pravda* stated that the increasingly complex international situation and the experience of recent years impel the socialist countries to seek greater solidarity and the strengthening of their technical-economic independence of the capitalist world. And it went on 'we have sufficient forces, sources of energy and raw materials, sufficient scientific and manpower potential to cope with any tasks, to storm any frontiers'. This language echoes what Tikhonov[9] said at the CMEA council meeting in Moscow last June, but *Pravda* appeared to give a rather tougher gloss to his words.

G. D. G. MURRELL

[9] Nikolai Tikhonov, Chairman of the Council of Ministers of the USSR.

No. 193

Letter from Mr Birch (Budapest) to Mr Montgomery, 21 December 1982
Confidential (FCO 28/4880, ENH 015/1)

Dear Alan,

Moves against the opposition in Hungary

1. In my letter of 13 December[1] about the opposition, I said an uneasy game of cat and mouse persisted between the regime and the dissidents. On 13 December

[1] Not printed. Mr Birch said that Hungary did not feature very prominently in dissident activities in Eastern Europe, probably because of the relatively liberal internal regime and the skill of the authorities in dealing with their opponents. But there was nevertheless an identifiable and active liberal opposition, the core of which probably numbered around 20-30 intellectuals united in

the cat pounced. The police raided the private bookshop run by Laszlo Rajk[2] and the apartments of four other dissident writers. The bookshop in Rajk's flat was stripped of all its *samizdat* material and duplicating equipment was confiscated. The names of 40 or so customers were taken. Material was also removed from the other four apartments. We have been told that the police were polite, explained the law under which they were acting and were anxious to avoid fracas. No one was arrested.

2. On 15 December a small and inconspicuous announcement appeared in *Népszabadság*:[3] 'The Budapest Police-Station has made investigations into an offence against the press regulations of the police. In the course of the investigations duplicating machines held illegally and writings produced without permission were seized. The persons who had stencilled the writings were reprimanded as ordained by the law and action was taken to confiscate the objects seized.' The same announcement was carried much more prominently in the MTI Bulletin[4] which is published in foreign languages.

3. I have discussed these events with a leading dissident. He said that the police action had certainly dealt a serious blow to opposition activities. The loss of duplicating equipment and paper would be hard to replace, though there were still supplies which had not been found by the police. News of the raid was likely to discourage people from handling *samizdat*, though he claimed there was a good deal of outrage in intellectual circles against the official action and that the resolve of the opposition would be strengthened.

4. The reasons for the move against the opposition are unclear. But the dissidents believe that the action was authorised by Kadar himself and that it had the following origins:

(*a*) Opposition activities were being more openly tolerated in Hungary than elsewhere in Eastern Europe. Kadar thus felt exposed when amongst his East European colleagues.

(*b*) The Russians told the Hungarians to act (it is certainly being put about in semi-official circles that the Hungarians were forced to bow unwillingly to Soviet pressure).

(*c*) Kadar wanted action taken before he met Andropov for the celebration of the 60th anniversary of the Soviet Union.

(*d*) The Romanians were accusing the HSWP of permitting the Hungarian opposition to foment trouble in Transylvania.

(*e*) The IMF loan[5] was safely in the bag and Hungary could afford a dent or two in its liberal image.

objecting to the authoritarian Hungarian regime, who challenged and revealed many of the abuses and prohibitions of life in Hungary. However they were more of an irritant than a threat to the regime, who were divided in their approach to them. Whilst the security services would probably like to see the dissidents put out of business, the more sensitive Party leaders feared the damage this might cause to Hungary's 'liberal' image and preferred to merely limit their activities.

[2] Architect and democratic opponent to the regime. From 1980 he was blacklisted and not allowed to work under his own name. In 1981, he co-founded the AB Publishing House and ran an illegal bookshop from his flat called 'Samizdat Boutique', which operated from January 1981 to January 1982.

[3] 'The People's Freedom' was the daily newspaper of the Hungarian Working People's Party.

[4] *Magyar Távirati Iroda*, the Hungarian News Agency.

[5] Hungary was admitted to the International Monetary Fund in May 1982 and in December was awarded an immediate credit of $80 million and further credits of $580 million.

5. We think the official action was most probably prompted by the impending Kadar/Andropov meeting though other considerations may have played a part. The time may also have been propitious for the hard liners to insist that action was taken to dampen opposition activity. There have been signs in the Party since the early autumn that economic hard times were not the moment to tolerate critics. The dissidents do not appear too dismayed and believe that the events will in the end lead to wider support for their calls for freedom of speech.

6. The ideological justification for the police action was given in an article by Peter Renyi[6] in *Népszabadság* 2 days before the raids took place. Renyi's article entitled 'There is a great deal at stake' focused on Gyorgy Konrad, the dissident writer currently in West Berlin, as an example of an internal opponent of socialism whose 'status' was in doubt.[7] Renyi argued that there could be 'no question of the internal opposition presenting itself as a moral factor that is independent of every power and is above the political struggle'. He went on charge that the real status of the opposition was determined by outside support, even though some dissidents did not welcome it. He warned the opposition to be careful 'once you have crossed the Rubicon that divides a critical approach from hostile activity'. Konrad was accused of being an accomplice of Radio Free Europe and Renyi said that he would have to decide what his status was—'whether he is outside or inside'.

7. Surprisingly, the dissidents do not appear to have seen this article as a warning that action was imminent. They do, of course, in retrospect and some believe that the statement that Konrad will have to decide 'whether he is outside or inside' to be a warning that residence in Hungary and criticism of the regime may no longer be compatible.

Yours ever,
J. A. BIRCH

[6] Deputy editor- in-Chief of *Népszabadság*.
[7] The novelist György Konrád, who wrote for *samizdat* journals, became one of the main opposition voices in Hungary. At the beginning of 1982 he went to Berlin for a year as a guest at the *Wissenschaftskolleg zu Berlin*. He gave interviews to Radio Free Europe and thus reached wider Hungarian audiences.

No. 194

Minute from Mr Pym to Mrs Thatcher, 23 December 1982
PM/82/111 Confidential (FCO 28/4980, ENP 051/4)

Poland: Martial Law

1. In the light of the vote in the Polish Parliament on 18 December to suspend martial law on 31 December, you may find it helpful if I set out briefly where we now stand, and the next steps we will be taking with our Allies and partners.

2. The measures entering into force on 31 December will remove the overwhelming majority of the martial law restrictions imposed on 13 December 1981. But certain features of martial law have already become permanent while others (such as trade union organisation and activity, including the right to strike, the running of the economy and censorship) will remain covered by new legislation or regulations which, at first sight, appear as stringent as the martial law restrictions they replaced.

3. It remains to be seen how many of the 200 or so original detainees will be released, and whether an amnesty will be offered to those serving sentences for offences committed during the period of martial law. The temporary re-arrest of Lech Walesa on 16 December, to stop him speaking at a ceremony to commemorate those killed in the 1970 disturbances, shows that the Polish authorities are determined to prevent any chance of opposition gaining momentum again.

4. In formal terms, therefore, we are faced by a situation in which the Poles have moved some way towards fulfilling the Western criteria set out in the NATO Declaration of 11 January. The actual situation, however, is less promising when measured either against our hopes or against the Polish authorities' declared intentions in the immediate aftermath of the imposition of martial law, which were to continue on the path of reform and renewal. The overall human rights situation in Poland is probably better than in most other Eastern European countries, but that is small comfort.

5. The key question will be how these latest measures are put into effect. In the NATO communiqué of 10 December, we stated that the actions of the Polish authorities would be judged by their practical effects.[1] The next steps in the Ten and NATO will be to review and assess the measures. This will take some time, and we may well have to wait weeks or months for the final lifting of martial law itself.[2] Until these assessments are completed, I do not think there can be any question of lifting our national measures which were announced in the House on 5 February.[3] To do so would, in my opinion, send quite the wrong sort of signal to both the Russians and the Poles. Equally, I do not think that any of us at the end of this year need any reminding of the importance of Alliance consultation and co-ordination over measures on Poland.

6. I know that a number of colleagues in OD had hoped that we might be able to move faster than this. I hope they will appreciate the reasons why we cannot. I will, of course, see that they are kept informed and consulted as necessary.

7. I am sending copies of this minute to colleagues in OD, the Home Secretary, the Minister of Agriculture, Fisheries and Food, and to Sir Robert Armstrong.

F. P.
(FRANCIS PYM)

[1] See Enclosure in No. 190.

[2] Martial law was finally lifted on 22 July 1983. Many of the political prisoners were not released until the general amnesty in 1986.

[3] See No. 142, note 4.

No. 195

Letter from Mr Cohen[1] (Warsaw) to Mr Tebbit, 24 December 1982
(FCO 28/4988, ENP 090/1)

Dear Kevin,

Poland: Tills are ringing

1. You, and no doubt every other reader of British newspapers, are probably fed up by now of almost daily reports of the bumper Christmas being enjoyed by shopkeepers all over the country. It would be, I think, an exaggeration to claim that the Polish consumer is in the same happy position as his counterpart in Britain. Nevertheless, in the past week or two the Polish media have been giving extensive coverage to reports of the goodies available in shops this year; and from my own observation, I would say that the shops are currently stocked with more goods that I can recall having seen in either of the two previous Christmases I have spent in Warsaw. Christmas trees are on sale everywhere and there seem copious supplies of tree decorations and Christmas lights. Consumer durables remain in fairly scarce supply although I have seen supplies of such desirable items as bicycles and sporting goods which were not available a few months ago. Toys too are plentiful. Our maid, for example, has bought my son as his Christmas present the East German equivalent of a Meccano set. In good socialist fashion, the instruction book tells him how to make trucks, tractors, oil drilling rigs and other useful items as befits a would-be socialist engineer. Models of a more obviously capitalist kind, e.g. motorcars, bicycles, are not presented and no doubt have to be left to the model builder's imagination to construct.

2. There is also much more food around than I can recall having seen at this time of the year. Fruit, root and salad vegetables, and tinned items, and even Coca-Cola can be bought. There is a wide range of cheese on sale including some American processed cheese available against production of a special children's ration coupon. Even the meat shops appear to be reasonably well-placed for those with the ration cards and the money available to make use of them.

3. No doubt one of the reasons why the shops appear relatively well stocked is because people do not on the whole have enough money to indulge in the hoarding endemic to the Polish character. This year's price increases have taken care of that. There are obviously problems and the supply of items such as shoes and a shortage of spare parts means that if a household durable breaks down it is very difficult to have it repaired. Nevertheless, for the Polish consumer with some funds available, this Christmas should be a lot less bleak than was the case last year. The authorities can probably congratulate themselves for having got their act together as far as the distribution and supply of goods for the shops this Christmas is concerned.

Yours ever,
M. R. Cohen

Best wishes for Christmas and the New Year.

[1] Commercial Secretary at HM Embassy.

INDEX